BEYONCÉ
ALL THE SONGS

BEYONCÉ
ALL THE SONGS
THE STORY BEHIND EVERY TRACK

BENOÎT CLERC

Contents

6 Foreword

8 Birth of an Icon

22 Destiny's Child

56 The Writing's On The Wall

94 Survivor

126 8 Days Of Christmas

144 Dangerously In Love

182 Destiny Fulfilled

208 B'Day

256 I Am…Sasha Fierce

294 4

324 Beyoncé

362 Lemonade

398 Everything Is Love

422 The Lion King: The Gift

440 Renaissance

468 Cowboy Carter

502 Compilations & Live

508 Glossary

510 Bibliography

516 Index

Beyoncé Knowles photographed by Cliff Watts in April 2013.

FOREWORD

The title of queen is usually attained only by unavoidable descent, which leads to a royal destiny that is set out in advance. Some women, however, earn this majestic adjective thanks to their position as a leader within a community, following a sporting exploit that leaves the competition far behind, or as the crowning glory of an artistic career studded with hits. The woman described in these pages climbed the rungs of royalty one by one, by dint of hard work and a fighting spirit, determined to attain the supreme position of monarch in a style of music of which she became, step by step, the muse and, finally, the queen. The music business is not kind to its female singers, even while many of them dream of becoming icons in their field. Whitney Houston was the idol of a generation, just as Mary J. Blige succeeded in earning the respect of her peers. Britney Spears made the whole world dance, while Christina Aguilera won listeners over thanks to an incomparable voice. But so far no other has managed to combine her talents and master the development of her own career as much as Beyoncé Knowles, alias Queen Bey.

A singer with multiple hits to her name, a super-rich businesswoman, philanthropic artist, successful actor, and devoted mother—none of these activities has ever frightened this artist, who has sold tens of millions of albums and can multi-task with natural ease, the fruit of work put in since her earliest childhood. Let us discover together the secrets behind the making of her many emblematic hits, such as *Single Ladies (Put a Ring on It)*, *Crazy in Love*, and *Texas Hold 'Em*, as well as those of her most intimate songs.

Grab your stetsons…and let the show begin!

Beyoncé Knowles photographed by Wyatt McSpadden in 2003.

BIRTH OF AN ICON

Life in the Knowles's family home at 2414 Rosedale Street, Houston, Texas, was lived to the soundtrack of vinyl records spinning on the household turntable. The house—dating from 1946 and bought in 1982 by the parents of the little girl who sang and danced in the living room—was the scene of a performance to which all those living nearby in the pleasant Third Ward neighborhood were accustomed. It was the year 1985 and, although those closest to the Knowles family often had a front-row seat at little Beyoncé's recitals, none was aware they were witnessing the first steps of one of the greatest stars of the 21st century.

A Texas family

It must be said that Beyoncé's parents supported their daughter's dreams of glory. Beyoncé Giselle Knowles was born on 4 September 1981 in the Park Plaza Hospital, Houston. Mathew, her father, had been born on 9 January 1951 in Gadsden, a segregationist town in Alabama sadly notorious for having been the scene of an act of unparalleled cruelty. On 11 February 1906, a 28-year-old African American named Bunk Richardson had been lynched by a group of 25 hooded individuals—hanged from the Louisville and Nashville Railroad Bridge, which crosses the Coosa River—for the rape of a white woman, which he did not commit. Like the 4,000 other victims of lynching in the United States since 1882, Richardson became the symbol of an America fractured by the sickening beliefs of a minority of its population. Supported by his mother, Lou Helen, a lawyer who worked to defend the rights of African Americans, Mathew Knowles made his Blackness into a strength, opposing appalling actions in order to champion his community. He soon became one of the first children of color to attend Litchfield Junior High School in Gadsden, even though a police presence was required to escort teenagers in the face of the displays of hate that daily disrupted the school's peace.

Mathew Knowles graduated from Nashville's prestigious Fisk University in 1974 with a BA in economics and a BSc. in business administration. He soon joined the Xerox company, which specialized in the sale of medical imaging peripherals, then moved on to Philips Medical Systems, where his salesman's skills made him the top seller of MRI machines and CT scanners for three years in succession. His situation allowed him to support his wife, Tina, who was born on 4 January 1954 in Galveston, Texas, when she told him of her wildest dream: to set up a large hair salon in Houston, catering to men and women of the city's African-American community. Located on Montrose Boulevard, Headliners opened in 1990 and became one of the most famous hair salons in Houston, both for the quality of its services and for the presence of four young women who soon began to put on improvised shows.

From Beyincé to Beyoncé

It's to her mother, Tina, that Beyoncé owes her highly original name. Celestine "Tina" Knowles was a Louisiana Creole who decided to pass on her maiden name, Beyoncé, to her elder daughter, so that the family name would not be lost after her marriage. Only the young Tina and her brother, Lumis Joseph "Skip", had benefited from this name, which had been misspelt by the registrar: on being asked to write Beyincé—the family name of their father, Lumis Albert Beyincé—he gave the

woeful reply: "Be happy that you're getting a birth certificate."[1] "My name was Celestine Beyoncé," Tina remembered, "which at that time was not a cool thing to have that weird name. I wanted my name to be Linda Smith."[2] When Celestine, who subsequently chose to be known as Tina, decided to give her daughter her maiden name, this elicited a strong reaction. "My family was not happy. My dad said, 'She's gonna be really mad at you, because that's a last name.' And I'm like, 'It's not a last name to anybody but you guys.'"[3] But in fact, proud of her roots, the future star went so far as to write "Beyincé" in capital letters on the sleeve of her eighth solo album, in 2024.

A happy childhood in Houston

From her earliest childhood Beyoncé Knowles was introduced to music by her parents—both of whom, in their youth, had taken part in talent shows. In high school Tina had even been one of the vocalists in a soul music group named The Veltones. Mathew played the piano, and introduced his daughter to the albums of Prince, Michael Jackson, and Luther Vandross. He completed her musical education with an unmissable weekly rendezvous in front of the television to enjoy the new releases featured on the legendary show *Soul Train*, then the flagship program for North American soul, funk, and disco music.

When a second daughter, Solange, was born in 1986, the family moved to the Parkwood neighborhood, where they lived comfortably at the heart of Texas society. Although extremely busy with their jobs, Tina and Mathew introduced their daughters to the cuisine of their beloved state, often treating them to fried chicken with red beans and rice, a specialty of Frenchy's at 4646 Scott Street, or the menus offered by the legendary Breakfast Klub at 3711 Travis Street. Weekends were a chance for the Knowles family to go to the rodeo, an event they all enjoyed—and an unmissable one for the city's inhabitants. "It was like the biggest family picnic; there was laughter and music everywhere and everyone dressed in their Texas finest," Beyoncé recalled years later. "I love watching all the people. We'd eat fried Snickers, funnel cakes, and fried turkey legs; the smell was the best mixture of spicy and sweet."[4] Solange Knowles also confirmed the privileged environment in which she and her older sister were raised. "Growing up on Parkwood was so inspiring because we got to see a little bit of everything. We grew up in the same neighborhood that produced Scarface, Debbie Allen, and Phylicia Rashad. So, culturally, it was as rich as it gets. People were warm. [...] I feel so happy that I got to grow up in a place where you could be the pastor's wife, you could be a lawyer, you could be a stripper on the side, you could be a schoolteacher."[5]

Beyoncé and her younger sister Solange in 1990.

Young Beyoncé in the expert hands of one of the hairdressers at Headliners.

Darlette Johnson lights the fuse

Although the young Beyoncé displayed a propensity for singing and dancing very early on, a Michael Jackson concert that her parents took her to made a profound impression on her. "I was [about] five years old," she explained later. "It was my first concert and it was his show, and I decided exactly my purpose. He's the reason I do what I do, because I would have never experienced that magic if it wasn't for him."[6]

From then on, little Beyoncé dreamed of being a singer, even though she revealed her ambition to no one, appearing shy and quiet at the St Mary primary school in Fredericksburg. "Because I was an introvert, I didn't speak very much as a child," she revealed in 2021. "I spent a lot of time in my head building my imagination. I am now grateful for those shy years of silence. Being shy taught me empathy and gave me the ability to connect and relate to people. I'm no longer shy, but I'm not sure I would dream as big as I dream today if it were not for those awkward years in my head."[7]

At the time, Beyoncé felt misunderstood by her classmates and remained very solitary during her schooling, while assiduously having dance lessons with Darlette Johnson. Although her performances caught her teacher's attention, there was another hidden talent the young girl possessed—which she would soon reveal to Johnson. "She was at the studio and she was the last one and her parents always came to get her, to pick her up, and I was just kinda sweeping around… and I was singing a song out of tune and Beyoncé finished the song for me and she hit a note and I said, 'Sing it again.' […] her parents came to pick her up, I said, 'She can sing! […] She really can sing.'"[8] From that moment on, Darlette Johnson ceaselessly encouraged the young Beyoncé, urging her to work on her voice as much as on her dance steps. "Beyoncé was quiet and reserved and didn't say much, but on the dancefloor she was a force to be reckoned with, and she had a golden voice. […] I told her, 'You are gonna be a world star. You are gonna be so big, the whole world is gonna know you.'"[9]

A little girl out to conquer the city

A great admirer of Stevie Wonder, En Vogue, and Donny Hathaway, Beyoncé Knowles now became aware of her own talent, but revealed it to no one except Darlette Johnson. The latter wasted no time in suggesting to Mathew and Tina that they enter their daughter in a talent contest that was soon to be held in St Mary's primary school—an invitation to which they readily agreed, for Johnson had told them of their daughter's potential. The song the little girl chose was John Lennon's *Imagine*, an anthem to peace in the world and equality among humankind. When told about this choice, Mathew Knowles

Beyoncé Knowles, LaTavia Roberson, LeToya Luckett, and Kelly Rowland: the final lineup of Girls Tyme.

considered that his daughter could interpret the song only if she had a real understanding of its lyrics. With this in mind, he took her to the underprivileged areas of the city, especially those where African Americans and Mexicans lived, in order to make her aware of the poverty that afflicted neighborhoods close to Parkwood, where the Knowles family lived a privileged existence. "While practicing *Imagine* in her room after that," Mathew Knowles said, "I could hear the difference from how she had sung it before. At least her interpretation of the song had changed. This would hone her ability to bring compassion and emotion, not only when singing *Imagine* but with every song she sang."[10]

When the day of the talent contest arrived, Tina and her husband were left open-mouthed by the performance of their daughter, who was normally so quiet and shy. "I was terrified and I didn't wanna do it," the singer recalled. "[...] I remember walking out and I was scared, but when the music started, I don't know what happened. I just...changed."[3] Beyoncé's performance got everyone's vote. As the supreme winner of the contest, the young girl became aware of the future that awaited her. "I was like, '"Oh, Lord, this is amazing.' So I knew I wanted to be a singer. I think I knew before that, but I'd never been on a stage before that."[3]

From then, Beyoncé Knowles went on to sweep the board at talent shows across the state, supported by her parents and Darlette Johnson. Each of her performances resulted in a victory, and her budding professionalism was noted by competition juries and audiences alike. In 1989, a year after winning a Sammy Davis Award, the young singer revisited the scene of her victory and excelled with her performance of *Home*, which Diana Ross had sung in the musical movie *The Wiz* in 1978. That day, with uncommon poise and panache, Beyoncé declared to the audience: "I would like to thank the judges for picking me, my parents, who I love—I love you, Houston!"[11] From then on, nothing seemed to stop her on her road to glory.

Girls Tyme sing their first notes

The enthusiasm generated by their daughter's performances led Beyoncé's parents to call on the services of a singing teacher. David Lee Brewer, newly graduated from the Cleveland Institute of Music and recently settled in Houston, got a call from Tina, asking him whether he would agree to audition their daughter with a view to her possibly attending his singing course. Brewer recalled his impression on encountering the budding artist: "What she let loose was one of the most impressive sounds I'd ever heard from a child. Something about it grabbed me and wouldn't let me go. The sound was molten gold, with a distinguished timbre. What's more,

12 BIRTH OF AN ICON

Beyoncé possessed a seemingly innate, physical connection to the music. This was more than just a voice, I thought to myself, it is a spirit. She and I bonded instantly over our mutual passion for singing."[12] With the support of her parents and Brewer's teaching, Beyoncé made multiple appearances at talent contests in Houston and the surrounding region, winning hands down each one she took part in.

Feeling that the young artist was ready to move up to the next stage in her career, Darlette Johnson invited Deborah LaDay and Denise Seals to come and hear Beyoncé in a concert she was performing in at the Evelyn Rubenstein Jewish Community Center in Houston. LaDay and Seals had recently founded D&D Management—an organization named for their two initials and aimed at supporting artists—and were looking for young female singers with a view to forming a group that could rival male ensembles fashionable at the time, such as Another Bad Creation, Boyz II Men, Kris Kross, New Edition, Color Me Badd, and New Kids on the Block. Stunned by Beyoncé's performance, Denise and Deborah invited her to two auditions, and then suggested she join the new group, which would consist of a trio of singers—Beyoncé, Staci LaToison, and Millicent LaDay—and the dancers LaTavia Roberson, Chris Lewis, Nicky Taylor, and Nicky's younger sister Nina. The group's name came easily to LaDay and Seals,

BEYONCÉ: ALL THE SONGS   13

Destiny's Child and actor Tahj Mowry on the set of the sitcom *Smart Guy* in 1998.

who were determined to give a feminine touch to the music scene of the time. They decided on Girls Tyme, because they believed that the time for girls had arrived.

Over the following months the group performed several concerts, most of them very successful. Denise Seals was the group's voice coach (replaced by Brewer after a time), Darlette Johnson was the choreographer, and Tina Knowles produced the stage costumes, while in the end management was entrusted to a newcomer, Andretta Tillman, who agreed to invest all her savings in the project. The year was 1991, and Tillman's first decision was to introduce to the girls a possible new recruit in the shape of Kelly Rowland, who was a great admirer of Whitney Houston. There was an immediate rapport between Beyoncé and Kelly, to the point that the latter very quickly moved into the Knowles's home, because her mother, Doris, although loving and devoted, was then employed by another family as a live-in childminder. Tirelessly working on their stage acts, the young women developed new choreographies inspired by those of The Jackson 5 or The Supremes, which they revealed in previews to the customers of Headliners, Tina Knowles's hair salon. Girls Tyme was soon enlivened by the arrival of the singer Ashley Támar Davis, and the group went on to feature various different line-ups, each as brilliant as the last.

The quality of their performances soon convinced Beyoncé's father, Mathew, who decided to involve himself fully in the project, sharing the team's management with Tillman. Mathew took numerous steps to find Girls Tyme partners who were on their level, as did Arne Frager, owner of the legendary Record Plant studios in Sausalito, California. At the time, Frager was looking for new, especially female, talent to compete with the success of male groups. At Mathew's request, he traveled to Houston and auditioned the girls at the Knowles's family home. He found the performance convincing, and invited Beyoncé and Ashley to come and record at Record Plant, accompanied by Andretta Tillman. Armed with a demo recording, Frager gained the support of Suzanne de Passe—a manager who could boast having once signed the Jackson brothers with Motown, where she worked at the time—who pointed him in the direction of one of her employees, Ruth Carson. Carson told Frager she would like to welcome Girls Tyme into the Suzanne de Passe Management stable, only to eventually withdraw her offer when she accepted a job offer from Sony Music and moved to New York. None of the negotiations undertaken by Mathew Knowles and Arne Frager led to the group landing a contract, for they always got the same reply: "Look, one of the reasons we don't want to sign these girls is you have three singers [Ashley had recently left the group] and you have four dancers, that's seven people. Then you've got their parents, which is another ten people. That's seventeen people that we got to deal with. We don't want to deal with that."[10] Nonplussed by this series of setbacks, Frager and Knowles decided to enter the group in a musical talent show screened every week on US television: *Star Search*.

The *Star Search* adventure

Dreaming of a potential victory that could bring them $100,000 and considerable visibility, in November 1992 the troupe flew to Orlando, Florida, to shoot the show, which was due to be aired the following February. From among the songs recorded at Record Plant, *That's the Way It Is in My City* was chosen, despite the reservations of Mathew, who feared that the jury, consisting of white men of a certain age, would hardly appreciate the song's hip-hop quality. Despite a performance of a quality worthy of the New York group Salt-N-Pepa, Girls Tyme did not win the competition, losing to the rock group Skeleton Crew. "Even when it hurt so bad, we're still smiling," Kelly Rowland recalled in 2001, "and when we walked offstage, everybody just broke down. Imagine 10- or 11-year-olds just breaking down and crying. Now that I'm thinking about it, I want to cry."[13]

Faced with the despair of his protégées, Mathew Knowles asked the show's star presenter Ed McMahon about the best way to help them. McMahon explained that none of the winners of *Star Search* had ever gone on to make a career, unlike the losers—some of whom, such as the members of Boyz II Men, had become very famous—who were motivated by the desire to assert their talent after such a defeat and

14 BIRTH OF AN ICON

Singer Mariah Carey was one of Mathew Knowles's models when he was preparing his protégées for the stage.

subsequently worked relentlessly to win over their audience. In no time at all, Mathew decided to quit his job at Xerox to devote himself totally to his daughter's career. "Seeing your daughter cry, I didn't want her or the rest of the ladies to give up on their dream, and so that's when I stepped in. […] I had to be the front sound man, I had to be the security, I had to be the road manager, I had to wear all of those hats, and so it allowed me to really understand almost every aspect of the day-to-day. I also used a lot of the business savvy that I had learned at Xerox, and that was understanding the customer and knowing how to work inside of a major company."[14]

A four-part group

The first step, then, was to restructure Girls Tyme around its singers, Beyoncé, Kelly Rowland, and LaTavia Roberson, who were soon joined by a newcomer, LeToya Luckett. Once the group's new setup had been finalized, Mathew moved heaven and earth to have his protégées signed up by a record label. With this in mind, he made numerous approaches and eventually caught the attention of the composer and producer Darryl Simmons, who had just signed the singer Monica, future star of contemporary R&B, to his company, Silent Partner Productions. Intrigued by these four undeniably talented singers, Simmons asked Mathew Knowles to send him a VHS video cassette introducing Girls Tyme, after which, in April 1993, he made the journey to Houston to meet them. The audition took place in the producer's hotel room, in the presence of his wife, Sherry, and Mathew. The four singers demonstrated their talent with a performance of Michael Jackson's *I Wanna Be Where You Are* and *Sunshine*, an original composition from their own repertoire. Darryl Simmons quickly offered the girls their first contract, inviting them to Atlanta to sign up with Silent Partner Productions and to work on promotion of the group, renamed The Dolls when they arrived in Georgia.

Chaperoned by LaTavia's mother, the girls stayed at the home of Simmons's assistant, and spent all day in Simmons's studio working on their demo recordings. Their new mentor introduced them to Sylvia Rhone, CEO of Elektra Entertainment Group, who offered them a contract, only to pull out a few months later in order to concentrate on her successful group En Vogue, in the process ending her long-standing collaboration with Simmons. "Sylvia dropped Darryl's company because he was too busy writing hit songs for everyone in the industry," Mathew Knowles explained. "He didn't have the time to give to his own artists."[15]

Mathew Knowles was inspired by the work of Berry Gordy, the founder of Motown, as he developed the career of the group that would become Destiny's Child.

The end of the dream

Although the breaking of the contract between The Dolls and Elektra inevitably plunged the girls into unprecedented disarray, Mathew Knowles refused to admit defeat and remained determined to prove to the whole world that his protégées had talent. Now unemployed, he became the group's sole manager and spared no expense to promote The Dolls—who once again changed their name, first to Borderline, then to Cliché—causing severe tension with his wife, Tina. "We lost our house shortly after my husband, Mathew, left his job to manage the girls under their first record deal," Tina revealed in 2003. "Then we lost that deal. Mathew would spend $5,000 of our money on a photoshoot, while I was working 16 hours a day to support us. I felt like the group was more important to him than his family. So we separated for six months. But we were miserable apart. We got back together and never let money separate us again."[16]

Although life was not easy for the Knowles family, now squeezed into a small apartment where Beyoncé and Kelly shared a bedroom, while Solange slept next to Tina, Mathew did not give up hope, devoting considerable energy to the group, who changed their name yet again, to Somethin' Fresh. To bring to fruition his plans for developing the quartet, Mathew drew inspiration from his idol Berry Gordy, founder of the legendary Motown label and an unparalleled discoverer of new talent. Accordingly, he set up his own production company for the promotion of artists, Music World Entertainment. "That's where I developed my concept, from Berry Gordy," Knowles said in 2001. "He doesn't get the credit he deserves. He had everything in-house. He had his choreographers, stylists, producers, and writers. He taught his artists etiquette. He had real artist development. And his artists were glamorous. That's really what the music world is all about."[17] Mathew employed the services of a model to teach his protégées how to walk in high heels, made them run in Memorial Park while singing in order to develop endurance, and organized a summer performance boot camp where they worked on dance and singing. "They were able to build their confidence, and they were able to understand what being an entertainer is versus being a singer," he explained. "We would sit and look at Mariah Carey, Whitney Houston, Michael Jackson, Madonna, Janet Jackson, and Tina Turner; those were the six artists that we studied. I would go and get every tape and performance that you can imagine, and we would literally sit down and study from the beginning of those performances."[18]

"This wasn't a parent or manager putting together a group to see about a record deal," Beyoncé explained. "This was young girls saying, 'This is what we want.'"[19] As regards his artists' development, Mathew Knowles felt they needed to change their name yet again. In order to do this, Tina opened a Bible and happened upon the word "destiny." After using this new name for a few months, the group found out there was already a female gospel group called Destiny, in Mississippi. It was thus decided to change the quartet's identity one last time and give them their definitive name: Destiny's Child.

Destiny's Child take on the record labels

Mathew Knowles sent off multiple promotional video cassettes of Destiny's Child, notably to Atlantic and Capital Records, which pointedly refused to hear any more about the four Texan singers. But when one of these VHS cassettes came into the possession of the singer, composer, and producer D'Wayne Wiggins, a founder member of the trio Tony! Toni! Toné!, he hastened to sign them up with his company Grass Roots Entertainment. Wiggins quickly turned out to be a godsend for Destiny's Child. In 1995 he introduced them to Teresa LaBarbera Whites, artistic director at Columbia, one of Sony

Destiny's Child in the studio in Houston, 1997.

Overleaf:
LaTavia Roberson, Beyoncé Knowles, LeToya Luckett, and Kelly Rowland ready to conquer the world, 1997.

Music's biggest labels. Whites invited the four girls to come and audition at Sony Music's offices in New York, where they sang two songs a cappella in front of an audience of company executives. The audition over, Destiny's Child returned to Houston, where they had to wait several weeks for news about their New York performance. The girls were in Tina Knowles's hair salon when they heard that Columbia was offering them a recording contract—which unleashed a wave of enthusiasm never seen before at Headliners. "We started screaming and crying right in the middle of the salon," Beyoncé said. "The ladies with their heads under the dryers looked at us like we were crazy, because they couldn't hear what all the yelling was about. We ran all around the shop, jumping up and down, holding our contract in the air for all the customers to see. It was a beautiful day at the beauty salon, that's for sure!"[20] The future looked bright for Destiny's Child, who then consisted of Beyoncé Knowles, Kelly Rowland, LaTavia Roberson, and LeToya Luckett.

BEYONCÉ: ALL THE SONGS   19

DESTINY'S CHILD

ALBUM

Destiny's Child

Second Nature • No, No, No Part 2 • With Me Part I • Tell Me • Bridges •
No, No, No Part 1 • With Me Part II • Show Me The Way • Killing Time • Illusion • Birthday •
Sail On • My Time Has Come (Dedicated To Andretta Tillman)

Released in the USA by Sony Music/Columbia: 17 February 1998 (album ref.: C 67728, CD ref.: CK 67728)
Best chart ranking in the USA: 67

The four talented singers in 1997, shortly before their first album was released.

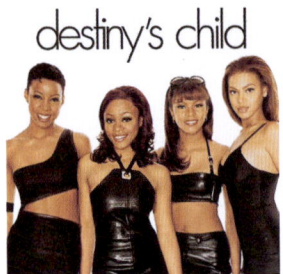

SHAPING THEIR DESTINY

If Destiny's Child had caught the attention of Columbia, one of Sony Music's most prestigious labels, it was because the days when groups of velvet-voiced young men reigned supreme over the music business were over. The time for girls had come at last, and it would not be long before they left their permanent mark on late 20th-century popular music with songs of quality. The bosses of record companies, who call the shots, had for some years offered their audiences numerous equally prestigious female groups who were technically proficient and charismatic—a far cry from the manufactured products of the middle years of the decade that was drawing to a close. Despite their undeniable talent, Destiny's Child nevertheless needed to compete with groups such as 702, made up of the sisters Irish and LeMisha Grinstead, and Kameelah Williams; Total, who were signed to Bad Boy Records, P. Diddy's label; the New York band SWV (Sisters with Voices); and Xscape, whose producer was Jermaine Dupri. But the most formidable of all were unquestionably Tionne "T-Boz" Watkins, Lisa "Left Eye" Lopes, and Rozonda "Chilli" Thomas who made up the group TLC; their second album, *CrazySexyCool*, released in 1994, had opened the way for a female branch of the style known as contemporary R&B, which had influenced this new generation of artists. Although Beyoncé Knowles and her associates were benefiting from the success of TLC's single *Creep*, released in October 1994, they nevertheless needed to contend with these hugely talented competitors who made brilliant songs.

A strong team

Destiny's Child were signed up by Columbia in December 1995. The contract, for seven albums, offered the group a budget of $85,000 for recording the first of these, and an advance on takings of almost $400,000, giving them considerable security after the numerous financial investments that the Knowles family had made in their effort to lead the quartet to success. Producing the record nevertheless took some considerable time, and the girls, who were then in ninth grade, attended lessons until January, after which they continued their studies by correspondence with private teachers. While they worked relentlessly on their choreography and vocal technique, Teresa LaBarbera Whites, who had been responsible for signing them to Columbia, sought out the best partners for her protégées. She had no difficulty obtaining a favorable response from the producers, composers, and songwriters of the time, easily securing the services of Vincent Herbert and Rob Fusari, Jermaine Dupri, the duo Tim & Bob (Tim Kelly and Bob Robinson), Benjamin Wright, and of course D'Wayne Wiggins, who had been a support from the outset.

Two years of toil

It would take Destiny's Child two years to finally complete the recording of their first album, as Kelly Rowland explained in *Soul Survivors. The Official Autobiography of Destiny's Child*, released in 2002: "Why did it take us so long to finish our album? Because it was our debut album and we wanted it to be perfect. [...] We were thinking about our sound, our image, our marketing strategy—basically, we were thinking about anything and everything."[20] It must be said that the four singers put in a phenomenal amount of work. "My mother taught me the principles of hard work, setting my own goals and

Tionne Watkins, Lisa "Left Eye" Lopes, and Rozonda Thomas are TLC, the main rival to Destiny's Child.

Will Smith plays Agent J in Barry Sonnenfeld's movie *Men in Black*.

visualizing my future," Beyoncé said in 2011. "From my early days with Destiny's Child, I understood I had to be focused and dedicated if I wanted true success. We were taught we needed a plan and the discipline to execute that plan to the fullest. I strongly believe if you work hard, whatever you want, it will come to you. I know that's easier said than done, but keep trying."[4]

Destiny's Child and *Men in Black*

Hard work paid off for Beyoncé, Kelly, LaTavia, and LeToya, for from 1997 onwards they made numerous appearances alongside developing artists. They were seen as extras in Jagged Edge's clip *Gotta Be*, released by So So Def Recording, Jermaine Dupri's label, and in the clip *Can't Stop* by Lil' O, for which they also recorded some backing vocals—making that song the very first official piece in Destiny's Child's discography. These collaborations prepared the public for the group's first full-length song, *Killing Time*, which was included on the soundtrack album of Barry Sonnenfeld's movie *Men in Black*, released in US cinemas on 2 July 1997. The international success of the film, starring Will Smith and Tommy Lee Jones, benefited *Killing Time*, as even though the song was not heard in the movie (only *Men in Black*, sung by Smith, featured in the final edit), it was excellent publicity for the upcoming release of Destiny's Child's first album.

Unfailing professionalism

The publicity Columbia put in place for Destiny's Child was in keeping with the success the record company hoped they would achieve. The group performed a series of promotional concerts with disconcerting ease, adapting to the most difficult conditions, as in Virginia, where they performed with aplomb in a promotional show on WJJS Radio in Roanoke. Lisa Ellis of Sony Music, who worked with them, bore witness to the singers' professionalism in a piece for *Billboard* magazine in 2006: "They were in a parking lot in front of a department store on a one-foot riser with a stage. Yet those girls came prepared like they were playing Madison Square Garden. They were

Boyz II Men at the height of their fame, Los Angeles, 1997.

Destiny's Child broadcasting from the Chicago radio station V103 FM in May 1999.

doing their own hair and makeup, complete with costume changes. Tina [Beyoncé's mother] literally sewed all the clothes back then. There were no lights and cameras. Just them and a crowd of people. And they killed it."[19]

When the group's first album—entitled simply *Destiny's Child*—appeared on 17 February 1998, it was an immediate success. The promotion gained momentum, and the four girls, then aged an average of 16, made headlines in the music press and were invited onto numerous American television shows. They showed great maturity in the interviews they gave, and demonstrated yet again that they were well prepared when a journalist asked them how they saw themselves in ten years' time: "We now own our record company," LaTavia predicted. "[…] Kelly has directed an extreme amount of videos now. LeToya is designing for everyone. I'm producing and writing, Beyoncé is running the record company, producing and writing also."[21]

A minor marketing error

Although they were able to bask in the success of their first album, driven by the singles *No, No, No* and *With Me*, Destiny's Child met Columbia's expectations only up to a point, for the company quickly identified a problem with the group's image. Influenced to a great extent by the soul music of The Supremes, on the record sleeve the four girls wore dresses unsuited to their young age, and even less to the dress code of contemporary R&B, which involved outfits closer to the world of sport than to the elegance of the Motown stars. Moreover, the album's sound lacked modernity, as Beyoncé explained a few years later: "The first record was successful but not hugely successful. It was a neo-soul record and we were 15 years old. It was way too mature for us."[22] Mathew Knowles confirmed: "We wanted to brand these girls as fresh hot teenagers. Though the album had some phenomenal songs, it didn't fit into the direction we were heading into."[15]

After playing as the supporting act for a Boyz II Men tour beginning on 28 August 1998 at Pyramid Arena in Memphis, Destiny's Child returned to work to correct this small error in communication and to win over the public in a lasting way, while the R&B wave swept through the United States and the whole world.

Tina Knowles decided to review her protégées' outfits in 1998 when their luggage was lost in transit between Houston and Cancún, Mexico, where they were to shoot an episode of the show *MTV Spring Break*. Borrowing a camouflage outfit from Wyclef Jean, who was also a guest on the show, Tina hurried off to buy identical material in order to hastily make stage costumes. From then on, Destiny's Child were never again seen dressed as they had been on the sleeve of their first album; their image finally came to fit with their musical world—and their youth.

BEYONCÉ: ALL THE SONGS 29

Kelly Rowland has always been considered part of the Knowles clan.

KELLY ROWLAND, BEYONCÉ'S KINDRED SPIRIT

Born on 11 February 1981 in Atlanta, Georgia, Kelendria Trene Rowland moved to Houston at the age of seven with her mother, Doris, who was fleeing from a violent husband. That was when she met the Knowles family, to whom Doris entrusted her daughter for a summer in order to work full-time as a child minder for a wealthy family. So much did Kelendria, who preferred to be known as Kelly, take to her host family that this set-up continued. The bond with Beyoncé, the elder of the Knowles sisters, grew especially strong, to the point that they became inseparable. "We never adopted her," Tina Knowles explained. "We never asked for custody. [...] Kelly's mother was a certified live-in nanny, and she moved from place to place. Her mother used to leave her job and bring Kelly across town for rehearsals every day. Her mom was in job transition, so Kelly came in to live with us for a couple of months. Kelly's mom had a key to our house and to our car. Most weekends she stayed with us. She has been a part of Kelly's life every day."[17]

Kelly quickly became passionate about singing, which she practiced every Saturday morning at St John's United Methodist Church in Houston, where the pastor, Rudy Rasmus, an emblematic figure in the city's African-American community, welcomed her alongside other future members of Destiny's Child. "I would definitely say church gives you a little more soul, especially when you're listening to the music, and the music here is amazing and it fills your heart and touches your soul. I've been singing since I was a kid and going to church just inspired me even more," Kelly declared in 2006.[23] A great admirer of Whitney Houston, she would go on to shine with Destiny's Child for her qualities as a singer, which made her personal career a colossal success. She even eclipsed Beyoncé's first venture as a soloist when *Dilemma*—a song in which Kelly accompanies the rapper Nelly—made the top of the *Billboard* 200, higher than *Work It Out*, her kindred spirit's first single. Even though *Crazy in Love*, a song from Beyoncé's first album, focused the media's attention on the latter a year later, Kelly Rowland enjoyed a prestigious career, selling several million albums between 2002 and 2024, on top of the more than 60 million sold with Destiny's Child. Her friendship with Beyoncé remained intact over the years. "Our relationship goes deeper than Destiny's Child," she told *Ebony* in 2000. "That's my sister, and I love her and I know she feels the same way about me. We have each other's back, no matter what."[24]

LaTavia Roberson in 1998.

PORTRAIT

LATAVIA ROBERSON: A YOUNG MODEL WITH A CATCHY FLOW

Born on 1 November 1981 in Houston, LaTavia Marie Roberson discovered singing and dancing at a very early age. She was spotted by a modeling agency and attracted attention in 1993 in an advertisement for the haircare brand Just for Me, aimed at African Americans. Her dance steps and hip-hop flow, worthy of Salt-N-Pepa, had caught the eye of her agent, who invited her to take part in an audition for a young female group then being formed. In 1989 she joined Girls Tyme, alongside Beyoncé, with whom she became friends. "Our relationship was wonderful. I was 8 years old when I auditioned for Destiny's Child. I was waiting in line next to Beyoncé, and that's when I met her. We made the group that became Girls Tyme, then we had several other names. Then I met Kelly in elementary school, and Beyoncé met LaToya in middle school two years later. We started working together and built a friendship."[25]

Following her departure from Destiny's Child in 2000, LaTavia entered a difficult period, falling into a severe depression triggered by the brutal break-up and the feeling that her future was slipping away. After struggling with drug addiction and breaking free of abuse, years later LaTavia appeared on the television show *R&B Divas: Atlanta*, alongside her old friend Kameelah Williams, formerly of the group 702, as well as Angie Stone, LaTocha Scott from Xscape, Faith Evans, and Nicci Gilbert from Brownstone.

Despite many personal and professional setbacks, she remained an important figure on the R&B scene in the 2000s, and even today speaks up for minorities. "When I did resurface, what I heard even in my darkest moments was to 'give back.' When I came back into the light, I've been doing just that. I ended up on *R&B Divas*, I've been doing a lot of speaking, philanthropy work, and things for the LGBT community. I'm in the studio working with some artists behind the scenes—to be the mogul behind putting out projects for other artists."[25]

After Destiny's Child, LeToya Luckett embarked on a successful acting career.

LETOYA LUCKETT: IN THE FOOTSTEPS OF WHITNEY HOUSTON

LeToya Nicole Luckett was born in Houston on 11 March 1981. Her introduction to singing was through the choir of Brentwood Baptist Church, where she secretly imitated her idols Janet Jackson and Whitney Houston. At school she met Beyoncé, with whom she soon joined Girls Tyme, the group that would later become Destiny's Child. It was when the group were signed by Columbia, in the winter of 1995, that tension first surfaced between LeToya and her three friends, with her mother Pamela demanding that her lawyer read the recording contract—a decision that seemed entirely legitimate but that displeased Mathew Knowles. Once she had broken away from the group that had launched her career, LeToya joined Capitol Records, with whom in 2006 she released her first solo album, *LeToya*, which went to the top of the *Billboard* 200 and earned her considerable success. After the release of her second album, *Lady Love*, in 2009, she turned to the cinema, appearing in *Preacher's Kid* and *Killers* in 2010, *From the Rough* in 2011, and *Lucky Girl* in 2015. She also worked in television, appearing in *Treme* in 2011 and *Single Ladies* in 2014.

LeToya subsequently released a series of quality singles (*Don't Make Me Wait* in 2014, *I'm Ready* and *Together* in 2015, then *Back 2 Life* in 2016), even though her renown would never equal that of her former colleagues in Destiny's Child. Like her friend LaTavia Roberson, LeToya Luckett became an active philanthropist, notably with regard to women who were victims of domestic violence.

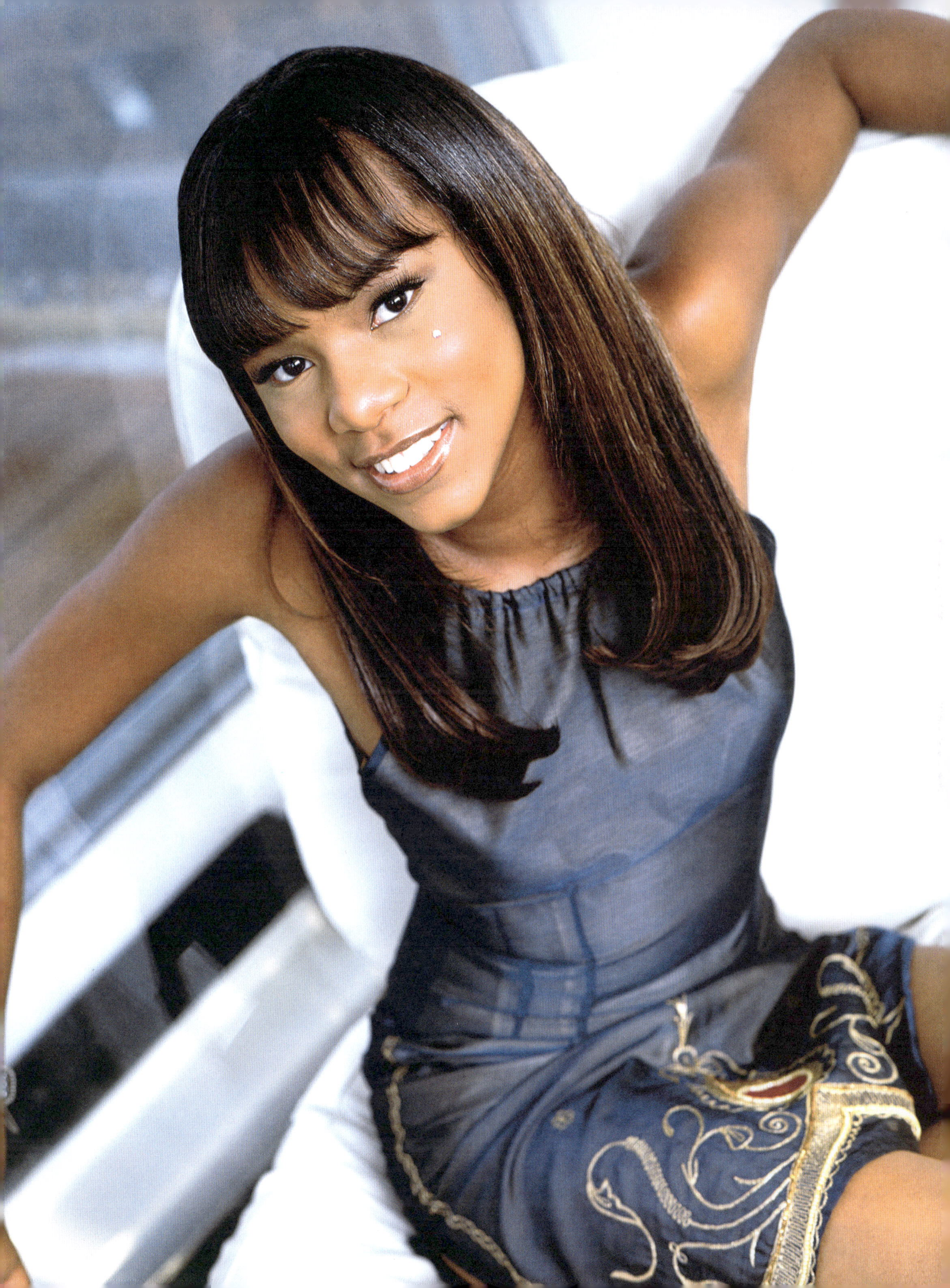

After sampling *Make Me Say It Again, Girl* on *Second Nature*, Beyoncé sang the song with The Isley Brothers in 2021.

SECOND NATURE

(Chris Jasper, Ernie Isley, Kymberli Armstrong, Marvin Isley, O'Kelly Isley, Ronald Isley, Terry T/5'09)

Musicians: Beyoncé Knowles: vocals, backing vocals / **Kelly Rowland:** vocals, backing vocals / **LeToya Luckett:** backing vocals / **LaTavia Roberson:** backing vocals / **Raymond McKinley:** bass guitar / **Lee Neal:** drums / **D'Wayne Wiggins:** guitar / **Jamie Hawkins:** Fender Rhodes / **Recording:** House of Music, Oakland: 1996 to 1998 / Pajama Studios, Oakland: 1996 to 1998 / **Technical team: Producers:** D'Wayne Wiggins, Jay Lincoln, Terry T / **Executive producer:** Mathew Knowles

With the first song of their official discography, Destiny's Child decided to pay homage to their soul roots, revisiting with their musicians the instrumental section of a classic by The Isley Brothers, *Make Me Say It Again, Girl*. The Isley Brothers song is a track in two sections entitled *Make Me Say It Again, Girl (Part I & II)*, recorded with their associate Chris Jasper. Here, it is completely re-recorded rather than sampled, which gives *Second Nature* unquestionable cachet, sustained by the lead vocals of Beyoncé Knowles. Raymond McKinley, legendary bass guitarist with Patti LaBelle, endows this first track with an irresistible groove. The choice of instruments used, such as the Fender Rhodes electric piano, is not insignificant, for Mathew Knowles and the producers, D'Wayne Wiggins, Jay Lincoln, and Terry T, were determined to give Destiny's Child's songs a soul quality that proudly contrasted with the ultra-modern R&B productions of rival artists at the time. "Live instrumentation was a big part of the thought process [of] going back to a kind of urbane sound that was similar to neo-soul," Mathew Knowles explained.[15] It is true that this first track on the album may remind the listener of the languor of *Welcome* or *Sumthin' Sumthin'*, from Maxwell's first album, *Maxwell's Urban Hang Suite*, released in 1996, as well as the soul hits of the 1970s, which artists positioned on their LPs between two explosive, danceable funk numbers. Destiny's Child would soon emulate this artistic trend in order to reach out to a younger audience, more partial to dance than to ballads with a sound that, at the time, seemed a touch outdated.

Wyclef Jean, gifted producer and founding member of the Fugees, contributed to the meteoric rise of Destiny's Child.

SINGLE

NO, NO, NO PART 2
(FEATURING WYCLEF JEAN)

(Barry White, Calvin Gaines, Mary Brown, Rob Fusari, Vincent Herbert/3'30)

Musicians: Beyoncé Knowles: vocals, backing vocals / **Kelly Rowland:** vocals, backing vocals / **LeToya Luckett:** backing vocals / **LaTavia Roberson:** backing vocals / **Wyclef Jean:** rap, backing vocals / **Recording** / Chung King Studios, New York: 1996 to 1998 / **Digital Services Recording Studios, Houston:** 1996 to 1998 / **Technical team:** Producers: Wyclef Jean, Che Greene, Jerry Duplessis / **Executive producer:** Mathew Knowles / **Recording engineers:** James Hoover, Warren Riker, Rawle Gittens / **Assistant recording engineer:** Storm Jefferson / **Released in the USA by Sony Music/Columbia:** 27 October 1997 (ref.: 38K 78618) / **Best chart ranking in the USA:** 3

It was unquestionably with this hit, remixed by the highly popular Wyclef Jean, that Destiny's Child gained admittance to the ranks of the greats. There are two versions of the song, which saw the light of day in the basement of a producer named Rob Fusari, a young man who a few years later would become the mentor of a certain Lady Gaga. *No, No, No Part I*, which appears a little later on the album, caught the attention of Teresa LaBarbera Whites when she was looking for hits for her protégées, Destiny's Child. Once the song had been found, recorded, and produced in a soul vein close to that of *Second Nature*, the team had the idea of offering the task of remixing it to Wyclef Jean of the Fugees—then world hip-hop superstars after the global success of their second LP, *The Score* (who could forget *Ready or Not*, *Fu-Gee-La*, and their version of Roberta Flack's *Killing Me Softly*?). Jean willingly accepted, charmed by the quartet's vocal prowess, and invited them to come and re-record their voice takes in New York, his remix being at a faster tempo than the original version. Destiny's Child then faced two insoluble problems. On the one hand, the budget allocated for recording their album had been practically exhausted and, on the other, Wyclef Jean's timetable was extremely tight: his plane needed to leave New York at 3pm. The session was thus held at breakneck speed, creating an unprecedentedly competitive atmosphere, which in turn produced Destiny's Child's signature vocal quality, especially that of Beyoncé, the lead singer in the song. Jean urged her to sing as quickly as possible, something she carried off in masterly fashion, as he recalled in 2017: "I knew they came from Texas. […] What if I could have Beyoncé sing in the double timing, almost like she's rhyming, like the dudes from Texas at the time? Everything was…double timing, but you never heard girls doing that."[26] Beyoncé followed Jean's shrewd advice and delivered an unforgettable performance of the song, which made an impact on the radio. *No, No, No Part 2* was released at the same time as *No, No, No Part 1*, the two singles thus increasing Destiny's Child's chance of making it on to the *Billboard* chart. The ploy paid off, and the group secured their first Top 10 place in the US charts.

HEADPHONES AT THE READY

The singer Barry White is credited on *No, No, No Part 2* because a sample from his instrumental piece *Strange Games & Things*, which features on the album *My Sweet Summer Suite* by his group Love Unlimited Orchestra, released in 1976, was used as the song's melodic base.

BEYONCÉ: ALL THE SONGS

SINGLE

WITH ME PART I
(FEATURING JD)

(Jermaine Dupri, Manuel Seal, Master P/3'22)

Musicians: Beyoncé Knowles: vocals, backing vocals / Kelly Rowland: vocals, backing vocals / LeToya Luckett: backing vocals / LaTavia Roberson: backing vocals / Jermaine Dupri: rap / **Recording:** KrossWire Studios, College Park, Georgia: 1996 to 1998 / **Technical team:** Producers: Manuel Seal, Jermaine Dupri / Executive producer: Mathew Knowles / Recording engineers: Brian Frye, Phil Tan / Released in the USA by Sony Music/Columbia: 20 January 1998 (CD single ref.: 666147 6) / **Best chart ranking in the USA:** did not make the charts

To say that Mathew Knowles and Teresa LaBarbera Whites managed to surround themselves with the best composers and producers of the day for Destiny's Child's first album would be understating the matter. After Wyclef Jean and Rob Fusari, it was the turn of Jermaine Dupri to come and work with this still-unknown group of Texan singers. Dupri owed his renown to the international success of the duo Kriss Kross, which he had set up and produced, and for whom he had created one of the hits of 1992, *Jump*. The star producer, who also boasted the recent triumph of the singles *Always Be My Baby* by Mariah Carey and *Just Kickin' It* and *Understanding* by Xscape, drew inspiration from another of his successes—Usher's *You Make Me Wanna*—in order to write *With Me Part I*. The youthful Destiny's Child sang the lyrics, which deal with romantic relationships, even though their experience of such things must have been limited in view of their age. "We didn't know what we were talking about," laughed LeToya Luckett of the song a few years later, "but it sounded good and people were rocking with it."[27] Featuring a sample from *Freak Hoes*, a song released on *Tru 2 da Game*—the fourth album by the New Orleans group TRU (The Real Untouchables), consisting of Master P, Silkk the Shocker, and C-Murder—*With Me Part I* was released as a single in January 1998, without, alas, repeating the success of *No, No, No Part 1* and *No, No, No Part 2*.

Jermaine Dupri would become one of the star producers of the R&B era.

D'Wayne Wiggins sampled Al Green during the production of *Bridges*.

TELL ME

(Bob Robinson, Tim Kelley/4'50)

Musicians: Beyoncé Knowles: vocals, backing vocals / **Kelly Rowland:** vocals, backing vocals / **LeToya Luckett:** backing vocals / **LaTavia Roberson:** backing vocals / **Anthony Papa Michael:** acoustic guitar / **Recording:** LaCoCo Studios, Atlanta: 1996 to 1998 / **Technical team:** Producers: Bob Robinson, Tim Kelley / **Executive producer:** Mathew Knowles / **Recording engineer:** John Frye

This was the first time the writers and composers Tim Kelley and Bob Robinson had worked with Destiny's Child. Known as Tim & Bob, the pair had started out working with the producer Dallas Austin, recording *Miss Thang*, the first album by the young performer Monica, then aged 12. The two artists had already offered songs to Destiny's Child when in 1993 Daryl Simmons signed the group to his company Silent Partner Productions. On learning they had just been signed by Columbia, Tim & Bob sent demos of their new songs to their contact at the record company, hoping they would catch the attention of Destiny's Child's entourage. The languorous *Tell Me* was chosen, and Beyoncé, LeToya, LaTavia, and Kelly immediately recorded it to feature on their first album.

BRIDGES

(Al Green, D'Wayne Wiggins, Michelle Hailey/4'03)

Musicians: Beyoncé Knowles: vocals, backing vocals / **Kelly Rowland:** vocals, backing vocals / **LeToya Luckett:** backing vocals / **LaTavia Roberson:** backing vocals / **D'Wayne Wiggins:** guitar, bass guitar, drums / **Carl Wheeler:** Fender Rhodes, synthesizers? / **Jay Lincoln:** Fender Rhodes, synthesizers? / **Vincent Lars:** saxophone / **Bill Ortiz:** trumpet / **Recording:** Live Oak Studios, Berkeley: 1996 to 1998 / House of Music, Oakland: 1996 to 1998 / **Technical team:** Producer: D'Wayne Wiggins / **Executive producer:** Mathew Knowles / **Recording engineer:** Dave Everingham

As he had done in *Second Nature*, producer D'Wayne Wiggins decided to use the instrumental part of a soul classic as the foundation for the song he was going to suggest to Destiny's Child. This time it was Al Green's *Simply Beautiful*, which the soul musician had recorded in 1971 for his fifth album, *I'm Still in Love with You*. Once again, this approach gave an undeniable cachet to the reinterpretation, which was enhanced by the powerful voices of the four young women, with Beyoncé Knowles leading the way. Wiggins himself played guitar, bass guitar, and drums in the piece, calling on the services of the saxophonist Vincent Lars and the trumpet player Bill Ortiz, who had accompanied Wiggins' group Tony! Toni! Toné! on their 1993–1995 tour, as a supporting act for Janet Jackson.

BEYONCÉ: ALL THE SONGS

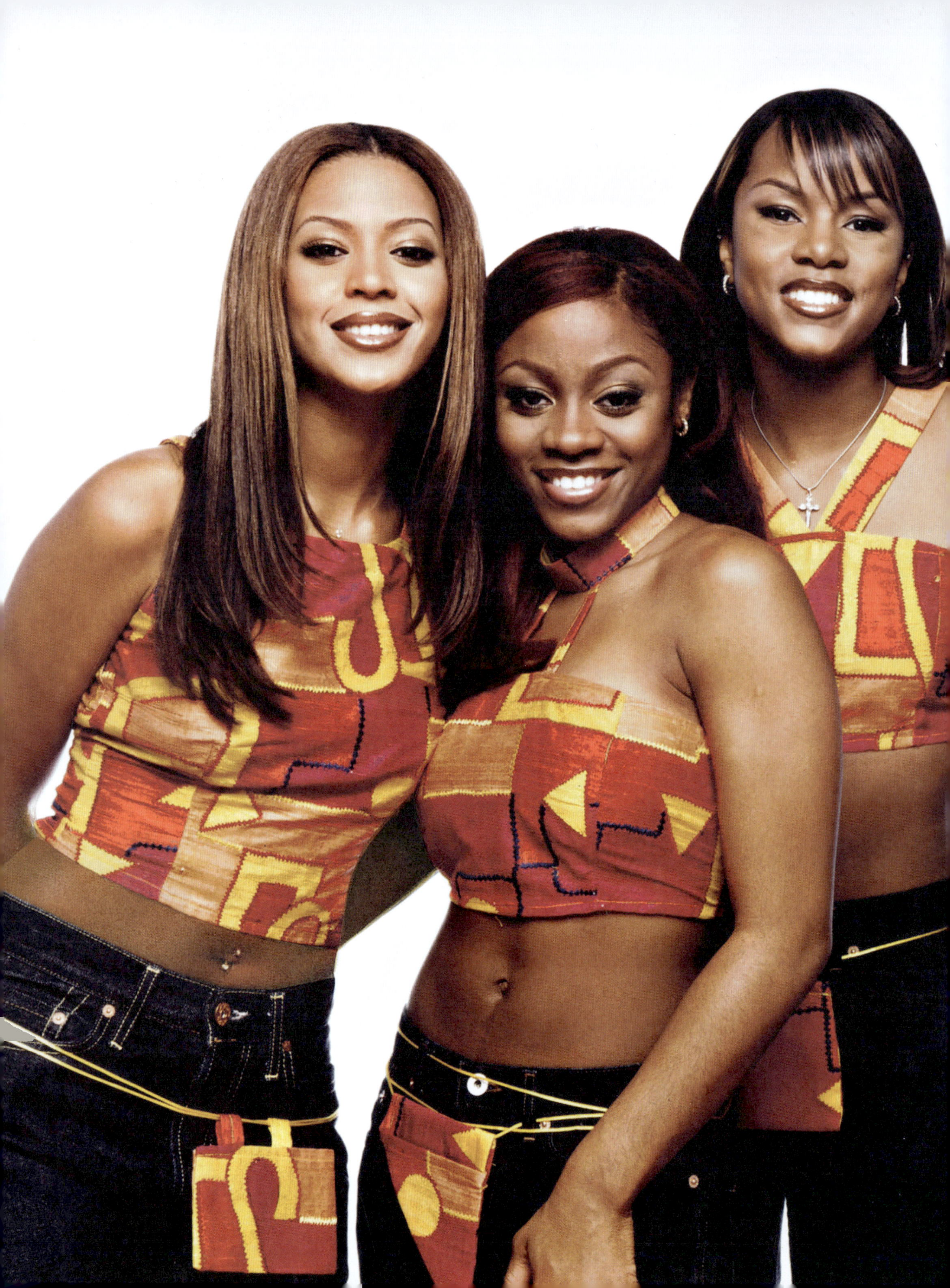

The Destiny's Child quartet in matching outfits, 1998.

NO, NO, NO PART 1

(Calvin Gaines, Mary Brown, Rob Fusari, Vincent Herbert/4'08)

Musicians: Beyoncé Knowles: vocals, backing vocals / **Kelly Rowland:** vocals, backing vocals / **LeToya Luckett:** backing vocals / **LaTavia Roberson:** backing vocals / **Recording:** Chung King Recording Studios, New York: 1996 to 1998 / **Technical team: Producers:** Rob Fusari, Vincent Herbert / **Executive producer:** Mathew Knowles / **Recording engineers:** Alex Olsson, Michael Roach / **Released in the USA by Sony Music/Columbia:** 27 October 1997 (ref.: 38K 78618) / **Best chart ranking in the USA:** 3

Before it shot to the top of the charts in October 1997, the song *No, No, No* had been created by a young producer no one had heard of before: Rob Fusari. Fusari, who worked on his demo recordings in the basement of his mother's house, formed a relationship with Vincent Herbert, a producer Teresa LaBarbera Whites had approached with a view to his working on Destiny's Child's first album. "One day he came to my mom's basement and I was working on the hook to *No, No, No*," Fusari recalled. "When I played it for him, he said, 'You've got to give me a copy of that. I'm working with this group who might be able to do that.' I gave him a cassette, and he calls me that night and says, 'We're cutting the record. And I've got a guarantee it will be their first single.'"[28] The song was subsequently reworked with Herbert and the writers Calvin Gaines and Mary Brown, before finally being re-recorded with the group in Manhattan. The two versions of *No, No, No* (*Parts 1* and *2*) were released in the same format and sent simultaneously to radio stations and MTV, two different clips having been shot for the occasion.

BEYONCÉ: ALL THE SONGS 41

Percy Robert Miller, aka Master P, one of the most prolific rappers of the 1990s.

WITH ME PART II
(FEATURING MASTER P)

(Beyoncé Knowles, Jermaine Dupri, Kelly Rowland, LaTavia Roberson, LeToya Luckett, Manuel Seal, Master P/4'14)

Musicians: Beyoncé Knowles: vocals, backing vocals / Kelly Rowland: vocals, backing vocals / LeToya Luckett: backing vocals / LaTavia Roberson: backing vocals / **Master P:** rap / **Recording:** ? / **Technical team:** Producers: Mean Green, Craig B, KLC, O'Dell / Executive producer: Mathew Knowles

As with *No, No, No*, the first song to be taken from the album, it was decided to release a song in two different forms as the group's second single. Initially produced by Jermaine Dupri and Manuel Seal, *With Me* was entrusted to the rapper Master P for him to come up with a reinterpretation, recording his voice in it in the process. "I gave them one of their first hit records," he said in 2013. "I'm definitely proud of them. To watch where she's at, it's amazing knowing that this was the same girl that was in my basement at my studio looking for records, and now she's able to reach her dreams."[29] "He was a very good person," said Destiny's Child's LeToya. "Everybody stereotypes him, saying he's this gangsta rapper...But he's not, he's a big teddy bear on the inside. He's a very sweet person, he's very professional. He's just a great person, a cool person, and someone who you can talk to."[30]

SHOW ME THE WAY

(Carl Breeding, Darcy Aldridge, Jeffrey Bowden/4'17)

Musicians: Beyoncé Knowles: vocals, backing vocals / Kelly Rowland: vocals, backing vocals / LeToya Luckett: backing vocals / LaTavia Roberson: backing vocals / Preston Crump: bass guitar / Carl Washington: additional instruments / **Recording:** Digital Services Recording Studios, Houston: 1996 to 1998 / Patchwerk Recording Studios, Atlanta: 1996 to 1998 / **Technical team:** Producer: Carl Washington / Executive producer: Mathew Knowles / Recording engineers: James Hoover, Mike Wilson / Arrangements: Darcy Aldridge

In *Show Me the Way*, a song totally rooted in the neo-soul wave of the late 1990s, producer Carl Washington evokes the synth-pop of Prince and the 1980s funk of Rick James and his girl band Mary Jane Girls. The song's rhythm and the placing of Beyoncé's voice evoke, in turn, the sensuality of Maxwell, the fine groove of Erykah Badu and Meshell Ndegeocello, and the heady melodies of the incomparable Brand New Heavies. Co-written by Carl Breeding, Jeffrey Bowden, and Darcy Aldridge, who had already worked together on albums for Jagged Edge, Kaycee, and Bobby Brown, the track is yet more proof that Mathew Knowles and Teresa LaBarbera Whites had a flair for surrounding themselves with the most influential hit-makers of the time.

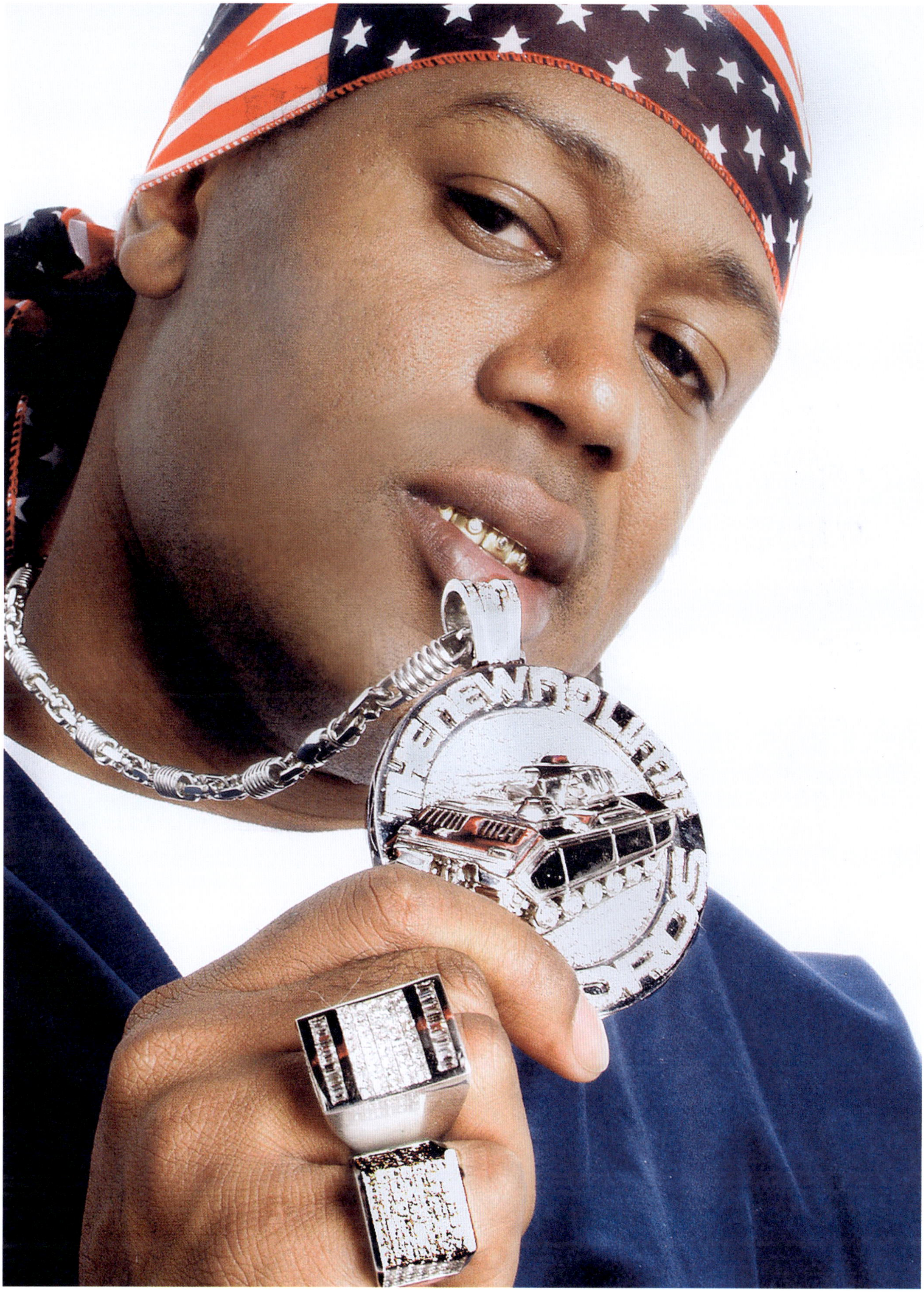

Before becoming a well-known producer, D'Wayne Wiggins (right) was a member of Tony! Toni! Toné! with his brother Charlie "Raphael Saadiq" Wiggins (center) and Timothy Christian Riley (left).

KILLING TIME

(D'Wayne Wiggins, Taura Stinson/5'07)

Musicians
Beyoncé Knowles: vocals, backing vocals
Kelly Rowland: vocals, backing vocals
LeToya Luckett: backing vocals
LaTavia Roberson: backing vocals
D'Wayne Wiggins: additional instruments
Lee Neal: percussion

Recording
House of Music, Oakland: 1996 to 1998
Pajama Studios, Oakland: 1996 to 1998

Technical team
Producer: D'Wayne Wiggins
Executive producer: Mathew Knowles
Recording engineers: Charles Brackins, Joey Swails
String arrangements: Benjamin Wright

Genesis

In 1997 a freshly made demo recording of *Killing Time* caught the attention of Randy Jackson, an artistic director at Columbia, and was due to be included on the soundtrack of a movie that was about to hit the cinemas: *Men in Black*, starring Will Smith and Tommy Lee Jones. The movie's international success in the summer of 1997 offered a welcome visibility to the four singers, whose renown continued to grow even before their first LP came out in February 1998. For her part, Beyoncé, now aged 17, learned a precious lesson in professionalism from working with the actor who played Agent J in the movie: "It can be hard sometimes, but I respect the fact that without fans, there'd be nothing. I learned that from Will Smith. We were just starting out and had a song on the *Men in Black* soundtrack. I met him at a publicity event for the film. I knew he was exhausted, but he looked at every person and said their names. He was so nice. I said to myself, 'that's the way I'm going to be'. I want to be as gracious as I possibly can be with my public, as my way of respecting their support and their love, because that's what it's all about."[32]

Production

Although it was never released as a single, *Killing Time* was nevertheless the very first song by Destiny's Child to reach the public. Taura Stinson, a member of the group Emage, who in 1993 wrote the hit *Gangsta Lean* for the Sacramento R&B trio DRS, co-wrote this song with caustic lyrics. Thanks to her fiancé, Alonzo Jackson (who had taken charge of production of the first demo recording by Girls Tyme in 1991, when the young singers had recorded at Arne Frager's Record Plant), Stinson, on arriving in New York, met the most influential artists of the time: A Tribe Called Quest, De La Soul, and Tony! Toni! Toné!, the new jack swing trio comprising Timothy Christian Riley, Raphael Saadiq, and D'Wayne Wiggins. It was during a meeting with Wiggins that their collaboration came about, as Stinson recalled in 2011. "We just came to a studio one day and he just had the guitar and it just came out. And the lyrics were totally different because I was actually writing about my ex boyfriend who was always high on weed. And so, the song was 'I'm waiting for you when you come back to reality.' So obviously we had to change some of the words once he actually put it on the group […]."[31]

FOR DESTINY'S CHILD ADDICTS

The promotion put in place by the inclusion of *Killing Time* on the soundtrack of *Men in Black* in the summer of 1997 stated that the group's first album, then in the process of production, would be named after a song on its track listing: *Bridges*. This was dropped a few months later in favor of the sober title *Destiny's Child*.

Wyclef Jean, Lauryn Hill, and Pras from the Fugees sold more than 22 million copies of their legendary 1996 album *The Score*.

ILLUSION
(FEATURING WYCLEF JEAN AND PRAS FROM REFUGEE CAMP)

(Ashley Ingram, Isaac Hayes, Leee John, Steve Jolley, Tony Swain/3'51)

Musicians
Beyoncé Knowles: vocals, backing vocals
Kelly Rowland: vocals, backing vocals
LeToya Luckett: backing vocals
LaTavia Roberson: rap, backing vocals
Wyclef Jean: rap
Pras: rap

Recording
?: 1996 to 1998

Technical team
Producers: Wyclef Jean, Jerry Duplessis, Pras
Executive producer: Mathew Knowles

Genesis
In order to grasp the impact that New Jersey trio Fugees had on popular culture with the release of their second album, *The Score*, in 1996, we should not see the record as another rap hit, but rather consider the unprecedented international triumph of a group that championed this musical aesthetic. Vocalist Lauryn Hill and rappers Wyclef Jean and Pras sold more than 22 million copies of this album, which was adored by an entire generation. Lauryn Hill went on to pursue a triumphant (but too short) career with the release of her only solo studio album, *The Miseducation of Lauryn Hill*, in 1998, while in the same year Pras also tried his luck with the album *Ghetto Supastar* and the single of the same name. For his part, Wyclef Jean became, alongside his personal discography, a producer known for his work with Whitney Houston (*My Love Is Your Love*, in 1998), Santana (*Maria Maria*, in 1999), and Mya (*Pussycats*, in 2000). It is therefore a crack team that features on *Illusion*, for the two men from Fugees are both producers and also rap with energy and elegance. To create the track, they delved into their record library and composed its structure based on several songs.

Production
First of all Beyoncé uses the melodic line of *Just an Illusion*, released by the British band Imagination in 1982, for her vocal line. On the instrumental side there is a sample from *Hung Up on my Baby* by Isaac Hayes, but also a line borrowed from *Mind Playing Tricks on Me*, by the Texas hip-hop group Geto Boys. Once envisaged as the third single from the *Destiny's Child* album, *Illusion* was eventually released in a promotional format, Columbia having decided to start production of the group's second album as soon as possible. At their label's request, the singers re-recorded their vocal parts for the version of the song remixed by Maurice Joshua, entitled *Illusion (Maurice's Radio Mix)*, which would set clubs dancing all over the world. This reinterpretation features a nod to another disco classic, *Best of My Love* by The Emotions. "It's not that we didn't love *Illusion*, but we were minors and it's the executives who make the decisions," said LaTavia Roberson, who had a rare vocal lead on the track. "The label wanted us to move on and create more age-appropriate music."[15]

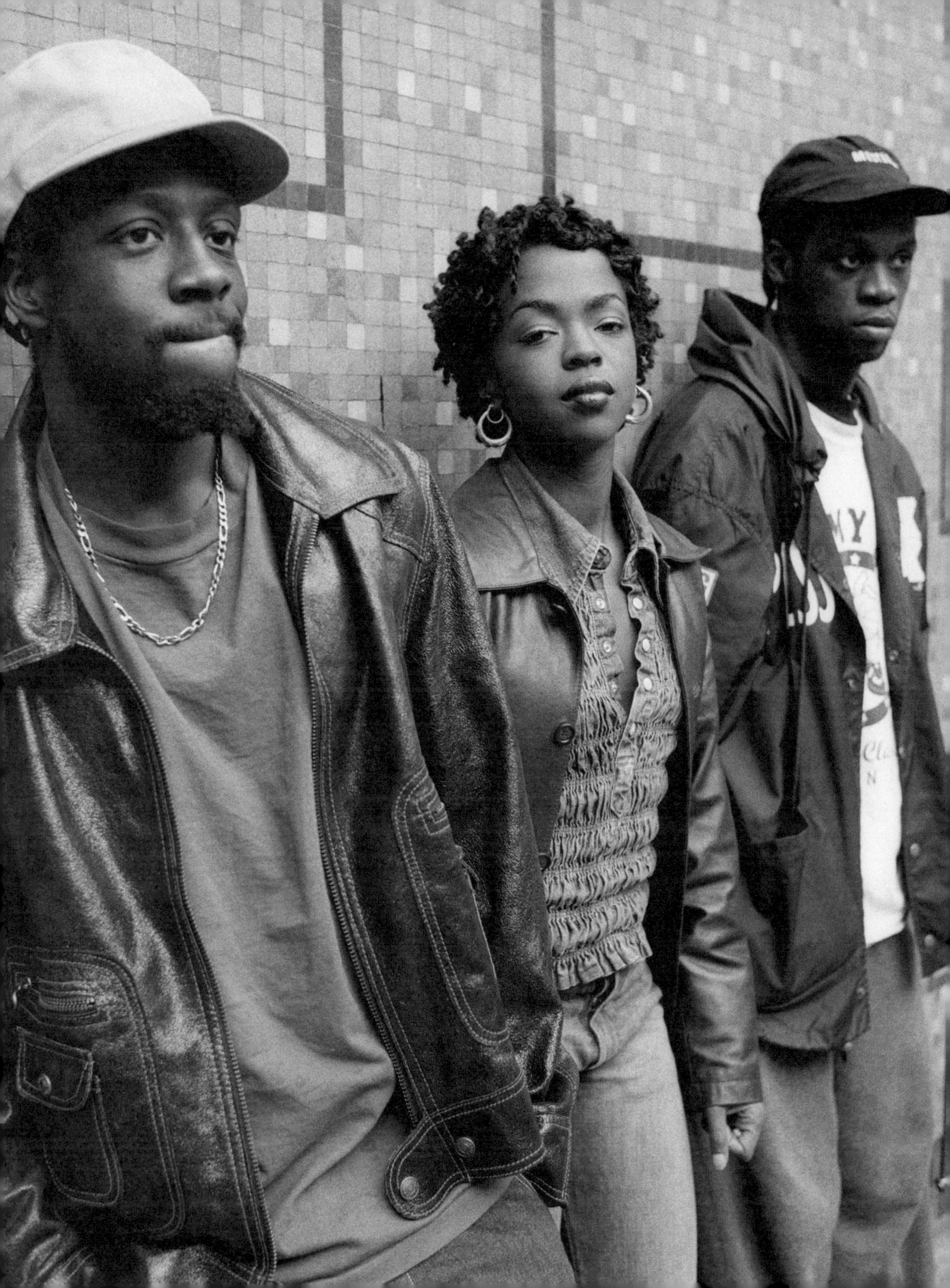

Kelly, Beyoncé, LeToya, and LaTavia in 1998.

The Commodores and their famous singer Lionel Richie in 1978.

BIRTHDAY

(Beyoncé Knowles, D'Wayne Wiggins, Kelly Rowland, LaTavia Roberson/5'13)

Musicians: Beyoncé Knowles: vocals, backing vocals / Kelly Rowland: vocals, backing vocals / LeToya Luckett: backing vocals / LaTavia Roberson: backing vocals / John "Jubu" Smith: guitar / Jay Lincoln: synthesizers / D'Wayne Wiggins: bass guitar, drums, synthesizers / **Recording:** Live Oak Studios, Berkeley: 1996 to 1998 / **Technical team:** Producer: D'Wayne Wiggins / Executive producer: Mathew Knowles / Recording engineer: Dave Everingham / String arrangements: Benjamin Wright

Who has never dreamed of closing their eyes on their birthday and hearing Beyoncé sing to them that all their wishes will come true? That is the fantasy that producer D'Wayne Wiggins created with *Birthday*, where sensuality is prominent, even though the singers were still very young to be singing about love. "I've heard a lot of people say that it might have been maybe before our time," LaTavia Roberson explained. "It was sensual, but we just suggested sensual things. But at that age, you start to think about certain things, per se. We were young girls that were coming into our own. We were young girls that were starting to experience things."[27]

SAIL ON

(Lionel Richie/4'04)

Musicians: Beyoncé Knowles: vocals, backing vocals / Kelly Rowland: vocals, backing vocals / LeToya Luckett: backing vocals / LaTavia Roberson: backing vocals / Kenny Demery: guitar / Cory Rooney: programming / **Recording:** The Hit Factory, New York: 1996 to 1998 / **Technical team:** Producers: Cory Rooney, Mark Morales / Executive producer: Mathew Knowles / Recording engineer: Ian Dalsemer

Cory Rooney and Mark Morales, producers of *Sail On*, were well known to lovers of R&B, having composed and produced *Real Love*, the single that propelled Mary J. Blige to the forefront of the hip-hop scene in 1992. Here, the inseparable hit-makers offered a reinterpretation of a 1970s soul standard: *Sail On* by Lionel Richie's group the Commodores, released in 1979 on the album *Midnight Magic*. The nod is emphasized, and the homage appreciated, but the numerous references to soul music's culture struggle to convince the listener that the young singers had managed to absorb their influences so as to produce a truly innovative piece of work. Momentum is lost here at the end of the album, and the hits *No, No, No Part 2* and *With Me Part II* already seem to be buried deep in the listener's memory. It is a safe bet that this was also the view of Columbia, who wasted no time in sending Destiny's Child to record new songs for their new album, which would prove to be a milestone in the history of pop music.

MY TIME HAS COME
(DEDICATED TO ANDRETTA TILLMAN)

(Reed Vertelney, Sylvia Bennett-Smith/4'23)

Musicians: Beyoncé Knowles: vocals, backing vocals / **Kelly Rowland:** vocals, backing vocals / **LeToya Luckett:** backing vocals / **LaTavia Roberson:** backing vocals / **Steve Forman:** percussion / **David Frank:** piano / **Recording:** Digital Services Recording Studios, Houston: 1996 to 1998 / **Castle Oak Studios, Calabasas:** 1996 to 1998 / **Manhattan Ave. Studios, Topanga:** 1996 to 1998 / **Technical team:** Producer: Sylvia Bennett-Smith / **Executive producer:** Mathew Knowles / **Recording engineers:** Eric Fischer, James Hoover, Mike Arnold, Paul Arnold

Although Destiny's Child enjoyed resounding success right from their first album, their path to glory was fraught with pitfalls—some harder to overcome than others. One of these was the loss of Andretta Tillman, their first manager, whose sudden death left a permanent mark on the young artists. A former employee of Houston Lighting and Power, Tillman had devoted herself to Destiny's Child's development, and—along with Denise Seals and Deborah LaDay of D&D Management—was one of the first to support them. After initiating the transformation of Girls Tyme into Destiny's Child in partnership with Mathew Knowles, Tillman was forced to entrust the group to him when illness prevented her from pursuing her career as a talent-spotter. Suffering from systemic lupus erythematosus, Andretta Tillman passed away on 16 May 1997, while her protégées were still recording their first album. Like Darlette Johnson, Tillman was a pivotal figure in the career of Beyoncé Knowles, and this last track on the album is dedicated to her. In addition, this was the first time the group had worked with the composer Sylvia Bennett-Smith, who also co-wrote the songs *Forever Starts Today* and *I Try*, which were recorded during the same period but remain unreleased.

Rapper Silkk the Shocker invited Destiny's Child to sing on his single *Just Be Straight With Me* in 1998.

SINGLE

CAN'T STOP
(LIL' O FEATURING DESTINY'S CHILD)

(Beyoncé Knowles, Carl Gladstone McIntosh, Derek Edwards, Jane Eugene, Oreoluwa Magnus-Lawson, Steve Orlando Nichol/3'49)

Musicians: Oreoluwa Magnus "Lil' O" Lawson: rap / Beyoncé Knowles: vocals, backing vocals / Kelly Rowland: backing vocals / LeToya Luckett: backing vocals / LaTavia Roberson: backing vocals / **Recording:** ? / **Technical team:** Producer: Derek "Grizz" Edwards / Executive producers: Bilal Allah, Mathew Knowles / *Can't Stop* (single) / Released in the USA by MCA Records: 1997 (ref.: MCADS-55356) / **Best chart ranking in the USA:** did not make the charts

Although the first song Destiny's Child released was *Killing Time*, included on the soundtrack of *Men in Black*, which was in cinemas during the summer of 1997, this collaboration with the rapper Lil' O was the first commercially available track featuring the young singers' voices. Recorded over a sample from *Hangin' on a String (Contemplating)*, released by the British group Loose Ends in 1985, *Can't Stop* was the first single by Lil' O, a young rapper of Nigerian descent who had been raised in Houston and whom Mathew Knowles discovered when he was launching his management company. Knowles quickly secured a contract for his protégé with MCA Records, at the time the world's biggest hip-hop label, whose catalog included such artists as New Edition, Mary J. Blige, and Jodeci. This amateur businessman, whose intuition was matched only by his commitment to his daughter's career, suggested to MCA that the single include backing vocals by Destiny's Child (who were still known as Cliché at the time), and—why not?—that they make an appearance in the clip. When *Can't Stop* was finally released, in 1997, Destiny's Child had already been signed by Columbia, and their career had taken off.

JUST BE STRAIGHT WITH ME
(SILKK THE SHOCKER FEATURING MASTER P, DESTINY'S CHILD, O'DELL, MO B. DICK)

(Silkk the Shocker, Master P, Destiny's Child, O'Dell, Mo B. Dick/4'21)

Musicians: Silkk the Shocker: rap / Master P: rap / O'Dell: rap / Mo B. Dick: rap / Beyoncé Knowles: vocals, backing vocals / Kelly Rowland: backing vocals / LeToya Luckett: backing vocals / LaTavia Roberson: backing vocals / **Recording:** ?: 1997 / **Technical team:** Producer: Craig B / Executive producer: Master P / Silkk the Shocker *Charge It 2 Da Game* (album) / Released in the USA by No Limit Records/Priority Records: 17 February 1998 (album ref.: P1 50716, CD ref.: P2 50716) / **Best chart ranking in the USA:** 57

Destiny's Child worked with numerous other artists before the release of their first album. Here, it is the rapper Silkk the Shocker who calls on the young women's services: in this new jack swing number they sing the choruses, which are largely inspired by those in *Just Be Good to Me* by S.O.S. Band, released in 1983 and produced by the inevitable Jimmy Jam and Terry Lewis (who were fired by Prince from his band The Time because of their work on the S.O.S. Band album—at the time Prince did not tolerate musical disloyalty). Although there is no mention of this minor borrowing on the sleeve of the single, it featured on the album *Charge It 2 Da Game*, which was a colossal success on its release, reaching number 3 on the *Billboard* 200 and the top spot on Top R&B/Hip-Hop Albums, thus drawing attention to Destiny's Child, who were decidedly omnipresent.

COLLABORATIONS

ONCE A FOOL
(DESTINY'S CHILD AND WILLIAM FLOYD)

(The Characters, Shamello/Buddah Epitome, William Floyd, Beyoncé/3'18)

Musicians: Beyoncé Knowles: vocals, backing vocals / **Kelly Rowland:** vocals, backing vocals / **LeToya Luckett:** vocals, backing vocals / **LaTavia Roberson:** vocals, backing vocals / **William Floyd:** rap / **Recording:** ?: 1998 / **Technical team: Producers:** Shamello/Buddah Epitome / **eMusic Presents NFL Jams (compilation)** / **Released in the USA by eMusic:** 29 September 1998 (CD ref.: 15095-3724-2)

A former American football star with the San Francisco 49ers, William "Bar None" Floyd had recently joined the Carolina Panthers in Charlotte when he worked with Destiny's Child in 1998. It must be said this was a substantial undertaking, for the project, initiated by eMusic, an avant-garde online music store launched in 1998, aimed to bring together R&B stars and famous American football players on a single compilation. Foxy Brown and Andre Rison, Boyz II Men and Garrison Hearst, and Faith Evans and Jeff Blake were all combinations capable of entrancing fans of both sport and pop. On the first track on the record there is even a certain Michael Jackson. But listeners should not be deceived. This is not the King of Pop slumming it with sports stars: it is Michael Dywane Jackson Dyson, former wide receiver with the Cleveland Browns and subsequently with the Baltimore Ravens. The members of Destiny's Child, always ready to lend their crystal-clear voices to an artistically worthwhile song, shared with William Floyd this track that is not without interest, and was perfectly in keeping with the R&B fashion of the time.

Timothy Mosley, aka Timbaland, a producer with a stellar discography, was one of the heavy hitters behind the rise of Destiny's Child.

GET ON THE BUS
(FEATURING TIMBALAND)

(Missy Elliott, Timbaland/4'46)

Musicians: Beyoncé Knowles: vocals, backing vocals / **Kelly Rowland:** vocals, backing vocals / **LeToya Luckett:** vocals, backing vocals / **LaTavia Roberson:** vocals, backing vocals / **Timbaland:** rap / **Recording:** Manhattan Center Studios, New York: 1998 / **Technical team:** Producers: Missy Elliott, Timbaland / **Recording engineer:** Senator Jimmy D / **Assistant recording engineer:** Todd Wachsmuth / **Why Do Fools Fall in Love: Music from and Inspired by the Motion Picture (compilation)** / Released in the USA by EastWest/Elektra Records/Goldmine Inc.: 8 September 1998 (CD ref.: 62265-2)

On 28 August 1998 American cinemas screened the new film by Gregory Nava, *Why Do Fools Fall in Love*, which told the story of the singer Frankie Lymon and his group, Frankie Lymon and The Teenagers. The renowned artist, who died from a heroin overdose at the age of 25, is played by Larenz Tate. Very quickly, two different soundtrack albums were made. While the first of these, *Why Do Fools Fall in Love: Original Versions from the Movie*, features the songs from the film, most of them drawn from the repertoire of North American music (it includes Little Richard, The Platters, and Otis Redding), the second, entitled *Why Do Fools Fall in Love: Music from and Inspired by the Motion Picture*, contains many songs that were merely inspired by the movie but didn't feature in it. This practice, much in vogue in the late 1990s and early 2000s, is in fact a ploy by record companies wishing to draw attention to their young stars and fill their coffers in the process. Numerous compilations of this kind packed the record shops, thus supporting the promotion of the films in question (for example, in no particular order, *Blade* in 1998, *M:I-2* in 2000, *8 Mile* and *Spider-Man* in 2002, and *School of Rock/Rock Academy* in 2003), and for the most part featuring unreleased songs by very popular artists. For their participation in *Why Do Fools Fall in Love: Music from and Inspired by the Motion Picture*, Destiny's Child called on the services of two influential and respected individuals: the rapper Missy Elliott and the producer Timbaland. Beyoncé's flow is fast and precise, and the track's instrumental element is hard-hitting. Unquestionably, what we are seeing is akin to an ugly duckling turning into a swan—or rather a very well-behaved young singer who had not assimilated her musical influences turning into a star of urban music with an immaculate, incisive style. For all these reasons, *Get on the Bus* is on several counts the song that bridged the gap between the timid *Destiny's Child* and the grandiose *The Writing's on the Wall*. The track also features as a bonus on the "international edition" of the latter, released in 1999.

SHE'S GONE
(MATTHEW MARSDEN FEATURING DESTINY'S CHILD)

(Daryl Hall, John Oates/3'50)

Musicians: Matthew Marsden: vocals / **Beyoncé Knowles:** backing vocals / **Kelly Rowland:** backing vocals / **LeToya Luckett:** backing vocals / **LaTavia Roberson:** spoken voice, backing vocals / **Stephen Dante:** backing vocals / **Recording:** Nomis Studios, London: 1998 / **Technical team:** Producers: Neville Henry, Karen Gibbs / **Executive producer:** John Williams / **Recording engineer:** Jim Lowe / **Assistant recording engineer:** Pete Frith / **Matthew Marsden *Say Who* (album)** / Released in the UK by Columbia/Viper Records: 26 October 1998 (CD ref.: 492529 2)

Does anyone today remember the MiniDisc format—that small audio disc launched by Sony in the early 1990s, which struggled to find favor with consumers despite its undeniable advantages over CDs that jumped in a Discman or cassettes that often became demagnetized? Perhaps Matthew Marsden—whose first album, *Say Who*, was released in Europe only in this unloved format—does. In the United Kingdom, on the other hand, where Marsden had been a star ever since appearing in the enormously popular television series *Coronation Street*, he enjoyed a launch to great fanfare in CD format, achieving considerable success in 1998. Columbia Records, which had just signed Destiny's Child, but also this young actor with a view to giving him a future career as a singer (a sweet baby face and resounding success will never fail to appeal to a record company), had the idea of bringing together its new recruits to boost the sales of both. Although it was a fine thought—above all from a financial point of view—it did not manage to save this feeble cover version of the single by Daryl Hall and John Oates which Atlantic had released in 1973. For Destiny's Child, however, the publicity was welcome, and introduced the group to the United Kingdom, where success awaited them.

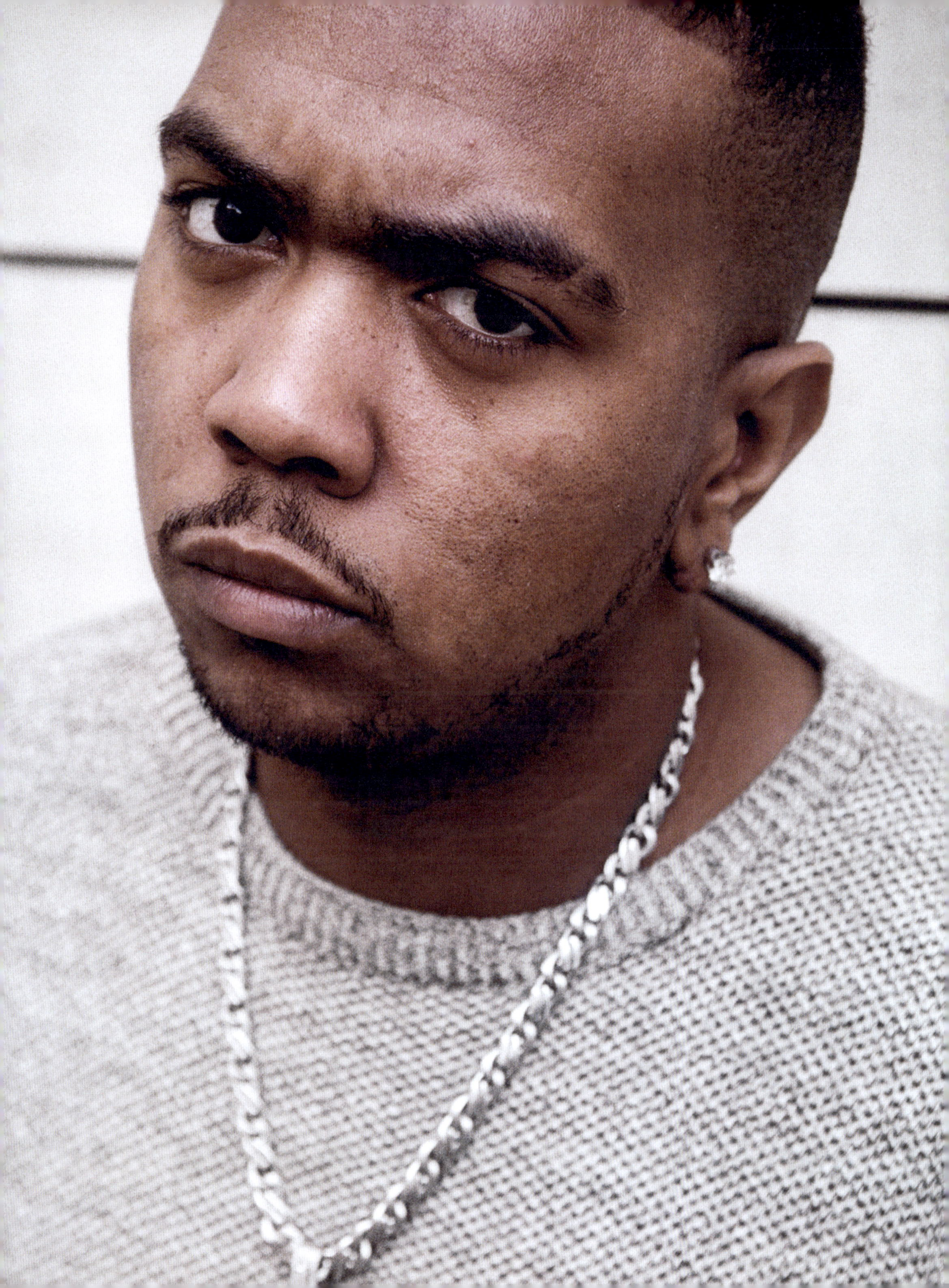

Wise Intelligent, Culture Freedom, and Father Shaheed from the group Poor Righteous Teachers in the streets of New York, 1990.

KNOW THAT

(Andre Robinson, Rachel Oden/4'27)

Musicians: Beyoncé Knowles: vocals, backing vocals / **Kelly Rowland:** vocals, backing vocals / **LeToya Luckett:** backing vocals / **LaTavia Roberson:** backing vocals / **Tim Shider:** synthesizers, bass guitar / **Recording:** Platinum Island Studio, New York: 1996 to 1998 / Digital Services Recording Studios, Houston: 1996 to 1998 / **Technical team:** Producer: Father Shaheed / **Executive producer:** Mathew Knowles / **Vocal arrangements:** Cha'n André / **Japanese edition of *Destiny's Child* (album)** / Released in Japan by Sony Records: 1 March 1998 (CD ref.: SRCS 8504)

With its introductory motif borrowed from Suzanne Vega's *Tom's Diner*, *Know That* is the result of Destiny's Child's collaboration with the producer Father Shaheed, DJ with the legendary New Jersey hip-hop group Poor Righteous Teachers. The song, which proudly proclaims the new jack swing that was in vogue at the start of the 1990s, also contains the quartet's neo-soul influences, especially thanks to the vocal arrangements by Cha'n André, who had previously worked on productions by Paula Abdul and Kaycee. It is a devilishly groovy song, in which the intrinsic sensuality of Destiny's Child is given full expression. In 1998, you had to travel to Japan and buy the Japanese edition of the album to be able to enjoy this bonus track.

YOU'RE THE ONLY ONE

(D'Wayne Wiggins, Taura Stinson/3'23)

Musicians: Beyoncé Knowles: vocals, backing vocals / **Kelly Rowland:** vocals, backing vocals / **LeToya Luckett:** backing vocals / **LaTavia Roberson:** backing vocals / **Recording:** ?: 1996 to 1998 / **Technical team:** Producers: Calvin Gaines, Mark Wilson, Vincent Herbert, Rob Fusari / **Executive producer:** Mathew Knowles / **European re-release of *Destiny's Child* (album)** / Released in Europe by Columbia: 3 September 2001 (ref.: COL 488535 9)

It is a shame that this extraordinarily groovy song was not included on the standard edition of *Destiny's Child*, but only on the album's European version. The funk guitar is reminiscent of *Lovely Jane* by Dag (1994), a burst of pop-funk unleashed on the world at a time when young people still listened to rock music. The straight rhythm put in place by the producers Calvin Gaines, Mark Wilson, Vincent Herbert, and Rob Fusari, accompanied by the aforementioned guitar, also recalls the instrumental tracks of the soundtrack to the video game Interstate '76, released by Activision in 1997, played by the session group Bullmark and born of the collaboration between the producers, Jason Slater and Kelly W. Rogers, and the video game developer.

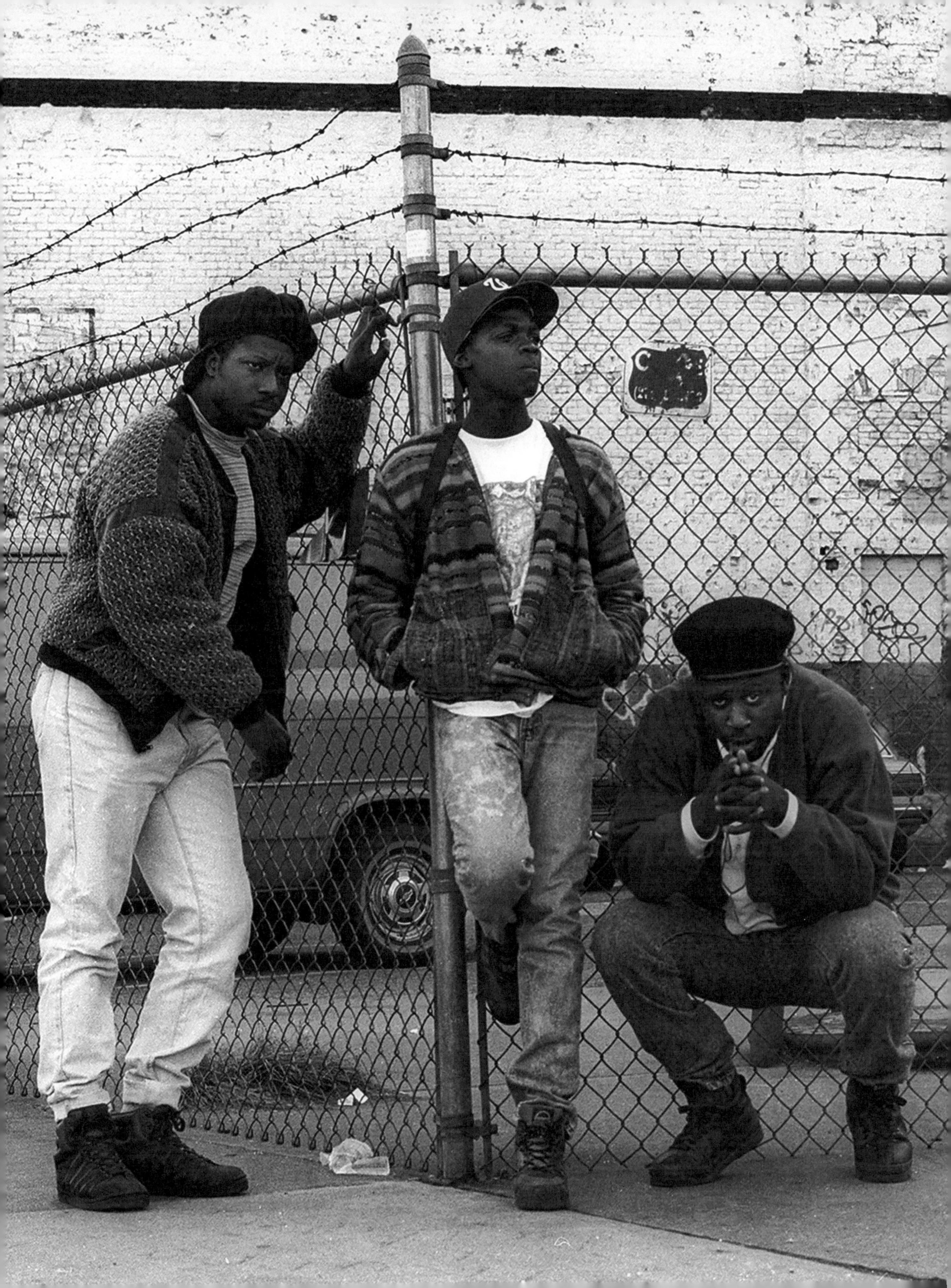

DESTINY'S CHILD

ALBUM

The Writing's On The Wall

Intro (The Writing's On The Wall) • So Good • Bills, Bills, Bills • Confessions •
Bug a Boo • Temptation • Now That She's Gone • Where'd You Go • Hey Ladies •
If You Leave • Jumpin', Jumpin' • Say My Name • She Can't Love You • Stay • Sweet Sixteen •
Outro (Amazing Grace…Dedicated to Andretta Tillman)

Released in the USA by Sony Music/Columbia: 14 July 1999 (album ref.: C2 69870, CD ref.: CK 69870)
Best chart ranking in the USA: 5

Destiny's Child 1999 version, more glamorous than ever.

THE CORONATION ALBUM

The commercial success of *Destiny's Child* encouraged Columbia to launch production of the group's second album. To that end, Teresa LaBarbera Whites went to the moon and back for her protégées, calling in the crème de la crème of songwriters, composers, and producers, all of whom were more than happy to write for the four promising artists. Among these top choices was one of the greatest American talents of the time, hit-maker Rodney "Darkchild" Jerkins, whose successes everyone was talking about. After turning Brandy & Monica into global superstars with the duet *The Boy Is Mine* in 1998, the studio wizard continued his ascent with the classic Whitney Houston number *It's Not Right But It's Okay* the same year. LaShawn Daniels—Jerkins' partner in this takeover of radio stations the world over following the success of *The Boy Is Mine*—was also brought in, as were Kevin "She'kspere" Briggs and his wife Kandi Burruss, the successful duo behind TLC's triumphant international hit *No Scrubs*, released on 2 February 1999. Rapper Missy Elliott and Chad "Dr. Ceuss" Elliott rounded off the team, joining regulars Darryl Simmons and D'Wayne Wiggins and newcomer Jovonn Alexander. Once this mind-blowing list had been approved by the record company's teams, Destiny's Child were finally ready to hit the recording studios.

Beyoncé in charge
As the album got underway, Beyoncé Knowles assumed the mantle of team leader, as well as co-composer, co-writer, and co-producer for most of the songs. "The label didn't really believe we were pop stars," she explained in 2016. "They underestimated us, and because of that, they allowed us to write our own songs and write our own video treatments. It ended up being the best thing, because that's when I became an artist and took control. It wasn't a conscious thing. It was because we had a vision for ourselves and nobody really cared to ask us what our vision was. So we created it on our own, and once it was successful, I realized that we had the power to create whatever vision we wanted for ourselves."[33] The four artists wanted to choose the themes for their songs, and got together very early on in the writing process to discuss the issues they would tackle in their lyrics. "It was really like waiting to exhale writing the songs," Beyoncé said later. "We all got together and just talked about how it is being in a relationship."[34] "When you listen to our album, every woman and every man will love it because it talks about real relationship issues," Kelly Rowland continued. "It deals with the side of love that people tend to run away from, like if a relationship is going to work out or if it isn't."[34]

Once the instrumentals were in the bag, the singers wrote during recording sessions with no prior preparation, inspired as never before by their own love affairs. The songs that emerged were modern and highly effective, clearly different from the neo-soul feel of the first album, and won them devoted audiences who loved the sensual, very danceable R&B that quickly invaded the airwaves.

1998–1999: the R&B wave comes crashing in
While they prepared this second album, Destiny's Child had plenty of inspiration but were also aware of the fierce competition they faced. In addition to the hits that made R&B popular from 1998 onwards, a succession of cult albums

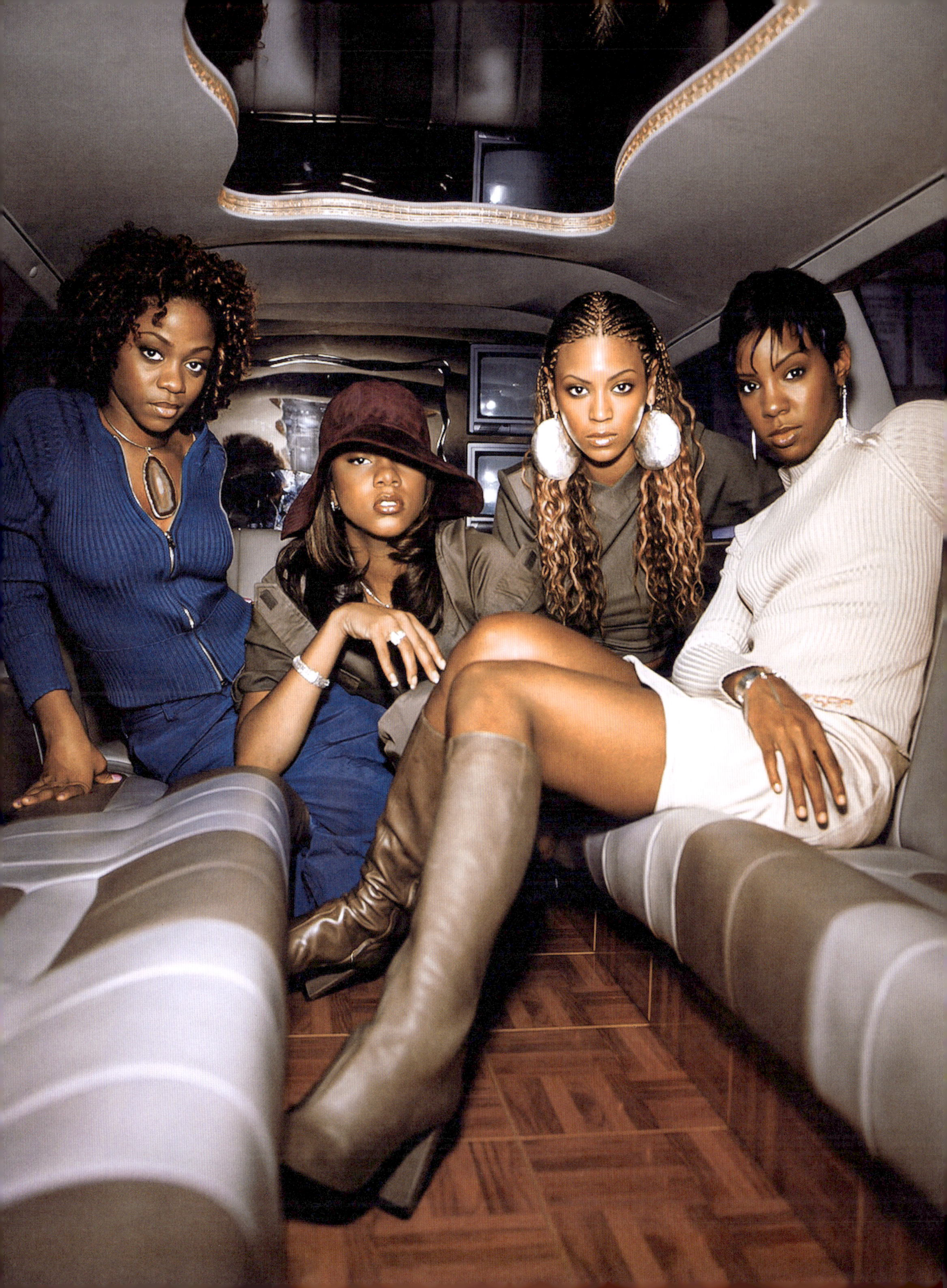

Beyoncé with her famous braids, which she wore again in 2016 on the cover for *Lemonade*.

Christina Aguilera became one of the stars of the R&B era with her 1999 hit *Genie in a Bottle*.

turned the late '90s into a golden age for this genre. The list of major albums produced between 1997 and 1999 is enough to make your head spin, but it's worth mentioning a few to show the sheer scale of the challenge our four Texans were facing: Janet Jackson's *The Velvet Rope*, Whitney Houston's *My Love Is Your Love*, Monica's *The Boy Is Mine*, Brandy's *Never Say Never*, Xscape's *Traces of My Lipstick*, TLC's *Fanmail*, Kelis's *Kaleidoscope*, Mariah Carey's *Rainbow*, Jennifer Lopez's *On the 6*, along with Christina Aguilera's first LP and 702's second album, were just some of the records the public could get their hands on and which all proved hugely successful thanks to their many timeless hits. Unperturbed by the competition, Destiny's Child carried on recording their album, whose title evokes the fighting spirit and serenity they felt as they geared up for the success that lay ahead of them. "Actually, *The Writing's on the Wall* is a cliché which means that something big is about to happen," explained LeToya Luckett in 1999. "And you can tell that in every song something big is about to happen in a relationship [...]. And also we hope that this album does well and it is a big turnout for us, so that's basically where the title came from."[35]

When the album was released on 14 July 1999, the four singers were not disappointed. Carried by the singles *Bills, Bills, Bills* and *Bug a Boo*, which were followed by the international hit *Say My Name*, the album met with a triumphant reception, hitting the Top 10 in the charts in Australia, Canada, New Zealand, Norway, the United Kingdom, and of course the United States, where it reached number five, and over the years went on to sell more than seven million copies. In 1999, Destiny's Child, hitherto young hopefuls on the soul music scene, joined the ranks of international superstars.

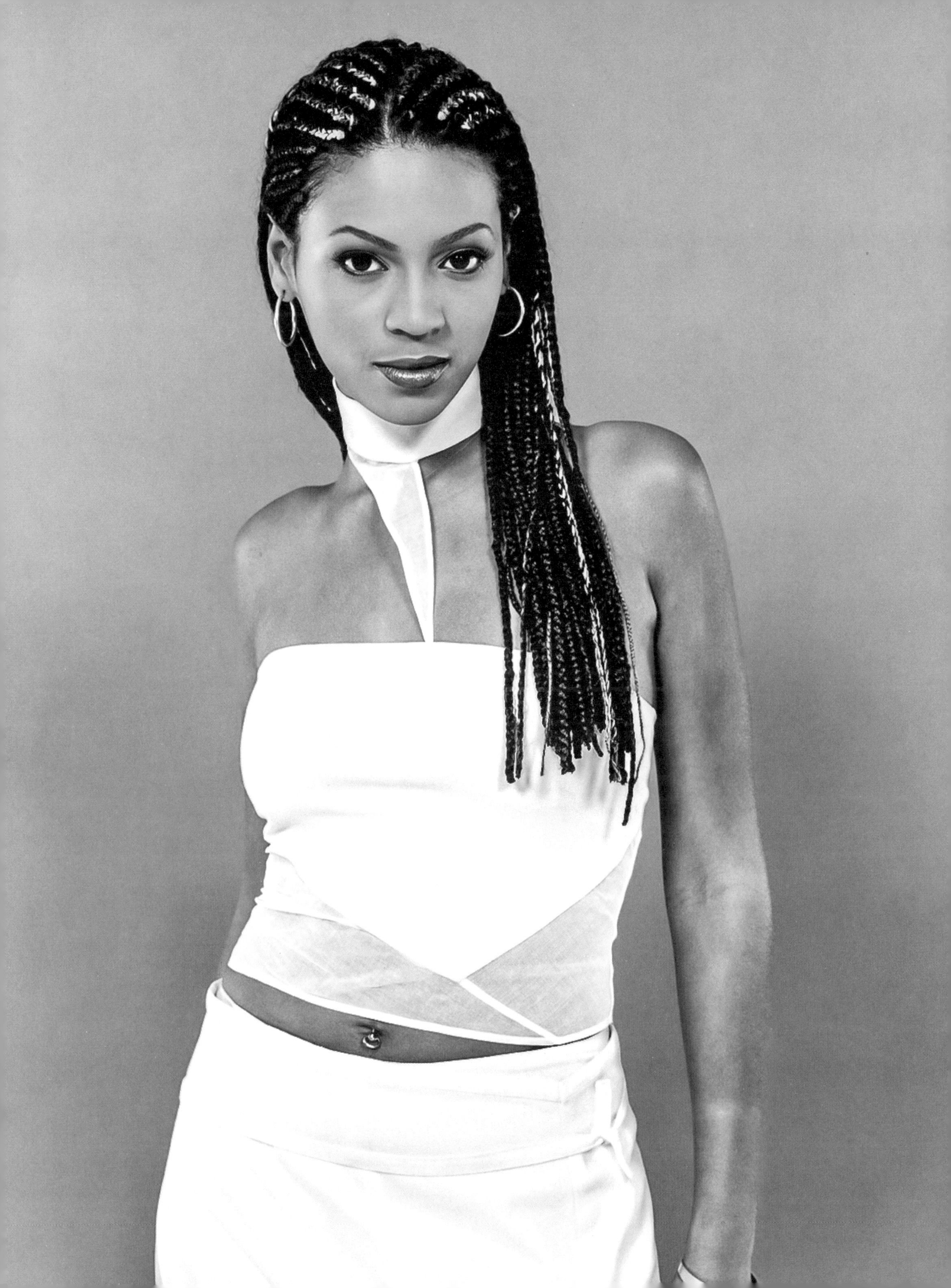

Michelle Williams, Beyoncé Knowles, Kelly Rowland, and Farrah Franklin, the final version of the Destiny's Child quartet.

Two clans within Destiny's Child

The dream that the young women were living would, however, be clouded by emerging tensions within the group. From the start of the tour—during which they opened for TLC from October to December 1999—two groups of two formed within the team. While Beyoncé and Kelly were fully committed to their careers, LeToya and LaTavia appeared to want to break free of the rules imposed by their manager, Mathew Knowles. On 15 December, they sent two letters through a Dallas lawyer, Randy Bowman, informing Knowles that they wanted to end their contract with him and hire their own manager while keeping their places in the band. This episode, which Knowles took very badly, added to the tensions that had arisen during the tour. LeToya and LaTavia had started dating respectively Brandon and Brian Casey, the twin brothers from the band Jagged Edge, who were present on some of the tour dates, and the two women were criticized for focusing more on their relationships than on their work. LeToya and LaTavia also started questioning the way profits were shared among the group, to the point that relations went from being close and full of warmth to being extremely frosty. "In interviews we couldn't say we were unhappy," Beyoncé explained in 2001, "because we didn't want to let our fans down, because they're our number one priority. So we agreed to act like everything was okay, even though it wasn't. They lost focus. They didn't want to do interviews, rehearse, or take voice lessons. Anybody that met us could see that me and Kelly were one group and they were another. It was obvious."[36] Following the episode of the lawyer's letters sent to Mathew Knowles, it was decided to part company with LeToya and LaTavia and find replacements for them as quickly as possible, especially as filming of the music video for *Say My Name* was scheduled for a few weeks later.

Enter Michelle Williams and Farrah Franklin

A helping hand from fate put Michelle Williams in Beyoncé Knowles's and Kelly Rowland's path in early 2000. The three singers had first met on 3 August 1999 at the Arco Arena in Sacramento. Michelle, who was a backing singer for Monica at the time, had enjoyed Destiny's Child's opening act and chatted to the band members at the sound checks a few hours earlier. In January the following year, Junella Segura, Destiny's Child's choreographer, who had also worked for Monica, suggested Michelle's name to Beyoncé and Kelly. A meeting was quickly arranged, during which the chemistry was instant: "When she walked into our living room, Kelly and I were sitting next to each other on the couch, and we just looked at each other. We were thinking the same thing: she's the one! We could tell instantly. Michelle has a real presence, and we could feel it even though she was standing in front of my coffee table and not on stage."[20]

With filming of the *Say My Name* video fast approaching, a second recruit was needed to reconstruct Destiny's Child. Kelly Rowland suggested auditioning Farrah Franklin, a young Los Angeles singer she had met almost a year earlier when shooting the *Bills, Bills, Bills* video, in which Franklin had played a customer in the hair salon used as the backdrop. The audition was a success. Michelle Williams and Farrah Franklin officially joined the band in February 2000 and managed to prepare their roles in the video in record time, brilliantly

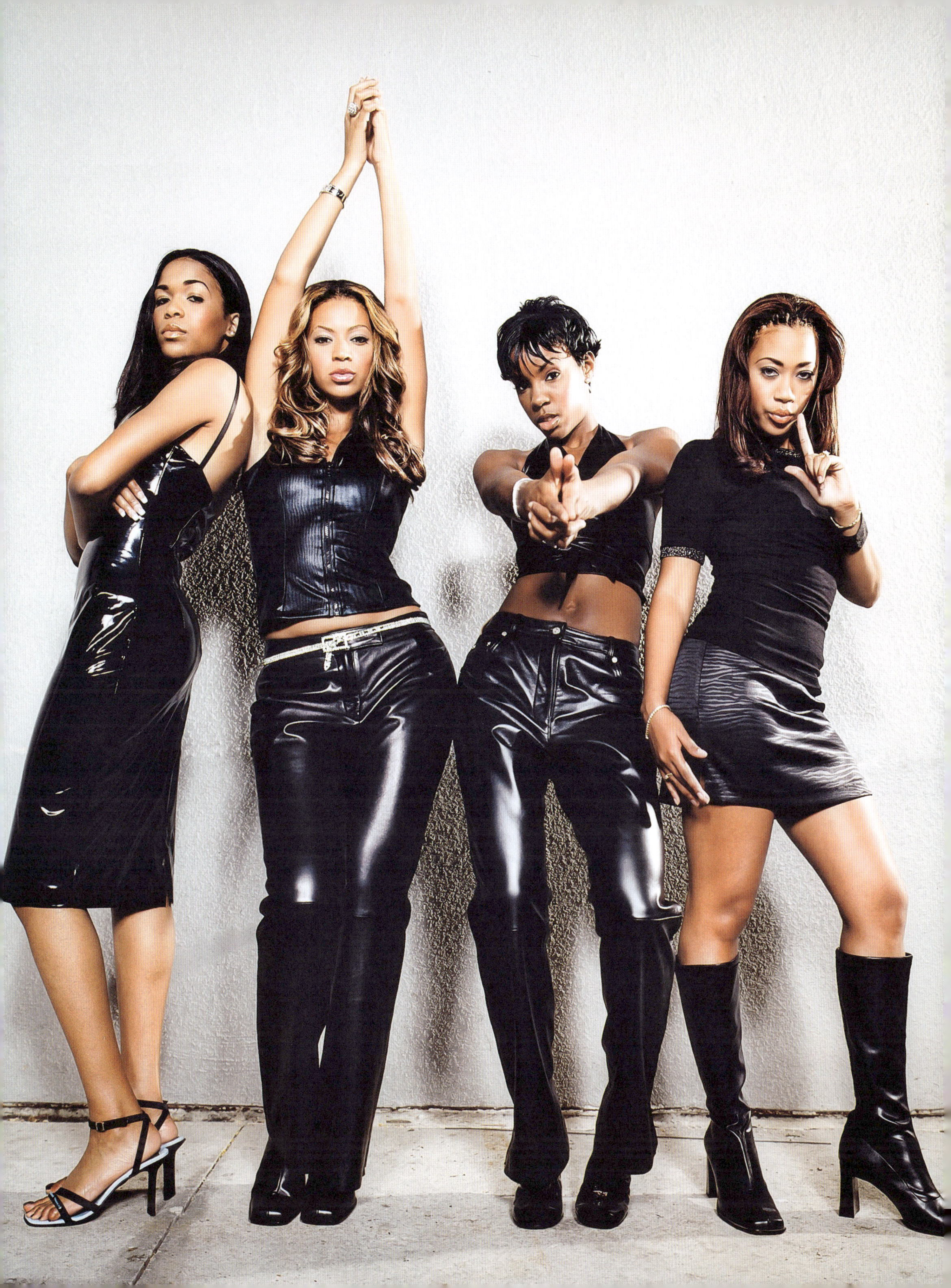

Michelle, Beyoncé, and Kelly with their manager and mentor Mathew Knowles.

FOR DESTINY'S CHILD ADDICTS

In February 1999, Beyoncé's fans could catch a glimpse of her as an extra in the video for *Happily Ever After*, the single from *Personal Conversation*, the singer Case's second album.

> In 1999, as Destiny's Child were on the brink of success, Mathew Knowles was already envisaging the day when the band members would have their own individual careers. "It is something that will happen, without question," he said at the time. "We've never made a secret of that being a goal. It's natural evolution for a group wherein you're dealing with strong vocalists."[37]

replacing LeToya Luckett and LaTavia Roberson. "They were consummate pros," said Mathew Knowles. "It had to be frightening, but they just rolled with it and did an amazing job."[37] "It was truly a tense time," added Stephanie Gayle, then director of marketing at Columbia. "We had worked so hard to get to this moment in time. There was so much at stake and so much riding on the shoulders of these young women. We at Columbia will always be impressed with how well they handled the transition."[37]

Destiny's Child in its final form

The calmness and serenity in Destiny's Child didn't last long because very soon Farrah Franklin began to rebel, notably against Mathew and Tina Knowles's demands that she undergo UV tanning sessions and dye her hair red, like LaTavia Roberson in the *Bills, Bills, Bills* video. While Michelle Williams had obvious chemistry with the rest of the band, the role of bad guy fell to Farrah, who also resented the idea of being just a backing singer behind Beyoncé. "She didn't fit in," Beyoncé would later say, "and everybody saw that—from people who didn't know us, to the people at the record label, to the fans. She is not a bad person; we just didn't click, and that's all."[20]

A series of setbacks sealed Farrah's fate in the band a few months after her arrival. First off, in spring 2000, she refused to travel from Los Angeles to Houston for an interview with MTV. She eventually relented, but this was not the case in July, when she did not travel to Seattle, where Destiny's Child were due to appear in a promotional show broadcast live online. Finally, on the 14th of that month, she refused to fly to Australia for two sold-out concerts. "That was such a huge thing for us," Mathew Knowles later explained. "It took us nine years to get on MTV. We'd worked so hard to get to that point. Whatever your problems, can't you hold off until you get back to the hotel? It showed how she'd only been in this for five months. That's what happens when you give somebody that kind of success in two weeks and they don't have to work for it."[38] But, against all the odds, the two Australian concerts in which Destiny's Child performed as a trio were so successful that they started to see their future in a new light. The chemistry between the three of them was unmistakable and Farrah's absence had allowed Michelle to occupy more space on stage and show off her vocal talents. They unanimously decided to wipe the slate clean and stop worrying about a fourth vocalist: Destiny's Child rose from the ashes as a trio.

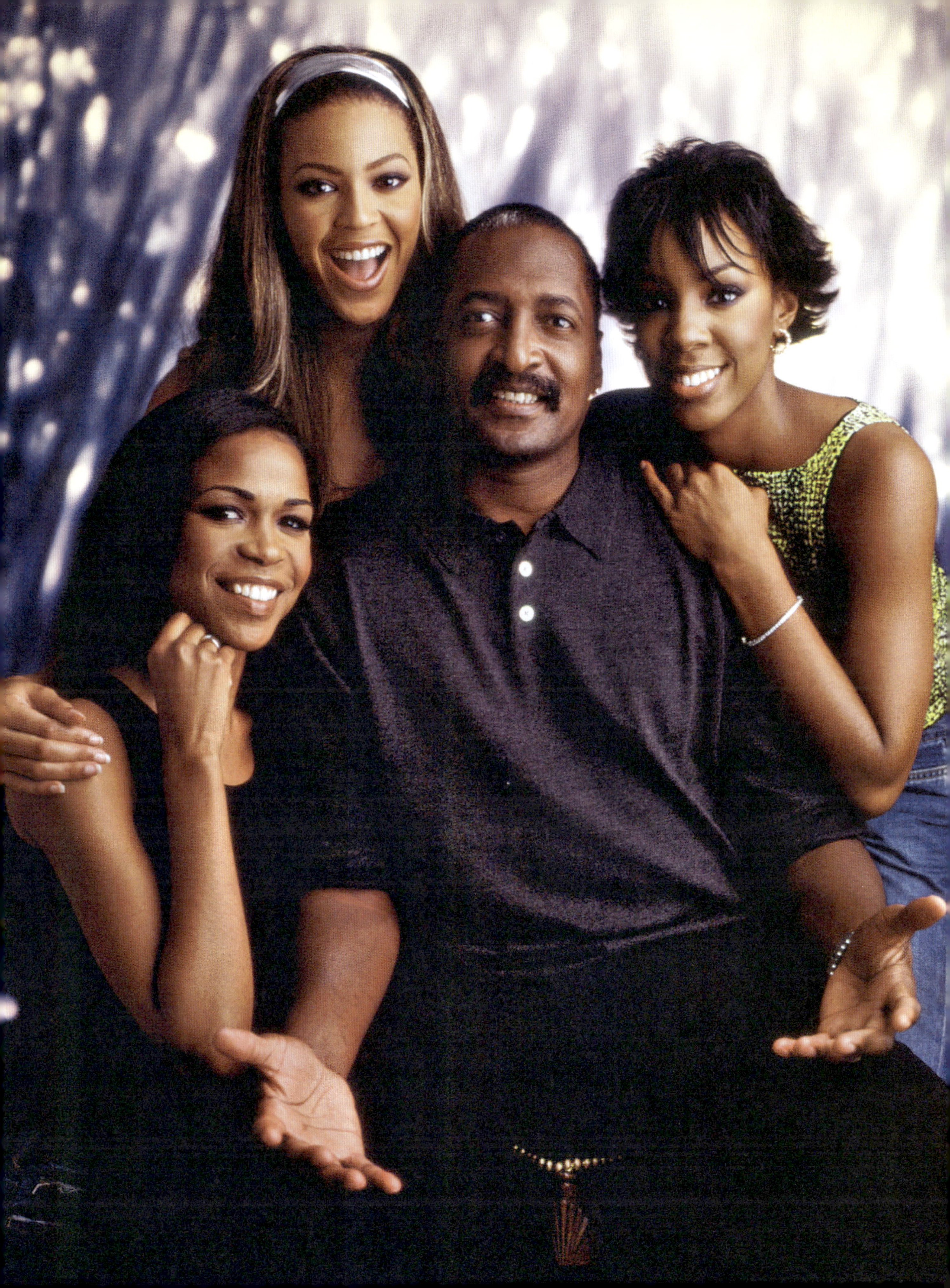

The deeply religious Michelle Williams became a permanent member of Destiny's Child.

MICHELLE WILLIAMS, FROM CHURCH PEWS TO *BILLBOARD*

Tenitra Michelle Williams was born in Rockford, Illinois, on 23 July 1979, to devout parents who introduced her to the Christian faith from an early age. She first demonstrated her singing talents at the age of seven in the St Paul Church of God in Christ, where she gave a brilliant rendition of an American gospel classic, *Blessed Assurance*, written by Fanny Jane Crosby and Phoebe Palmer Knapp in 1873. Inspired by the repertoires of Yolanda Adams, Kirk Franklin, Commissioned, The Clark Sisters, Hezekiah Walker, and Marvin Winans, young Michelle soon joined two groups in her parish: United Harmony and Chosen Expression, in which she stood out for her vocal performances and confidence on stage. Although talented, she chose to follow a standard educational path and didn't plan to pursue a career as a performer. "I was really doing it for fun," she said in 2004. "I was at college and wanted to be an attorney. I come from a family of high achievers, doctors, nurses, so it was important to get a good education."[39]

Despite this lofty goal, something happened that would change her plans. "A friend of mine who I hadn't talked to in years was playing for Monica. [...] 'So what are you doing?' I told him, 'Nothing. But if Monica needs a background vocal, give me a call!' I was just playing around but he called me a week later and said she was having auditions in Atlanta and to get there. I got there and I auditioned and got the part."[40]

It was when Michelle Williams was on the road with the singer of *The First Night* and *Angel of Mine* that she met Beyoncé Knowles and Kelly Rowland, who in January 2000 asked her to join Destiny's Child. Alongside her role in the successful trio, Michelle would also return to her first love, releasing four solo albums, the first two of which, the gospel-style *Heart to Yours* in 2002 and *Do You Know* in 2004, were a hit with the Christian community in the United States. "Some people will do gospel when their career fails," the singer observed, "but I chose to do it at the height of the popularity of Destiny's Child. And, I didn't want to do it because it was a fad. I wanted to do it because it's in me. It's in my heart."[41]

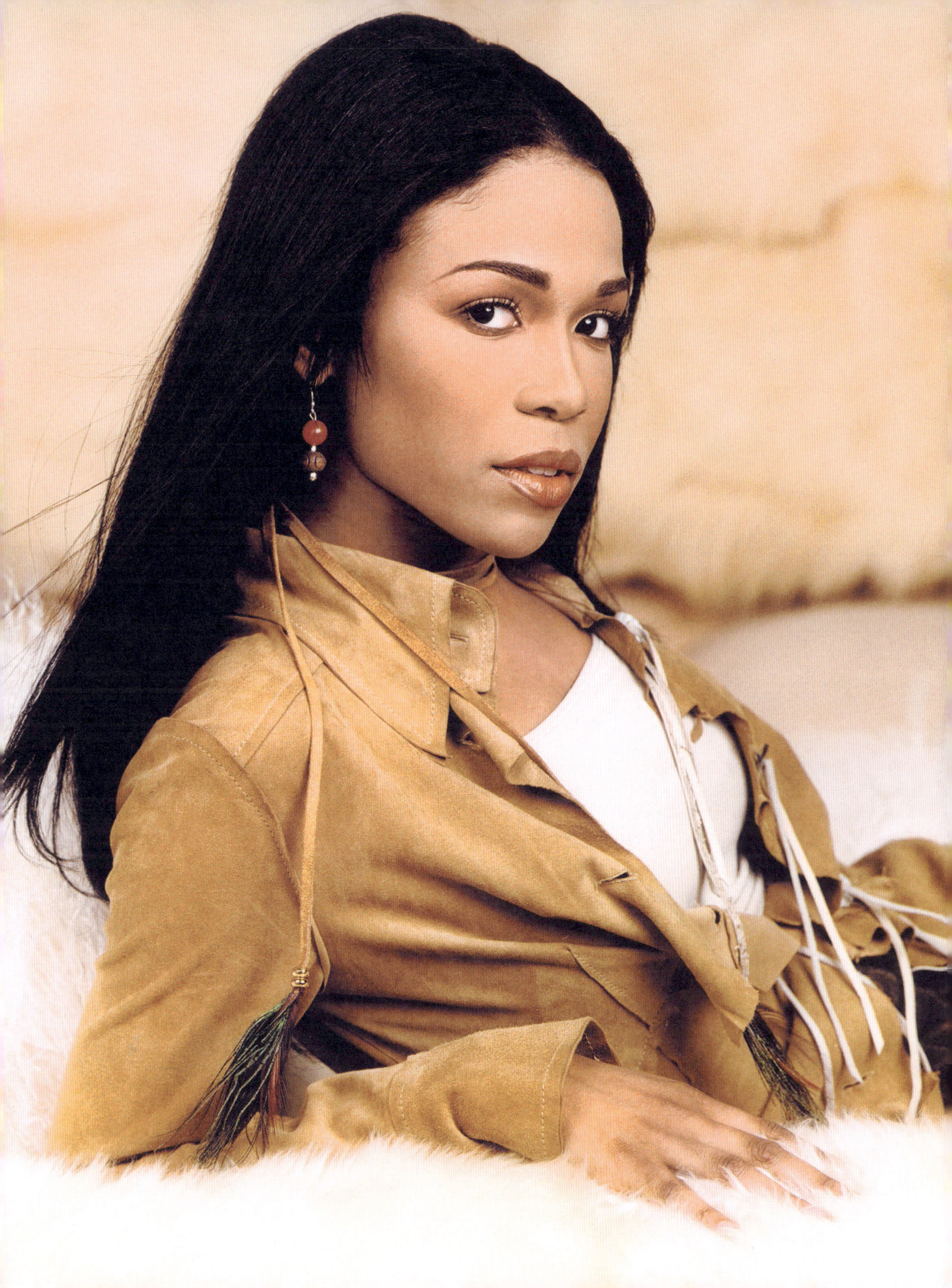

LaTavia Roberson, Kelly Rowland, Beyoncé Knowles, and LeToya Luckett in London at the launch of Maxwell's album *Embrya*.

INTRO (THE WRITING'S ON THE WALL)

(Beyoncé Knowles, Kelly Rowland, LeToya Luckett, LaTavia Roberson/2'05)

Musicians: Beyoncé Knowles: vocals, backing vocals / Kelly Rowland: vocals, backing vocals / LeToya Luckett: backing vocals / LaTavia Roberson: backing vocals / Anthony Hardy: additional instruments / Donald Holmes: additional instruments / Gerard Thomas: additional instruments / **Recording:** Digital Services Recording Studios, Houston: October 1998 to April 1999 / **Technical team: Producers:** Beyoncé Knowles, Anthony Hardy, Donald Holmes, Gerard Thomas / **Executive producers:** Mathew Knowles, Kevin "She'kspere" Briggs / **Recording engineer:** Michael Calderon

Destiny's Child introduced their new album with a touch of humor, a story about an Italian family reunion worthy of a scene from the Francis Ford Coppola trilogy *The Godfather*. With rather shaky Sicilian accents, the singers—re-named LeToya Barzini, Kelly Steracki, Beyoncé Corleone, and LaTavia Menser for the occasion—sing about four families coming together to sign a mutual non-aggression pact in a parable of the sisterly bonds that appeared to unite the four young women. While this narrative is somewhat disconcerting on first listen, it was even more so when the album was released, as LaTavia and LeToya had disembarked the Destiny's Child ship without having had a chance to enjoy the album's phenomenal success.

> Beyoncé seems to have a particular fondness for the world of *The Godfather*, as in 2020 she filmed some sequences for her movie *Black Is King* in the sumptuous Beverly Hills property that was used for Francis Ford Coppola's film. In 2017, she sang *Family Feud* with Jay-Z, in which the rapper appears as a mafia boss on a par with Vito Corleone.

SO GOOD

(Beyoncé Knowles, Kandi Burruss, Kelly Rowland, Kevin Briggs, LaTavia Roberson, LeToya Luckett/3'13)

Musicians: Beyoncé Knowles: vocals, backing vocals / Kelly Rowland: vocals, backing vocals / LeToya Luckett: backing vocals / LaTavia Roberson: backing vocals / Kevin "She'kspere" Briggs: additional instruments / **Recording:** SugarHill Recording Studios, Houston: October 1998 to April 1999 / Triangle Sound, Atlanta: October 1998 to April 1999 / **Technical team: Producer:** Kevin "She'kspere" Briggs / **Executive producer:** Mathew Knowles / **Recording engineers:** Dan Workman, Kevin "She'kspere" Briggs

It is with a hint of bitterness towards those who had failed to encourage her that Beyoncé sings the lyrics to *So Good*, an R&B diatribe in which she settles scores with all kinds of hypocrites who had crossed her path since her group hit the top of the *Billboard* charts. "Everybody in life has that, and that's things you have to go through in life," she said to journalists at the time, "and I know that's why we wrote the song *So Good*, which is on the album, [...] whose lyrics are saying, 'Don't smile in my face now because I know about, back in the days before I was in Destiny's Child how you'd said we will never make it, how you'd said I was all that, how you'd said all that negative people say about you, and now that you're successful and they're in your face and they want to be "Hey hey hey!", "Oh girl, you're my best friend", "You're my cousin".' It's just saying that by the grace of God, I'm doing good."[42]

While the many producers and composers on *The Writing's on the Wall* were acclaimed for the quality of their work, the one who really worked the magic was the brilliant Dan Workman, recording engineer on *So Good* and *Bug a Boo*. Workman, who owned SugarHill Recording Studios in Houston and would be back on 2001's *Survivor*, then 2003's *Dangerously in Love*, remembers meeting Beyoncé when she came with her father Mathew to scout SugarHill for the *Writing's on the Wall* sessions. "This is a real vocalist," he told J. Randy Taraborrelli, author of the biography *Becoming Beyoncé: The Untold Story*. "You could tell she knew her way around a studio. The way she intuitively used the microphone and asked for feedback showed a level of professionalism far beyond her years...While it felt a little weird having this teenager drive the session, she was so good I was blown away by the whole thing."[43]

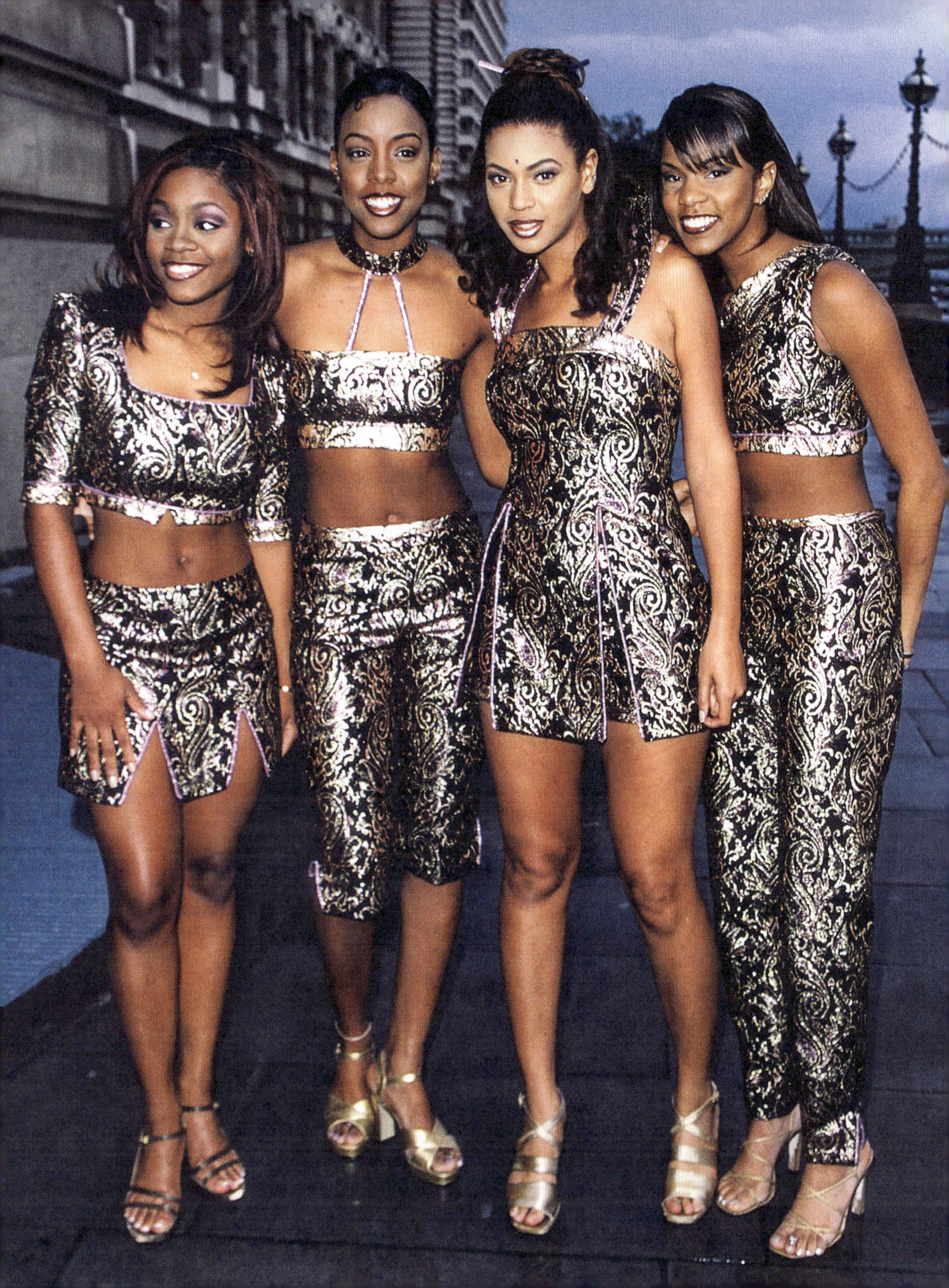

Kandi Burruss, Tameka Cottle, LaTocha Scott, and Tamika Scott from the group Xscape, 1993.

SINGLE

BILLS, BILLS, BILLS

(Beyoncé Knowles, Kandi Burruss, Kelly Rowland, Kevin Briggs, LeToya Luckett/4'16)

Musicians
Beyoncé Knowles: vocals, backing vocals
Kelly Rowland: vocals, backing vocals
LeToya Luckett: backing vocals
LaTavia Roberson: backing vocals
Kevin "She'kspere" Briggs: additional instruments

Recording
Digital Services Recording Studios, Houston: October 1998 to April 1999
DARP Studios, Atlanta: October 1998 to April 1999

Technical team
Producers: Beyoncé Knowles, Kevin "She'kspere" Briggs
Executive producers: Mathew Knowles, Kevin "She'kspere" Briggs
Recording engineers: Kevin "She'kspere" Briggs, Michael Calderon, Vernon Mungo
Assistant recording engineer: Claudine Pontier

Single
Released in the USA by Sony Music/Columbia: 31 May 1999 (CD single ref.: 38K 79175)
Best chart ranking in the USA: 1

Genesis

When Teresa LaBarbera Whites invited Kevin "She'kspere" Briggs and Kandi Burruss, one of the singers with Xscape, to come and work for Destiny's Child, she could never have imagined the impact it would have on the careers of her four protégées. The year was 1998 and the duo (the former a producer and the latter a songwriter and composer) had just penned TLC's future hit *No Scrubs*, a virulent, feminist anthem about men who didn't take care of their girlfriends. But the song hadn't yet been released when the two artists (who also happened to be a couple) got down to work. Inspiration therefore came naturally rather than being influenced by the subsequent colossal success of TLC's single. Just after meeting up with Mathew Knowles to discuss a possible collaboration, Burruss and Briggs were in a Texan supermarket, which is where they first got the idea for *Bills, Bills, Bills*. "He started beatboxing it to me," said Burruss of Briggs. "He actually started thinking of the hook and singing, 'Can you pay my bills? Can you pay my automo' bills?' I was like, 'I like that.'"[44] Although Burruss was inspired by the theme, she was bothered by the image that such lyrics might conjure up. "We don't want them to seem like they're just gold digger-type of girls," she told him, "so why don't we put the story behind it in the verse?"[44] She took her inspiration from a previous relationship she'd had—with Brandon Casey, one of the singers in the group Jagged Edge, who was then dating none other than LaTavia Roberson. "The part that was a clear inspiration—using my phone and pretending like he didn't use it, driving my car and not putting any gas in it—that was real stuff that had happened to me!"[45] Burruss said. Brandon Casey, who had already inspired the lyrics of *No Scrubs*, would once again be hauled over the coals in *Bills, Bills, Bills* without anyone telling LaTavia that the song referred to her boyfriend.

Production

Beyoncé's flow has the same feel as that of *No, No, No Part 2*, recorded with Wyclef Jean for the group's first album. "Destiny's Child was the first group to do that fast 'rapping singing,'" Michelle Williams explained in 2001. "Now everybody and their momma is doing it. Other female groups' style and image are like ours. That's fine. It just means that people are watching."[46] To complete the song's lyrics, which were largely inspired by Kandi Burruss's own story, the Destiny's Child singers added their own experiences to the tale. "When I got with the girls at the studio, we were singing them the idea," Burruss confirmed. "I had the melody of how I felt like the verse should go, and we came together for the lyrics."[47]

Kandi Burruss's feminist salvo would attract some comments directed at Destiny's Child from certain men who didn't appreciate the themes. After *Bills, Bills, Bills* came out, the rap band Sporty Thievz quickly released the thunderous *(Why, Why, Why) No Billz*, in response. When the Texan girls were asked about the vitriol this expressed, they replied innocently: "If you're all in a relationship it needs to be a fifty-fifty thing but we're old-fashioned and like on the first date it's nice if the guy pays for the movie that one time, but later on we don't mind paying for anything."[35]

BEYONCÉ: ALL THE SONGS   71

The inimitable rap artist and producer Missy Elliott, who became one of Beyoncé's frequent collaborators.

CONFESSIONS
(FEATURING MISSY ELLIOTT)

(Donald Holmes, Gerard Thomas, Missy Elliott/4'57)

Musicians
Beyoncé Knowles: vocals, backing vocals
Kelly Rowland: vocals, backing vocals
LeToya Luckett: backing vocals
LaTavia Roberson: backing vocals
Missy Elliott: rap

Recording
The Hit Factory, New York: October 1998 to April 1999
The Enterprise, Burbank: October 1998 to April 1999

Technical team
Producers: Missy Elliott, Lenny Holmes, Gerard Thomas
Executive producer: Mathew Knowles
Recording engineers: Brian Springer, Jimmy Douglass

Genesis

On 5 April 1999, the group 702 released one of that year's biggest hits, *Where My Girls At?* Behind this R&B anthem (yet another one!) was rapper Missy Elliott. Songwriter, composer, and producer, Elliott is a leading figure in women's rap who has always called for equal power-sharing between men and women (remember 1999's corrosive *She's a Bitch* and 2001's *One Minute Man*). She has written for the biggest artists in American hip-hop and R&B, including Ginuwine, Aaliyah, Mariah Carey, Lil' Kim, Total, Mya, and Whitney Houston. Asked to collaborate with Destiny's Child, she gave the four singers a track called *Confessions*, written in her highly recognizable style. In the song, Beyoncé confesses to her boyfriend that she's been unfaithful and tells her story complete with juicy details.

Production

Missy Elliott was the standard-bearer of a new type of hip-hop in which female artists finally found their space and were sometimes as sexist as male rappers. Here she brilliantly attempts to push Destiny's Child into the same playing field, encouraging them to sing this tasty morsel in which the man and not the woman is the victim of infidelity. "They all had something special," Missy said in 2018 of the four singers. "And Beyoncé, she knew exactly how to attack a record. When I heard Bey singing the verses, I was like, 'Oh they gonna go far.' And it's funny when I think back on it because you rarely get women having to confess. It's always the guy who ends up having to confess. That was a different kind of twist for a female to be like, 'Look, I basically kicked it with Mike when you was gone, this went down and that went down.'"[48] The coming together of Beyoncé and Missy Elliott undoubtedly bore fruit, to the extent that Beyoncé's lyrics would become barbed on the albums *Survivor* and *Dangerously in Love*.

1999

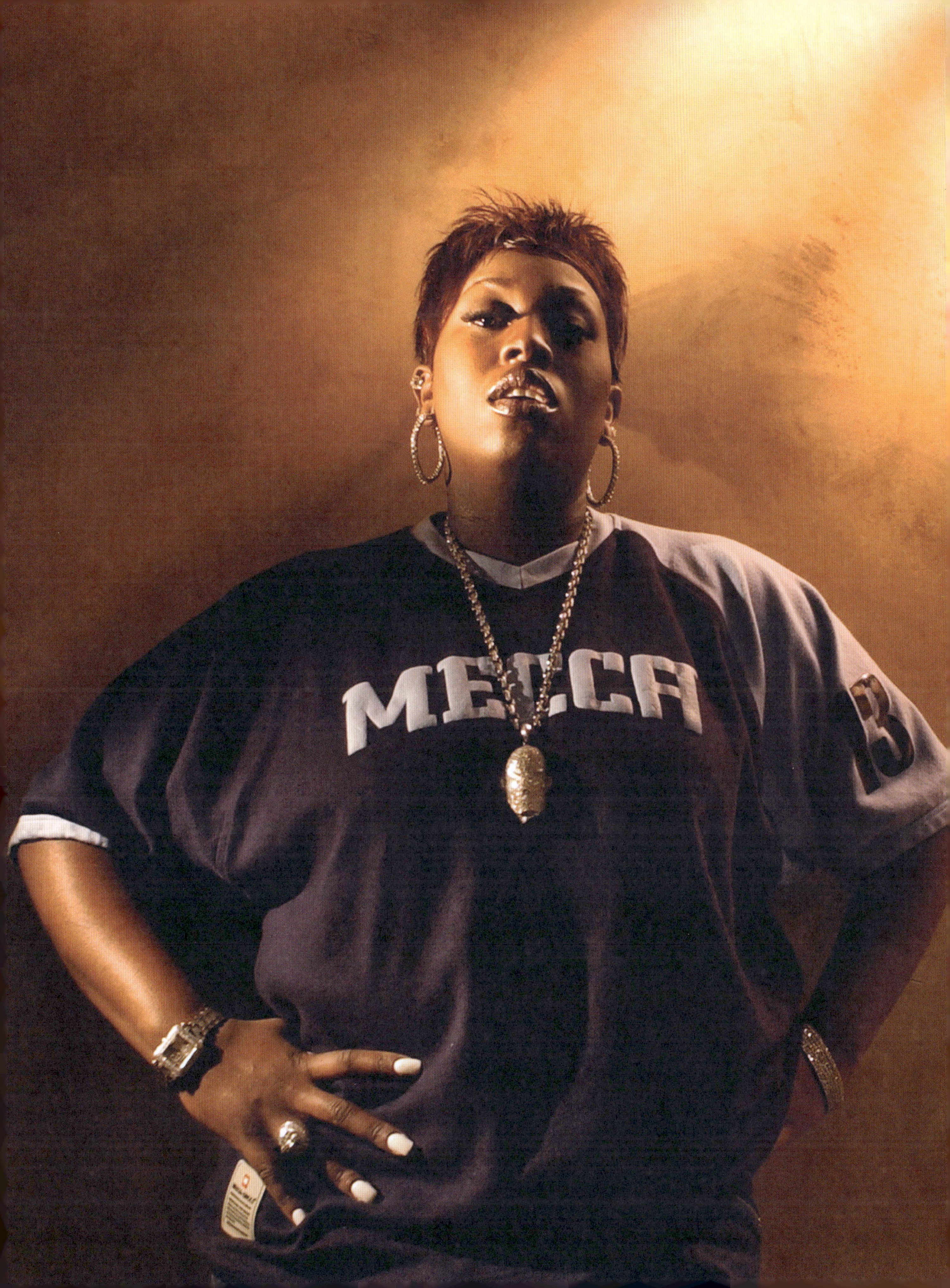
MECCA

Michelle, Beyoncé, Kelly, and Farrah in 2000.

SINGLE

BUG A BOO

(Beyoncé Knowles, Kandi Burruss, Kelly Rowland, Kevin Briggs, LaTavia Roberson, LeToya Luckett/3'31)

Musicians
Beyoncé Knowles: vocals, backing vocals
Kelly Rowland: vocals, backing vocals
LeToya Luckett: backing vocals
LaTavia Roberson: backing vocals
Kevin "She'kspere" Briggs: additional instruments

Recording
SugarHill Recording Studios, Houston: October 1998 to April 1999
Triangle Sound, Atlanta: October 1998 to April 1999

Technical team
Producers: Kevin "She'kspere" Briggs, Kandi Burruss
Executive producers: Kevin "She'kspere" Briggs, Mathew Knowles
Recording engineers: Dan Workman, Ramon Morales

Single
Released in the USA by Sony Music/Columbia: 7 September 1999 (promotional CD single ref: CSK 42499)
Best chart ranking in the USA: 33

Genesis

Destiny's Child sing about a time that under-twenties wouldn't have known in this song written by the duo of Kandi Burruss and Kevin "She'kspere" Briggs. *Bug a Boo*, the first track the couple brought to the four Texan singers (preceding *Bills, Bills, Bills* and *So Good*), depicts a young woman's frustration with the constant calls and emails from an intrusive boyfriend, and lists all kinds of devices that no longer exist. *You make me wanna throw my pager out the window/Tell MCI to cut the phone poles/Break my lease so I can move/'Cause you a bug a boo, a bug a boo.* Bugaboo is a word used in fantasy books to describe an imaginary creature that comes in the night and scares children, but here Burruss changes the meaning and spelling. "Me personally, I use a lot of slang, so certain words that I felt like are cool words I just try to take them and make cool songs out of 'em. Same way with *No Scrubs*, I'll just use a slang term that I use with friends. 'Bug-a-Boo', that's a saying I say all the time. I cannot stand when I let a person go through to voicemail, and they keep hanging up and calling back. Or you tell them, 'Hey, call me back in 5 minutes' and they call back in exactly 4.5 minutes, like 'Damn, such a bug-a-boo! Back up off me!'"[49]

Production

Recorded during the first work session between Kandi Burruss, Kevin "She'kspere" Briggs, and Destiny's Child, *Bug a Boo* is a testament to Burruss' expertise with the artists she works with. She came to the studio with the instrumental and the main hook for the song to get first impressions from her employers and initially kept the melody and the lyrics to herself.

"When they was listening to the tracks, at first I was being quiet and letting them say their opinions," she said, "but they were listening to those tracks and kinda of like, 'I don't like this, I don't know about that'. When the track for *Bug a Boo* played they were like, 'don't know about this', because, you know, if you just listen to that track and they had never heard the song or the concept over it, you'll be thinking, 'What can somebody sing over this?' I remember I was like, 'Do y'all mind if I sing to you the idea that I was thinking?' and they was like 'Cool', so I started singing."[49] As she had only written a verse and a chorus, Burruss left space for the singers to add their own ideas to the track, knowing full well they would want to contribute to the writing of the final lyrics. *Bug a Boo* went on to reach number 30 on the *Billboard* 200, but was released only as a promotional CD single in the United States.

In 1999, *Bug a Boo* was one of a series of songs that reflected the anxieties of a generation as new technologies increasingly took hold and took over. As the entire planet prepared for the Y2K bug in the year 2000, the girls from TLC sang about the virtual relationship they had with their fans in a song called *Fanmail*, on the album of the same name released in 1999.

Beyoncé Knowles in a shot taken by photographer Ola Bergman in Stockholm, December 1999.

TEMPTATION

(Beyoncé Knowles, Kandi Burruss, Anthony Ray, Carl Wheeler, Kelly Rowland, D'Wayne Wiggins, LaTavia Roberson, LeToya Luckett/4'05)

Musicians: Beyoncé Knowles: vocals, backing vocals / **Kelly Rowland:** vocals, backing vocals / **LeToya Luckett:** backing vocals / **LaTavia Roberson:** backing vocals / **Charles Spikes:** guitar / **D'Wayne Wiggins:** guitar, bass / **Terry T:** bass, programming, synthesizers / **Recording:** House of Music, Oakland: October 1998 to April 1999 / Digital Sound, Houston: October 1998 to April 1999 / **Technical team:** Producers: Terry T, D'Wayne Wiggins / **Executive producer:** Mathew Knowles / **Recording engineers:** Chuck Walpole, Joey Swails, Michael Calderon

A ballad was clearly needed to extinguish the fire after the dance-floor numbers at the start of the album. Mission accomplished with *Temptation*, a track akin to other soulful tracks that were released as the millennium drew to a close, songs such as Jagged Edge's *Let's Get Married*, Ginuwine's *So Anxious*, Case's *Happily Ever After*, and Blaque's *808*, all hits whose sole purpose was to sell the idea of being in love to a teenaged audience. Producers Terry T and D'Wayne Wiggins are at the helm here, sampling two songs by the latter's band Tony! Toni! Toné!, *Feels Good* and *Whatever You Want*, both taken from the 1990 album *The Revival*. *Temptation* also includes an extract from *Posse on Broadway*, released by Sir Mix-a-Lot on his 1988 album *Swass*.

NOW THAT SHE'S GONE

(Aleese Simmons, Donnie Boynton, Ken Fambro, Lonnie Simmons, Tara Geter/5'35)

Musicians: Beyoncé Knowles: vocals, backing vocals / **Kelly Rowland:** vocals, backing vocals / **LeToya Luckett:** backing vocals / **LaTavia Roberson:** backing vocals / **Recording:** Digital Sound, Houston: October 1998 to April 1999 / Doppler Studios, Atlanta: October 1998 to April 1999 / **Technical team:** Producers: Donnie Boynton, Ken Fambro / **Executive producer:** Mathew Knowles / **Recording engineers:** Blake Eiseman, James Hoover, Kenny Stallworth / **Vocal arrangements:** LaTrelle Simmons

While *Temptation* was about love relationships seen through the prism of seduction, *Now That She's Gone* is a song about a cat-and-mouse game between two lovers. Now 18, Beyoncé appears comfortable with this theme, which features prominently on the album. Some journalists nevertheless criticized Tina and Mathew Knowles for not giving their daughter the freedom that every young adult needs to gradually become independent. Tina Knowles defended herself against the accusations in September 2001's issue of *Ebony*: "What mother wouldn't want her daughter to have a boyfriend? I'm no different from any other mother. I want my kids to be happy. I don't want them to be lonely. [...] If I were saying to them, 'No, you don't need a boyfriend! You need to concentrate on your career', how long do you think they would put up with that?"[17] Not long, that's for sure.

1999

76 THE WRITING'S ON THE WALL

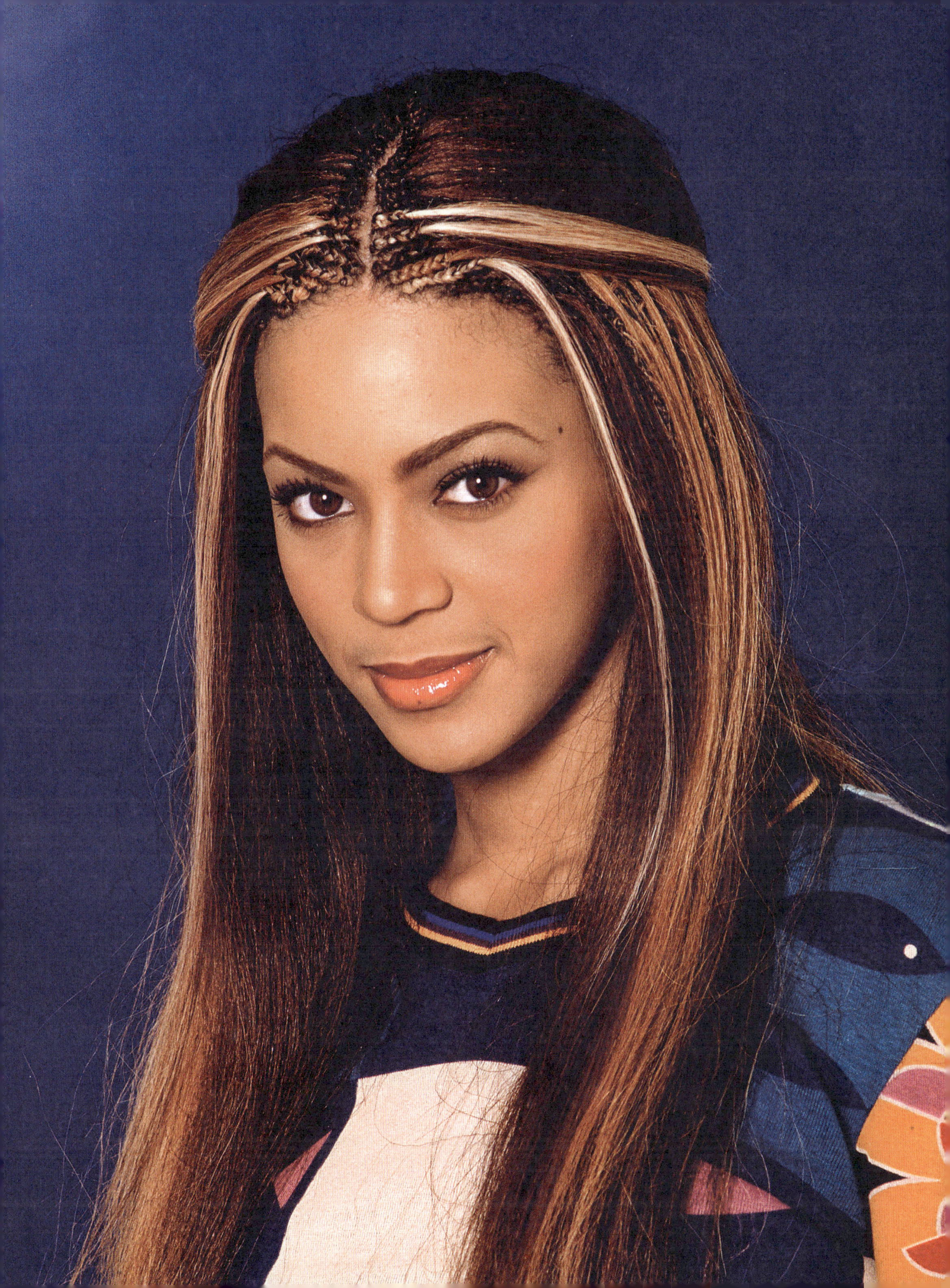

The members of TLC at the height of their fame following the release of their third album, *Fanmail*, in 1999.

WHERE'D YOU GO

(Beyoncé Knowles, Chris Stokes, Kelly Rowland, LaTavia Roberson, LeToya Luckett, Platinum Status / 4'15)

Musicians: Beyoncé Knowles: vocals, backing vocals / Kelly Rowland: backing vocals / LeToya Luckett: backing vocals / LaTavia Roberson: vocals, backing vocals / **Recording:** Madhouse Recordings, Los Angeles: October 1998 to April 1999 / **Technical team: Producers:** Beyoncé Knowles, Chris Stokes, Platinum Status / **Executive producer:** Mathew Knowles

Where'd You Go is without a doubt one of the most accomplished songs on *The Writing's on the Wall*. The trio of producers known as Platinum Status, consisting of Kelton Kessee, Marques Houston, and Tony Scott, strike the perfect balance between ultra-modern R&B grooves and a poignant verse melody, topped off with one of the album's best choruses. Only *Say My Name* could possibly claim a higher position on the podium than this irresistible hit. Oddly, the song was never put forward as a single, perhaps because Destiny's Child didn't see its obvious potential. For once, Beyoncé Knowles shares lead vocals with LaTavia Roberson. Beyoncé, who once again demonstrates her virtuosity here, was much criticized at the time for her dominance in the group. "I have to work double-time, because everybody in the audience is trying to say that the only reason I got something is because of my dad," she observed in 2001. "I've got to be extra tight. I have to prove myself every day. It's really unfair, because nobody else had to do that. It's not Sisqo's fault when he sings lead. It's not Coko's fault that she sang lead. The haters make me feel bad about singing lead, when that should be something that I'm happy about. Sometimes I wish my father wasn't the manager, so people would just stop attacking me. Whenever something goes wrong in the group, it's my fault. Blame Beyoncé. Somebody left the group, it's Beyoncé's fault. Kelly broke her toes, it's Beyoncé's fault."[36]

HEY LADIES

(Beyoncé Knowles, Kandi Burruss, Kelly Rowland, Kevin Briggs, LaTavia Roberson, LeToya Luckett / 4'16)

Musicians: Beyoncé Knowles: vocals, backing vocals / Kelly Rowland: vocals, backing vocals / LeToya Luckett: backing vocals / LaTavia Roberson: backing vocals / Kevin "She'kspere" Briggs: additional instruments / **Recording:** SugarHill Recording Studios, Houston: October 1998 to April 1999 / Triangle Sound, Atlanta: October 1998 to April 1999 / **Technical team: Producers:** Kevin "She'kspere" Briggs, Beyoncé Knowles, Kandi Burruss / **Executive producers:** Mathew Knowles, Kevin "She'kspere" Briggs / **Recording engineers:** Kevin "She'kspere" Briggs, Ramon Morales

Talented composer and songwriter Kandi Burruss and her partner in crime Kevin "She'kspere" Briggs co-wrote this new feminist anthem with the goal of giving women the power they should have had from the start to decide their own destiny. Here again, they offer an alternative to male dominance in R&B and in society in general. Though not consciously aware of it, Burruss spearheaded a pivotal movement in pop music, with songs tackling this kind of subject invading the airwaves in subsequent years (TLC's *Unpretty*, Toni Braxton's *He Wasn't Man Enough*, *Stronger* by Britney Spears, and Christina Aguilera's *Can't Hold Us Down*). "I was just writing songs inspired by relationships or things that I had wondered. It was just me and my personality on record. I didn't know people were going to look at it as this big girl empowerment movement. I didn't know that when I was doing it. I'm constantly writing about things that I am going through at that time. For me, if I'm mad or the dude pissed me off or whatever, then I'm talking about it when I'm in the studio. *No Scrubs* and *Bills, Bills, Bills* were inspired by the same dude. *Hey Ladies* was a different guy I was dating. He had erm, he kinda um, he cheated on me with this chick […]. So, for me I was kinda venting on certain songs."[49] Women were speaking out and flexing their muscles in 1999, and that was a very good thing.

1999

78 THE WRITING'S ON THE WALL

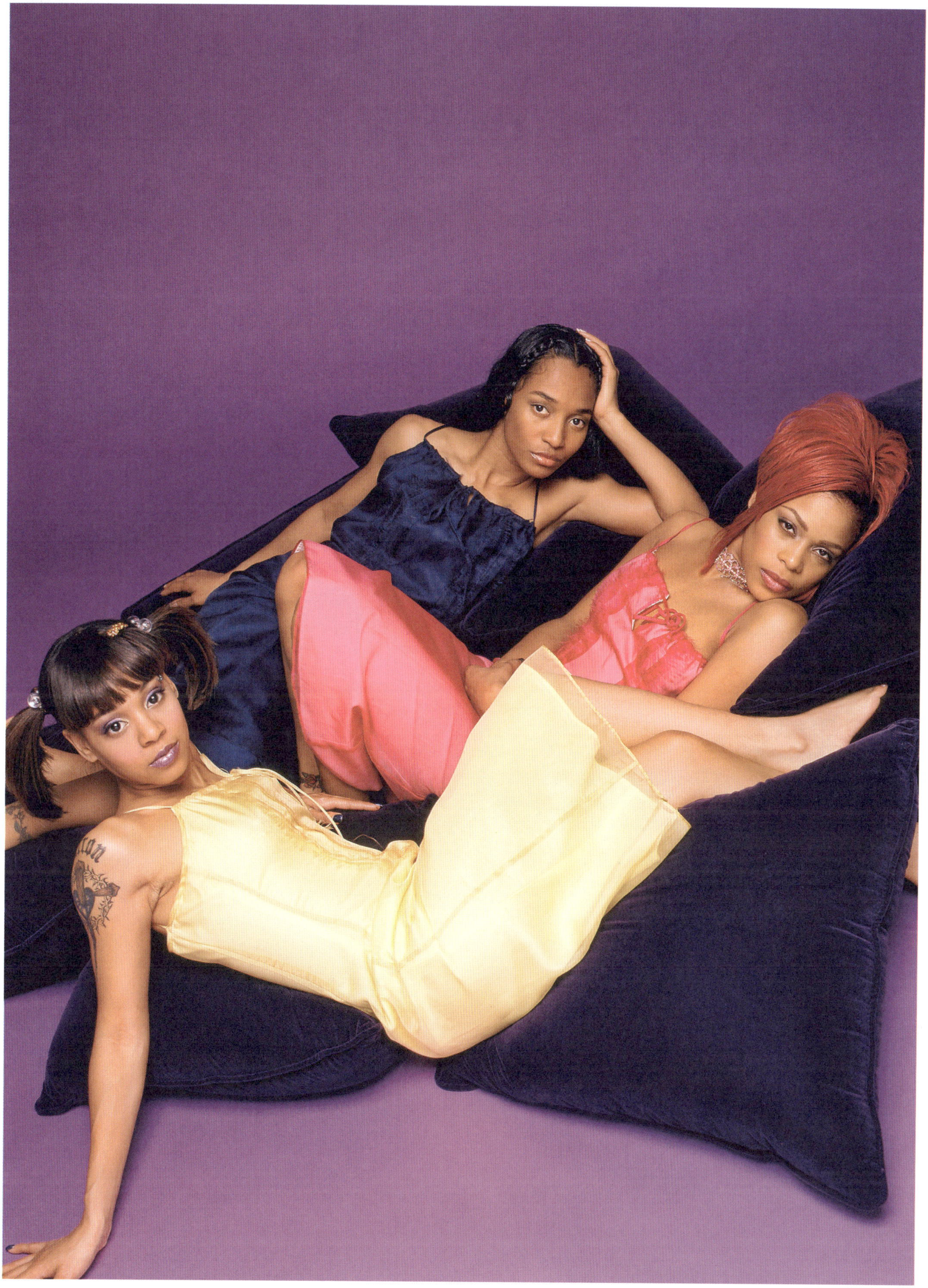

Raphael "Tweety" Brown, Terry "T-Low" Brown, and Robert Lavelle "R. L." Huggar from the group Next, in Chicago, June 2000.

IF YOU LEAVE
(FEATURING NEXT)

(Chad Elliott, Nycolia Turman, Oshea Hunter, Robert L. Huggar/4'35)

Musicians: Beyoncé Knowles: vocals, backing vocals / **Kelly Rowland:** vocals, backing vocals / **LeToya Luckett:** backing vocals / **LaTavia Roberson:** backing vocals / **Raphael Brown:** vocals, backing vocals / **Robert L. Huggar:** vocals, backing vocals / **Terrance Brown:** vocals, backing vocals / **Recording:** Electric Lady, New York: October 1998 to April 1999 / **Dallas Sound Lab, Dallas:** October 1998 to April 1999 / **Technical team: Producers:** Chad "Dr. Ceuss" Elliott, Oshea Hunter / **Executive producer:** Mathew Knowles / **Recording engineers:** Andre DeBourg, Chris Bell

Although the R&B trio Next, consisting of brothers Raphael and Terry (or Terrance) Brown and Robert L. Huggar, disappeared from circulation after the release of their last album *The Next Episode* in 2002, it is worth mentioning the colossal success they had when their single *Too Close,* from their debut album *Rated Next,* was released in January 1998. It was number 1 on the *Billboard* 200 for five consecutive weeks, following on from *Butta Love,* which had been a big hit the previous year, reaching number 1 on the R&B charts in the United States. While Arista Records and its legendary founder, Clive Davis, had predicted a triumphant career for the group, alas, this wouldn't come to pass: record labels had failed to anticipate the wave of boy bands (Backstreet Boys, *NSYNC, Take That), which at the time was doing away with all the male groups who sang about love in a soulful, sensual way, as Next, Boyz II Men, and Jagged Edge had done so well. But in 1998, the three boys from Next were still riding high, and the decision to invite them to sing alongside the girls on *The Writing's on the Wall* was both clever and lucrative.

SINGLE

JUMPIN', JUMPIN'

(Beyoncé Knowles, Chad Elliott, Rufus Moore/3'50)

Musicians: Beyoncé Knowles: vocals, backing vocals / **Byron Rittenhouse:** spoken voice / **Recording:** 353 Studio, New York: October 1998 to April 1999 / **24/7 Studio, Houston:** October 1998 to April 1999 / **Technical team: Producers:** Beyoncé Knowles, Chad "Dr. Ceuss" Elliott, Jovonn Alexander / **Executive producer:** Mathew Knowles / **Recording engineers:** Andre DeBourg, David Donaldson / **Released in the USA by Sony Music/Columbia:** 14 July 2000 (CD maxi single ref.: 44K 79446) / **Best chart ranking in the USA:** 3

Jumpin', Jumpin' was the final single taken from *The Writing's on the Wall,* released in the United States on 14 July 2000. It was also the last single to include Farrah Franklin on the cover and in the music video, as she was encouraged to leave the group shortly after the song was released. The track, produced by Jovonn Alexander and Chad Elliott, and composed by the latter and Rufus Moore, was sent to Mathew Knowles without a single lyric. It was Beyoncé herself who wrote the words for the piece, though when she came up with *Ladies leave your man at home/The club is full of ballers and their pockets full grown,* she was no doubt influenced by songwriter Kandi Burruss. Beyoncé recorded all the vocal parts for the track in a single session, thus proving to the world that she didn't need anyone else in order to create a hit. When Destiny's Child released their remix album *This Is the Remix* in 2002, it featured a reworking of the track by producer Jermaine Dupri. "Yeah, it just came out of nowhere," Dupri explained. "They asked us to do the remix and I was like…I think it was a Columbia thing, once again. We were all on the same label, Destiny's Child had a hit and they wanted Bow Wow to break. The label was actually thinking, 'Put Bow Wow on this Destiny's Child song, and JD, you do the remix. Come up with it.' So we just branded it out with So So Def and did what we had to do."[50] Li'l Bow Wow, a young rapper who released his first album in 2000, later talked about his deep admiration for Beyoncé and her colleagues: "They have gained the respect of all music lovers. They care about their music and message and it shows. They are doing something that they love and they put their all into their performances."[46]

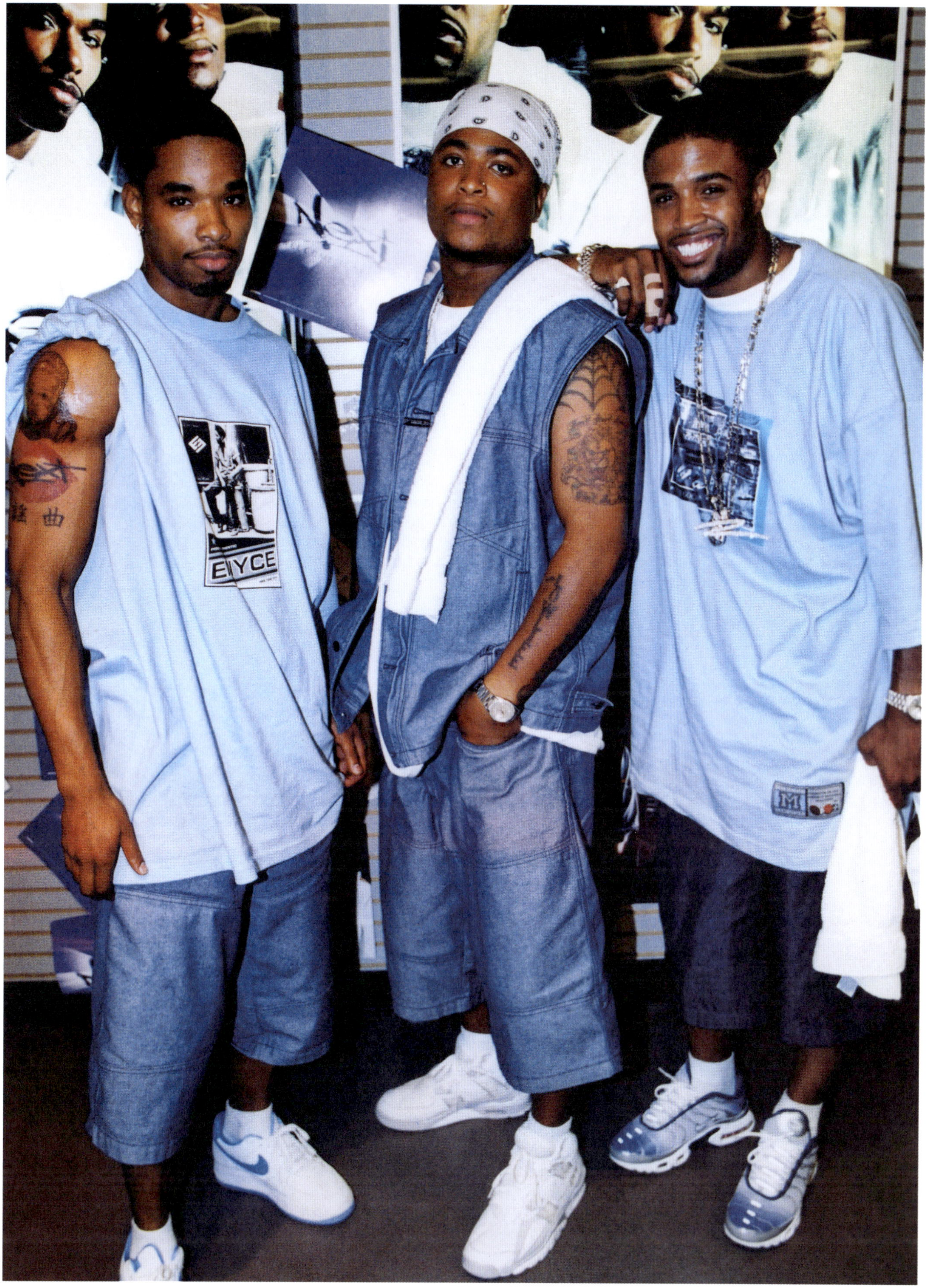

Destiny's Child are all smiles, shortly before the disagreements that would lead to Farrah Franklin's departure.

SINGLE

SAY MY NAME

(Beyoncé Knowles, Fred Jerkins III, Kelly Rowland, LaShawn Daniels, LaTavia Roberson, LeToya Luckett, Rodney Jerkins/4'31)

Musicians
Beyoncé Knowles: vocals, backing vocals
Kelly Rowland: vocals, backing vocals
LeToya Luckett: backing vocals
LaTavia Roberson: backing vocals
Rodney Jerkins: spoken voice

Recording
Pacifique Studio, North Hollywood: October 1998 to April 1999

Technical team
Producers: Beyoncé Knowles, Rodney Jerkins, LaShawn Daniels
Executive producer: Mathew Knowles
Recording engineers: Brad Gildem, LaShawn Daniels

Single
Released in the USA by Sony Music/Columbia: 29 February 2000 (CD ref.: 38K 79342)
Best chart ranking in the USA: 1

Genesis

Rodney Jerkins was a writer, composer, and producer of genius, and definitely no novice when he set to work for Destiny's Child. The man behind Brandy & Monica's *The Boy Is Mine*, Whitney Houston's *It's Not Right But It's Okay*, and Jennifer Lopez's *If You Had My Love* had become an institution when it came to turning his clients into superstars. This is certainly what Teresa LaBarbera Whites was thinking when she asked him to come in during the production of *The Writing's on the Wall*, to which he would contribute what would become Destiny's Child's most famous track. But this hit was also the fruit of the producer's collaboration with his brother, lyricist Fred Jerkins III, and LaShawn Daniels, a brilliant all-rounder who also co-wrote and co-produced the track. Daniels drew on his own experience to bring to life the woman who asks her partner to say her name after she is worried by a sudden change in his voice as they chat on the phone. "I would be places, I would be at work, and if [my girlfriend] would call or hear anyone laughing, or speaking, or doing anything in the background, she'd be like, 'Who is that?' Then she'd be like, 'Well, say my name then, and tell me that you love me.' [The song] was actually the premise of what I would go through, and we had the conversation of 'how embarrassing is that?' Beyoncé was in a relationship at that time, and she could relate well to the situation."[51]

Production

After recording the initial version, Beyoncé, who by then was captain of the Destiny's Child ship, was not satisfied with the track, which she felt was messy and cacophonous. Rodney Jerkins, the main producer, was not satisfied either, so he decided to go back to the drawing board while the team was preparing to mix the album. "Wait a minute," he said, "you have to give me a couple of hours. I have to make this track as exciting as the song…"[51] "It wasn't going to make the album," Beyoncé recalls, "and then when we were doing the photo shoot for the record my dad came in to the studio and said, 'Rodney's done a new mix of that song that you hate but you just have to take a listen to it.' He played the mix to us and we couldn't even focus on anything. He had turned it into an amazing, timeless R&B record. It was just excellent. It was one of the best songs we ever had, one of the best he's ever produced."[22]

1999

82 THE WRITING'S ON THE WALL

FOR DESTINY'S CHILD ADDICTS

The famous three-beat choreography performed by Destiny's Child in the *Say My Name* video was improvised on the day of shooting, as the two new recruits, Michelle Williams and Farrah Franklin, were unable to do the initially planned routine while wearing stilettos. That didn't stop the video from going down in history and fans copying their idols' jerky movements.

HEADPHONES AT THE READY

The male voice that can be heard from 2'50 onwards on *Say My Name* is that of Rodney "Darkchild" Jerkins, the track's co-producer and co-writer. While fans mostly remember the hook *Darkchild Na-Na*, Jerkins confessed in 2018 on his Instagram page that what he had recorded was in fact *Darkchild Nine-Nine*, referring to 1999, the year the track was recorded.

Part-pop, part-R&B, singer Pink has had a highly successful career.

SHE CAN'T LOVE YOU

(Beyoncé Knowles, Kelly Rowland, Kandi Burruss, Kevin Briggs, LaTavia Roberson, LeToya Luckett/4'05)

Musicians: Beyoncé Knowles: vocals, backing vocals / Kelly Rowland: vocals, backing vocals / LeToya Luckett: backing vocals / LaTavia Roberson: backing vocals / Kevin "She'kspere" Briggs: additional instruments / **Recording:** Triangle Sound, Atlanta: October 1998 to April 1999 / Digital Services Recording Studios, Houston: October 1998 to April 1999 / SugarHill Recording Studios, Houston: October 1998 to April 1999 / **Technical team:** Producers: Kevin "She'kspere" Briggs, Beyoncé Knowles, Kandi Burruss / **Executive producers:** Mathew Knowles, Kevin "She'kspere" Briggs / **Recording engineers:** Ramon Morales, Kevin "She'kspere" Briggs

Kevin "She'kspere" Briggs once again works wonders on this Hispanic-sounding track, which resurrects the classical guitar as the backdrop to an effective groove already adopted by Carlos Santana in 1998 on *To Zion* by Lauryn Hill, ex-Fugees frontwoman turned R&B queen following the release of her album *The Miseducation of Lauryn Hill*. With lyrics from Kandi Burruss, Beyoncé sings of heartbreak, as she tries to convince her man that the other woman who has captured his heart won't love him as well as she does. Burruss has spoken on many occasions about Beyoncé's professionalism, and the 18-year-old needed lessons from no one when it came to recording her vocal lines. "A lot of times, when we were going to the studio with people, I'm the one telling them what they need to sing," Burruss revealed in 2021, "what harmony they need to do, what part they need to stack, but I didn't have to do that with her. She was in there coming up with parts, coming up with harmonies, telling her other group members what she heard them doing, and what she wanted them to do."[44]

STAY

(Daryl Simmons/4'51)

Musicians: Beyoncé Knowles: vocals, backing vocals / Kelly Rowland: vocals, backing vocals / LeToya Luckett: backing vocals / LaTavia Roberson: backing vocals / Sonny Lallerstedt: guitar / Ronnie Garrett: bass / Daryl Simmons: synthesizers, programming / Tony Williams: programming / **Recording:** Silent Sound Studios, Atlanta: 1995, October 1998 to April 1999 / **Technical team:** Producers: Daryl Simmons / **Executive producer:** Mathew Knowles / **Recording engineer:** Thom "TK" Kidd / **Assistant recording engineers:** Kevin Lively, Stephanie Vonarx

In 1995, Chrissy Conway, Sharon Flanagan, and Alecia Moore from the group Choice flew to Atlanta, where producer Daryl Simmons was waiting for them. The three women were planning to record their first album there in the hope of landing a record contract. Their endeavors were in vain and only the track *Key to My Heart* appealed to Antonio "L.A." Reid (legendary founder of LaFace Records, alongside Kenneth "Babyface" Edmonds, and a regular collaborator of Darryl Simmons), who placed it on the soundtrack for the film *Kazaam*, directed by Paul Michael Glaser in 1996. Although Reid declined to produce Choice, he did urge one of the group's three singers, Alecia Moore, to join his label and change her name to Pink. The rest is pop history, with the *So What* singer now one of the biggest stars of American music. When Mathew Knowles got back in touch with Darryl Simmons in 1998, he told him he needed a ballad for the new Destiny's Child album. The latter pulled *Stay*—which he had produced for Choice—back out of the bag and recovered the tape that had been sitting on the shelves at his Silent Sound Studios in Atlanta. Adopted by Beyoncé, the song would feature on *The Writing's on the Wall* in 1999.

Jody Watley, the iconic singer with Shalamar from 1977 to 1983.

SWEET SIXTEEN

(Beyoncé Knowles, D'Wayne Wiggins, Jody Watley, Kelly Rowland/4'12)

Musicians: Beyoncé Knowles: vocals, backing vocals / **LaTavia Roberson:** vocals, backing vocals / **Kelly Rowland:** vocals, backing vocals / **LeToya Luckett:** backing vocals / **Raymond McKinley:** bass / **D'Wayne Wiggins:** guitar, synthesizers, programming / **Vincent Lars:** saxophone / **Bill Ortiz:** trumpet / **Recording:** House of Music, Oakland: October 1998 to April 1999 / **Live Oak Studios, Berkeley:** October 1998 to April 1999 / **Digital Sound, Houston:** October 1998 to April 1999 / **Technical team:** Producers: D'Wayne Wiggins, Beyoncé Knowles / **Executive producer:** Mathew Knowles / **Recording engineers:** James Hoover, Joey Swails

In 1998, Jody Watley, who was the singer with Shalamar between 1977 and 1983 (the vocals in *A Night to Remember*, that's her), was about to record her sixth solo album with producer D'Wayne Wiggins. While she was waiting on the curbside at the airport, a song theme popped into her mind. "I was thinking about girls who try to grow up too fast, teen pregnancy and many of the ramifications that come after, someone I knew was devastated when learning his daughter was pregnant at 15 and that was in my consciousness as well, I also thought about one of my nieces who'd say she couldn't wait to be grown."[52] As soon as they got to the studio, Wiggins quickly laid the track, called *16*, down on tape, planning for it to appear on *Flower*, Watley's next album. Some time later, when Wiggins was asked to work with Destiny's Child, he offered the song to the group, who immediately took it on, renamed it *Sweet Sixteen*, and in the process forgot to credit the composer in the booklet that accompanied the record's first pressing. This was later corrected after Watley's lawyer got involved.

HEADPHONES AT THE READY

Although not credited in the liner notes for *The Writing's on the Wall*, the reference to Thelma Houston's *Do You Know Where You're Going To* (1973) is easy to spot in the choruses of *Sweet Sixteen*.

OUTRO
(AMAZING GRACE... DEDICATED TO ANDRETTA TILLMAN)

(John Newton, William Walker/2'39)

Musicians: Beyoncé Knowles: vocals, backing vocals / **Kelly Rowland:** vocals, backing vocals / **LeToya Luckett:** backing vocals / **LaTavia Roberson:** backing vocals / **Recording:** Digital Sound, Houston: October 1998 to April 1999 / **Technical team:** Producer: Beyoncé Knowles / **Executive producer:** Mathew Knowles / **Recording engineer:** James Hoover / **Arrangements:** Beyoncé Knowles

This interpretation of *Amazing Grace*, an 18th-century Christian hymn, is dedicated to Andretta Tillman, who had died in 1997. It closes the album as if to remind the listener that, behind her group's sensual songs, Beyoncé is a woman of faith whose belief in God is unshakeable. Michelle Williams, who joined the band after the album had been recorded, would say more about their Christian faith in 2002: "Beyoncé, Kelly, and I go to church every Sunday that we can. We read our Bibles lots of times instead of going to a party. We get on our tour bus and have church in the back of the bus. We surround ourselves with Christians and people who are Spirit-filled. We trust God and he still speaks to us. We know that he does. [...] I know what God has done in my life and I know that God is still with me and he still loves me. I'm here to testify about that."[40]

BEYONCÉ: ALL THE SONGS 85

STIMULATE ME
(DESTINY'S CHILD WITH MOCHA)

(Aleesha Richards, R. Kelly, Mocha/4'14)

Musicians: Beyoncé Knowles: vocals, backing vocals / **Kelly Rowland:** vocals, backing vocals / **LeToya Luckett:** vocals, backing vocals / **LaTavia Roberson:** backing vocals / **Mocha:** rap / **Roy Hamilton:** programming / **Blake Chaffin:** programming / **Bryon Rickerson:** programming / **Joey "The Don" Donatello:** programming / **Recording:** Chicago Trax Recording, Chicago: 1999 / **Technical team:** Producer: R. Kelly / **Recording engineers:** Blake Chaffin, Joey "The Don" Donatello / **Assistant recording engineers:** Andy Gallas, Bryon Rickerson, Ian Mereness / **Life: Music Inspired by the Motion Picture** (compilation) / Released in the USA by Rock Land Records/Interscope Records: 16 March 1999 (album ref.: INT2-90314, CD ref.: NTD-90373)

Following on from *Get on the Bus*, an original number that Destiny's Child crafted for the soundtrack to the Gregory Nava film *Why Do Fools Fall in Love*, the young ladies treat us to this R&B nugget exclusively available on the soundtrack to *Life*, a Ted Demme comedy starring Eddie Murphy and Martin Lawrence. The task of producing a record to pay tribute to feature films (one of those famous "music inspired by the movie" compilations) was entrusted to the crème de la crème of hit-makers at the time, namely Wyclef Jean, Jerry "Wonda" Duplessis, and especially the famous R. Kelly, who was then surfing the wave of the colossal success of his 1996 single, *I Believe I Can Fly*. Some 25 years before the profession disowned him in the wake of multiple criminal charges that landed him a 30-year prison sentence in 2022, Kelly wrote a track for Destiny's Child that was smooth, sensual, and with a groove that would eclipse the other star of *Life: Music Inspired by the Motion Picture*: the velvet-voiced singer Maxwell, whose single *Fortunate* (also written and produced by R. Kelly) is the real star of the record. Also worthy of note are the remarkable contributions from Kelly Rowland and LeToya Luckett—here every bit as good as Beyoncé—and the rapper Mocha, real name Aleesha Richards.

NO MORE RAINY DAYS

(Rob Fusari, Vincent Herbert, Calvin Gaines, Beyoncé Knowles, LaTavia Roberson, Kelly Rowland/4'27)

Musicians: Beyoncé Knowles: vocals, backing vocals / **Kelly Rowland:** vocals, backing vocals / **LeToya Luckett:** vocals, backing vocals / **LaTavia Roberson:** backing vocals / **Recording:** Encore Studios, Burbank: November 1998 / **Technical team:** Producers: Vincent Herbert, Rob Fusari / **The PJs: Music from & Inspired by the Hit Television Series** (compilation) / Released in the USA by Hollywood Records/Touchstone Television/Imagine Television: 30 March 1999 (CD ref.: HR-62170-2)

This time, we need to turn to the series *The PJs* for a new track from the Texans, produced by Vincent Herbert and Rob Fusari, who had already worked on the group's first album, creating the hit *No, No, No Part 2*. This compilation brings together the cream of hip-hop (Snoop Dogg, Raekwon), funk (George Clinton, Earth, Wind and Fire), and R&B (Jermaine Dupri, Raphael Saadiq), offering a salvo of previously unreleased songs, like the many other original soundtracks produced at the time. Less surprising than *Stimulate Me*, *No More Rainy Days* is still a rarity that fans will enjoy.

CRAZY FEELINGS
(MISSY ELLIOTT FEATURING BEYONCÉ OF DESTINY'S CHILD)

(Missy Elliott, Timothy Mosley/4'35)

Musicians: Missy Elliott: vocals, backing vocals / **Beyoncé Knowles:** vocals, backing vocals / **Recording:** Master Sound Studios, Virginia Beach: 1998 to 1999 / **Technical team:** Executive producers: Missy Elliott, Timbaland / **Recording engineer:** Senator Jimmy D / **Missy Elliott Da Real World** (album) / Released in the USA by EastWest: 22 June 1999 (album ref.: 7559-62232-1, CD ref.: 7559-62232-2)

If there is one female rapper who stands out for her creativity and unique style, it's the great Missy Elliott, who had already worked with Destiny's Child on the sultry *Confessions*. Appearing alongside her was a privilege, especially as the tracklist of her album *Da Real World* reveals the presence of Redman, Big Boi, Lady Saw, Lil' Kim, Aaliyah, and a newcomer by the name of Eminem—his contribution to *Busa Rhyme* makes it worth rushing out to buy the album just for that. Among the hits *She's a Bitch* (Missy is notorious for telling it like it is) and *All n My Grill*, we find *Crazy Feelings*, composed by Elliott and her favored collaborator Timothy "Timbaland" Mosley, one of the best-known producers of the 1990s and 2000s. Note here that Beyoncé, not Destiny's Child, is the featured artist, a sign that her artistic emancipation was becoming ever more likely.

Sexy vest, bulging muscles, and velvety voice are all part of ex-Boyz II Men Marc Nelson's arsenal.

AFTER ALL IS SAID AND DONE
(BEYONCÉ AND MARC NELSON)

(Gordon Chambers, Phil Galdston/4'16)

Musicians: Beyoncé Knowles: vocals, backing vocals / Marc Nelson: vocals, backing vocals / Warryn "Baby Dub" Campbell: programming, additional instruments / **Recording:** Pacific Recording, North Hollywood: 1999 / **Technical team:** Producer: Warryn "Baby Dub" Campbell / Recording engineer: Anthony Jeffries / **The Best Man (Music from the Motion Picture) (compilation)** / Released in the USA by Sony Music Soundtrax/Columbia: 12 October 1999 (CD ref.: CK 69924)

This charmingly old-fashioned ballad was recorded by Beyoncé and singer Marc Nelson—a founding member of the most famous of male R&B groups, Boyz II Men—to be included in yet another film soundtrack. This time it was for *The Best Man*, a romantic comedy by Malcolm D. Lee, produced by his cousin, director Spike Lee. Once again, the cream of the crop answered the call, with the compilation featuring tracks from The Roots, Maxwell, Faith Evans, Meshell Ndegeocello, and Ginuwine. Queen Lauryn Hill even supplies a posthumous duet with Bob Marley, covering a top track from the king of reggae's 1977 album, *Exodus: Turn Your Lights Down Low*.

WOMAN IN ME
(JESSICA SIMPSON FEATURING DESTINY'S CHILD)

(Anders Bagge, Meja Beckman/3'52)

Musicians: Jessica Simpson: vocals, backing vocals / Beyoncé Knowles: vocals, backing vocals / Kelly Rowland: backing vocals / LeToya Luckett: backing vocals / LaTavia Roberson: backing vocals / Tim Heintz: synthesizers / Robbie Nevil: electric guitar / **Recording:** Blue Wave Studio, Vancouver: 1998 / **Technical team:** Producer: Robbie Nevil / **Jessica Simpson *Sweet Kisses* (album)** / Released in the USA by Columbia: 23 November 1999 (CD ref.: CK 69096)

With its slight resemblance to Mariah Carey's *Dreamlover* (1993), *Woman in Me* is the work of Jessica Simpson, a newcomer on the alternative R&B scene, preaching virtue and virginity as fundamental values of youth, just like her young comrade Britney Spears, whose first album, *Baby One More Time*, would soon propel the blonde singer to international stardom. Beyoncé is a discreet presence on this track—overshadowing her host would have been so easy that she seems to have wisely decided to remain in the background. Like a bridesmaid who wouldn't dare wear white to her best friend's wedding, Beyoncé simply embellishes this unremarkable track while her three Destiny's Child colleagues provide perfectly controlled backing vocals.

BEYONCÉ: ALL THE SONGS

The talented and much-missed Aaliyah in 1994, promoting her first album, *Age Ain't Nothing But a Number*.

PERFECT MAN

(Beyoncé Knowles, Eric Seats, Rapture Stewart/3'47)

Musicians: Beyoncé Knowles: vocals, backing vocals / Kelly Rowland: backing vocals / LeToya Luckett: backing vocals / LaTavia Roberson: backing vocals / **Recording:** Soundtrack Studios, New York: 1999 / **Technical team:** Producers: Eric Seats, Rapture Stewart / Recording engineer: Michael Conrader / **Romeo Must Die (The Album) (compilation)** / Released in the USA by Warner Bros Records: 14 March 2000 (album ref.: 7243 8 49052 1 7, CD ref.: 7243 8 49052 2 4)

Then it was the turn of the film *Romeo Must Die* to be given a soundtrack featuring previously unreleased tracks, rarities, and delicious duets. Directed by Andrzej Bartkowiak, the feature-length film notably shone a spotlight on the acting talents of singer Aaliyah, whose first two albums, *Age Ain't Nothing But a Number* (1994) and *One in a Million* (1996), had shot her to R&B superstardom. For their contribution to this compilation, Destiny's Child enlisted the help of producer Rapture Stewart, whose main achievement at the time had been co-writing the international hit *Where My Girls At?* for 702.

GOOD TO ME
(MARY MARY WITH DESTINY'S CHILD)

(Curtis Mayfield, Erica Atkins, Trecina Atkins, Warryn Campbell/4'09)

Musicians: Erica Atkins-Campbell: vocals, backing vocals / Trecina Atkins-Campbell: vocals, backing vocals / Beyoncé Knowles: vocals, backing vocals / Kelly Rowland: backing vocals / LeToya Luckett: backing vocals / LaTavia Roberson: backing vocals / Charlie "Little Charlie" Bereal: electric guitar / Warryn "Baby Dubb" Campbell: additional instruments / **Recording:** The Hit Factory, New York: 1999 / Hartmann Way Sound Studios, West Hills: 1999 / **Technical team:** Producer: Warryn "Baby Dubb" Campbell / Recording engineer: Kevin Crouse / **Mary Mary Thankful (album)** / Released in the USA by Sony Music/Columbia: 2 May 2000 (ref.: 497985 2)

Among the hits that made the R&B era legendary was the danceable *Shackles (Praise You)* by the duo Mary Mary, comprising sisters Erica and Tina Atkins. Released on their first album *Thankful* (2000), for a time the track dominated FM airwaves around the world and it remains a classic of the genre to this day. Born in Inglewood, California, the two singers would always regard their singing as intimately associated with the passion for gospel they had inherited from their parents. "Singing in choirs allowed our voices to blend in a really cool way," they explained in 2014, "and that's what makes the Mary Mary magic."[53] Produced by the talented Warryn "Baby Dubb" Campbell, who was still relatively unknown at the time, the Californian duo's first album was an instant success when it was released. Sensing that Campbell would become one of America's essential hit-makers in the years to come (thanks to his work on *Songs in A Minor* by Alicia Keys, Brandy's *Full Moon*, and Kanye West's *Late Registration*), Teresa LaBarbera Whites and Mathew Knowles invited him to work with Destiny's Child and once again their intuition seemed to be bang on. With its zouk-like rhythm, his nod to Curtis Mayfield's *Give Me Your Love*, and the electric guitar score performed by Charlie "Little Charlie" Bereal, *Good to Me* showcased the virtuosity of the Atkins sisters and of their four guests, with Beyoncé front and center in the mix, affording the young Texan a welcome soul platform. *Thankful* went on to win the Grammy Award for Best Contemporary R&B Gospel Album, selling over two million copies in the United States.

Memphis Bleek, Amil, and Beanie Sigel, the inner circle of rapper Jay-Z (third from left).

BIG MOMMA'S THEME
(DA BRAT AND VITA FEATURING DESTINY'S CHILD)

(Bryan-Michael Cox, Da Brat, Jermaine Dupri, Tiheem Crocker, Tamara Savage/3'14)

Musicians: Da Brat: rap / Vita: rap / Beyoncé Knowles: vocals, backing vocals / Kelly Rowland: backing vocals / LeToya Luckett: backing vocals / LaTavia Roberson: backing vocals / **Recording:** SouthSide Studios, Atlanta: 1999 / Digital Services Recording Studios, Houston: 1999 / **Technical team: Producers:** Jermaine Dupri, Bryan-Michael Cox / **Recording engineers:** Brian Frye, Brian Remenick, James Hoover, John Horesco IV / **Big Momma's House: Music from the Motion Picture (compilation)** / Released in the USA by Sony Music Soundtrax/So So Def: 30 May 2000 (album ref.: C2 61076, CD ref.: CK 61076)

One more soundtrack notched up for Destiny's Child, who once again surrounded themselves with the most popular artists and producers of the moment. On the compilation that accompanied Raja Gosnell's comedy *Big Mamma*, we find rising and established R&B stars including Missy Elliott, Monica, Li'l Bow Wow, Jagged Edge, Chanté Moore, and Marc Nelson, alongside producers Jermaine Dupri, Kevin Briggs, Warren G, and Bryan-Michael Cox. Admittedly an intimate affair, it is nonetheless wonderfully crafted and gives a broad overview of productions of that era. Although there was a glut of these movie soundtracks, they all offered fans previously unreleased songs, most of which emerged from prestigious collaborations. Albums to be added to your collection ASAP.

I GOT THAT
(AMIL FEATURING BEYONCÉ OF DESTINY'S CHILD)

(Amil Whitehead, Shawn Carter, Tamy Lester Smith, Samuel J. Barnes, Leshan Lewis, Makeda Davis, Jean-Claude Olivier/3'19)

Musicians: Amil: rap / Beyoncé Knowles: vocals, backing vocals / **Recording:** The Hit Factory, New York: 2000 / Platinum Post Studios, Orlando: 2000 / **Technical team: Producers:** Leshan David "L.E.S." Lewis, Poke and Tone / **Executive producers:** Damon Dash, Kareem "Biggs" Burke, Shawn Carter / **Recording engineers:** Mark Mason, Steve Sauder / **Amil All Money Is Legal (album)** / Released in the USA by Sony Music/Roc-A-Fella Records/Columbia: 29 August 2000 (album ref.: C 62048, CD ref.: CK 63936)

After guesting on Jay-Z's *Can I Get A…* on his album *Vol. 2… Hard Knock Life*, rapper Amil joined Roc-A-Fella Records, the New York hip-hop magnate's stable. At the request of Mathew Knowles, Jay-Z invited Beyoncé to participate on Amil's first album *All Money Is Legal*. The young Texan laid down her vocals on the corrosive *I Got That*, which Jay-Z co-wrote and which sampled *Seventh Heaven*, recorded by Gwen Guthrie in 1983. Jay-Z was so impressed by Beyoncé's professionalism during the sessions that he was soon back in touch with Mathew to discuss a possible duet with her, a project that came to pass two years later with the single *03 Bonnie & Clyde*. Besides being impressively effective, *Can I Get A…* also enjoys the status of being the first collaboration between Jay-Z and his future wife, Beyoncé Knowles.

Rapper Cam'Ron joined Jay-Z's label Roc-A-Fella in 2001.

THUG LOVE
(50 CENT FEATURING DESTINY'S CHILD)
(Curtis Jackson, Rashad Smith, Joshua M. Schwartz, Brian Kierulf, Nycolia Turman/3'12)

Musicians: 50 Cent: rap / **Beyoncé Knowles:** vocals, backing vocals / **Kelly Rowland:** backing vocals / **LeToya Luckett:** backing vocals / **LaTavia Roberson:** backing vocals / **Recording:** Bearsville Studios, Bearsville: 2000 / **Technical team:** Producers: Brian Kierulf, Joshua M. Schwartz, Rashad Smith / Recording engineer: Jason Goldstein / **50 Cent *Power of the Dollar* (EP)** / Released in the USA by Columbia: 12 September 2000 (ref.: 44K 79479)

Among the rappers on the rise in 1999, 50 Cent was indisputably one of the most talented. His smooth, Nate Dogg-style vocals, his unmistakably sharp flow, and his past as a kid trying to find his way on the streets of Queens made him a fully formed artist. This didn't escape the notice of Columbia Records, who invited him to record his first album, *Power of the Dollar*, in 1999. Scheduled for release on 4 July 2000, the album included a remarkable duet with Destiny's Child, *Thug Love*, released on 21 September 1999. But nothing would go to plan. In May 2000, with the music video due to be filmed several days later, 50 Cent—real name Curtis James Jackson III—was the victim of a shooting in which he was hit by nine 9mm bullets. Immediately dropped by Columbia Records, *Power of the Dollar* would become one of the most famous bootlegs of the 2000s, and, in 2002, 50 Cent would sign with Shady Records and Aftermath Entertainment, the labels owned respectively by Eminem and Dr. Dre. Only an EP version of *Power of the Dollar* was released on 12 September 2000, but it did feature the succulent *Thug Love*. As for 50 Cent, he went on to become one of the biggest rappers of the 2000s and 2010s, thanks to his singles *In Da Club*, *P.I.M.P.*, and *Candy Shop*.

DO IT AGAIN
(CAM'RON FEATURING DESTINY'S CHILD AND JIMMY JONES)
(Cameron Giles, Beyoncé Knowles, Jim Jones, Darrell Branch/4'07)

Musicians: Cam'Ron: rap / **Jimmy Jones:** rap / **Beyoncé Knowles:** vocals, backing vocals / **Kelly Rowland:** backing vocals / **LeToya Luckett:** backing vocals / **LaTavia Roberson:** backing vocals / **Recording:** Battery Studios, New York: 1999 / The Cutting Room Recording Studios, New York: 1999 / Hit Factory, Miami: 1999 / **Technical team:** Producers: Darrell "Digga" Branch / Recording engineers: Sharon Kearney, Tim Donovan / **Cam'Ron *S.D.E.* (album)** / Released in the USA by Epic: 19 September 2000 (album ref.: E2 69873, CD ref.: EK 69873)

Before joining Jay-Z's label Roc-A-Fella Records, rapper Cam'Ron recorded two albums for Epic: *Confessions of Fire* in 1998 and *S.D.E.* two years later. The latter stood for *Sports, Drugs, and Entertainment*, thus making it fairly clear that the East Harlem-born rapper intended to offer an edgy, uncompromising style of rap. It was on this second LP that Beyoncé and her three bandmates were invited to sing, adding a few heartfelt lines to this cheery rap produced by Darrell "Digga" Branch. It was a collaboration that wouldn't be repeated in the foreseeable future, as over the years Cam'Ron and Jay-Z—who by then was Beyoncé's husband—became sworn enemies after a power struggle at Roc-A-Fella Records led to the two men putting out a memorable series of diss-tracks—songs on which a rapper verbally attacks or criticizes other artists.

COLLABORATIONS

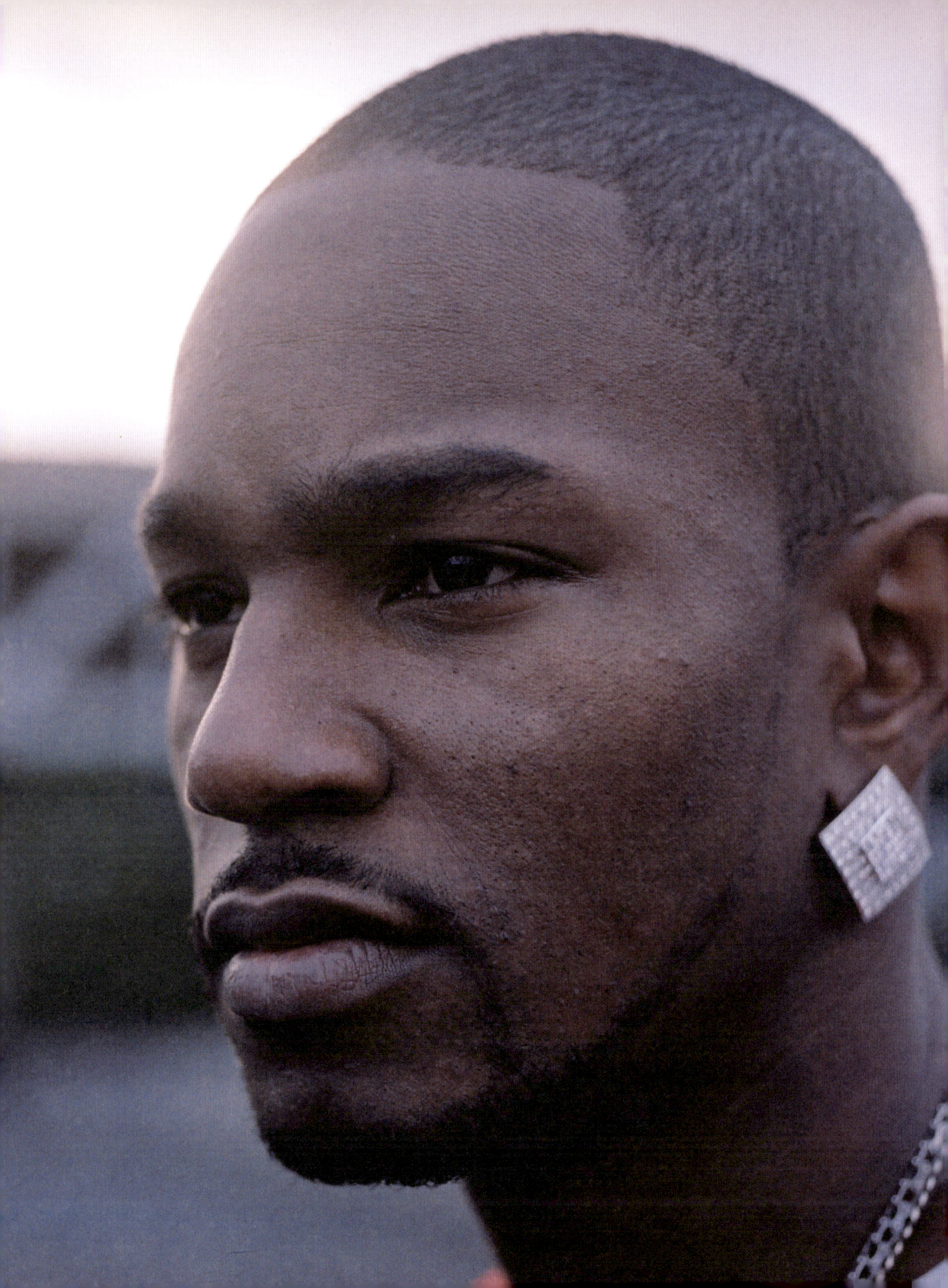

Mary Wilson, Florence Ballard, and Diana Ross were The Supremes, the iconic Motown trio.

CAN'T HELP MYSELF

(Babyface, Daryl Simmons/4'53)

Musicians
Beyoncé Knowles: vocals, backing vocals
Kelly Rowland: vocals, backing vocals
LeToya Luckett: vocals, backing vocals
LaTavia Roberson: vocals, backing vocals
Recording
Silent Sound Studios, Atlanta: 1999
Technical team
Producer: Daryl Simmons

Destiny's Child *B-Sides* (promotional CD)
Distributed in the US by Columbia: 1999 (ref.: CSK 42717)

Genesis

If there is such a thing as a magic formula for churning out hits, it has to be in the hands of the trio comprising Antonio "L.A." Reid, Kenneth "Babyface" Edmonds, and Daryl Simmons. In 1999, working as a group or in pairs, the three men were behind a series of hits that were the envy of all the big-name American producers. *On Our Own* by Bobby Brown, *End of the Road* by Boyz II Men, *Knocked Out* by Paula Abdul, and *Queen of the Night* by Whitney Houston were some of the many trophies on the walls at LaFace Records, the label created by L.A. and Babyface in 1989. When Babyface and Simmons got involved with Destiny's Child, the result was a fabulous soul track, reminiscent of the languorous Boyz II Men but also of the sheer chemistry of the legendary Motown trio, The Supremes. Although Beyoncé has always claimed to have been influenced by Diana Ross's group, what she took from them was more related to sisterhood than to soul. "The reason is because I loved being in a group. I do love sisterhood," she said in 2006 about Destiny's Child. "All of us—and not just me, this is about Kelly and Michelle also—whatever was best for the group, no matter whether it was best for us individually, would let something go. That element of compromise and sacrifice taught me a lot about myself and about friendship."[22]

Production

It was in a collegial spirit that *Can't Help Myself* was recorded, with the group's four singers each having a rare platform at the heart of the song. Daryl Simmons, at the helm here, gives the track a very 1990s feel and the personal stamp of the man who wrote Boyz II Men's *End of the Road* is instantly recognizable. Simmons created his hits using the Yamaha S80 synthesizer, a very effective instrument launched by the Japanese company in 1999 to compete with Korg's famous Triton and Trinity synths. "The S80 sounds inspire me to sit there until I come up with something," he said. "I usually start with either a warm electric piano or an acoustic piano sound. I don't like to spend time editing sounds, because I don't want to stop and risk losing my ideas. That's why the S80 pianos are great: you just push a couple of buttons, and you have the right one within seconds. The S80 is also great for setting up a quick beat without having to stop everything to hook up a drum machine. When I have an idea, I want to get it down right away."[54]

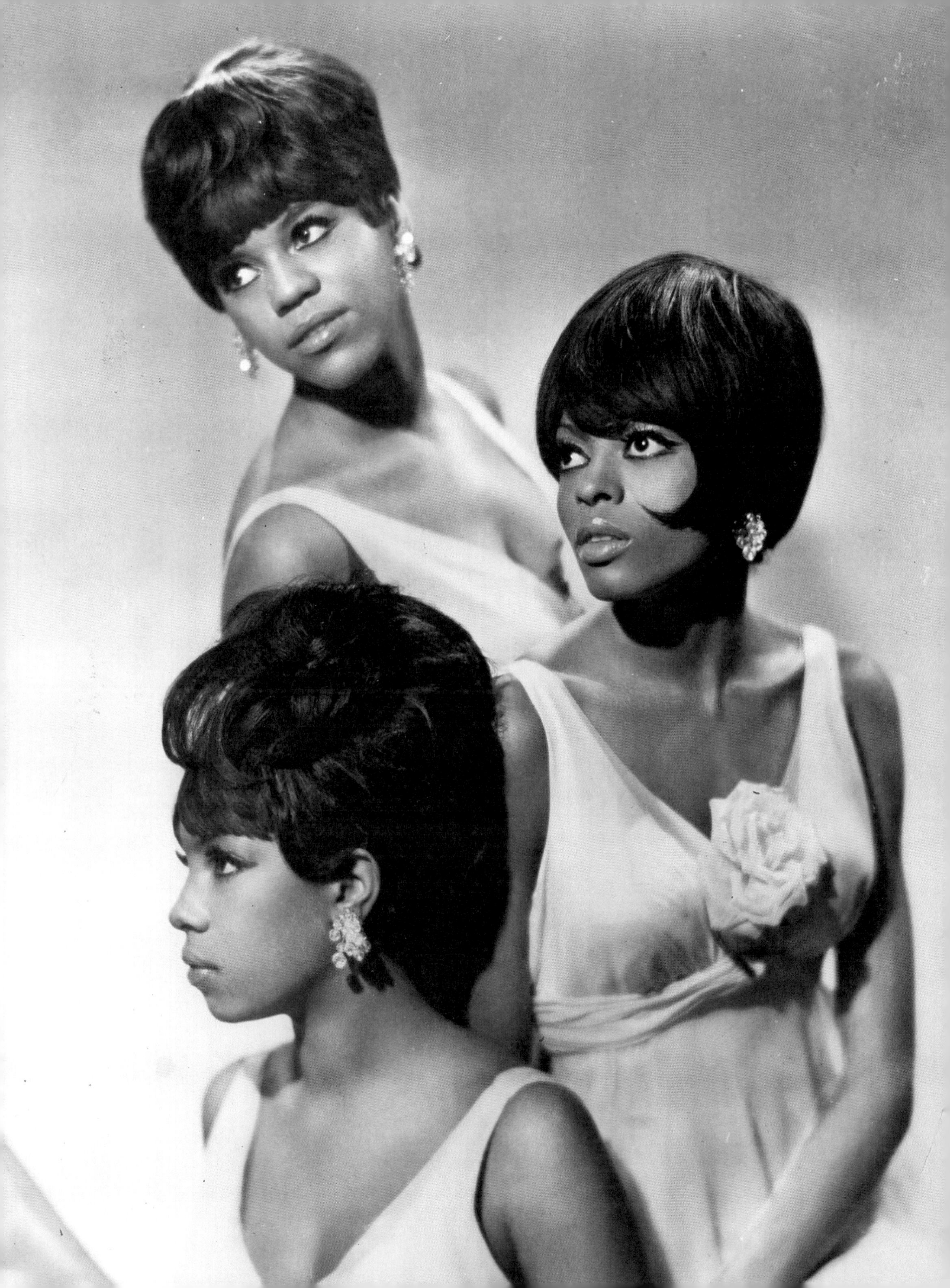

DESTINY'S CHILD

ALBUM

Survivor

Independent Women Part I • Survivor • Bootylicious • Nasty Girl • Fancy • Apple Pie À La Mode • Sexy Daddy • Perfect Man • Independent Women Part II • Happy Face • Dance With Me • My Heart Still Beats • Emotion • Brown Eyes • Dangerously In Love • The Story Of Beauty • Gospel Medley (Dedicated To Andretta Tillman): You've Been So Good / Now Behold The Lamb / Jesus Loves Me / Total Praise • Outro (DC-3) Thank You

Released in the USA by Sony Music/Columbia: 25 April 2001 (LP ref.: C2 61063, CD ref.: CK 61063)
Best chart ranking in the USA: 1

Having survived the internal conflict that shook the group, Destiny's Child picked themselves up and headed for even greater fame.

THE THREE AMAZONS OF R&B

The first concert Destiny's Child gave as a trio was on 18 July 2000 at the Hordern Pavilion in Sydney, Australia. Against all expectations, the three singers exuded an unprecedented energy during their performance, as much the result of the synergy between them as of the audience's welcome. "It was a bit scary," Beyoncé confided, "but we refused to let our differences with LeToya and LaTavia break up the group. As a music fan myself, I hate to see my favorite groups dissolve because of one or two changes. I prefer to see what will happen when they try to keep things going."[37] The day after the concert, the group decided their future lay in this line-up, and told Mathew Knowles, who immediately approved of their taking this risk. "It's part of the business," he confirmed. "The two best groups of all times, The Temptations and The Supremes, had people leave. The Temptations had 17 different members. So when you compare that with Destiny's Child, it's not a major deal."[46]

Mathew's Angels

On the return of Beyoncé, Kelly, and Michelle from their promotional trip to Australia, the decision to continue as a trio was confirmed. Another piece of good news came when Mathew Knowles informed them that Sony Pictures wanted to include one of their new songs, *Independent Women*, on the soundtrack of the movie adaptation of the television series *Charlie's Angels*, due to be released the following October. The cherry on the cake was that the clip of the song—for which release as a single seemed inevitable—featured not only the three singers but also the three stars of the movie: Drew Barrymore, Cameron Diaz, and Lucy Liu. It was July, and only a few weeks remained for Destiny's Child to prepare the release of this single so eagerly awaited by fans. When *Independent Women Part I* came out, on 29 August 2000, it was a colossal success and went straight to the top of the charts in many countries, including the United States, the United Kingdom, New Zealand, and Australia. In the song, the members of Destiny's Child revealed themselves to be strong women, determined to take charge of their destiny and asserting their independence from men. Boosted by the international success of their new single, they went ahead with recording their third album, the release of which was planned for the following April.

The Destiny's Child brand

Recording of *Survivor* started before the group's tour as the supporting act to Christina Aguilera—whose single *Genie in a Bottle* was selling outstandingly well—and was subject to ever-increasing rigor on the part of Destiny's Child, who worked tirelessly to prepare their big comeback. Mathew Knowles, for his part, was covering all bases, hoping the success of *Independent Women Part I* would do a lot to secure his protégées' future. "We started building the brand of Destiny's Child," he said. "After the second record, we said we would take the marketing dollars from Sony, and then we would go and find at least one strategic partner to partner up with [so] we could also have greater marketing dollars, and we could all go together marching in the same direction for success."[18] In 2004, Mathew Knowles elaborated further on his strategy when speaking to *Texas Monthly*: "When you sell a product, you first have to design and build it, but also you have

2001

96 SURVIVOR

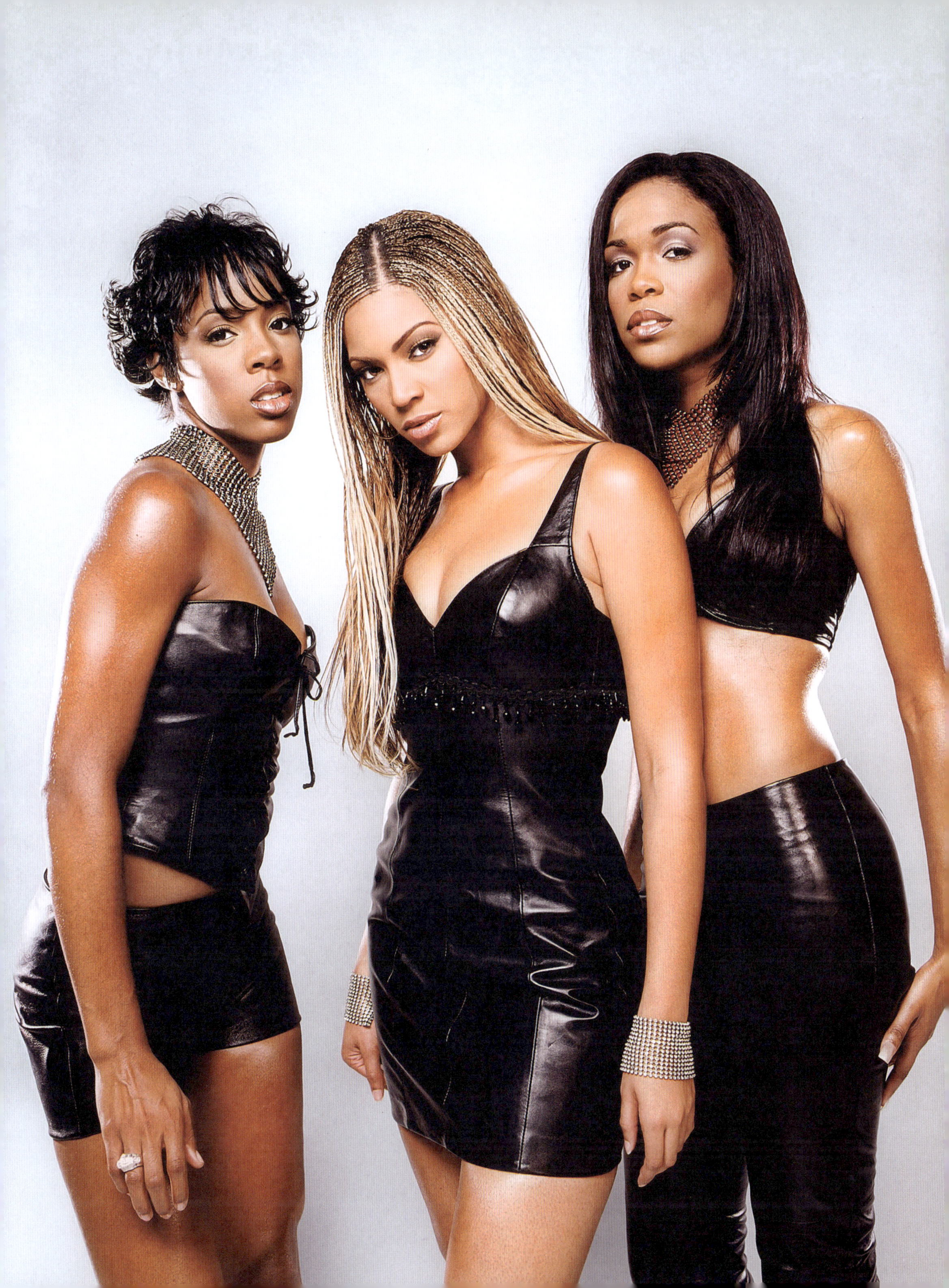

2001

to figure out the needs of the customer. When we put the group together, we had a plan. We figured out our demographic, our customers, our imaging, what type of songs we're going to sing. It's not by accident that we write songs like *Independent Women* and *Survivor*—female-based empowerment songs. That's our customer base."[11] In addition to the two songs mentioned, many others on the record contain a message aimed at women, urging them to build self-confidence, to persevere in the face of adversity, or commit to being proud of their body and their personality. As Beyoncé put it: "We were like, 'All the songs from this point on are gonna be about surviving something. It wasn't talking about relationships as much, like the last album.'"[55]

A procession of producers

To help them make their new album, Destiny's Child called on the services of D'Wayne Wiggins, Rob Fusari, Eric Seats, Rapture Stewart, and Ken "K-Fam" Fambro, who were joined by a long list of producers: Cory Rooney, Poke and Tone, Anthony Dent, Falonte Moore, Damon Elliott, Bill Lee, Calvin

98 SURVIVOR

Kelly, Beyoncé, and Michelle striking a *Charlie's Angels* pose.

Walter Afanasieff, one of the many artists who contributed to *Survivor*.

Gaines, Carsten Schack and Kenneth Karlin of the duo Soulshock & Karlin, Walter Afanasieff, Mark J. Feist, and Erroll "Poppi" McCalla Jr, with whom Beyoncé would later work again. The recording of *Survivor* also marked the moment when Beyoncé broke free once and for all from the diktats of outside producers: she was now co-producer of all the songs on the record. The atmosphere in the studio was assiduous, with each member of the group able to take part in putting the vocal lines together, even though Beyoncé Knowles and Kelly Rowland would perform most of them. Fun and relaxation reigned during the sessions, as Michelle Williams recalled: "We were just writing and eating, writing and eating in the studio. Chips, candy, smoothies, ordering a lot of Boston market rotisserie chicken, the sweet potato casserole, corn bread. Of course Popeyes—which gave us life-membership cards during the *Survivor* era."[56]

2001—the year of Destiny's Child

From the start of 2001, promotion of the three singers began. On 20 January they attended the inauguration of the Republican president George W. Bush, even though they declared that they did not belong to a political party or support Bush—nor his defeated Democratic rival, Al Gore. "It wasn't political," Tina Knowles explained. "The agreement was that the organizers would take down all the signs and everything that was politically connected and that they [the trio] would just perform for the kids."[57] On 6 March, *Survivor*, Destiny's Child's new single, was released, barely a month before the album. It was a success: the clip revealed the three singers as Amazons prepared to confront anyone who tried to belittle or wound them. Never before had Beyoncé shown herself to be so combative, as if the conflicts and breakups within Destiny's Child had unleashed in her a survival instinct of which she had hitherto been unaware. As she had written the song's lyrics, her talent as a songwriter was revealed too, and it now seemed as if nothing could stop her rise as an artist.

When the album *Survivor* was released, on 25 April, the world had eyes only for Destiny's Child, a trio of women who had succeeded in sweeping away the competition with an album that was committed, danceable, and touching at the same time. It sold almost 700,000 copies in a week in America alone. One thing was certain: Beyoncé's dazzling success was

Beyoncé and her famous low-rise jeans, emblematic of the R&B look in the early noughties.

The unexpected death of Lisa "Left Eye" Lopes in 2002 marked the end of the rivalry between Destiny's Child and TLC.

only just beginning. "The other day at home I was looking at our plaques and awards and they all seem to say, like, '2001,'" Michelle Williams said a few months after the album's release. "So I know that fifteen years down the line, people will be able to say, 'Gosh, 2001! That was a hot year for you.' So it's very amazing and we've been blessed to [have] accomplished things and be giving so many things and be acknowledged for so many things we have done through the years."[35]

The world of R&B was in mourning on 25 August 2001, when American media announced the death of the singer Aaliyah in a plane crash at Marsh Harbour, in the Abaco Islands in the Bahamas. Eight months to the day later, the charismatic Lisa "Left Eye" Lopes of TLC left us, killed in a car accident in Honduras, thus bringing to an end the legendary rivalry between TLC and Destiny's Child.

2001

100 SURVIVOR

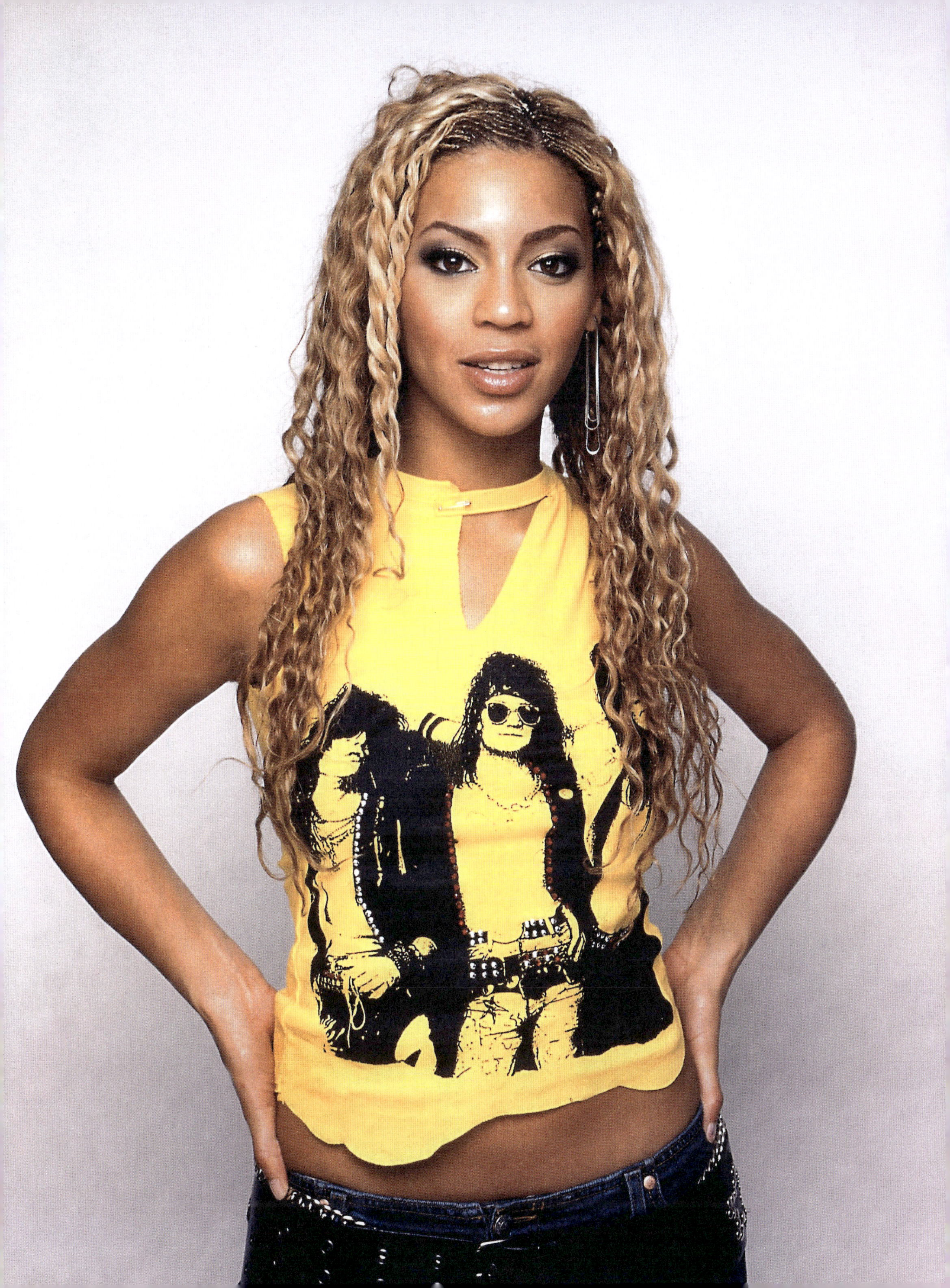

SINGLE

INDEPENDENT WOMEN PART I

(Beyoncé Knowles, Jean-Claude Olivier, Samuel J. Barnes/3'41)

Musicians
Beyoncé Knowles: vocals, backing vocals
Kelly Rowland: vocals, backing vocals
Michelle Williams: backing vocals

Recording
Lobo Studios, Deer Park: 2000
TK Disc Studios, Honolulu: 2000
SugarHill Recording Studios, Houston: 2000

Technical team
Producers: Beyoncé Knowles, Cory Rooney, Poke and Tone
Executive producer: Mathew Knowles
Recording engineers: Manelich Sotolongo, Ramon Morales, Troy Gonzalez

Single
Released in the USA by Sony Music Soundtrax: 5 December 2000
(maxi single CD ref.: 44K 79493)
Best chart ranking in the USA: 1

HEADPHONES AT THE READY

Beyoncé was accustomed to catchy motifs, and spent some time seeking a way to fill in the audible gaps at the start of each verse. "Well, there was a space in the song, so I needed a word. I went through 'listen' and 'check it out' and then … 'question'! Yeah! That's the best one."[61]

Genesis

When, in 2000, Sony Pictures put the final touches to the production of *Charlie's Angels*, adapted from the legendary 1970s' television series and directed by McG, the movie's musical director, John Houlihan, quickly had the idea of working with Destiny's Child, Sony Music/Columbia's goose that laid the golden eggs. Mathew Knowles, who was to the three singers what the character of Charlie Townsend is to the heroines of the series, sent Houlihan the demo recording of a song freshly recorded by Beyoncé, whose theme matched the movie's girl-power element pretty well. In *Independent Women Part I*, the trio sing about women's financial autonomy, encouraging them to free themselves of their dependence on men. "That song is intended to be an anthem to women who stand on their two feet, without needing a man to hold them up," Beyoncé explained.[37] She also saw the song, which is in the vein of feminist R&B songs of the period, as a sequel to *The Writing's on the Wall*, which had elicited much press comment. "That came out of *Bills, Bills, Bills*," she said in another interview. "That song was misunderstood. The song started off cool with this guy, but then he would use our car and not fill up the tank and use our phone to dial long-distance. But the chorus is so big that people didn't hear those words—they thought we were being gold-diggers. That always frustrated me, so I wrote *Independent Women*, you know."[58]

As the rappers of Salt-N-Pepa had done in 1990 with the very feminist *Independent* on their album *Blacks' Magic*, where they take a similar line to Destiny's Child, the latter pursued their quest for freedom and declared loud and clear their liberation from male power, which would become one of the recurring themes in Beyoncé's discography. John Houlihan, for his part, could only congratulate himself on having agreed to include the song in the movie, for the two were inextricably linked on their release—images of the Charlie's Angels Drew Barrymore, Lucy Liu, and Cameron Diaz were even included in the clip, which was made by the director Francis Lawrence between August and September 2001. "Destiny's Child was a dream act," Houlihan said. "From the very get-go of that song, Beyoncé is giving a shoutout to the actors by name: 'Lucy Liu, Cameron D, my girl Drew.' To have the lyrics 'Charlie, how your Angels get down like that' in the chorus was a best-case scenario."[59] A multi-million-dollar scenario, for the movie

Drew Barrymore, Cameron Diaz, and Lucy Liu are the fearsome funny women in McG's film.

earned Sony Pictures more than $264 million, while *Independent Women Part I* entered the *Guinness Book of World Records* as the song by a female group that had spent longest at number 1 in the *Billboard* chart.

Production

Although the lyrics of *Independent Women Part I* are by Beyoncé, its music is the work of three talented composers and producers from the heyday of Sony Music in previous years. Two of these were the duo Poke and Tone, real names Jean-Claude Olivier and Samuel J. Barnes, the former renowned for his work on the hits *If I Ruled the World (Imagine That)* by Nas and Lauryn Hill (1996), *Men in Black* by Will Smith (1997), and *(Holy Matrimony) Letter to the Firm* by Foxy Brown, which features on the much-loved soundtrack to Quentin Tarantino's *Jackie Brown*, released in 1997. The other master was Cory Rooney, who had already produced *Sail On* on *Destiny's Child*. Rooney, the son of none other than Herb Rooney, occasionally a producer for The Isley Brothers, had an equally impressive CV. He was behind the first hit by Mary J. Blige, *Real Love* (1992), and his reputation had been boosted by the success of Jennifer Lopez's *If You Had My Love* (1999). As someone accustomed to turning everything he touched into gold, Rooney explained his approach to writing on the Universal Audio website in 2003: "It's not just the beat of the record, everything is important. The melody can't be too complicated, it has to have a great hook that's commercial enough for people to catch the first time they hear it. I feel like I can 'design' a hit record. Writing gives me a big advantage, it goes hand in hand with producing."[60]

SINGLE

SURVIVOR

(Anthony Dent, Beyoncé Knowles, Mathew Knowles/4'14)

Musicians
Beyoncé Knowles: vocals, backing vocals
Kelly Rowland: vocals, backing vocals
Michelle Williams: vocals, backing vocals
Redd: synthesizers
Karren Berz: violin

Recording
Chase Studios, Atlanta: 2000
The Enterprise, Burbank: 2000

Technical team
Producers: Anthony Dent, Beyoncé Knowles
Executive producer: Mathew Knowles
Recording engineers: Anthony Dent, Orlando Calzada, Brian Springer
Assistant recording engineer: Rich Balmer

Single
Released in the USA by Sony/Columbia: 6 March 2001
(single ref.: 38 079582)
Best chart ranking in the USA: 2

FOR DESTINY'S CHILD ADDICTS

For the shoot of the *Survivor* clip, the three members of Destiny's Child used wigs identical to their hairstyles in order to avoid having to dry their hair when it got wet. At the very end of the clip, when they rush to the helicopter that has come to save them from the shipwreck they have been involved in, Kelly Rowland's wig has been blown away by the wind from the aircraft's rotor blades. "They think we're running away from the helicopter because the sand is beating us," Beyoncé laughed, "but we're running after her wig!"[62]

HEADPHONES AT THE READY

Mathew Knowles is credited as co-writer of *Survivor*, but his involvement in the song is unconnected either to the lyrics or to the instrumental part. In fact, he asked the singers to add, at the end of each line in the choruses, the famous "What?", which stuck in the minds of listeners…and which brought him plentiful royalties in the process.

Genesis

The spring of 2000 saw the start of the first tour by the former star of the show *The All-New Mickey Mouse Club*, singer Christina Aguilera, who had just had a spectacular success with her single *Genie in a Bottle*. The numerous groups invited to be supporting acts on the tour included Destiny's Child, who were then in the midst of writing their third album. As the trio were on a bus to the airport, heading to an upcoming concert, the radio broadcast a program in which the presenter commented ironically on their situation, comparing it to a famous television show set on an island where contestants are eliminated one after the other. As Beyoncé recalled, the radio was saying, "'Destiny's Child is like the *Survivor* series, we're trying to see which member is gonna end up the last on the island, which one is gonna get voted off.' It was a joke. It was actually cute and it inspired me to write a song. I was like 'We can use a negative thing to turn to a positive thing and do a whole *Survivor* video and laugh at them, and make fools out of them.' And that's what we did."[62] Written on board the aircraft that was taking them to their next tour date, the lyrics to *Survivor* quickly became universal, aimed at those who are forced to struggle in their lives. "It's a positive song," Beyoncé said, "and it's something we can relate to and something that a lot of people can relate to, not only people that's been through things in groups but surviving cancer, AIDS, and racism, and all different things that happen in life."[62]

Production

With its backing vocals reminiscent of those in *Gangsta's Paradise*, a 1995 hit by the rapper Coolio, *Survivor* remains unquestionably the most famous song by Destiny's Child when they were a trio (nicknamed DC-3 by their fans). Its instrumental part is the work of the producer and composer Anthony Dent, who had previously worked with Puff Daddy, Jay-Z, Mya, and Faith Evans. Before Dent even knew what the song was about, he intuitively wanted to write a powerful, danceable track for the three singers, with a forceful sound and incisive production. "It was an aggressive track, the music part of it was before the lyrics, so I didn't know it was *Survivor*. I kind of did the music […] with her in mind, with an aggressive rap music collaboration," Dent said. "I can't say exactly was going in, I knew what was on my mind, […] I just wanted the

Destiny's Child in military fatigues, ready to let rip at their detractors.

music to be aggressive."[63] Even sharper than the original version, the remix, featuring the rapper Da Brat and renamed *Survivor (remix extended version)*, later featured on a maxi single containing various reinterpretations of the song by the producers Victor Calderone, Charlie Rosario, Maurice Joshua, and Kay Fingers.

After the 9/11 attacks on 11 September 2001, the song *Survivor* acquired a new life, with many Americans re-appropriating it as bearing witness to their resilience in the face of the acts that had plunged their country into mourning. "I remember *Survivor* having an anthemic second life [as the nation was] getting past the terrorist attacks," recalled John Houlihan, the musical director for the movie *Charlie's Angels*. "*Survivor* went from being a personal power song to being a tool for national grief in a way to show solidarity and strength."[56]

BEYONCÉ: ALL THE SONGS   105

SINGLE

BOOTYLICIOUS

(Beyoncé Knowles, Falonte Moore, Rob Fusari, Stevie Nicks/3'27)

Musicians
Beyoncé Knowles: vocals, backing vocals
Kelly Rowland: vocals, backing vocals
Michelle Williams: vocals, backing vocals

Recording
SugarHill Recording Studios, Houston: 2000
Sound on Sound, New York: 2000

Technical team
Producers: Beyoncé Knowles, Falonte Moore, Rob Fusari
Executive producer: Mathew Knowles
Recording engineer: Dan Workman

Single
Released in the USA by Sony Music/Columbia: 17 July 2001
(CD single ref.: 38K 79629)
Best chart ranking in the USA: 1

Genesis

One of the goals Destiny's Child set themselves in 2000, while working on their album *Survivor*, was to encourage women to be proud of themselves and of their bodies. Beyoncé, who wrote almost all the lyrics for the record, throws herself into this with the outspoken *Bootylicious*, made for the dancefloor and with words inspired by her personal experience. "Some days I look in the mirror and feel good but others I'm just like 'ugh!' I've got hips and thighs; people will tell me to lose five pounds. This is typical of most women, so I wrote a song about just being proud of your body and loving what you've got."[64] In order to do this, Beyoncé invented a word: "bootylicious." "If you've got a big booty, then it's OK," said Michelle Williams. "Put on some pants and be confident."[13] The song made number 1 in the *Billboard* chart on its release as a single in 2001, and earned an extraordinary privilege: the word "bootylicious" was included in the *Oxford English Dictionary*, to the astonishment of its inventor. "I still can't believe it!" laughed Beyoncé in 2010. "It's hilarious. I actually wish it was another word that I created. I wish it didn't have 'booty' in it."[65]

Production

Bootylicious was created in the basement of Rob Fusari, the hit-maker who had been responsible for *No, No, No Part 2* in 1997. Fusari, now enjoying the international success of the hit *Wild Wild West*, which he had produced for Will Smith in 1999, was approached again by Teresa LaBarbera Whites and Mathew Knowles, to whom he sent some 30 demo recordings during the pre-production stage of *Survivor*. Four were retained: they would later become *Apple Pie à la Mode*, *Happy Face*, *Outro (DC-3) Thank You*, and *Bootylicious*. For the last of these Fusari wanted to sample the guitar riff from the introduction of *Eye of the Tiger* by the group Survivor (you couldn't make it up). Not having the record to hand, he made do with the album *Bella Donna* (1981) by Stevie Nicks, inimitable vocalist with Fleetwood Mac, where he found the single *Edge of Seventeen*, introduced by a similar riff played by guitarist Waddy Wachtel. On her first listening, Beyoncé was delighted by the piece, for which she wanted to write as soon as possible lyrics on a subject she had in mind for some time. Fusari reserved it for her (the hip-hop group Bell Biv Devoe also wanted it), but told Mathew Knowles he wanted to

FOR DESTINY'S CHILD ADDICTS

Although only the introduction to *Edge of Seventeen* was sampled for *Bootylicious*, the legendary Stevie Nicks had pride of place in the clip of the song, for she was invited to the shooting and even appears for a few seconds, guitar in hand, at the start of the video. "They gave me a chance to pretend like I was playing guitar," she laughed. "I don't think anybody ever gave me that chance ever again."[68]

Stevie Nicks was one of the singers in Fleetwood Mac, a group she joined in 1975 along with her then partner, Lindsey Buckingham.

re-record the introductory motif himself. "I figured I'd put the guitar loop on there temporarily," Fusari explained, "[…] because I'd learned, after sampling Stevie Wonder's *I Wish* for Will Smith's *Wild Wild West*, that I didn't want to lose 50 percent of the publishing. I vividly remember telling Mathew Knowles, 'Mathew, you got to book me into your studio and let me replay that riff.' He didn't want to do it. So 50 percent got cut for one note. That whole experience was bittersweet for me."[28]

Only once she was in the studio with the recording engineer Dan Workman did Beyoncé write the lyrics for the song, which she then recorded immediately with Michelle and Kelly. "Beyoncé would be driving over to the studio listening to all these tracks that had been sent to her, and she would pick out her favorite," Workman remembered. "When she got here, she would immediately start writing lyrics for the song and finish it right there in front of me. For the song *Bootylicious* she wrote all the lyrics for it right in [SugarHill Recording Studios'] Studio A. Then she taught the song to Kelly and Michelle, and all three of them worked on the vocals together."[66] "When I was cutting that song," he concluded, "I definitely had the sense of 'Oh my gosh, this is one of those moments.' I knew it was going to be a hit record. I've had that maybe twice in my career. It was just greatness."[67]

BEYONCÉ: ALL THE SONGS 107

James McShane, singer with the group Baltimora at the time of their 1985 hit *Tarzan Boy*.

NASTY GIRL

(Anthony Dent, Beyoncé Knowles, Maurizio Bassi, Naimy Hackett/4'17)

Musicians: Beyoncé Knowles: vocals, backing vocals / Kelly Rowland: vocals, backing vocals / Michelle Williams: vocals, backing vocals / **Recording:** Chase Studios, Atlanta: 2000 / Digital Services Recording Studios, Houston: 2000 / **Technical team:** Producers: Anthony Dent, Beyoncé Knowles / **Executive producer:** Mathew Knowles / **Recording engineer:** James Hoover

HEADPHONES AT THE READY

At 3'00 in *Nasty Girl*, Beyoncé launches into a tune familiar to those who know 1980s pop. It is the vocal motif of *Tarzan Boy*, sung by the Italian singer-songwriter Baltimora in 1985. With a commendable sense of fair play, Destiny's Child credited Maurizio Bassi and Naimy Hackett, who created that hit, as co-writers of *Nasty Girl*.

2001

In this song Beyoncé settles scores with young women dressed in a manner she deems far too vulgar. That is the message of *Nasty Girl*, stunningly produced by Anthony Dent, who also made the song *Survivor*. Even though the message seems offensive to women who want to dress as they like (a paradox with regard to which Beyoncé would have to evolve over the years), the three singers stood their ground in interviews, determined to get their own back on those seductive young women who had crossed their path. "The song has a positive message to it," Beyoncé explained. "It lets people know that it's about how you carry yourself in your clothes."[69] She had no objection, she went on to say, to a girl dressing sexily, perhaps showing a bit of cleavage, so that people noticed and thought she looked good. "But then you see a girl who's a little nasty and on top of that, and the way she's acting is nasty. That's what the song is about."[69] Given that ultimately the concept of vulgarity is highly subjective, let us give the benefit of the doubt to those young women whom the three singers attack head-on. The critics wasted no time in coming down heavily on the group, who were well known for their skimpy outfits. "Destiny's Child is about being sexy but always classy," Beyoncé hit back. "Our clothes may be revealing, but you'll never see one of our boobs popping out. I'm hoping people won't get mad about that song!"[64]

108 SURVIVOR

FANCY

(Beyoncé Knowles, D'Wayne Wiggins, Jonathan Rotem/4'12)

Musicians: Beyoncé Knowles: vocals, backing vocals / Kelly Rowland: backing vocals / Michelle Williams: backing vocals / D'Wayne Wiggins: guitar / Jonathan Rotem: additional instruments / **Recording:** Digital Services Recording Studios, Houston: 2000 / House of Music, Oakland: 2000 / **Technical team:** Producers: Beyoncé Knowles, D'Wayne Wiggins / Executive producer: Mathew Knowles / Recording engineers: James Hoover, Terry T

There is a rancor in *Fancy* that indicates rivalry between two young women. Co-produced by Beyoncé and D'Wayne Wiggins, the song is built around a typical 1990s groove, which inevitably gives a somewhat old-fashioned feel to the track—one could swear it had been recorded by En Vogue, a pioneering female R&B group. Once again, Beyoncé took care of writing the song's lyrics, even though the studio work remained a family affair. "They took their time to pick lyrics and make sure they had the right clever words," Wiggins recalled. "[…] They shared the energy, they supported each other, and they would just take a song and dissect it and put it back together again. For *Fancy*, it took [only] about 30 or 45 minutes to change the hook."[59] Jonathan Rotem, a future superstar producer, was also a co-writer of the song. He explained his way of working when writing it: "Back then, I was making beats on one keyboard and one drum machine. I can hear now that sonically *Fancy* was a smaller sound: I can hear it was just made on one keyboard and one drum machine, max. […] There was a real purity to that song."[59]

APPLE PIE À LA MODE

(Beyoncé Knowles, Falonte Moore, Rob Fusari/2'58)

Musicians: Beyoncé Knowles: vocals, backing vocals / Kelly Rowland: backing vocals / Michelle Williams: backing vocals / **Recording** / Sound on Sound, New York: 2000 / Digital Services Recording Studios, Houston: 2000 / The Enterprise, Burbank: 2000 / **Technical team:** Producers: Beyoncé Knowles, Falonte Moore, Rob Fusari / Executive producer: Mathew Knowles / Recording engineers: James Hoover, Kent Huffnagle

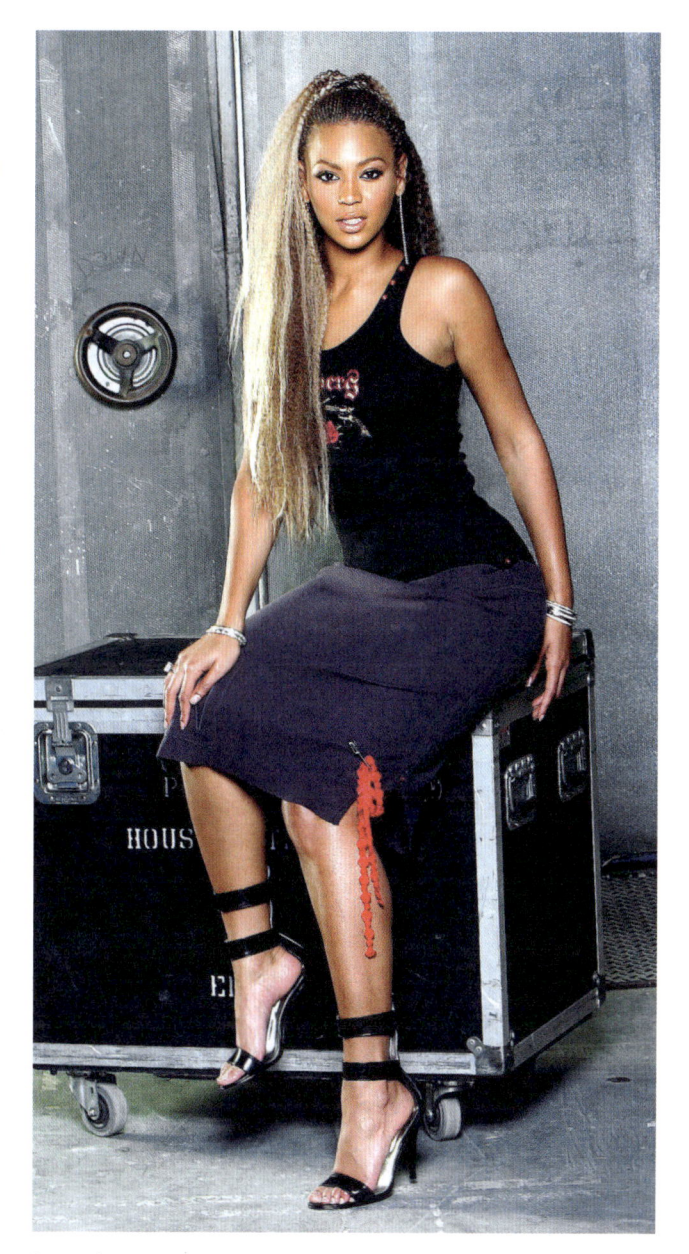

Beyoncé Knowles posing at the Houston Films & Productions studios in November 2001.

Comparing a young man who just walked into a nightclub where she was with her friends to an apple pie à la mode—that is, served with ice cream, a typical American dish—Beyoncé now revealed herself as a woman who owned her desire, and had left behind the prudishness of her younger years. Although she was to acknowledge her transition to adulthood and her sensuality more clearly in her first solo album in 2003, she seemed ill at ease when talking about desire and sensuality to journalists, as if reality and the world of her songs were still clearly separate. "Well, we never talk about…um, sexuality," she said in 2001. "That's private. Everybody has their own preference and we're not trying to put our beliefs on anybody. There's a lot of people that have sex before marriage, and who are we to tell them that that's wrong?"[61] Co-produced by Rob Fusari, the song aims to be danceable and benefits from highly effective production. "It was great working with Beyoncé," the hit-maker said in 2005. "She's an extremely gifted artist, and she's the real deal as a songwriter."[70]

Producer Damon Elliott modernized the Destiny's Child sound by introducing a reggaeton feel.

SEXY DADDY

(Anthony Dent, Beyoncé Knowles, Maurizio Bassi, Naimy Hackett/4'17)

Musicians: Beyoncé Knowles: vocals, backing vocals / Kelly Rowland: vocals, backing vocals / Michelle Williams: vocals, backing vocals / **Recording:** Digital Services Recording Studios, Houston: 2000 / The Enterprise, Burbank: 2000 / **Technical team: Producers:** Beyoncé Knowles, Damon Elliott / **Executive producer:** Mathew Knowles / **Recording engineers:** James Hoover, Damon Elliott / **Assistant recording engineer:** Wassin Zreik

Damon Elliott, son of the legendary singer Dionne Warwick, was the producer at the controls of the avant-garde *Sexy Daddy*, which combines the sensuality of R&B with the harmonizing voices typical of DC-1 (nickname of the first version of Destiny's Child), but also with a reggaeton rhythm that Beyoncé would use again in *Baby Boy* in 2003. To bring his productions to life, Elliott mostly used his beloved Korg Triton synthesizer, which he complemented with samples contained in his MPC3000. Launched by the Japanese company Akai in 1994, the MPC3000 is the little brother of the legendary MPC60 which, since 1988, had enabled users to record sound, retain it in the machine, and re-use it as desired using pads contained in the upper part of the device. This is how the sample technique—widely used by musicians, especially in hip-hop—was born. For *Sexy Daddy*, Damon Elliott went off the beaten track, using his favorite instrument in an unexpected way. "I use the MPC3000, I have for years," he said in 2009. "That's my baby. You know, I have four of them, two that travel with me and two that stay stationary [...]. When I was working with Beyoncé's and Destiny's samples, I sampled a vacuum cleaner. [...] I used the vacuum cleaner like as a bassline, you know, and it tweaked in and worked out really well. [...] And I didn't know if I'd have to pay Hoover the rights. So hopefully Hoover don't come after me."[71]

PERFECT MAN

(Beyoncé Knowles, Eric Seats, Rapture Stewart/3'41)

Musicians: Beyoncé Knowles: vocals, backing vocals / Kelly Rowland: backing vocals / Michelle Williams: backing vocals / **Recording:** Soundtrack Studios, New York: 2000 / **Technical team: Producers:** Eric Seats, Rapture Stewart, Beyoncé Knowles / **Executive producer:** Mathew Knowles / **Recording engineer:** Michael Conrader

The duo Key Beats—consisting of the producers Rapture Stewart and Eric Seats, and famous for having made one of the biggest R&B hits of 1999, *Where My Girls At?* by 702—were also responsible for the innovative *Perfect Man*, in which samples blend with the melody, sung almost exclusively by Beyoncé. But the squabbles of not so long ago, caused especially by Beyoncé's leadership and her vocal omnipresence in the group's songs, now seemed to belong in the past; the three singers had drawn a line under their quarrels to make their group rise from the ashes, as Michelle Williams described to *Jet* in May 2001. "With the three of us in the group there is no envy and no jealousy about who is going to sing lead and who is going to sing what. We support one another. We know who sounds the best at doing what."[46]

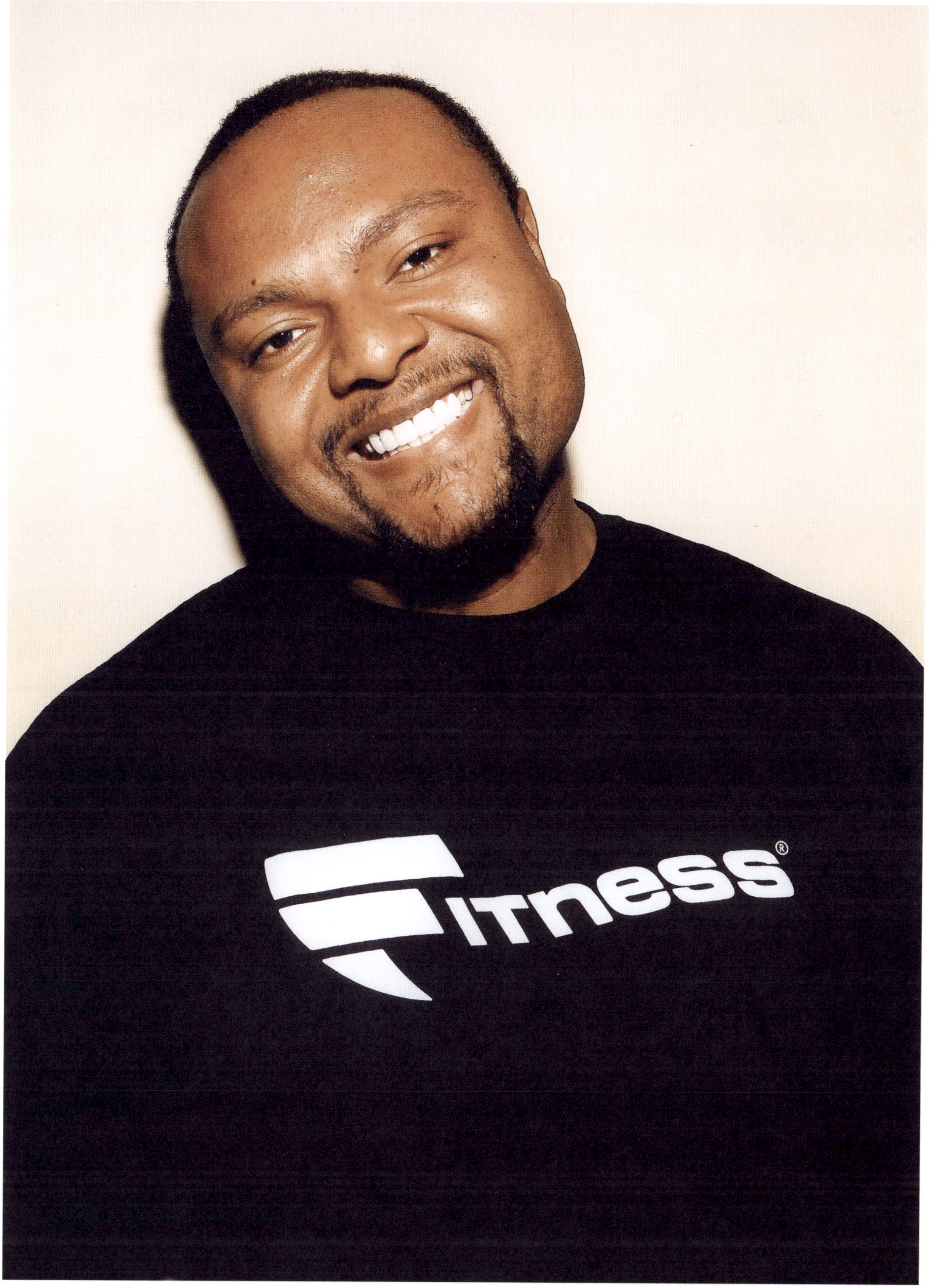
Fitness®

INDEPENDENT WOMEN PART II

(Beyoncé Knowles, David Donaldson, Eric Seats, Frank Comstock, Rapture Stewart / 3'45)

Musicians: Beyoncé Knowles: vocals, backing vocals / **Kelly Rowland:** backing vocals / **Michelle Williams:** backing vocals / **David Donaldson:** synthesizers / **Eric Seats:** additional instruments / **Rapture Stewart:** additional instruments / **Recording:** Chung King Studios, New York: 2000 / 24/7 Studio, Houston: 2000 / **Technical team: Producers:** Beyoncé Knowles, Eric Seats, Rapture Stewart / **Executive producer:** Mathew Knowles / **Recording engineer:** Michael Conrader

Starting with a sample from the credits of the cartoon *Peabody's Improbable History*, composed by Frank Comstock at the end of the 1950s, this second segment of *Independent Women*, logically enough entitled *Independent Women Part II*, has in common with *Part I* only the theme of women's autonomy, dear to Beyoncé's heart. The young woman reveals herself to be a man-eater when she sings: "*What you think about a girl like me?/Got my own car and spend my own money/Only ring your celly when I'm feelin' lonely/When it's all over, please get up and leave.*" Beyoncé was unquestionably independent. But it must be said that, despite her group's success, she struggled to make her mark as a songwriter in a music business still largely run by men. "Well, you get respect, but it's hard in the industry for critics to give you your props," she told the website VH1.com in 2002. "Guys can go onstage and take off their shirts and girls are going to scream, scream, scream. But girls can get on the stage and they have to work extra hard. And for writers, it's very, very hard. And me being young, it's ridiculously hard. To this day people do not know that my name is [listed] last [in credits], even if I write the majority of the songs, or they don't even want to give me 'co-produced' credit."[69]

Kelly, Beyoncé, and Michelle, inseparable in Houston, 2001.

HAPPY FACE

(Beyoncé Knowles, Bill Lee, Calvin Gaines, Falonte Moore, Rob Fusari/4'19)

Musicians: Beyoncé Knowles: vocals, backing vocals / **Kelly Rowland:** vocals, backing vocals / **Michelle Williams:** vocals, backing vocals / **Nunzio Signore:** guitar / **Recording:** Sound on Sound, New York: 2000 / Digital Services Recording Studios, Houston: 2000 / **Technical team:** Producers: Bill Lee, Calvin Gaines, Falonte Moore, Beyoncé Knowles, Rob Fusari / **Executive producer:** Mathew Knowles / **Recording engineer:** James Hoover

Although clearly the weak link in *Survivor, Happy Face* was at one time envisaged as the third single from the album, at the end of the summer of 2001, before being replaced by the Bee Gees' cover *Emotion*. The song, which is luminous and full of hope, came to Beyoncé one morning, when the previous evening she had gone to sleep feeling down. "In the song, I say there are plenty of people who don't like me, but there are ten times more who love me, and aside from that, I love myself. The song talks about waking up to the sun shining and outside is a beautiful day. […] I thought, Why am I complaining? I'm so blessed. Even if I didn't make it in the music industry, I'm lucky just to be alive and healthy, to have my family, and to have friends like Kelly and Michelle."[20]

DANCE WITH ME

(Beyoncé Knowles, Kenneth Karlin, Soulshock/3'43)

Musicians: Beyoncé Knowles: vocals, backing vocals / **Kelly Rowland:** backing vocals / **Michelle Williams:** backing vocals / **Carsten Schack:** additional instruments / **Kenneth Karlin:** additional instruments / **Recording:** Signet Sound, Los Angeles: 2000 / **Technical team:** Producers: Soulshock & Karlin, Beyoncé Knowles / **Executive producer:** Mathew Knowles / **Recording engineer:** William Malina

Another great catch for the Destiny's Child team, who this time brought in the Danish producers Soulshock & Karlin, otherwise known as Carsten Schack and Kenneth Karlin. The pair had enjoyed a boost to their reputation following the success of the single *Heartbreak Hotel*, initially written for TLC but adopted in 1998 by the superstar Whitney Houston for her album *My Love Is Your Love*. Also responsible for the magnificent *You Don't Know* by 702 the following year, the duo who transformed everything they touched into gold were no beginners when they worked with Beyoncé, Michelle, and Kelly. In this song, Beyoncé sings about the pleasure of having fun with her friends, and asks an attractive young man to come and dance with her. Although this subject matter brings rather a light touch to the album's feminist vein, the singer did not hesitate to temper its casual nature in an interview, emphasizing that it was more important to have real talent than to be beautiful, because beauty fades: "There have been millions of beautiful bands that have come and gone, but if you don't have any substance and talent behind it, then after one or two albums there's another beautiful band there to take your place."[69]

MY HEART STILL BEATS
(FEATURING BEYONCÉ)

(Beyoncé Knowles, Walter Afanasieff/4'08)

Musicians: Beyoncé Knowles: vocals, backing vocals / **Kelly Rowland:** backing vocals / **Michelle Williams:** backing vocals / **Walter Afanasieff:** bass guitar, synthesizers, programming / **Robert Conley:** programming / **Greg Bieck:** synthesizers, programming / **Recording:** Wally World Studios, Los Angeles: 2000 / The Hit Factory, New York: 2000 / **Technical team:** Producers: Beyoncé Knowles, Walter Afanasieff / **Executive producer:** Mathew Knowles / **Recording engineer:** Greg Bieck / **Assistant recording engineers:** Michael McCoy, Pete Krawiec / **Arrangements:** Walter Afanasieff

"Even if the name Walter Afanasieff means nothing to you, it's a safe bet you know his songs." That is the best way of introducing this American producer of Brazilian descent, responsible for a series of *Billboard* hits like few before him. Keyboard player on Whitney Houston's *I'm Your Baby Tonight* in 1990, multi-instrumentalist on Mariah Carey's *Hero* and *Without You* in 1993, co-writer of the inescapable *All I Want for Christmas Is You*, also by Mariah Carey, in 1994, and co-producer of *My Heart Will Go On*, recorded by Céline Dion for the soundtrack of James Cameron's movie *Titanic* in 1997, he is a true hit-maker. It was on a track quite similar to Céline Dion's hit that Afanasieff asked Beyoncé to sing. The rest of the group were not invited to the recording session—justifying the note "featuring Beyoncé" alongside the song's title.

EMOTION

(Barry Gibb, Robin Gibb/3'56)

2001

Musicians: Beyoncé Knowles: vocals, backing vocals / **Kelly Rowland:** backing vocals / **Michelle Williams:** backing vocals / **Erroll "Poppi" McCalla Jr:** programming / **Recording:** The Enterprise, Burbank: 2000 / SugarHill Recording Studios, Houston: 2000 / **Technical team: Producers:** Mark J. Feist, Mathew Knowles / **Executive producer:** Mathew Knowles / **Recording engineers:** Brian Springer, Dan Workman / **Best chart ranking in the USA:** 10

Composed in 1977 by the brothers Barry and Robin Gibb for the Australian singer Samantha Sang, *Emotion* has all the features of a hit by The Bee Gees, a group they formed with their brother Maurice. In 1998 the producer Mark J. Feist offered the Filipino singer Regine Velasquez a reinterpretation of the song, which featured on her album *Drawn*. This cover caught the attention of Mathew Knowles, who in turn introduced it to his daughter and encouraged her to perform it with Kelly Rowland and Michelle Williams. Feist used the instrumental part produced for Velasquez without changing a note, and gave it to Destiny's Child, who made it their own with brio. Beyoncé later confessed that she and her friends worried about doing cover songs, in case what they produced wasn't as good as the original. But in this case, she said, "…instead of trying to compete, we did it differently and added our Destiny's Child flavor to it."[69] *Emotion* got to number 10 on the *Billboard* Hot 100 even though it had been released only in a promotional format in the United States—distributed to the media as a CD but also as a double maxi single, accompanied by a series of remixes made by Victor Calderone, Maurice Joshua, and The Neptunes, the group consisting of Pharrell Williams and Chad Hugo.

Destiny's Child borrowed the single *Emotion* from the legendary Bee Gees.

BROWN EYES

(Beyoncé Knowles, Walter Afanasieff/4'36)

Musicians: Beyoncé Knowles: vocals, backing vocals / **Kelly Rowland:** backing vocals / **Michelle Williams:** backing vocals / **Walter Afanasieff:** bass guitar, synthesizers, programming / **Greg Bieck:** synthesizers, programming / **Robert Conley:** programming / **Recording:** Wally World Studios, Los Angeles: 2000 / The Hit Factory, New York: 2000 / **Technical team: Producers:** Beyoncé Knowles, Walter Afanasieff / **Executive producer:** Mathew Knowles / **Recording engineers:** David Gleeson, Greg Bieck / **Assistant recording engineers:** Michael McCoy, Pete Krawiec

This song, the second on which Beyoncé and Walter Afanasieff worked together, bears the hallmark of the composer/producer, who here again plays a synthesizer with a very 1990s sound, modeled on the Rhodes electric piano, though without its characteristic warmth of tone. Although the composer's skills as a hit-maker are apparent, these sounds do not work in Destiny's Child's favor—the music seems suddenly to have come straight from the soundtrack of an early 1990s film. But aside from this ultimately highly subjective issue, the track offers Beyoncé a playground worthy of her talents as a singer: she manages to push a slightly old-fashioned instrumental part into the background, thanks to her vocal prowess. Is that not the mark of a great artist?

DANGEROUSLY IN LOVE

(Beyoncé Knowles, Erroll "Poppi" McCalla Jr/5'06)

Musicians: Beyoncé Knowles: vocals, backing vocals / **Kelly Rowland:** backing vocals / **Michelle Williams:** backing vocals / **Dan Workman:** guitar / **John "Jab" Broussard:** guitar / **Recording:** SugarHill Recording Studios, Houston: 2000 / The Enterprise, Burbank: 2000 / **Technical team: Producers:** Beyoncé Knowles, Erroll "Poppi" McCalla Jr / **Executive producer:** Mathew Knowles / **Recording engineers:** Dan Workman, Brian Springer

Before becoming a favored associate of Destiny's Child and working with them on their album *8 Days of Christmas*, Erroll "Poppi" McCalla Jr endured some rebuffs from Mathew Knowles, to whom he tried to give many demo recordings when they met in Houston, where they both lived at the end of the 1990s. It took the intervention of the rapper Missy Elliott, a friend of McCalla, for the Knowles clan to start taking an interest in his work. "Missy played some of my music for them when they became excited about meeting me!" McCalla said in 2021. "As soon as they got back to Houston, I received a call from their A&R on a 3-way call with Mr. M. Knowles while en route from the airport. They wanted to meet me that evening and we made arrangements, met that evening, then started working together in the studio within days!"[72] During the first sessions together, McCalla created rhythmic lines over which Beyoncé wrote lyrics and melodies. These included *8 Days of Christmas* (which would be released in October 2001 on the album of that name), *Dot* (which features on the soundtrack of *Charlie's Angels*), *Independent Women*, and *Dangerously in Love*. The latter would give its name to Beyoncé's first solo album in 2003.

THE STORY OF BEAUTY

(Beyoncé Knowles, Ken Fambro/3'31)

Musicians: Beyoncé Knowles: vocals, backing vocals / **Kelly Rowland:** vocals, backing vocals / **Michelle Williams:** vocals, backing vocals / **Recording:** Stay Tuned Studio, Atlanta: 2000 / The Enterprise, Burbank: 2000 / **Technical team: Producers:** Beyoncé Knowles, Ken "K-Fam" Fambro / **Executive producer:** Mathew Knowles / **Recording engineer:** Brian Springer

The Story of Beauty is important in many respects. Aside from the careful production by Ken Fambro, the song relates the suffering of a young woman who has been raped by her stepfather. It was inspired by a young Destiny's Child fan who had written Kelly Rowland a letter in which she expressed her admiration for her, and also opened up about the violence of which she had been a victim. Beyoncé seized upon this distressing story to write the lyrics of the song, which the three singers performed with emotion. "It's letting her know that it's not her fault, and she can go on with her life," Michelle Williams explained in 2001.[13] With its sadly still topical message, *The Story of Beauty* found a new echo 17 years after its release with the emergence of the #MeToo movement, which fought to make the voices of women who had been victims of sexual violence—whether physical or psychological—heard.

Kirk Franklin, gospel singer and choirmaster, wrote *Now Behold the Lamb*, one of the songs on *Gospel Medley*.

GOSPEL MEDLEY
(DEDICATED TO ANDRETTA TILLMAN): YOU'VE BEEN SO GOOD/NOW BEHOLD THE LAMB/JESUS LOVES ME/ TOTAL PRAISE

Beyoncé Knowles, Kirk Franklin, Richard Smallwood/3'24

Musicians: Beyoncé Knowles: vocals, backing vocals / Kelly Rowland: vocals, backing vocals / Michelle Williams: vocals, backing vocals / **Recording:** SugarHill Recording Studios, Houston: 2000 / **Technical team:** Producer: Beyoncé Knowles / Executive producer: Mathew Knowles / Recording engineer: Dan Workman

If there was one thing the three members of Destiny's Child shared, it was their unshakeable faith in God, which they all demonstrated during their childhood, singing in their respective parish churches. In dedicating this medley of gospel songs to the sadly missed Andretta Tillman, who had been the group's very first manager a few years earlier, Destiny's Child here offered a digression, in which their three voices seemed to soar to the heavens. Of the four songs making up this potpourri only the first, *You've Been So Good*, was written specially for it. *Now Behold the Lamb* is by the singer and rapper Kirk Franklin, *Jesus Loves Me* is a traditional hymn, and the last, *Total Praise*, is by the American gospel singer Richard Smallwood. "[If] I'm confused about something I ask God to reveal the answers to my questions, and he does," Beyoncé said in 2001. "[…] You know, through God, I'm learning how to appreciate the good and the bad. That's why in *Gospel Medley* […], we thank God for our struggles, for our trials and tribulations, because they've made us who we are. If everything was perfect you would never learn and you would never grow."[57]

OUTRO (DC-3) THANK YOU

(Beyoncé Knowles, Bill Lee, Calvin Gaines, Kelly Rowland, Michelle Williams, Rob Fusari/4'04)

Musicians: Beyoncé Knowles: vocals, spoken voice, backing vocals / Kelly Rowland: vocals, spoken voice, backing vocals / Michelle Williams: vocals, spoken voice, backing vocals / **Recording:** Sony Music Studios, New York: 2000 / **Technical team:** Producers: Beyoncé Knowles, Rob Fusari, Bill Lee, Calvin Gaines / Executive producer: Mathew Knowles / Recording engineer: Jim Caruana

The only track on which all three members of Destiny's Child are credited, *Outro (DC-3) Thank You* is not a song, strictly speaking. Over an instrumental recording by Rob Fusari, Bill Lee, and Calvin Gaines, the three singers congratulate and thank one another, each listing the others' qualities at length. "It's really funny, 'cause some people have criticized that *Thank You* thing," Beyoncé said in 2002. "Whenever you do something different, people have something to say 'cause they don't understand it. I think we have made music history with this album, and I think people will start doing a lot more things like *Survivor*."[69] The recording session, run by Dan Workman, was completed in record time. The three singers recorded under live conditions, all grouped around the same microphone, which demanded great concentration, as well as managing their distance from the mic in order to achieve balance between their recorded voices. "I know that when we all wrote the song we were very emotional," Kelly Rowland recalled, "because it was written for each other and ourselves. It was kind of hard to record it, because we got choked up."[69]

2001

116 SURVIVOR

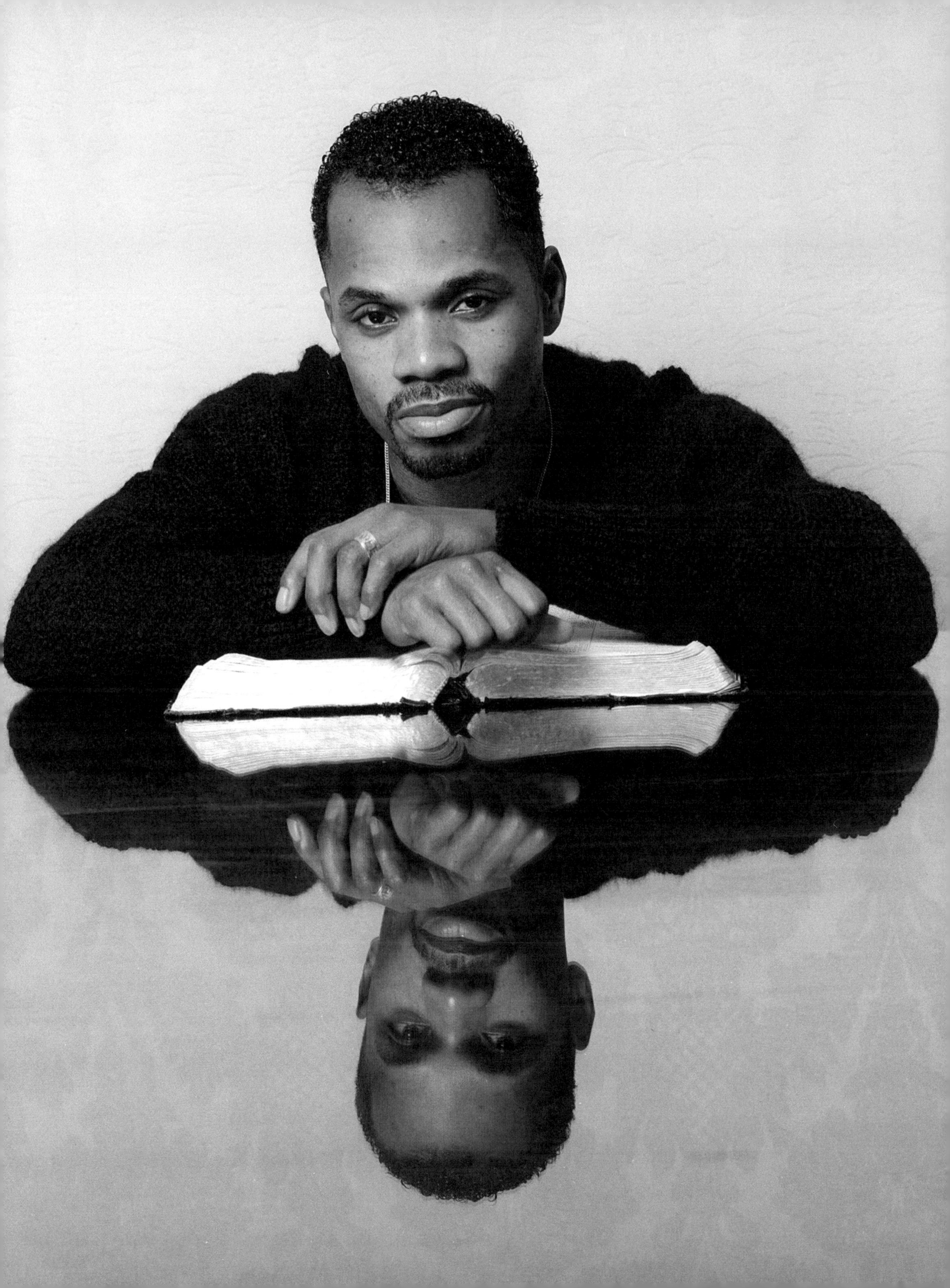

Photo session for the April 2001 issue of British magazine *Smash Hits*.

MY SONG

(Beyoncé Knowles, D'Wayne Wiggins, Jonathan Rotem/4'02)

Musicians
Beyoncé Knowles: vocals, spoken voice, backing vocals
Kelly Rowland: vocals, spoken voice, backing vocals
Michelle Williams: vocals, spoken voice, backing vocals
D'Wayne Wiggins: electric guitar
Jonathan Rotem: additional instruments

Recording
Digital Services Recording Studios: 2000
The Hit Factory, New York: 2000
House of Music, Oakland: 2000

Technical team
Producers: Beyoncé Knowles, D'Wayne Wiggins
Recording engineers: James Hoover, Joey Swails

Love: Destiny (EP)
Distributed in Target stores by Columbia: 10 July 2001 (CD ref.: CSK 16813)
Best chart ranking in the USA: did not make the charts

Genesis

Even though *Survivor* had been released almost three months earlier, in July 2001 the American chain store Target sold a special edition of the album, accompanied by an unreleased EP entitled *Love: Destiny*. The record contained many remixes of songs from *The Writing's on the Wall*: *Bug a Boo featuring Wyclef Jean (Refugee Camp Remix)*, *So Good (Digital Black-N-Groove Club Mix)*, *Say My Name featuring Timbaland and Static (Timbaland Remix)*, and *Jumpin', Jumpin' featuring Jermaine Dupri, Da Brat, and Lil' Bow Wow (So So Def Remix)*. Two more, from *Survivor*, also featured on the compilation's track listing: *Bootylicious (Love: Destiny Version)* and *Survivor (Victor Calderone Club Mix)*, and a new, unreleased track, *My Song*, formed the introduction to the record, to attract fans—and drive them to buy their idols' album a second time.

Production

Co-produced by the faithful D'Wayne Wiggins, the song is meticulously crafted, giving free rein to Beyoncé and her friends, who deliver a performance equal to those on the album where the song was originally meant to feature. Many such outtakes were to appear online over time. During the specific period corresponding to *Survivor*, these included, in no particular order, *Everything, Girl Like Me, Hold My Beer, I Gotta Leave You, I've Tried, Like Dat, Love Me Not, Paranoia,* and *This Love*—all posted illegally by unscrupulous bootleggers, but delighting fans. *My Song* was saved at the last minute from unofficial distribution by being included on *Love: Destiny*. To this day, fans still await a compilation bringing together Destiny's Child's numerous outtakes…

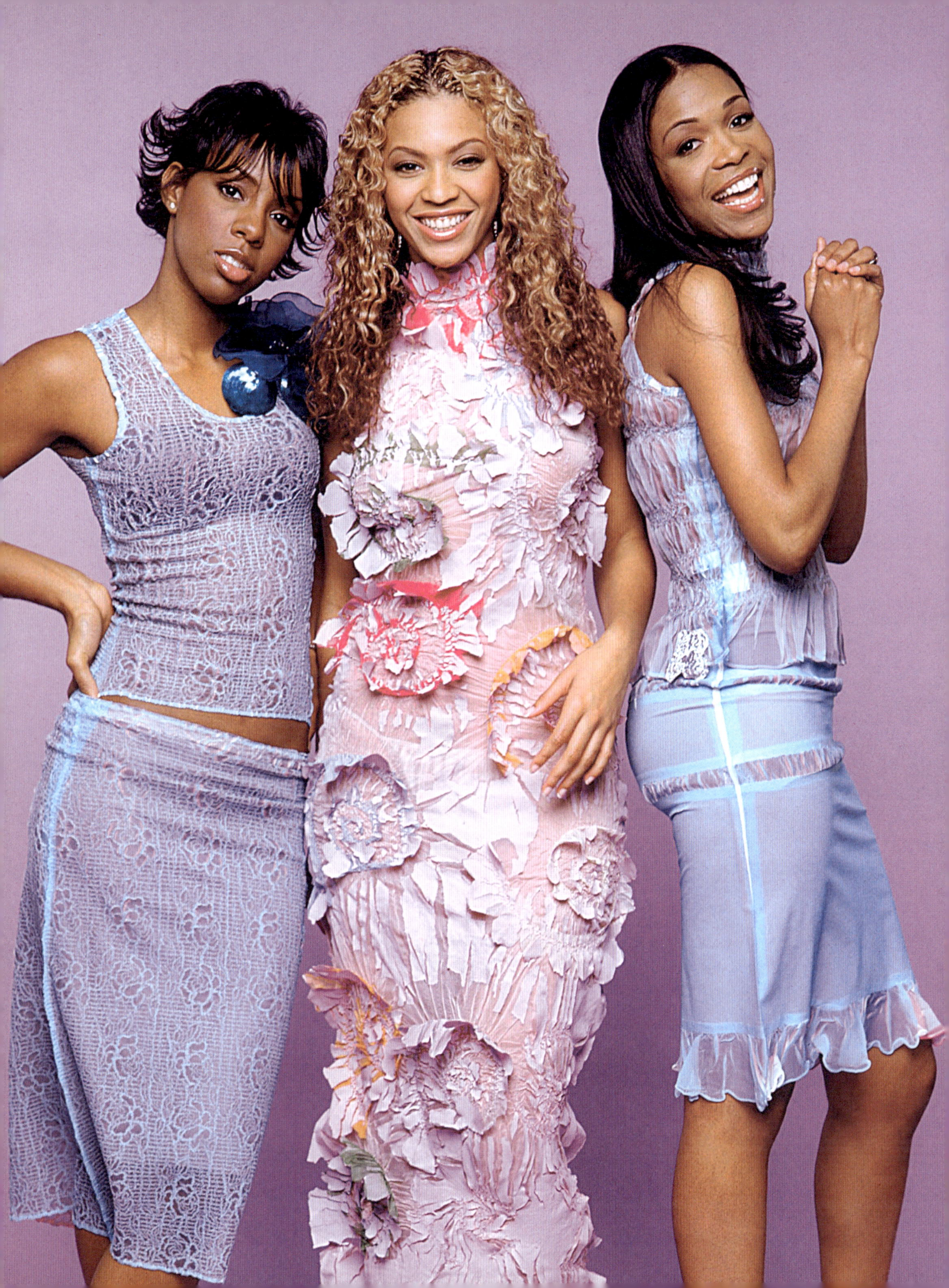

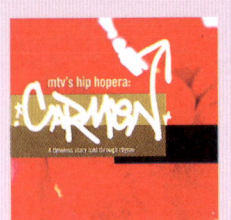

MTV's Hip Hopera: Carmen (compilation)
Released in the USA by Columbia: 25 June 2001 (CD ref.: 5033242000, maxi single ref.: 44 79620)

MTV's Hip Hopera: Carmen (2001)

1. **The Introduction**—Da Brat
2. **Survivor**—Destiny's Child
3. **Boom**—Royce Da 5'9"
4. **What We Gonna Do**—Rah Digga
5. **If Looks Could Kill (You Would Be Dead)**—Beyoncé Knowles & Mos Def & Sam Sarpong*
6. **Cards Never Lie**—Beyoncé Knowles & Wyclef Jean & Rah Digga*
7. **The Last Great Seduction**—Beyoncé Knowles & Mekhi Phifer*
8. **B.L.A.Z.E.**—Casey Lee & Rah Digga & Joy Bryant
9. **Black & Blue**—Mos Def & Mekhi Phifer
10. **Stop That!**—Beyoncé Knowles & Mekhi Phifer*
11. **Blaze Finale**—Casey Lee
12. **Immortal Beloved (Outro)**—Da Brat
13. **Bootylicious**—Destiny's Child

* *MTV's Hip Hopera: Carmen* features tracks by several artists; only those performed by Beyoncé are discussed here.

TELEVISION

CARMEN— HIP-HOP VERSION

While the recording of *Survivor* was progressing, Beyoncé was offered an audition for a television film produced by Graig Hutchison, to be broadcast on the American music channel MTV. Directed by Robert Townsend (who made *Hollywood Shuffle* in 1987 and *The Five Heartbeats* in 1991), the project aimed to offer an ultra-modern reinterpretation of Georges Bizet's opera *Carmen*, which had premiered on 3 March 1875 at the l'Opéra-Comique in Paris. This was not the first time such a project had been tried. The director and his screenwriter, Michael Elliot, made no secret of the fact they were inspired by *Carmen Jones*, a movie adaptation by Otto Preminger, which had been screened in cinemas in October 1954 and had been a great success at the time. What was new, though, was the casting, which comprised the cream of rap and R&B singers of the day—Mos Def, Rah Digga, Wyclef Jean, Da Brat, Jermaine Dupri, and Lil' Bow Wow; among the actors whose involvement in the movie was confirmed, Mekhi Phifer was to play the lead. Beyoncé was given the title role, and traveled to Los Angeles for the shooting. "MTV came to a Destiny's Child show with the script," she explained, "and at the time, acting wasn't something I was planning to do. […] We're not going to be the number one group in the world forever—so you have to have something else to fall back on. I did *Carmen* because I liked the script and I thought it was really cool. It was a great experience."[57]

Alone in LA

Aside from taking her first steps as an actor, Beyoncé took advantage of this period in Los Angeles to step outside her comfort zone, living alone in California, far from her family and friends. "My life, my job and responsibilities, and the pressures I've had have forced me to mature faster," she said in 2003. "When I had to do the movie *Carmen* at 18, I matured the most. It doesn't seem like a big film, but I was away from home, away from everything. Besides a new job, I had to make friends in a new city […] I had to depend on myself, and I had to grow. After that, I felt more confident, like I could accomplish anything."[16] *Carmen: A Hip Hopera* was broadcast on MTV 8 May 2001, and the soundtrack, *MTV's Hip Hopera: Carmen*, was released on 25 June.

IF LOOKS COULD KILL (YOU WOULD BE DEAD)
(BEYONCÉ KNOWLES, MOS DEF, SAM SARPONG)

(Sekani Williams/2'05)

Musicians: Beyoncé Knowles: vocals, backing vocals / Mos Def: rap / Sam Sarpong: rap / **Recording:** Doppler Studios, Atlanta: 2000 to 2001 / The Hit Factory, New York: 2000 to 2001 / Mirror Image Recorders, New York: 2000 to 2001 / Music Grinder Studios, Los Angeles: 2000 to 2001 / Right Track Recording, New York: 2000 to 2001 / SouthSide Studios, Atlanta: 2000 to 2001 / ULB Studios, New York: 2000 to 2001 / **Technical team:** Producer: Kip Collins / Recording engineers: Kip Collins, Larry Ferguson, Samie Barela

When Carmen Brown appears on the screen, the eyes of Lieutenant Frank Miller (Mos Def) and his young colleague Nathaniel (Sam Sarpong) are fixed on this beauty. A rap of seduction follows, produced by Kip Collins and written by Sekani Williams. "It was important to find a lyricist that could just make this all make sense but at the same time still be dope," the writer, Michael Elliot, said. "And it's a credit to Sekani, he did his thing."[73] While Carmen's red dress made an impression on viewers, the three actors' rap did as well, thanks to its meticulous production, perfectly suited to Beyoncé's precise flow.

CARDS NEVER LIE
(BEYONCÉ KNOWLES, WYCLEF JEAN, RAH DIGGA)

(Kip Collins, Sekani Williams/2'42)

Musicians: Beyoncé Knowles: vocals, backing vocals / Wyclef Jean: rap, vocals / Rah Digga: rap / **Recording:** Doppler Studios, Atlanta: 2000 to 2001 / The Hit Factory, New York: 2000 to 2001 / Mirror Image Recorders, New York: 2000 to 2001 / Music Grinder Studios, Los Angeles: 2000 to 2001 / Right Track Recording, New York: 2000 to 2001 / SouthSide Studios, Atlanta: 2000 to 2001 / ULB Studios, New York: 2000 to 2001 / **Technical team:** Producer: Kip Collins / Recording engineers: Andy Grassi, Kip Collins, Larry Ferguson, Samie Barela

When Carmen sits down at the table of the fortune-teller, played by Wyclef Jean, it is clear that the scene will live up to our expectations. Carmen hears dire predictions about her future: ruin, sorrow, and death. There follows a duet of high quality, in which Wyclef's warm, Caribbean-accented voice blends brilliantly with Beyoncé's. *Cards Never Lie* was also offered to British fans of Destiny's Child, on the maxi single of *Bootylicious*, released on 23 July 2001.

THE LAST GREAT SEDUCTION
(BEYONCÉ KNOWLES AND MEKHI PHIFER)

(Kip Collins, Sekani Williams/2'22)

Musicians: Beyoncé Knowles: vocals, rap / Mekhi Phifer: rap / **Recording:** Doppler Studios, Atlanta: 2000 to 2001 / The Hit Factory, New York: 2000 to 2001 / Mirror Image Recorders, New York: 2000 to 2001 / Music Grinder Studios, Los Angeles: 2000 to 2001 / Right Track Recording, New York: 2000 to 2001 / SouthSide Studios, Atlanta: 2000 to 2001 / ULB Studios, New York: 2000 to 2001 / **Technical team:** Producer: Kip Collins / Recording engineers: Kip Collins, Larry Ferguson, Samie Barela

For the scene in which Carmen tries to seduce Sergeant Derek Hill, played by Mekhi Phifer, Beyoncé did her best to prepare the role of the man-eater she was not in real life. "The seduction scene was the hardest thing for me to do," Beyoncé recalled. "When I read the script, I loved it, but when I read the seduction scene, I was like 'I can't do it'. Basically I got to get in my little outfit and take off my robe and dance around… We have to kiss like fifty times."[74] "I survived, it was not that bad," she said after the shooting. "You know my co-workers will be messing with me but we got through, we're cool, we're cool."[74]

STOP THAT!
(BEYONCÉ KNOWLES AND MEKHI PHIFER)

(Kip Collins/1'58)

Musicians: Beyoncé Knowles: rap / Mekhi Phifer: rap / **Recording:** Doppler Studios, Atlanta: 2000 to 2001 / The Hit Factory, New York: 2000 to 2001 / Mirror Image Recorders, New York: 2000 to 2001 / Music Grinder Studios, Los Angeles: 2000 to 2001 / Right Track Recording, New York: 2000 to 2001 / SouthSide Studios, Atlanta: 2000 to 2001 / ULB Studios, New York: 2000 to 2001 / **Technical team:** Producer: Kip Collins / Recording engineers: Kip Collins, Larry Ferguson, Samie Barela

This hard-hitting rap exchange between Mekhi Phifer and Beyoncé marks the end of the passionate relationship between Sergeant Derek Hill and Carmen Brown. "We wanted to push the envelope a bit with the musical numbers," said director Robert Townsend. "I was concerned about the raps at first, but we were really intent on making a smooth transition from dialogue to raps."[75] Beyoncé, who had never rapped before, played along with brio, displaying a skill she had not revealed until that point. "That was another thing I was nervous about. But instead of trying to be a rapper, I just talked like I normally talk, but to the beat."[73]

The first signs that Kelly Rowland and Beyoncé were moving away from Destiny's Child came with the single *Have Your Way*, released under both their names.

DOT

(Beyoncé Knowles, Erroll "Poppi" McCalla Jr/3'50)

Musicians: Beyoncé Knowles: vocals, backing vocals / **Kelly Rowland:** backing vocals / **Michelle Williams:** backing vocals / **Farrah Franklin:** backing vocals / **Recording:** ?: 2000 / **Technical team: Producers:** Beyoncé Knowles, Mathew Knowles, Erroll "Poppi" McCalla Jr / **Executive producer:** McG / **Recording engineer:** Dan Workman / *Charlie's Angels: Music from the Motion Picture* (compilation) / Released in the USA by Sony Music Soundtrax: 24 October 2000 (CD ref.: CK 61064)

Recorded at the same time as *Independent Women Part I*, *Dot* featured with it on the soundtrack of *Charlie's Angels* in October 2000. It was probably because of its caustic lyrics that the song was withdrawn from the track listing of *Survivor*, for in it Beyoncé reveals herself to be a strong woman prepared to confront those who criticize her. "*Shut up! No one said to open your mouth/Shut up! If you do not like me how about/Shut up! Why waste your energy on me?/Shut up! Is it 'cause you wanna be me?*" she sings, over an instrumental accompaniment by Erroll McCalla, who worked with Destiny's Child at the time but who is not always credited for his work on their records. "Thinking back, I don't even have all my credits corrected to date for so much work that I've done in the music industry, it's insane," the musician and producer said in 2021. "This is still happening to date in 2021 and is incredibly disrespectful to creators as they are depending on this to secure future work. I've really never been the type to care too much about it, just pay me correctly, and I'll shut up, lol," he added, referring to the "shut up" in the song.[72] *Dot* also featured on the soundtrack to *Lakeview Terrace*, a film by Neil LaBute released in 2008.

HAVE YOUR WAY
(BEYONCÉ AND KELLY FROM DESTINY'S CHILD)

(?/3'58)

Musicians: Beyoncé Knowles: vocals / **Kelly Rowland:** vocals / **Recording:** ? / **Technical team:** Producer: Fred Jerkins III / *His Woman His Wife (The Soundtrack)* (compilation) / Released in the USA by GospoCentric Records: 2000 (CD ref.: 606949054724)

The unreleased *Have Your Way* features on the soundtrack of the made-for-television film *His Woman His Wife*, directed by David E. Talbert and featuring Malik Yoba and Yvette Nicole Brown. The song is credited not to Destiny's Child, but to "Beyoncé & Kelly from Destiny's Child," as if to indicate that the work of the two singers on the song is a parenthesis in the group's recorded work. Produced by Fred Jerkins III, one of the composers of *Say My Name*, *Have Your Way* is not without merit, but does not have the qualities of an effective single. The song also features on the compilation *Spirit Rising Vol. 2: Inspirational*, produced by Columbia in 2003 in collaboration with Music World Music, Mathew Knowles's label.

HEADPHONES AT THE READY

R&B fans will doubtless see some similarities between the harmonies in *Dot* and those in the choruses of the Christina Aguilera single *Can't Hold Us Down*, produced by Scott Storch and released in July 2003.

COLLABORATIONS

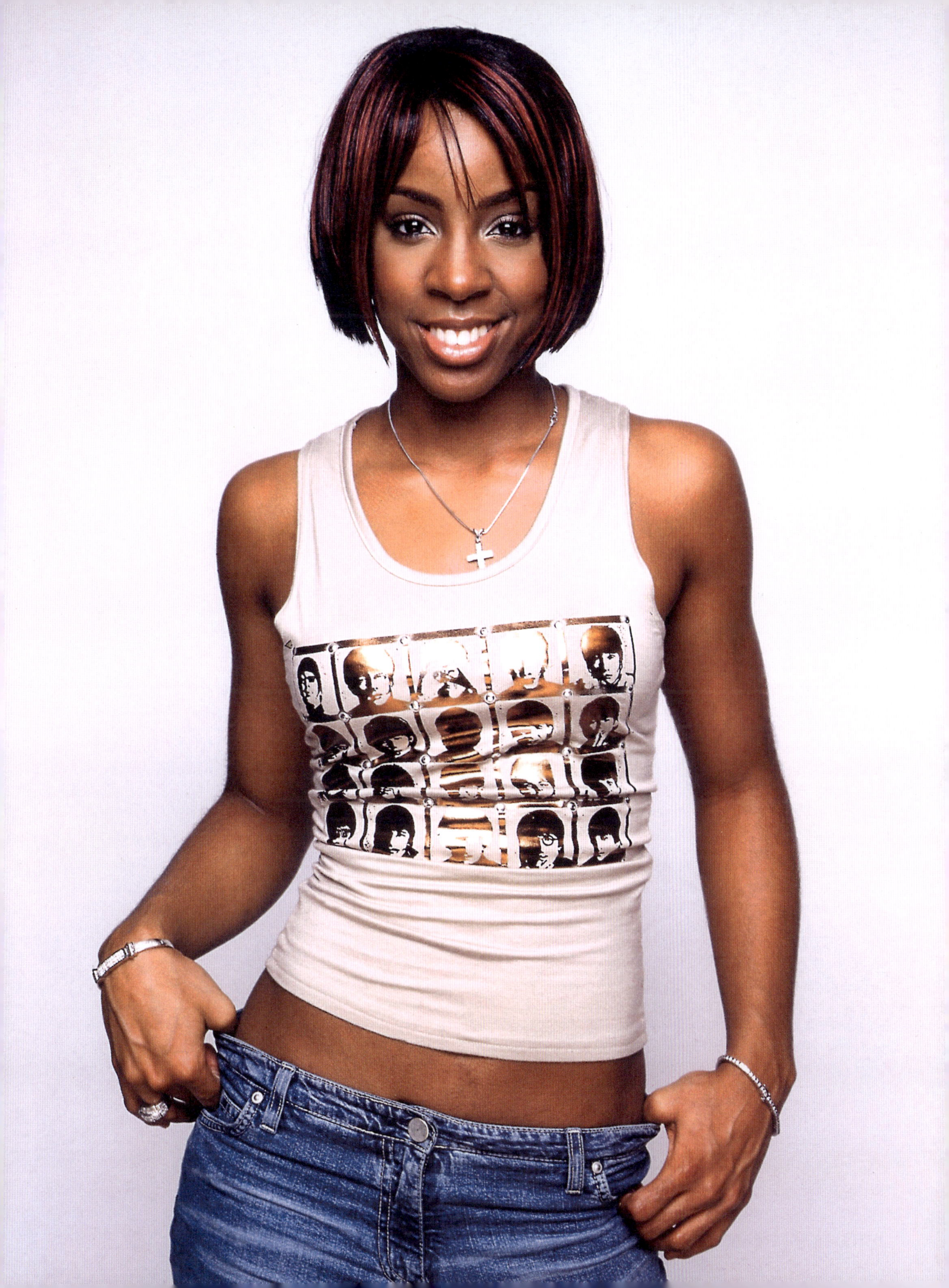

Harking back to the glory days of charity songs, the track *What's Going On* involved a whole host of superstars, including the indispensable Britney Spears.

COLLABORATIONS

WHAT'S GOING ON
ALL-STAR TRIBUTE/ARTISTS AGAINST AIDS WORLDWIDE

(Alfred Cleveland, Marvin Gaye, Renaldo Benson/4'20)

Musicians: P. Diddy: spoken voice / **Jermaine Dupri:** spoken voice / **Bono:** vocals, backing vocals / **Gwen Stefani:** vocals, backing vocals / **Aaron Lewis:** vocals, backing vocals / **Nona Gaye:** vocals, backing vocals / **Backstreet Boys:** vocals, backing vocals / **Christina Aguilera:** vocals, backing vocals / **Britney Spears:** vocals, backing vocals / **Jennifer "J-Lo" Lopez:** vocals, backing vocals / **Destiny's Child:** vocals, backing vocals / **Ja Rule:** rap / **Nelly Furtado:** vocals, backing vocals / **Michael Stipe:** vocals, backing vocals / **Alicia Keys:** vocals, backing vocals / ***NSYNC:** vocals, backing vocals / **Mary J. Blige:** vocals, backing vocals / **Darren Hayes:** vocals, backing vocals / **Nelly:** rap / **Nas:** rap / **Eve:** rap / **Fred Durst:** rap / **Wyclef Jean:** electric guitar / **Billy Odum:** electric guitar / **LaMarquis "ReMarqable" Jefferson:** bass guitar, synthesizers / **Ahmir "Questlove" Thompson:** drums / **Rickey Johnson:** synthesizers / **Omar Phillips:** percussion / **Recording:** Battery Studios, New York: 5 to 7 September 2001 / **Technical team:** Producers: Jermaine Dupri, LaMarquis "ReMarqable" Jefferson / **Executive producers:** Leigh Blake, Bono / **Recording engineers:** Brian Frye, Franny G, John Horesco IV, Phil Tan / **Assistant recording engineers:** Charles McCrorey, Richard J. Tapper, Shane Stoneback, Yen-Hue Tan / ***Artists Against AIDS Worldwide/All Star Tribute—What's Going On (single)*** / Released in the USA by Columbia/Play-Tone: 30 October 2001 (maxi single CD ref.: CK 86199, single ref.: 44 79675)

From 5 to 7 September 2001, the cream of American pop gathered at Battery Studios in New York to record a new version of Marvin Gaye's *What's Going On*. On the initiative of Bono, the U2 vocalist who had long promoted humanitarian causes, and supported by the association Artists Against AIDS Worldwide (AAAW), founded by Leigh Blake, already known for her work for the Red Hot Organization, the project aimed to raise funds to fight AIDS. The virus was ravaging some regions of Africa at the time, with almost 5,000 people dying every day from the disease. Produced by Jermaine Dupri, the cover of this Motown classic brought together Gwen Stefani, of the group No Doubt, Britney Spears, Christina Aguilera, and also the three singers of Destiny's Child. "The song we've done is all about mobilization and action," said singer Nona Gaye, Marvin Gaye's daughter, "because the missing ingredient has been political will. We are all asking—What's Going On? President Bush and other political leaders have made clear that the answer to the questions is incomplete without considering Global poverty and AIDS. Those at risk from AIDS in Africa are the very poorest and cannot be forgotten. The congress and the administration should work together to provide $1 billion dollars of emergency money to fight AIDS in Africa."[76] Bad things never happen on their own: the single's release came just after the terrorist attacks on the World Trade Center, which led Columbia and the AAAW to share the profits from the record's sales with the United Way September 11th Fund, a foundation set up to help the victims of the attacks and their families.

124 COLLABORATIONS

THE TRUTH

DESTINY'S CHILD

ALBUM

8 Days Of Christmas

8 Days Of Christmas • Winter Paradise • A "DC" Christmas Medley • Silent Night •
Little Drummer Boy • Do You Hear What I Hear? • White Christmas •
Platinum Bells • O' Holy Night • Spread A Little Love On Christmas Day •
This Christmas • Opera Of The Bells

Released in the US by Sony Music/Columbia: 30 October 2001 (CD ref.: CK 86098)
Best chart ranking in the USA: 34

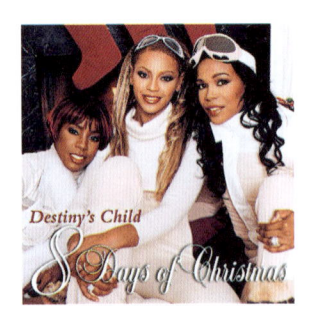

Destiny's Child in Chanel ski wear, ready to hit the slopes of success.

A CHRISTMAS WITH DESTINY'S CHILD

The Total Request Live Tour, organized by the MTV music channel, kicked off on 18 July 2001 at the Pepsi Arena in Albany, New York. It was Destiny's Child's first headlining tour, although in reality they shared it with 3LW, Dream, St. Lunatics, Eve, Nelly, and Jessica Simpson. After 39 triumphant performances, the tour came to an abrupt end following the 9/11 terrorist attacks, except for one final date at Honolulu's Blaisdell Arena that remained unchanged. That autumn, Beyoncé's group was due to begin the Destiny's Child World Tour in support of the album *Survivor*, but this was also postponed to a later date. After participating in The Concert for New York City in New York on 20 October and United We Stand: What More Can I Give in Washington—organized by Michael Jackson and featuring artists including Mary J. Blige, Jennifer Lopez, and Usher—on 21 October, Destiny's Child decided to focus on another project, namely, releasing an album of Christmas songs that they had recorded on the road during their 2001 spring tour.

An R&B Christmas

Two years had passed since Destiny's Child planned to release an album of American standards for the festive season. It was a long-standing tradition in the US, where all artists worthy of their name released a Christmas album at some point. Before Destiny's Child, many American performers had followed this custom, including Frank Sinatra (*A Jolly Christmas from Frank Sinatra* in 1957), The Beach Boys (*The Beach Boys' Christmas Album* in 1964), Mariah Carey (*Merry Christmas* in 1994), and, more recently, Christina Aguilera (*My Kind of Christmas* in 2000). *8 Days of Christmas*—consisting of four original songs and eight covers—was released on 30 October 2001 and Destiny's Child immediately began promoting it. Although the album's very modern arrangements undeniably made it much more original than other albums of the same stripe, it failed to satisfy fans because what they really wanted was to see their favorite group live in concert. They had to wait until April 2002 for the tour to resume.

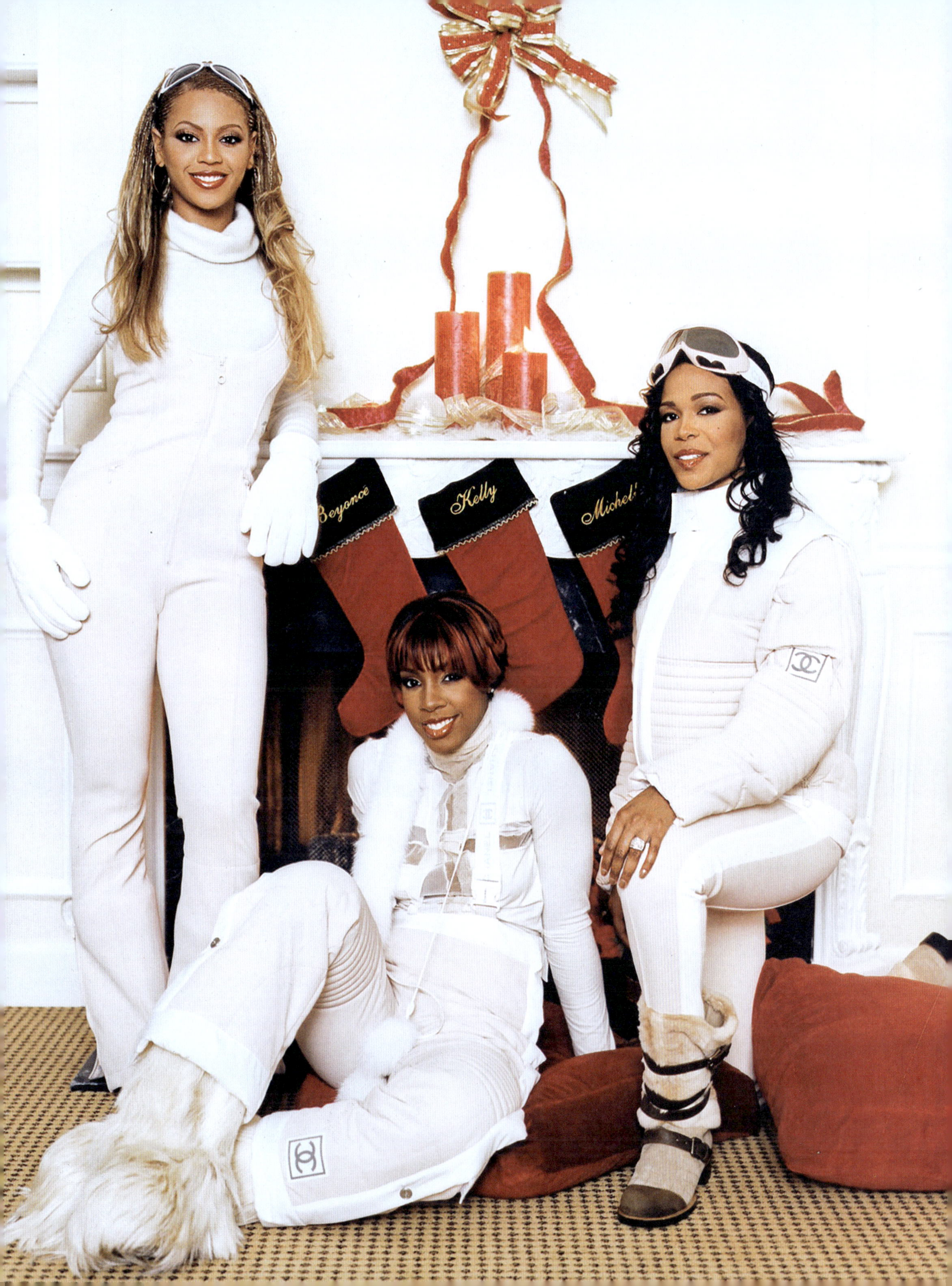
Beyoncé
Kelly

Kelly, Beyoncé, and Michelle photographed by Antoine Verglas, 2001.

Three Destiny's Child singers go solo

The fans' joy was short-lived, however, as our three singers used their world tour to publicly announce the group would be taking a hiatus. "Destiny's Child put out four albums in four years, which is unbelievable. That doesn't happen a lot," Beyoncé explained. "We've been working, Kelly and I, since we were nine, nonstop. So I think Destiny's Child is going to take a little break."[77]

But behind the decision lay another plan, namely, the women's desire to develop their respective careers. Michelle Williams was the first to release a solo album, *Heart to Yours*, on 16 April 2002, in the gospel style she had loved since childhood. Kelly Rowland had already released the track *Angel*, produced by Rob Fusari and Falonte Moore, in February 2001 on the soundtrack to Chris and Paul Wietz's film *Down to Earth*. On 25 June 2002, Rowland had an international hit when *Dilemma*, her duet with rapper Nelly, was released; on it she delivers a chorus that people remember to this day. Beyoncé was also working on writing her first solo album, but in 2002 she was more focused on films, having landed the role of Foxxy Cleopatra in the third instalment of the adventures of the blundering spy Austin Powers, portrayed by Mike Myers at the peak of his career. When *Austin Powers in Goldmember* hit cinemas on 26 July 2002, Beyoncé Knowles was crowned queen of pop, a status cemented by the release of her first solo album a year later.

2001

FOR DESTINY'S CHILD ADDICTS

The three Destiny's Child singers weren't the only ones to go solo. On 26 December 2002 Beyoncé's younger sister Solange Knowles also released her first solo album, entitled *Solo Star* and featuring productions from Damon Elliott, Chris Stokes, Timbaland, The Neptunes, and Beyoncé herself.

BEYONCÉ: ALL THE SONGS 131

8 DAYS OF CHRISTMAS

(Beyoncé Knowles, Errol McCalla Jr/3'31)

Musicians: Beyoncé Knowles: vocals, backing vocals / **Kelly Rowland:** spoken voice, vocals, backing vocals / **Michelle Williams:** backing vocals / **Recording:** Manta Sound, Toronto: 1999 to 2000 / **Technical team:** Producers: Beyoncé Knowles, Errol McCalla, Mathew Knowles / **Executive producer:** Mathew Knowles / **Recording engineer:** John Naslen / **Assistant recording engineer:** Stephen Stephanie

Before appearing on the album of the same name, the song *8 Days of Christmas* was presented to fans on the European reissue of *The Writing's on the Wall*, released by Columbia on 27 November 2000. "Actually I wrote the song two years ago when we went in the studio to do some Christmas something," Beyoncé explained on the *106 & Park* show in 2001. "That's what started the idea of doing a Christmas album."[78] While the singer seems a little materialistic as she details the gifts her boyfriend gives her in the days leading up to 25 December, Beyoncé once again reveals her talents as a songwriter, with the melody on the track proving particularly catchy. It was produced by Errol McCalla with, on the console, John Naslen, former member of the successful Canadian rock band Lighthouse turned recording engineer at Toronto's Manta Sound Studios. Although Destiny's Child performed *8 Days of Christmas* many times when the album was released, it only appeared in the US as a promotional record.

WINTER PARADISE

(Beyoncé Knowles, Falonte Moore, George Michael, Rob Fusari/3'36)

Musicians: Beyoncé Knowles: vocals, backing vocals / **Kelly Rowland:** vocals, backing vocals / **Michelle Williams:** vocals, backing vocals / **Recording:** Digital Services Recording Studios, Houston: 2000 to 2001 / **Technical team:** Producers: Beyoncé Knowles, Falonte Moore, Rob Fusari / **Executive producer:** Mathew Knowles / **Recording engineer:** James Hoover

The reason that, on first listen, the chorus of *Winter Paradise* sounds familiar is that it's built around the harmonic line of the verses in *Father Figure*, one of British singer George Michael's best-known songs, released as a single in December 1987 and featured on *Faith*, his first solo album. *Father Figure* had a gospel feel, a genre that the Destiny's Child singers loved and which suited the spirit of their Christmas album. This was undoubtedly why they chose to pay homage in this way. Whether or not the 1980s smash hit consciously inspired Beyoncé and her producers Falonte Moore and Rob Fusari, George Michael is nonetheless credited on the track, as it wasn't the best time to be sued for plagiarism. Throughout her career, Beyoncé has always been rigorous about credits, apart from a few minor exceptions that earned her some scathing remarks from uncredited rights holders, such as the singer Kelis, who accused her of sampling her song *Milkshake* (2003) on the track *Energy* in 2022.

A "DC" CHRISTMAS MEDLEY

(Gene Autry, Haven Gillespie, J. Fred Coots, Jack Rollins, Johnny Marks, Oakley Haldeman, Steve Nelson, traditional/3'59)

Musicians: Beyoncé Knowles: vocals, backing vocals / **Kelly Rowland:** vocals, backing vocals / **Michelle Williams:** vocals, backing vocals / **Frankie Romano:** guitar / **Recording:** Digital Services Recording Studios, Houston: 2000 to 2001 / **Technical team:** Producers: Beyoncé Knowles, Falonte Moore, Rob Fusari / **Executive producer:** Mathew Knowles / **Recording engineer:** James Hoover

Originality out and classics in with this medley of well-known Christmas songs thrown into a pot, seasoned with R&B and reggae sauce, and served up by our three singers sporting Mother Christmas hats to promote the album. The dish turned out to be somewhat indigestible and was denigrated by many music critics. It is a higgledy-piggledy mix that includes *Santa Claus Is Coming to Town* by J. Fred Coots and Haven Gillespie (1934), *Frosty the Snowman* by Steve Nelson and Jack Rollins (1950), *Have a Holly Jolly Christmas* by Johnny Marks (1962), *Here Comes Santa Claus* by Gene Autry (1947), and the traditional tunes *Jingle Bells* and *Deck the Halls*.

While this pot-pourri of legendary American Christmas songs wasn't the most convincing of Beyoncé's productions, she showed her loyalty to her parish much more effectively by discreetly donating $500,000 to St John's Methodist Church in Houston, which she had attended in her youth. So Destiny's Child can be forgiven this particular Christmas melody, which doesn't seem to have spoiled the Christmas spirit.

Beyoncé Knowles singing (with Kelly Rowland and Michelle Williams) at the traditional turning on of the Christmas tree lights at New York's Rockefeller Center, 28 November 2001.

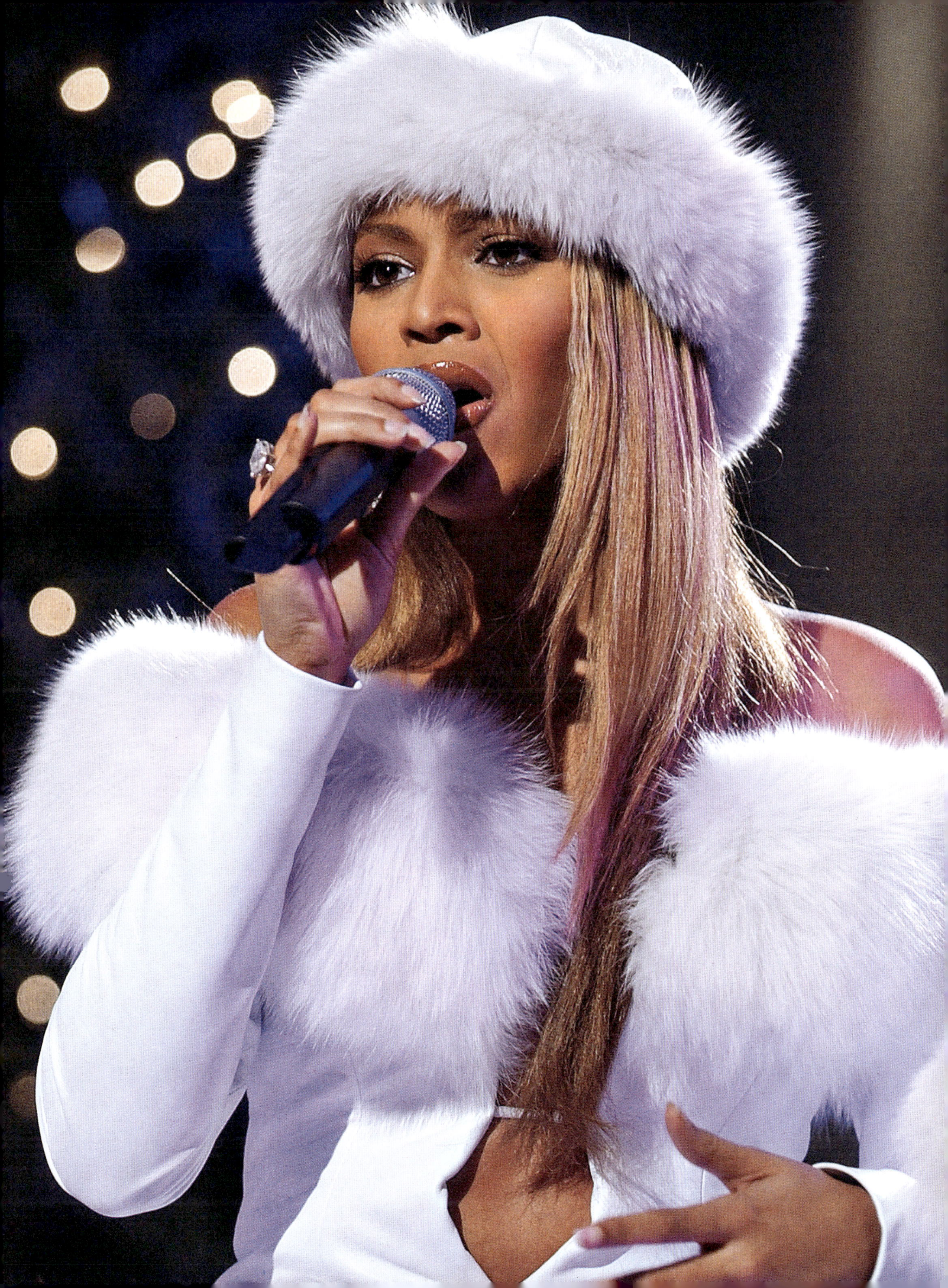

SILENT NIGHT
(FEATURING BEYONCÉ KNOWLES)

(Beyoncé Knowles/3'41)

Musicians: Beyoncé Knowles: vocals, backing vocals / Michael Morales: acoustic guitar / **Recording:** Studio M, San Antonio: 2000 to 2001 / **Technical team:** Producer: Beyoncé Knowles / **Executive producer:** Mathew Knowles / **Recording engineer:** Marius Perron III

Stripped of any artifice, this reworking of *Silent Night* is without a doubt the album's best song, carried by Beyoncé's powerful, crystal-clear voice as she solos her way through the track's many harmonies, accompanied on acoustic six-string by Michael Morales, a singer and guitarist who had his moment of glory with the 1989 single *Who Do You Give Your Love To?* Although *Silent Night* is credited here to Beyoncé Knowles, it was actually composed by Franz Xaver Gruber in 1818 to lyrics written by Joseph Mohr in 1816. *Silent Night* is one of the major classics and slots perfectly into the tracklist of this Christmas album.

LITTLE DRUMMER BOY
(FEATURING SOLANGE)

(Harry Simeone, Henry Onorati, Katherine K. Davis/3'36)

Musicians: Beyoncé Knowles: vocals, backing vocals / Kelly Rowland: vocals, backing vocals / Michelle Williams: vocals, backing vocals / Solange Knowles: vocals, backing vocals / **Recording:** The Enterprise, Los Angeles: 2000 to 2001 / **Technical team:** Producers: Alonzo Jackson, Beyoncé Knowles / **Executive producer:** Mathew Knowles / **Recording engineer:** Asif Ali / **Assistant recording engineer:** Juan Ramirez / **Vocal arrangements:** Beyoncé Knowles

Even though the prize for most disconcerting version of this Christmas classic goes to the Bing Crosby/David Bowie duet performed on the *Bing Crosby's Merrie Olde Christmas* special on 30 November 1977, the Destiny's Child rendition of this 1941 Katherine Kennicott Davis composition based on a traditional Czech song takes on the challenge of delivering the most surprising cover. Destiny's Child are joined here by Solange Knowles, Beyoncé's younger sister, whose debut album was under production at the time.

DO YOU HEAR WHAT I HEAR?
(FEATURING KELLY ROWLAND)

(Gloria Shayne, Noël Regney/3'47)

Musicians: Kelly Rowland: vocals, backing vocals / Beyoncé Knowles: backing vocals / Michelle Williams: backing vocals / **Recording:** Sony Music Studios, New York: 2000 to 2001 / **Technical team:** Producers: Alan Floyd, Wirlie Morris / **Executive producer:** Mathew Knowles / **Recording engineers:** David Swope, Pablo Arraya / **Assistant recording engineer:** Jaime Gudewicz / **Vocal arrangements:** Kelly Rowland, Kim Burse

Behind this R&B track about the Nativity story lies a fascinating tale. Like many men from Alsace during the Second World War, Noël Regney was forcibly enlisted into the German army but was secretly active in the Resistance. In 1952, he left his homeland for the United States, where he pursued a career as a composer for television and advertising. In October 1962, he and his wife, pianist Gloria Shayne, wrote *Do You Hear What I Hear?*, at a time when the Americans and Soviets were on the verge of an unprecedented war over intercontinental ballistic missiles in Cuba. At his producer's request, Regney composed a song that ended up being covered several hundred times. "I had thought I'd never write a Christmas song," he would say years later. "Christmas had become so commercial. But this was the time of the Cuban Missile Crisis. In the studio, the producer was listening to the radio to see if we had been obliterated. En route to my home, I saw two mothers with their babies in strollers. The little angels were looking at each other and smiling. All of a sudden, my mood was extraordinary."[79] Kelly Rowland had the privilege of singing this song solo, inspired by her idol Whitney Houston's version, which featured on the Special Olympics Productions charity album *A Very Special Christmas* released on 12 October 1987.

The original performer of *White Christmas*, Bing Crosby, seen here with Rosemary Clooney filming *The Bing Crosby—Rosemary Clooney Show* in 1960.

WHITE CHRISTMAS

(Irving Berlin/1'42)

Musicians: Beyoncé Knowles: vocals, backing vocals / Kelly Rowland: vocals, backing vocals / Michelle Williams: vocals, backing vocals / **Recording:** Morrisound Recording, Tampa: 2000 to 2001 / **Technical team: Producers:** Beyoncé Knowles, Damon Elliott / **Executive producer:** Mathew Knowles / **Recording engineer:** Tom Morris / **Assistant recording engineer:** Robert Valdez / **Vocal arrangements:** Beyoncé Knowles

White Christmas was composed by Irving Berlin in 1942 for the musical film *Holiday Inn*, directed by Mark Sandrich, and became a Christmas classic after Bing Crosby performed it in that movie. Destiny's Child offer a much more modern version here, even if producer Damon Elliot has retained the original flavor. "Usually when you hear the Christmas songs," Beyoncé explained to MTV News, "they're kind of corny. But you could hear this album all year round."[80]

PLATINUM BELLS

(Jay Livingston, Ray Evans/1'26)

Musicians: Beyoncé Knowles: vocals, backing vocals / Kelly Rowland: vocals, backing vocals / Michelle Williams: vocals, backing vocals / **Recording:** Morrisound Recording, Tampa: 2000 to 2001 / **Technical team: Producers:** Beyoncé Knowles, Damon Elliott / **Executive producer:** Mathew Knowles / **Recording engineer:** Tom Morris / **Assistant recording engineer:** Robert Valdez / **Vocal arrangements:** Beyoncé Knowles

Destiny's Child tackle another track popularized by Bing Crosby with this ultramodern version of *Silver Bells*, which Crosby and Carol Richards had performed in 1950. No violin or vibraphone here, just the beat from the Korg Triton synthesizer, played by the expert hands of producer Damon Elliott, on a mission to create an R&B version of this classic. The fact that *8 Days of Christmas* was recorded on the move in various studios in the United States, Canada, and Japan during the Total Request Live Tour meant that many recording engineers contributed to the Destiny's Child sound. For *Platinum Bells*, recorded mostly at Morrisound Recording in Tampa, Tom Morris was on the console. What an experience that must have been for this seasoned technician, who until then had mostly specialized in music that can only be described as extreme. Before getting involved with the Destiny's Child Christmas R&B, Morris had tended to work with bands such as Morbid Angel, Iced Earth, Coroner, and Necrosis. But versatility being the mark of the greats, we take our hats off to this all-round recording engineer.

BEYONCÉ: ALL THE SONGS

O' HOLY NIGHT
(FEATURING MICHELLE WILLIAMS)

(Erron Williams, Kim Burse, Michelle Williams/4'24)

Musicians: Michelle Williams: vocals, backing vocals / Derrick Coleman: backing vocals / Kevin Turner: acoustic guitar / Sharay Reed: bass / **Recording:** Chicago Trax Recording, Chicago: 2000 to 2001 / Studio M, San Antonio: 2000 to 2001 / The Enterprise, Burbank: 2000 to 2001 / **Technical team:** Producer: Erron Williams / Executive producer: Mathew Knowles / Recording engineers: Tucker Allen, Byron Rickerson, Dylan Dresdow, Larry Sturm / **Assistant recording engineer:** Brian Summer / **Arrangements:** Erron Williams, Kim Burse, Michelle Williams

Like Kelly Rowland on *Do You Hear What I Hear?* and Beyoncé on *Silent Night*, Michelle Williams steps up here with a solo track, a reworking of *O' Holy Night* written by French (atheist) poet Placide Cappeau in 1843, set to music by composer Aldolphe Adam in 1847, and performed the same year by opera singer Emily Laurey. Although now in the public domain, the song deserved to be credited here to its original authors. This didn't happen, as the names on the album's liner notes are Michelle Williams, her brother Erron, who produced the song, and Kim Burse, A&R executive at Columbia.

SPREAD A LITTLE LOVE ON CHRISTMAS DAY

(Bernard Edwards Jr, Beyoncé Knowles/3'41)

Musicians: Beyoncé Knowles: vocals, backing vocals / Kelly Rowland: vocals, backing vocals / Michelle Williams: vocals, backing vocals / **Recording:** Sony Music Studios, New York: 2000 to 2001 / The Hit Factory, New York: 2000 to 2001 / **Technical team:** Producers: Beyoncé Knowles, Bernard "Focus" Edwards Jr, Ric Wake / Executive producer: Mathew Knowles / Vocal arrangements: Beyoncé Knowles

Listening to *Spread a Little Love on Christmas Day* makes you feel it's a shame that the whole album doesn't consist of original songs. Beyoncé excels in writing these hits, especially when supported by talented producers, as is the case here with Bernard Edwards Jr, aka "Focus," son of the famous bassist and co-founder of the group Chic. You might catch yourself nodding along or even dancing to this Christmas groove produced by such a powerhouse duo. The album's main inspiration is more Hitsville U.S.A.—the name given to Motown's first headquarters—than Lapland, where Father Christmas hangs out, as Beyoncé revealed on MTV. "There

Focus is one of the best-known hip-hop producers in the US and has worked with Dr. Dre, Kendrick Lamar, and Eminem.

Beyoncé pays tribute to Donny Hathaway with this cover of his 1970 single, *This Christmas*.

hasn't been a Christmas album like this—it's kind of a 2000 version of *Motown Christmas*," she added, referring to the compilation produced by the famous Detroit label in 1973, featuring standards performed by Stevie Wonder, Diana Ross & The Supremes, and The Jackson 5. "There's nothing traditional about the album, even with the traditional songs. We totally remade them, and we have some really different harmonies and arrangements."[81]

THIS CHRISTMAS

(Donny Hathaway, Nadine McKinnor/3'38)

Musicians: Beyoncé Knowles: vocals, backing vocals / **Kelly Rowland:** vocals, backing vocals / **Michelle Williams:** vocals, backing vocals / **Recording:** Sony Music Studios, Tokyo: 2000, June 2001 / **Technical team: Producers:** Bill Lee, Calvin Gaines, Beyoncé Knowles, Rob Fusari / **Executive producer:** Mathew Knowles / **Recording engineer:** Ramon Morales / **Assistant recording engineer:** Motonori Sasaki / **Vocal arrangements:** Beyoncé Knowles

Here Beyoncé tackles a monument of American culture in a tribute to one of her idols, singer Donny Hathaway. *This Christmas*, composed in 1970 when the soul singer was just twenty-five years old, would become the first Christmas song written by an African American, as well as a classic of the genre, covered over the years by The Temptations, Diana Ross, and Christina Aguilera. Produced by the trio of Bill Lee, Calvin Gaines, and Rob Fusari, who had been behind the tracks *Happy Face* and *Outro (DC-3) Thank You* on *Survivor*, *This Christmas* was completed in June 2001, when Beyoncé, Michelle, and Kelly took advantage of a promotional trip to Japan to record their vocals for the track at Sony Music Studios in Tokyo.

OPERA OF THE BELLS

(Beyoncé Knowles/4'34)

Musicians: Beyoncé Knowles: vocals, backing vocals / **Recording:** SugarHill Recording Studios, Houston: 2000 to 2001 / Flyte Tyme, Minneapolis: 2000 to 2001 / **Technical team: Producer:** Beyoncé Knowles / **Executive producer:** Mathew Knowles / **Recording engineer:** Ramon Morales / **Arrangements:** Beyoncé Knowles

Although credited to Beyoncé Knowles, *Opera of the Bells* is in fact a reworking of *Carol of the Bells*, one of the most famous Christmas songs, composed by Mykola Léontovitch in 1914 and based on a traditional Ukrainian song called *Shchedryk*, usually sung at New Year. But Beyoncé didn't just settle for changing the original lyrics of this anthem, which is particularly striking for its three main notes, its minor key, and its triplets that swing like carillon bells high up in the belfry. Here she delivers one of her most memorable vocal performances, and the harmonies written for the track—performed a cappella—are quite simply stunning. Singer Ariana Grande later praised the work that went into recording this classic. "That's where I discovered my range," she said in 2015. "I grew up listening to Destiny's Child. I would try so hard to mimic Beyoncé's little runs and ad-lib things. They are so precise. It's like math. Remember the Destiny's Child version of *Carol of the Bells*? I took it apart, put it in GarageBand, and dissected it all. That's how I learned about harmonies and runs and ad-libs. Thank you, Destiny's Child!"[82]

BEYONCÉ: ALL THE SONGS 137

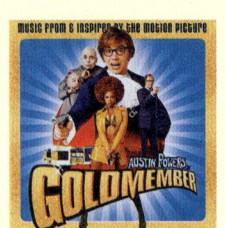

Music from & Inspired by the Motion Picture
Austin Powers in Goldmember (compilation)
Released in the US by Maverick: 16 July 2002 (CD ref.: 9 48349-2)

Afro cut and schoolboy humor in the third Austin Powers secret agent movie.

Austin Powers in Goldmember (2002)

1. **Work It Out**—Beyoncé Knowles*
2. **Miss You (Dr. Dre Remix 2002)**—The Rolling Stones
3. **Boys (Co-Ed Remix)**—Britney Spears
4. **Groove Me**—Angie Stone
5. **Shining Star**—Earth, Wind & Fire
6. **Hey Goldmember**—Foxxy Cleopatra*
7. **Ain't No Mystery**—Smash Mouth
8. **Evil Woman**—Soul Hooligan
9. **1975**—Oakenfold
10. **Hard Knock Life (Ghetto Anthem—Dr. Evil Remix)**—Dr. Evil
11. **Daddy Wasn't There**—Ming Tea
12. **Alfie (What's It All About, Austin?)**—Susanna Hoffs

* *Music from & Inspired by the Motion Picture Austin Powers in Goldmember* features tracks by several artists; only those performed by Beyoncé are discussed here.

BEYONCÉ KNOWLES IS FOXXY CLEOPATRA

Beyoncé chose a highly original franchise for her film debut when she joined the cast of the third instalment in the zany adventures of British secret agent Austin Powers. Portrayed by the irresistible Mike Myers, Powers is a colorful, sexually insatiable character who makes a joke out of everything. His adventures, parodying those of another famous agent of Her Majesty, Ian Fleming's charismatic James Bond, had already been the subject of two gag-filled films: *Austin Powers: International Man of Mystery* in 1997 and *Austin Powers: The Spy Who Shagged Me* in 1999. Filming for the third instalment of this saga, which had become a cult, began in 2000, this time with a tale of Powers' reunion with his father as well as his legendary battle with Dr. Evil and other characters, most of them played by Myers himself.

Producer John Lyons and director Jay Roach were looking for a new Austin Powers girl who would live up to the unforgettable Elizabeth Hurley and Heather Graham who had appeared in the first and second films respectively. A famous celebrity agent suggested the leading light of R&B. "We knew that we were searching for a young Black actress," Lyons explained. "I was originally a casting director and always loved looking at musicians for parts, and I remember Sharon Sheinwold Jackson, the agent, telling me that the lead singer for Destiny's Child was really special."[83] A meeting was quickly arranged between Beyoncé and the film production team, who fell for the charms of the aspiring actress whose work they had admired in the TV film *Carmen: A Hip Hopera*.

A nod to Blaxploitation

It was on the rooftop patio of the Chateau Marmont Hotel in Los Angeles that Roach, Lyons, Myers, and Beyoncé met to discuss the possibility of including the singer in the film's cast list. The female character who would act as the foil to Austin Powers was heavily inspired by two heroines of 1970s Blaxploitation films: Pam Grier in the *Foxy Brown* saga and Tamara Dobson in *Cleopatra Jones*. After two auditions, Beyoncé was offered the first film role of her career, playing the character Foxxy Cleopatra. Unforgettable in the part, she shone alongside Mike Myers and performed two songs for the film's soundtrack: *Hey Goldmember* and *Work It Out*.

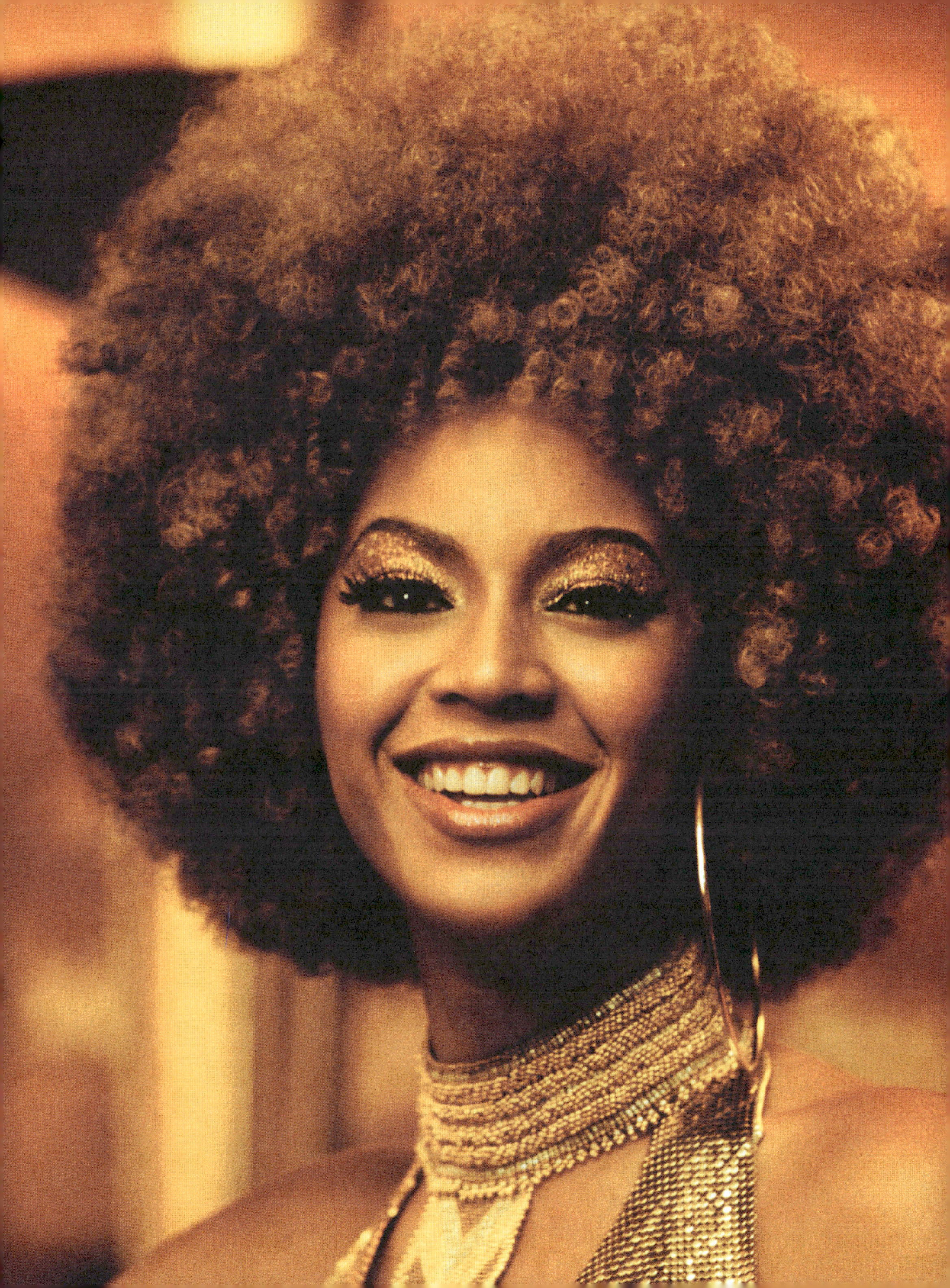

The irresistible and too-rarely-seen Mike Myers playing the larger-than-life Austin Powers.

FOR FOXXY CLEOPATRA ADDICTS

Solange Knowles is one of the backing singers on *Hey Goldmember* and was originally supposed to be dancing alongside her sister in the scene that features the song. When Tina Knowles read the lyrics for the track—which, let's face it, are a bit naughty—she categorically refused to allow Solange to appear in the film, despite the fact her daughter's costume had already been made.

WORK IT OUT
(Pharrell Williams, Chad Hugo, Beyoncé Knowles/3'22)

Musicians: Beyoncé Knowles: vocals, backing vocals / **Recording:** ?, Los Angeles: 2001 / **Technical team:** Producers: Pharrell Williams, Chad Hugo / **Executive producer:** Mathew Knowles

Produced by The Neptunes, the super-talented duo of Pharrell Williams and Chad Hugo, and released to promote the film *Austin Powers in Goldmember, Work It Out* was the first solo single of Beyoncé's career. The song—whose verses may remind some listeners of The Jackson 5's 1974 track *Dancing Machine*—was distributed in a promotional format, but failed to make the *Billboard* Hot 100, despite Columbia's best efforts. Unlike Madonna, who scored a hit with *Beautiful Stranger* from the soundtrack to *Austin Powers: The Spy Who Shagged Me* in 1999, Beyoncé found herself with a complete flop on her hands with *Work It Out*. Why was it so badly received? The track's very Seventies' aesthetic—which references both The JB's and the funky salvos of their inflammatory leader, James Brown, as well as the Hohner Clavinet electric piano in Stevie Wonder's hit *Superstition*—was a throwback to a decade that no longer seemed to appeal to R&B fans. They were looking for something more modern in a genre defined by constant renewal. Nonetheless, *Work It Out* is one of the most accomplished songs in Beyoncé's repertoire, made for the dance floor in Studio 69, the nightclub where the sparkling Foxxy Cleopatra makes her first appearance in the film.

HEY GOLDMEMBER
(FOXXY CLEOPATRA FEATURING DEVIN AND SOLANGE)
(Harry Wayne Casey, Richard Finch, Mike Myers, Paul Myers/2'44)

Musicians: Beyoncé Knowles: vocals, backing vocals / Solange Knowles: backing vocals / Devin Vasquez: backing vocals / **Recording:** ?, Los Angeles: 2000 to 2001 / **Technical team:** Producers: Beyoncé Knowles, Damon Elliott

Beyoncé Knowles, alias Foxxy Cleopatra, sweeps into the film and sets the dance floor at Studio 69 alight—note the cheeky number change in this obvious reference to the legendary Studio 54 in 1970s New York—with the very danceable *Hey Goldmember*, which producer Damon Elliott based on a number of disco classics.

"For *Hey Goldmember*, we decided to mash up three KC and The Sunshine Band songs," explained John Houlihan, music supervisor on the film. "We went to Mike's hilarious brother, Paul Myers, and he wrote the lyrics."[83] Solange Knowles was invited to join the recording session in Los Angeles and contributed backing vocals to the track, as did singer Devin Vasquez, an up-and-coming artist at the Columbia stable. "It's not a serious song—it's really funny and crazy," Beyoncé said at the time. "I'm not a singer in the movie, but it makes me feel a little bit more comfortable that the first time people see me I'm up there [dancing], doing what they are used to seeing me do."[84]

CINEMA

140 AUSTIN POWERS IN GOLDMEMBER (2002)

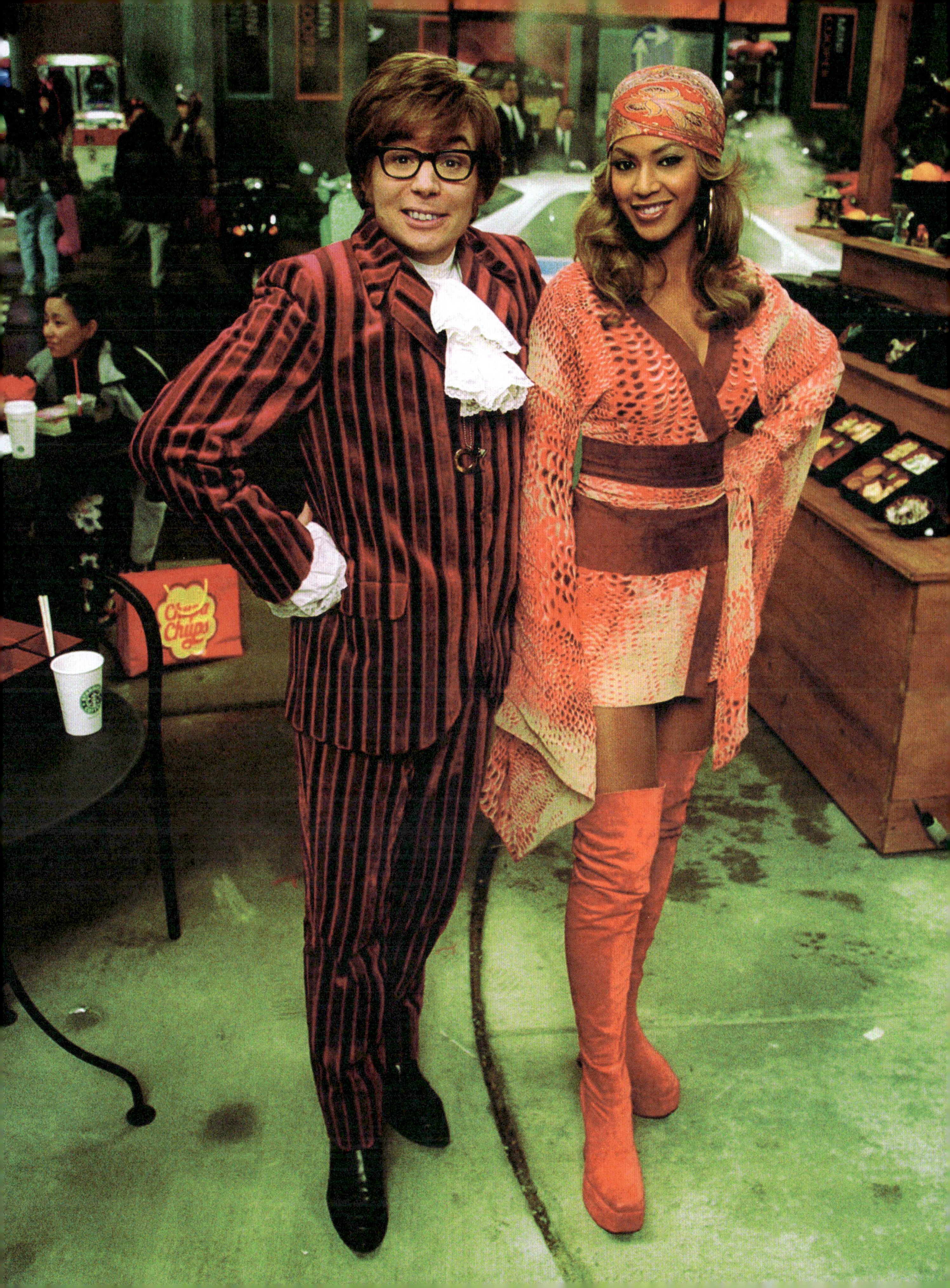
Chupa Chups

THE PROUD FAMILY THEME SONG
(SOLANGE FEATURING DESTINY'S CHILD)

(Kurt Farquhar, Gerald Harbour/2'18)

Musicians: Solange Knowles: vocals, backing vocals / **Beyoncé Knowles:** backing vocals / **Kelly Rowland:** backing vocals / **Michelle Williams:** backing vocals / **Recording:** ? / **Technical team: Producers:** Beyoncé Knowles, Kurt Farquhar / *The Proud Family (Songs from the Hit TV Series)* **(compilation)** / Released in the US by Walt Disney Records: 20 April 2004 (CD ref.: 61088-7)

In 2001, when director Bruce W. Smith noticed there had been very few animated series about African-American families, he launched production of *The Proud Family* for broadcast on the Disney Channel. When the first episode went out on 15 September 2001, viewers discovered that the theme tune was performed by Solange Knowles and Destiny's Child. *The Proud Family Theme Song* was composed and produced by Kurt Farquhar, a talented all-rounder who had also created the soundtracks to *The Sinbad Show* and *The Corner*. The song later appeared on a compilation from the series, and also as a bonus track on the European edition of the *8 Days Of Christmas* album. In 2022, when a new version of *The Proud Family* became available on the Disney+ Channel, the privilege of re-recording the theme tune went to singer Joyce Wrice. At Halloween that year, as if to remind people of their fondness for the program, Beyoncé and her husband Jay-Z, accompanied by their children, posted a photo on Instagram of them dressed up as the Proud family.

The Proud Family, with the theme tune sung by the Knowles clan and friends.

The Bama Boyz concocted *Home for the Holidays*, which works equally well on ski runs and dancefloors.

RUDOLPH THE RED-NOSED REINDEER

(Johnny Marks/2'31)

Musicians: Beyoncé Knowles: vocals, backing vocals / **Kelly Rowland:** vocals, backing vocals / **Michelle Williams:** vocals, backing vocals / **Recording:** Sunrise Studios, Houston: 2000 to 2001 / **Technical team:** Producers: Beyoncé Knowles, Erroll "Poppi" McCalla Jr / **Executive producer:** Mathew Knowles / **Rudolph the Red-Nosed Reindeer (promotional single)** / Distributed in the US by Sony Music/Columbia: 3 January 2002

In 1939, the American department store chain Montgomery Ward asked author Robert L. May to invent a character for a coloring book for its customers. May came up with Rudolph, the little reindeer who saved Christmas. Several million copies of the book were sold, which prompted May to ask his brother-in-law, composer Johnny Marks, to write a song inspired by his character. *Rudolph the Red-Nosed Reindeer*, performed by Gene Autry in 1949, was a massive hit and became an American classic. Among the countless versions of the song, the one by Destiny's Child was released in a promotional format in 2002 and featured on the reissue of *8 Days of Christmas* in 2005.

HOME FOR THE HOLIDAYS

(Beyoncé Knowles, Solange Knowles, Eddie "E-Trez" Smith III, Jesse J. Rankins, Jonathan D. Wells/3'10)

Musicians: Beyoncé Knowles: vocals, backing vocals / **Kelly Rowland:** vocals, backing vocals / **Michelle Williams:** vocals, backing vocals / **Recording:** ?: 2004 to 2005 / **Technical team:** Producers: Beyoncé Knowles, Solange Knowles, The Bama Boyz / **Executive producer:** Mathew Knowles / **8 Days Of Christmas—2005 Reissue (album)** / Released in the US by Sony Music/Columbia: 18 October 2005 (CD ref.: CK 97767)

The reissue of *8 Days of Christmas* in the run-up to Christmas 2005 was an opportunity for Destiny's Child to offer their fans two songs not featured on the first version of the album, released four years earlier: *Rudolph the Red-Nosed Reindeer* (released only in promotional format at the time) and *Home for the Holidays*, concocted by The Bama Boyz, a trio of producers comprising Eddie "E-Trez" Smith III, Jesse J. Rankins, and Jonathan D. Wells, who had come to the attention of Mathew Knowles in 2003. The track should not be confused with *(There's No Place Like) Home for the Holidays*, a Christmas classic composed by Robert Allen and Al Stillman in 1954, and popularized by Perry Como the same year.

BEYONCÉ: ALL THE SONGS

ALBUM

Dangerously in Love

CD VERSION

Crazy In Love • Naughty Girl • Baby Boy • Hip Hop Star • Be With You • Me, Myself And I • Yes • Signs • Speechless • That's How You Like It • The Closer I Get To You • Dangerously in Love 2 • Beyoncé Interlude • Gift From Virgo • Daddy

---

VINYL/ALBUM VERSION

Crazy In Love • Naughty Girl • That's How You Like It • Baby Boy • Hip Hop Star • Be With You • Me, Myself And I • Yes • Signs • Speechless • The Closer I Get To You • Dangerously in Love 2 • Beyoncé Interlude • Gift From Virgo • Daddy

---

Released in the USA by Sony Music/Columbia: 23 July 2003 (album ref.: C2 86286, CD ref.: CK 86386)
Best chart ranking in the USA: 1

Beyoncé spreads her wings in 2003 for the promotion of her first solo album.

FOR BEYONCÉ ADDICTS

While posing for Markus Klinko, who shot the cover photo for her first album, Beyoncé refused to wear a skirt, claiming it felt too red carpet. The photographer recalls: "I said, 'I believe that this should be paired with denim. What if you wear mine?' I had on these Dolce & Gabbana men's jeans. And she said, 'Okay,' and so I went and took them off, and they fit her like a glove."[90]

BEYONCÉ TAKES FLIGHT

2003

Developing the individual careers of the members of Destiny's Child was always part of the Knowles clan's project. In 2000, when the group launched production of their forthcoming album *Survivor*, Beyoncé was already revealing her plans on MTV: "We are negotiating solo projects for all three of us. They're all going to come out at the same time. We're going to all do different types of music and support each other's albums. Basically, they're not going to compete with each other. And we'll come back and do another album for Destiny's Child, and hopefully it will broaden our audience, so it will help us all out."[85] Michelle Williams was first up with her gospel album *Heart to Yours* on 16 April 2002, closely followed by Kelly Rowland and *Simply Deep* on 22 October. While her two friends and colleagues enjoyed success (appreciation for the former and in the charts for the latter), Beyoncé suffered the first real setback of her career, with the flop of her first solo single: *Work It Out*, taken from the soundtrack to the film *Austin Powers in Goldmember*, was released to general indifference on 11 June 2002. But as failure wasn't part of the singer's plans, she forced the hand of destiny by reuniting with an East Coast rapper who had vowed to work with her again after inviting her to sing on his protégée Amil's album in 2000. His name? Shawn Corey Carter, aka Jay-Z.

A calculated risk

As had happened with *Dilemma*, a smash hit by the rapper Nelly released in June with a guest appearance from Kelly Rowland, Jay-Z and Beyoncé supplied the perfect symbiosis of hip-hop and R&B with the release of the single *03 Bonnie & Clyde* in October 2002. The track was an international hit, reaching number 4 on the *Billboard* Hot 100 and number 2 in the British and Australian charts, giving Beyoncé a considerable boost. She continued production of her first solo album with renewed enthusiasm, even though the fear of being alone in front of her audiences worried her at the time. "It's hard to leave a group when you love each other and there's nothing going wrong. It's easy when you hate each other and you can't stand to be in the same room, but when you still share dressing rooms, still share a tour bus, still love each other and still take that risk and you don't have to, because you're still selling records. […]. I took that risk and it was very scary."[86]

An album with multiple influences

Seeking to push beyond her comfort zone, Beyoncé decided to record her first album far from Houston, at South Beach Studios in Miami, where she hoped to be find inspiration in the sweet ocean vibes. "I wanted to be around the ocean," she explained at the time. "And I basically stayed at this hotel; downstairs was the studio, and that's what I did. I went from upstairs to downstairs to around the corner to work out, back to the hotel. And I had the best time."[87] Apart from the comfortable location, Beyoncé did not view production of this album as a moment of respite in her career. Quite the contrary—she saw it as another opportunity to show the world that she was now the sole captain on board the Beyoncé ship. After hitting the heights of R&B with Destiny's Child, she wanted to work with as many producers—unknowns included—as possible, hoping to benefit from the energy and drive of people who had everything to prove. "I wanted to get new fresh people. I believe people that haven't really done

146   DANGEROUSLY IN LOVE

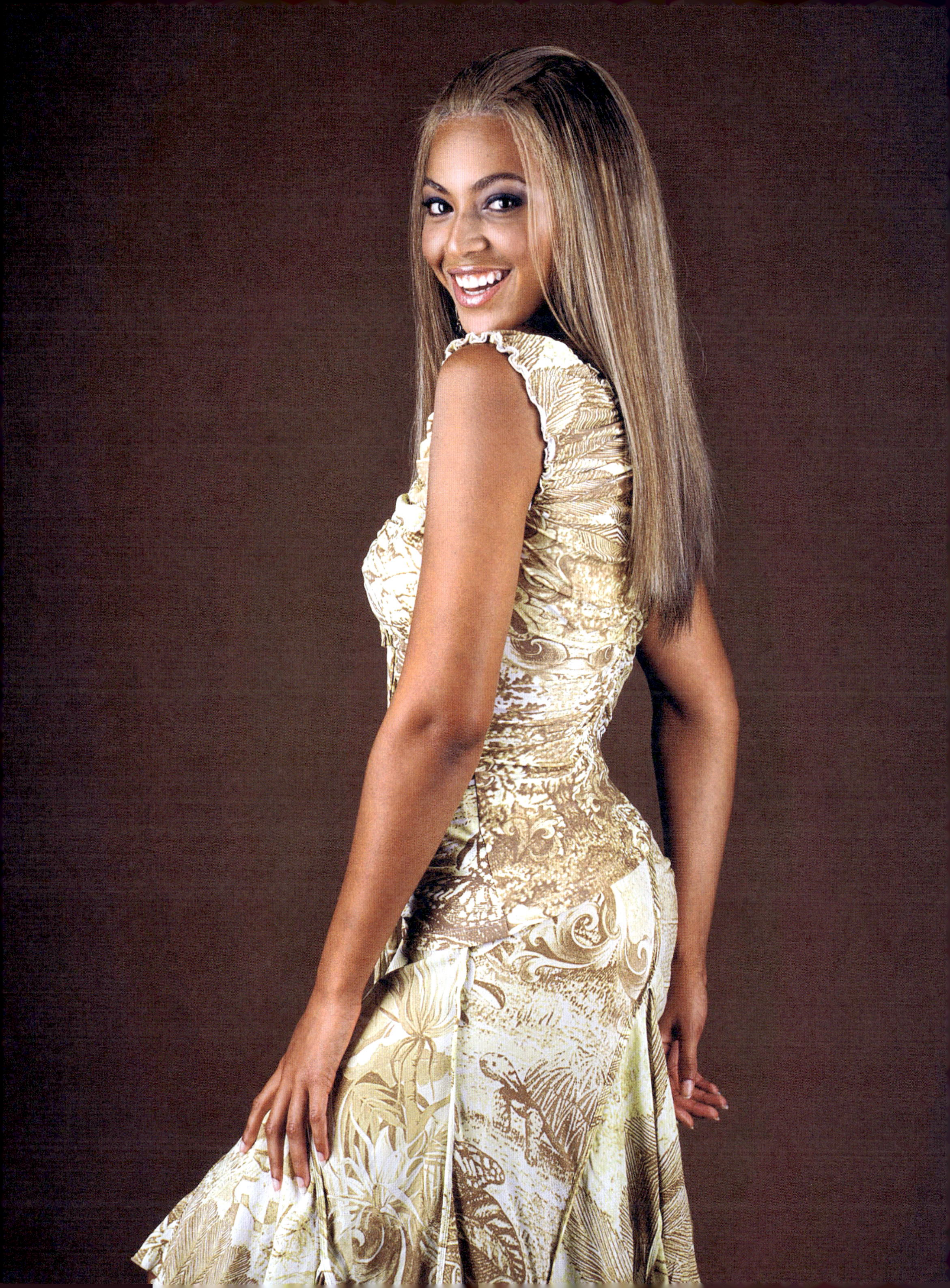

148 **DANGEROUSLY IN LOVE**

Beyoncé on stage at the 2003 MTV Europe Music Awards in Edinburgh.

that much with other artists aren't jaded and they are so hungry, they have new fresh ideas […]. I wanted to find the new sound and I wanted also my album to not sound like anybody else's."[88] With that aim in mind, Beyoncé set about meeting people the length and breadth of the United States. "I had meetings and interviews with every producer from the East Coast and every producer from the West Coast," she explained to the British *Guardian* newspaper in 2003, "all day for two days, every 30 minutes someone else."[58] Among those lucky enough to get their names on the production schedule were Rich Harrison and Scott Storch, who were joined by a number of faces already familiar to fans: Missy Elliott, Bernard Edwards Jr, and Errol McCalla Jr. Beyoncé also wanted to feature various collaborations on the album and invited dancehall king Sean Paul to sing with her on *Baby Boy*; Big Boi, half of the duo OutKast, on *Hip Hop Star*; and Jay-Z on the album's first single, *Crazy in Love*. "I worked with Jay-Z on his album, so I asked him to do the same,"[87] Beyoncé revealed. As a result, people quickly began to assume she was dating the rapper, but that's not what she wanted to talk about. "I feel like because I sing and because I dance and act and I write music doesn't mean things that a stranger would ask me I have to tell them. But I'm very comfortable with everything in my life. I just like to keep certain things private."[87]

Beyoncé's transformation into a global star
On 18 March 2003, just before her unconfirmed relationship with Jay-Z hit the headlines in the tabloids and celebrity press, Beyoncé was savoring the success of her single *Crazy in Love*, recorded as a duet with the rapper. By now, she was a pop culture icon and had partnered up with major brands,

Jay-Z and Beyoncé at the time of their first duet and their first secret dates.

> In 2003, every appearance by Beyoncé created a stir, such as when she appeared on stage at the MTV Video Music Awards on 28 August 2003, and delivered a stunning performance alongside Jay-Z, before leaving with no fewer than three trophies. The following year, she dazzled audiences when she appeared with Prince at the Grammy Awards.

2003

including L'Oréal, Estée Lauder, and Pepsi, following in the footsteps of one of her idols who had once been an ambassador for the soft-drinks brand. "Well… Michael Jackson. I mean, for one, it's an historical thing," she was quoted as saying in an article in *The Face* in 2003. "[…] L'Oréal, the pictures are beautiful and… why not? It's just a cool thing to be able to do. I go to Japan, France, I have l'Oréal ads in different places, so, y'know, people can see me there. And, all around, it just makes you…a bigger star."[89]

The release of *Dangerously in Love* on 23 July 2003 continued Beyoncé's transformation into an international star, no longer corralled into the R&B enclosure that had made her famous. It was the album's many music styles that made it such a success, selling 317,000 copies and topping the *Billboard* 200 the week it was released. "It wasn't the most commercial album, which was something that I did consciously. Because Destiny's Child sold 33 million records, big pop albums, we've already done that. I can't satisfy a five-year-old and a 55-year- old, men and women, the critics and the fans—there's no way. So I said, 'I'm gonna satisfy myself.'"[89] With these tracks, which are much sexier than fans were used to, Beyoncé reveals a new side to herself, proud of the 21-year-old woman she has become and not afraid to play the seduction game in this, her first solo album. The album cover features a photo by Markus Klinko, inspired by an image of French supermodel Laetitia Casta that had appeared in *The Web* in 2000 and caught Beyoncé's eye. It shows Beyoncé at her most sensual, now seemingly unstoppable. Whenever the young lady who was now a global star spoke to the media, she no longer concealed her true ambitions. "I wanna be remembered, and I wanna be respected," she said in *The Face* in May 2003. "And I wanna be an icon."[89] Beyoncé's wishes would soon be granted.

> The European leg of the *Dangerously in Love* world tour took place between 3 and 19 November 2003. Accompanied by a live band, Beyoncé delivered some of her most authentic live performances, which were released in April 2004 on the *Beyoncé: Live at Wembley* DVD recorded at Wembley Arena, London, on 10 November 2003.

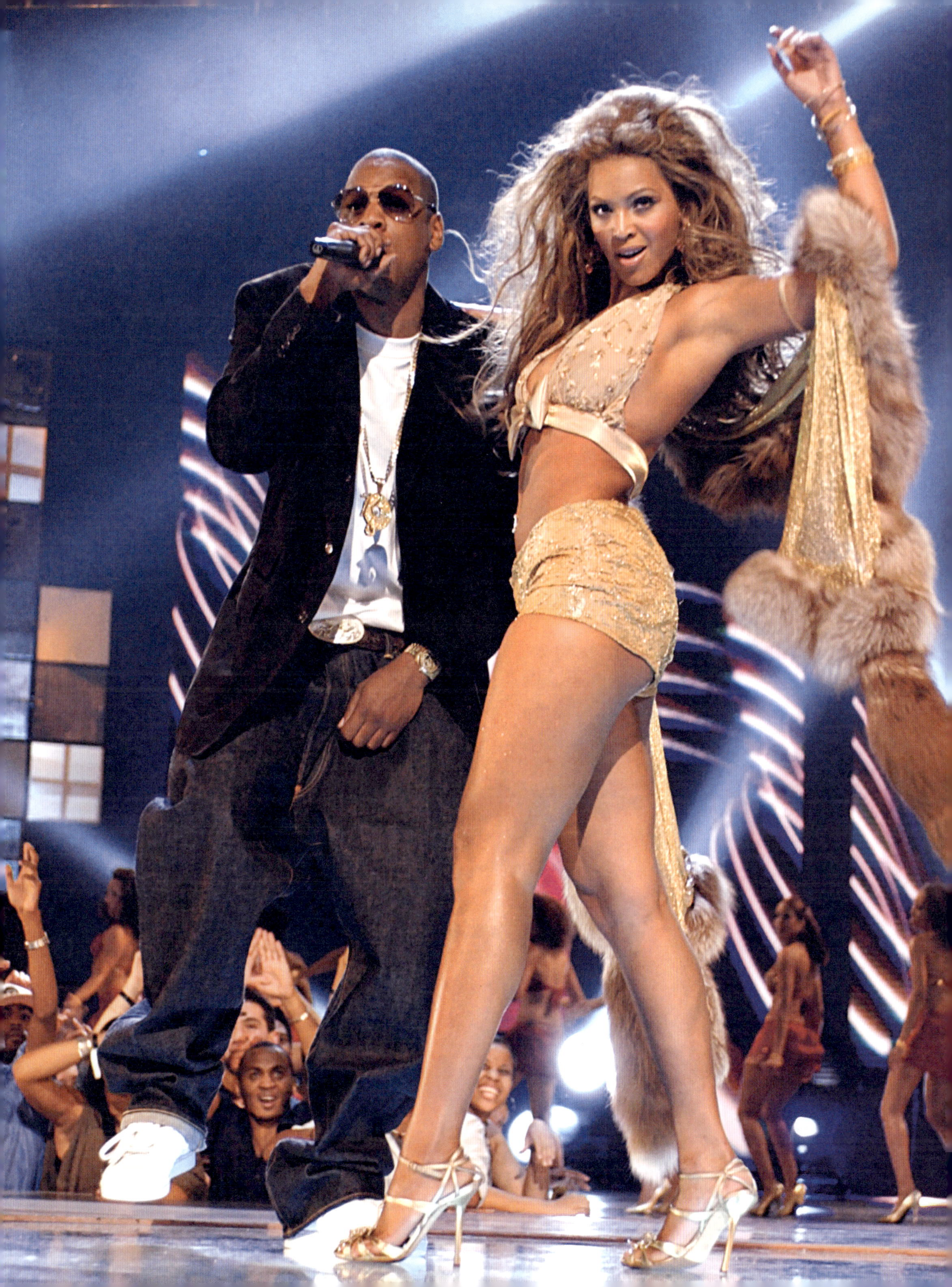

Jay-Z, music industry magnate, director of a successful company, and gifted producer.

JAY-Z, BEYONCÉ'S ALTER EGO

Shawn Corey Carter was born on 4 December 1969 in New York. His father Adnis abandoned the family home when Shawn was only 11, and he was raised by his mother Gloria in the Marcy Houses, a city-run housing development of over 1,700 apartments in Brooklyn's Bedford-Stuyvesant neighborhood. The lack of a father figure made Shawn angry and bitter and he sometimes mixed with unsavory characters. His childhood was fraught with difficulties, which he managed to overcome by taking refuge in music, a passion he would soon share with his mentor, the rapper Jaz-O, four years his senior. Through his collaborations with other artists, Shawn—who called himself Jazzy, then Jay-Z—sang about the streets, the social status to which he aspired, and his loyalty to friends and family, the foundations on which he built his work and his social self.

The king of East Coast sound

Since the release of his first album, *Reasonable Doubt*, in 1996, Jay-Z had made a name for himself with his cutting style and unique flow. He had further developed this in his two subsequent albums, 1997's *In My Lifetime, Vol. 1* and 1998's *Vol. 2...Hard Knock Life*. The latter features the single *Hard Knock Life (Ghetto Anthem)*, which went on to become a global hit and a hip-hop anthem that ranks alongside Tupac Shakur's *California Love,* Dr. Dre's *Still D.R.E.*, and Snoop Dogg's *Who Am I (What's My Name)?* As he rose to become a big-name rapper, Jay-Z also became a seasoned businessman, establishing Roc-A-Fella Records with his friends Damon Dash and Kareem Burke. Under this label he released both his own albums and those of artists such as Christión, Memphis Bleek, Rell, Beanie Sigel, and Cam'Ron. Jay-Z steadily grew his business interests, opening the 40/40 Club in Manhattan on 18 June 2003 with Desiree Gonzalez and Juan Perez, acquiring the Armadale vodka brand, and launching his own clothing line, Rocawear.

Renowned for his artistic talents and business acumen, Jay-Z was one of the biggest figures in contemporary music at the start of the new millennium. Inevitable, then, that he would end up working with Beyoncé, with whom he released the single *03 Bonnie & Clyde* on 12 November 2002.

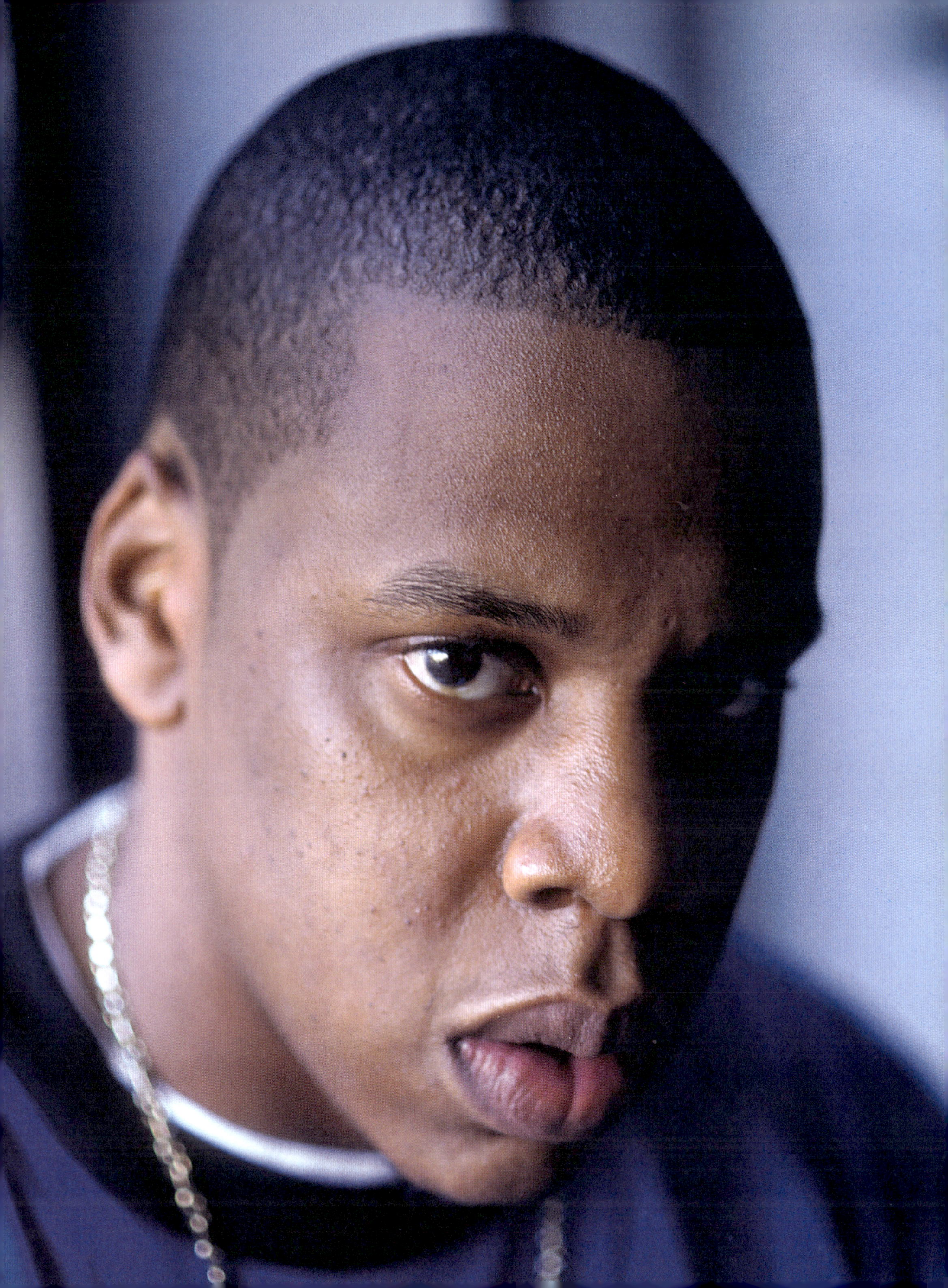

SINGLE

CRAZY IN LOVE
(FEATURING JAY-Z)

(Beyoncé Knowles, Eugene Record, Rich Harrison, Shawn Carter/3'56)

Musicians
Beyoncé Knowles: vocals, backing vocals
Jay-Z: rap
Rich Harrison: additional instruments

Recording
Sony Music Studios, New York: 2002 to 2003
The Hit Factory, New York: 2003

Technical team
Producer: Rich Harrison
Executive producers: Beyoncé Knowles, Mathew Knowles
Recording engineers: Jim Caruana, Pat Thrall

Single
Digital distribution on iTunes: 14 May 2003
Best chart ranking in the USA: 1

Genesis

For her first solo album, Beyoncé wanted to surround herself with bold producers. That was certainly the case with Rich Harrison, who had just worked with Kelly Rowland on her album *Simply Deep*. Harrison presented Beyoncé with an instrumental based on a sample from *Are You My Woman (Tell Me So)*, released by the Chi-Lites on their 1970 album *I Like Your Lovin' (Do You Like Mine?)*. Interviewed about the album, Beyoncé explained what she had liked about *Crazy in Love*: "I thought the track was so different because it was a great mixture of live with hip-hop and soul and it's a great club track."[88] When singer and producer got together to record the vocal line, Beyoncé struggled to find inspiration for the lyrics. She decided to take a break and go buy a birthday gift for Kelly Rowland, but told Harrison that she couldn't leave the building dressed as she was: "I was looking crazy with my clothes. And I kept saying, 'I'm looking crazy right now.' I wanted to go out […] but I didn't want to leave the studio because I was scared that people were going to take pictures of me."[58] Inspired by the artist's concerns about how she looked, Harrison came up with the hook for the song, *Got me looking so crazy right now*, to which he added the now famous line of sounds that comes after the chorus. "*Crazy in Love* is very different from anything I've done and very different from most R&B songs," Beyoncé observed. "[…] The song is about a person who is in a relationship and they are at the point where they are so in love they are looking kind of crazy, doing things they don't normally do."[91]

Production

With the song earmarked to be her first single finished, Beyoncé still felt that it was lacking something. So she decided to call in rapper Jay-Z, with whom she had recently worked on the single *03 Bonnie & Clyde*. "He came to the studio at 3 a.m. the night before I serviced it to the radio. I just thought it was such a great mixture of old school and new school."[92] "We work really well together in the studio," she added. "Hip-hop and R&B always is a great collaboration…There's a male point of view, and a female point of view. Men relate; women relate."[87] Alongside this now legendary track, the music video, shot in Los Angeles and directed by Jake Nava, also symbolizes Beyoncé's transformation into the sexy, independent woman

Beyoncé wearing her iconic shorts in the *Crazy in Love* video.

that she has remained throughout her career. Thanks to the choreography by LaVelle Smith Jr and Frank Gatson Jr, the video shows Beyoncé at her most sensual yet, dressed in her now-iconic super-short shorts and perched on her indispensable stilettos. "I had just turned 21 […]," Beyoncé explained in 2011. "I wanted to be a female version of James Dean and wear an iconic white T-shirt and jean shorts. I always think about wearing something a fan could buy and make her own; as a young girl I remember seeing so many artists, and then I'd try to dress like them."[93] With its sultry video, prestigious guest star, and bold production, *Crazy in Love* would definitively launch Beyoncé's solo career, and the hits kept on coming, whatever artistic experimentation she tried. "I always thought it was an incredible song. I wasn't sure that people were going to understand it because it was so different—it doesn't sound like anything else…But it's a great song and people get it. I guess they were happy to hear something fresh."[94] The 11 million people who bought *Dangerously in Love* would have no trouble agreeing with their idol's opinion.

BEYONCÉ: ALL THE SONGS 155

Queen of disco Donna Summer, cited twice by Beyoncé: in 2003's *Naughty Girl* and 2022's *Summer Renaissance*.

HEADPHONES AT THE READY

Does the vocal line in the intro to *Naughty Girl* ring a bell? It wouldn't be surprising if it did, because this wasn't the first time a female R&B singer reused the famous hook from Donna Summer's 1975 hit single, *Love to Love You Baby*. TLC had already paid tribute to Summer at 1'20 of their song *I'm Good at Being Bad* on their 1999 album *Fanmail*.

SINGLE

NAUGHTY GIRL

(Angela Beyincé, Beyoncé Knowles, Donna Summer, Giorgio Moroder, Pete Bellotte, Robert Waller, Scott Storch/3'29)

Musicians: Beyoncé Knowles: vocals, backing vocals / **Recording:** South Beach Studios, Miami: 2002 to 2003 / **Technical team: Producers:** Beyoncé Knowles, Scott Storch / **Executive producers:** Beyoncé Knowles, Mathew Knowles / **Recording engineer:** Carlos Bedoya / **Single:** Released in the USA by Columbia/Sony Music Soundtrax/Music World Music: 20 April 2004 (CD single ref.: 38K 76853) / **Best chart ranking in the USA:** 3

The spellbinding *Naughty Girl* came into being thanks to the work of star producer Scott Storch. Initially planned as the first single from *Dangerously in Love*, it was ultimately replaced by *Crazy in Love*. "When I first met Scott, we just clicked," Beyoncé recalled, "he was just a very humble person and I was already a fan of his productions."[95] Storch was an iconic figure on the American hip-hop scene, having worked with some of the genre's biggest artists, including The Roots, Xzibit, Busta Rhymes, Snoop Dogg, Eve, and Mobb Deep. No one, apart from perhaps Jay-Z or Dr. Dre, could boast such a resumé. Although Beyoncé had said she wanted to surround herself with amateur producers for her album, thankfully she made an exception for Storch, because *Naughty Girl* turned out to be the best song on it in more ways than one. First of all, its Arabian feel was just right for the period, as is shown by hit singles such as Jay-Z's *Big Pimpin'* (2000), Nas and Bravehearts' *Oochie Wally* (2000), Missy Elliott's *Get Ur Freak On* (2001), and *Addictive* by Truth Hurts (2002), which all had the *de rigueur* Middle Eastern touch. Then there are Beyoncé's vocal lines, sensual enough to melt an iceberg, perfectly complementing the lyrics in which she is sexier than ever. The chemistry between the singer and her producer was such that two other songs—*Baby Boy* and *Me, Myself and I*—emerged from their week's work, which launched production of the album. "When I was in the studio," Storch later revealed, "I was thinking to myself so many times, this is the best singer I've ever worked with and probably will ever work with."[96]

FOR BEYONCÉ ADDICTS

In the *Naughty Girl* video, the man whom Beyoncé seduces is none other than the singer Usher. It was an amazing reunion between the rapper and the woman he once "baby-sat," as he explained in 2023: "I was at Daryl Simmons' house. He was working with them at the time, and I just happened to be over there and they were working on a session. I kind of found my way into being their like, I don't know, chaperone, nanny, or something like that."[97]

2003

156　DANGEROUSLY IN LOVE

Beyoncé and Sean Paul's dance moves did not please Jay-Z.

SINGLE

BABY BOY
(FEATURING SEAN PAUL)

(Beyoncé Knowles, Robert Waller, Sean Paul Henriques, Shawn Carter/4'04)

Musicians: Beyoncé Knowles: vocals, backing vocals / Sean Paul: vocals / **Recording:** South Beach Studios, Miami: 2002 to 2003 / The Hit Factory, New York: 2002 to 2003 / **Technical team: Producers:** Beyoncé Knowles, Scott Storch / **Executive producers:** Beyoncé Knowles, Mathew Knowles / **Recording engineers:** Carlos Bedoya, Pat Thrall / **Single:** Digital distribution on iTunes: 3 August 2003 / **Best chart ranking in the USA:** 1

In 2003, if there was one singer it was impossible to ignore, it was Sean Paul. The Jamaican, who had achieved international success with his singles *Gimme the Light* (2002) and *Get Busy* (2003), specializes in a style that blends dancehall, hip-hop, and reggaeton. He was the one that all female singers of the time wanted to work with, his deep, husky voice a perfect foil to the ladies' delicate vocals—listen to Blu Cantrell's *Breathe (Rap Version)* (2003) for proof. While Scott Storch and Beyoncé were putting the finishing touches to *Baby Boy*, they had the idea of inviting Paul to add his inimitable flow to the song. Paul sent Storch an initial recording of his vocal part before finally joining the team at South Beach Studios in Miami to record a verse and a few well-delivered ad libs. They all got on and worked well together, so much so that *Baby Boy* was in the running to be released as a single a few months later. "She's amazing, a focused person, very talented,"[98] Paul later said of his employer. "He went into the studio, he killed it, and it turned out great,"[95] she said of him. While the song, which was released as a single in August 2003, was a testimony to the chemistry between the two stars, it didn't please Jay-Z, whose relationship with Beyoncé wasn't yet official. He saw red when the two performed *Baby Boy* on stage together at the MTV Video Music Awards on 28 August 2003. He didn't like seeing the Jamaican and the Texan dancing together in such a suggestive manner and forbade Beyoncé to work with Sean Paul again; this led to an argument and to the couple briefly splitting up. Despite the issues and quarrels caused by this collaboration, *Baby Boy* is still, over 20 years later, one of Beyoncé's most sensual and danceable tracks. Even now when Sean Paul is asked about his rumored relationship with Beyoncé, he laughs and replies bluntly: "Nah! I wish I did! She's beautiful."[99]

HEADPHONES AT THE READY

Although it has become his signature intro to songs, the Jamaican singer isn't saying his own name at 0'09 of *Baby Boy*. While the whole world clearly hears "Sean Paul," he is in fact saying, "Chanderpaul," in reference to the Guyanese cricketer Shivnarine Chanderpaul. What was a vocal hook at the start of the singer's career became an oft-repeated joke, and a well-kept secret for many years!

BEYONCÉ: ALL THE SONGS

Big Boi and André 3000 of the successful duo OutKast.

HIP HOP STAR
(FEATURING BIG BOI AND SLEEPY BROWN)

(Antwan Patton, Beyoncé Knowles, Bryce Wilson, Makeda Davis, Shawn Carter/3'42)

Musicians: Beyoncé Knowles: vocals, backing vocals / Big Boi: rap / Sleepy Brown: rap / **Recording:** Baseline Studios, New York: 2002 to 2003 / Stankonia Studios, Atlanta: 2002 to 2003 / **Technical team: Producers:** Beyoncé Knowles, Bryce Wilson, Big Boi / **Executive producers:** Beyoncé Knowles, Mathew Knowles / **Recording engineers:** Guru, Chris Carmouche, Vincent Alexander

"It's a very different hip-hop song," Beyoncé remarked of *Hip Hop Star*, "[…] but it's very rock'n'roll, […] almost Broadway, sounds like Marilyn Monroe mixed with rocking hip, well I can't describe it but it's very different."[88] The reason this is a unique track is that it is co-produced and performed by Big Boi who, along with the charismatic and eccentric rapper André 300, made up the duo OutKast. The sound of the two musicians who hail from Atlanta is instantly recognizable, thanks in no small part to the bold combination of music genres that made hits of their singles *Ms. Jackson* in 2000 and *Hey Ya!* in 2003. With the artistic audacity that characterizes her, and her habitual poise, Beyoncé gives this unusual song all she has, adding another rich layer to the album that is a far cry from the uniform, bland R&B tracks that were starting to invade FM radio stations in 2003.

BE WITH YOU

(Angela Beyincé, Beyoncé Knowles, William Collins, Gary Cooper, George Clinton Jr, Rich Harrison, Shuggie Otis/4'20)

Musicians: Beyoncé Knowles: vocals, backing vocals / Rich Harrison: additional instruments / **Recording:** Sony Music Studios, New York: 2002 to 2003 / **Technical team: Producers:** Beyoncé Knowles, Rich Harrison / **Executive producers:** Beyoncé Knowles, Mathew Knowles / **Recording engineer:** Jim Caruana

Be with You was produced by Rich Harrison, who had already worked on *Crazy in Love*, and is constructed around the chord progression of the choruses in *I'd Rather Be with You*, a 1976 track from Bootsy Collins' group, Bootsy's Rubber Band. The vocal line features another of Harrison's 1970s influences: the main sequence from *Strawberry Letter 23*, composed by Shuggie Otis in 1971 but made popular by The Brothers Johnson in 1977, before being introduced to a whole new generation of music lovers on the soundtrack to Quentin Tarantino's *Jackie Brown* 20 years later. Studying the credits for the song reveals that a certain Angela Beyincé helped compose it. Beyoncé's cousin had already been credited as a songwriter on *Naughty Girl,* and would work with our singer on many occasions, namely on the tracks *Get Me Bodied, Upgrade U,* and *Why Don't You Love Me.*

SINGLE

ME, MYSELF AND I

(Beyoncé Knowles, Robert Waller, Scott Storch/5'01)

Musicians: Beyoncé Knowles: vocals, backing vocals / **Recording:** South Beach Studios, Miami: 2002 to 2003 / **Technical team: Producers:** Beyoncé Knowles, Scott Storch / **Executive producers:** Beyoncé Knowles, Mathew Knowles / **Recording engineer:** Carlos Bedoya / **Single:** Released in the USA by Columbia: 19 October 2003 (CD single ref.: 38K 76911) / **Best chart ranking in the USA:** 4

Women breaking away from male domination had been a recurrent theme in Beyoncé's songs for several years. *Me, Myself and I* is no exception and slots nicely into her best protest songs, such as *Bills, Bills, Bills, Hey Ladies, Survivor,* and *Independent Women Part I*. In this case, the Texan urges women trapped in toxic relationships to get out, to trust only their instincts and to learn to be on their own, which, she says, is often better than being in a bad relationship. "Usually women feel stupid and silly and they blame themselves 'cause you have all the signs most of the time, but you love the guy so you don't want to see them go," Beyoncé said. "And in this song, it's kind of like a celebration of the breakup, because I like to look at it when something like that happens that the guy kind of taught you a lesson and now you know yourself and now you know better than those excuses."[100] "It talks about women basically listening to their inner voice and knowing that they will never disappoint themselves,"[101] she added in another interview. Columbia chose *Me, Myself and I*, entirely written and composed by Beyoncé and Scott Storch at South Beach Studios in Miami, as the third single from *Dangerously in Love*, because they wanted to show a different side to Beyoncé, presenting her as a singer with a timeless style and voice.

Former bassist for James Brown, the outlandish Bootsy Collins had numerous solo hits.

YES

(Bernard Edwards Jr, Beyoncé Knowles, Shawn Carter/4'19)

Musicians: Beyoncé Knowles: vocals, backing vocals / **Focus:** additional instruments / **Recording:** COE.BE.3 Studios, Stone Mountain: 2002 to 2003 / South Beach Studios, Miami: 2002 to 2003 / **Technical team: Producers:** Beyoncé Knowles, Focus / **Executive producers:** Beyoncé Knowles, Mathew Knowles / **Recording engineers:** Focus, Carlos Bedoya

Once again, Beyoncé rebels against her demanding boyfriend, who can't bear it when she refuses to do something he wants. However, she gives her lyrics broader meaning, speaking out against people in general's inability to say no. "I can sign a million autographs and the first time I have to say: 'Sorry, I'm gonna miss my plane,' it's like I never signed the other million. That happens all the time with all different situations of life. That's why I thought it was such a good concept."[102] The track emerged from Beyoncé's collaboration with Bernard Edwards Jr, aka Focus, the artist behind *Spread a Little Love on Christmas Day* on the *8 Days of Christmas* album.

SIGNS
(FEATURING MISSY ELLIOTT)
(Craig Brockman, Missy Elliott, Nisan Stewart/4'57)

Musicians: Beyoncé Knowles: vocals, backing vocals / **Missy Elliott:** rap / **Recording:** Sony Music Studios, New York: 2002 to 2003 / The Hit Factory Criteria, Miami: 2002 to 2003 / **Technical team: Producers:** Craig Brockman, Nisan Stewart, Missy Elliott, Beyoncé Knowles / **Executive producers:** Beyoncé Knowles, Mathew Knowles / **Recording engineer:** Jim Caruana

Beyoncé's relationship with rapper Missy Elliott goes beyond the professional. "[She's] a friend of mine, I completely respect her," Beyoncé says. "She's so different from everyone else. She's not afraid to do daring things, she's not afraid to say what's on her mind. She'll say and do anything that's in her head. She's like completely ahead of her time."[88] "Destiny's Child are incredible as a group," said the woman in question, "but now it's like you see the maturity in Beyoncé. Now she's this grownup woman like [how] you witnessed Aaliyah from *Back & Forth* to *More Than a Woman*. Her album is incredible."[103] Beyond the mutual back pats, the two artists have enjoyed a solid and prolific partnership. From *Confessions* on *The Writing's on the Wall* in 1999 to Beyoncé's contribution to Elliott's repertoire (*Crazy Feelings* on *Da Real World* in 1999, and *Nothing Out There for Me* on *Under Construction* in 2002), it's safe to say that sparks fly when the two women get together. As she does on *Gift from Virgo* six tracks later and on *Virgo's Groove* in 2022, here Beyoncé sings about her belief in astrology and in her star sign, Virgo—a theme that crops up regularly in interviews over the years.

SPEECHLESS
(Andreao Heard, Angela Beyincé, Beyoncé Knowles, Sherrod Barnes/6'00)

Musicians: Beyoncé Knowles: vocals, backing vocals / **Recording:** Soho Studios, New York: 2002 to 2003 / Patchwerk Recording Studios, Atlanta: 2002 to 2003 / South Beach Studios, Miami: 2002 to 2003 / **Technical team: Producers:** Andreao Heard, Beyoncé Knowles, Sherrod Barnes / **Executive producers:** Beyoncé Knowles, Mathew Knowles

"It's a serious album, a romantic album," Beyoncé declared when *Dangerously in Love* was released. "There are some songs that talk about making love, but it talks about all different steps of relationships, from the first time you meet a guy and you're attracted to him to the first time you tell him no. Everything. First time you say you love someone, first time he disappoints you. It just talks about everything that women go through."[104] While this first solo album as a whole reflects the different stages in a relationship, *Speechless* takes us straight to the first time a couple make love, with the song's inherent eroticism largely down to the singer's sensual performance, the electric guitar that cuts in, the slow tempo, and the growling bass that accentuates the effect. Beyoncé makes it clear that she is now a woman and is determined to savor the pleasures of womanhood. "As soon as I heard the track it inspired me. It's very sexy, very sensual. The sort of ballad that I've never done before. This song is definitely a population increaser!"[105]

THAT'S HOW YOU LIKE IT
(FEATURING JAY-Z)
(Brian Bridgeman, Delroy Andrews, Eldra DeBarge, Etterlene Jordan, Randy DeBarge, Shawn Carter/3'39)

Musicians: Beyoncé Knowles: vocals, backing vocals / **Jay-Z:** rap / **Recording:** Baseline Studios, New York: 2002 to 2003 / **Technical team: Producers:** Beyoncé Knowles, D-Roy, Mr. B / **Executive producers:** Beyoncé Knowles, Mathew Knowles / **Recording engineer:** Guru

In 2003, Beyoncé and Jay-Z were doing their best to deny they were in a relationship, but the temperature inevitably rises on *That's How You Like It*, a duet that sounded to fans like a confession. No one was fooled by their denials, as they were regularly seen together in public, claiming they were just good friends to conceal their closer involvement. This song nonetheless gives some clues that point to their budding romance, especially when Jay-Z explicitly refers to the two lovebirds when he sings *Young Hova and the letter B* (Hova being one of the rapper's nicknames)—the story within a story is obvious. The song's lyrics weren't all written by Beyoncé: she borrows a few lines, or at least a few turns of phrase, from *I Like It,* released by the family band DeBarge in August 1982.

Beyoncé in a shot by photographer Todd Plitt, August 2003.

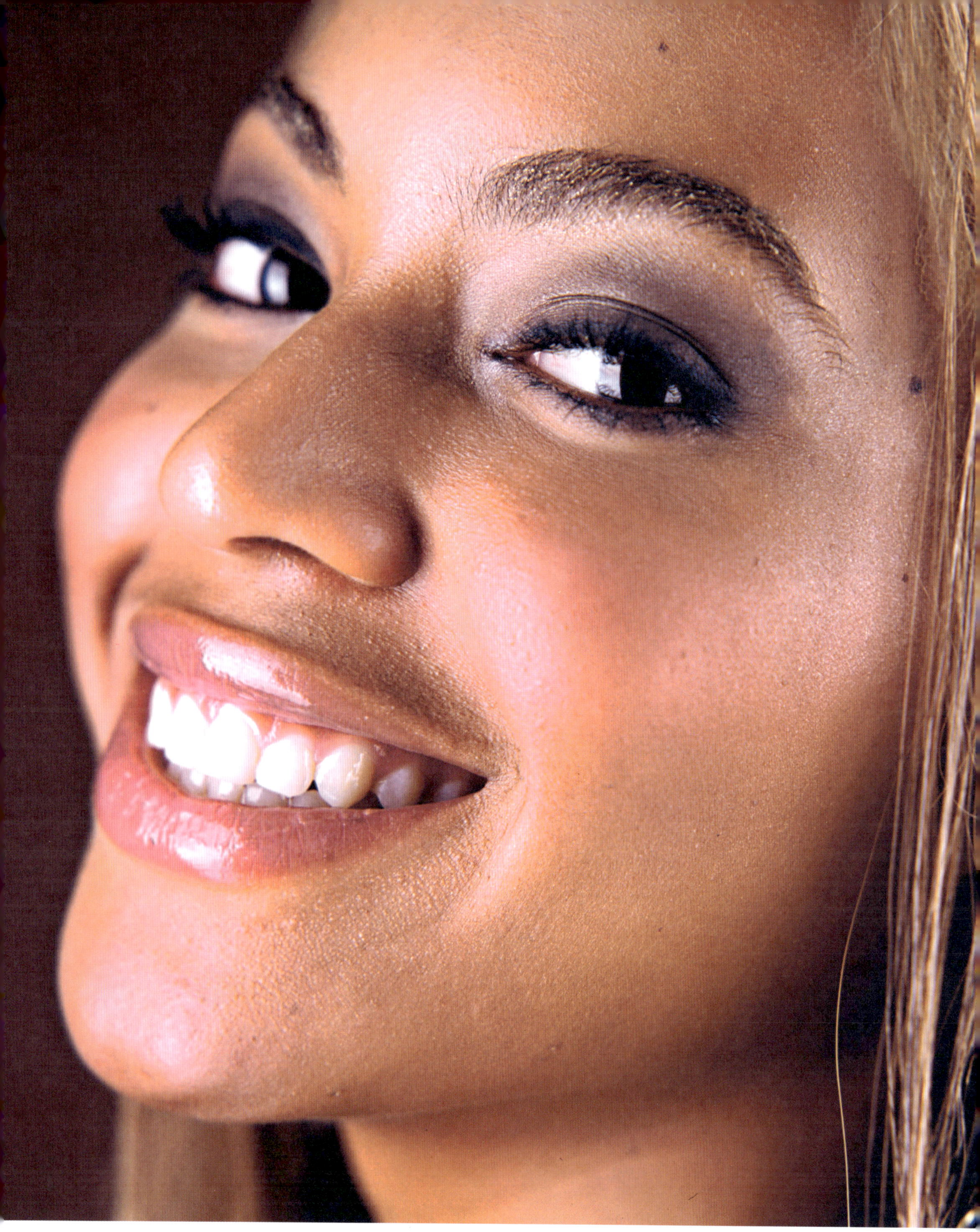

One-time backing singer for David Bowie, Luther Vandross spread his wings and took flight.

THE CLOSER I GET TO YOU
(FEATURING LUTHER VANDROSS)

(James Mtume, Reggie Lucas/4'58)

Musicians: Beyoncé Knowles: vocals, backing vocals / **Luther Vandross:** vocals / **Brenda White-King:** backing vocals / **Candace Thomas:** backing vocals / **Cissy Houston:** backing vocals / **Tawatha Agee:** backing vocals / **Phil Hamilton:** guitar / **Byron Miller:** bass / **Ivan Hampden:** drums / **Nat Adderley Jr:** electric piano / **Bashiri Johnson:** percussions / **Skip Anderson:** synthesizers, programming / **Al Brown:** conductor / **Recording:** The Hit Factory, New York: 2002 to 2003 / Right Track Recording, New York: 2002 to 2003 / **Technical team:** Producer: Nat Adderley Jr / **Executive producers:** Beyoncé Knowles, Mathew Knowles / **Recording engineers:** Stan Wallace, Ray Bardani / **Arrangements:** Nat Adderley Jr, Skip Anderson / **String arrangements:** Nat Adderley Jr / **Vocal arrangements:** Luther Vandross

Although its old-fashioned feel is in direct contrast to the artistic modernity Beyoncé claimed to be seeking in 2003, this cover of the classic by soul master and crooner Luther Vandross is a testament to Beyoncé's independence, as she defies conventional wisdom to perform this duet with one of her idols. *The Closer I Get to You*, first recorded by Roberta Flack with Donny Hathaway in 1977, was Flack's second-biggest hit after 1973's celebrated *Killing Me Softly with His Song*. Performing this song with Luther Vandross saw Beyoncé achieve one of her wildest dreams, as she revealed in 2003: "Luther Vandross […] is just a wonderful artist that is an icon and I completely admire and look up to him. And he helped me make history. I think that song is one of the most beautiful songs on my record and it showcases my voice and I had no idea that the collaboration with us two, our voices will complement each other so well."[88]

DANGEROUSLY IN LOVE 2

(Beyoncé Knowles, Errol McCalla Jr/4'53)

Musicians: Beyoncé Knowles: vocals, backing vocals / **Dan Workman:** guitar / **John "Jab" Broussard:** guitar / **Recording:** SugarHill Studios, Houston: 2002 to 2003 / The Enterprise, Burbank: 2002 to 2003 / **Technical team:** Producers: Beyoncé Knowles, Errol "Poppi" McCalla Jr / **Executive producers:** Beyoncé Knowles, Mathew Knowles / **Recording engineers:** Brian Springer, Dan Workman

The hidden sides of relationships are at the heart of Beyoncé's first solo album, which explores the different facets of romance, as she explained when the album was released. The tracklisting included a sequel to the song *Dangerously in Love* from *Survivor*, unsurprisingly called *Dangerously in Love 2*. "I said *Dangerously in Love* because I feel like when love is real, it's a little scary and that scary feeling feels a little dangerous."[88] "There's something exciting when anything in life is a little scary, you know, and that's what I mean by dangerous,"[100] she added in another interview. Errol McCalla Jr, who co-produced the first version, is back at the helm here. There are very few differences between the two versions apart from the new instrumental part, more modern and more of its time—two years in show business being the equivalent of a millennium when it comes to music productions. McCalla had originally written the song for Usher when he presented it to Shakir Stewart at Hitco Music Publishing, the record label owned by the famous producer L. A. Reid. On Stewart's advice, the song was offered to Beyoncé instead. With her first album under production, it was Beyoncé herself who asked McCalla to rework the *Dangerously in Love* instrumental.

FOR BEYONCÉ ADDICTS

Lyndall Locke, one of Beyoncé's ex-boyfriends, still tells anyone who will listen that *Dangerously in Love* was written for him at the time that the two were dating. "She sang this song to me that she said was about us. […] When I hear it today, it really hit me hard."[43]

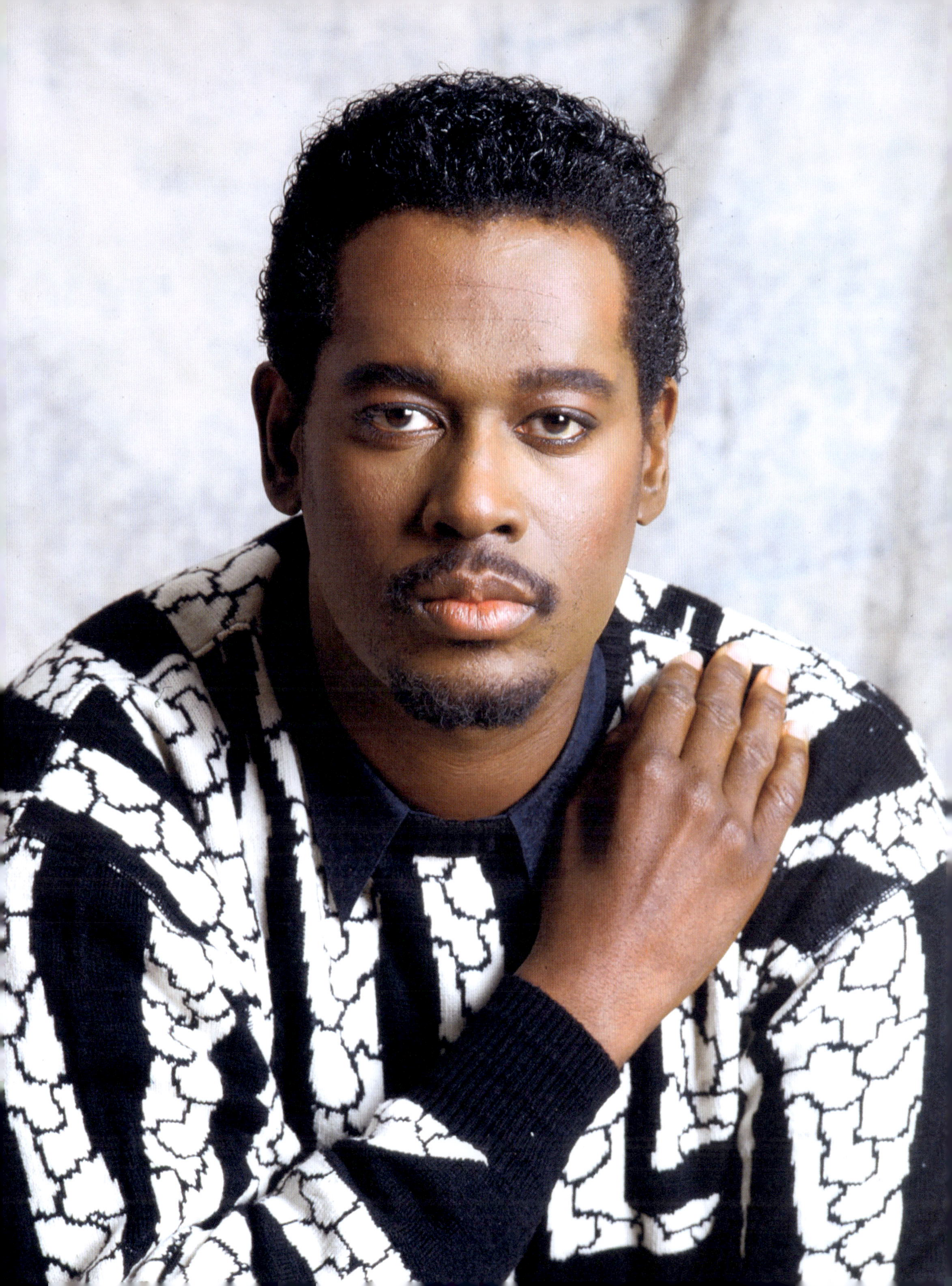

Lauryn Hill's interludes on her first solo album influenced Beyoncé in the production of *Dangerously in Love*.

BEYONCÉ INTERLUDE

(Beyoncé Knowles/0'18)

Musicians: Beyoncé Knowles: spoken voice / **Recording:** South Beach Studios, Miami: 2002 to 2003 / **Technical team:** Producer: Beyoncé Knowles / **Executive producers:** Beyoncé Knowles, Mathew Knowles / **Recording engineer:** Carlos Bedoya

One listen to this short poem in which Beyoncé reveals her passion for a mysterious stranger and there can be no doubt about it: she is well and truly in love. While the text is clearly Beyoncé's, no information is given about who composed the background instrumentals. The interlude is reminiscent of the ones on the great Lauryn Hill's debut album in 1998, in which Ras Baraka, future mayor of Newark, can be heard asking students how they feel about love in a recording made in Hill's house in South Orange, New Jersey. "There were chairs set up in the living room and a bunch of kids were there," Baraka recalled. "She told me she wanted to discuss the concept of love. There was a blackboard and I wrote the letters 'LOVE' and we just went into the whole discussion."[106] There's no doubt that these famous interludes must have influenced Beyoncé, a huge admirer of Lauryn Hill's work.

GIFT FROM VIRGO

(Beyoncé Knowles, Shuggie Otis/2'44)

Musicians: Beyoncé Knowles: vocals, backing vocals / **Recording:** Patchwerk Recording Studios, Atlanta: 2002 to 2003 / **Technical team:** Producer: Beyoncé Knowles / **Executive producers:** Beyoncé Knowles, Mathew Knowles

It is over a sample—or rather the whole of the original recording—of *Rainy Days*, released by Shuggie Otis in 1974, that Beyoncé declares her love for someone, whom we guess is Jay-Z, with numerous references in the lyrics to their romance. "Because I'm older now, I just talked about something that everybody feels, and that's love. I wanted to do something timeless. And I wanted to do something more vulnerable. Because I wrote so many songs that talked about strength and being powerful that I think people lost touch with [the fact that] I could get hurt, and I could fall in love, and I can feel things that everyone else goes through."[87]

DADDY

(Beyoncé Knowles, Mark Batson/4'58)

Musicians: Beyoncé Knowles: vocals, backing vocals / Mark Batson: bass, drums, piano / Nioka Workman: cello / Judith Insell-Staack: viola / Marlene Rice: violin / **Recording:** ?: 2002 / **Technical team:** Producers: Beyoncé Knowles, Mark Batson / **Executive producers:** Beyoncé Knowles, Mathew Knowles / **Recording engineers:** Michael McCoy, Mark Batson / **Assistant recording engineer:** Jon Belec / **String arrangements:** Mark Batson

Before becoming a star producer for Eminem, Dr. Dre, The Game, Alicia Keys, Nas, and 50 Cent, Mark Batson worked with Beyoncé on the final song on *Dangerously in Love*, which appeared only as a hidden track at the end of the album on all versions worldwide except in the USA, where it was part of the official tracklisting. The track is Beyoncé's tribute to her father, Mathew, for whom she feels unconditional love and admiration, and whose praises she sings in the song, recounting memories of her happy childhood. She hesitated before including it on the album, not knowing whether revealing her feelings to this extent was the right thing to do. "I actually didn't write it for the album. I didn't want to put it on it. I just kind of did it for him. And he was speechless. He didn't know what to say or how to react really, because it is really a heavy song."[100] Shortly before appearing on *Dangerously in Love*, *Daddy* was uploaded onto the iTunes Store in the United States on 23 June 2003. It also featured on the soundtrack to Tyler Perry's 2007 film *Daddy's Little Girls*.

164 **DANGEROUSLY IN LOVE**

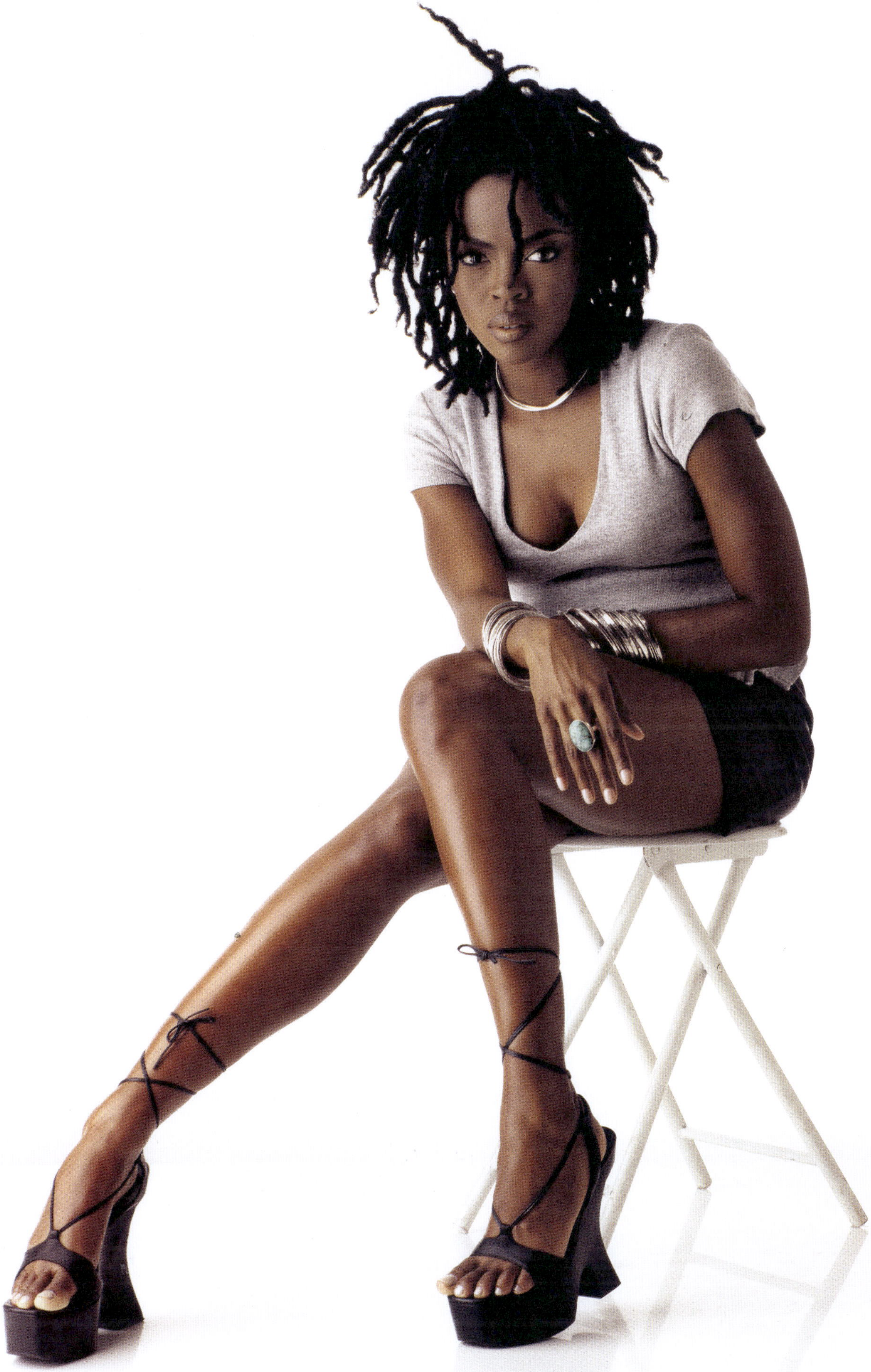

Tupac Shakur, aka 2Pac, in Oakland, 7 January 1992.

03 BONNIE & CLYDE
(JAY-Z FEATURING BEYONCÉ KNOWLES)

(Darryl Harper, Kanye West, Prince, Ricardo Rouse, Shawn Carter, Tupac Shakur, Tyrone Wrice/3'25)

Musicians
Jay-Z: rap
Beyoncé Knowles: vocals, backing vocals
Eric "E-Bass" Johnson: acoustic guitar, bass, synthesizers
Kanye West: programming
Recording
Baseline Studios, New York: 2002
Technical team
Producer: Kanye West
Executive producers: Damon Dash, Kareem "Biggs" Burke, Shawn Carter
Recording engineers: Gimel "Young Guru" Keaton, Shane "Bermuda" Woodley

Jay-Z "The Blueprint²: The Gift & The Curse" (album)
Released in the USA by Roc-A-Fella Records: 12 November 2002
(LP ref.: 440 063 381-1, CD ref.: 440 063 381-2)

HEADPHONES AT THE READY

The reason Prince is credited on the track is that, in Beyoncé's vocal line at 2'18, there is a nod to the song *If I Was Your Girlfriend*, which featured on Prince's 1987 album *Sign o' the Times*.

FOR BEYONCÉ ADDICTS

The release of *03 Bonnie & Clyde* triggered a war of words between Jay-Z and singer Toni Braxton. This was because *More than a Woman*, Braxton's fifth album, also contains a cover version of Tupac's *Me and My Girlfriend*, recorded before the Jay-Z and Beyoncé version and entitled *Me & My Boyfriend*. The angry words flew back and forth, but no one will ever know if, as Braxton claimed, Jay-Z and Kanye West stole the idea for the track from her.

Genesis

It's 2002. Kanye West, a successful rapper and producer who is close to Jay-Z, with whom he worked on *The Dynasty: Roc La Familia* in 2000 and *Jay-Z—The Blueprint* in 2001, can't believe his ears when he hears a track from Tupac Shakur's latest studio album. *The Don Killuminati: The 7 Day Theory*, released under Shakur's new name, Makaveli, had come out on 5 November 1996, less than two months after he was murdered in Las Vegas. One of the album's tracks caught Kanye's attention: "I went to *Me and My Girlfriend* and was like, 'Oh, sh--, this joint would be crazy for [Jay-Z] and Beyoncé.' He had told me a week before that he needed a joint for him and Beyoncé."[107] He looked into it and quickly proposed a reworked version of the song to Jay-Z, who renamed it *03 Bonnie & Clyde* in reference to the legendary American bandits. Released on Jay-Z's album *The Blueprint²: The Gift & The Curse* in November 2002, the song became an international hit, and played an important part in Beyoncé's career, not least for bringing her into the world of hip-hop, from which she had thus far kept her distance, despite a number of collaborations that included MTV's *Carmen: A Hip Hopera*. "He has taught me about hip-hop," she said about Jay-Z in 2006. "I loved it as a child, but my mom wouldn't let me listen to the cussing. Now I understand it. It is a reality."[22]

Production

To create the instrumental for *03 Bonnie & Clyde*, Kanye West went to 127 West 26th Street, Manhattan, home of Jay-Z's sanctuary, Baseline Studios. There, he met up with Eric "E-Bass" Johnson, an incredibly talented musician who plays on most of his compositions. "[E] came through," West recalled. "I programmed the drums in 10 minutes, and then he played all the different parts. [...] I brought it to [Jay-Z] that night, he heard it, he thought of the video treatment before he thought of the rap. He just knew it was gonna be the one."[107]

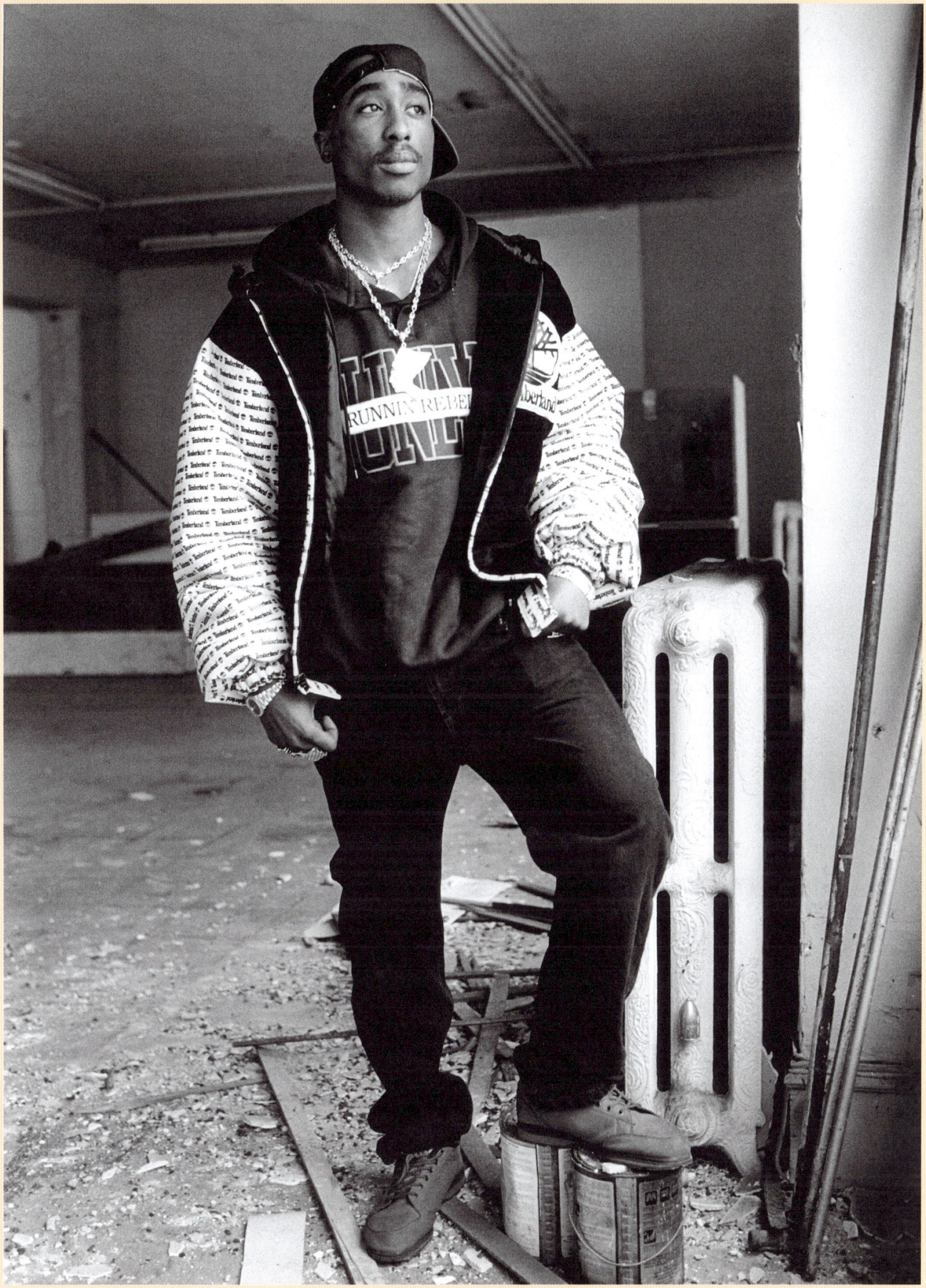
RUNNIN' REBEL
Timberland

NOTHING OUT THERE FOR ME
(MISSY ELLIOTT FEATURING BEYONCÉ KNOWLES)

(Craig Brockman, Missy Elliott, Nisan Stewart/3'05)

Musicians: Missy Elliott: spoken voice, rap, vocals / **Beyoncé Knowles:** spoken voice, rap, vocals, backing vocals / **Tweet:** vocals, backing vocals / **Recording:** The Hit Factory Criteria, Miami: 2002 / Patchwerk Recording Studios, Atlanta: 2002 / **Technical team:** Producers: Craig Brockman, Missy Elliott, Nisan Stewart / **Executive producers:** Missy Elliott, Timbaland / **Recording engineers:** Josh Butler, Mike Wilson / **Assistant recording engineers:** Cory Williams, Justin Phillips / **Missy Elliott "Under Construction" (album):** Released in the USA by Elektra: 12 November 2002 (LP ref.: 62813-1, CD ref.: 62813-2)

Missy Elliott was one of Beyoncé's key collaborators. When she was working on the production of her fourth studio album, she invited the Texan to sing and rap—although it's more spoken voice than rap—on the track *Nothing Out There for Me*. Elliott later recalled that she didn't hesitate to push Beyoncé beyond her comfort zone. "I said: 'Hey, I want you to rap a little bit.' And she was like: 'Miss, if I sound crazy, don't put this out!' And I said: 'Trust me, B, I'm not gonna allow you to sound crazy.' She went in there and now she's rapping better than me!"[108] The chemistry happened in a legendary Miami venue known as the Criteria Studios. Central to the Miami Sound of the 1970s, the studios were bought in 1999 by the Hit Factory Group, which owned a number of others around the United States. After several months of refurbishment, the recording complex reopened in 2000 under the name The Hit Factory Criteria Miami.

NAIVE
(SOLANGE FEATURING DA BRAT AND BEYONCÉ KNOWLES)

(Beyoncé Knowles, Da Brat, HR Crump, Mathew Knowles/3'46)

Musicians: Solange Knowles: vocals, backing vocals / **Beyoncé Knowles:** vocals, backing vocals / **Da Brat:** rap / **Recording:** Digital Services Recording Studios: 2002 / The Enterprise, Burbank: 2002 / **Technical team:** Producers: Beyoncé Knowles, HR Crump / **Solange "Solo Star" (album):** Released in the USA by Columbia/Music World Music: 26 December 2002 (CD ref.: CK 86354)

Five years her junior, Solange Knowles isn't just Beyoncé's little sister. She is also an accomplished artist who released four albums between 2002 and 2019 and appeared in several films and TV series. When production of her first album *Solo Star* got underway in 2001, a collaboration with Beyoncé was inevitable. With an instrumental composed by producer HR Crump, *Naive* also features rapper Da Brat, one of Beyoncé's earliest collaborators. "I'm very proud of my sister and protective of her," Beyoncé said in 2003. "Solange is the one person I will fight for. Don't talk about my sister; don't play with me about my sister. If you do, you'll see another side of me."[109] *Naive* appeared as a hidden track on *Solo Star,* along with *This Song's for You* and *Feelin' You Pt. 2 (H-Town Screwed Mix)*.

KEEP GIVING YOUR LOVE TO ME

(Adonis Shropshire, Beyoncé Knowles, Richard Frierson, Ryan Leslie/3'08)

Musicians: Beyoncé Knowles: vocals, backing vocals / **Ryan Leslie:** all instruments / **Recording:** Daddy's House, New York: 2002 to 2003 / **Technical team:** Producers: Sean "P. Diddy" Combs, Ryan Leslie, Younglord / **Recording engineers:** Roger Che, Chip Karpells, Eric Lynch / **Assistant recording engineers:** Lynn Montrose, Alexis Seaton / **"Bad Boys II—The Soundtrack" (compilation):** Released in the USA by Universal/Bad Boys Records: 15 July 2003 (LP ref.: B0000716-01, CD ref.: B0000716-02)

You could say that Beyoncé's destiny was linked to that of actor Will Smith. *Killing Time* was released on the soundtrack to the film *Men in Black* in the summer of 1997 and was the very first Destiny's Child song to be presented to the public. Six years later, Beyoncé popped up on the soundtrack to another Smith blockbuster, *Bad Boys II,* with a track produced by the threesome of P. Diddy, Ryan Leslie, and Younglord. The compilation album is packed with absolute gems such as Jay-Z's *La-La-La*, produced by Pharrell Williams's band The Neptunes, *Realest Niggas*, performed as a duet by 50 Cent and the late great The Notorious B.I.G., and *Gangsta Shit* by Snoop Dogg. Beyoncé, who, along with Mary J. Blige, is the only female artist on the album, sets sparks flying with this powerful, melodic track.

Solange and Beyoncé Knowles in 2003.

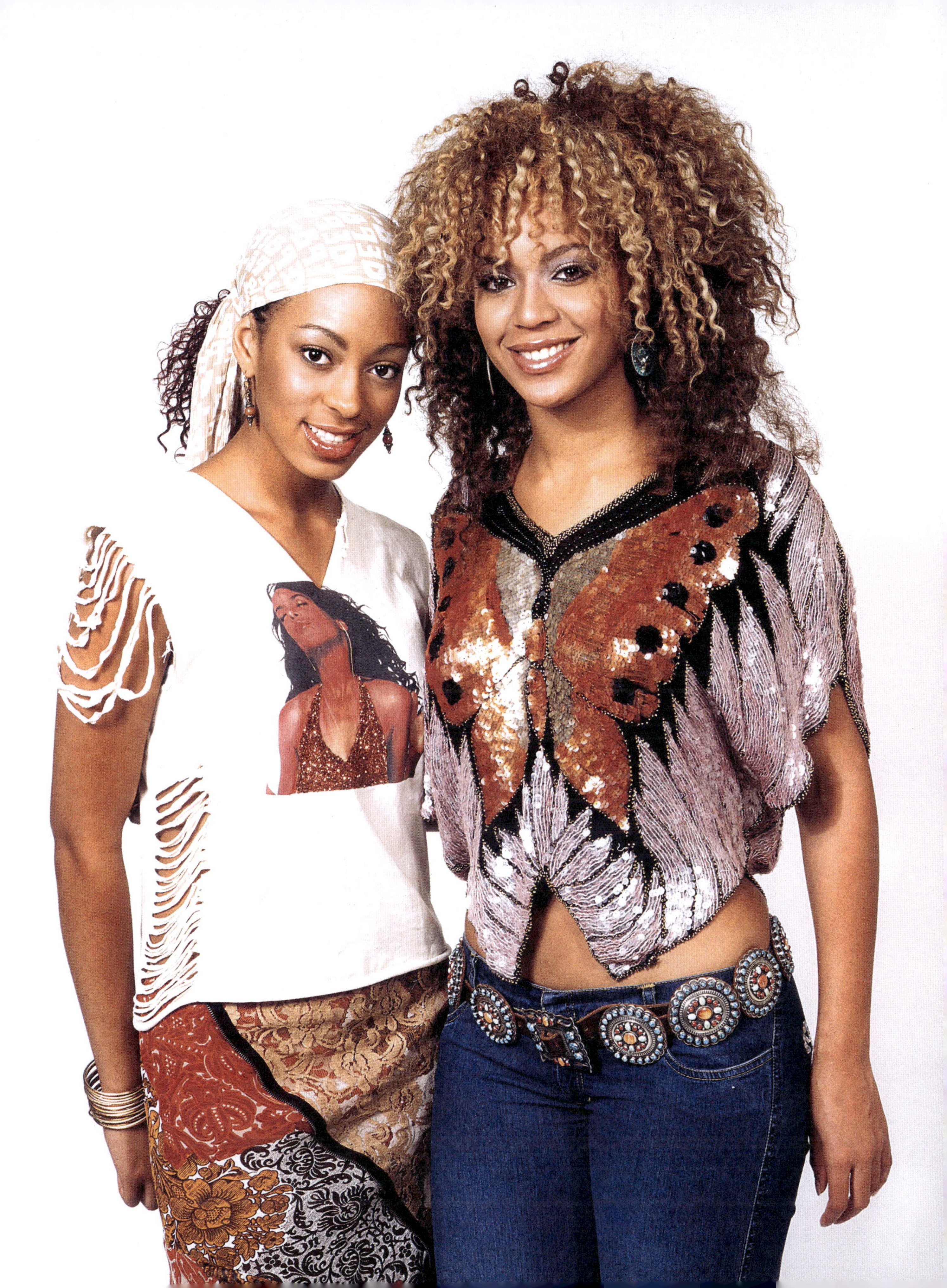

Members of IAM, the legendary rap group from Marseilles: Kephren, Shurik'n, Imhotep, Akhenaton, Freeman, and Khéops.

COLLABORATIONS

BIENVENUE
(IAM FEATURING BEYONCÉ)

(Akhenaton, Shurik'n, Deni Hines/4'27)

Musicians: Akhenaton: rap / Shurik'n: rap / Beyoncé Knowles: vocals, backing vocals / Khéops: scratching / Slim Pezin: guitar, bass / Raoul Duflot-Verez: synthesizers / Deyan Pavlov: conductor / Bulgarian Symphony Orchestra: orchestra / **Recording:** Studios Zgen, Avignon: 2003 / Studio La Cosca, Marseille: 2003 (IAM vocals) / Studio Claudia Sound, Paris: 2003 / Bulgarian Radio Studios, Sofia: 2003 (strings) / Sony Music Studios, New York: 2003 (Beyoncé vocals) / **Technical team: Producer:** Akhenaton / **Recording engineers:** Philippe Amir (Studios Zgen), Eric Chevet (Studio La Cosca), Nabil Ghrib (Studio La Cosca), Didier Lizé (Bulgarian Radio Studios), Maxime Lefèvre (Studio Claudia Sound) / **String arrangements:** Bruno Coulais / **IAM *"Revoir un Printemps"* (album): Released in France by Hostile Records:** 16 September 2003 (LP ref.: 7243 5 92934 1 7, CD ref.: 7243 5 93578 2 9)

Seen from outside France, Beyoncé's collaboration with a group from Marseille might seem surprising. But that's only if you don't know how big a role IAM played in popularizing hip-hop in France, producing some of the best of the genre since it first arrived there in the early 1980s. The two masterminds behind the group—Philippe "Akhenaton" Fragione and Geoffroy "Shurik'n" Mussard—wrote arguably some of the best lyrics in the genre and were also renowned for their inimitable flow with a Mediterranean tinge. In 2003, when IAM were recording their eagerly awaited fourth album (their previous one, *L'Ecole du Micro D'Argent*, had become a benchmark in French hip-hop with sales of 1.6 million copies), they asked Beyoncé to work with them. As they were about to fly to the United States to meet up with her, an Air France strike grounded their plane. Beyoncé therefore recorded her vocals at Sony Music Studios in New York and sent them to IAM in France, who added them to their track. "When we suggested it to her, we were expecting an artist of her stature to ask to be paid for featuring on the track. She said: 'No, I don't want anything, just your permission to use the track on my album.' So, we did an exchange. That was really classy of her."[110] So, as well as appearing on the tracklisting of *Revoir un Printemps*, *Bienvenue* also featured on the French and Belgian editions of *Dangerously in Love*. It's worth another listen, if only to hear the unparalleled sounds of one of the world's greatest hip-hop groups.

170 COLLABORATIONS

What More Can I Give appeared to be jinxed and did not achieve the success of *We Are the World*, another famous charity song co-written by Michael Jackson in 1985.

WHAT MORE CAN I GIVE
(UNITED WE STAND)

(Michael Jackson/3'36)

Musicians: *NSYNC: vocals / 3LW: vocals / Anastacia: vocals / Rubén Blades: vocals / Mariah Carey: vocals / Aaron Carter: vocals / Nick Carter: vocals / Cristian Castro: vocals / Céline Dion: vocals / Joy Enriquez: vocals / Gloria Estefan: vocals / Juan Gabriel: vocals / Billy Gilman: vocals / Hanson: vocals / Julio Iglesias: vocals / Michael Jackson: vocals / Bryton James: vocals / Beyoncé Knowles: vocals / Ziggy Marley: vocals / Ricky Martin: vocals / Michael McCary: vocals / Reba McEntire: vocals / Brian McKnight: vocals / Luis Miguel: vocals / Mya: vocals / Laura Pausini: vocals / Tom Petty: vocals / Carlos Santana: vocals / Alejandro Sanz: vocals / Jon Secada: vocals / Shakira: vocals / Shawn Stockman: vocals / Olga Tañón: vocals / Thalía: vocals / Justin Timberlake: vocals / Luther Vandross: vocals / Usher: vocals / **Recording:** ?: 1996 to 2001 / **Technical team: Producer:** Michael Jackson / **Recording engineer:** Bruce Swedien / **Promotional single** distributed by Sony Music in the USA: 2001 (CD ref.: none) / Streaming broadcast on MusicForGiving.com: 27 October 2003

This track, which Michael Jackson wrote under the working title *Heal L.A.* during the recording sessions for his ninth album *HIStory: Past, Present and Future, Book I*, has had many lives. It wasn't included on the album, but acquired its definitive title and humanist lyrics after the King of Pop met Nelson Mandela on 25 March 1999 while visiting Cape Town to announce two charity concerts. With lyrics that paid tribute to the victims of the war in Kosovo, the song once again failed to make it onto the singer's discography when it was left off the album *Invincible* in 2001. Following the terrorist attacks on the World Trade Center on 11 September of that year, Jackson rewrote the lyrics and invited other stars to perform alongside him, in an attempt to replicate the success of *We Are the World*, a single he had co-written with Lionel Richie in 1985 to raise funds for the famine in Ethiopia. But as his relationship with his record label Sony Music had seriously deteriorated, the song was distributed only as a promotional track. It wasn't until October 2003, two years after it had been produced, and thanks to the Clear Channel Communications platform, that the single finally became available as a download, along with a music video of the artists who participated in the project.

The year 2001 wasn't the most propitious time for Michael Jackson (with rumors swirling about his relationships with young children added to his battles with his record label) and he struggled to match the success of *We Are the World*. Despite everything, he still had the backing of the American music industry, and artists rushed to sing on *What More Can I Give*, with support for victims of the New York terrorist attacks outweighing the accusations against Jackson. R&B and hip-hop were well represented by artists such as Mya, Usher, Justin Timberlake, and Beyoncé, while pop at the start of the millennium was covered by Anastacia, Céline Dion, and Julio Iglesias. However, the song was soon forgotten by the public, as were some of the performers.

BEYONCÉ: ALL THE SONGS 171

Beyoncé on stage at Wembley Arena, London, on 10 November 2003.

I CAN'T TAKE NO MORE

(Beyoncé Knowles, Mario Winans, Mike Jones/4'46)

Musicians: Beyoncé Knowles: vocals, backing vocals / **Recording:** Sony Music Studios, New York: 2002 / **Technical team:** Producer: Mario Winans / **Downloadable track free with pre-orders of Dangerously in Love:** 2 June 2003

In the run-up to the release of *Dangerously in Love*, Beyoncé was everywhere promoting it. On 14 June 2003, she was on stage at the Henry Ford II World Center in Dearborn, Michigan, where she gave her first solo performance, to mark the hundredth anniversary of the company founded by the famous businessman Henry Ford. This commemoration gave Beyoncé the opportunity to reunite with Kelly Rowland and Michelle Williams, as well as to appear with her younger sister, Solange Knowles. In the meantime, Sony Music launched pre-sales of the album on sonymusicstore.com, an approach to distribution that would be widely adopted by record labels in the future. Sony also offered customers who had pre-ordered the album a link to download a previously unreleased track by their idol: *I Can't Take No More*, produced by Mario Winans, who also worked with P. Diddy, Jennifer Lopez, and Whitney Houston. This well-crafted song never appeared on any of Beyoncé's physical records, and slumbers on in old computers around the world or on iPods thrown into the backs of drawers and long forgotten by their owners.

MY FIRST TIME

(Beyoncé Knowles, Chad Hugo, Pharrell Williams/4'25)

Musicians: Beyoncé Knowles: vocals, backing vocals / **Recording:** ?: 2003 to 2004 / **Technical team:** Producers: Pharrell Williams, Chad Hugo / **"Live at Wembley" Bonus Disc (album):** Released in the USA by Columbia: 26 April 2004 (DVD + CD ref.: CVD 58627)

The release, in April 2004, of Beyoncé's first live DVD, filmed at her Wembley Arena concert in London on 10 November 2003, was an opportunity for Sony to offer fans rare or previously unreleased content. The CD that came with the DVD featured three songs—*My First Time*, *What's It Gonna Be*, and *Wishing on a Star*—that have never been included on an album, as well as three remixes of Beyoncé's latest singles: *Krazy in Luv (Maurice's Nu Soul Remix)*, *Baby Boy (Junior's World Mixshow)*, and *Naughty Girl (Calderone Quayle Club Mix)*. For the production of *My First Time*, Beyoncé reunited with The Neptunes, the duo consisting of Chad Hugo and Pharrell Williams, with whom she had worked on 2001's *Work It Out*.

WHAT'S IT GONNA BE

(Beyoncé Knowles, Corte Ellis, Kandice Love, Karrim Mack, Larry Troutman, LaShaun Owens, Roger Troutman/3'35)

Musicians: Beyoncé Knowles: vocals, backing vocals / **Recording:** ?: 2003 to 2004 / **Technical team:** Producers: Beyoncé Knowles, Soul Diggaz / **"Live at Wembley" Bonus Disc (album):** Released in the USA by Columbia: 26 April 2004 (DVD + CD ref.: CVD 58627)

What's It Gonna Be was not a new release, as it had already appeared on the Japanese edition of *Dangerously in Love* in 2003. The song, which arose from Beyoncé's collaboration with the three-man production team Soul Diggaz, had also come out as a single on 29 July 2003, with a second version being released in 2004 as part of Beyoncé's partnership with French cosmetics brand L'Oréal. On the back of the CD, buyers would also find a two-dollar voucher that could be redeemed against future L'Oréal purchases.

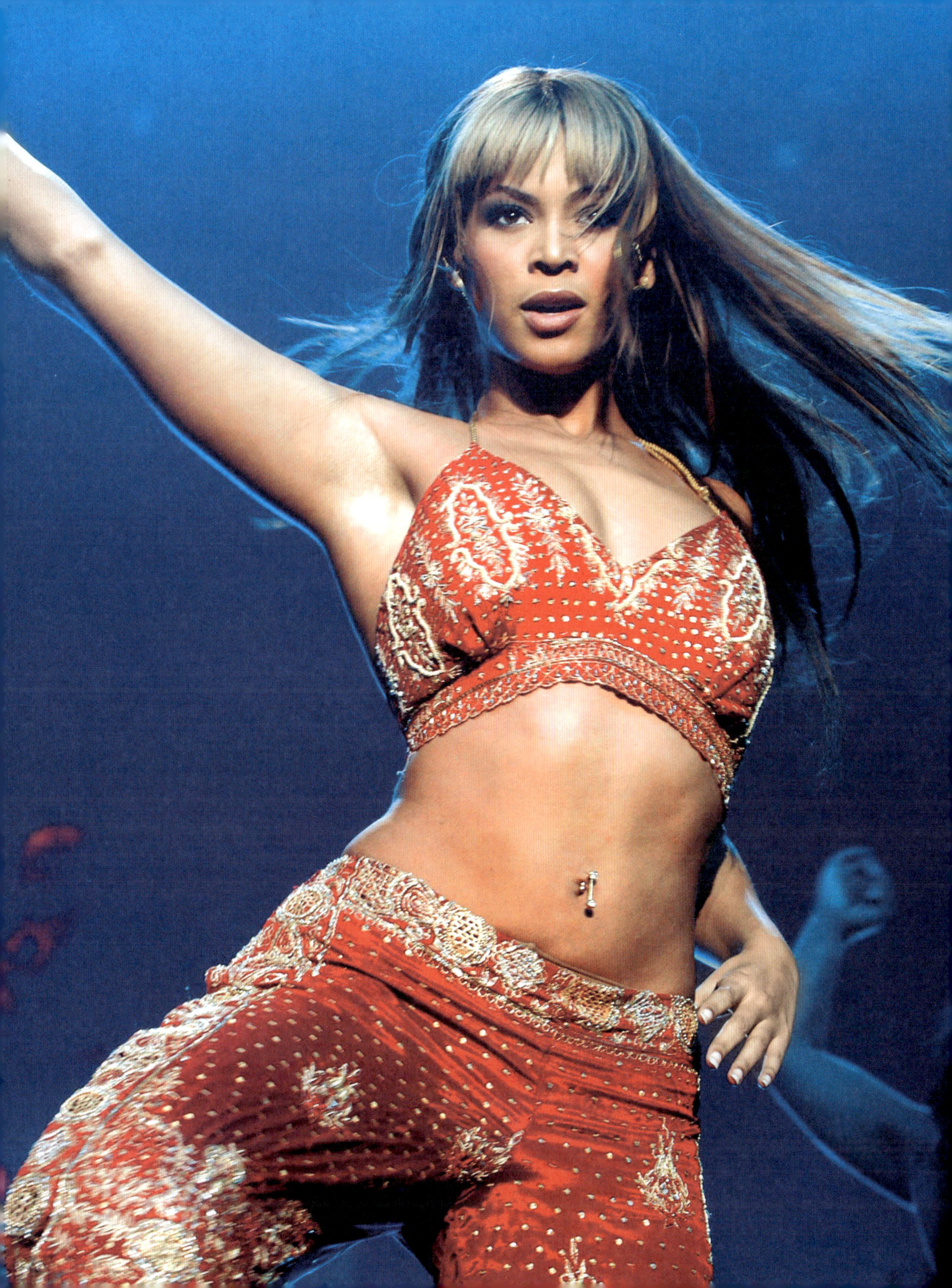

This cover version of 50 Cent's *In Da Club* marked Dr. Dre's first foray into Beyoncé's discography. The second was 2017's *Walk on Water*, a duet with Eminem.

WISHING ON A STAR

(Billie Rae Calvin/4'09)

Musicians: Beyoncé Knowles: vocals, backing vocals / **Recording:** ?: 2003 to 2004 / **Technical team:** Producer: ? / **"Live at Wembley" Bonus Disc (album):** Released in the USA by Columbia: 26 April 2004 (DVD + CD ref.: CVD 58627)

Wishing on a Star is a soul classic par excellence. It was composed in 1977 by Billie Rae Calvin, formerly a singer with The Undisputed Truth. The same year, the group Rose Royce—who had achieved their first international hit in 1976 with *Car Wash*, carried by the inimitable voice of their lead singer Gwen Dickey—recorded the song and released it on their second album, *In Full Bloom*. But this hit could just as easily have been a success for another singer, as Dickey explained: "*Wishing on a Star* wasn't written for Rose Royce. It was written for Barbra Streisand. At that time she was recording an album and she had chosen the song to go on it and then for whatever reason she decided she had enough songs and wasn't going to have *Wishing on a Star* on her album."[111] Covered by many artists, the Rose Royce hit was given a hip-hop makeover by Jay-Z that appeared on the British and European versions of his second album, *In My Lifetime, Vol. 1*, before Beyoncé then re-recorded it as a bonus track on her *Live at Wembley* DVD in 2004. The same year, the song appeared on the promotional CD put out by the Tommy Hilfiger brand for the launch of its new fragrance, True Star, with Beyoncé as the face of the campaign. The CD, called *True Star (A Private Performance)* also contained the duet *Naive*, which Beyoncé had recorded with her sister Solange in 2002. An a cappella version of *Wishing on a Star* was also recorded for the TV advertising campaign. In 2005, the full version appeared on the soundtrack to the film *Roll Bounce*, directed by Malcolm D. Lee.

SEXY LIL' THUG

(Curtis James Jackson III, Andre Romelle Young, Michael Elizondo, Beyoncé Knowles/4'33)

Musicians: Beyoncé Knowles: vocals, backing vocals / DJ Quik: programming / **Recording:** Teamwork Studios, Long Island: June 2002 (original version) / ?: 2003 (remix and Beyoncé vocals) / **Technical team:** Producers: Dr. Dre, Mike Elizondo (original version), Errol McCalla Jr. (remix)

Some songs are destined to become hits and *In Da Club*, with instrumentals produced by Dr. Dre and his loyal partner Mike Elizondo in 2002, was one of them. The song was initially offered to D12—a supergroup featuring the virtuosic Eminem and his protégés Proof, Bizarre, Mr. Porter, Kuniva, and Swifty McVay—whose second album, *D12 World*, was under production. The Detroit collective's spectacular debut album *Devil's Night*, released in 2001, had garnered attention for its many cutting-edge tracks, all bearing the stamp of their leader (*Pistol Pistol, Ain't Nuttin' But Music*, and most of all the formidable *Blow My Buzz*, indisputably one of the best hip-hop tracks of the 2000s). However, their ability to sniff out a hit failed them when they refused the instrumental from *In Da Club* because they couldn't work out a way to adapt their incisive flow to the track. In the end, it was given to 50 Cent, who had just signed to the Shady/Aftermath stable, a conglomerate comprising Eminem's label and that of his mentor Dr. Dre. 50 Cent, real name Curtis James Jackson III, put his mark on the track, using it to bring a positive note to the tracklisting of his debut album *Get Rich or Die Tryin'*, whose songs are tinged with a violence redolent of the performer's turbulent past. When *In Da Club* was released as a single on 7 January 2003, it became an instant cult hit and remains one of the best-known songs in the history of hip-hop, as well as a great party anthem.

In 2003, when Beyoncé was writing her first solo album, she recorded a new version of *In Da Club*, retaining the entire instrumental line but adding a host of new harmonies and a brand new vocal line. Renamed *Sexy Lil' Thug*, the track was earmarked for *Dangerously in Love*, but the idea was dropped in favor of keeping the original songs. This remix, produced by Errol McCalla Jr, offers a very feminine version of 50 Cent's hit and reveals the full extent of Beyoncé's talent, as she stood on the cusp of international success with *Dangerously in Love*. Although the song wasn't officially released, it nonetheless peaked at number 67 on *Billboard*'s Hot R&B/Hip-Hop Singles & Tracks on 5 April 2003. That week, the top spot was occupied by...*In Da Club* by 50 Cent!

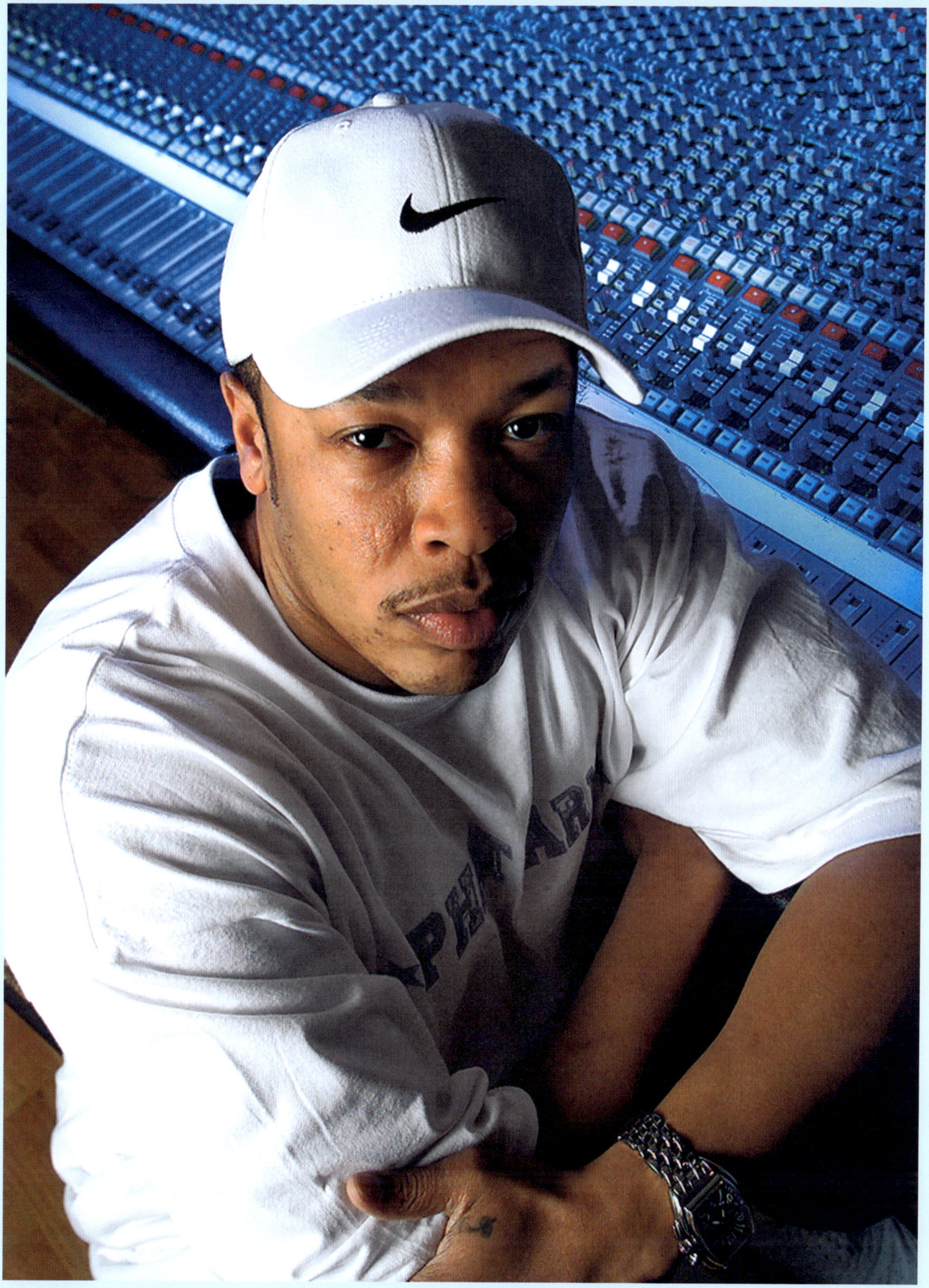

Music from the Motion Picture The Fighting Temptations (compilation)
Released in the USA by Sony Music Soundtrax/Columbia:
9 September 2003 (CD ref.: CK 90286)

Cuba Gooding Jr and Beyoncé Knowles filming *The Fighting Temptations*.

The Fighting Temptations (2003)

1. **Fighting Temptation**—Beyoncé, Missy Elliott, MC Lyte, and Free*
2. **I Know**—Destiny's Child
3. **Rain Down**—Angie Stone and Eddie Levert Sr (of The O'Jays)
4. **To Da River**—T-Bone, Zane, and Montell Jordan
5. **I'm Getting Ready**—Ann Nesby
6. **The Stone**—Shirley Caesar and Ann Nesby
7. **Heaven Knows**—Faith Evans
8. **Fever**—Beyoncé*
9. **Everything I Do**—Beyoncé and Bilal*
10. **Loves Me Like a Rock**—The O'Jays
11. **Swing Low, Sweet Chariot**—Beyoncé*
12. **He Still Loves Me**—Beyoncé and Walter Williams Sr (of The O'Jays)*
13. **Time to Come Home**—Beyoncé, Angie Stone, and Melba Moore*
14. **Don't Fight the Feeling**—Solange
15. **Summertime**—Beyoncé*

* *Music from the Motion Picture The Fighting Temptations,* features tracks by several artists; only those performed by Beyoncé are discussed here.

THE FIGHTING TEMPTATIONS: A FIVE-STAR CAST TO ACCOMPANY BEYONCÉ

In 2003, for her second film role, Beyoncé Knowles chose the antithesis of her part in *Austin Powers in Goldmember*. Ditching the glitz for a more human, more authentic character, she joined Cuba Gooding Jr, LaTanya Richardson, and Mike Epps in the cast of *The Fighting Temptations*, a Jonathan Lynn film about the adventures of Darrin Hill, a top New York advertising executive who returns to his hometown of Monte Carlo, Georgia, to attend the funeral of his Aunt Sally. He discovers that she has bequeathed him $150,000 on condition that he leads the local choir to victory in a regional contest. He meets some colorful characters and falls for the charms of a talented local singer, Lilly (played by Beyoncé Knowles), who helps him put his plan into action. "The 'Goldmember' clothes were ridiculous," said Beyoncé. "Every day it was like playing dress-up. They had all of the cool fabrics and everything. It was great. [But in] this movie [my character] is a real person. She's very earthy, she's very bohemian."[112]

Music in the background

As Lauryn Hill had done before her, in Bill Duke's *Sister Act 2: Back in the Habit* in 1993, Beyoncé uses a film role to let those who don't yet know that she is a fantastic singer. She is surrounded on set by a whole host of soul and R&B stars, including Faith Evans, Angie Stone, Melba Moore, Montell Jordan, and Mary Mary. But for her second big-screen role, Beyoncé decided to take a back seat and to learn from her colleague Cuba Gooding Jr, for whom she has boundless admiration. "I consciously did an urban film," she told *Savoy* in 2003, "because that's where it all started for me. I also didn't want to be the star of the film because I'm still learning to be an actress. It was also a conscious decision to play a real black woman with real issues. It was my choice to wear braids with no makeup where I could cry and make ugly faces […] and wear flat shoes with jeans and long dresses—nothing sexy."[113]

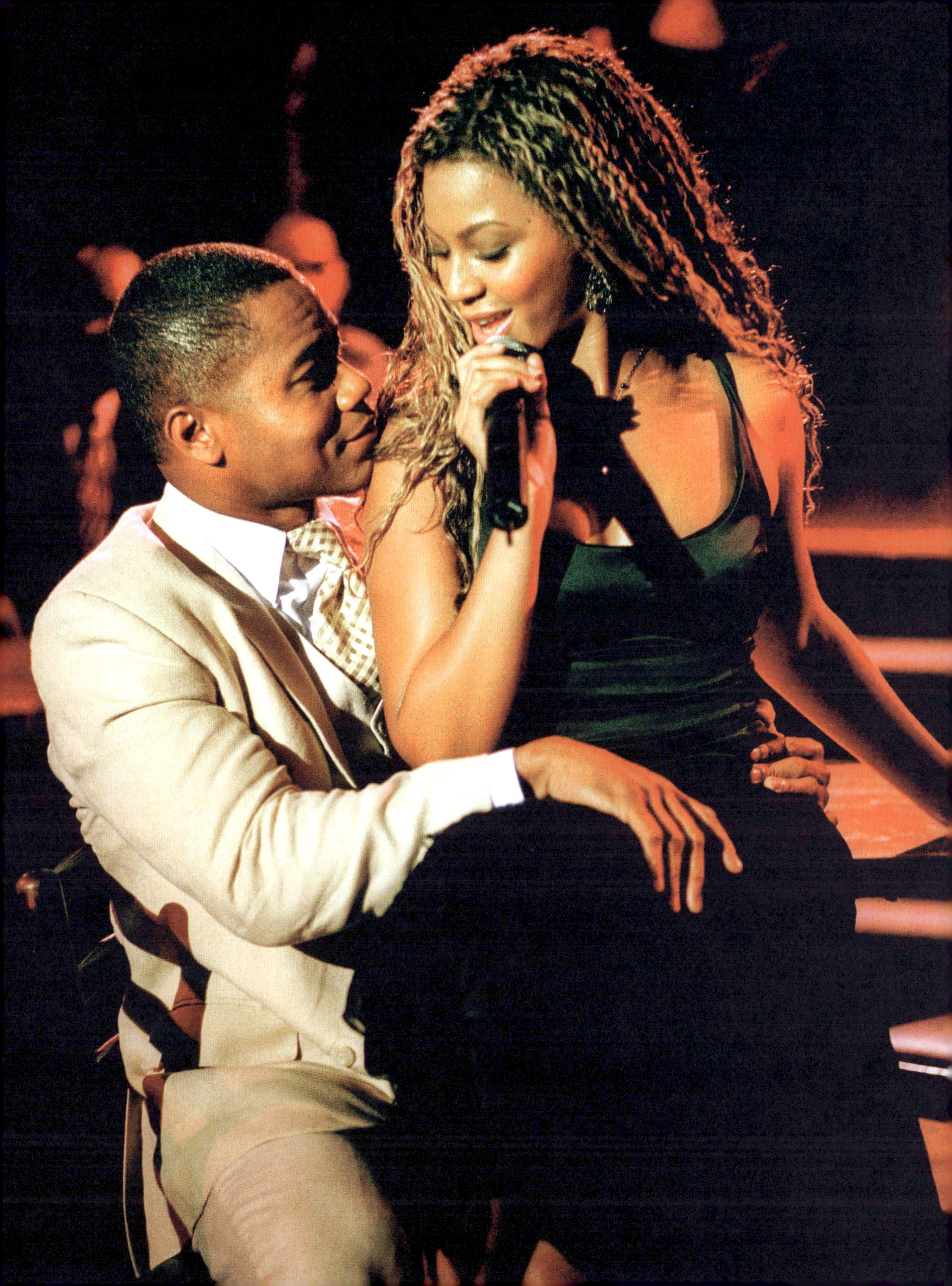

CINEMA

New York rap artist MC Lyte made a noteworthy guest appearance in *The Fighting Temptations*.

FIGHTING TEMPTATION
(BEYONCÉ, MISSY ELLIOTT, MC LYTE, FREE)

(Gene Pistilli, Jonathan Burks, Karrim Mack, LaShaun Owens, Lana Moorer, Marie Wright, Walter Murphy, Missy Elliott/3'51)

Musicians: Beyoncé Knowles: vocals, backing vocals / Missy Elliott: rap / MC Lyte: rap / Free: rap / **Recording:** ? / **Technical team: Producers:** Missy Elliott, Soul Diggaz, Beyoncé Knowles / **Executive producer:** Mathew Knowles

Used as a promotional single for the film, *Fighting Temptation* was also officially released in Europe, where it passed pretty much under the radar. Yet the song was a potential hit in many ways. It was produced by Soul Diggaz, a trio consisting of Corte Ellis, Karrim Mack, and LaShaun Owens, with whom Missy Elliott had just worked on her album *This Is Not a Test!*, and it also features the aforementioned rapper along with the explosive MC Lyte and Free. *Fighting Temptation* was built on a sample from *I Like Funky Music*, performed by Uncle Louie in 1979; it should be listened to as a matter of urgency and added to your playlist of Beyoncé's lesser-known but most accomplished songs, not least for the talent of its female rappers at a time when these women were determined to bare their fangs and confront the all-powerful male rappers. "Once you hear the song, and all the music in this film," Beyoncé said to a journalist for *Jet* in 2003, "you can't help but fall in love with it."[114] A statement with which the author of this book very much agrees.

178 THE FIGHTING TEMPTATIONS (2003)

I KNOW
(DESTINY'S CHILD)

(Corte Ellis, Jully Black, Karrim Mack, LaShaun Owens, Beyoncé Knowles/3'43)

Musicians: Beyoncé Knowles: vocals, backing vocals / **Kelly Rowland:** vocals, backing vocals / **Michelle Williams:** vocals, backing vocals / **Recording:** Sony Music Studios, New York: 2003 / **Technical team: Producers:** Soul Diggaz, Beyoncé Knowles / **Recording engineer:** Jim Caruana

Let it be said that Destiny's Child hadn't yet had their last word. The production of *The Fighting Temptations* soundtrack, supervised by Mathew Knowles, was an opportunity for Beyoncé's group to remind their audiences that they were still there. "We were never gone," Kelly Rowland assured MTV.com journalists in April 2003. "We've always been together."[115] "We've actually done some things together," added Michelle Williams. "We just recently did the Trumpet Awards together. We did a European tour last April to June and we had a ball, the time of our lives over there. We keep in touch with each other [even though] we're all doing our own thing."[115] For their big return to the studio, the three friends recorded a track called *I Know* that Beyoncé had rejected for the tracklisting of *Dangerously in Love*. "I just thought it sounded like a Destiny's Child song,"[115] she said. That was enough to arouse the curiosity of fans, who would soon rediscover their idols on a record and even on stage.

FEVER

(Eddie Cooley, John Davenport/4'32)

Musicians: Beyoncé Knowles: vocals, backing vocals / **Romeo Antonio:** guitar / **Tim Landers:** bass / **Joe Pusateri:** drums / **Damon Elliott:** programming, percussions, synthesizers / **Greg Curtis:** piano / **Jimmy "Z" Zavala:** saxophone, flute, harmonica / **Recording:** The Enterprise, Burbank: 2003 / **Technical team: Producers:** Damon Elliott, Beyoncé Knowles / **Recording engineer:** Dave Pensado

Beyoncé's first appearance on screen in *The Fighting Temptations* is identical to those in *Carmen: A Hip Hopera* and *Austin Powers in Goldmember*: she's singing in a club and surprises the male protagonist with her talent and charm. Here, however, Beyoncé is performing an American classic, *Fever*, written by Eddie Cooley and Otis Blackwell (aka John Davenport) in 1956 for Little Willie John, although the most famous rendition of the song has always been the one by Peggy Lee two years later. In the scene Beyoncé once again plays on her sensuality, as she admitted to *Vibe* in October 2002: "I want to make sure people realize that this is me and that I have other parts to my personality."[116] So it was Beyoncé's turn to offer her take on the song for the soundtrack to *The Fighting Temptations* in 2003; she even sang it on *The Tonight Show With Jay Leno* on 17 September. In 2010, *Fever* would be used on the advertising campaign for Beyoncé's perfume, *Heat*. "I want women to feel sexy, strong, empowered," she wrote on beyonceparfums.com, a website that was launched for the occasion, "and I want them to feel like they can conquer anything. When they walk into a room, I want them to feel like they can leave a lasting impression on everyone they walk past."[117] *Fever* was distributed as a download on 8 February 2010, and appeared a year later on *Heat Limited Edition CD*, an EP that was distributed in Europe to anyone who bought the fragrance.

EVERYTHING I DO
(BEYONCÉ AND BILAL)

(James Harris III, Terry Lewis, James Wright/4'22)

Musicians: Beyoncé: vocals, backing vocals / **Bilal:** vocals, backing vocals / **IZ:** drums, percussions / **James Wright:** synthesizers / **Alex "Godson" Richbourg:** programming / **Recording:** Doppler Studios, Atlanta: 2003 / The Village Recorder, Los Angeles: 2003 / **Technical team: Producers:** Jimmy Jam, Terry Lewis, James Wright / **Recording engineer:** Blake Eiseman / **Assistant recording engineer:** Matt Marrin

Among the celebrities who appeared on *The Fighting Temptations*, neo soul singer Bilal gave us a memorable duet with Beyoncé on *Everything I Do*, produced by the omnipresent Jimmy Jam and Terry Lewis, former members of Prince's inner circle who broke away from his rule in the mid-1980s to pursue their own careers. The song is soft and sensual, like many of the album's other tracks. "You'll definitely get emotional," Beyoncé promises. "You might become happy or even sad, your heart will get full. All the songs are touching and spiritual, and that's what the movie itself is like."[114]

The choir, directed by Cuba Gooding Jr, and Beyoncé performing for inmates of the county jail in the film *The Fighting Temptations*.

SWING LOW, SWEET CHARIOT

(Wallace Willis/2'05)

Musicians: Beyoncé Knowles: vocals, backing vocals / **Recording:** Doppler Studios, Atlanta: 2003 / **Technical team: Producers:** Beyoncé Knowles, Loretha Jones / **Recording engineer:** Ralph Cacciurri / **Arrangements:** Keith Lancaster, Wayburn Dean

This Christian anthem, which has its roots in African-American culture, was written by a former slave, Wallace Willis, in the mid-nineteenth century, at the end of the American Civil War. It talks about hope, the chariot in question being that of the prophet Elijah, who in the Bible used it to cross the Jordan River before ascending to Heaven. Here, Beyoncé revisits this traditional song with its powerful message, performing it in the film for prisoners in the county jail, accompanied by the choir she is trying to lead to victory.

HE STILL LOVES ME
(WALTER WILLIAMS SR AND BEYONCÉ)

(James Harris III, Terry Lewis, James Wright/4'22)

Musicians: Beyoncé Knowles: vocals, backing vocals / **Walter Williams Sr:** vocals, backing vocals / **Angie Stone:** vocals, backing vocals / **Eddie Levert Sr:** vocals, backing vocals / **Melba Moore:** vocals, backing vocals / **Montell Jordan:** vocals, backing vocals / **Ricky Watford:** guitar / **Bobby Ross Avila:** bass, synthesizers / **James Wright:** Hammond organ, synthesizers / **IZ:** drums, percussions / **Alex "Godson" Richbourg:** programming / **Recording:** Doppler Studios, Atlanta: 2003 / The Village Recorder, Los Angeles: 2003 / **Technical team: Producers:** Jimmy Jam, Terry Lewis / **Recording engineer:** Blake Eiseman / **Assistant recording engineer:** Matt Marrin

He Still Loves Me is an example of the perfect symbiosis between gospel and R&B styles. Performed by a dream team led by Beyoncé and Walter Williams Sr from The O'Jays and featuring prestigious choir members in the shape of Angie Stone, Melba Moore, and Montell Jordan, the song is rhythmic and extraordinarily moving. Every actor in *The Fighting Temptations* was chosen for their ability to sing as well as act, said Loretha Jones, executive producer of the film's music. "For example, the O'Jays, who are singing legends, landed the role of the barbers who sing the Paul Simon song *Love Me Like a Rock*. They'd never acted before, but because the story lends itself to what they do naturally, it didn't take long for them to become comfortable with the acting process."[114] For Beyoncé, working alongside such renowned singers was an unforgettable experience. "I was listening to them work together. And they've been in the group so long, and I love that. I hope for us, Destiny's Child, to be like that. I was just sittin' back like, that is how it's supposed to be."[87]

Legendary producers Jimmy Jam and Terry Lewis, the "Blues Brothers" of funk and soul.

TIME TO COME HOME
(BEYONCÉ, MELBA MOORE, ANGIE STONE)

(James Harris III, Terry Lewis, James Wright, Beyoncé/3'52)

Musicians: Beyoncé Knowles: vocals, backing vocals / Melba Moore: vocals, backing vocals / Angie Stone: vocals, backing vocals / Ricky Watford: guitar / IZ: drums / Alex "Godson" Richbourg: programming / Rosalie Washington: tambourine / **Recording:** Doppler Studios, Atlanta: 2003 / The Village Recorder, Los Angeles: 2003 / **Technical team:** Producers: Jimmy Jam, Terry Lewis, James Wright / Recording engineers: Matt Marrin, Blake Eiseman

Production of *Time to Come Home* was entrusted to Jimmy Jam and Terry Lewis, former members of the group The Time who became superstars thanks to their work for Janet Jackson, Mariah Carey, Boyz II Men, Mary J. Blige, and Usher. The song is a skillful blend of gospel and R&B, and fits in perfectly with the scene in the film where the actors and dancers show off their talents at a Sunday mass. Alongside Beyoncé are two illustrious singers, Melba Moore and Angie Stone—the first a soul music legend and seasoned actress, and the second riding high on the success of her second album, *Mahogany Soul*, released in 2001, which stood out for the single *Brotha Part II*, performed with rapper Eve and soul diva Alicia Keys.

SUMMERTIME
(BEYONCÉ FEATURING P. DIDDY)

(Adonis Shropshire, Angela Beyincé, Beyoncé Knowles, Mario Winans, Sean Combs, Steven Jordan, Varick Smith/3'54)

Musicians: Beyoncé Knowles: vocals, backing vocals / P. Diddy: rap / Paul Logus: guitar / Stevie J.: guitar / Mario Winans: various instruments / **Recording:** Daddy's House Recordings, New York: 2003 / **Technical team:** Producers: Stevie J., Sean Combs, Mario Winans / Recording engineer: Roger Che

Not featured in the film, *Summertime* was produced by Sean "P. Diddy" Combs, Mario Winans, and Stevie J. P. Diddy, who was already a superstar, also appears on the track with a modest but effective rap. Winans would go on to have a huge hit in 2004 with his single *I Don't Wanna Know*, built around a sample of *Boadicea* by Irish singer Enya, an instrumental segment that the Fugees had already successfully used on their 1996 single *Ready or Not*. The third of the producers, Stevie J., played an important role at P. Diddy's Bad Boy Records as a member of The Hitmen, a collective of composers and producers within the label who worked for in-house artists. Stevie J. notably wrote for The Notorious B.I.G. and also produced P. Diddy's biggest commercial success, *I'll Be Missing You* in 1997.

DESTINY'S CHILD

ALBUM

Destiny Fulfilled

Lose My Breath • Soldier • Cater 2 U • T-Shirt • Is She the Reason • Girl •
Bad Habit • If • Free • Through With Love • Love

Released in the USA by Sony Urban Music/Columbia: 8 November 2004 (CD ref.: CK 92595)
Best chart ranking in the USA: 2

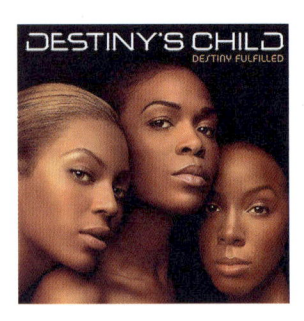

Now all grown up, Destiny's Child produced here a more mature album, still as sensual as ever.

FAREWELL FROM DESTINY'S CHILD

2004

The success of *Dangerously in Love*, with 317,000 copies flying off the shelves in the days following its release in July 2003 (and over 11 million records sold worldwide from the time of release to 2025), sealed Beyoncé's status as an international star. Her involvement in the Pepsi ad campaign, followed by an invitation to perform *The Star-Spangled Banner* at the 38th Super Bowl on 1 February 2004, completed her childhood dream of becoming an icon.

Dividing her time between her sumptuous apartment in Miami and the one she had just acquired in New York, her lifestyle was identical to that of the stars she had admired as a young singer with Girls Tyme. Her romance with Jay-Z was blossoming although shrouded in secrecy, as she did not want details of her private life to become public. Then, just as her solo career seemed underway and Columbia were impatiently awaiting her second album, she took an astonishing decision.

The original plan had been to follow up *Dangerously in Love* with an album featuring the many songs that were not selected for the first one—that is, until Beyoncé changed her mind after performing with Kelly Rowland and Michelle Williams on stage at Reggae Sumfest in Montego Bay, Jamaica. Destiny's Child were sharing the bill with Third World, Sean Paul, Tanto Metro and Devonte, T.O.K., and Beenie Man. The sheer chemistry between the three girls on stage that night led them to consider an official reunion. "It was incredible," Beyoncé said later. "The energy was beautiful. We started talking about what we should do, what our look should be and what the album should sound like."[118] In interviews, she constantly talked of the bonds she had with her two friends and colleagues. "I love Destiny's Child and I am a member of the group. We haven't broken up. We're going to continue to tour and record and be a group. [...] We all decided a long time back to explore solo projects and I'm the third member of the group to release my own record. Things like working apart keep the fire going and keep the fans eager for you."[105]

So in 2004, with Beyoncémania in full swing, the decision was made to return to the studio to record a follow-up to *Survivor*, which had come out three years earlier.

Talking before writing

The reunion between our three singers was marked by the desire to take the time they needed to write songs. After choosing a selection of demos from the many sent in by various composers and producers, Beyoncé, Kelly, and Michelle spent several days sitting on the studio couches discussing them and talking about the themes that meant a lot to them: human relationships, gender equality, and, of course, their own romantic relationships. They recorded their conversations so as not to forget the slightest detail. "We were running our mouth, catching up," Kelly Rowland revealed. "It was non-stop energy. And that helped us out on the album, conceptually and creatively."[119] "We're talking and singing about what we love and relate to," added Michelle Williams. "There's no song on this album that we didn't experience."[119] "I think there's ten hours of tape with us talking and, man, there's some good scandal on there—I hope no one gets a hold of that tape!" concluded Beyoncé.[120]

184 DESTINY FULFILLED

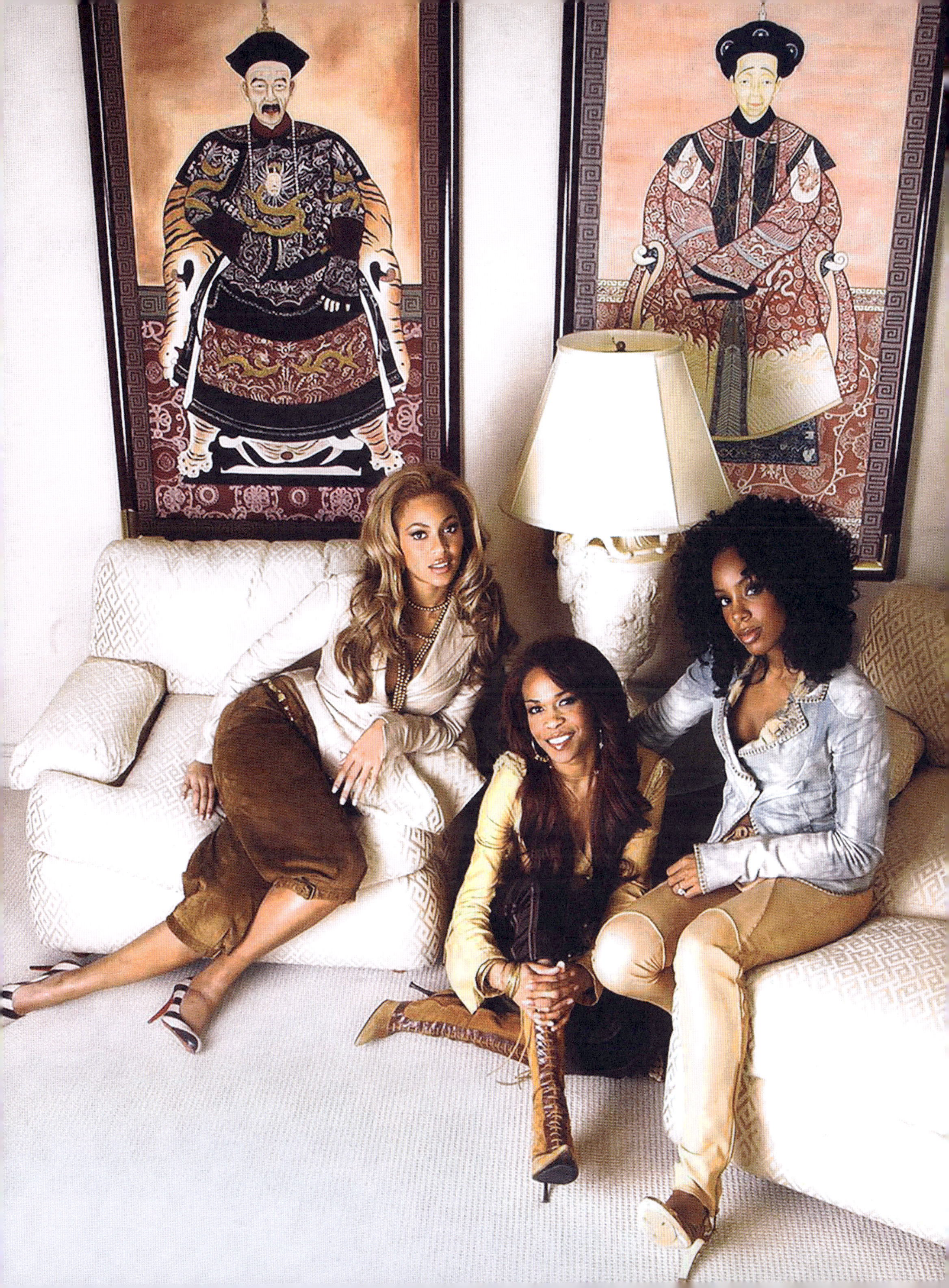

Beyoncé and Tina Knowles, founders of the House of Deréon brand.

Destiny's Child performing the American national anthem at the NBA All-Star Game in Houston on 19 February 2006.

FOR BEYONCÉ ADDICTS

In 2005, in partnership with her mother, Beyoncé launched her ready-to-wear fashion line, House of Deréon, named after her maternal grandmother, Agnèz Deréon. "To me, this is the greatest way to enter into the fashion world," Beyoncé said at the time. "Inspired by my grandmother, working with my mother, and pursuing a dream we have all had for many years—establishing an important fashion company."[122]

2004

A destiny fulfilled

On 8 November 2004, having already sold close to 12 million copies of their previous albums, Destiny's Child released their fifth: *Destiny Fulfilled*. Although they were very much hoping it would be a hit, that wasn't their real motivation, as Beyoncé explained at the time. "Obviously, it would feel good to be No. 1, but we're not thinking competitively. We did this record for ourselves, not to sell a million the first week out. That doesn't mean as much to us as just the fact that three friends got back together to do another record."[119]

The album's release was followed by the launch of the Destiny Fulfilled...and Lovin' It tour, which kicked off on 9 April 2005 at the Hiroshima Sun Plaza Hall in Japan and ended on 10 September at General Motors Place in Vancouver, Canada. What the fans didn't yet know was that it would be their favorite group's last tour. On 11 June 2005, on stage at the Palau Sant Jordi in Barcelona, Spain, the trio announced to the crowd that this would be their last performance on European soil. The following day, an official press release was sent to MTV.com, announcing that Destiny's Child were to split once the tour was over. "We have been working together as Destiny's Child since we were nine, and touring together since we were 14. After a lot of discussion and some deep soul-searching, we realized that our current tour has given us the opportunity to leave Destiny's Child on a high note, united in our friendship and filled with an overwhelming gratitude for our music, our fans, and each other. After all these wonderful years working together, we realized that now is the time to pursue our personal goals and solo efforts in earnest."[121] Never before had an R&B group been so successful; in the space of five albums, Destiny's Child had managed to top the list of the highest-earning female groups in the history of American music. The legendary group having breathed its last, Beyoncé had just one goal in mind: to become the queen of world pop.

Despite the split, the members of Destiny's Child reunited on stage at the Toyota Center in Houston on 19 February 2006 to sing the American national anthem for the 2006 NBA All-Star Game.

DESTINY FULFILLED

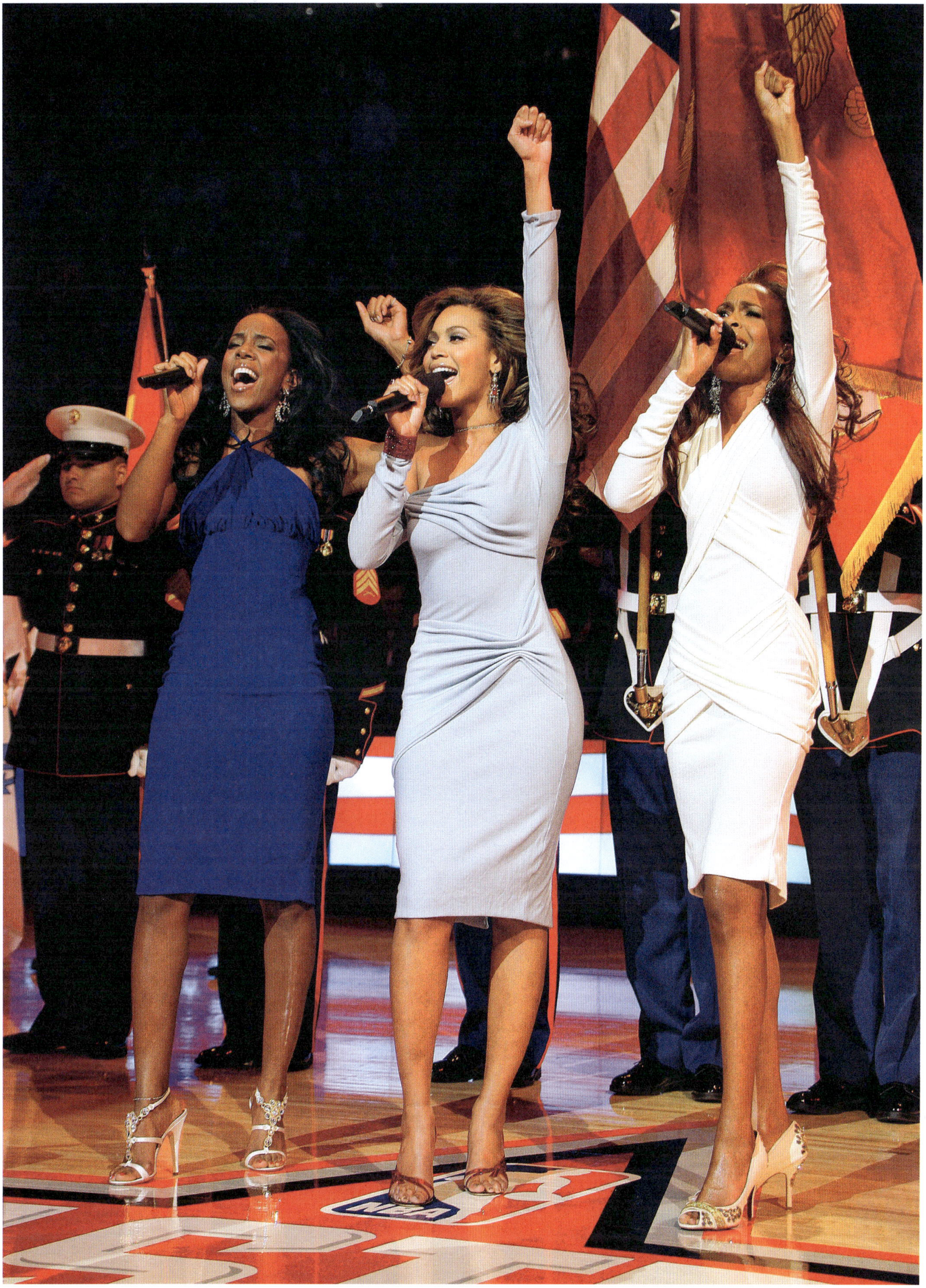
NBA

Tens of millions of TV viewers enjoyed Beyoncé's performance of *The Star-Spangled Banner* on 1 February 2004.

THE STAR SPANGLED BANNER
(FROM THE SUPER BOWL XXXVIII PERFORMANCE)

(John Stafford Smith, Francis Scott Key, Ralph Tomlinson/2'35)

Musicians
Beyoncé Knowles: vocals
Orchestra

Recording
Reliant Stadium, Houston: 1 February 2004

Technical team
?

Single
Digital distribution by Sony Urban Music: 1 February 2004
Best chart ranking in the USA: did not make the charts

Fifty stars for Beyoncé

On 1 February 2004, the 38th Super Bowl took place in Houston, Texas, and there was no American artist more fitting to sing the national anthem—traditionally performed before the start of the match—than Houston-born Beyoncé Knowles. While the world mostly remembers the Justin Timberlake/Janet Jackson scandal when the former ripped off the latter's bustier, exposing her right nipple on American television and causing a deluge of complaints to the CBS switchboard, Beyoncé's performance also left a lasting impression. Occurring as it did just a few days before, on 8 February, she won five Grammy Awards for her album *Dangerously in Love* and lit up the stage alongside Prince at the Staples Center in Los Angeles, her Super Bowl appearance was confirmation of the aura shining over her.

Behind the R&B singer is a diva

Columbia made a deliberate decision to present Beyoncé to the world in a more traditional way, wanting to prove that their goose who laid golden eggs was not just an R&B artist but a singer whose voice was an integral part of the American music landscape. The choice of *Me, Myself and I* as the third single from *Dangerously in Love* confirmed this desire to reveal a new Beyoncé. Will Botwin, one of the label's key executives, explained the approach to *Billboard* magazine: "She felt she needed to show that side of herself. Everyone knew she could move. With the choice of *Me, Myself & I* and the TV appearances, we established the other side."[119]

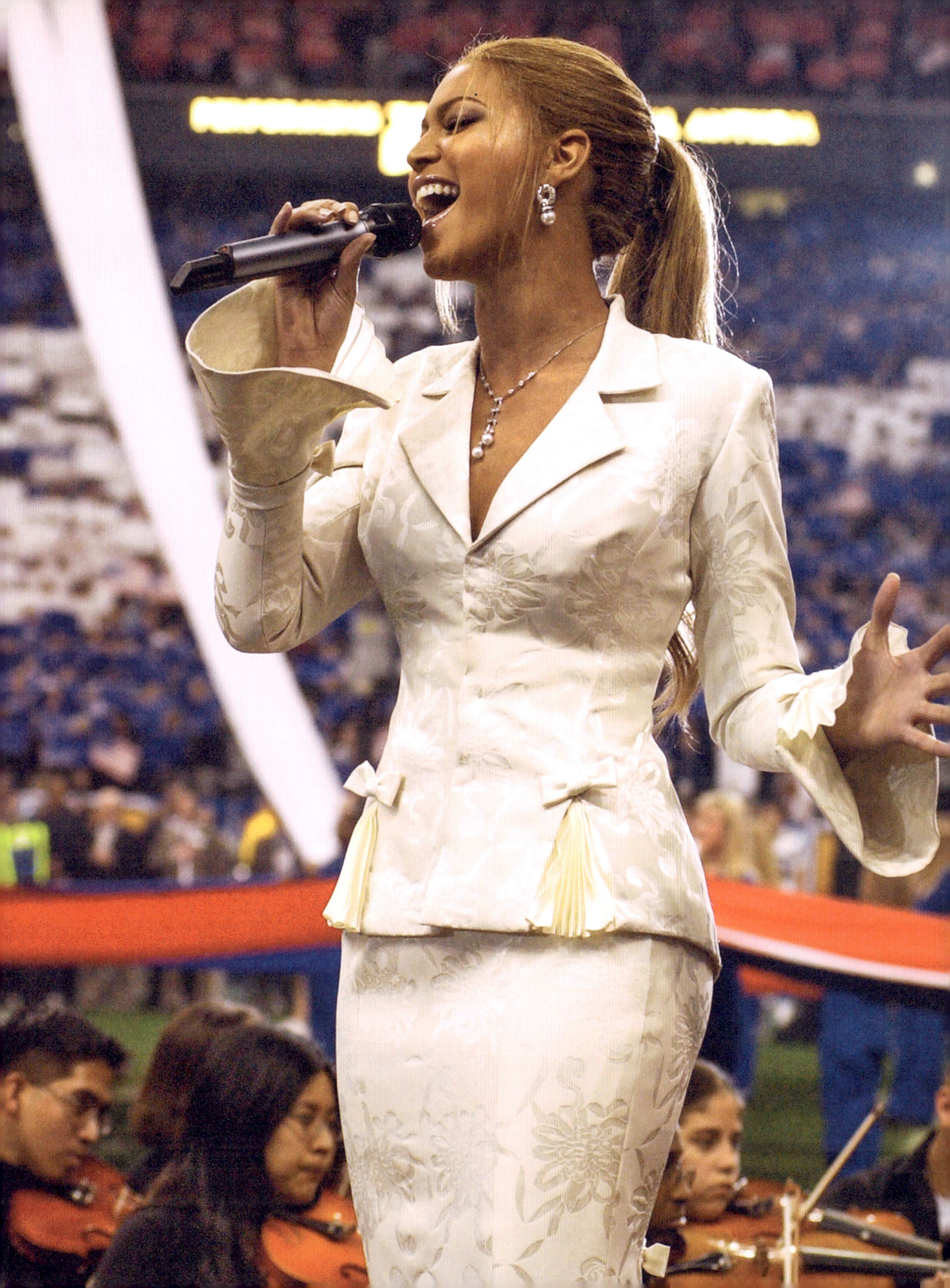

Michelle, Kelly, and Beyoncé filming the video for *Lose My Breath*.

SINGLE

LOSE MY BREATH

(Beyoncé Knowles, Fred Jerkins III, Kelly Rowland, LaShawn Daniels, Michelle Williams, Rodney Jerkins, Shawn Carter/4'02)

Musicians
Beyoncé Knowles: vocals, backing vocals
Kelly Rowland: vocals, backing vocals
Michelle Williams: vocals, backing vocals
Rodney "Darkchild" Jerkins: additional instruments

Recording
Darkchild Entertainment, Trenton: 2004
Sony Music Studios, New York: 2004

Technical team
Producers: Beyoncé Knowles, Rodney "Darkchild" Jerkins, Sean Garrett
Executive producers: Beyoncé Knowles, Kelly Rowland, Mathew Knowles, Michelle Williams
Recording engineers: Jeff Villanueva, Jim Caruana

Single
Released in the USA by Sony Urban Music/Columbia: 5 October 2004 (CD single ref.: 38K 70096)
Best chart ranking in the USA: 3

2004

Genesis
Rodney "Darkchild" Jerkins, who had contributed greatly to the success of the legendary *Say My Name*, was once again at the helm for this first single from *Destiny Fulfilled*. "He said, 'You know what? I'm gonna get that first single,' and he was working on his machines, trying to make tracks or whatever and he got it," Michelle Williams recounted in 2004. "*Lose My Breath*, when we heard that instrumental, the drums, we're like 'Wow, that's so different, that's so unique.'"[123] The faithful LaShawn Daniels, co-producer of *Say My Name,* was also involved, and always happy to work with Beyoncé, Kelly, and Michelle. "I'm one of the guys who believes that women are extremely smarter than men. I think if you empower a woman, you empower the world."[51]

Production
Daniels also spoke of Beyoncé's astonishing virtuosity when it came to delivering the vocal lines for *Lose My Breath*, standing next to him in the control room in front of the microphone, rather than on her own in the recording booth as is usually the case. One of the most catchy lines in the song, *Can you keep up?*, which leads into the chorus, was suggested by Jay-Z, who was invited to contribute to the track's development. "I told him we heard this crazy track and it's going to have everyone losing their breath," Beyoncé explained, "and he was like, 'I got it, *Can you keep up?*' He actually came up with the chorus without even hearing the track."[124] Accompanying the song was a flashy video, directed by Marc Klasfeld, who had produced the videos for Sum 41's *Fat Lip, Still Waiting*, and *The Hell Song*, Vanessa Carlton's *A Thousand Miles*, and The Foo Fighters' *Times Like These*. "It's really a dance-off between a more sophisticated 'in-fashion' Destiny's Child versus a more 'street' Destiny's Child," Beyoncé said, "and in the end a third Destiny's Child even more fierce takes over. It's a lot of hard work for us because we have to learn three routines for the same song. People will be shocked because it's different for us. They've never seen us really dance."[124]

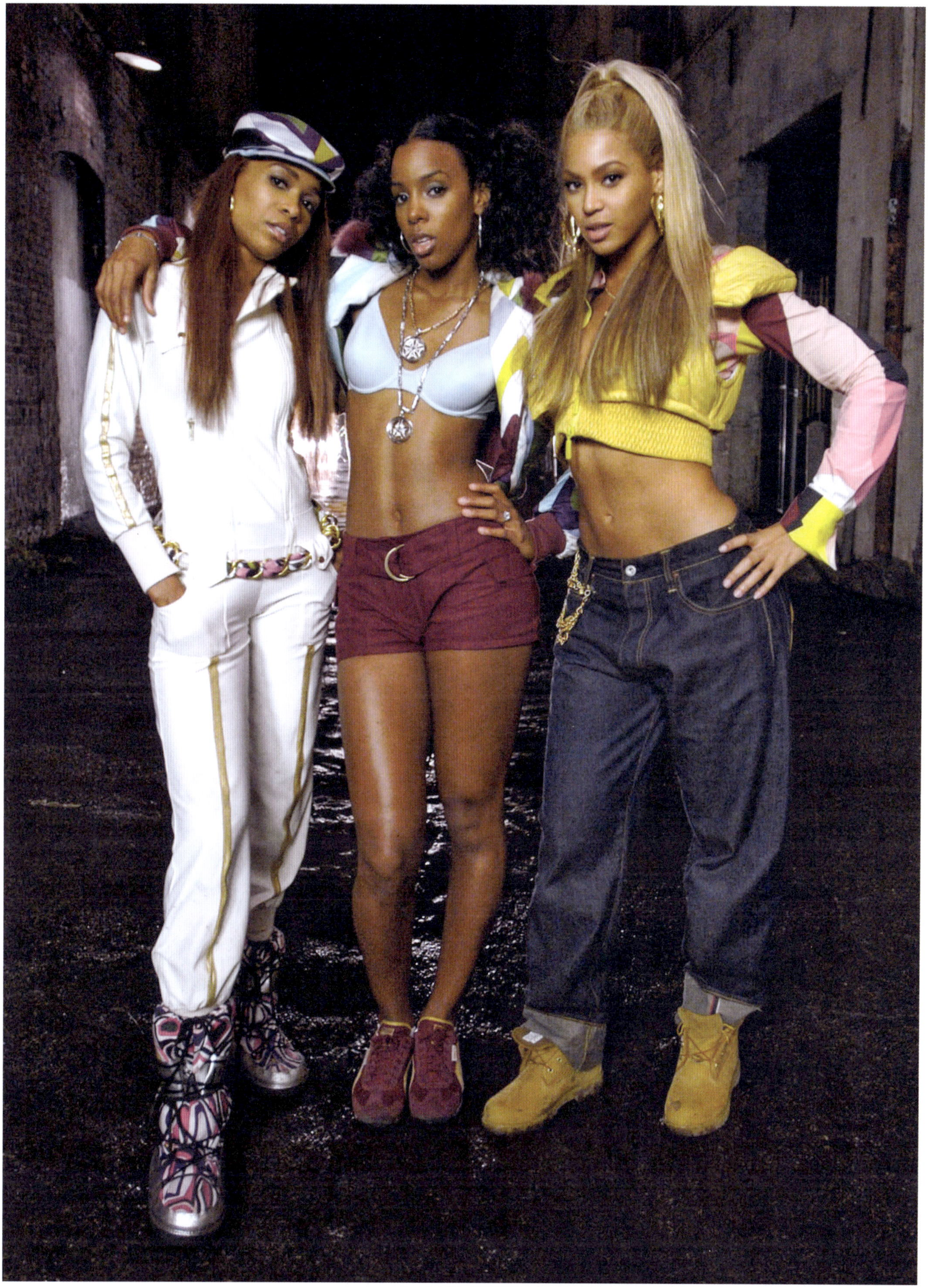

SINGLE

SOLDIER
(FEATURING T.I. AND LIL WAYNE)

(Beyoncé Knowles, Clifford Harris, Dwayne Carter, Kelly Rowland, Michelle Williams, Rich Harrison, Sean Garrett/5'25)

Musicians
Beyoncé Knowles: vocals, backing vocals
Kelly Rowland: vocals, backing vocals
Michelle Williams: vocals, backing vocals
T.I.: rap
Lil Wayne: rap

Recording
Sony Music Studios, New York: 2004
Silent Sound Studios, Atlanta: 2004
Cash Money Studios, New Orleans: 2004

Technical team
Producers: Beyoncé Knowles, Rich Harrison
Executive producers: Beyoncé Knowles, Kelly Rowland, Mathew Knowles, Michelle Williams
Recording engineers: Jim Caruana, Fabian Marasciullo, Tom Tapley

Single
Released in the USA by Sony Urban Music/Columbia: 9 November 2004 (CD single ref.: 38K 70702)
Best chart ranking in the USA: 3

Genesis

The selection process for tracks on the album was done blind, as the three singers chose to listen to work sent in by multiple producers without knowing who they were. By a stroke of luck, the three women were once again drawn to a Rich Harrison track, stripped down and spectacularly effective, a far cry from Rodney Jerkins' and LaShawn Daniels' *Lose My Breath*. Sean Garrett, who composed the song, explained how it came about: "I wrote *Soldier* on the way to the studio in a taxi. I said I got this hook that's nuts and I would come in and sing it to the girls and they would say, 'I like that.'"[125] Beyoncé, Kelly, and Michelle then got together and wrote the lyrics, in which they open up about the man in their lives. "What was great about that was they all liked guys from the streets," adds Garrett. "Each verse was a representation of the guy they were actually into."[125] "*Soldier* is basically talking about what you want is a soldier that is going to stand up for you," Kelly Rowland explained at the time. "A man that is just about it, you know what I mean? And we actually really get into detail about the kind of men that we like, whether he's from the East Coast or the West Coast or the South side with gold grills…I know everybody's got a little preference, and Destiny's Child, we want a soldier."[126]

Production

The second single from *Destiny Fulfilled* hit the third spot on the *Billboard* Hot 100 when it was released, cementing the trio's status as a mainstay of American R&B, and, more importantly, giving welcome visibility to its two guest stars, rappers T.I. and Lil Wayne. Fresh from the success of their respective singles *Bring Em Out* and *Go D.J.*, both men's careers received a boost from the success of *Soldier*, as the latter testified: "That shit was big, man. That shit was Destiny's Child, *Soldier*. It was poppin'."[127] Lil Wayne later performed with Kelly Rowland on the 2011 track *Motivation*, then supported Solange Knowles on 2016's *Mad*, but we can catch him again with Beyoncé in 2008 on Usher's *Love in This Club, Pt. II*.

Lil Wayne, a big-name guest on the single *Soldier*.

BEYONCÉ: ALL THE SONGS 193

An elegant Beyoncé in a shot by Jim Cooper, November 2004.

SINGLE

CATER 2 U

(Beyoncé Knowles, Kelly Rowland, Michelle Williams, Ric Rude, Robert Waller, Rodney Jerkins/4'07)

Musicians
Beyoncé Knowles: vocals, backing vocals
Kelly Rowland: vocals, backing vocals
Michelle Williams: vocals, backing vocals
Tim Stewart: guitar

Recording
2nd Floor Studios, Orlando: 2004
Sony Music Studios, New York: 2004

Technical team
Producers: Beyoncé Knowles, Ric Rude, Rodney "Darkchild" Jerkins
Executive producers: Beyoncé Knowles, Kelly Rowland, Mathew Knowles, Michelle Williams
Recording engineers: Jeff Villanueva, Jim Caruana

Single
Digital distribution Sony Urban Music/Columbia: 7 June 2005
Best chart ranking in the USA: 14

Genesis

Cater 2 U, the third single from *Destiny Fulfilled*, was distributed only digitally in the United States, along with a promotional CD single sent to the media. That didn't stop it reaching a respectable 14th place on the *Billboard* charts when it was released, despite proving slightly polemic. Observers were concerned about the lyrics, as Beyoncé sings about being totally devoted to her man: *Let me help you/Take off your shoes/ Untie your shoe strings/Take off your cufflinks/What you wanna eat, boo?/Let me feed you/Let me run your bathwater/ Whatever your desire, I'll supply ya*. People found this confusing from someone who had set herself up as the standard-bearer for independent women. When asked about this by *Cosmopolitan* magazine in 2006, Beyoncé replied: "I thought [the members of Destiny's Child] felt like characters…like we were so strong that we couldn't have our hearts broken or we wouldn't do things for a man. But we're human."[128]

Production

Robert Waller, who wrote this track (and *Me, Myself and I* before that), spoke of the professionalism the three singers displayed when recording it. "They are always trying to be better in addition to the initial talent they have and the strong people behind them. It wasn't a game, about trying to be cute or stepping on each other's toes. They were all committed to a common goal: success."[129] The virtuosic Tim Stewart, Jessica Simpson's guitarist, delivered a few six-string lines on the track, and would soon be accompanying two other divas close to Beyoncé: Lady Gaga and Rihanna.

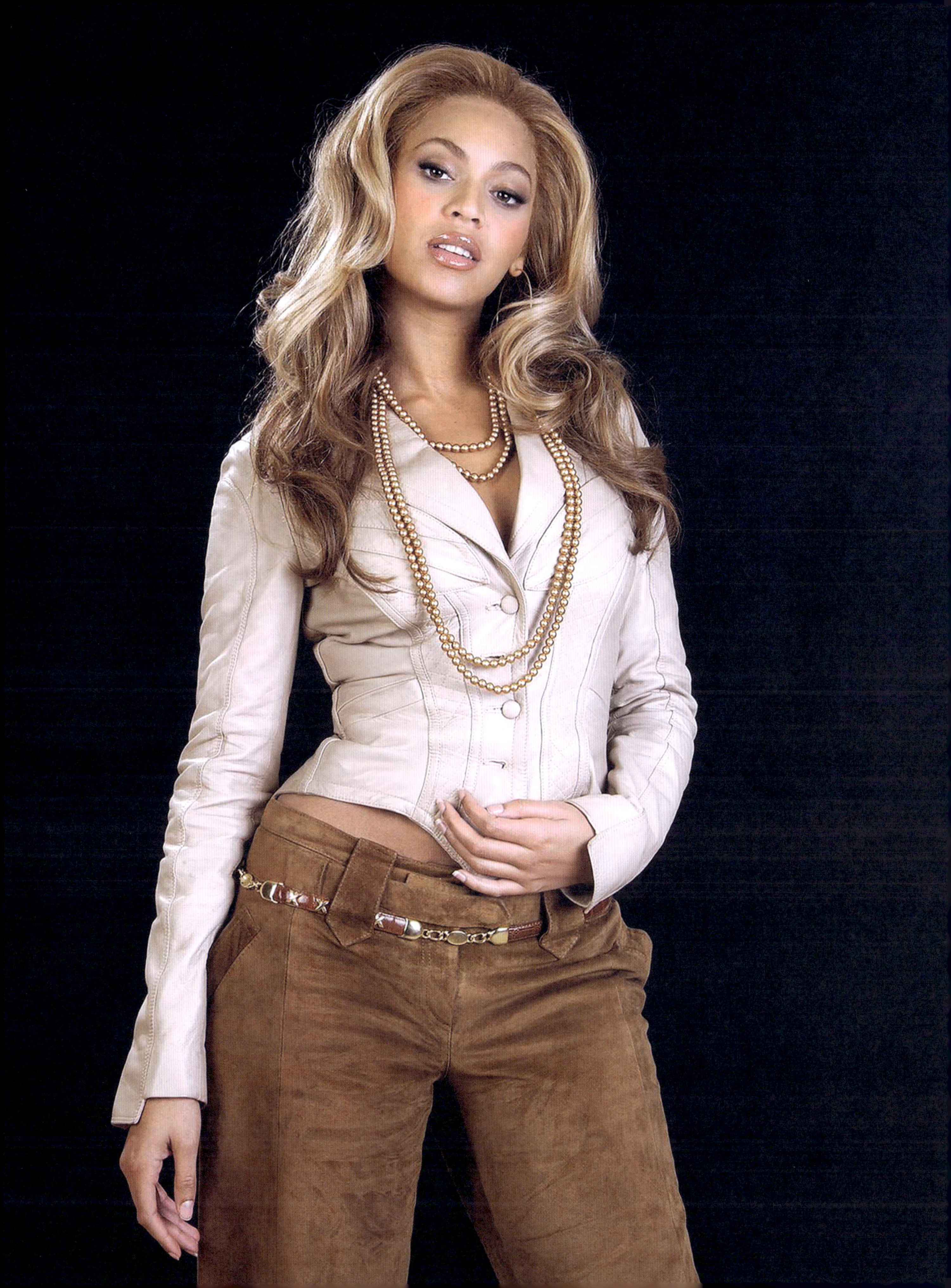

Kelly Rowland in April 2004.

T-SHIRT

(Andre Harris, Angela Beyincé, Beyoncé Knowles, Kelly Rowland, Michelle Williams, Sean Garrett, Vidal Davis/4'40)

Musicians: Beyoncé Knowles: vocals, backing vocals / **Kelly Rowland:** vocals, backing vocals / **Michelle Williams:** vocals, backing vocals / **Recording:** Studio 609, Philadelphia: 2004 / Sony Music Studios, New York: 2004 / **Technical team:** Producers: Beyoncé Knowles, Sean Garrett, Andre Harris, Vidal Davis / **Executive producers:** Beyoncé Knowles, Kelly Rowland, Mathew Knowles, Michelle Williams / **Recording engineers:** Jim Caruana, Vincent DiLorenzo

Andre Harris and Vidal Davis—the songwriting duo Dre and Vidal—co-wrote and produced this wickedly sexy track, in which the three singers imagine undressing a man who appears in their dreams at night. Working alongside them was the faithful Sean Garrett, who brought so much to the group's songs, as Kelly Rowland testifies: "The energy that he brought to this project was so amazing, and he was so excited. He brought the male perspective out 'cause of course people are so used to hear our side. This time they heard a male perspective as well, which was really cool because it's kind of balanced."[123]

IS SHE THE REASON

(Beyoncé Knowles, Gene McFadden, John Whitehead, Kelly Rowland, Michelle Williams, Patrick Douthit, Sean Garrett, Victor Carstarphen/4'47)

Musicians: Beyoncé Knowles: vocals, backing vocals / **Kelly Rowland:** vocals, backing vocals / **Michelle Williams:** vocals, backing vocals / **Recording:** Sony Music Studios, New York: 2004 / **Technical team:** Producers: Beyoncé Knowles, 9th Wonder, Sean Garrett / **Executive producers:** Beyoncé Knowles, Kelly Rowland, Mathew Knowles, Michelle Williams / **Recording engineer:** Jim Caruana

Is She the Reason was constructed around a sample from *I Don't Know No One Else to Turn to*, written by Victor Carstarphen, John Whitehead, and Gene McFadden in 1977 and recorded the same year by Melba Moore on her album *A Portrait of Melba*. Vocally, the song is centered around Kelly Rowland and Michelle Williams, just as Beyoncé intended. "I wanted to make sure Kelly and Michelle were heard," she said. "I wanted people to hear how beautiful and strong their voices are, how much they've matured."[119] It was during a three-day session that producer Patrick "9th Wonder" Douthit created *Is She the Reason*, as he explained in 2004: "I just flipped a Melba Moore sample, and I didn't know it was going to be an R&B joint. I had no idea. I played that record and Beyoncé said, 'I like your beats, but your beats need bridges in them because this is R&B. I want our music to sound like The Emotions, the group from the '70's.' So I tried to figure out a way to make them sound like The Emotions, but keep it up to date. Now one of my favorite R&B groups is SWV, so I was like 'Why don't I try to SWV these girls?' That's what *Is She the Reason* is."[130]

GIRL

(Angela Beyincé, Beyoncé Knowles, Don Davis, Eddie Robinson, Kelly Rowland, Michelle Williams, Patrick Douthit, Sean Garrett/3'44)

Musicians: Beyoncé Knowles: vocals, backing vocals / **Kelly Rowland:** vocals, backing vocals / **Michelle Williams:** vocals, backing vocals / **Recording:** Sony Music Studios, New York: 2004 / **Technical team:** Producers: Beyoncé Knowles, 9th Wonder / **Executive producers:** Beyoncé Knowles, Kelly Rowland, Mathew Knowles, Michelle Williams / **Recording engineer:** Jim Caruana

Produced by 9th Wonder, *Girl* includes a sample from *Ocean of Thoughts and Dreams*, performed by The Dramatics in 1977. Lyrically, it is one of Destiny's Child's deepest songs, with words directly inspired by a painful relationship Kelly Rowland was then involved in. Rowland's friends use the lyrics, written by the threesome and Beyoncé's cousin Angela Beyincé, to express their unconditional support for her, although it took her years to admit that she was the subject of the song. "I remember *Girl*. That was my life," Rowland admitted in 2020. "I was living that toxic relationship. It was real—it was literally Michelle, Mama T [Kelly's nickname for Tina Knowles], Bey, Solange, and Angie trying to talk me out of this toxic relationship."[131]

BAD HABIT

(Bryan-Michael Cox, Kelly Rowland, Kendrick Dean, Solange Knowles/3'54)

Musicians: Kelly Rowland: vocals, backing vocals / **Beyoncé Knowles:** backing vocals / **Michelle Williams:** backing vocals / **Bryan-Michael Cox:** synthesizers, programming / **Wyldcard:** synthesizers / **Recording:** Sony Music Studios, New York: 2004 / **Technical team: Producers:** Solange Knowles, Bryan-Michael Cox, Kendrick Dean / **Executive producers:** Beyoncé Knowles, Kelly Rowland, Mathew Knowles, Michelle Williams / **Recording engineer:** Jim Caruana

Before building up a collection of Grammy Awards and hits (*Shortie Like Mine* for Bow Wow, *Can't Help But Wait* for Trey Songz, and *Be Without You* for Mary J. Blige), composer and producer Bryan-Michael Cox was a friend of Beyoncé's, having got to know her and LeToya Luckett at high school. "There were other girls in the school acting like they were going to be stars, all crazy, pretentious and stuck-up," Cox recalls, "but Beyoncé was a sweetheart. You knew she was going to be a star; everybody knew."[132] Strange, then, that he enjoyed a succession of hits from 1999 onwards and worked with the crème de la crème of R&B (Usher, Toni Braxton, Ginuwine, Jagged Edge, Alicia Keys, and Jermaine Dupri), but that it wasn't until 2004 that the young prodigy was granted the ultimate privilege of contributing to a Destiny's Child album. This, despite the fact that he was one of the first to work with the young women back when they were still known as Destiny. It's Kelly Rowland who gets the chance to be lead singer on *Bad Habit*, one of the best tracks on *Destiny Fulfilled*. "I always pushed for that 'cause I always thought Kelly was an incredible singer," Cox declared in 2014.[133]

IF

(Beyoncé Knowles, Charles Jackson, Dana Stinson, Kelly Rowland, Marvin Yancy, Michelle Williams/4'15)

Musicians: Beyoncé Knowles: vocals, backing vocals / Kelly Rowland: vocals, backing vocals / Michelle Williams: vocals, backing vocals / **Recording:** Sony Music Studios, New York: 2004 / **Technical team:** Producers: Rockwilder, Juanita Wynn, Beyoncé Knowles, Big Drawers / Executive producers: Beyoncé Knowles, Kelly Rowland, Mathew Knowles, Michelle Williams / Recording engineer: Jim Caruana

A long-time collaborator of Redman and Busta Rhymes, producer Dana "Rockwilder" Stinson had already worked with Destiny's Child, creating the remarkable remix of *Bootylicious* that features on the *This Is the Remix* compilation, released on 12 May 2002. Here, he gives the three girls a platform commensurate with their talents, authoring a gospel-sounding track that gives each of them a verse featuring their signature vocal style. Rockwilder built the instrumental on a sample from Natalie Cole's 1975 recording *Inseparable*, having always wanted to rework that song's intro. His collaboration with Destiny's Child gave him the opportunity to make a very old dream come true, as he told *The Donnie Houston Podcast* in 2020. "I used to pull that record back when I was seven years old. I used to love the fact that it had that beginning like that. [...] So when Beyoncé asked me, 'How long you did this?' I said, 'I did this when I was seven years old.' I always wanted to keep the record going like that."[134]

FREE

(Beyoncé Knowles, Big Drawers, Dana Stinson, Fonce Mizell, James Carter, Kelly Rowland, Larry Mizell, Michelle Williams/4'51)

Musicians: Beyoncé Knowles: vocals, backing vocals / Kelly Rowland: vocals, backing vocals / Michelle Williams: vocals, backing vocals / **Recording:** Sony Music Studios, New York: 2004 / **Technical team:** Producers: Beyoncé Knowles, Rockwilder / Executive producers: Beyoncé Knowles, Kelly Rowland, Mathew Knowles, Michelle Williams / Recording engineer: Jim Caruana

Free is the second track Rockwilder produced for *Destiny Fulfilled*, this time borrowing a sample from *Night Whistler*, composed by Larry Mizell, James Carter, and Fonce Mizell, and performed by Donald Byrd in 1975. Although he had achieved huge success working with many of the greats, the producer's ultimate accolade came after working with Destiny's Child. "I went to a Grammy party and Beyoncé told me that Prince came to this show in Atlanta when they did the film in Atlanta of the Destiny's tour and his two favorite records on the album was *If* and *Free*."[134] What better compliment for a soul and R&B producer than one from the kid from Minneapolis himself?

THROUGH WITH LOVE

(Beyoncé Knowles, Kelly Rowland, Mario Winans, Michelle Williams, Sean Garrett/3'35)

Musicians: Beyoncé Knowles: vocals, backing vocals / Kelly Rowland: vocals, backing vocals / Michelle Williams: vocals, backing vocals / **Recording:** Big3 Records, St Petersburg: 2004 / **Technical team:** Producers: Beyoncé Knowles, Mario Winans / Executive producers: Beyoncé Knowles, Kelly Rowland, Mathew Knowles, Michelle Williams / Recording engineer: Eric Hunter

Although Beyoncé sings that she's through with love, by now everyone knew she was living a romantic idyll with rapper Jay-Z. Kelly Rowland and Michelle Williams take turns to join her on the song to emphasize the theme: the difficulty of getting over a toxic relationship. It's a safe bet that the lyrics were inspired by Rowland's own experience, as was the case with *Girl*. "*Through with Love* is one of the most amazing songs I honestly think that we've ever done," said Kelly. "It has so much emotion, so much passion in it."[123] "*Through with Love*, it takes you through so much, it's anger, into loneliness and kinda desperateness and then finding yourself in loving yourself all over again,"[123] Beyoncé added.

LOVE

(Angela Beyincé, Beyoncé Knowles, Erron Williams, Kelly Rowland, Michelle Williams/4'32)

Musicians: Beyoncé Knowles: vocals, backing vocals / Kelly Rowland: vocals, backing vocals / Michelle Williams: vocals, backing vocals / **Recording:** Sony Music Studios, New York: 2004 / **Technical team:** Producers: Beyoncé Knowles, Erron Williams / Executive producers: Beyoncé Knowles, Kelly Rowland, Mathew Knowles, Michelle Williams / Recording engineer: Jim Caruana

For the final track on *Destiny Fulfilled*, Destiny's Child gave Michelle's brother Erron Williams the chance to demonstrate his talents as a producer and composer. This languid instrumental left the women no choice but to sing of love, which had become their preferred theme after leaving the

Michelle Williams sang about her Christian faith in her subsequent gospel albums.

loud and proud feminist songs behind them. "It's about how love has inspired us," said Michelle. "My brother [Erron] produced it, and the harmonies are absolutely bananas!"[118] After producing *O' Holy Night* on *8 Days of Christmas*, followed by his younger sister's album *Heart to Yours*, Erron Williams pursued his own career while keeping a protective eye on Michelle. "I had to become someway defensive because you have people who don't like her success or they don't like her as a person for whatever reason,"[135] he said in 2021. The 60 million Destiny's Child albums sold since Michelle joined the group without a doubt make her a highly successful R&B and gospel singer.

BEYONCÉ: ALL THE SONGS 199

Founding member of the Black Eyed Peas, will.i.am went on to become a major producer.

WE WILL ROCK YOU
(PEPSI "GLADIATOR" SOUND TRACK REMIX 2004) (BEYONCÉ, BRITNEY SPEARS, PINK)

(Brian May/3'10)

Musicians: Britney Spears: vocals, backing vocals / **Beyoncé Knowles:** vocals, backing vocals / **Pink:** vocals, backing vocals / **Freddie Mercury:** backing vocals, claps, stomps / **Brian May:** electric guitar, bass, backing vocals, claps, stomps / **John Deacon:** claps, stomps / **Roger Taylor:** claps, stomps / **Susie Webb:** backing vocals / **Zoe Nicholas:** backing vocals / **Recording:** Patchwork Studios, Culver City: 2004 / **Sunrise Sound Studios, Houston:** 2004 / **Technical team:** Producers: Justin Shirley-Smith, Brian May / **Recording engineers:** Justin Shirley-Smith / **Assistant recording engineers:** Giacomo De Caterini, Ricky Graham, Joshua J. Macrae, Kris Fredriksson / **"Pepsi Music 2004 (Dare for More)" (promotional EP):** Released in the USA by Jive: 31 May 2004 (CD ref.: PI/BS/2004A)

In 2003, when Pepsi launched its latest ad campaign, the head of advertising, David Foulds, decided to call in a long-time collaborator, the director Tarsem Singh, who had been behind the brand's "Foosball" and "Shirt" campaigns in 2000. Singh had made a name for himself with his work on the music video for R.E.M.'s *Losing My Religion* in 1991 and was ready to take on the challenge Foulds set him: using a new version of the legendary *We Will Rock You*, first recorded by Queen in 1977, for a performance by the three biggest stars of American music at that time, namely Beyoncé, Britney Spears, and Pink. We already know about Beyoncé's success; as for the others, Spears was at the peak of her career after the triumphant reception of her fourth album *In the Zone* (2003), featuring the singles *Toxic* and *Me Against the Music*, while Pink had enjoyed hits with her songs *Just Like a Pill* and *Family Portrait* in 2002, and *Trouble* in 2003. The script for the ad goes like this: three female gladiators are thrown into a Roman arena, under the watchful eye of an emperor played by the singer Enrique Iglesias, whose hits *Bailamos* and *Rhythm Divine* (1999), *Be With You* (2000), and *Hero* (2001) made him the fourth star to appear in what must have been an astronomically expensive advert. The three women embody modern-day feminism and a spirit of revolt against an omnipresent patriarchy, rebelling against their sovereign as they blast out *We Will Rock You*, cheered on by a delirious crowd. Rerecorded in part by Brian May himself (Queen purists might spot May and Roger Taylor in the crowd at 1'39), the song features verses performed by the three pop stars, with backing vocals supplied by Susie Webb and Zoe Nicholas from The Brian May Band. As well as providing the soundtrack to the advert, *We Will Rock You (Pepsi "Gladiator" Sound Track Remix 2004)* was distributed on a promotional EP, *Pepsi Music 2004 (Dare for More)*, which contributed to the success of the now-legendary advert.

I KNOW
(DESTINY'S CHILD–WILL.I.AM)

(Beyoncé Knowles, Corte Ellis, Jully Black, Karriem Mack, LaShaun Owens/3'50)

Musicians: Beyoncé Knowles: vocals, backing vocals / **Kelly Rowland:** vocals, backing vocals / **Michelle Williams:** vocals, backing vocals / **will.i.am:** vocals, rap / **Recording:** The Hit Factory, New York: 2003, 2004 / **Technical team:** Producers: Beyoncé Knowles, Soul Diggaz, will.i.am / **"Unity (The Official Athens 2004 Olympic Games Album)" (compilation):** Released in the USA by EMI/Capitol Music: 2004 (CD ref.: 72434-73083-2-1)

Holding the 2004 Summer Olympics in Athens, Greece, was highly symbolic, as it was the first time the modern games had returned to the place they had been created in 1896, under the aegis of the International Olympic Committee founded by Pierre de Coubertin. It was also an opportunity for the world to unite at a time when conflicts raged across the globe. Record label EMI produced three albums for the occasion: *Harmony—The Official Athens 2004 Olympic Games Classical Album*, featuring many classical artists; *Phos—The Official Athens 2004 Olympic Games Greek Album*, featuring Greek singers; and finally, *Unity (The Official Athens 2004 Olympic Games Album)*, with duets sung by artists of diverse origins to promote fraternity among nations. "The unity album is much more than a simple collection of songs," Gianna Angelopoulos-Daskalaki, President of the Athens 2004 organizing committee, said at the time. "It is a message that calls for participation, friendship, and peace."[136] Destiny's Child put forward the song *I Know*, originally recorded for the soundtrack to Jonathan Lynn's 2003 film *The Fighting Temptations*. The track was entrusted to will.i.am, the brains behind the Black Eyed Peas, and was remixed with additional vocals from the famous rapper, who was basking in the success of his group's hits *Where Is the Love?*, *Shut Up*, *Hey Mama*, and *Let's Get It Started*.

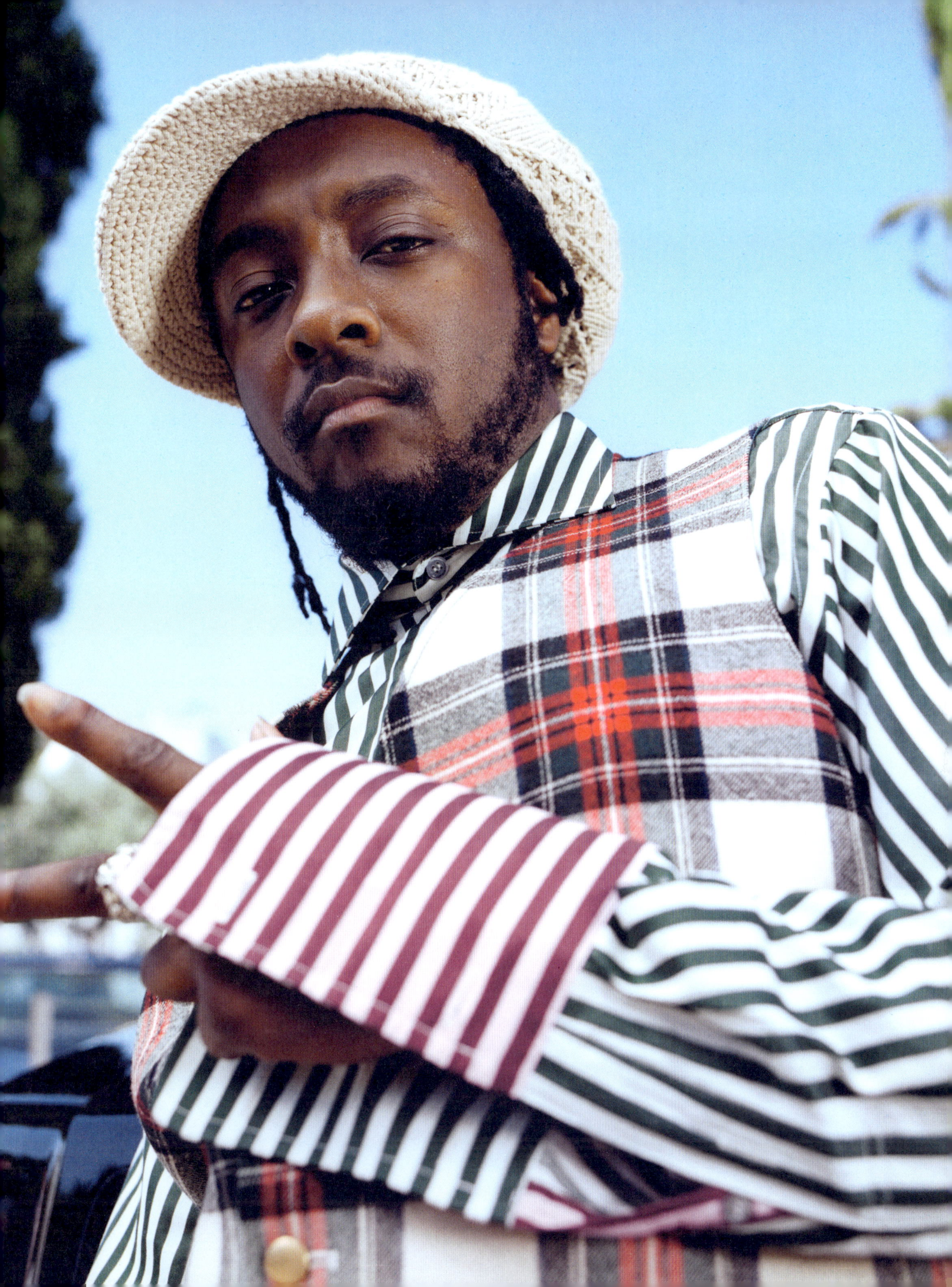

Kitten Kay Sera, famous for her love of pink, is the kind of colorful character that the city of Los Angeles produces.

Singer Dionne Warwick in 1983.

SO AMAZING
(BEYONCÉ AND STEVIE WONDER)
(Luther Vandross, Marcus Miller/4'12)

Musicians: Beyoncé Knowles: vocals / Stevie Wonder: vocals, harmonica / **Rob Bacon:** acoustic guitar / **Raphael Saadiq:** bass / **Bobby Ozuna:** percussion / **Tim Riley:** piano, drums / **Charles Veal:** violin / **The South Central Orchestra:** strings / **Recording:** Blakeslee Recording Studio, Los Angeles: 2005 / Sony Music Studios, New York: 2005 (Beyoncé vocals) / **Technical team:** Producers: Raphael Saadiq, Jake and the Phatman, Beyoncé Knowles / **Recording engineers:** James Tanksley, Jim Caruana, Daniel Romero, Glenn Standridge, Johnny Tanksley, Reggie Dozier / **Assistant recording engineers:** Charles Brungardt, Geoffrey Rice / **String arrangements:** Benjamin Wright / **"So Amazing: An All-Star Tribute to Luther Vandross" (compilation):** Released in the USA by J Records: 20 September 2005 (LP ref.: 82876-62472-1, CD ref.: 82876-62472-2)

Never really having recovered from the stroke he suffered on 16 April 2003, soul legend Luther Vandross passed away on 1 July 2005, surrounded by his family. *Dance with My Father*—the last album by the man who had sung backing vocals on David Bowie's *Young Americans* in 1974—had won four Grammy Awards in 2004, and sold 442,000 copies in the week after its release. This was largely thanks to its tracklisting, which comprised duets with prestigious guests including Beyoncé, Busta Rhymes, and Queen Latifah. Vandross's death, which many had feared would not be long in coming as he struggled to recover, saddened the American music world. In summer 2005, producers Jimmy Jam and Terry Lewis led the efforts to produce an album of Vandross covers, featuring artists such as Mary J. Blige, Usher, Aretha Franklin, Elton John, and Donna Summer. Also on the list of prestigious names were Beyoncé and Stevie Wonder, who gave listeners a top-class duet with their cover version of *So Amazing*, originally written by Vandross and Marcus Miller for Dionne Warwick in 1983, before the former reappropriated it in 1986 for his album *Give Me the Reason*. Beyoncé, who had re-recorded *The Closer I Get to You* with Vandross in 2002–3, also appears in the video for *Dance with My Father*, a song performed by Céline Dion for the album of the same name, when Vandross was recovering from his stroke. "I'm a part of this project because I got the wonderful opportunity to work with Luther," Beyoncé said in 2003. "When I was in the studio with him, I fell in love. He is such a special person, I just wanted to be here for him. I've been praying for him and am so happy that he's doing well."[137] Sadly, two years later, Vandross took his final bow, leaving behind him a body of work that is as legendary as he was.

202 COLLABORATIONS

ALL THAT I'M LOOKIN' FOR
(KITTEN K. SERA FEATURING BEYONCÉ AND KELLY ROWLAND)

(Wolfram de Marco, Kelly Kidd/3'52)

Musicians: *Kitten K. Sera:* vocals, backing vocals / *Beyoncé Knowles:* backing vocals / *Kelly Rowland:* backing vocals / **Recording:** ?: 2005 / **Technical team:** Producers: Wolfram de Marco, Kelly Kidd / Executive producer: Christian Andreason / **"Recording Artists for Hope—The Katrina CD Vol. 1" (compilation):** Available on Spotify: 6 December 2005

The devastation caused by Hurricane Katrina after it hit New Orleans on 29 August 2005 was considerable: 1,836 people lost their lives and over 140,000 residents of the city found themselves homeless. Images of this natural disaster were beamed around the globe and, across America, humanitarian aid was organized to help the people of Louisiana. The action taken by composer Christian Andreason stands out. First, he decided to donate the profits from his song *Call My Name* to the victims of the disaster, before setting his sights higher. "I had another idea…" he said. "I realized that there are literally hundreds of awesome recording artists out there who feel just as I do, who also want to help; so I thought rather than just releasing my own single, why not work with other artists so they can release a single of their own too? So I set out to put together a collection of outstanding songs from the best artists I either knew personally or could find (who held their own licensing rights)…super fast!"[138] These artists included Kitten K. Sera, aka The Pink Lady of Hollywood, famous for wearing only pink and having only pink possessions. Her track features two big-name backing singers: Beyoncé Knowles and Kelly Rowland, who were always ready to support a charitable cause. Despite the good intentions, the song was only briefly available on the streaming platform Spotify on 6 December 2005 before being permanently withdrawn from the website. It's now practically impossible to listen to this track, except on the KatrinaCD.com website, which Andreason created at the time to promote the compilation, and which is still online.

GOT'S MY OWN

(Beyoncé Knowles, Kelly Rowland, Michelle Williams, Sean Garrett, LaShawn Daniels, Rodney Jerkins, Angela Beyincé, Fred Jerkins III/3'59)

Musicians: Beyoncé Knowles: vocals, backing vocals / **Kelly Rowland:** vocals, backing vocals / **Michelle Williams:** vocals, backing vocals / **Rodney Jerkins:** spoken voice / **Recording:** ? : 2004 / **Technical team: Producers:** Beyoncé Knowles, Rodney Jerkins / **Executive producers:** Beyoncé Knowles, Kelly Rowland, Mathew Knowles, Michelle Williams / ***"Destiny Fulfilled Japanese Edition"*** **(album): Released in the USA by Sony Music Japan:** 10 November 2004 (ref.: SICP 700)

Michelle Williams says it loud and clear in this track: money's not enough, I need something more. By proudly declaring their financial independence and personal success, the members of Destiny's Child are harking back to the themes that made them leading lights of the feminist R&B movement in the late 1990s, a position shared with the trio who made up TLC. Produced by Rodney Jerkins and Beyoncé, *Got's My Own* appeared on the B-side (a slightly anachronistic term, given that it is a CD single) of *Girl* in Australia, Europe, and the United Kingdom. The track would also feature on the Japanese version of *Destiny Fulfilled* in November 2004.

GAME OVER

(Beyoncé Knowles, Kelly Rowland, Michelle Williams, Sean Garrett, Patrick Douthit, Michael Burton, Phillip Terry/4'03)

Musicians: Beyoncé Knowles: vocals, backing vocals / **Kelly Rowland:** vocals, backing vocals / **Michelle Williams:** vocals, backing vocals / **Recording:** Sony Music Studios, New York: 2004 / **Technical team: Producers:** Beyoncé Knowles, Patrick "9th Wonder" Douthit, Erron Williams / **Executive producers:** Beyoncé Knowles, Kelly Rowland, Mathew Knowles, Michelle Williams / **Recording engineers:** Jim Caruana / ***"Destiny Fulfilled Japanese Edition"*** **(album): Released in the USA by Sony Music Japan:** 10 November 2004 (ref.: SICP 700)

Patrick "9th Wonder" Douthit recorded *Game Over*, which features on the Japanese edition of *Destiny Fulfilled*, during the session that also produced *Is She the Reason* and *Girl*. With

Producer and DJ 9th Wonder, who produced some great work on *Destiny Fulfilled*.

a sample from Dee Dee Sharp Gamble's *Flashback*, the B-side of her 1977 single *Nobody Could Take Your Place*, *Game Over* is a nu soul nugget far removed from the sort of danceable R&B numbers we were used to hearing from Destiny's Child. "That was one of the best sessions I ever have been in, man," 9th Wonder said. "The girls were real cool, real laid-back, and hilarious, and they're God-fearing girls. Beyoncé would sing all night long. We'd be in that joint sleeping. Sean Garrett wrote those songs, and made it real special. And the records we cut are the records we kept."[130]

WHY YOU ACTIN'

(Beyoncé Knowles, Kelly Rowland, Michelle Williams, Paul Allen, James Moss, Marcus Devine, Angela Beyincé/4'28)

Musicians: Beyoncé Knowles: vocals, backing vocals / Kelly Rowland: vocals, backing vocals / Michelle Williams: vocals, backing vocals / PAJAM: additional instruments / **Recording:** Sony Music Studios, New York: 2004 / Silent Sound Studios, Atlanta: 2004 / Cash Money Studios, Miami: 2004 / 2nd Floor Studios, Los Angeles: 2004 / Studio 609, Philadelphia: 2004 / Big3 Records, St. Petersburg: 2004 / SGC Studio, Detroit: 2004 / **Technical team: Producers:** Beyoncé Knowles, James Moss, Paul "PDA" Allen, Marcus "Da Heat Mizer" Devine / **Executive producers:** Beyoncé Knowles, Kelly Rowland, Mathew Knowles, Michelle Williams / **Recording engineers:** James Moss, Paul "PDA" Allen, Jim Caruana, Todd Kozey / **Assistant recording engineers:** Rod Levens, Willie Wood / **"Destiny Fulfilled Japanese Edition" (album):** Released in the USA by Sony Music Japan: 10 November 2004 (ref.: SICP 700)

Marcus "Da Heat Mizer" Devine, a composer and producer who had worked with Ashanti, Ginuwine, Aaliyah, Xscape, Monica, and Brownstone, was behind this nu soul track that features on the CD single of *Lose My Breath* in Australia and the United Kingdom, as well as on the Japanese edition of *Destiny Fulfilled*. This studio wizard comes from Detroit, Michigan, and is joined here by a crack team who goes by the name of PAJAM—Paul "PDA" Allen, James "J. Moss" Moss, and Walter "Stone" Kearney, although only the first two contributed to this project. PAJAM specialize in soul and gospel music, and also appear in the credits to Michelle Williams' second album, *Do You Know*, released in 2004, leading us to believe that she was the one who put their names forward to work on *Destiny Fulfilled*.

MY MAN
(DESTINY'S CHILD FEATURING BEYONCÉ)

(Angela Beyincé, Beyoncé Knowles, Robert Waller, Scott Storch/3'34)

Musicians: Beyoncé Knowles: vocals, backing vocals / **Recording:** South Beach Studios, Miami: 2002 to 2003 / **Technical team: Producers:** Beyoncé Knowles, Scott Storch / **Executive producers:** Beyoncé Knowles, Kelly Rowland, Mathew Knowles, Michelle Williams / **"Destiny Fulfilled Walmart and Sam's Club Edition" (album):** Released in the USA by Sony Urban Music/Columbia: 16 November 2004 (longbox ref.: CK 92915)

On 16 November 2004, the Walmart retail chain, along with its subsidiary Sam's Club, whose members pay an annual subscription fee that gives them access to promotional offers, offered an exclusive version of *Destiny Fulfilled*. It included two previously unreleased tracks, *My Man* and *2 Step*, as well as a remix of *Survivor* called *Survivor (Remix Feat/Da Brat) (Extended Version)*; a rare track called *What It's Gonna Be*, which had already featured on the *Live at Wembley* album in April 2004; and finally *Independent Women Part II*, from *Survivor*. *My Man*, produced by Scott Storch during the South Beach Studio sessions in Miami from which *Naughty Girl*, *Baby Boy*, and *Me, Myself and I* also emerged, was briefly considered for *Dangerously in Love*—which is why Beyoncé was lead vocalist—before being included on *Destiny Fulfilled*.

BEYONCÉ: ALL THE SONGS

2 STEP

(Beyoncé Knowles, Kelly Rowland, Michelle Williams, Robert Waller, Scott Storch, Stephen Garrett/3'24)

Musicians: Beyoncé Knowles: vocals, backing vocals / Kelly Rowland: vocals, backing vocals / Michelle Williams: vocals, backing vocals / **Recording:** ? : 2004 / **Technical team:** Producers: Beyoncé Knowles, Scott Storch / Executive producers: Beyoncé Knowles, Kelly Rowland, Mathew Knowles, Michelle Williams / **"Destiny Fulfilled Walmart and Sam's Club Edition" (album):** Released in the USA by Sony Urban Music/Columbia: 16 November 2004 (longbox ref.: CK 92915)

Lucky owners of this special edition of *Destiny Fulfilled*, distributed by Walmart and Sam's Club in 2004, could enjoy the best track recorded for the album, but unfortunately withdrawn from it at the last minute. *Step 2* is a success in every way. Its thumping beat, addictive minimalism, and catchy melody are the work of composer Stephen Ellis Garrett, better known as Static Major. This prodigy, a former member of The Swing Mob—an early 1990s musical collective that included future R&B stars such as Missy Elliott, Timbaland, Ginuwine, and Tweet—was by now a well-known songwriter, particularly after his involvement in Aaliyah's 2008 single *Try Again*. A young man with a bright future ahead of him, Static Major sadly died on 25 February 2008 at the age of 33 in his hometown of Louisville, Kentucky, due to complications following a medical procedure.

FEEL THE SAME WAY I DO

(Beyoncé Knowles, Kelly Rowland, Michelle Williams, Rodney Jerkins, Fred Jerkins III, LaShawn Daniels, Ricky Lewis/4'06)

Musicians: Beyoncé Knowles: vocals, spoken voice, backing vocals / Kelly Rowland: vocals, backing vocals / Michelle Williams: vocals, backing vocals / Rodney Jerkins: spoken voice / **Recording:** Sony Music Studios, New York: 2005 / **Technical team:** Producers: Rodney Jerkins, Beyoncé Knowles, Ric Rude / Recording engineers: Jeff Villanueva, Jim Caruana / **"#1's" (compilation):** Released in the USA by Sony Urban Music/Columbia: 21 October 2005 (ref.: CK 97765)

Columbia's release of the *#1's* compilation provided the opportunity to give fans three previously unreleased songs, including *Feel the Same Way I Do*, produced by the ever-loyal Rodney "Darkchild" Jerkins. This is a song about a young woman who tells her lover about feelings she hadn't expected during one of their frequent nights together, and asks him if he feels the same way. Beyoncé has come of age, no longer shy of talking about sexuality in her songs and encouraging women to express their own personalities. "I really am [on their side]. I mean, I'm a woman, so I definitely am," she said in 2004. "I encourage women to have high self-esteem and to look at their inner beauty, but I don't wanna preach to anyone."[139] With sounds that are not unlike Motown soul, particularly thanks to the Coral Sitar, a Danelectro guitar that simulates the sound of the famous Indian string instrument and that featured on *No Matter What Sign You Are* by Diana Ross and The Supremes (1969) and *Signed, Sealed, Delivered (I'm Yours)* by Stevie Wonder (1970), two hits from the Detroit label.

STAND UP FOR LOVE
(2005 WORLD CHILDREN'S DAY ANTHEM)

(Amy Foster-Gillies, David Foster/4'45)

Musicians: Beyoncé Knowles: vocals, backing vocals / Kelly Rowland: vocals, backing vocals / Michelle Williams: vocals, backing vocals / Dean Parks: guitar / Nathan East: bass / Vinnie Colaiuta: drums / Jochem van der Saag: organ, programming / David Foster: piano, synthesizers / Paulinho da Costa: percussion / Jules Chaikin: conductor / **Recording:** Chartmaker Studios, Malibu: 2005 / The Record Plant, Los Angeles: 2005 / Fox Studios, Los Angeles: 2005 / **Technical team:** Producers: David Foster, Humberto Gatica / Executive producers: Beyoncé Knowles, Kelly Rowland, Michelle Williams, Mathew Knowles / Recording engineers: Humberto Gatica, Neil Devor, Alejandro Rodriguez / Assistant recording engineer: Jason Larien / String arrangements: David Foster, Bill Ross / **"#1's" (compilation):** Released in the USA by Sony Urban Music/Columbia: 21 October 2005 (ref.: CK 97765) / **Best chart ranking in the USA:** did not make the charts

On 27 September 2005, a brand new single from Destiny's Child was broadcast on the radio and just under a month later it was released on the *#1's* compilation. Composed by Canadian David Foster and his daughter Amy Foster-Gillies, *Stand Up for Love (2005 World Children's Day Anthem)* celebrates childhood and urges people to support the disadvantaged. The track was created to mark World Children's Day, established by the Ronald McDonald House Charities Foundation in 2002 (not to be confused with the World Children's Day founded by UNICEF in 1954). "On our tour, we met many of the children and families who are

Although *Destiny Fulfilled* was Destiny's Child's swansong, its members will always be friends.

assisted by the funds raised through World Children's Day," said Beyoncé. "We really recorded this song for them and all of the people who stand up and help. We'll never be able to repay those kids for what they've taught us. We hope they love this song and it helps raise awareness of World Children's Day at McDonald's."[140] "I think that's one of the best songs that we've done collectively," said Michelle Williams. "Vocally, it's incredible."[141] The version that had been sent to the media was a promotional single to help publicize the compilation.

BEYONCÉ: ALL THE SONGS 207

ALBUM

B'Day

Déjà Vu • Get Me Bodied • Suga Mama • Upgrade U • Ring The Alarm • Kitty Kat •
Freakum Dress • Green Light • Irreplaceable • Resentment •
Check On It (Bonus Track) / Encore For The Fans (Interlude) / Listen / Get Me Bodied (Extended)

Released in the USA by Sony Urban Music/Columbia: 5 September 2006
(LP ref.: 82876 88132 1, CD ref.: 82876 88132 2)
Best chart ranking in the USA: 1

Beyoncé, more invincible than ever, on the cover for the single *Ring the Alarm*.

IN THE FOOTSTEPS OF DIANA ROSS

2006

The disbanding of Destiny's Child coincided with a totally new project for Beyoncé: playing the part of Diana Ross, lead singer of The Supremes, in the movie *Dreamgirls*, which Bill Condon was about to direct. It was adapted for the big screen from the stage musical of the same name, which had opened on Broadway in 1981. Being surrounded by iconic actors such as Jamie Foxx, Eddie Murphy, and Danny Glover, Beyoncé decided to immerse herself in her part, that of Deena Jones (Diana Ross's counterpart), so much so that the recording of a new album, which she was contractually obliged to deliver to Sony Music, was postponed for a time. "I was Deena for six months and I refused to go into the studio 'cause I didn't want to get myself confused with this character. I wanted to live and breathe Deena, I didn't even watch TV during that time," she said.[142] When the shooting of *Dreamgirls* was finished, Beyoncé was able to allow herself some time off in the company of the person with whom she now officially shared her life, the rapper Jay-Z. "It's very easy," she told Corey Moss of MTV.com. "[...] We respect each other. If I have any suggestions, he respects it. If he has any suggestions, I respect it. It's just, I don't know, easy."[143]

A closely guarded secret

Although the holiday the two stars allowed themselves in spring 2006 was well earned—Jay-Z was in the midst of recording his ninth album, *Kingdom Come*, due to be released in November—Beyoncé was keen to get back into the studio as soon as possible, even though she had no goal beyond writing and recording some new songs. "When I was on my vacation, I told everyone, 'Please, let me be, don't ask me to do anything, don't call me, let me go away, and relaxing, get my mind back and kinda come back to my body.' I've been in Deena's body, the character, for so long. And while I was there, I couldn't relax."[144] Beyoncé therefore cut short her holiday in order to hasten back to New York. She asked Columbia to reserve Sony Music Studios in Manhattan so that she could work there from April, and invited three of the producers who had helped her become an international star—Rodney Jerkins, Sean Garrett, and Rich Harrison—to join her. She installed each one in a separate recording studio, and they then set to work. They were soon joined by other talented beatmakers: Pharrell Williams, Kasseem "Swizz Beatz" Dean, Cameron Wallace, and Ne-Yo, as well as Tor Erik Hermansen and Mikkel Storleer Eriksen, who comprised the duo Stargate. The work rate was intense, each producer working in a different studio and Beyoncé running from one to the other to listen to their ideas, before going back to work on lyrics with her cousin Angela Beyincé and Makeba Riddick, a hit-maker from Jay-Z's label Roc Nation. "We worked together every day, pulling 14-hour days," Riddick said. "I see the reason why she is the biggest artist of our generation: Her work ethic is unlike anything I've ever seen. She would tell us to be there at 11 o'clock in the morning and we would be there until, like, four or five in the morning. But she would be there before 11 a.m. When we got there, she was already there, working. Her concepts were so incredible. I never saw an artist have so much of her own vision and know exactly what they want to say. She would say, 'I have this crazy idea for this song, check out this situation.' We would be talking, bugging out—three hours later, then comes the song."[142]

210 **B'DAY**

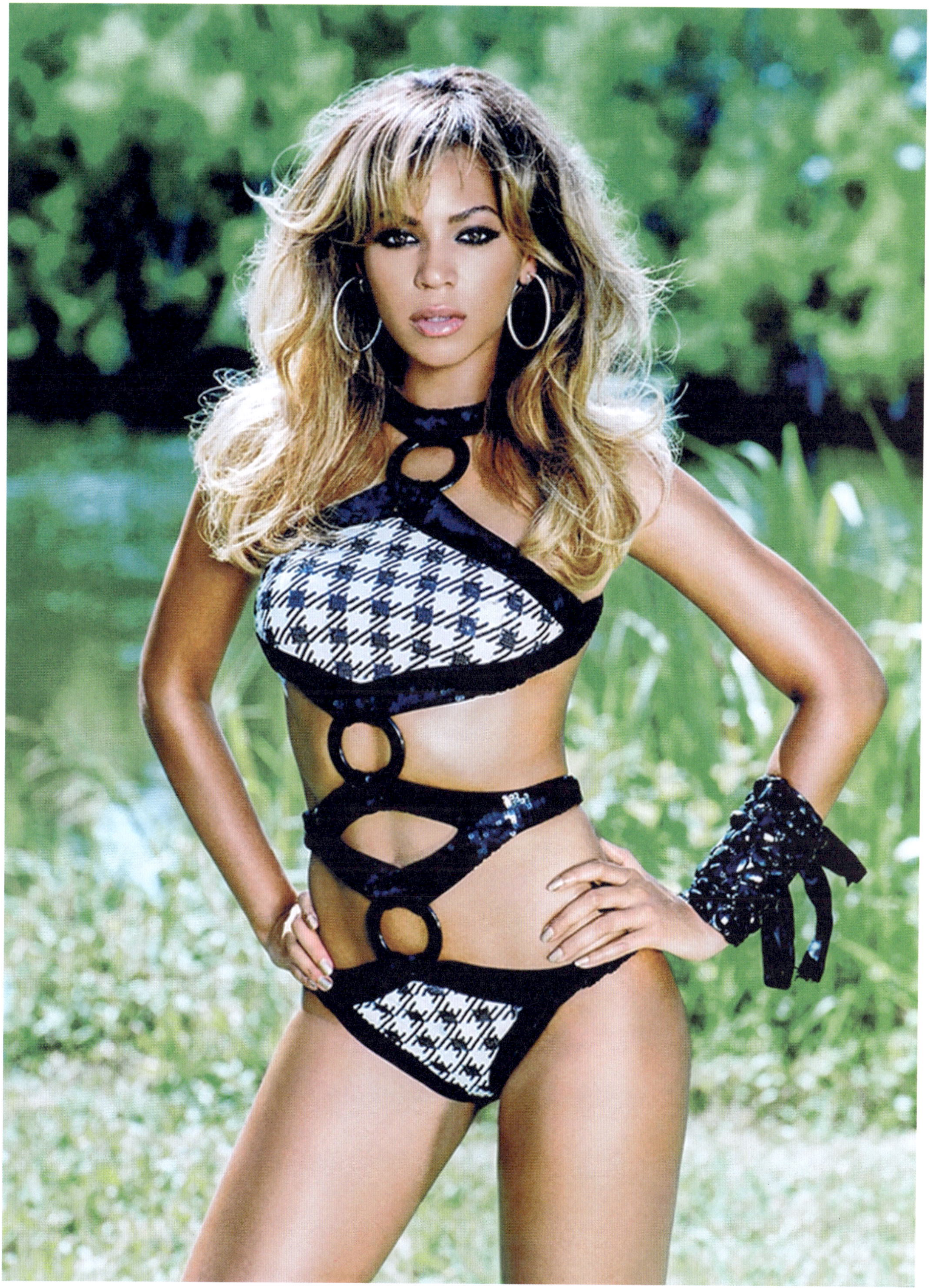

Beyoncé plays Deena Jones, a character based on singer Diana Ross, in the film *Dreamgirls*.

Having recently found out about her Nigerian descent, Beyoncé went to Lagos on 7 October 2006 to take part in the ThisDay Music Festival, part of the celebrations for the 46th anniversary of the country's independence. There, she delivered a touching performance of the Nigerian national anthem, which she had learned in just two hours. "Thousands of people were singing along. They went crazy! It made the whole trip worthwhile."[148]

Ever-present Deena Jones

Such was the competitive spirit in Sony Music Studios that Beyoncé's second album was completed in just two weeks, with release planned for the following September. Beyoncé ran the entire project—not only on the artistic side but also financially, for she funded the album's recording out of her own pocket, without even informing her father and manager, Mathew Knowles. The making of this new record bore witness to Beyoncé's fighting spirit: her songs became more aggressive, more often than not featuring assertive lyrics, thus turning a page on *Destiny Fulfilled*—where the lyrics frequently described burgeoning love—and revealing instead a young woman for whom romantic relationships, and failed ones, no longer held any secrets.

Most of the album's lyrics were inspired by Beyoncé's experience of shooting *Dreamgirls*. "The record is really aggressive," she said at the time. "I'm very happy, I'm very content in my life, but Deena felt like she was trapped and she was married and she was in this relationship for so long and it was all the things I wanted to say while I was doing the movie, all the things I wanted the character to say. So I'm speaking for every woman that's kind of been in a relationship for a long time. It's supposed to empower women, to have the extra boost to say all the things that they feel in their heart. So it's really a strong album and it really makes women feel like they're powerful and it kind of makes you want to get your power back."[144]

B'Day and its spinoffs

Having been made in record time, *B'Day* was released worldwide on 4 September 2006, Beyoncé's 25th birthday, and in the United States on 5 September. The title referenced her nickname, Bey, but also the American term "b-day," short for birthday. It was illustrated with photographs by Max Vadukul, and preceded by the single *Déjà Vu*, recorded as a duet with Jay-Z and produced by Rodney Jerkins. A slew of equally effective singles followed that hit, including the now classic *Ring the Alarm*, *Irreplaceable*, *Get Me Bodied*, and *Green Light*. In April 2007 a deluxe edition of the album was released, adding songs that had not made *B'Day*'s initial tracklisting, including *Beautiful Liar*, featuring a legendary pairing of Beyoncé and the Colombian singer Shakira. Beyoncé was now paying close attention to the clips of her songs, and offered her fans a DVD entitled *B'Day Anthology Video Album*, containing all the videos that had been shot for them. Astonishingly, there were eight of these, the making of which Beyoncé described as "overwhelming but such an amazing experience." Despite initial resistance from the studio, which thought two would be enough, Beyoncé brought in the best possible creative people, with the result that all eight videos were, in her opinion, incredible. "I can't decide which one is my favorite," she said in an interview at the time.[145]

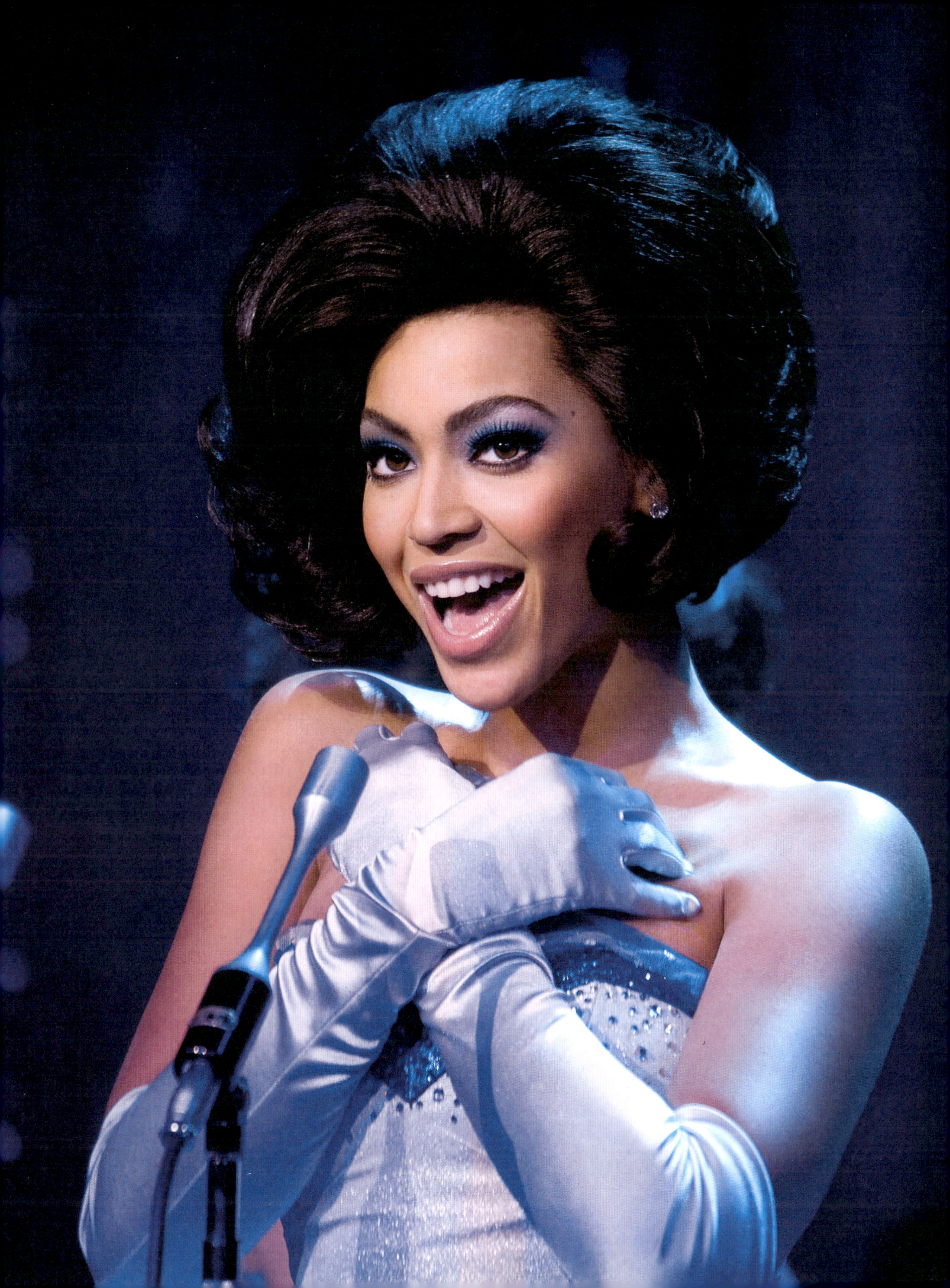

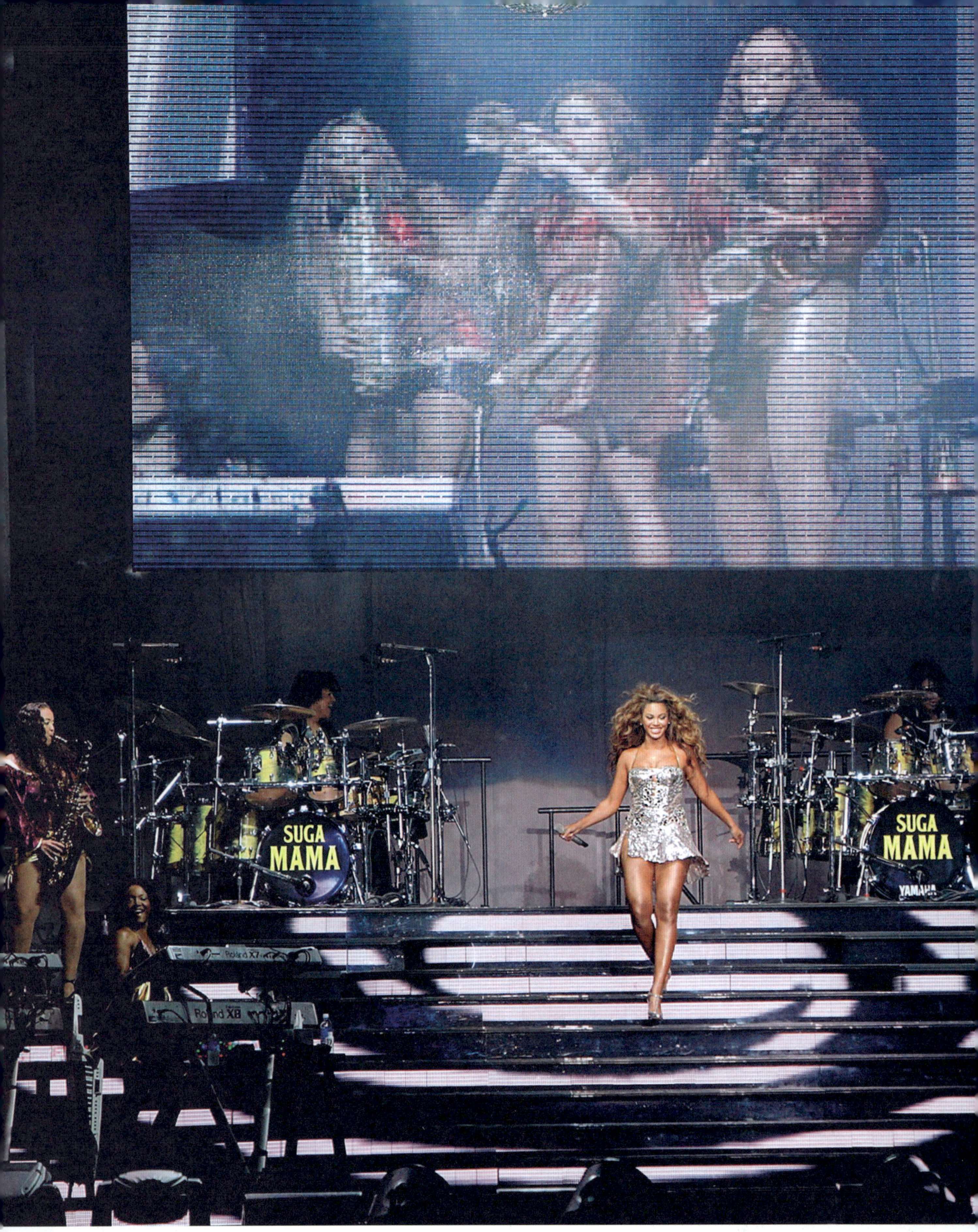
SUGA
MAMA
SUGA
MAMA
YAMAHA

Beyoncé and her band Suga Mama on stage at the Essence Music Festival in New Orleans, 6 July 2006.

The Beyoncé Experience

On 10 April 2007 the insatiable and tireless Beyoncé embarked on her second international tour. The Beyoncé Experience started in Japan, at the Tokyo Dome, and visited Australia, Europe, Africa, North America, and Mexico, before returning to Asia, ending at Zhongshan Soccer Stadium, Taipei, Taiwan, on 12 November. A huge project, exhausting for the singer, The Beyoncé Experience presented the artist on stage surrounded by an all-female group named Suga Mama, once again emphasizing the newly discovered power of women vis-à-vis men. "I wanted to get together a group of fierce, talented, hungry, beautiful women and form an all-girl band. I'm all about female empowerment. I'm all about pushing the envelope. I know it's my responsibility to do something different. I said, 'I want a band, I want something different.' I had worldwide auditions; people flew in from Atlanta, Houston, Israel, all over the world. It was extremely difficult, [there are] so many talented women [...] When they were playing, I said, 'I want to see y'all battle.' I brought in two of every instrument and that's how I chose. You see the one that really wants it. It was so entertaining, the energy, seeing the girls battle...God, it was the best. It was magical."[146]

FOR BEYONCÉ ADDICTS

Although today she has become the queen of social media, in 2007 Beyoncé had a profound aversion to the internet, as the told the magazine *Vibe*. "I don't go to the internet. I absolutely do not. I have my Blackberry, but unless I'm approving videos or approving song mixes, I don't go. I don't buy anything online, I'm scared."[147]

BEYONCÉ: ALL THE SONGS 215

Beyoncé sparkling at the 2006 BET Awards ceremony in Los Angeles.

SINGLE

DÉJÀ VU
(FEATURING JAY-Z)

(Beyoncé Knowles, Delisha Thomas, Keli Nicole Price, Makeba Riddick, Rodney Jerkins, Shawn Carter/4'00)

Musicians
Beyoncé Knowles: vocals, backing vocals
Jay-Z: rap
Rodney "Darkchild" Jerkins: additional instruments
Jon Jon Webb: bass guitar
Aaron "Goody" Goode: trombone
Allen "Al Geez" Arthur: saxophone
Ronald Judge: trumpet

Recording
Sony Music Studios, New York: April 2006
The Record Plant, Los Angeles: 2006

Technical team
Producers: Beyoncé Knowles, Rodney "Darkchild" Jerkins
Executive producers: Beyoncé Knowles, Mathew Knowles
Recording engineers: Rodney "Darkchild" Jerkins, Jeff Villanueva, Jim Caruana, Jun Ishizeki, Rob Kinelski
Assistant recording engineer: Jon Jon Webb
Brass arrangements: Rodney "Darkchild" Jerkins

Singlel
Released in the USA by Columbia/Sony Urban Music: 24 June 2006
(CD single ref.: 82876 88435 2)
Best chart ranking in the USA: 4

Genesis

In early spring 2006 producer Rodney "Darkchild" Jerkins had a call from Beyoncé. She asked him to get back to work so that she could quickly offer him some new songs, because a recording session—to which Jenkins was invited—was set for April. A few days before the session, as he was driving with the bass player Jon Jon Webb to buy some Slurpees at the local 7-Eleven, Jenkins had a daring idea. "I told Jon-Jon, 'Man, what if we gave Beyoncé some Michael Jackson-type stuff?' I worked with Michael and I'm a big fan, but Beyoncé was probably the only female artist that was challenging herself in a way that Michael would, and that could really entertain in that way. We were listening to the *Off the Wall* album, listening to *Don't Stop 'Til You Get Enough*. My studio was not even five minutes from 7-11, and on our way back, we went right to the studio and I started going 'da, da'—that little guitar line, with a guitar sound I had on my keys."[149] Webb immediately grabbed his Fender Jazz Bass Marcus Miller Signature, plugged it into his Aguilar preamp and Neve console, and brought the song to life with his bass line, which had an addictive groove. As for the lyrics, they were written by Delisha Thomas and Makeba Riddick, the latter having recorded her voice on the demo that would soon be given to Beyoncé. The clip of *Déjà Vu* was shot in Louisiana, home to Beyoncé's Creole roots. "We shot this in New Orleans right after Hurricane Katrina," Beyoncé said, "and the choreography was almost tribal in my mind. There's something spiritual about Louisiana, where my family is from, and I thought of Josephine Baker. She had a way of dancing that was almost possessed. I used her as a reference and combined her with Brigitte Bardot. My hair, the bustier: it's very Bardot. I love to mix things that you wouldn't put together—like Baker and Bardot. They both had that French influence, which is really strong in Louisiana."[93]

Production

Jon Jon Webb's bass line is unquestionably the centerpiece of the song. "The bass line just came to me, or more accurately through me," Webb explained. "I wasn't thinking of a specific player or style. I just wanted to use my creativity and my fingers to touch listeners."[150] Since this musical sequence created the tone of the song, Beyoncé demanded that it feature real instruments, with the exception of the drum

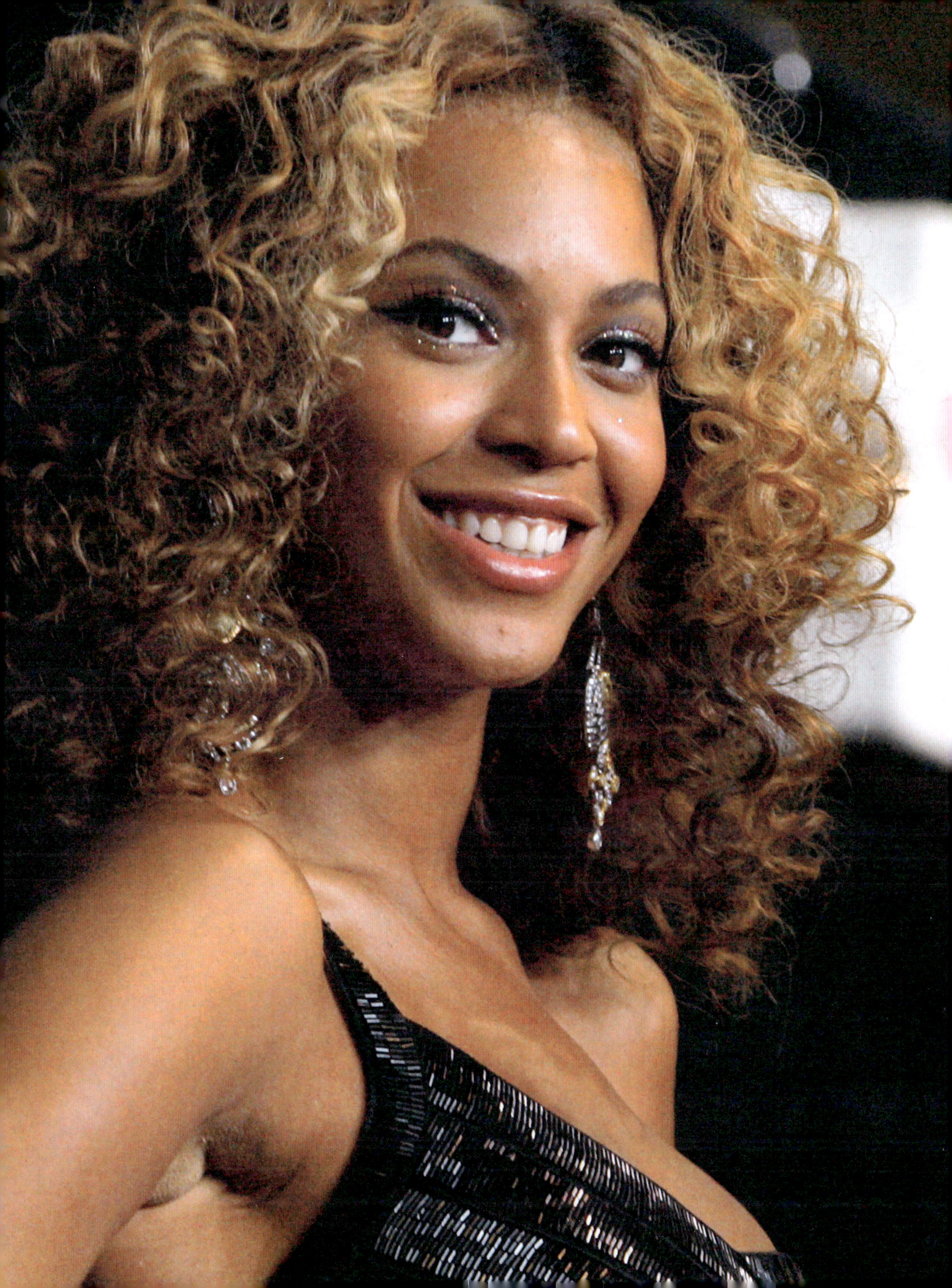

Beyoncé studied Josephine Baker's choreography for the *Déjà Vu* video and was inspired by the iconic banana belt for her stage costumes.

machine, a TR-808, which she requested for the piece and to which she refers in the intro, saying, "8-O-8" to introduce it. "When I recorded *Déjà Vu*…I knew that even before I started working on my album, I wanted to add live instruments to all of my songs," Beyoncé said in June 2019. "It's such a balance, it has live congas, live horns, live bass. It's still young, still new and fresh, but it has the old soul groove. The energy is incredible. It's the summer anthem, *I Pray*. I feel it. It's already broken records. Rodney Jerkins is incredible, Jay of course is on it, he blessed the song, I'm happy with it."[146] Indeed, a distinguished guest came to rap in the song, namely Jay-Z, Beyoncé's boyfriend and a rap superstar, whose artistic influence can be heard throughout the album. "Actually, I never planned for him to be on *Déjà Vu*," Beyoncé said. "But once he heard it, I saw his lips start moving. So I was like, 'Would you like to go into the studio and record what you just did?'"[151] "I remember when Jay first went in the booth," Jenkins said. "He was trying to catch the beat, 'cause the beat is a little unconventional. So he was trying to catch that rhythm. Jay doesn't write his words down on paper, of course. He just goes in there. He was sitting down in the chair, listening to it over and over again. And then he went to the booth and he laid it down, and it was a different rap. He wasn't happy with it. So he went in there and he laid something completely different. And we thought it was perfect. And he's like, 'Nah.' And then he went back in and did another version. That's the one you guys hear."[149]

FOR BEYONCÉ ADDICTS

The bass guitarist Divinity Roxx, a close friend of Jon Jon Webb, was brought in to join Suga Mama, the group that would accompany Beyoncé on the Beyoncé Experience tour. In concert, Roxx played the legendary bass line of *Déjà Vu* brilliantly, armed with her two favorite instruments: a five-string Fodera NYC Empire and a Modulus Flea 4. "I use my fingers and try to stay as close to Jon Jon's original line as possible," she said.[150] What is funny is that at the beginning of clip of the song Beyoncé mimes Webb's bass playing with an invisible pick, although he definitely played with his fingers for the record.

2006

218   B'DAY

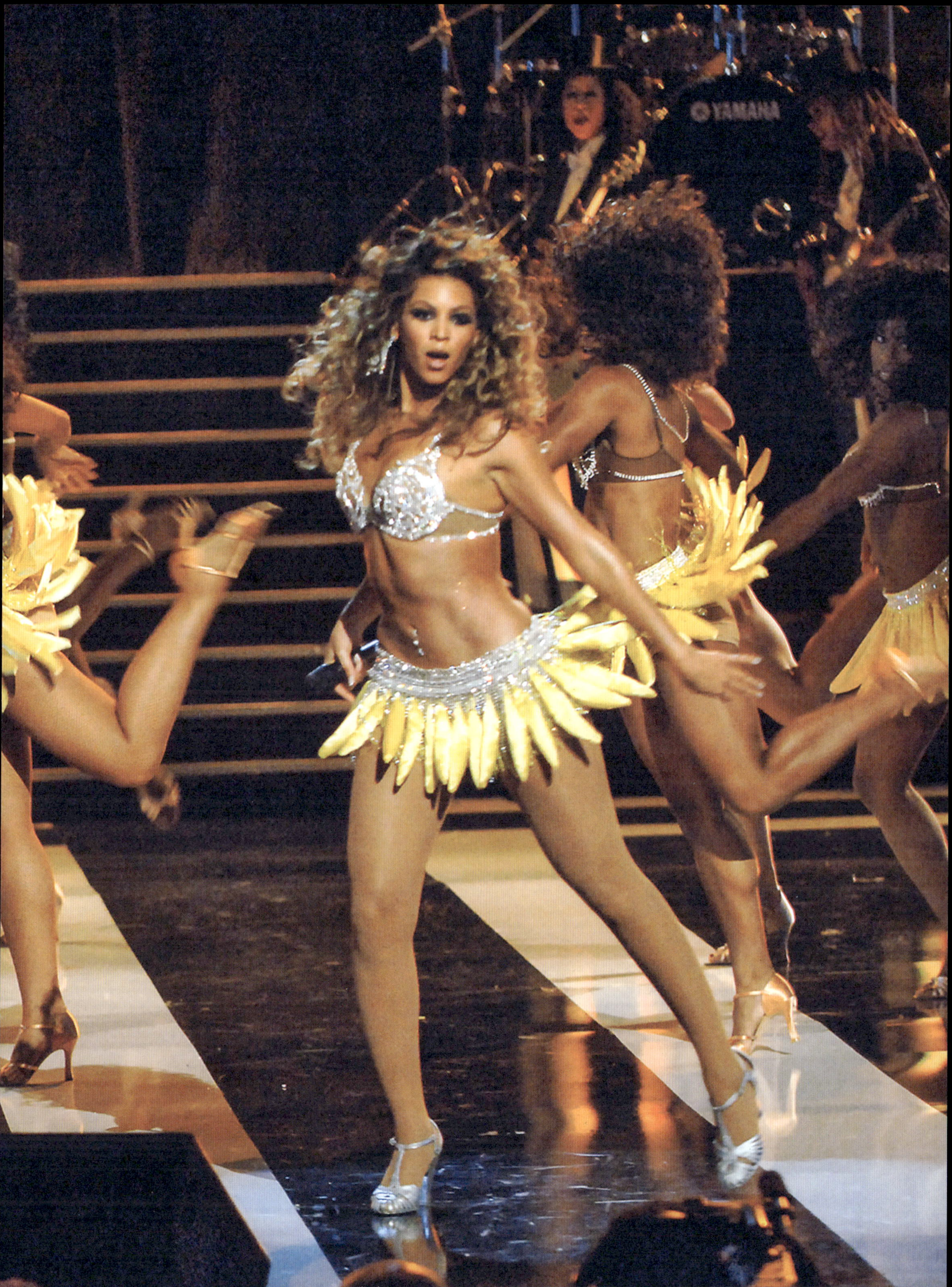
YAMAHA

The strange, uncomfortable costume Beyoncé wore for her performance of *Get Me Bodied* at the 2007 BET Awards.

SINGLE

GET ME BODIED

(Angela Beyince, Beyoncé Knowles, Kasseem "Swizz Beatz" Dean, Makeba Riddick, Sean Garrett, Solange Knowles/3'25)

Musicians: Beyoncé Knowles: vocals, backing vocals / **Recording:** Sony Music Studios, New York: April 2006 / **Technical team: Producers:** Beyoncé Knowles, Sean Garrett, Swizz Beatz / **Executive producers:** Beyoncé Knowles, Mathew Knowles / **Recording engineer:** Jim Caruana / **Assistant recording engineer:** Rob Kinelski / **Single: Released in the USA by Columbia:** 10 July 2007 (CD single ref.: 88697 13225 2) / **Best chart ranking in the USA:** 46

Produced by Beyoncé, Sean Garrett, and Swizz Beatz, this formidable song has only one goal: to make us dance! Initially intended to be the second single from *B'Day*, it was not finally released in that format until 10 July 2007. On the B-side was its extended version, featuring numerous vocal motifs by the singer, as if to prepare the listener for the explosion that would be triggered by the release of the titanic *Single Ladies (Put a Ring on It)* in October 2008. *Get Me Bodied (Extended Version)* thus featured on the deluxe version of *B'Day*, which contained numerous unreleased songs. Its clip, made by Beyoncé and Anthony Mandler, brought in three distinguished guests: Michelle Williams, Kelly Rowland, and Solange Knowles were invited to take part in the shooting. Beyoncé later revealed that she had had these three in mind when she wrote the lyric that mentioned her "three best friends"; between takes of the recording, the women laughed so much together that "It really sets the tone of the video, because you feel like you're there for part of the experience."[145] The clip is avowedly a homage to a scene from Bob Fosse's movie *Sweet Charity*, released in 1969, in which Shirley MacLaine attends a cabaret performance featuring 1960s dances that are now dated: the Frug, the Aloof, the Heavyweight, and the Big Finish. Reflecting on what had inspired the clip, Beyoncé observed that it was "kind of like an instructional video," because it showed how to do all these vintage dances, with influences ranging from Jamaica to Fosse-style movement. "That's the inspiration," she said, referring to *Sweet Charity*. "I love all of that—it's still relevant and it's how many years old? Forty?"[145]

FOR BEYONCÉ ADDICTS

In March 2011, Beyoncé joined the First Lady of the United States, Michelle Obama, in her national campaign against obesity. To support the Let's Move! initiative launched by Obama, Beyoncé re-recorded *Get Me Bodied*, changing the lyrics so as to exhort young Americans to take exercise. Renamed *Move Your Body*, the song was accompanied by a clip made by Melina Matsoukas, which showed Beyoncé fitter than ever, and deeply committed to that noble cause.

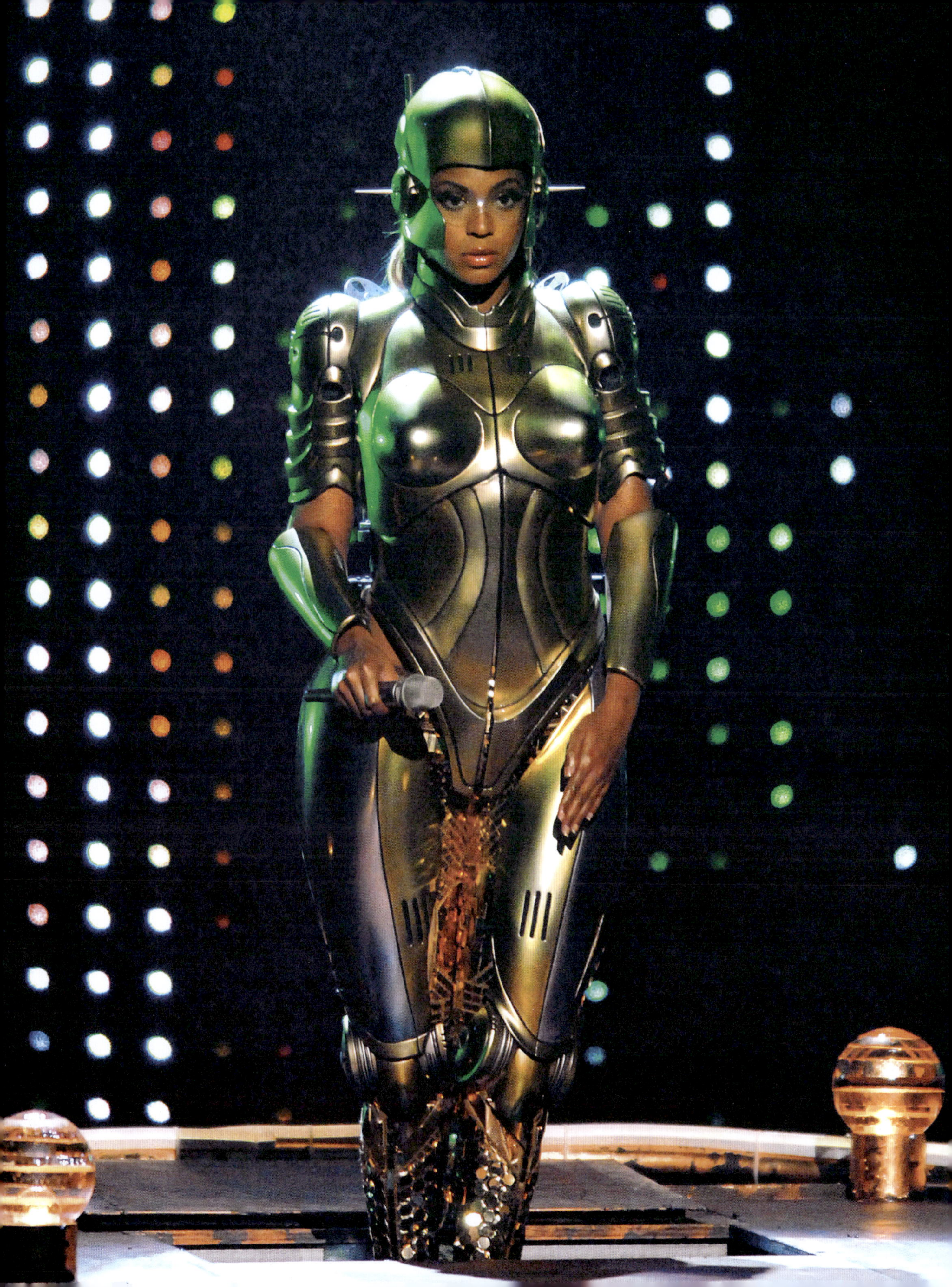

Betty Wright and her track *Girls Can't Do What the Guys Do* influenced the single *Upgrade U*, a duet with Jay-Z.

SUGA MAMA

(Beyoncé Knowles, Chuck Middleton, Makeba Riddick, Rich Harrison/3'25)

Musicians: Beyoncé Knowles: vocals, backing vocals / **Recording:** Sony Music Studios, New York: April 2006 / **Technical team: Producers:** Beyoncé Knowles, Rich Harrison / **Executive producers:** Beyoncé Knowles, Mathew Knowles / **Recording engineer:** Jim Caruana / **Assistant recording engineer:** Rob Kinelski

Before it became the name of the all-female group accompanying Beyoncé on The Beyoncé Experience, *Suga Mama* was one of the most funk songs on *B'Day*. This was due to producer Rich Harrison's use of a sample from the group Jake Wade and The Soul Searchers, borrowed from their song *Searching for Soul, Part 1*, released in 1968 by Mutt Records. A sampling specialist endowed with unparalleled musical knowledge, Harrison was nicknamed the Indiana Jones of soul by the Fox News journalist Roger Friedman in his account of *B'Day*, published in August 2006. Although the song was not released as a single, it was nevertheless accompanied by a clip made by Melina Matsoukas and Beyoncé herself, which would later be included on the DVD *B'Day Anthology Video Album*, like most of the songs on the album. In it, Beyoncé rides a mechanical rodeo bull with extraordinary ease, especially between 3'02 and 3'05, when the machine's speed seems to increase dangerously. Indeed, Melina later suggested that the man operating the bull was "playing a little game," deliberately making it go faster with each new take.[145] Beyoncé unhesitatingly adopted all sorts of positions, then repeatedly fell off. When the film was edited, one of the falls was retained for the final seconds of the video. To make shooting easier, it was decided to film the sequence speeded up, Beyoncé singing the words twice as fast as on the record; the image was then slowed down during editing.

UPGRADE U
(FEATURING JAY-Z)

(Angela Beyincé, Beyoncé Knowles, Clarence Reid, Jay-Z, Makeba Riddick, MK, Sean Garrett, Solange Knowles, Willie Clarke/4'32)

Musicians: Beyoncé Knowles: vocals, backing vocals / **Jay-Z:** rap / **Recording:** Sony Music Studios, New York: April 2006 / **Technical team: Producers:** Beyoncé Knowles, Cameron Wallace, Kasseem "Swizz Beatz" Dean / **Executive producers:** Beyoncé Knowles, Mathew Knowles / **Recording engineer:** Jim Caruana / **Assistant recording engineer:** Rob Kinelski

Although the song's instrumental part was composed by Cameron Wallace and Swizz Beatz before its lyrics were written, their use of the sample from Betty Wright's *Girls Can't Do What the Guys Do* (1968) in the introduction doubtless inspired the three writers, Angela Beyincé, Makeba Riddick, and Beyoncé herself, when they worked on the words. The song paints the portrait of a strong woman telling her man to allow himself to be improved, as if thumbing her nose at the all-powerful male domination that was still rampant in the world of hip-hop, even though Ms Knowles had been working to wipe it out for some years already. In the video of the song, Beyoncé, made up to look like her boyfriend Jay-Z, mimics in barely exaggerated fashion the face-pulling often overdone by rappers. Having asked Jay-Z to leave because it was embarrassing to perform in this way with him in the room, Beyoncé confessed, "It was exciting being a guy, it gave me an excuse to pretend that I was a little gangster. I could do whatever I wanted—I could slouch, be a little more tough, be a little more aggressive, say whatever I wanted." Facing up to the prospect of her fans being shocked to see her acting like this, she added, "I really am a little bit of a tomboy—the way I work, the way I treat my job, the way I focus is kind of masculine."[145]

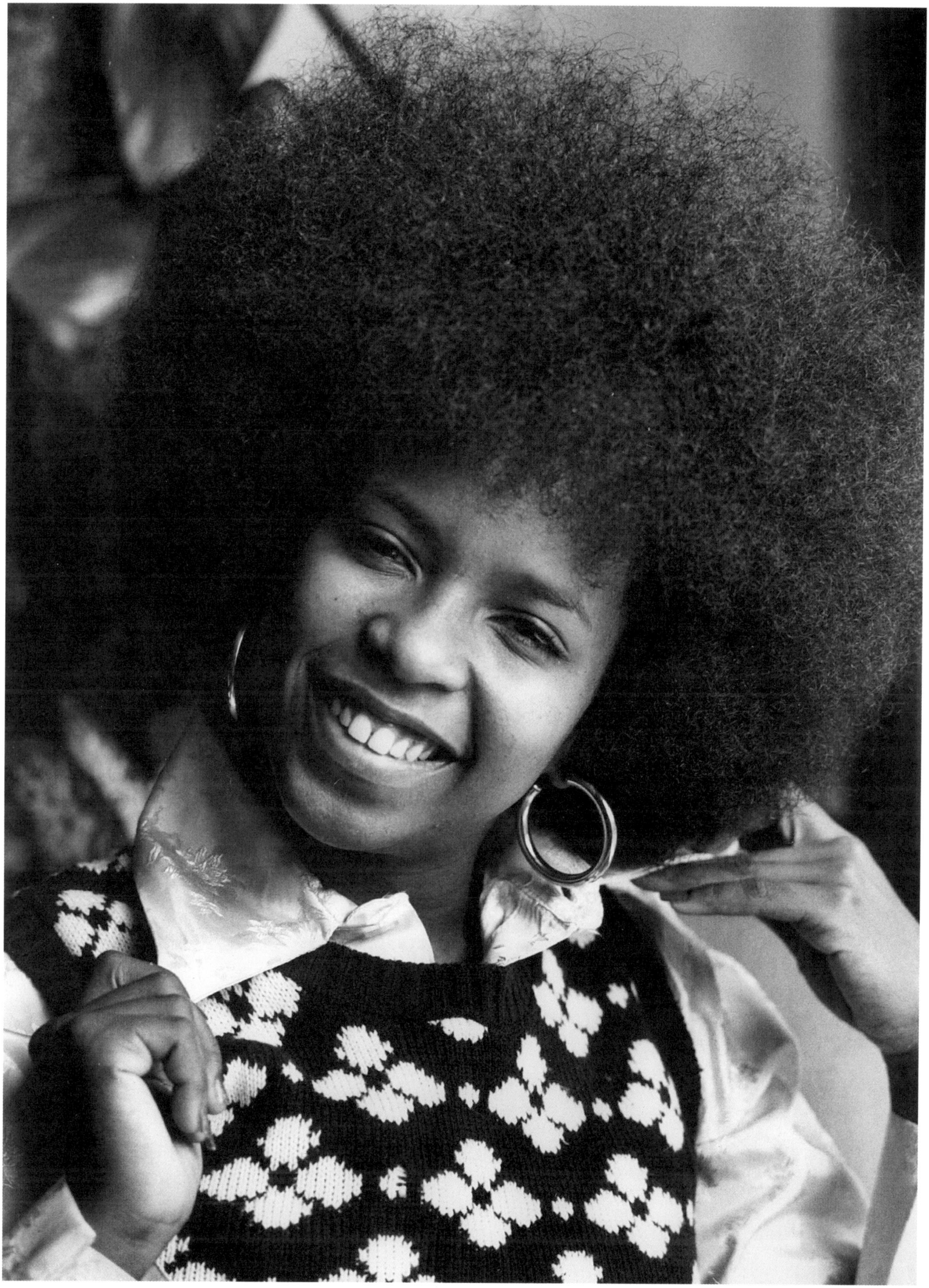

Friend or foe? Beyoncé and Rihanna share a talent for performance.

SINGLE

RING THE ALARM

(Beyoncé Knowles, Kasseem "Swizz Beatz" Dean, Sean Garrett/3'23)

Musicians
Beyoncé Knowles: vocals, backing vocals

Recording
Sony Music Studios, New York: April 2006

Technical team
Producers: Beyoncé Knowles, Swizz Beatz
Executive producers: Beyoncé Knowles, Mathew Knowles
Recording engineer: Jim Caruana
Assistant recording engineer: Rob Kinelski

Single
Released in the USA by Columbia/Sony Urban Music: 10 September 2006 (CD single ref.: 88697 02086 2)
Best chart ranking in the USA: 11

> While performing the very energetic *Ring the Alarm* on stage at the Amway Arena in Orlando on 24 July 2007, Beyoncé had a spectacular fall, after her feet got caught in the long coat she was wearing. Having fallen head first and violently banged her chin, she continued her choreography in a natural manner, once again displaying unparalleled professionalism.

Genesis

When *Ring the Alarm*, the second single from *B'Day*, was released in September 2006, the music industry was in turmoil. Was the romance between Beyoncé and Jay-Z hanging by a thread? Rumors swirled around a supposed relationship between the rapper and his protégée, the young Rihanna, who was on the point of becoming a global superstar. Although these rumors were never confirmed, the lyrics of *Ring the Alarm* sowed disquiet in the minds of the press and listeners. It must be said that the words of the song seem to confirm this hearsay. In them, Beyoncé informs her partner that she will not allow him to leave her for another woman, and takes the opportunity to disparage his supposed lover. "*Tell me how should I feel when I know what I know/ And my female intuition telling me you're a dog?/People told me 'bout the flames, I couldn't see through the smoke,*" she sings with obvious rage, sustained by Swizz Beatz's production. The song was accompanied by a clip showing Beyoncé in various scenes, one of which pays homage to the legendary sequence of Sharon Stone being interrogated in Paul Verhoeven's *Basic Instinct* (1992). "I am very proud of this song," Beyoncé said in August 2006, "and I believe the video is one of the best I have ever done. [...] My thoughts about releasing *Green Light* and *Get Me Bodied* [were] to go first to the international market, but the vibrancy of *Ring the Alarm* is something I wanted the whole world to see and hear right now."[152]

Production

The making of this powerful, aggressive song (the sound of the alarm siren quickly becomes deafening and disturbing) was the result of the collaboration between Beyoncé and Swizz Beatz. "That's just one of the many presents I gave her for her *B'Day*," he said in 2006. "I have the most tracks on her album as a single producer, and just wait till you hear the other three. I've never heard a singer singing on tracks like this. It hasn't been done in R&B—yet."[153] The other songs Swizz Beatz produced on the album are *Get Me Bodied*, *Upgrade U*, and *Check on It*.

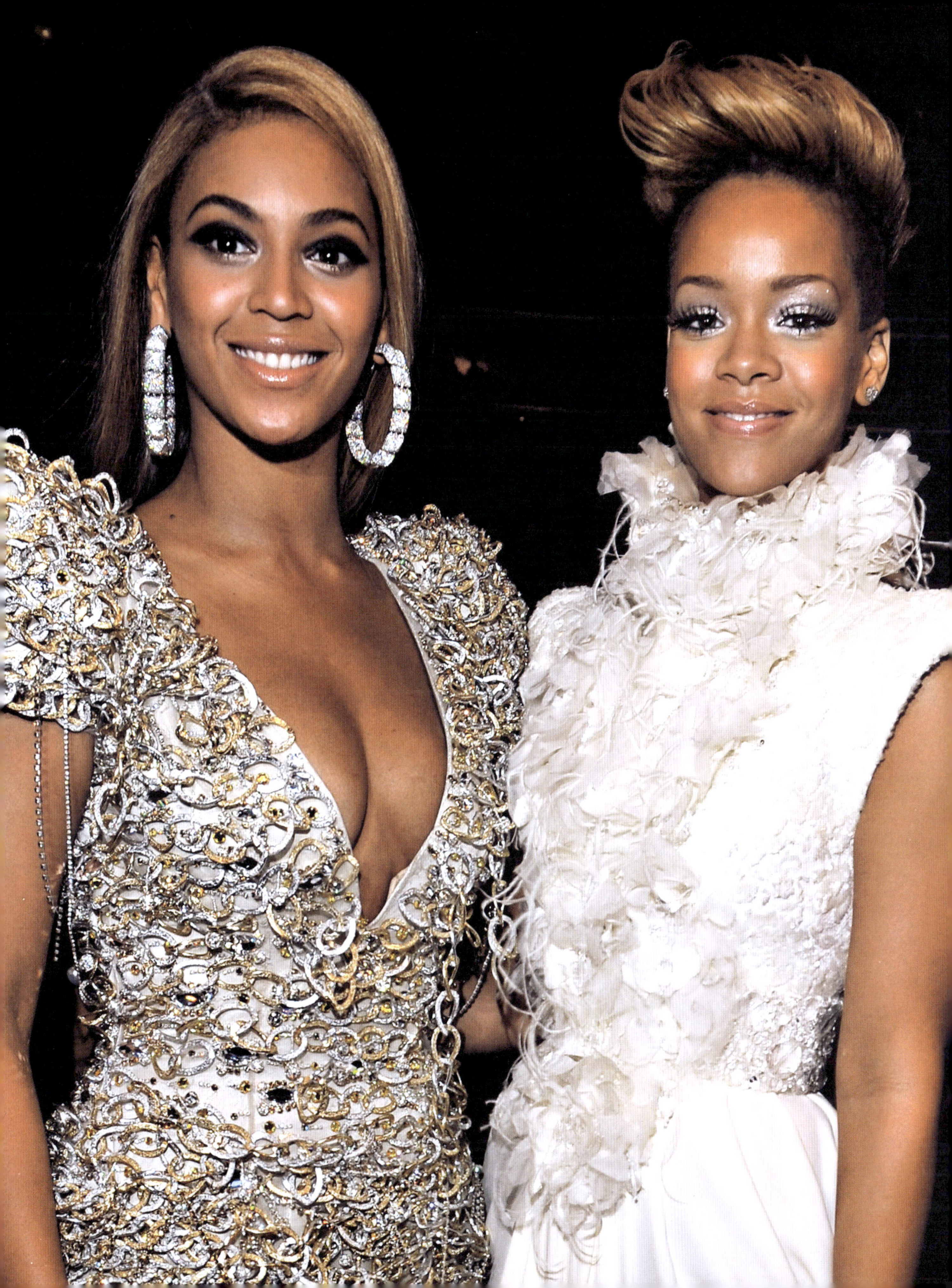

KITTY KAT

(Beyoncé Knowles, Pharrell Williams, Shawn Carter/3'55)

Musicians: Beyoncé Knowles: vocals, backing vocals / **Recording:** Sony Music Studios, New York: April 2006 / The Record Plant, Los Angeles: 2006 / **Technical team:** Producers: Beyoncé Knowles, The Neptunes / **Executive producers:** Beyoncé Knowles, Mathew Knowles / **Recording engineers:** Andrew Coleman, Geoff Rice, Jim Caruana / **Assistant recording engineer:** Rob Kinelski

Even though the animal's trainers were present on stage, handling the cat used in filming *Kitty Kat*—a languorous song produced by The Neptunes, the duo made up of Chad Hugo and Pharrell Williams—was no simple matter. The third video shot for the DVD *B'Day Anthology Video Album*, that of *Kitty Kat*, shows Beyoncé with a feline look, as she sings of her loneliness because her lover is out with friends and she is left at home. "And you're like, 'No more of this. It's time to go,'" she said. "We had the oversized kitty cat [in the video], which was so cute! I had to pretend it was there, because I was really in front of the green screen."[145]

FREAKUM DRESS

(Beyoncé Knowles, Makeba Riddick, Rich Harrison/3'20)

Musicians: Beyoncé Knowles: vocals, backing vocals / **Recording:** Sony Music Studios, New York: April 2006 / Great Divide Studios, Aspen: 2006 / **Technical team:** Producers: Beyoncé Knowles, Rich Harrison / **Executive producers:** Beyoncé Knowles, Mathew Knowles / **Recording engineers:** Jamie Rosenberg, Jim Caruana / **Assistant recording engineer:** Rob Kinelski

"I'm very happy and calm and in a good place in my life," Beyoncé said in August 2006. "[*B'Day*] is very empowering—it's a record women need to hear."[142] According to her, female power unquestionably lies in seduction, as conveyed in this song that sings the praises of an outfit before which a man will inevitably succumb. "You know, when your man starts taking you for granted and you put on that one dress that makes him go, 'Wow', and not want you to leave the house."[154] Determined to raise the temperature, Beyoncé called on the services of the faithful Rich Harrison and produced a danceable number, the clip of which sustained its sensual quality. For the occasion, Tina Knowles made 30 dresses, sometimes while shooting was in progress. Only one accessory seen in the video did not come from Beyoncé's mother's wardrobe: the glasses the singer wears at 2'54, which were borrowed from her make-up artist, Francesca Tolot.

GREEN LIGHT

(Beyoncé Knowles, Pharrell Williams, Sean Garrett/3'29)

Musicians: Beyoncé Knowles: vocals, backing vocals / **Recording:** Sony Music Studios, New York: April 2006 / The Record Plant, Los Angeles: 2006 / **Technical team:** Producers: Beyoncé Knowles, The Neptunes / **Executive producers:** Beyoncé Knowles, Mathew Knowles / **Recording engineers:** Andrew Coleman, Jim Caruana / **Assistant recording engineer:** Rob Kinelski

Close observers of the work of producer Pharrell Williams could pick his style out of a thousand. For example, the percussions used in *Green Light* could be heard again in 2013 in Robin Thicke's *Blurred Lines*, an international hit that had a global impact because of its lively tempo, the appearance of the supermodel Emily Ratajkowski topless, and the legal action for plagiarism that its authors lost in 2018 for having used, without declaring it, a highly recognizable sample from Marvin Gaye's *Got to Give Up* (1977). Inspired by the clip of Robert Palmer's *Addicted to Love* (1985), that of *Green Light* reveals a Beyoncé who is more rock'n'roll than ever, wielding an electric guitar, even though the song contains no guitar line. According to the singer, that is a nod to Vanity 6, the legendary all-female band of the 1980s, produced by Prince in 1982. Speaking about the clip, Beyoncé, who could play a bit of guitar but didn't feel she was good enough to do it in public, said: "The guitar felt good in my hands—I want to learn to play now, for real. And the band [in the video] is my real band. [...] I love being around females. They inspire me, make me stronger, and there's something special about us jamming."[145]

For the *Green Light* video, Beyoncé was inspired by the sensuality of the all-female group Vanity 6, produced by Prince in 1982.

SINGLE

IRREPLACEABLE

(Amund Bjørklund, Beyoncé Knowles, Espen Lind, Mikkel S. Eriksen, Shaffer Smith, Tor Erik Hermansen/3'47)

Musicians
Beyoncé Knowles: vocals, backing vocals
Espen Lind: acoustic guitar
Amund Bjørklund: acoustic guitar
Mikkel S. Eriksen: additional instruments
Tor Erik Hermansen: additional instruments

Recording
Sony Music Studios, New York: April 2006

Technical team
Producers: Shaffer "Ne-Yo" Smith, Beyoncé Knowles, Stargate
Executive producers: Beyoncé Knowles, Mathew Knowles
Recording engineers: Geoff Rice, Jim Caruana
Assistant recording engineer: Rob Kinelski

Single
Released in the USA by Columbia/Sony Urban Music: 23 October 2006 (CD single ref.: 88697 02377 2)
Best chart ranking in the USA: 1

Genesis

The Scandinavian countries have long proved the depth of their expertise in matters of songwriting and record production. During the 2000s one of the most famous ambassadors for Swedish pop was none other than Max Martin, a superstar producer whose track record included a dizzying list of hits, including *Baby One More Time* by Britney Spears, *I Kissed a Girl, Teenage Dream*, and *California Gurls* by Katy Perry, and *So What* by Pink. Norwegians Tor Erik Hermansen and Mikkel S. Eriksen, who make up the duo Stargate, were also much talked about in 2006. As they were working on some new songs, the pair received from their friend Jay Brown, head of Jay-Z's label Roc Nation, a piece of advice that would turn their lives upside down: he suggested they write a pop song, but give the leading role to a folk guitar. "We were up for it straight away, we love acoustic guitars," Eriksen recalled. "One of the differences between us and a lot of US producers is that we're much more melodic, we use more real instruments, more chords, we have bridges…so it was very natural for us to use acoustic guitars."[155] Using a sample of guitar recorded by their friends Espen Lind and Amund Bjørklund, of the production team Espionage, the two artists put together their song and presented it to the singer Ne-Yo, who wrote the lyrics and melody, starting with what would become one of the most famous phrases in Beyoncé's repertoire: *To the left, to the left*. Although Ne-Yo initially wanted to perform the song himself, he received a visit at his studio from Larry Jackson of Apple Music, who advised him to endow the song with a female voice. Ne-Yo then thought of suggesting the song to Shania Twain or Faith Hill, but when Beyoncé heard *Irreplaceable* the die was cast—she demanded she record it for her new album. Initially, Stargate were told that the song would not be retained on the tracklisting of *B'Day*. "We knew that it was so different to anything else she was doing, or anyone else was doing for that matter. There was nothing like it; it wouldn't fit on urban, it wouldn't fit on pop, it didn't seem to fit anywhere."[155] Only when producer Swizz Beatz intervened did Beyoncé appreciate the song for its true value: he told her she would be mad not to include it on her album. *Irreplaceable* was an immediate hit with the public, spending six weeks at number 1 in the *Billboard* charts, and was nominated for Song of the Year at the 2008 Grammy

The Norwegian duo Stargate consists of Tor Erik Hermansen (left) and Mikkel S. Eriksen.

Awards. "I love *Irreplaceable*," Beyoncé said. "I think it's important to have those songs. I've had so many people come up to me in tears saying, 'I experienced my first breakup. If it wasn't for the song, I wouldn't be strong enough to not call. I wouldn't know how much I'm worth.' I'm happy to be a part of that. I wrote *Independent Women* and *Bootylicious* and *Survivor*, and it helped women with their self-esteem. I'm happy to continue to do that."[156]

Production

As soon as she was given the song, Beyoncé asked Stargate to give it a more hip-hop beat. To do this, Eriksen and Hermansen used a Roland TR-808 drum machine, already heard in *Déjà Vu*. When the pair went to New York to record the singer's voice, the least that could be said is that they were unnerved by her legendary charisma, as Hermansen testified: "She is so beautiful that you can't really look straight at her. You have to look to the left of her or something so you don't get distracted. She's just magnetic and, really, the most humble. There's never any drama. She always finishes her stuff. [...] She never leaves anything half-finished."[157] Jason Goldstein, who had the Midas touch in the studio and was in charge of mixing the album, revealed some technical details regarding his work on the song. The acoustic guitar, the song's centerpiece, was connected to an analog flanger effect from a TC Electronic TC 1210 rack, while Beyoncé's voice was covered with a slight delay from an Echo Farm plug-in made by Line 6 and an Oxford compression plug-in. Thanks to their typically Scandinavian know-how, the two members of Stargate gave Beyoncé one of the greatest hits of her career.

Songwriter and soul singer Curtis Mayfield in 1972.

RESENTMENT

(Beyoncé Knowles, Candice C. Nelson, Curtis Mayfield, Walter Millsap III/4'40)

Musicians
Beyoncé Knowles: vocals, backing vocals
Candice Nelson: additional instruments
Walter Millsap III: additional instruments
Recording
Sony Music Studios, New York: April 2006
Lair Studios, Los Angeles: 2006
Technical team
Producers: Beyoncé Knowles, Walter Millsap III, Candice C. Nelson
Executive producers: Beyoncé Knowles, Mathew Knowles
Recording engineers: Dave Lopez, Jim Caruana, Walter Millsap III
Assistant recording engineer: Rob Kinelski

Genesis

In 2003, the landmark documentary *The "Real" Beckhams*, produced by Caroline Mandell, appeared. It is an intimate look at the life of the UK's most glamorous couple, David and Victoria Beckham. Among the songs that accompany the film, which would be offered to buyers of the DVD when it came out a few months later, is *Resentment*, which the former Spice Girl had recorded for her third album, in the process of being written at the time. Since that album was soon abandoned, the song lay dormant on a hard disc belonging to its composer, the versatile Walter Millsap III, who had been a recording engineer for Alicia Keys and songwriter for Jennifer Lopez, and would later be Lady Gaga's musical director. A close friend of Timbaland, Millsap had built the song around a sample from *Think*, one of the titles on Curtis Mayfield's soundtrack for the movie *Super Fly*, directed by Gordon Parks Jr and released in 1972. When word got around that Beyoncé was at the pre-production stage of her new solo album, the song was offered to her, and her interpretation of it was the most interesting track on the record, bathed in a melancholy suited to its subject matter: a woman singing about her partner's infidelity and lies. "The song on my new album I am proudest of is probably *Resentment*," Beyoncé said in 2014. "I feel like vocally I've grown, I feel like all the chord changes and the beautiful harmonies and the lyrics is something that I really am proud of."[158]

Production

Walter Millsap III was an ambassador for the Japanese brand Yamaha, and used various items of its studio equipment (here a Motif XS-8 synthesizer, his favorite Yamaha instrument). He demonstrated an irreproachable ethic when it came to working with stars of Beyoncé's caliber. "When an artist has an idea, and you're able to interpret it and make it come to life, it's like a baby being born," he explained. "That's what makes it worthwhile. I think I find the most joy in satisfying others and making them happy. So when my job is to make you happy, and your job is to hire me so you can be happy, it all adds up!"[159]

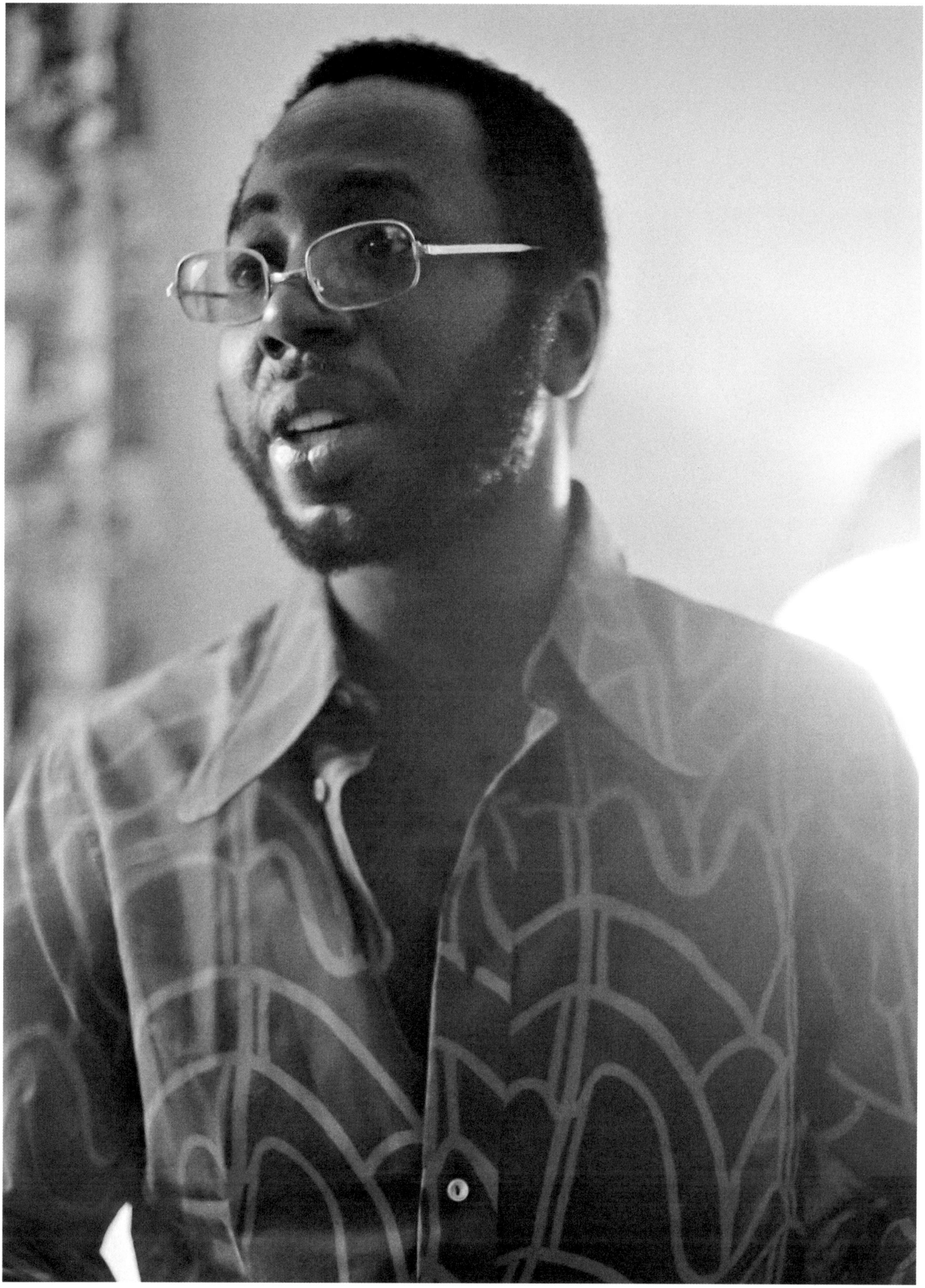

CHECK ON IT
(BEYONCÉ FEATURING BUN B AND SLIM THUG)

(Beyoncé Knowles, Stayve Thomas, Sean Garrett, Kasseem Dean, Angela Beyincé/3'32)

Musicians: Beyoncé Knowles: vocals, backing vocals / **Bun B:** rap / Slim Thug: rap / **Recording:** Sony Music Studios, New York: 2005 / Henson Recording Studios, Hollywood: 2005 / **Technical team: Producers:** Beyoncé Knowles, Swizz Beatz / **Recording engineers:** Jim Caruana, Nathan Jenkins / **Assistant recording engineers:** Geoffrey Rice, Matt Serrecchio / **"#1's" (compilation):** Released in the USA by Sony Urban Music/Columbia: 21 October 2005 (ref.: CK 97765)

When Beyoncé joined the cast of *The Pink Panther*, a new movie directed by Shawn Levy and starring Steve Martin and Kevin Kline, it was planned to include two of her songs on the CD of the film's soundtrack, complementing the instrumental score by composer Christophe Beck. *Check on It* had been added to the track listing for the Destiny's Child compilation *#1's*, on 21 October 2005, then retrieved from Columbia's archives when it was considered for inclusion in *The Pink Panther*. Although it is heard in the movie, in the end it did not feature on the disc, which consists exclusively of music by Beck. In order to promote the song, *Check on It* was accompanied by a video made by Hype Williams. "I thought this video was gonna have to be really simple and I knew we didn't have a lot of time to shoot it," Beyoncé said, "so I wanted to get the absolute best director and I spoke with Hype and we're on the same page."[160]

A WOMAN LIKE ME

(Charmelle Cofield, Ron Lawrence, Beyoncé Knowles/4'16)

Musicians: Beyoncé Knowles: vocals, backing vocals / **Recording:** Sony Music Studios, New York: 2006 / **Technical team: Producers:** Ronald Lawrence, Beyoncé Knowles, Charmelle Cofield / **Digital distribution by Columbia/Sony Urban Music:** September 2006

As production of *The Pink Panther* was in full swing, the movie's team was working on a song that the character Xania, played by Beyoncé, would sing in one scene. *A Woman Like Me* was sent to her while she was working on her part, but she decided to revise the arrangements so as to give it an R&B rhythm which, it must be said, fits rather well with the predominant string parts. Beyoncé also revised the lyrics of the song which, like *Check on It*, was meant to be included on the soundtrack CD. Alas, also like *Check on It*, *A Woman Like Me* would be sold only online. Built around a sample of

Beyoncé on the set of *The Pink Panther* in 2005.

> The producer and rapper Shaffer "Ne-Yo" Smith, who wrote *Hollywood*, got his nickname from a famous science-fiction movie. "It was given to me by a producer friend of mine, and his name is Big D. Evans. He said, 'In my opinion, you see music the way Neo sees the Matrix' from the movie *The Matrix*. That's a reference from that movie."[162]

string arrangements from *Hammerhead* and *Great Day*, two compositions by Simon Haseley, the song was effective, as Beyoncé confirmed in 2006: "It had the strength of a Tina Turner song but the drama of a Bond tune. It definitely fit the character."[161]

SINGLE

HOLLYWOOD
(JAY-Z FEATURING BEYONCÉ)

(Reggie Perry, Shaffer Smith/4'17)

Musicians: Jay-Z: rap / Beyoncé Knowles: vocals, backing vocals / **Recording:** Sony Music Studios, New York: 2006 / **Technical team:** Producer: Syience / Executive producer: Shawn Carter / Recording engineer: Gimel "Young Guru" Keaton / Assistant recording engineer: Jason Agel / **Jay-Z Kingdom Come (album):** Released in the USA by Roc-A-Fella Records: 21 November 2006 (LP ref.: B0008045-01, CD ref.: B0008045-02)

In inviting his girlfriend Beyoncé to come and sing on his new single, Jay-Z was offering his fans a plunge into a star system from which he seemed to be taking a step back. *When your friends is Chris and Gwyneth/When your girl is more famous than Juventus/Then it's time to get all your windows tinted*, the rapper sings, slipping in a humorous allusion to one of the star couples of the time, Coldplay's vocalist Chris Martin and the actor Gwyneth Paltrow. Composed by Reggie "Syience" Perry and Shaffer "Ne-Yo" Smith, *Hollywood* has a more danceable and less gangsta approach than the hip-hop we are used to hearing from Jay-Z, but it fits perfectly with Beyoncé's very tuneful phrasing. The latter offered her fans a re-interpretation of the song, entitled *Welcome to Hollywood*, on the deluxe version of her album *B'Day*, in April 2007.

PRAY
(JAY-Z)

(Deleno Matthews, Alan Hawkshaw, Levar Coppin, Sean Combs, Shawn Carter/3'56)

Musicians: Jay-Z: rap / James Lewis: guitar, bass guitar / Mario Winans: drums, synthesizers / Aaron J. Johnson: clarinet, trombone / Beyoncé Knowles: spoken voice, backing vocals / A.J. Walker: vocals / Adonis Shropshire: vocals / Carmen Cameron: vocals / Cheri Dennis: vocals / Jayms Madison: vocals / Leisa Johnson: vocals / Shannon Jones: vocals / **Recording:** Daddy's House, New York: 2007 / Roc The Mic, New York: 2007 / **Technical team:** Producers: Levar Ryan Coppin, P. Diddy, Sean Cane / Executive producers: Antonio "L. A." Reid, Shawn Carter / Recording engineers: Gimel "Young Guru" Keaton, Steve "Rock Star" Dickey, Victor Abijaoudi II / Assistant recording engineer: Andy Geel / **Jay-Z American Gangster (album):** Released in the USA by Roc-A-Fella Records: 6 November 2007 (LP ref.: B0008045-01, CD ref.: B0010229-02)

The rapper Jay-Z was decidedly prolific, having regaled his audience with an album per year since 1996 (with the exception of 2006). The year 2008 saw the release of *American Gangster*, a concept album inspired by the movie of the same name, made by Ridley Scott in 2007 and starring Russell Crowe and Denzel Washington. For *Pray*, Beyoncé was invited to recite monologues which were inserted at various points in the song, even though she was not credited in the album's sleeve notes. This was also the case with another song on the album, *Roc Boys (And the Winner Is)…*, on which Beyoncé sang a few discreet backing vocals alongside Kanye West between 2'56 and 3'03. It seemed that Beyoncé and Jay-Z, the two superstar lovebirds, had become inseparable, to the great joy of their fans.

BEYONCÉ: ALL THE SONGS

Colombian singer Shakira in 2002, following the international success of her fifth album, *Laundry Service*.

SINGLE

BEAUTIFUL LIAR
(BEYONCÉ AND SHAKIRA)

(Amanda Ghost, Beyoncé Knowles, Ian Dench, Mikkel S. Eriksen, Tor Erik Hermansen/3'19)

Musicians
Beyoncé Knowles: vocals
Shakira: vocals
Boujemaa Razgui: ney
Naser Musa: oud
Omar Al-Musfi: percussion
Denaun Porter: programming
Visitante: programming
Hanna Khoury: violin, viola
Mikkel S. Eriksen: additional instruments
Tor Erik Hermansen: additional instruments

Recording
Battery Studios, New York: 2006
La Marimonda, Nassau: 2006
Futura Productions, Boston: 2006
The Hit Factory Criteria, Miami: 2006
Sony Music Studios, New York: 2006

Technical team
Producers: Beyoncé Knowles, Stargate, Eduardo Cabra, Shakira
Recording engineers: Gustavo Celis, Jim Caruana, John Weston, Roberto Almodovar, Stargate
Assistant recording engineers: David Stearns, Rob Kinelski
Arrangements: Shakira, Stargate
String arrangements: Kareem Roustom, Shakira

Irreemplazable **(EP)**
Released in the USA by Sony Urban Music/Columbia/Music World Music: 27 August 2007 (CD ref.: 88697 12804 2)
Best chart ranking in the USA: 3

Genesis
In 2006 the Norwegian duo Mikkel S. Eriksen and Tor Erik Hermansen, known as Stargate, presented one of their productions to their manager, Tyran "Ty Ty" Smith. The latter immediately imagined the song being performed as a duet by the two biggest pop stars of the time, Beyoncé and Shakira. "We presented it to Beyoncé, who loved it and added her own twist to the lyrics and then recorded a version of it, but they could not get Shakira to feature on the song in time for the release of *B'Day*," Eriksen recalled.[163] It was several months before the Colombian singer found the time to record her vocal lines, and asked her musicians to enhance the piece with Middle Eastern instruments such as the oud and the ney. The song became an international hit on its release as a single and its addition to the new edition of *B'Day* in April 2007. It was also on Beyoncé's EP *Irreemplazable*, which brought together various of her songs reinterpreted in Spanish.

Production
"This song is very simple," Mikkel Eriksen explained. "Most of the time we have more chords in a song, because we find it hard writing a great song on just one chord. But if you do it right, you can make it work, and this song is an example."[163] With its insistent tempo and Arabian motif, both reminiscent of the 50 Cent and Olivia hit *Candy Shop*, released in 2005, *Beautiful Liar* is a song in the spirit of the time. But when the two Stargate partners finished producing the piece, they lacked the most important elements to make a hit out of an instrumental number. "We didn't have a lyric or a top melody," Eriksen explained, "so various writers had a stab at finishing the song. The first two or three attempts weren't good enough, and then [manager Tyran "Ty Ty" Smith] had the idea of putting us together with Amanda [Ghost] and Ian [Dench], who we hadn't heard of."[163] Ghost, who had recently worked on the James Blunt hit single *You're Beautiful,* explained that Beyoncé "approached me through her husband, Jay, because we had been introduced and were talking about working together. He arranged a meeting and she said would I write a song for her? And I said I don't know anything about urban music. But she likes so many different styles, as does Jay-Z. The reason they wanted me was because I wasn't from that world and we started a friendship up."[164]

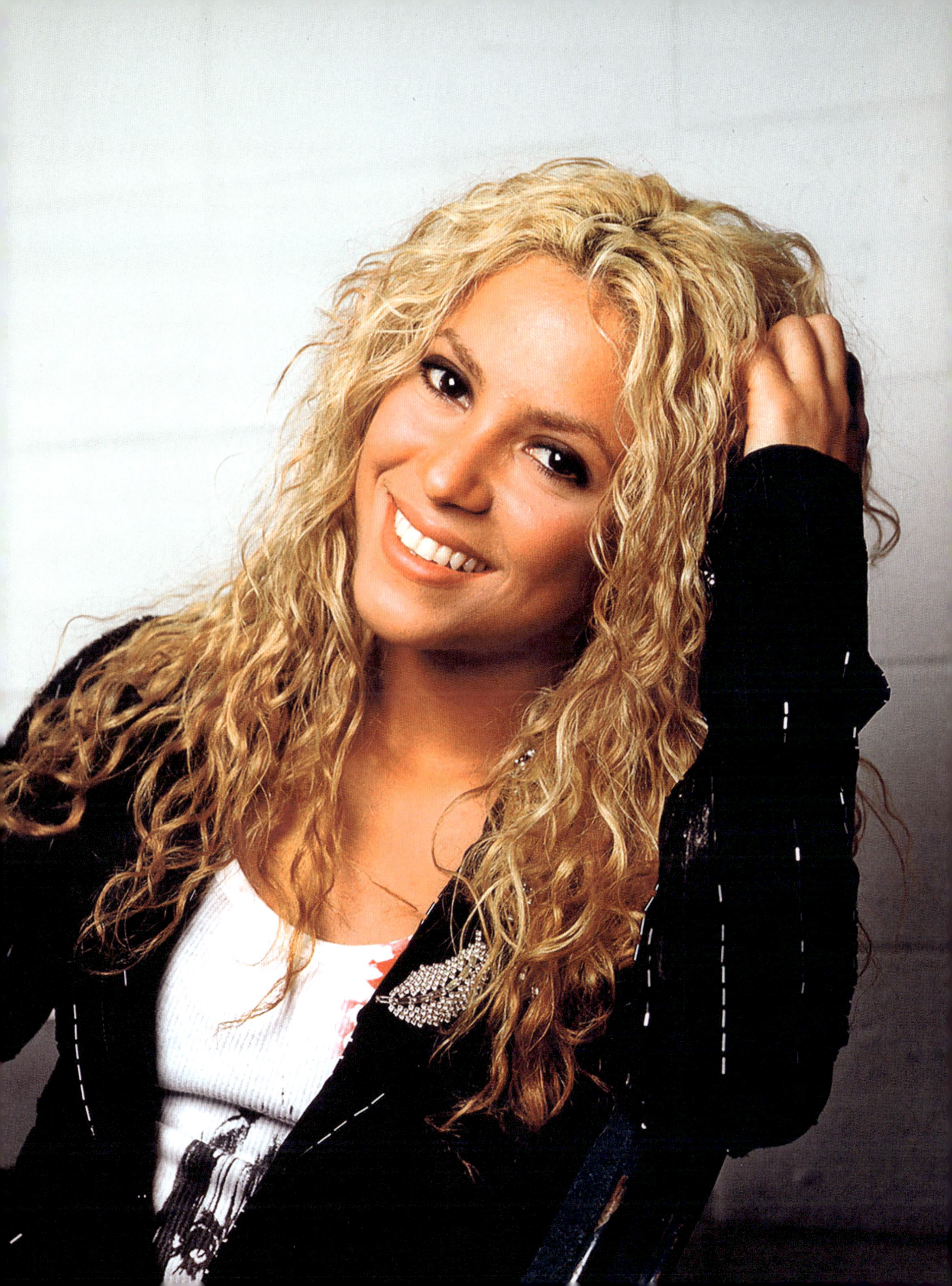

Alejandro Fernández in 2005, promoting his 14th album, *México–Madrid: En Directo Y Sin Escalas*.

AMOR GITANO
(BEYONCÉ AND ALEJANDRO FERNÁNDEZ)

(Beyoncé Knowles, Jaime Flores, Reyli Barba/3'48)

Musicians: Beyoncé Knowles: vocals / Alejandro Fernández: vocals / Jasmin Cruz: backing vocals / Rudy Perez: backing vocals, classical guitar, programming / Paco "El Sevillano": vocals / Rene Luis Toledo: classical guitar / Clay Perry: programming / **Recording:** The Beach House Recording Studios, Miami Beach: 2007 / Roc The Mic, New York: 2007 / **Technical team:** Producers: Beyoncé Knowles, Rudy Perez / Recording engineer: David Lopez / Assistant recording engineer: Shane Woodley / Arrangements: Rudy Perez / **Irreemplazable (EP):** Released in the USA by Sony Urban Music/Columbia/Music World Music: 27 August 2007 (CD ref.: 88697 12804 2) / **Best chart ranking in the USA:** 105

Like many artists before her, in 2007 Beyoncé decided to offer her Latin-American fans reinterpretations of her songs in Spanish, including *Irreplaceable*, *Listen*, and *Beautiful Liar*. She admitted at the time that, although she had done Spanish at school, she couldn't speak more than a few words. But at the Grammy Awards on 27 February 2002, Destiny's Child had joined with the Spanish singer Alejandro Sanz to sing a composition of his, *Quisiera Ser*. "[…] our Latin fans were so excited, they were like, 'When are you going to do more?'" Beyoncé observed.[145] Rather than rush into the project with inadequate Spanish, she enlisted the help of Rudy Perez [also co-producer of the EP], intending to do one song. But, she added, after praising her tutor's patience, "We did it phonetically and I was pretty good at it, and before you knew it, I had six of them." One of the songs was *Amor Gitano*, a duet with the Mexican singer Alejandro Fernández, a superstar in Latin America. "I loved working with Alejandro on *Amor Gitano*," Beyoncé recalled. "When I was asked to record with him, I immediately said yes. He is extremely talented."[165] *Amor Gitano* featured on the EP *Irreemplazable* and on the deluxe version of *B'Day*, as well as on Fernández's album *Viento a Favor*, released in 2007. The song also became the signature theme of the TV soap opera *El Zorro: la espada y la rosa*, which was broadcast from February 2007 on the Spanish-language network Telemundo, and met with considerable success worldwide at the time.

Singer Justin Timberlake once again proves his talent with a second album made for night clubs.

UNTIL THE END OF TIME
(JUSTIN TIMBERLAKE DUET WITH BEYONCÉ)

(Justin Timberlake, Nate Hills, Timothy Mosley/5'22)

Musicians: Justin Timberlake: vocals, backing vocals / **Beyoncé Knowles:** vocals, backing vocals / **Nate "Danja" Hills:** programming, synthesizers / **Timbaland:** programming, synthesizers / **The Benjamin Wright Orchestra Richard Adkins:** violin; Peggy Baldwin: cello; Brian Benning: violin; Charlie Bisharat: violin; Ida Bodin: double bass; Kevin Brandon: bass guitar; Mark Cargill: violin; Susan Chatman: violin; Phillipa Clarke: violin; Jeff Clayton: flute; Salvator Cracchiolo: trumpet; Yvette Devereaux: violin; Ernie Ehrhardt: cello; James Ford: trumpet; Pam Gates: violin; Valarie King: flute; Songa Lee-Kitto: violin; Marisa McLeod: violin; Giovanna Moraga: cello; Patrick Morgan: viola; Michele Nardone: viola; Cameron Patrick: viola; Kathleen Robertson: violin; Jimbo Ross: viola; Nancy Stein-Ross: cello; Mari Tsumura: violin / **Benjamin Wright:** conductor / **Recording:** Thomas Crown Studios, Virginia Beach: 2005 to 2006 / Capitol Studios, Hollywood: 2005 to 2006 (strings) / **Technical team: Producers:** Timbaland, Justin Timberlake, Nate "Danja" Hills / **Recording engineers:** Jimmy Douglass, Ethan Willoughby, Lisa Hampton, Khaliq Glover / **String arrangements:** Benjamin Wright / **Justin Timberlake FutureSex/LoveSounds Deluxe Edition (album): Released in the USA by Jive/Zomba:** 27 November 2007 (CD ref.: 88697-17391-2)

FutureSex/LoveSounds, Justin Timberlake's second studio album, is a most interesting record. Produced by hit-makers of the caliber of Timbaland and Rick Rubin, it showcases sounds that are sometimes futuristic and sometimes vintage, and the juxtaposition of these two opposites offers fans of the former *NSYNC vocalist a very danceable record. After its eagerly awaited launch on 12 September 2006, Timberlake released, on 27 November 2007, a deluxe version, enhanced with reinterpretations of three of his songs: *SexyBack*, remixed by Wayne Williams; *Sexy Ladies*, with the superstar rapper 50 Cent; and finally the languorous *Until the End of Time*, performed as a duet with Beyoncé. Fans of Prince will doubtless appreciate the nod to his music, so much do the settings of the Linn LM-1 drum machine, chosen by Timbaland and his associate Nate "Danja" Hills, pay homage to the musician from Minneapolis's *1999* and *Purple Rain* periods. The American website Rap-Up—a benchmark in urban music in the United States—made no mistake when it stated shortly before the Timberlake/Beyoncé duet was released as a single: "We're sure this will rocket up the charts though. JT + Beyoncé = Certified hit."[166] Indeed, the song sold more than 500,000 at a time of unprecedented crisis in record sales, the result of the advent in 2003 of illegal downloading from the internet. So, a success for this coming together at the top of US pop music, even though the song did not stand out for its originality, in terms of either writing or performance.

BEYONCÉ: ALL THE SONGS 237

British singer Des'ree in 1991. Her 1994 song, *You Gotta Be*, was a global hit.

OUTTAKES

WELCOME TO HOLLYWOOD

(Beyoncé Knowles, Reggie Perry, Shaffer Smith, Shawn Carter/3'18)

Musicians: Beyoncé Knowles: vocals, backing vocals / **Recording:** Sony Music Studios, New York: 2006 / **Technical team:** Producer: Syience / **Executive producer:** Shawn Carter / **Recording engineer:** Gimel "Young Guru" Keaton / **Assistant recording engineer:** Jason Agel / ***B'Day Deluxe Edition* (album):** Released in the USA by Sony Urban Music/Columbia: 3 April 2007 (CD ref.: 82876 89492 2)

A pared-down version of most of the pieces rapped by her boyfriend Jay-Z, Beyoncé's reinterpretation of his *Hollywood* showcases her vocal lines, but offers nothing new compared to the vitriolic description of Los Angeles that the star rapper, who also went by the name Hova, had originally recorded.

FLAWS AND ALL

(Beyoncé Knowles, Shaffer Smith, Shea Taylor, Solange Knowles/4'10)

Musicians: Beyoncé Knowles: vocals / **Recording:** Roc The Mic, New York: 2006, 2007 / **Technical team:** Producers: Beyoncé Knowles, Shea Taylor, Ne-Yo / **Recording engineers:** Jim Caruana, Michael Tocci, Robert "LB" Dorsey, Shane Woodley, Colin Miller / ***B'Day Japanese Deluxe Edition* (album):** Released in the USA by Columbia: 4 April 2007 (CD ref.: SICP 1389~90)

Under contract to Def Jam, the legendary hip-hop label founded by Rick Rubin in 1984, the rapper Ne-Yo was working on writing his first album in 2006. Alongside his own recordings, he also composed for other artists, including Britney Spears, for whom he was asked to quickly write a few song suggestions. When he played the instrumental part of *Flaws and All*—which he and his associate Shea Taylor had just finished for Spears—to Tyran "Ty Ty" Smith, a close associate and friend of Jay-Z, the former's reaction was decisive. A few days after taking a copy of *Flaws and All* to Beyoncé so she could listen to it, Ty Ty asked Ne-Yo specifically not to suggest it to Britney Spears—for Beyoncé had wanted to save the song for herself. The same went for *Question Existing*, which had been written for Spears but was finally offered to Rihanna for her album *Good Girl Gone Bad* (2007). The lyrics of *Flaws and All*, written by Beyoncé and her sister Solange, are a genuine declaration of the singer's love for Jay-Z, in which she apologizes for sometimes neglecting him and thanks him for loving her for who she is, with her good qualities and her faults. The clip, made by the singer and Cliff Watts, emphasized Beyoncé's natural side. It was shot in Super 8 format and without makeup, for Beyoncé wanted to reveal herself as never before, echoing the poses of three of her idols: Marilyn Monroe, Brigitte Bardot, and Barbra Streisand. "The whole time it's like a silent movie and I'm being myself," she said. "It's not performing. I reveal a side of myself no one's ever seen. I'm silly and goofy and not…trying to be a diva, or trying to be a star—just me."[147]

STILL IN LOVE (KISSING YOU)

(Beyoncé Knowles, Des'ree Weekes, Timothy Atack/4'36)

Musicians: Beyoncé Knowles: vocals / **Recording:** Roc The Mic, New York: 2006, 2007 / **Technical team:** Producers: Beyoncé Knowles, Nellee Hooper / **Recording engineers:** Andy Todd, Jim Abbiss, Shane Woodley / **String arrangements:** Craig Armstrong / ***B'Day Deluxe Edition* (album):** Released in the USA by Sony Urban Music/Columbia: 3 April 2007 (CD ref.: 82876 89492 2)

Collectors, get shopping! Because the very first version of *B'Day Deluxe Edition*—bearing the reference number 82876 89492 2—included a song that was withdrawn from subsequent editions of the record following a legal case in the federal court of the southern district of New York in 2007. Rewind to summer 2006, when Beyoncé was wrapping up the recording of her second solo album. She decided to record one last song during the sessions, a cover of *Kissing You*, which had propelled the singer Des'ree to success when it featured in Baz Luhrmann's movie *Romeo + Juliet* in 1996 and became an instant classic. "I've always loved that song," Beyoncé explained in April 2007. "It gives you this emotion—I don't care who you are, you just feel it. And it meant a lot for me to do this."[145] Emotion, perhaps, but surely also anger, must have been what Des'ree felt on learning that her flagship song was going to be distributed commercially by Beyoncé. Des'ree, who did not appreciate the famous Texan appropriating her hit, nor probably the fact that she had changed the title to *Still in Love (Kissing You)*, immediately took legal action against her through her publisher, Royalty Network. As a result, the cover was withdrawn not only from later editions of *B'Day Deluxe Edition*, but also from the DVD *B'Day Anthology Video Album*, which featured a clip of the song shot by Cliff Watts in Super 8 format. *Still in Love (Kissing You)* does not appear on streaming platforms, having simply disappeared from the album's tracklisting on most official sites.

Rodney "Darkchild" Jerkins in 2008; in 2000 he had been one of the producers on Say My Name.

my own director and do my own production. It's exciting. I always try to find new dancers. I was given an opportunity and I like to give new people opportunity...so I have auditions all across America. It'll be the same type of show: broken down with me singing, big production, and dancers and a band, the whole nine."[156]

BACK UP

(Anesha Birchett, Angela Beyincé, Antea Birchett, Delisha Thomas, Fred Jerkins III, LaShawn Daniels, Beyoncé Knowles, Rodney "Darkchild" Jerkins/3'30)

Musicians: Beyoncé Knowles: vocals / Kenneth Whalum III: saxophone / Keyon Harrold: trumpet / Saunders H. Sermons II: trombone / **Recording:** Sony Music Studios, New York: April 2006 / The Record Plant, Los Angeles: 2006 / **Technical team:** Producers: Beyoncé Knowles, Rodney "Darkchild" Jerkins / Recording engineers: Jeff Villanueva, Colin Miller / **B'Day Circuit City Exclusive Version** (album): Distributed in Circuit City shops by Sony Urban Music/Columbia: 5 September 2006 (CD ref.: 82876 89493 2)

WORLD WIDE WOMAN

(Angela Beyincé, Beyoncé Knowles, LaShawn Daniels, Makeba Riddick, Sean Garrett/3'41)

Musicians: Beyoncé Knowles: vocals / Sean Carrington: guitar / James Cheeks: saxophone / Marcus Strickland: saxophone / Keyon Harrold: trumpet / Marvin Thompson: trombone / **Recording:** Sony Music Studios, New York: April 2006 / The Record Plant, Los Angeles: 2006 / **Technical team:** Producers: Beyoncé Knowles, Rodney "Darkchild" Jerkins / Recording engineer: Jeff Villanueva / **B'Day Japanese Deluxe Edition** (album): Released in the USA by Columbia: 4 April 2007 (CD ref.: SICP 1389~90)

A woman of the world? An international star? These are expressions that perfectly fit Beyoncé, who describes herself here as a "world wide woman"—a play on "world wide web." Produced by Rodney Jerkins, the song featured on the North American version of B'Day Deluxe Edition in April 2007. At exactly that time, Beyoncé's actions matched her words, for it was then that she embarked on her second international tour, thus proving that conquering the world remained one of her favorite pastimes. "I love to tour," she said in December 2006. "I love to perform every night. It's kinda like I get to be

As she was starting the production of B'Day, Beyoncé invited producer Rodney Jerkins to join her at Sony Music Studios in New York. Among other things, she asked him to suggest some instrumental music influenced by the sounds of New Orleans, where incidentally the clip of Déjà Vu would be filmed and the photographs for the album sleeve taken. "We were doing a lot of ideas around that, and the horns," Jerkins explained, "but at the same time, we wanted to give that urban street edge. So we tried to get that combination. That's really where that tune started from, from that inspiration that she gave us."[167] Back Up would not be retained for the album, nor for the deluxe edition a year later; it appeared only on an edition distributed exclusively through Circuit City shops, which specialized in the sale of electronic equipment—something which, understandably, disappointed Jerkins. "That's common in our industry," he admitted, philosophically, "where some songs make the cut, some don't. It's bad when it doesn't make the cut and you don't get in on the project. But in that scenario, we got the first single with Déjà Vu and Jay Z, so it worked out anyways."[167]

Beyoncé promoting Samsung's B'Phone in 2007.

CREOLE

(Beyoncé Knowles, Ed Bland, Makeba Riddick, Rich Harrison/3'52)

Musicians: Beyoncé Knowles: vocals / **Recording:** Sony Music Studios, New York: 2007 / **Technical team:** Producers: Beyoncé Knowles, Rich Harrison / **Executive producers:** Beyoncé Knowles, Mathew Knowles / **Recording engineer:** Jim Caruana / **Assistant recording engineer:** Rob Kinelski / **B'Day Japanese Deluxe Edition (album):** Released in the USA by Columbia: 4 April 2007 (CD ref.: SICP 1389~90)

Of the songs Rich Harrison produced for *B'Day*, some, such as *Suga Mama* and *Freakum Dress*, passed the test for selection, whereas Beyoncé, who was the producer on the sessions, left others on the shelf. This is what happened with *Creole*, which is built around a sample of *Skunk Juice* by The Pazant Brothers (1968), and references the singer's origins, both in its title and in its Louisiana sound quality—for Beyoncé had asked her producers to come up with instrumental pieces influenced by the music of New Orleans. Rather than featuring on the album, *Creole* was offered to Japanese fans on the exclusive *B'Day Japanese Deluxe Edition*, released in Japan in April 2007. On her tour there, Beyoncé did not forget to thank her admirers, whose devotion had never diminished with the passing years: "I would like to thank all the Japanese fans for all of their support. They have been supporting Destiny's Child and me as a solo artist for nine years now, and every time that I am here I feel so welcome and I feel very grateful that they appreciate what I do."[168]

632-5792

(?/4'28)

Musicians: Beyoncé Knowles: vocals, backing vocals / **Ashley Davis:** vocals, backing vocals / **Kelly Rowland:** vocals, backing vocals / **Recording:** The Record Plant, Sausalito: 1991 / **Technical team:** Producer: Arne Frager / **Executive producer:** Mathew Knowles / **Available on the Samsung Beyoncé Special Edition B'Phone:** 11 October 2007

On 4 November 2007 the South Korean brand Samsung launched a limited version of its SGH-300 mobile phone. Distributed exclusively in Walmart and Sprint stores, it had a name to sweep Beyoncé fans off their feet. "The B'Phone offers an attractive and glamorous update to our music-centric lineup, along with content you can't find anywhere else on a mobile phone," said Peter Skarzynski, senior vice-president at Samsung Telecommunications America.[169] Indeed, thanks to a partnership with the singer, lucky buyers of the B'Phone could enjoy, via an MP3 interface—a widespread audio format in the mid-2000s—an unreleased song by their idol, recorded at the time of Girls Tyme. "When I was ten," Beyoncé explained, "I recorded a song called *632-5792*—a phone number. It's a little embarrassing but it's cute. There's a recording of that song on the phone exclusively for my fans. I wanted to make sure people got a feel for who I really am. It's only through this phone that you can get this close to my life."[170] The song reappeared in 2019 on the compilation *Destiny's Child: The Untold Story Presents Girls Tyme*, which Mathew Knowles released and which brought together all the songs recorded by Girls Tyme during the 1991 sessions at The Record Plant.

BEYONCÉ: ALL THE SONGS

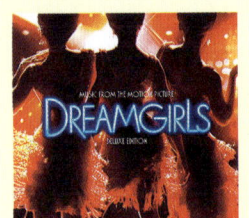

Music from the Motion Picture Dreamgirls—Deluxe Edition
(compilation)
Released in the USA by Sony Urban Music/Columbia/Music World
Music: 5 December 2006 (CD ref.: 88697 02012 2)

NB: The version of *Music from the Motion Picture Dreamgirls* described here is the *Deluxe Edition* version.

Jennifer Hudson, Beyoncé Knowles, and Anika Noni Rose, three dreamgirls inspired by The Supremes.

Dreamgirls (2006)

1. I'm Lookin' for Something
2. Goin' Downtown
3. Takin' the Long Way Home
4. Move*
5. Fake Your Way to the Top*
6. Big (jazz instrumental)
7. Cadillac Car*
8. Steppin' to the Bad Side*
9. Love You I Do
10. I Want You Baby*
11. Family*
12. Dreamgirls*
13. Heavy*
14. It's All Over*
15. And I Am Telling You I'm Not Going
16. I'm Somebody*
17. When I First Saw You
18. Patience
19. I Am Changing
20. Perfect World
21. I Meant You No Harm/Jimmy's Rap
22. Lorrell Loves Jimmy/Family (reprise)*
23. Step on Over*
24. I Miss You Old Friend
25. Effie, Sing My Song
26. One Night Only
27. One Night Only (disco)*
28. Listen*
29. Hard to Say Goodbye*
30. Dreamgirls (finale)*
31. Curtain Call
32. Family (end title)*
33. When I First Saw You (duet)*
34. One Night Only (dance mix)*
35. And I Am Telling You I'm Not Going (dance mix)
36. Patience (composer demo)

* *Music from the Motion Picture Dreamgirls* features tracks by several artists; only those performed by Beyoncé are discussed here.

CINEMA

PLAYING THE PART OF DIANA ROSS

When she discovered in 2005 that the musical *Dreamgirls*, an early 1980s Broadway hit that traces the career of Diana Ross and The Supremes, was going to be adapted for the big screen, Beyoncé was beside herself. "I've been hearing about *Dreamgirls* since I was 15," she said. "I've never seen it, because I was born the year it was on Broadway, but I've seen the bootleg. I've been hearing about Deena and everything about her, because my choreographer's obsessed with her. And they told me they were doing this movie and I said, 'Oh my God, I have to have this movie.'"[171] Even though Beyoncé had an international reputation and had played movie roles that were well received by the critics, the director, Bill Condon, initially hesitated to give her the key part in the film—that of Deena Jones, loosely based on Diana Ross. "At first they weren't sure if I could play the part," Beyoncé said, "because I haven't done anything like it on film and I knew I could do it, I just never had the chance to do it."[171] Accompanied by a drama teacher, Ivana Chuban, Beyoncé eventually landed the part, and joined a superb cast that included Eddie Murphy, Jamie Foxx, and Danny Glover. Beyoncé shared top billing with Anika Noni Rose, who had just won a Tony Award for her role in the musical *Caroline, or Change* by Tony Kushner and Jeanine Tesori, but also with a former unsuccessful competitor in the TV show *American Idol*, Jennifer Hudson. Although Hudson won universal approval for her part in the movie—overshadowing Beyoncé as a result—the latter considered her participation in *Dreamgirls* one of the most important experiences of her career. "I got the movie and I'm so excited, because I'm finding myself and I get to play a character with range," Beyoncé said shortly before *Dreamgirls'* release. "I'm 15 in the beginning and I grow up to be 36 and in the beginning there's nothing glamorous about Deena and she kind of butterflies into this diva and I have dramatic scenes and emotional scenes and very funny scenes and it's all these colors and I'm so excited because people are gonna get to see me act for the first time."[172]

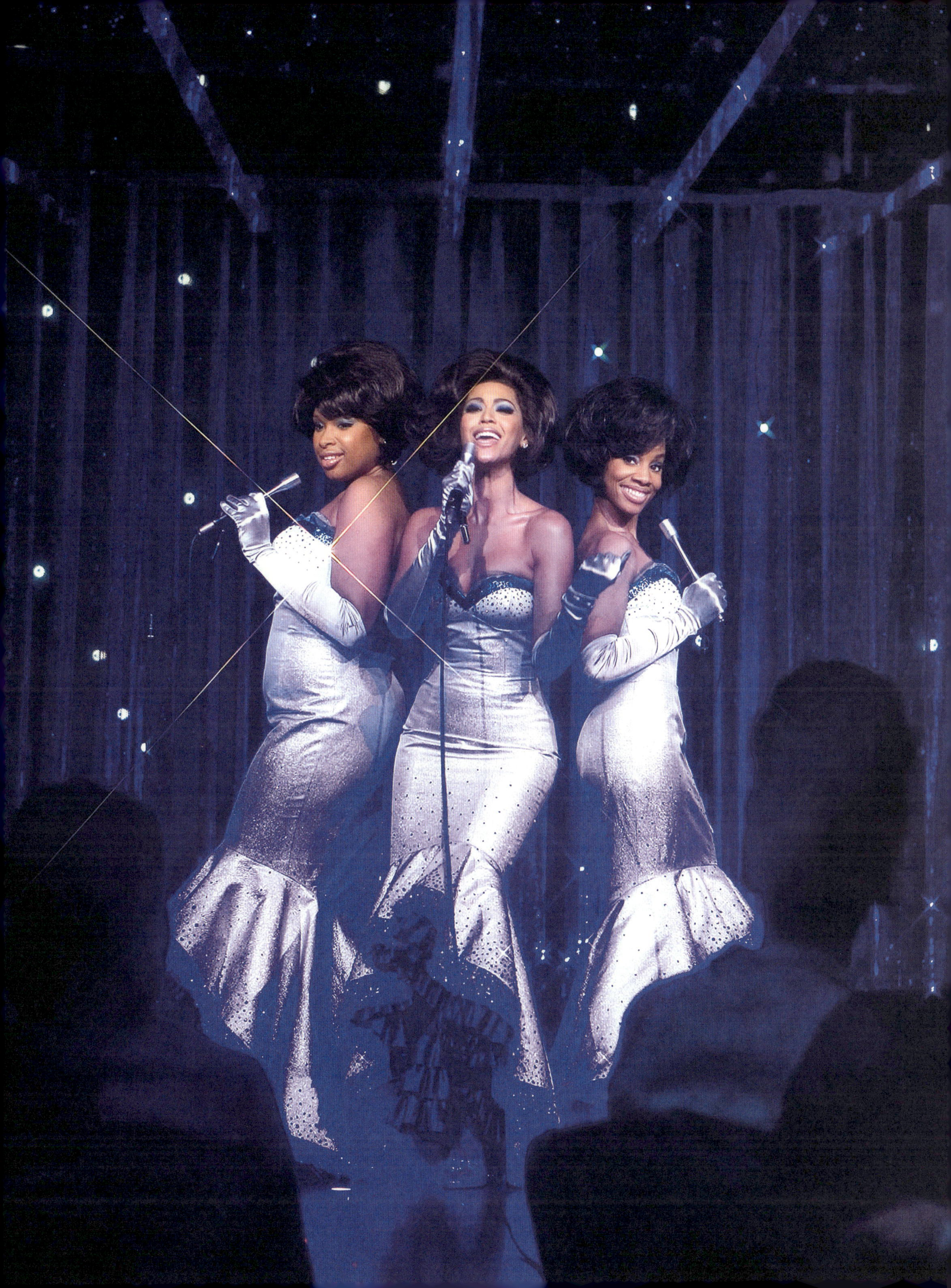

MOVE
(JENNIFER HUDSON, BEYONCÉ KNOWLES, ANIKA NONI ROSE)

(Henry Krieger, Tom Eyen/2'08)

Musicians: Beyoncé Knowles: vocals, backing vocals / Jennifer Hudson: vocals, backing vocals / Anika Noni Rose: vocals, backing vocals / Darrell Crooks, Eric Jackson, Michael Thompson: guitar / Nathan East?, James Johnson?, Harvey Mason Jr?: bass guitar / Glendon Campbell?, Gordon Campbell?, Ricky Lawson?, Harvey Mason Jr?, Anthony Moore?: drums / Harvey Mason Sr: drums, percussion, piano / Randy Spendlove: guitar, piano / John Beasley?, Tim Carmon?, Eric Griggs?, Greg Phillinganes?, Kevin Randolph?: piano / Damon Thomas: piano / Wayne Bergeron, Gary Grant, Jerry Hey: trumpet / Frederick Fiddmont, Daniel Higgins: saxophone / William Reichenbach, Steve Holtman: trombone / **Recording:** The Underlab, Los Angeles: 2004 to 2006 / **Technical team: Producers:** Harvey Mason Jr, Damon Thomas, Randy Spendlove, Matt Sullivan / **Executive producers:** Bill Condon, Mathew Knowles, Glen Brunman / **Recording engineers:** Chris Spilfogel, Dabling Harward / **Assistant recording engineers:** Aaron Renner, Aaron Walk, Bryan Smith, Bryan Walk, Kevin Mills, Paul Smith, Riley Mackin, Sheldon Yellowhair / **Arrangements:** The Underdogs

The soundtrack to *Dreamgirls*, which had been produced by The Underdogs, a duo made up of Harvey Mason Jr and Damon Thomas, was part of a trend during 2006 that had started with the international success of the album *Back to Black* by the British singer Amy Winehouse. It consisted of reproducing to perfection the sound of the 1960s soul artists who were the glory of the Motown label of Detroit. To do this, Mason and Thomas did not skimp on the means used, employing Berry Gordy's entire soul arsenal: brass instruments, impeccable bass guitar and drum rhythms, and three-part vocal harmonies. Used in a scene in which The Dreamettes take part in a musical talent contest, *Move* has all the features of the hits formerly sung by The Supremes, when they still called themselves The Primettes. Mason and Thomas, who were accustomed to making hits, here produced their first movie soundtrack. "We knew we wanted to do films," Thomas explained. "But we wanted to wait for a great opportunity."[173]

FAKE YOUR WAY TO THE TOP
(EDDIE MURPHY, ANIKA NONI ROSE, JENNIFER HUDSON, BEYONCÉ KNOWLES)

(Henry Krieger, Tom Eyen/3'54)

Musicians: Eddie Murphy: vocals / Beyoncé Knowles: backing vocals / Jennifer Hudson: backing vocals / Anika Noni Rose: backing vocals / Darrell Crooks, Eric Jackson, Michael Thompson: guitar / Nathan East?, James Johnson?, Harvey Mason Jr?: bass guitar / Glendon Campbell?, Gordon Campbell?, Ricky Lawson?, Harvey Mason Jr?, Anthony Moore?: drums / Harvey Mason Sr?: drums, percussion, piano / Randy Spendlove?: guitar, piano / John Beasley?, Tim Carmon?, Eric Griggs?, Greg Phillinganes?, Kevin Randolph?: piano / Damon Thomas?: piano, Hammond organ / Wayne Bergeron, Gary Grant, Jerry Hey: trumpet / Frederick Fiddmont, Daniel Higgins: saxophone / **Recording:** The Underlab, Los Angeles: 2004 to 2006 / **Technical team: Producers:** Harvey Mason Jr., Damon Thomas, Randy Spendlove, Matt Sullivan / **Executive producers:** Bill Condon, Mathew Knowles, Glen Brunman / **Recording engineers:** Chris Spilfogel, Dabling Harward / **Assistant recording engineers:** Aaron Renner, Aaron Walk, Bryan Smith, Bryan Walk, Kevin Mills, Paul Smith, Riley Mackin, Sheldon Yellowhair / **Arrangements:** The Underdogs

There is something of Otis Redding and Wilson Pickett in this astonishing interpretation of *Fake Your Way to the Top* by the legendary Eddie Murphy, in the role James "Thunder" Early. Accompanied by his backing vocalists, Deena Jones, Effie White, and Lorrell Robinson—played by Beyoncé, Jennifer Hudson, and Anika Noni Rose—Murphy here makes his big comeback to film, displaying all his skill as an actor, singer, and dancer. It is great art, and a renewed pleasure to see the actor who had previously played the legendary Axel Foley, the nonchalant police inspector in *Beverly Hills Cop*. Murphy later returned to his cult character with the fourth movie in the series, released in 2024.

CADILLAC CAR
(EDDIE MURPHY, ANIKA NONI ROSE, JENNIFER HUDSON, BEYONCÉ KNOWLES, RORY O'MALLEY, LAURA BELL BUNDY, ANNE WARREN)

(Henry Krieger, Tom Eyen/2'22)

Musicians: Eddie Murphy: vocals / Beyoncé Knowles: backing vocals / Jennifer Hudson: backing vocals / Anika Noni Rose: backing vocals / Rory O'Malley: backing vocals / Laura Bell Bundy: backing vocals / Anne Warren: backing vocals / Darrell Crooks, Eric Jackson, Michael Thompson: guitar / Nathan East?, James Johnson?, Harvey Mason Jr?: bass guitar / Glendon Campbell?, Gordon Campbell?, Ricky Lawson?, Harvey Mason Jr?, Anthony Moore?: drums / Harvey Mason Sr: drums, percussion, piano / Randy Spendlove: guitar, piano / John Beasley?, Tim Carmon?, Eric Griggs?, Greg Phillinganes?, Kevin Randolph?: piano / Damon Thomas: piano / Wayne Bergeron, Gary Grant, Jerry Hey: trumpet / Frederick Fiddmont, Daniel Higgins: saxophone / **Recording:** The Underlab, Los Angeles: 2004 to 2006 / **Technical team: Producers:** Harvey Mason Jr, Damon Thomas, Randy Spendlove, Matt Sullivan / **Executive producers:** Bill Condon, Mathew Knowles, Glen Brunman / **Recording engineers:** Chris Spilfogel, Dabling Harward / **Assistant recording engineers:** Aaron Renner, Aaron Walk, Bryan Smith, Bryan Walk, Kevin Mills, Paul Smith, Riley Mackin, Sheldon Yellowhair / **Arrangements:** The Underdogs

As in some other movies set in 1960s America, discrimination against African Americans is an underlying theme. Although the Motown groups were for the most part enormously successful in the United States, it took a long time to establish in the public's mind a kind of music championed by a community that had suffered decades of segregation. The sequence in the film accompanied by this explosive song is the perfect illustration of this, as Eddie Murphy explained when talking about his character. *"Cadillac Car* is a song that he writes and thinks can be a big hit. We record it at his car dealership and it becomes a hit. But just before it breaks out to become a really big record, a white group cuts the song, and turns it into a bubble gum pop hit, and ours falls off the charts. Then we start playing dirty."[174]

STEPPIN' TO THE BAD SIDE
(JAMIE FOXX, KEITH ROBINSON, HINTON BATTLE, EDDIE MURPHY, ANIKA NONI ROSE, JENNIFER HUDSON, BEYONCÉ KNOWLES)

(Henry Krieger, Tom Eyen/4'55)

Musicians: Jamie Foxx: vocals / Eddie Murphy: vocals / Keith Robinson: vocals / Hinton Battle: vocals / Beyoncé Knowles: vocals / Jennifer Hudson: vocals / Anika Noni Rose: vocals / Darrell Crooks, Eric Jackson, Michael Thompson: guitar / Nathan East?, James Johnson?, Harvey Mason Jr?: bass guitar / Glendon Campbell?, Gordon Campbell?, Ricky Lawson?, Harvey Mason Jr?, Anthony Moore?: drums / Harvey Mason Sr: drums, percussion, piano / Randy Spendlove: guitar, piano / John Beasley?, Tim Carmon?, Eric Griggs?, Greg Phillinganes?, Kevin Randolph?: piano / Damon Thomas: piano / Wayne Bergeron, Gary Grant, Jerry Hey: trumpet / Frederick Fiddmont, Daniel Higgins: saxophone / **Recording:** The Underlab, Los Angeles: 2004 to 2006 / **Technical team: Producers:** Harvey Mason Jr, Damon Thomas, Randy Spendlove, Matt Sullivan / **Executive producers:** Bill Condon, Mathew Knowles, Glen Brunman / **Recording engineers:** Chris Spilfogel, Dabling Harward / **Assistant recording engineers:** Aaron Renner, Aaron Walk, Bryan Smith, Bryan Walk, Kevin Mills, Paul Smith, Riley Mackin, Sheldon Yellowhair / **Arrangements:** The Underdogs

Following the success of Taylor Hackford's 2004 movie *Ray*, in which Jamie Foxx played a Ray Charles character more authentic than the original, the actor easily secured a place in the cast of *Dreamgirls*, playing Curtis Taylor Jr, a manipulative manager whose only goal is to grow his personal fortune. As he had done with *Ray*, Foxx sang on the soundtrack of *Dreamgirls*, sharing the microphone with Eddie Murphy. Although his character recalled Berry Gordy, the founder of Motown, Foxx denied that the latter had any influence on the role he was playing. "It's not about Berry Gordy at all, this character is made up of different music people that I've met in the industry in the past three years. Berry Gordy did something that nobody pointed out. Berry Gordy said, if we're gonna get this black music into the white world, we're going to have to do it in an eloquent way. So we're gonna have etiquette class, we're gonna teach you how to conduct an interview, we're going to teach you how to dance—so they did a lot of things in forming those artists, and Berry had to have endearing qualities about him, or else he wouldn't have lasted as long as he did, especially at that time."[175]

BEYONCÉ: ALL THE SONGS   245

I WANT YOU BABY
(EDDIE MURPHY, ANIKA NONI ROSE, JENNIFER HUDSON, BEYONCÉ KNOWLES)

(Henry Krieger, Tom Eyen/2'53)

Musicians: Eddie Murphy: vocals / Beyoncé Knowles: backing vocals / Jennifer Hudson: backing vocals / Anika Noni Rose: backing vocals / Darrell Crooks, Eric Jackson, Michael Thompson: guitar / Nathan East?, James Johnson?, Harvey Mason Jr?: bass guitar / Glendon Campbell?, Gordon Campbell?, Ricky Lawson?, Harvey Mason Jr?, Anthony Moore?: drums / Harvey Mason Sr: drums, percussion, piano / Randy Spendlove: guitar, piano / John Beasley?, Tim Carmon?, Eric Griggs?, Greg Phillinganes?, Kevin Randolph?: piano / Damon Thomas: piano / Wayne Bergeron, Gary Grant, Jerry Hey: trumpet / Frederick Fiddmont, Daniel Higgins: saxophone / Gayle Levant: harp / Orchestra / **Recording:** The Underlab, Los Angeles: 2004 to 2006 / Capitol Studios, Los Angeles: 2005 to 2006 (strings) / Henson Recording Studios, Los Angeles: 2005 to 2006 (strings) / The Record Plant, Los Angeles: 2005 to 2006 (strings) / **Technical team:** Producers: Harvey Mason Jr, Damon Thomas, Randy Spendlove, Matt Sullivan / Executive producers: Bill Condon, Mathew Knowles, Glen Brunman / Recording engineers: Chris Spilfogel, Dabling Harward, Jess Sutcliffe, Scott Campbell, Troy Halderson / Assistant recording engineers: Aaron Renner, Aaron Walk, Bryan Smith, Bryan Walk, Kevin Mills, Paul Smith, Riley Mackin, Sheldon Yellowhair / **Arrangements:** The Underdogs

Motown did not produce only cheerful, rousing hits, such as The Marvelettes' *Please Mr. Postman* (1961), The Supremes' *Baby Love* (1964), and Marvin Gaye's *How Sweet It Is (To Be Loved by You)* (1964). As *I Want You Baby* revealed, the musical world of Berry Gordy's label was imbued with an artful mix of emotions, and the ballads produced non-stop in Hitsville U.S.A., Gordy's headquarters, frequently expressed the feeling of love in all its forms. Naturally, when James Early and The Dreamettes performed the languorous *I Want You Baby* before a mostly white audience who laughed at racist jokes by the warm-up act but took offense at the sensuality emanating from the character played brilliantly by Eddie Murphy, the songs that came to mind were *The Tracks of My Tears*, sung by Smokey Robinson and The Miracles in 1965, the inevitable *What Becomes of the Brokenhearted* by Jimmy Ruffin (1966), and *Just My Imagination (Running Away with Me)* by The Temptations (1971). That was one of the main virtues of *Dreamgirls*: it succeeded in conveying the resplendent destiny of a label that championed the African-American community at a time when discrimination and hatred of anything "other" were deeply rooted.

FAMILY
(JAMIE FOXX, JENNIFER HUDSON, BEYONCÉ KNOWLES, KEITH ROBINSON, ANIKA NONI ROSE)

(Henry Krieger, Tom Eyen/3'22)

Musicians: Keith Robinson: vocals, spoken voice / Jennifer Hudson: vocals, backing vocals / Beyoncé Knowles: backing vocals / Anika Noni Rose: backing vocals / Jamie Foxx: spoken voice / Darrell Crooks, Eric Jackson, Michael Thompson: guitar / Nathan East?, James Johnson?, Harvey Mason Jr?: bass guitar / Glendon Campbell?, Gordon Campbell?, Ricky Lawson?, Harvey Mason Jr?, Anthony Moore?: drums / Harvey Mason Sr: drums, percussion, piano / Randy Spendlove: guitar, piano / John Beasley?, Tim Carmon?, Eric Griggs?, Greg Phillinganes?, Kevin Randolph?: piano / Damon Thomas: piano / Gayle Levant: harp / Orchestra / Choir / **Recording:** The Underlab, Los Angeles: 2004 to 2006 / Capitol Studios, Los Angeles: 2005 to 2006 (strings) / Henson Recording Studios, Los Angeles: 2005 to 2006 (strings) / The Record Plant, Los Angeles: 2005 to 2006 (strings) / **Technical team:** Producers: Harvey Mason Jr, Damon Thomas, Randy Spendlove, Matt Sullivan / Executive producers: Bill Condon, Mathew Knowles, Glen Brunman / Recording engineers: Chris Spilfogel, Dabling Harward, Jess Sutcliffe, Scott Campbell, Troy Halderson / Assistant recording engineers: Aaron Renner, Aaron Walk, Bryan Smith, Bryan Walk, Kevin Mills, Paul Smith, Riley Mackin, Sheldon Yellowhair / **Arrangements:** The Underdogs

Beyoncé and Anika Noni Rose are only backing singers in this song, performed as a duet by Keith Robinson and Jennifer Hudson. Robinson described the bond between him and his partner, both young actors on the point of becoming stars: "I think that both of us being new, that gave us some kinship and a basic camaraderie that we innately knew each other before we got here. I think we both represented the young artist who was getting a shot at [stardom] being around all these heavyweights and making their mark. It felt like we were really like brother and sister. We became really close and I'm just really proud of her. I have done a lot of TV and film, but for her and it being her first time, she really had an innate sensibility."[176]

Actors Keith Robinson and Jennifer Hudson filming *Dreamgirls*.

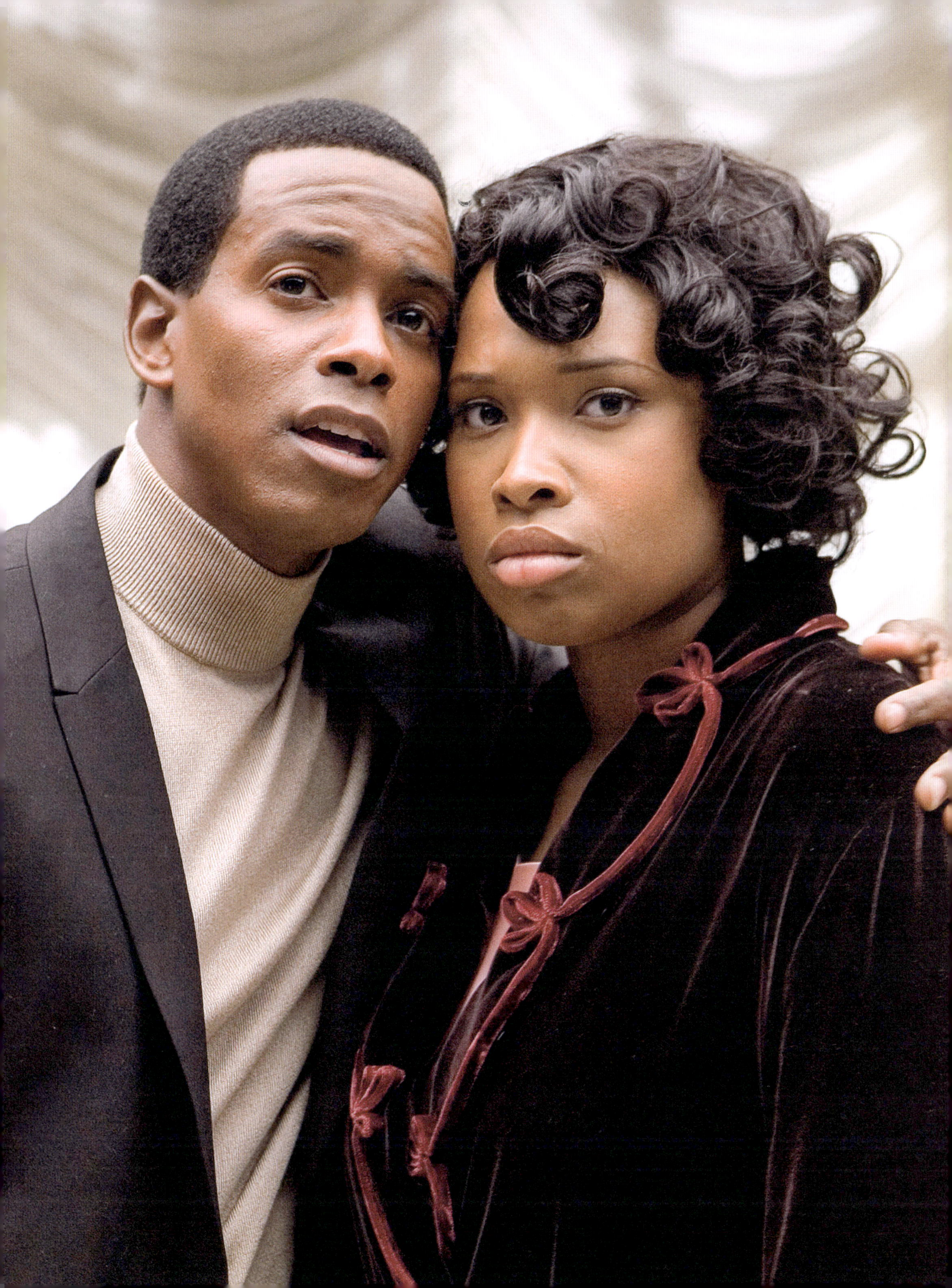

Jamie Foxx plays Curtis Taylor Jr, a character based on Berry Gordy, founder of the Motown label.

DREAMGIRLS
(BEYONCÉ KNOWLES, JENNIFER HUDSON, ANIKA NONI ROSE)

(Henry Krieger, Tom Eyen/3'20)

Musicians: Beyoncé Knowles: vocals / Jennifer Hudson: vocals, backing vocals / Anika Noni Rose: vocals, backing vocals / Darrell Crooks, Eric Jackson, Michael Thompson: guitar / Nathan East?, James Johnson?, Harvey Mason Jr?: bass guitar / Glendon Campbell?, Gordon Campbell?, Ricky Lawson?, Harvey Mason Jr?, Anthony Moore?: drums / Harvey Mason Sr: drums, percussion, piano / Randy Spendlove: guitar, piano / John Beasley?, Tim Carmon?, Eric Griggs?, Greg Phillinganes?, Kevin Randolph?: piano / Damon Thomas: piano / Wayne Bergeron, Gary Grant, Jerry Hey: trumpet / Frederick Fiddmont, Daniel Higgins: saxophone / Orchestra / Choir / **Recording:** The Underlab, Los Angeles: 2004 to 2006 / Capitol Studios, Los Angeles: 2005 to 2006 (strings) / Henson Recording Studios, Los Angeles: 2005 to 2006 (strings) / The Record Plant, Los Angeles: 2005 to 2006 (strings) / **Technical team:** Producers: Harvey Mason Jr, Damon Thomas, Randy Spendlove, Matt Sullivan / **Executive producers:** Bill Condon, Mathew Knowles, Glen Brunman / **Recording engineers:** Chris Spilfogel, Dabling Harward, Jess Sutcliffe, Scott Campbell, Troy Halderson / **Assistant recording engineers:** Aaron Renner, Aaron Walk, Bryan Smith, Bryan Walk, Kevin Mills, Paul Smith, Riley Mackin, Sheldon Yellowhair / **Arrangements:** The Underdogs

When the three young women were starting out—as The Dreams, a group of which Deena Jones became the soloist—they performed the movie's title song, *Dreamgirls*, in the vein of a hit by The Supremes, shortly before Berry Gordy decided to rename them Diana Ross and The Supremes in 1967. It is this highlighting of Diana Ross that comes through in this scene, in which Beyoncé imitates to perfection the slightest mannerism of her idol, right down to echoing the star's legendary shoulder movements, following the rhythm while she is singing. Beyoncé had the good fortune to meet Ross at a party organized by Clive Davis, a legendary producer at Columbia, at the 2006 Grammy Awards. "I had pictures of her all over my movie trailer, and there she was, right in front of me. I was terrified. Then she tapped me on the shoulder and told me she was happy I was doing *Dreamgirls*. I thought I would pass out."[177]

HEAVY
(JENNIFER HUDSON, BEYONCÉ KNOWLES, ANIKA NONI ROSE)

(Henry Krieger, Tom Eyen/1'33)

Musicians: Beyoncé Knowles: vocals, backing vocals / Jennifer Hudson: backing vocals / Anika Noni Rose: backing vocals / Darrell Crooks, Eric Jackson, Michael Thompson: guitar / Nathan East?, James Johnson?, Harvey Mason Jr?: bass guitar / Glendon Campbell?, Gordon Campbell?, Ricky Lawson?, Harvey Mason Jr?, Anthony Moore?: drums / Harvey Mason Sr: drums, percussion, piano / Randy Spendlove: guitar, piano / John Beasley?, Tim Carmon?, Eric Griggs?, Greg Phillinganes?, Kevin Randolph?: piano / Damon Thomas: piano / Wayne Bergeron, Gary Grant, Jerry Hey: trumpet / Frederick Fiddmont, Daniel Higgins: saxophone / **Recording:** The Underlab, Los Angeles: 2004 to 2006 / **Technical team:** Producers: Harvey Mason Jr, Damon Thomas, Randy Spendlove, Matt Sullivan / **Executive producers:** Bill Condon, Mathew Knowles, Glen Brunman / **Recording engineers:** Chris Spilfogel, Dabling Harward / **Assistant recording engineers:** Aaron Renner, Aaron Walk, Bryan Smith, Bryan Walk, Kevin Mills, Paul Smith, Riley Mackin, Sheldon Yellowhair / **Arrangements:** The Underdogs

The sequence in which The Dreams record *Heavy* reveals the growing rivalry between Effie White and Deena Jones. Like a story within a story in the movie, the scene reproduces, in part, the very real competition between Jennifer Hudson and Beyoncé during the film's shooting and promotion. In fact, even though Beyoncé was an international star in 2006, the press only had eyes for Hudson, whose performance was considered outstanding, and who had the good fortune to perform the most famous song in *Dreamgirls*: *And I Am Telling You I'm Not Going,* formerly sung by Jennifer Holliday, who first played Effie White on Broadway. "It's really unfortunate that everyone is saying I'm jealous of Jennifer," Beyoncé declared in 2006. "It hurts my heart because it's so clichéd. [...] Because I'm a star they just automatically assume that I'm not humble enough to sit down and take a back seat, which I am. I knew that the character that I played wasn't the star. Deena wasn't the underdog. She didn't have the struggle and the pain and the dramatic scenes that Effie had, and I was fine with that. I'm already a star. I already have nine Grammys. Everyone knows I can sing. I did this because I wanted people to know that I can act and I can play someone so different from myself."[178]

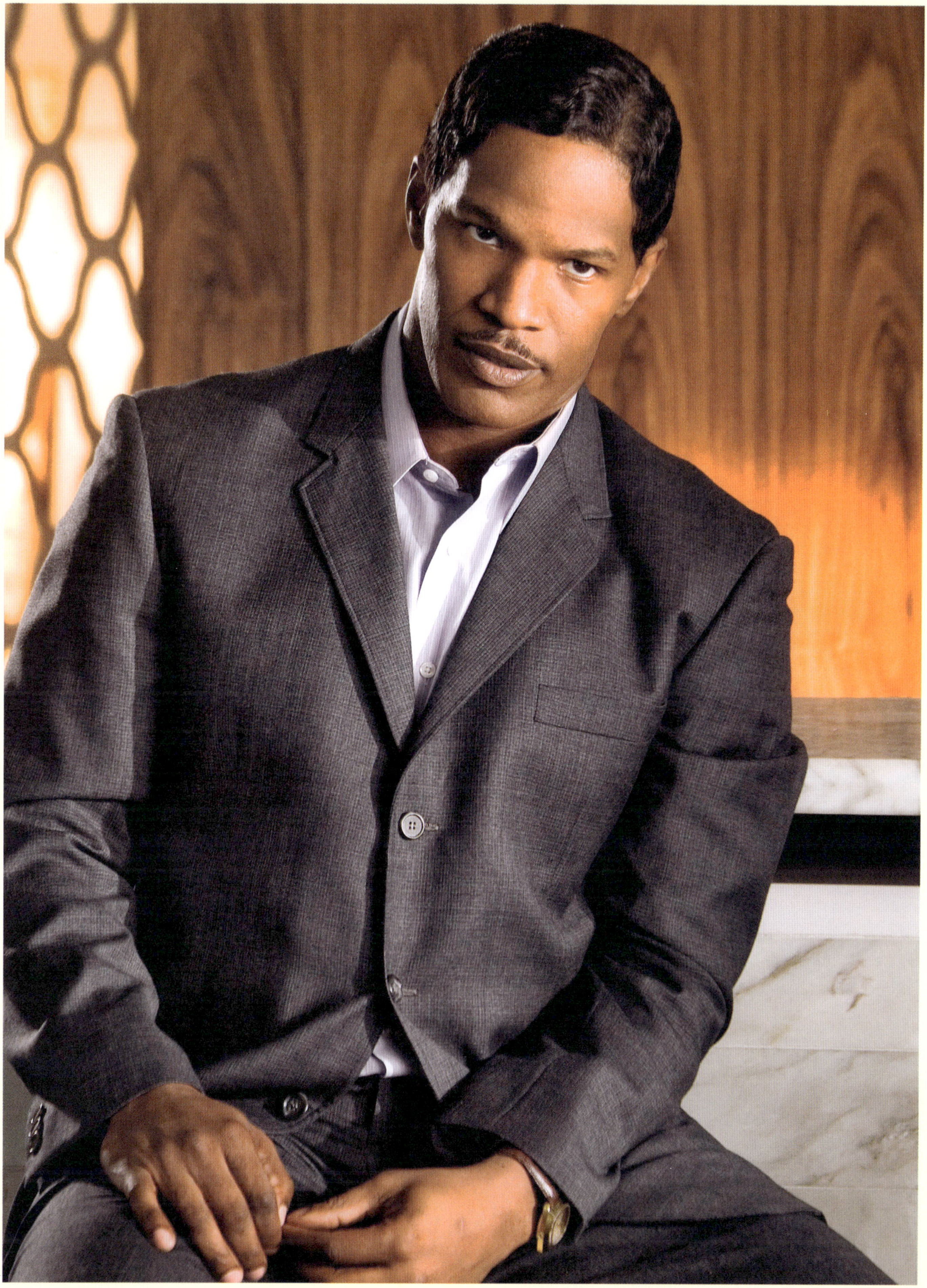

Beyoncé portraying a highly believable Diana Ross.

IT'S ALL OVER
(JENNIFER HUDSON, JAMIE FOXX, BEYONCÉ KNOWLES, ANIKA NONI ROSE, KEITH ROBINSON, SHARON LEAL)

(Henry Krieger, Tom Eyen/3'41)

Musicians: Beyoncé Knowles: spoken voice, vocals, backing vocals / Jennifer Hudson: spoken voice, vocals, backing vocals / Anika Noni Rose: spoken voice, vocals, backing vocals / Sharon Leal: spoken voice, vocals, backing vocals / Jamie Foxx: spoken voice, vocals, backing vocals / Keith Robinson: spoken voice, vocals, backing vocals / Darrell Crooks, Eric Jackson, Michael Thompson: guitar / Nathan East?, James Johnson?, Harvey Mason Jr?: bass guitar / Glendon Campbell?, Gordon Campbell?, Ricky Lawson?, Harvey Mason Jr?, Anthony Moore?: drums / Harvey Mason Sr: drums, percussion, piano / Randy Spendlove: guitar, piano / John Beasley?, Tim Carmon?, Eric Griggs?, Greg Phillinganes?, Kevin Randolph?: piano / Damon Thomas: piano / Wayne Bergeron, Gary Grant, Jerry Hey: trumpet / Frederick Fiddmont, Daniel Higgins: saxophone / Orchestra / **Recording:** The Underlab, Los Angeles: 2004 to 2006 / Capitol Studios, Los Angeles: 2005 to 2006 (strings) / Henson Recording Studios, Los Angeles: 2005 to 2006 (strings) / The Record Plant, Los Angeles: 2005 to 2006 (strings) / **Technical team:** Producers: Harvey Mason Jr, Damon Thomas, Randy Spendlove, Matt Sullivan / **Executive producers:** Bill Condon, Mathew Knowles, Glen Brunman / **Recording engineers:** Chris Spilfogel, Dabling Harward, Jess Sutcliffe, Scott Campbell, Troy Halderson / **Assistant recording engineers:** Aaron Renner, Aaron Walk, Bryan Smith, Bryan Walk, Kevin Mills, Paul Smith, Riley Mackin, Sheldon Yellowhair / **Arrangements:** The Underdogs

It's All Over is without a doubt one of the high points of *Dreamgirls*. Over the most soul—even very funk—instrumental accompaniment, emotions become heated and scores are settled in a verbal sparring match between the movie's key characters. The rift between Effie White and her colleagues is now confirmed, and each person raises their voice to make their arguments in this formidable dogfight. This is where the viewer is introduced to Effie's replacement, Michelle Morris, played by the talented Sharon Leal. "*Dreamgirls* was my first big movie," Leal said in 2021. "That was probably the biggest highlight of my career, because that just seemed like such a long shot. I hadn't done feature film before, and all of a sudden I was working alongside some of the industry's biggest names. I kind of felt like a silent, stalker fan on the set."[179]

I'M SOMEBODY
(BEYONCÉ KNOWLES, SHARON LEAL, ANIKA NONI ROSE)

(Henry Krieger, Tom Eyen/1'29)

Musicians: Beyoncé Knowles: vocals, backing vocals / Sharon Leal: backing vocals / Anika Noni Rose: backing vocals / Darrell Crooks, Eric Jackson, Michael Thompson: guitar / Nathan East?, James Johnson?, Harvey Mason Jr?: bass guitar / Glendon Campbell?, Gordon Campbell?, Ricky Lawson?, Harvey Mason Jr?, Anthony Moore?: drums / Harvey Mason Sr: drums, percussion, piano / Randy Spendlove: guitar, piano / John Beasley?, Tim Carmon?, Eric Griggs?, Greg Phillinganes?, Kevin Randolph?: piano / Damon Thomas: piano / Wayne Bergeron, Gary Grant, Jerry Hey: trumpet / Frederick Fiddmont, Daniel Higgins: saxophone / Orchestra / **Recording** / The Underlab, Los Angeles: 2004 to 2006 / Capitol Studios, Los Angeles: 2005 to 2006 (strings) / Henson Recording Studios, Los Angeles: 2005 to 2006 (strings) / The Record Plant, Los Angeles: 2005 to 2006 (strings) / **Technical team:** Producers: Harvey Mason Jr, Damon Thomas, Randy Spendlove, Matt Sullivan / **Executive producers:** Bill Condon, Mathew Knowles, Glen Brunman / **Recording engineers:** Chris Spilfogel, Dabling Harward, Jess Sutcliffe, Scott Campbell, Troy Halderson / **Assistant recording engineers:** Aaron Renner, Aaron Walk, Bryan Smith, Bryan Walk, Kevin Mills, Paul Smith, Riley Mackin, Sheldon Yellowhair / **Arrangements:** The Underdogs

Performed by Deena Jones and The Dreams in the movie, *I'm Somebody* has an important place in the plot because it reveals the singer's new, more disco, side. Diana Ross's musical change of direction during the 1970s was indeed remarkable, for she managed to go from queen of soul to disco icon, making albums as beloved as *The Boss*, produced by Nickolas Ashford and Valerie Simpson in 1979, and, above all, *Diana*, made by the masters of disco Nile Rodgers and Bernard Edwards in 1980 and featuring numerous hits, including the unforgettable *Upside Down*.

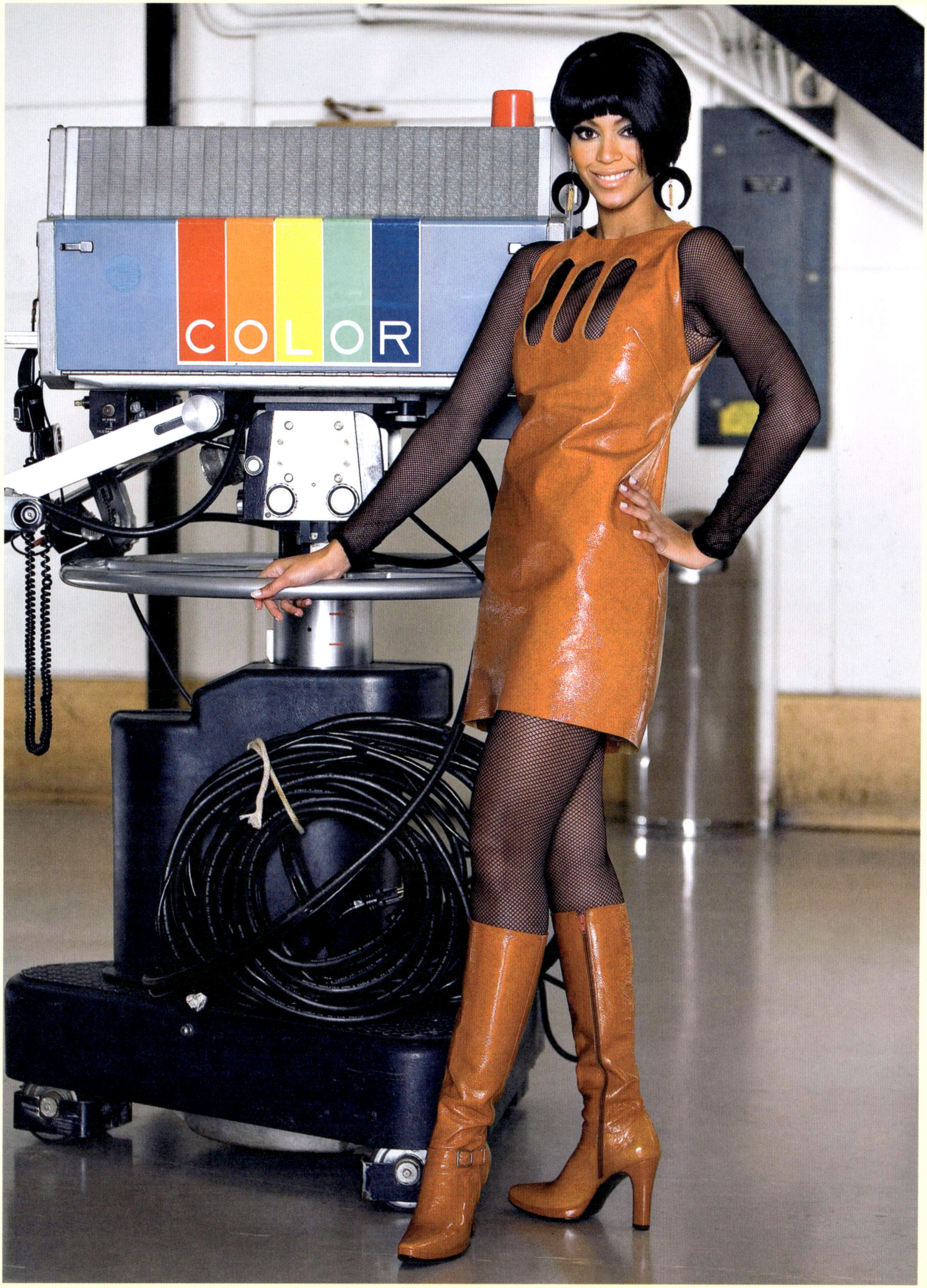
COLOR

Superstar Diana Ross in 1975, before her transition to disco.

STEP ON OVER
(BEYONCÉ KNOWLES, SHARON LEAL, ANIKA NONI ROSE)

(Henry Krieger, Tom Eyen/0'23)

Musicians: Beyoncé Knowles: vocals, backing vocals / **Sharon Leal:** backing vocals / **Anika Noni Rose:** backing vocals / **Darrell Crooks, Eric Jackson, Michael Thompson:** guitar / **Nathan East?, James Johnson?, Harvey Mason Jr?:** bass guitar / **Glendon Campbell?, Gordon Campbell?, Ricky Lawson?, Harvey Mason Jr?, Anthony Moore?:** drums / **Harvey Mason Sr:** drums, percussion, piano / **Randy Spendlove:** guitar, piano / **John Beasley?, Tim Carmon?, Eric Griggs?, Greg Phillinganes?, Kevin Randolph?:** piano / **Damon Thomas:** piano / **Orchestra** / **Recording** / The Underlab, Los Angeles: 2004 to 2006 / Capitol Studios, Los Angeles: 2005 to 2006 (strings) / Henson Recording Studios, Los Angeles: 2005 to 2006 (strings) / The Record Plant, Los Angeles: 2005 to 2006 (strings) / **Technical team:** Producers: Harvey Mason Jr, Damon Thomas, Randy Spendlove, Matt Sullivan / **Executive producers:** Bill Condon, Mathew Knowles, Glen Brunman / **Recording engineers:** Chris Spilfogel, Dabling Harward, Jess Sutcliffe, Scott Campbell, Troy Halderson / **Assistant recording engineers:** Aaron Renner, Aaron Walk, Bryan Smith, Bryan Walk, Kevin Mills, Paul Smith, Riley Mackin, Sheldon Yellowhair / **Arrangements:** The Underdogs

Accompanied by the thunderous rhythm of a guitar with a wah-wah pedal, Deena Jones and The Dreams reveal the trio's new sound, more incisive than ever. The reference to one of the most famous wah-wah passages in the history of cinema—that of *Theme from Shaft*, written and sung by Isaac Hayes in 1971 for the Gordon Parks-directed movie *Shaft*—is impossible to miss, and the truth is plain to see (and hear): Deena Jones is taking full ownership of her transition to a more disco style, abandoning the soul of her beginnings.

ONE NIGHT ONLY (DISCO)
(BEYONCÉ KNOWLES, ANIKA NONI ROSE, SHARON LEAL)

(Henry Krieger, Tom Eyen/3'10)

Musicians: Beyoncé Knowles: vocals, backing vocals / **Sharon Leal:** backing vocals / **Anika Noni Rose:** backing vocals / **Darrell Crooks, Eric Jackson, Michael Thompson:** guitar / **Nathan East?, James Johnson?, Harvey Mason Jr?:** bass guitar / **Glendon Campbell?, Gordon Campbell?, Ricky Lawson?, Harvey Mason Jr?, Anthony Moore?:** drums / **Harvey Mason Sr:** drums, percussion, piano / **Randy Spendlove:** guitar, piano / **John Beasley?, Tim Carmon?, Eric Griggs?, Greg Phillinganes?, Kevin Randolph?:** piano / **Damon Thomas:** piano / **Wayne Bergeron, Gary Grant, Jerry Hey:** trumpet / **Frederick Fiddmont, Daniel Higgins:** saxophone / **Orchestra** / **Recording:** The Underlab, Los Angeles: 2004 to 2006 / Capitol Studios, Los Angeles: 2005 to 2006 (strings) / Henson Recording Studios, Los Angeles: 2005 to 2006 (strings) / The Record Plant, Los Angeles: 2005 to 2006 (strings) / **Technical team:** Producers: Harvey Mason Jr, Damon Thomas, Randy Spendlove, Matt Sullivan / **Executive producers:** Bill Condon, Mathew Knowles, Glen Brunman / **Recording engineers:** Chris Spilfogel, Dabling Harward, Jess Sutcliffe, Scott Campbell, Troy Halderson / **Assistant recording engineers:** Aaron Renner, Aaron Walk, Bryan Smith, Bryan Walk, Kevin Mills, Paul Smith, Riley Mackin, Sheldon Yellowhair / **Arrangements:** The Underdogs

With its crescendo leading the listener from a slow introduction to the point where it takes flight in the most danceable way, the disco version of *One Night Only* is an obvious reference to one of Diana Ross's greatest hits of the 1970s, *Love Hangover*. Produced by Hal Davis in 1975 for the album *Diana Ross*, which was released the following year, *Love Hangover* is the perfect example of the most authentic music of the disco era. A sensual anthem stretching over almost eight minutes, it's ideally suited to the dancefloor, but in no way betrays the fundamentals of disco, which was soon to be decried the world over—namely a devilishly sexy voice, an unforgettable tune, and the use of real instruments, played with mastery and breathtaking precision and feeling.

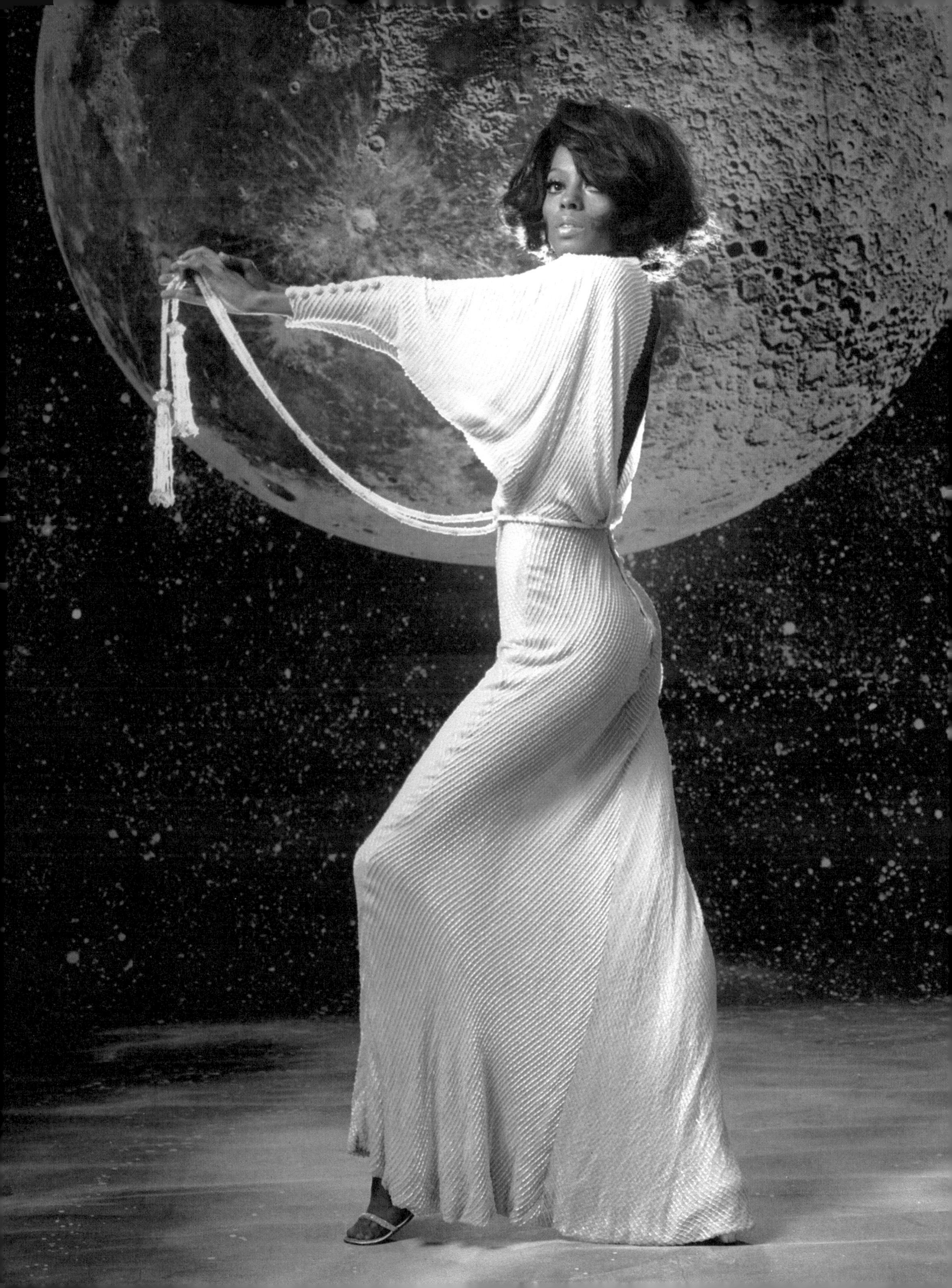

SINGLE

LISTEN

(Scott Cutler, Henry Krieger, Beyoncé Knowles, Anne Preven/3'40)

Musicians: Beyoncé Knowles: vocals, backing vocals / Michael Thompson: electric guitar / James Johnson: bass guitar / Nathan East: bass guitar / Ricky Lawson: drums / Tim Carmon: piano / Harvey Mason Jr: percussion / Darrell Crooks, Eric Jackson, Michael Thompson: guitar / Nathan East?, James Johnson?, Harvey Mason Jr?: bass guitar / Glendon Campbell?, Gordon Campbell?, Ricky Lawson?, Harvey Mason Jr?, Anthony Moore?: drums / Harvey Mason Sr: drums, percussion, piano / Randy Spendlove: guitar, piano / John Beasley?, Tim Carmon?, Eric Griggs?, Greg Phillinganes?, Kevin Randolph?: piano / Damon Thomas: piano / Orchestra / **Recording:** The Underlab, Los Angeles: 2004 to 2006 / Capitol Studios, Los Angeles: 2005 to 2006 (strings) / Henson Recording Studios, Los Angeles: 2005 to 2006 (strings) / The Record Plant, Los Angeles: 2005 to 2006 (strings) / **Technical team:** Producers: Harvey Mason Jr, Damon Thomas, Randy Spendlove, Matt Sullivan / **Executive producers:** Bill Condon, Mathew Knowles, Glen Brunman / **Recording engineers:** Chris Spilfogel, Dabling Harward, Jess Sutcliffe, Scott Campbell, Troy Halderson / **Assistant recording engineers:** Aaron Renner, Aaron Walk, Bryan Smith, Bryan Walk, Kevin Mills, Paul Smith, Riley Mackin, Sheldon Yellowhair / **Arrangements:** The Underdogs

While *Dreamgirls* was coming together, with the soundtrack of the 1982 musical as its connecting thread, its director, Bill Condon, felt his movie needed an original song. The piece's original composer, Henry Krieger, was therefore brought in, and set to work to give the movie its flagship number. "*Listen* was the song that took the most time and hard work," he explained, "because we needed to fashion something in the musical vernacular of Beyoncé while at the same time adhere to what the movie needed story-wise. That song took a while to write because, generally speaking, I don't write Beyoncé songs. I teamed up with Scott Cutler, who did a lot of musical innovation on the song…and Anne Preven, who wrote the lyrics. We would show Beyoncé what we were doing and she would ask for maybe a little of this and a little of that. It was a group effort and a lot of fun."[180] "It was important for Deena's character," Beyoncé added, "because she was so controlled [throughout] the whole movie—so manipulated—and finally, when she stands up for herself, it's so effective. I love the record. I think it's something that's still relevant now. Everyone has a moment when they decide they're taking control of their life."[156]

HARD TO SAY GOODBYE
(BEYONCÉ KNOWLES, ANIKA NONI ROSE, SHARON LEAL)

(Henry Krieger, Tom Eyen/2'37)

Musicians: Beyoncé Knowles: vocals, backing vocals / Sharon Leal: vocals, backing vocals / Anika Noni Rose: vocals, backing vocals / Darrell Crooks, Eric Jackson, Michael Thompson: guitar / Nathan East?, James Johnson?, Harvey Mason Jr?: bass guitar / Glendon Campbell?, Gordon Campbell?, Ricky Lawson?, Harvey Mason Jr?, Anthony Moore?: drums / Harvey Mason Sr: drums, percussion, piano / Randy Spendlove: guitar, piano / John Beasley?, Tim Carmon?, Eric Griggs?, Greg Phillinganes?, Kevin Randolph?: piano / Damon Thomas: piano / Orchestra / **Recording:** The Underlab, Los Angeles: 2004 to 2006 / Capitol Studios, Los Angeles: 2005 to 2006 (strings) / Henson Recording Studios, Los Angeles: 2005 to 2006 (strings) / The Record Plant, Los Angeles: 2005 to 2006 (strings) / **Technical team:** Producers: Harvey Mason Jr, Damon Thomas, Randy Spendlove, Matt Sullivan / **Executive producers:** Bill Condon, Mathew Knowles, Glen Brunman / **Recording engineers:** Chris Spilfogel, Dabling Harward, Jess Sutcliffe, Scott Campbell, Troy Halderson / **Assistant recording engineers:** Aaron Renner, Aaron Walk, Bryan Smith, Bryan Walk, Kevin Mills, Paul Smith, Riley Mackin, Sheldon Yellowhair / **Arrangements:** The Underdogs

Ending the film with a flourish was the obvious thing to do, with this sequence sung by Beyoncé, playing a Diana Ross more authentic than the original. Everything about Beyoncé's expression evokes her idol as she performs *Hard to Say Goodbye* with Anika Noni Rose and Sharon Leal. Henry Krieger described his impression of the singer: "It had been decided that the film was going to be done and we all hoped that she would join us, and, then, she did. I'll tell you a story: I hadn't met her yet and I was sitting at the piano, just waiting to do a little bit of cleanup from the vocal director. Then, she came in, and, with her hand outstretched, she said, 'Henry, I am so happy to meet you! This is an honor,' and all that. And, I said, 'Oh, my God. This is going to be easy and fun'—and it was. She couldn't have been an easier person to work with."[181]

DREAMGIRLS (FINALE)
(JENNIFER HUDSON, BEYONCÉ KNOWLES, ANIKA NONI ROSE, SHARON LEAL)

(Henry Krieger, Tom Eyen/2'33)

Musicians: Beyoncé Knowles: vocals, backing vocals / Sharon Leal: vocals, backing vocals / Anika Noni Rose: vocals, backing vocals / Jennifer Hudson: vocals, backing vocals / Darrell Crooks, Eric Jackson, Michael Thompson: guitar / Nathan East?, James Johnson?, Harvey Mason Jr?: bass guitar / Glendon Campbell?, Gordon Campbell?, Ricky Lawson?, Harvey Mason Jr?, Anthony Moore?: drums / Harvey Mason Sr: drums, percussion, piano / Randy Spendlove: guitar, piano / John Beasley?, Tim Carmon?, Eric Griggs?, Greg Phillinganes?, Kevin Randolph?: piano / Damon Thomas: piano / Orchestra / **Recording:** The Underlab, Los Angeles: 2004 to 2006 / Capitol Studios, Los Angeles: 2005 to 2006 (strings) / Henson Recording Studios, Los Angeles: 2005 to 2006 (strings) / The Record Plant, Los Angeles: 2005 to 2006 (strings) / **Technical team:** Producers: Harvey Mason Jr, Damon Thomas, Randy Spendlove, Matt Sullivan / Executive producers: Bill Condon, Mathew Knowles, Glen Brunman / Recording engineers: Chris Spilfogel, Dabling Harward, Jess Sutcliffe, Scott Campbell, Troy Halderson / Assistant recording engineers: Aaron Renner, Aaron Walk, Bryan Smith, Bryan Walk, Kevin Mills, Paul Smith, Riley Mackin, Sheldon Yellowhair / **Arrangements:** The Underdogs

In the scene showing Deena Jones and The Dreams being reunited with Effie White, it is hard not to notice some similarities between the characters on the screen and Destiny's Child. You could swear that what you were seeing in the movie was Latavia Roberson or LeToya Luckett—even Farrah Franklin—joining her former colleagues and friends on stage. There is inevitably an element of personal experience on Beyoncé's part in this sequence, even though she did not mention it at the time. A similar Destiny's Child reunion did not actually take place until 3 January 2024, when LeToya posted on her Instagram page a photograph taken backstage at Beyoncé's Renaissance World Tour. It shows herself, Latavia, Kelly Rowland, and Michelle Williams alongside Beyoncé. A dream team that we dream of seeing sing together one day.

WHEN I FIRST SAW YOU (DUET)
(JAMIE FOXX, BEYONCÉ KNOWLES)

(Henry Krieger, Tom Eyen/3'03)

Musicians: Jamie Foxx: vocals, backing vocals / Beyoncé Knowles: vocals, backing vocals / Darrell Crooks, Eric Jackson, Michael Thompson: guitar / Nathan East?, James Johnson?, Harvey Mason Jr?: bass guitar / Glendon Campbell?, Gordon Campbell?, Ricky Lawson?, Harvey Mason Jr?, Anthony Moore?: drums / Harvey Mason Sr: drums, percussion, piano / Randy Spendlove: guitar, piano / John Beasley?, Tim Carmon?, Eric Griggs?, Greg Phillinganes?, Kevin Randolph?: piano / Damon Thomas: piano / Orchestra / **Recording:** The Underlab, Los Angeles: 2004 to 2006 / Capitol Studios, Los Angeles: 2005 to 2006 (strings) / Henson Recording Studios, Los Angeles: 2005 to 2006 (strings) / The Record Plant, Los Angeles: 2005 to 2006 (strings) / **Technical team:** Producers: Harvey Mason Jr, Damon Thomas, Randy Spendlove, Matt Sullivan / Executive producers: Bill Condon, Mathew Knowles, Glen Brunman / Recording engineers: Chris Spilfogel, Dabling Harward, Jess Sutcliffe, Scott Campbell, Troy Halderson / Assistant recording engineers: Aaron Renner, Aaron Walk, Bryan Smith, Bryan Walk, Kevin Mills, Paul Smith, Riley Mackin, Sheldon Yellowhair / **Arrangements:** The Underdogs

This two-part version of *When I First Saw You*, which Jamie Foxx sings earlier in the movie with Beyoncé, is a little nod to *Endless Love*, a song Diana Ross performed as a duet with Lionel Richie in 1981. Foxx had an emotional memory of working with Beyoncé, as he declared some time after the filming of *Dreamgirls*: "I think Beyoncé was incredible in the sense that she took it serious. She took it serious in the sense that she knew this was her opportunity to do something special as far as her acting muscles were considered. When you think about it, you know she can sing. You know the music is going to blow you away. What she had to do was connect that drama, and I think her turns that she did in the acting fuels the music. So when she's singing you really feel it."[182]

ALBUM

I Am...Sasha Fierce

If I Were A Boy • Halo • Disappear • Broken-Hearted Girl • Ave Maria • Satellites • Single Ladies (Put a Ring on It) • Radio • Diva • Sweet Dreams • Video Phone

Released in the USA by Music World Music/Columbia: 18 November 2008 (CD ref.: 88697 41735 2)
Best chart ranking in the USA: 1

Beyoncé Knowles as Sasha Fierce, on stage in Berlin in 2009.

THE TWO FACES OF BEYONCÉ

Despite the international success of *B'Day*, criticism of the songs on the album caught Beyoncé's attention. Indeed the press, though supportive of her cause, did not fail to point out a marked difference in the record's production—largely influenced by the working methods of Jay-Z at his company Roc Nation, as well as by the rapper's sound, more incisive and angry than that which listeners were accustomed to hearing from the former Destiny's Child vocalist. This state of affairs provoked an immediate reaction from Beyoncé, who went back to work in December 2007 with the ambitious aim of offering her fans a concept album that would reveal the two sides of her personality. In the first part of the disc the discreet, timid Beyoncé sings her ballads and pop songs, while the rest gives prominence to her alter ego, whose name was invented by her cousin, Angela Beyincé. "Sasha Fierce, I usually use when I'm really nervous and when I'm on the stage and I have to do uptempo songs and I have to be really sexy in my dance videos," Beyoncé explained. "But, you know, it's interesting because the older I get, the more Sasha Fierce comes out all the time […] It's the same person. It's just kind of my alter ego and the stronger version of myself."[183]
"Usually when I hear the chords, when I put on my stilettos. Like the moment right before when you're nervous," she added in another interview. "Then Sasha Fierce appears, and my posture and the way I speak and everything is different."[184]

A breath of fresh air

In order to bring this ambitious project to fruition, Beyoncé wanted to take her time—no longer using the methods she had employed in making *B'Day*, when there was a pervasive feeling of urgency at Sony Music Studios in New York. For almost ten months she put the finishing touches to her songs in the company of her faithful producers Rodney "Darkchild" Jerkins and Kenneth "Babyface" Edmonds, or of the duo Stargate. But the desire for something new led Beyoncé to recruit talents who were able to write real songs for her, featuring effective, catchy melodies—which had been missing, according to some in the music press, from the tracklisting of *B'Day*. It was among the younger pop generation that she sought the composers and songwriters BC Jean, Toby Gad, and Ryan Tedder of the pop group OneRepublic. The same went for producers, with the arrival of Terius "The-Dream" Nash, Jim Jonsin, Dave McCracken, and Ian Dench. During the recording of her new album Beyoncé was driven by this desire for revival, demonstrating a maturity that she was determined to fully own. "When I started the record, I knew that, artistically, I had to grow. Even though I've been very successful and very fortunate, I want to still be challenged and still be nervous and still be anxious about all the things that make my career exciting."[185] Working mostly at Roc the Mic Studios in New York, and having received the instrumental

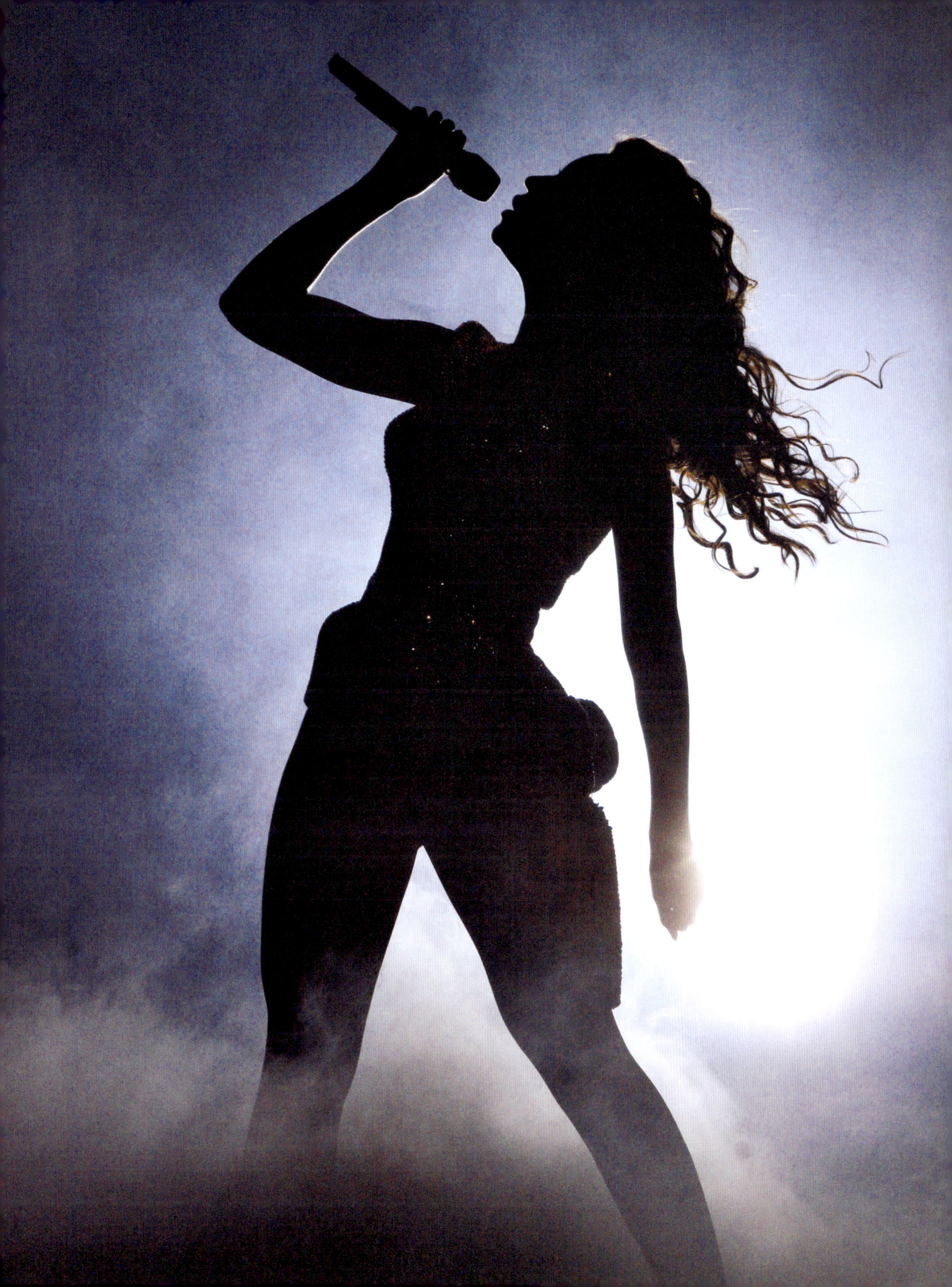

Above: In *Obsessed*, Beyoncé portrays a woman prepared to do anything to defend her family.
Opposite: Playing the role of Etta James on the set of *Cadillac Records*.

passages from her numerous associates, Beyoncé recorded more than 70 songs, which made up her next album, *I Am… Sasha Fierce*, soon scheduled for release on 18 November 2008.

Back to the cinema

The year 2008 was also when Beyoncé returned to the big screen, appearing in two feature films. *Cadillac Records*, directed by Darnell Martin, related the saga of Chicago's Chess Records label, where the singer Etta James made her name; she is played in the movie by Beyoncé. "It was a challenge for me emotionally because Etta had a lot of challenges in her life, things that I've never experienced. I had to really dig deep so that I could have the right performance and represent her well. One thing she taught me is her fearlessness; she was Etta all the time."[185] Also in 2008 Beyoncé portrayed another strong character, in the thriller *Obsessed*, directed by Steve Shill. Here she shared top billing with Idris Elba, playing a wife prepared to do anything in order to stop an intrusive young female colleague of her husband being given free rein. Like *Cadillac Records*, *Obsessed* was co-produced with the production company Beyoncé had just formed, Parkwood Entertainment—named after the affluent area of Houston where the Knowles family had lived when she was a child.

A risk that paid off

I Am…Sasha Fierce came out on 18 November 2008, preceded, on 7 October, by the simultaneous release of the two singles *If I Were a Boy* and *Single Ladies (Put a Ring on It)*. Each portraying one of the two sides of the artist's character, these songs were a colossal success and paved the way for the album, which went to the top of the charts on its release. The singles *Halo* and *Sweet Dreams* confirmed this success: *I Am…Sasha Fierce* sold more than 10 million in a few months and, like *Dangerously in Love* before it, became one of the best-selling albums of the early 21st century. To prepare her fans for the conceptual aspect of her album, Beyoncé had first of all written a letter to her admirers through her label, Columbia, in which she opened up unreservedly: "I have poured my heart and soul into it. It is my baby. It is the most time I have spent on any project since my first records

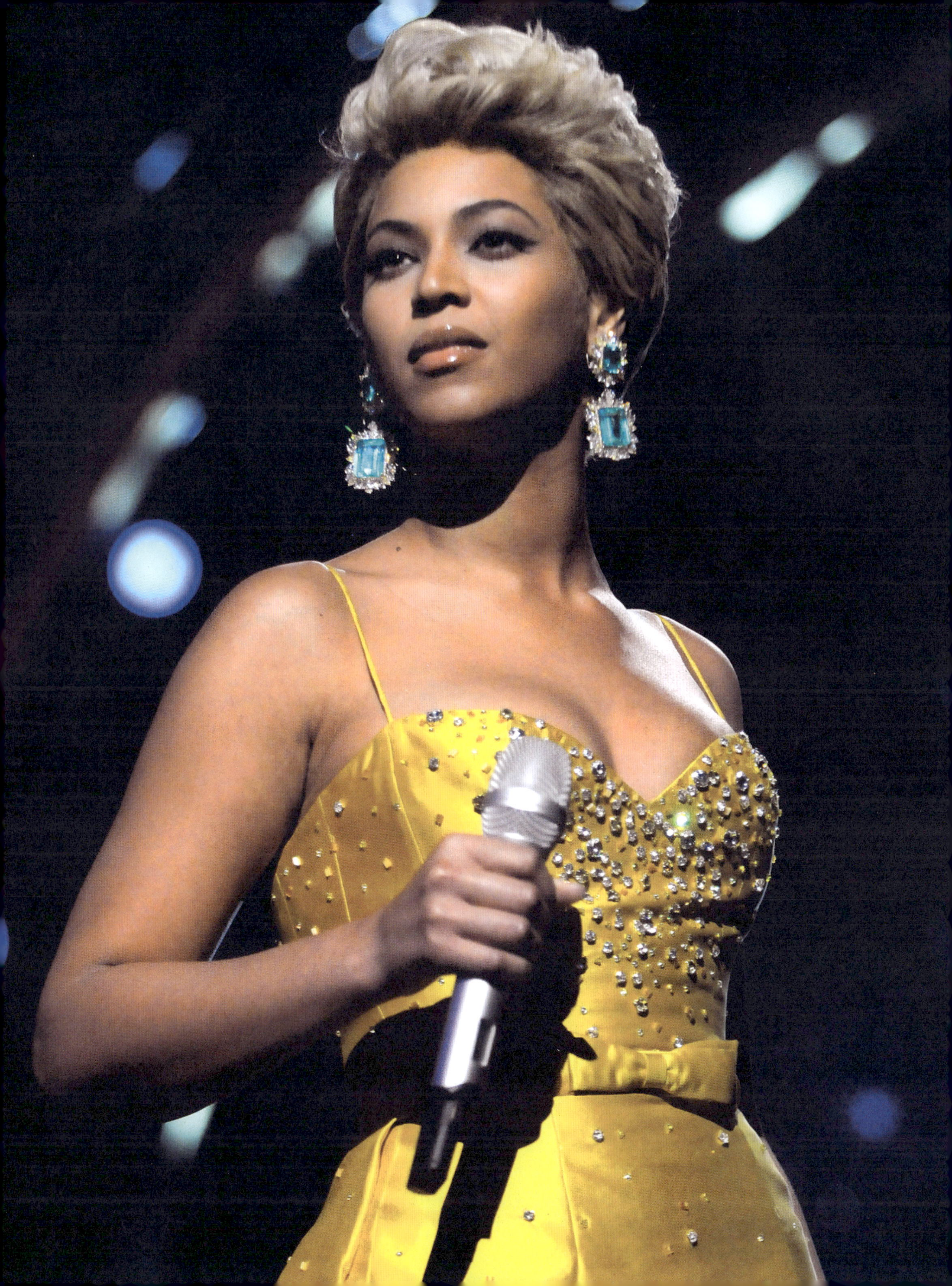

The Carters at the MTV Europe Music Awards in Berlin, 5 November 2009.

Beyoncé and Usher at the inauguration of President Barack Obama, 20 January 2009.

as a member of Destiny's Child when I was 15 years old. I have recorded over 70 songs and have created a sound that reveals all of me. I am in a different place right now, and I wanted people to see the many sides of me. [...] I have taken risks here. I am not afraid…There is no label or tag on my sound. It's me, and I am so excited to share it with the world."[186] Alongside this message, a website was set up to arouse the curiosity of fans. Its address—whoissashafierce.com—asked a question that intrigued visitors, who were invited to call 917-288-9229 to take part in a mysterious game. "One lucky person with the correct answer will be randomly chosen to receive a personal message from Sasha Fierce when she is ready to unveil her identity. The same lucky individual will also receive a gift bag valued at $500," the website promised.[187]

Mrs Carter

The year 2008 also saw the wedding of Jay-Z and Beyoncé, on 4 April in New York. It was a very private ceremony, attended by some 40 of their closest friends and held—in total secrecy—at their 13,500-square-foot (1,255-square-metre) apartment in the Tribeca neighborhood of Manhattan. Accompanied once again by her all-female group Suga Mama, Beyoncé confirmed her commitment to feminism at the announcement of her I Am…Tour, which would feature more than a hundred concerts performed across six continents and run from 26 March 2009 to 18 February 2010. Also in 2009 Beyoncé openly declared her enthusiasm following Barack Obama's election to the presidency. "I'm so proud," she said. "You know, I've always said it, I never thought I would live for this, to see this moment. And I'm very happy with the progress our country has already made. And being someone that's traveled around the world, I had never seen the enthusiasm in people that are not Americans."[183] With the release on 20 October 2009 of the platinum edition of *I Am…Sasha Fierce*, containing unpublished songs from the album's recording sessions, Beyoncé was able to savor its colossal success, which came with an extraordinary fortune, earning her more than $87 million between July 2008 and July 2009. Before, Beyoncé had been a star who was respected and admired; now she was an artist who was idolized the world over, and enjoyed exceptional credibility with the public. "I want to be an icon," she declared in 2008.[188] Unquestionably, that goal had now been attained.

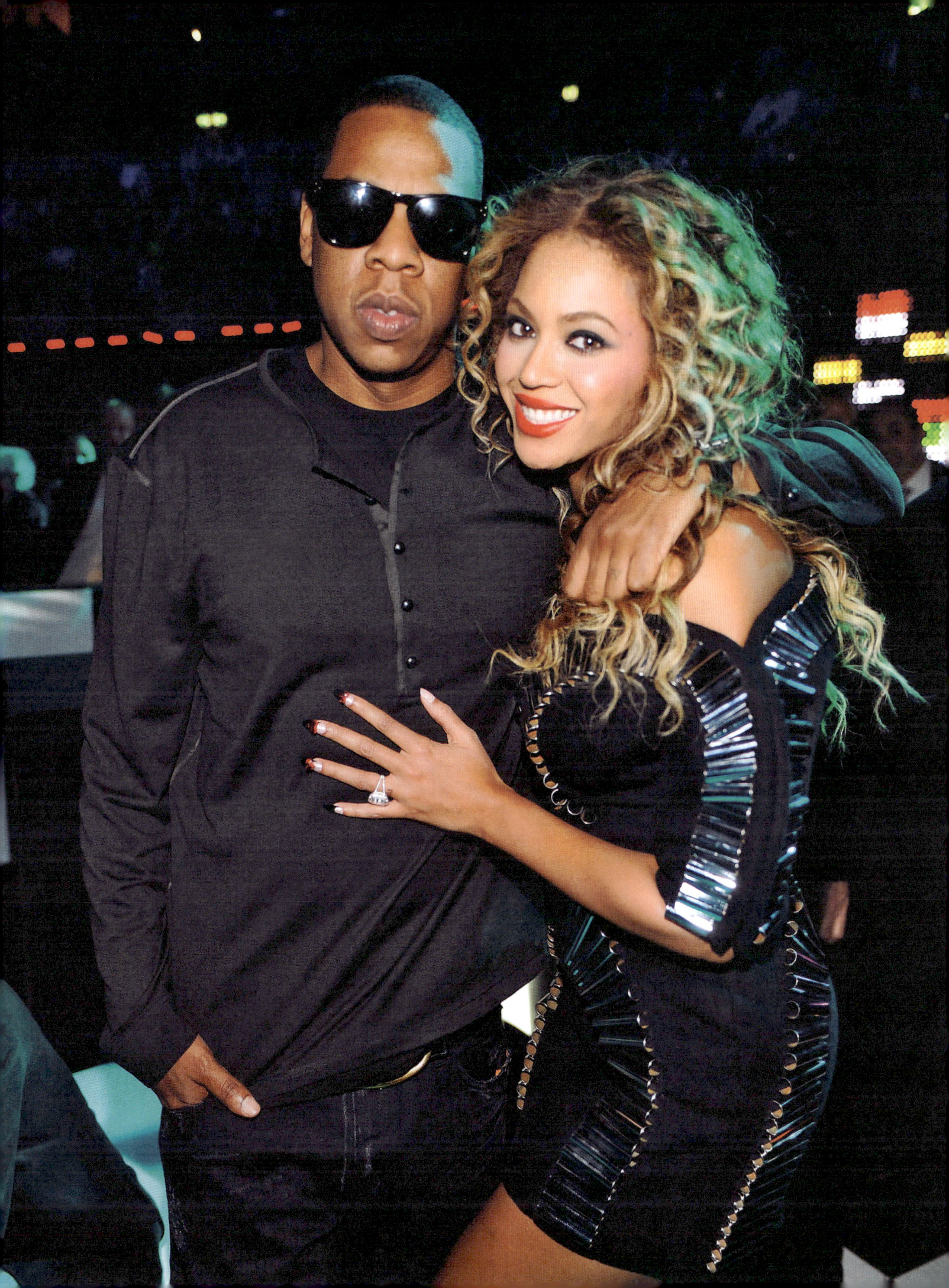

Brittany Jean Carlson went from obscurity to glory after co-writing *If I Were a Boy* with Toby Gad.

SINGLE

IF I WERE A BOY

(BC Jean, Toby Gad/4'10)

Musicians
Beyoncé Knowles: vocals, backing vocals
Jens Gad: drums
Syience: acoustic guitar, programming
Toby Gad: additional instruments

Recording
Strawberrybee Productions, New York: 2008 to 2009
GAD Studios, Ibiza: 2008 to 2009
Roc the Mic Studios, New York: 2009 (overdubs, vocals)

Technical team
Producers: Beyoncé Knowles, Toby Gad
Executive producers: Beyoncé Knowles, Mathew Knowles
Recording engineers: Toby Gad, Jim Caruana (vocals)

Single
Digital release by Columbia/Music World Music: 7 November 2008 (ref.: none)
Best chart ranking in the USA: 3

Genesis

Toby Gad—who had just had an international hit with *Big Girls Don't Cry*, a single he wrote and produced for Fergie, the vocalist of Black Eyed Peas—was looking for new talents he could take under his wing. Then on the social network MySpace he came across a 20-year-old singer named BC Jean, and soon suggested they work together. BC Jean—real name Brittany Jean Carlson—was also a writer and composer who was influenced by the pop music of Alanis Morissette and No Doubt. At their first work session, in New York in the autumn of 2008, Gad and Jean wrote nine songs together, but it was the tenth that was to change the young woman's life. "Toby [Gad] and I were walking around Times Square," she said, "and there was an amazing smell coming from this pizzeria. I was doing the diet thing and was like, 'Mmm, you smell that? If I were a boy, I would totally eat that.' And he said, 'What did you say?' And I said, 'I wish I were a boy so I could eat pizza and popcorn and wear baggy clothes.' He asked me what else I would do and I said, 'I'd be a better man than my ex-boyfriend.'"[189] Jean's painful breakup with her boyfriend was undoubtedly the best thing that could have happened to her, for when she and Gad returned to the studio they made *If I Were A Boy* into a demo, ready to send to record labels, which Toby Gad went on to do in order to get his protégée a contract.

Production

As Beyoncé was starting preproduction of her third solo album in December 2008, Max Gousse, artistic director at Columbia, invited Toby Gad to take part in the writing sessions. Shut up in a studio alone with Beyoncé for two days, Gad showed her some of his songs. "Before we started writing, I played her a few songs including *If I Were a Boy*. When Beyoncé heard it, she jumped up and said, 'I want to record this song right now—I love it.'"[190] *If I Were a Boy* was the subject of numerous covers over the years, although the one that made the most impact was that recorded by the country star Reba McEntire in 2010.

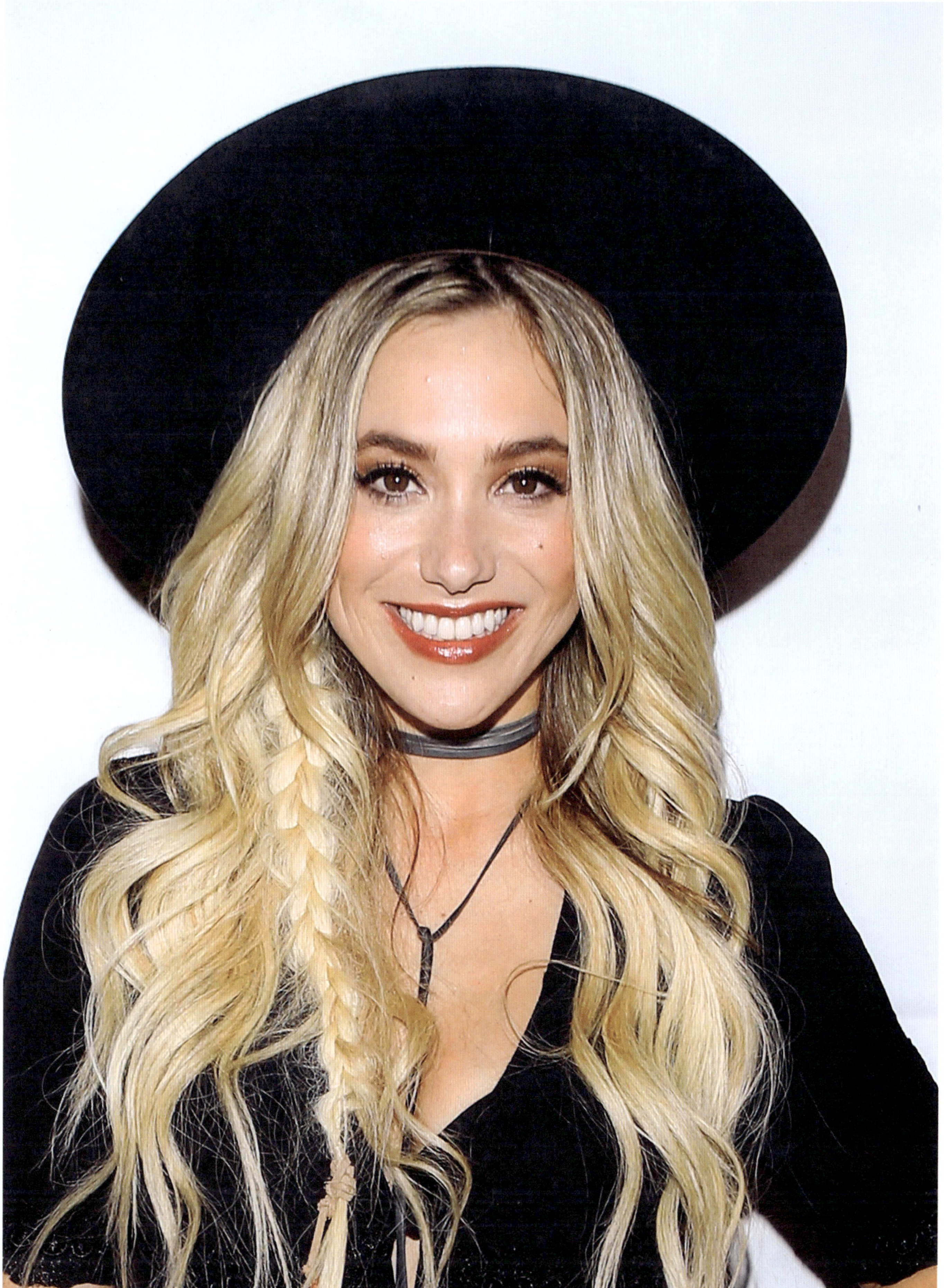

Ryan Tedder, vocalist with OneRepublic and author of *Halo*, a global hit for Beyoncé.

SINGLE

HALO

(Beyoncé Knowles, Evan Bogart, Ryan Tedder/4'22)

Musicians
Beyoncé Knowles: vocals, backing vocals
Ryan Tedder: additional instruments

Recording
Mansfield Studios, Los Angeles: 2008 to 2009
Germano Studios, New York: 2008 to 2009
Roc the Mic Studios, New York: 2009 (vocals)

Technical team
Producers: Beyoncé Knowles, Ryan Tedder
Executive producers: Beyoncé Knowles, Mathew Knowles
Recording engineers: Ryan Tedder, Jim Caruana (vocals)
Assistant recording engineer: Christian Baker

Single
Released in the USA by Columbia/Music World Music: 20 January 2009 (ref.: 88697 49296 2)
Best chart ranking in the USA: 5

FOR BEYONCÉ ADDICTS

For the singer's admirers, the success of *Halo* will always be associated with an incident that has attained cult status. On 22 July 2013, while Beyoncé was on stage at the Bell Centre in Montreal, Canada, performing *Halo* in front of almost 20,000 people, her hair was caught in a fan. Thanks to the cool head of one of her bodyguards, who managed to deal with the problem, and to Beyoncé's outstanding professionalism, the concert continued after this incident.

Genesis

A former DJ, rapper, agent to the stars, and artistic director with a record label, Evan Bogart had more than one string to his bow. The success of *SOS*, a song built around a sample from *Tainted Love* by Soft Cell which had won Rihanna renown in 2006, drove him to concentrate on his new passion: writing international hits. Bogart was very close to Ryan Tedder—vocalist with OneRepublic, a group he had himself signed to his artistic agency APA—and liked to work with him; the two men often wrote together. Between 25 April and 28 May 2008, OneRepublic was forced to cancel several concerts, because Tedder had torn his Achilles tendon playing basketball. "On his first day back in LA I was going to take over some food and hang out with him," Bogart recalled. "When I got there, he was like, 'Dude, we should write. We should write a song,' and I'm like, 'Well, you're not supposed to be writing. You're supposed to be in bed.' Eventually we ended up in his studio and, with him on crutches, we wrote *Halo*."[191] Certain that they had a hit, the pair sent the song to Jay Brown, managing director of Jay-Z's label Roc Nation, hoping to secure a place for it on Beyoncé's next album. After waiting several weeks and receiving no reply from the singer, Ryan Tedder sent a copy to Simon Cowell, to be shown to Cowell's protégée Leona Lewis, whom he had just signed to his label Syco. But Cowell did not even have time to imagine counting the millions of dollars the song would have earned before Beyoncé hastened to secure it, demanding it be kept for her album. The international success of this pop marvel spoke for itself, much to the chagrin of Simon Cowell and Leona Lewis.

Production

Halo was perfectly suited to the concept Beyoncé wanted for the calmer part of her album. Tedder and Bogart had been inspired to write it by a famous American folk musician, whose first studio album, *Trouble*, had encountered great success in 2004. "The idea was always, 'Let's write a song that embodies Ray LaMontagne,'" Bogart explained. "He has a song called *Shelter*, which is beautiful. And it's a song to this girl which is like, 'I will always shelter you.' And I said, 'We should write a Ray LaMontagne *Shelter* kind of song for Jay-Z and Beyoncé.' Ryan then started playing some angelic chords. I said, 'What about *Halo*?' Three hours later we had

Halo done."[191] Although the song was a huge success, the singer Kelly Clarkson complained of the resemblance between *Halo* and her song *Already Gone*, also written by Ryan Tedder. In his defense, the latter made it clear that his two creations were well and truly different, and nothing detracted from the triumph of Beyoncé's single.

A new version of *Halo*, which Beyoncé this time performed with Chris Martin, singer with the British group Coldplay, featured in 2010 on the charity album *Hope for Haiti Now*, which raised funds following the earthquake that struck the country on 12 January of that year.

2008

Amanda Ghost, author of numerous lyrics on *I Am …Sasha Fierce*.

DISAPPEAR

(Amanda Ghost, Beyoncé Knowles, Dave McCracken, Hugo Chakrabongse, Ian Dench/4'29)

Musician: Beyoncé Knowles: vocals, backing vocals / **Recording:** Roc the Mic Studios, New York: 2008 to 2009 / **Technical team: Producers:** Amanda Ghost, Beyoncé Knowles, Dave McCracken, Ian Dench / **Executive producers:** Beyoncé Knowles, Mathew Knowles / **Recording engineers:** Jim Caruana, Marcos Tovar

Hugo Chakrabongse, great-great-grandson of Chulalongkorn, the King of Siam (now Thailand) who reigned from 1868 to 1910, was a star in his own country, where he had lived since the age of 17 after a childhood spent in London. Following a bad experience with Island Records, which ended with his artist's contract being broken, Chakrabongse took advantage of a meeting with the writer Amanda Ghost to show her some of his songs. One of these, *Disappear*, caught the attention of the young woman, who had written the lyrics to *Beautiful Liar* for Beyoncé and Shakira in 2006. When Ghost was invited to work with Beyoncé in early 2008, the latter was immediately charmed by *Disappear*. "We spent three weeks together in New York working on the new record and we had the most incredible time," Ghost recalled. "She has a complete, almost laser-like focus on what she is and what she can do."[192]

BROKEN-HEARTED GIRL

(Beyoncé Knowles, Kenneth "Babyface" Edmonds, Mikkel S. Eriksen, Tor Erik Hermansen/4'39)

Musicians: Beyoncé Knowles: vocals, backing vocals / **Mikkel S. Eriksen:** additional instruments / **Tor Erik Hermansen:** additional instruments / **Recording:** Roc the Mic Studios, New York: 2008 to 2009 / **Technical team: Producers:** Beyoncé Knowles, Stargate / **Executive producers:** Beyoncé Knowles, Mathew Knowles / **Recording engineers:** Mikkel S. Eriksen, Jim Caruana (vocals)

Mikkel S. Eriksen and Tor Erik Hermansen, who comprised the duo Stargate, were now part of Beyoncé's inner circle. When the latter embarked on the production of *I Am … Sasha Fierce*, the two Norwegians were naturally invited to suggest some songs, one of which, *Broken-Hearted Girl*, caught the artist's attention. Eriksen explained that they had originally written it as an R&B track with Babyface Edmonds, who "changed one chord" and contributed the lyrics, before adding "a falsetto voice that we recorded as a demo. From there we proceeded to change the entire backing track around his vocal. We changed the chords, everything, and this is where that four to the floor piano emerged." Like many of Stargate's songs, *Broken-Hearted Girl* is in a minor key, in this case D minor. "We probably lean towards more a moody, melodic expression," Eriksen concluded.[163]

268 I AM…SASHA FIERCE

FOR BEYONCÉ ADDICTS

As she was preparing to give a concert in the Port Ghalib hotel complex in Egypt, in November 2009, Beyoncé visited Cairo to see the pyramids of Giza. There, she underwent an unprecedented spiritual experience. "I started singing *Ave Maria* inside the pyramid," she recalled in 2011. "The depth of the tomb was so clear. My voice sounded so pure. It was inconceivable. I could have stayed in there forever. All I could do was say, Thank you, Lord, for this experience."[4]

Portrait of the Austrian composer Franz Schubert (1797–1828).

AVE MARIA

(Amanda Ghost, Beyoncé Knowles, Ian Dench, Makeba Riddick, Mikkel S. Eriksen, Tor Erik Hermansen/3'42)

Musicians: Beyoncé Knowles: vocals, backing vocals / Ian Dench: acoustic guitar / Mikkel S. Eriksen: additional instruments / Tor Erik Hermansen: additional instruments / **Recording:** Roc the Mic Studios, New York: 2008 to 2009 / **Technical team:** Producers: Beyoncé Knowles, Stargate / Executive producers: Beyoncé Knowles, Mathew Knowles / Recording engineer: Mikkel S. Eriksen

Although he is not credited, because his score has long been in the public domain, the Austrian composer Franz Schubert very clearly influenced Beyoncé's *Ave Maria*, whose chorus melody, title, and harmonic progression played in arpeggios owe everything to his composition, and to the later piano arrangement by Hungarian composer Franz Liszt. Undeniably, Beyoncé pulls off a feat in tackling this classic, whose production was entrusted to Stargate and lyrics to Amanda Ghost, Makeba Riddick, and Ian Dench, with help from Beyoncé herself. "[Beyoncé and I] were talking about how much we loved the Schubert *Ave Maria*," Ghost recalled. "We had both recently got married, and it turned out we had both come up the aisle to that song. So I said wouldn't it be great to try and rewrite it. And the lyric is very much about her. She talks about being surrounded by friends but she's alone: 'How can the silence seem so loud?' and then 'There's only us when the lights go down'. I think that's probably the most personal line on the whole album about her and Jay, because they are very real, and they're very much in love, and it must be pretty tough to have that love when you're incredibly famous."[193]

SATELLITES

(Amanda Ghost, Beyoncé Knowles, Dave McCracken, Ian Dench/3'07)

Musician: Beyoncé Knowles: vocals, backing vocals / **Recording:** Roc the Mic Studios, New York: 2008 to 2009 / **Technical team:** Producers: Amanda Ghost, Beyoncé Knowles, Dave McCracken, Ian Dench / Executive producers: Beyoncé Knowles, Mathew Knowles / Recording engineers: Jim Caruana, Marcos Tovar

By her own account, *I Am…Sasha Fierce* is the most authentic album Beyoncé has recorded; she opens up in each song as never before. "When I knew that certain things I wanted to say, I couldn't say myself, I invited other writers to come in," she explained in 2009. "Lyrically, it's the best album I've ever had. If a song didn't say anything or mean anything to me, I didn't put it on the record."[185] It must be said that her romantic life had a considerable impact on her songs, and her marriage to Jay-Z is central to the lyrics of *I Am…Sasha Fierce*. "We learn from each other," she said in 2006. "We both work hard, and we're focused and professional. Just being around that helps the other person."[151]

BEYONCÉ: ALL THE SONGS 269

Beyoncé dances in *Single Ladies (Put a Ring on It)* on stage at the American Music Awards in Los Angeles, 23 November 2008.

SINGLE

SINGLE LADIES (PUT A RING ON IT)

(Beyoncé Knowles, Terius Nash, Thaddis Harrell, Christopher Stewart/3'13)

Musician
Beyoncé Knowles: vocals, backing vocals

Recording
Roc the Mic Studios, New York: 2008 to 2009

Technical team
Producers: Beyoncé Knowles, Terius "The-Dream" Nash, Christopher "Tricky" Stewart
Executive producers: Beyoncé Knowles, Mathew Knowles
Recording engineers: Brian "B-LUV" Thomas, Kuk Harrell, Jim Caruana (vocals)

Single
Digital release by Columbia/Music World Music: 13 October 2008 (ref.: none)
Best chart ranking in the USA: 1

Genesis

The lineup for the Heart of the City Tour, which began on 22 March 2008 at the American Airlines Arena in Miami, was highly prestigious. The lucky holders of a ticket for this series of concerts could hear two of the greatest American hip-hop and R&B artists, Jay-Z and Mary J. Blige. But since young talents are always lying in wait to dethrone their elders, it was the rapper who performed the first part of the concerts, The-Dream, who needed to be watched closely. Jay-Z, whose talent for spotting future stars was obvious to everyone, had judged correctly: between two concerts, he asked the young man—whose real name is Terius Nash—to meet Beyoncé and take part in the writing sessions which were taking place at Roc the Mic Studios in New York. It must be said that with him, but also with Christopher "Tricky" Stewart and Thaddis "Kuk" Harrell, Jay-Z had had a colossal success the previous year with *Umbrella* by Rihanna. So the team of writers, composers, and producers could not miss the opportunity to build on that. The-Dream duly took himself to Roc the Mic Studios to join the other producers, among them Timbaland and Stargate, who were already at work, and who had formerly worked, each in their own studio, on writing *B'Day*. All were focused on the same goal: delivering to Beyoncé the first single of her future album. It was also the goal of The-Dream, who joined the team, proudly declaring: "I don't know who has or think they have the first single on B, but it's over with, I got the first single."[194] "I had not wrote a record," the producer went on to explain. "I didn't know what I was going to write. I ain't heard a beat, nothing. I literally backed myself into this corner."[194] But, boldness having been at the root of many a hit, that night The-Dream recorded a first piece, then embarked on making a second, which was to win him the Song of the Year award at the 2009 Grammys: *Single Ladies (Put a Ring on It)*. Soon joined by his associates Christopher "Tricky" Stewart and Thaddis "Kuk" Harrell, The-Dream produced an anthem to dance, with a savage, jerky tempo reminiscent of *Get Me Bodied*, which Swizz Beatz and Sean Garrett had written for *B'Day* in 2006—perfectly suited to the second part of the album, which would be devoted to revealing the fiery temperament of Beyoncé's alter ego, Sasha Fierce. The inspiration for the song's lyrics, co-written by Beyoncé, came to The-Dream via the singer herself, who had recently married

270 I AM…SASHA FIERCE

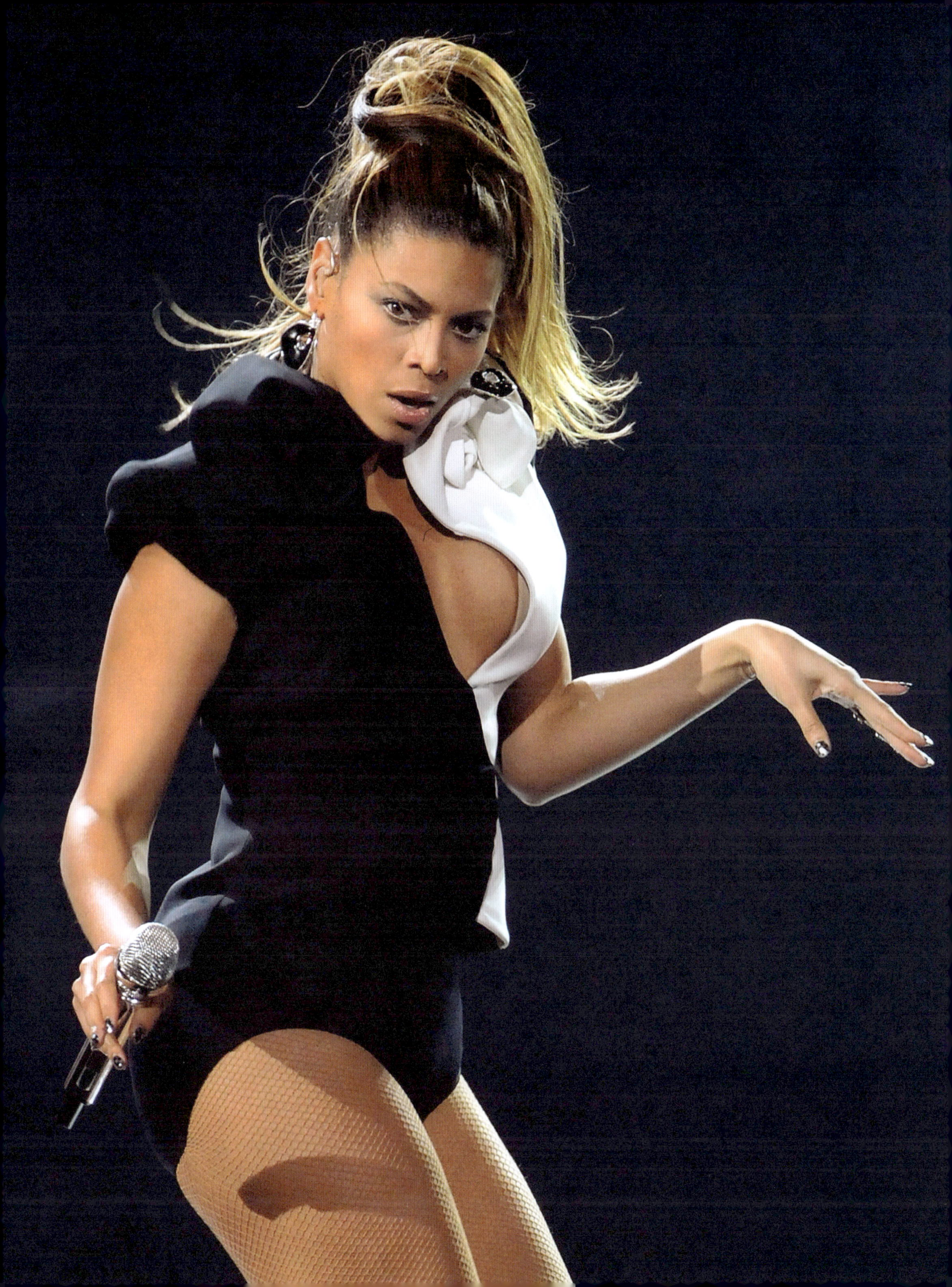

Jay-Z but wore no wedding ring. "It was the only public statement that they ever made about marriage," Christopher "Tricky" Stewart explained. "When we went into the studio she didn't have a ring on or anything, because at that point they were still really hiding it. That's where Dream got that concept from."[195] The-Dream added: "I thought it was a subject that most women wanted to talk about because most of us men are scared as s— to be bound to a commitment."[195] And Beyoncé concluded: "That song is all about: 'I've been with you all this time, you're taking too long and now I'm looking hot and you see it and you gotta suffer because you shoulda put a ring on it.'"[185] For all men who are delaying popping the question, the message is clear: don't leave it too long, guys!

An iconic clip

The international success of *Single Ladies (Put a Ring on It)* owed as much to Beyoncé's vocal performance as to the song's legendary clip, directed by Jake Nava, who had already made those of *Crazy in Love* and *Beautiful Liar*. It was filmed immediately after the clip accompanying *If I Were a Boy*, so that it could be released at the same time (the two singles appeared together in order to show the two facets of Beyoncé). The simplicity of the *Single Ladies (Put a Ring on It)* video enabled the viewer to focus on the impressive choreography executed by the singer and her two dancers. Although this was the work of Frank Gatson and JaQuel Knight, the inspiration for it initially came to Beyoncé from a video of an

Beyoncé on stage with her dancers at the MTV Video Music Awards in New York, 13 September 2009.

we can from the tapes," Knight explained.[197] "Out of all my videos, it was the least expensive and took the least amount of time," Beyoncé said in 2009. "And it ended up being the most iconic. I absolutely didn't expect that—I don't think anyone did."[198]

Production

Although it was the product of The-Dream's imagination, *Single Ladies (Put a Ring on It)* is the result of close collaboration with Christopher "Tricky" Stewart. The beat was created using an MPC 3000, on which the pair recorded an abrasive synthesizer line. The hand claps were suggested to The-Dream by Beyoncé's southern background and her love of church choirs, in which she had so often taken part. "I can see the paper fans in the church and the wooden benches and the reverend and the baptisms that are going and knowing what's happening after that," the producer explained. "That's everything I get from one sound."[199] Boldness was to the fore during this night session at Jay-Z's Roc the Mic Studios in New York, as can be heard in the song, whose production is the exact opposite of the gentle ballads at the start of the album. As the producers each worked on instrumental sequences they would suggest to Beyoncé, the explosion of that of *Single Ladies (Put a Ring on It)*, played at full volume through the complex's Augspurger loudspeakers, left no room for doubt: The-Dream, "Tricky" Stewart, and Thaddis "Kuk" Harrell definitely had their hit.

episode of *The Ed Sullivan Show* dating from 1969, in which the actor Gwen Verdon danced to music by Lalo Schifrin. The sequence, entitled "Mexican Breakfast", was directed by Bob Fosse, who had already given Beyoncé the inspiration for the clip of *Get Me Bodied*. "I saw a video on YouTube," she explained. "They had a plain background and it was shot on the crane; it was 360 degrees, they could move around. And I said, 'This is genius.' We kept a lot of the Fosse choreography and added the down-south thing—it's called J-setting, where one person does something and the next person follows."[196] "We even had [dancer and Broadway performer] Desmond Richardson come in and teach us some Fosse movements, signature Fosse pieces, and we just continued to study what

FOR BEYONCÉ ADDICTS

Although the clip of *Single Ladies (Put a Ring on It)* has become legendary, the parody of it made by Justin Timberlake, Bobby Moynihan, and Andy Samberg, broadcast on *Saturday Night Live* in November 2008, is equally so. The three actors had shaved their legs and put on leotards to accompany the singer in her dance routine. "It was so hilarious. It was very difficult to stay focused," she said in 2009.[183]

The producer Rico Love in New York, 2005.

RADIO

(Beyoncé Knowles, Dwayne Nesmith, James Scheffer, Rico Love/3'39)

Musician: Beyoncé Knowles: vocals, backing vocals / **Recording:** The Boom Boom Room, Los Angeles: 2008 to 2009 / Roc the Mic Studios, New York: 2008 to 2009 / **Technical team: Producers:** D-Town, Jim Jonsin, Rico Love / **Executive producers:** Beyoncé Knowles, Mathew Knowles / **Recording engineers:** Jim Caruana, Jim Jonsin

Behind its festive face, *Radio* is Beyoncé's homage to the years of her youth, during which she spent more time listening to her radio than partying with her friends, as she confirmed in 2009: "In my household, I didn't go to all of the parties and I didn't do all the things that a lot of the other teenage girls did because I was so in love with my radio and my music. I was so in love with this radio and my parents were happy that I was into something positive. I try to make uptempo records that feel good but underneath they're still saying something. *Sasha Fierce* is a collection of the kinds of songs that I'm usually known for and I love just as much as the more intimate side of me."[185] The producer Jim Jonsin, who was involved with *Radio*, recalled working with Beyoncé: "She's an incredible vocalist and one of the hardest-working artists in show business, not to mention a positive inspiration for women. Young people these days need strong role models and she's that person. For all the fame and fortune she has been blessed with, Beyoncé acts like she's just the girl next door. She's a real and pure soul."[200]

SINGLE

DIVA

(Beyoncé Knowles, Sean Garrett, Shondrae Crawford/3'21)

Musician: Beyoncé Knowles: vocals, backing vocals / **Recording:** Silent Sound Studios, Atlanta: 2008 to 2009 / Patchwerk Recording Studios, Atlanta: 2008 to 2009 / Bangladesh Studios, Atlanta: 2008 to 2009 / Roc the Mic Studios, New York: 2009 (vocals) / **Technical team: Producers:** Beyoncé Knowles, Sean Garrett, Shondrae Crawford, Miles Walker / **Executive producers:** Beyoncé Knowles, Mathew Knowles / **Recording engineers:** Miles Walker, Jim Caruana / **Assistant recording engineers:** Kory Aaron, Michael Miller / **Single:** Digital release by Columbia/Music World Music: 20 January 2009 (ref.: none) / **Best chart ranking in the USA:** 19

As he was doing a training session in his favorite Los Angeles club, the producer Shondrae "Bangladesh" Crawford had a brilliant idea. He had just had a hit with *A Milli*, the hip-hop anthem he had written for Lil Wayne; now he wanted to make a similar song, but this time for a female artist. And not just any female artist: none other than Beyoncé. Once production was complete, Bangladesh sent the recording to his associate Sean Garrett, for him to put the finishing touches to it. "I did this one song for her that's gonna shake the clubs up," Garrett explained.[201] As for the lyrics, Beyoncé embraced them, singing that she is not a diva, even though her definition of that word fits perfectly with her personality: "A true diva is graceful and talented and strong and fearless and brave and someone with humility."[192] No one would deny that these are exactly the singer's attributes.

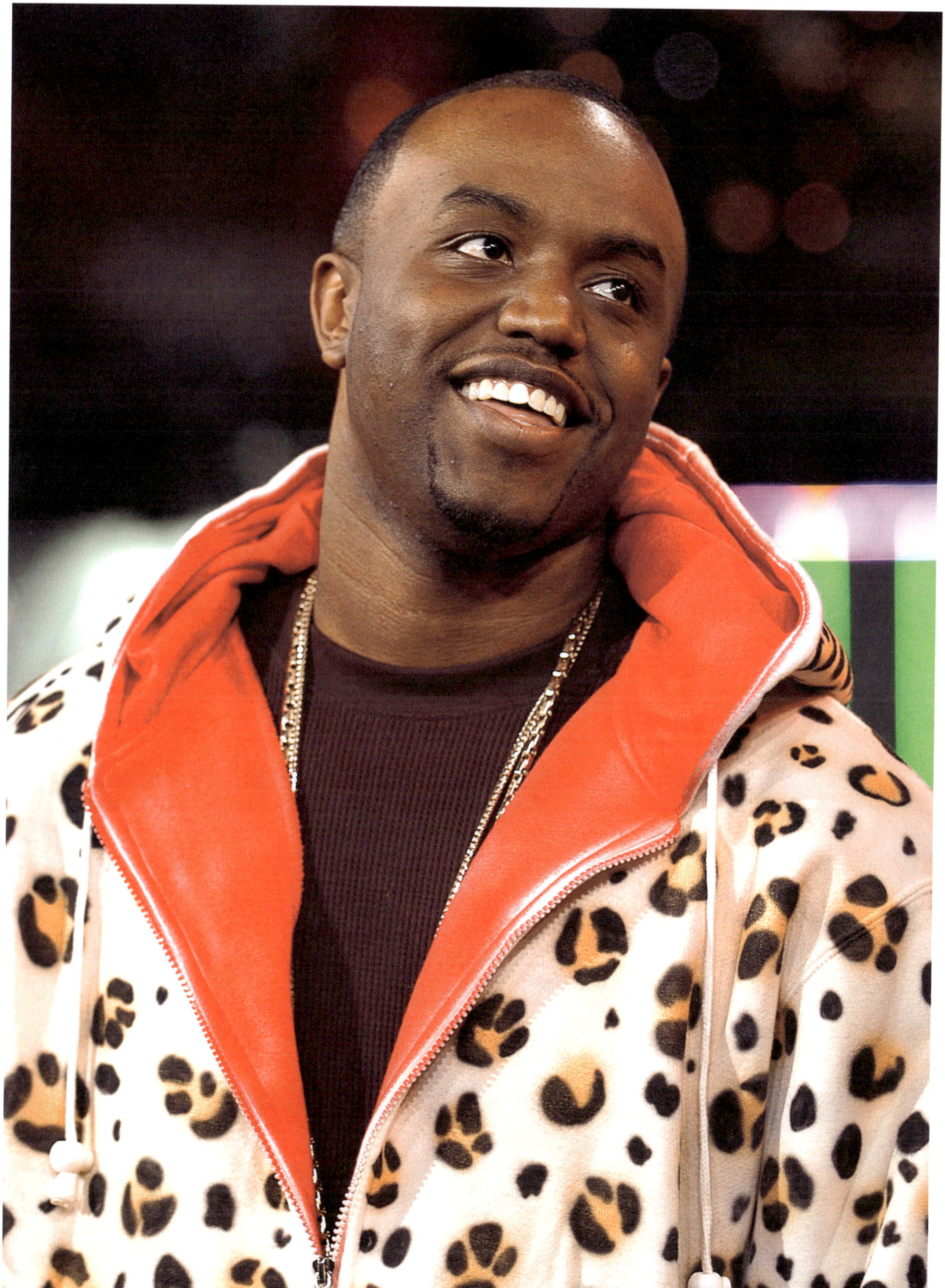

Beyoncé Knowles, aka Sasha Fierce, on stage at the MTV Europe Music Awards in Berlin, 5 November 2009.

SINGLE

SWEET DREAMS

(Beyoncé Knowles, James Scheffer, Rico Love, Wayne Wilkins/3'28)

Musicians: Beyoncé Knowles: vocals, backing vocals / Rico Love: backing vocals / **Recording:** South Beach Studios, Miami Beach: 2008 to 2009 / **Technical team: Producers:** Beyoncé Knowles, Jim Jonsin, Rico Love, Wayne Wilkins / **Executive producers:** Beyoncé Knowles, Mathew Knowles / **Recording engineer:** Jim Caruana / **Single:** Digital release by Columbia/Music World Music: 2 June 2009 (ref.: none) / **Best chart ranking in the USA:** 10

Listening to *Sweet Dreams*, you can tell that the R&B era of the early 1990s was well and truly over, and that pop and EDM (electronic dance music) had replaced its groove. Although the EDM hits by Calvin Harris, Avicii, and David Guetta would not arrive until the next decade, the last of these, who had encountered huge success from the start of the 2000s with a more house style, became one of the big names of EDM thanks to working with Sia, Bebe Rexha, and one Kelly Rowland. As Beyoncé was recording her third solo album in 2008, the arrival on the scene of a new contender for the title of Queen of American Pop put her, if not in danger, at least in a state of permanent vigilance. With her first album, *The Fame*, the young Stefani Germanotta, aka Lady Gaga, offered a totally irresistible cocktail of pop, dance, and synth-pop, and the crazy series of hits from this album and its 2009 deluxe version *The Fame Monster* would—one imagines—have put Queen B, as her fans liked to call her, into a cold sweat. As she was preparing to attend a concert on the Heart of the City Tour, which Jay-Z shared with Mary J. Blige, Beyoncé stopped in at the studio of the producer Rico Love. The latter played her a song he had just been working on, whose pop and dance quality immediately charmed her. "I played her *Sweet Dreams* and she loved it so much that she just jumped in the booth and sang it," Love explained. "I don't think she even recorded the song in an hour and a half, if that."[202] "She wasn't prepared to record," the producer added, "but heard the song and said, 'Let's do it.' It's actually my background vocals in the hook. She liked the way it sounded so we kept it."[203] Effective and melodious, on its release *Sweet Dreams* was a serious competitor to *Just Dance*, *Paparazzi*, *Poker Face*, *Bad Romance*, and *Alejandro*, to name but a few of the hits Lady Gaga made in 2008 and 2009. However, there was never anything less than friendship between the two women, who in 2009 made a superb duet, *Telephone*, as a demonstration of the good terms they were on.

VIDEO PHONE

(Angela Beyincé, Beyoncé Knowles, Sean Garrett, Shondrae Crawford/3'35)

Musician: Beyoncé Knowles: vocals, backing vocals / **Recording:** Silent Sound Studios, Atlanta: 2008 to 2009 / Patchwerk Recording Studios, Atlanta: 2008 to 2009 / Bangladesh Studios, Atlanta: 2008 to 2009 / Roc the Mic Studios, New York: 2009 (vocals) / **Technical team: Producers:** Beyoncé Knowles, Sean Garrett, Shondrae Crawford, Miles Walker / **Executive producers:** Beyoncé Knowles, Mathew Knowles / **Recording engineers:** Miles Walker, Jim Caruana (vocals) / **Assistant recording engineers:** Kory Aaron, Michael Miller

No one under the age of 20 can have experienced the time—the era before smartphones, before it was common to take photographs or shoot videos on a mobile telephone, as such technological marvels were still called in those days—that Beyoncé is referring to in *Video Phone* when she asks her boyfriend to film her with his camera, given that he can't possess her. Before it was re-recorded in 2009 as a duo with Lady Gaga (seriously, why this passion for phones?) and flopped, *Video Phone* was the work of producers Shondrae "Bangladesh" Crawford and Sean Garrett, the former having made way for the latter, who eagerly played the song to Beyoncé. Bangladesh recalled: "We were working on *Diva* at the time and when [Sean] played *Videophone* he was just telling me she loves this beat. It wasn't a beat that was really on my radar. Like, as a producer you have your favorite beat and you only let certain people hear that. And *Videophone* wasn't one of those beats. So when he played it and he said, 'She loves this beat' I was surprised."[204]

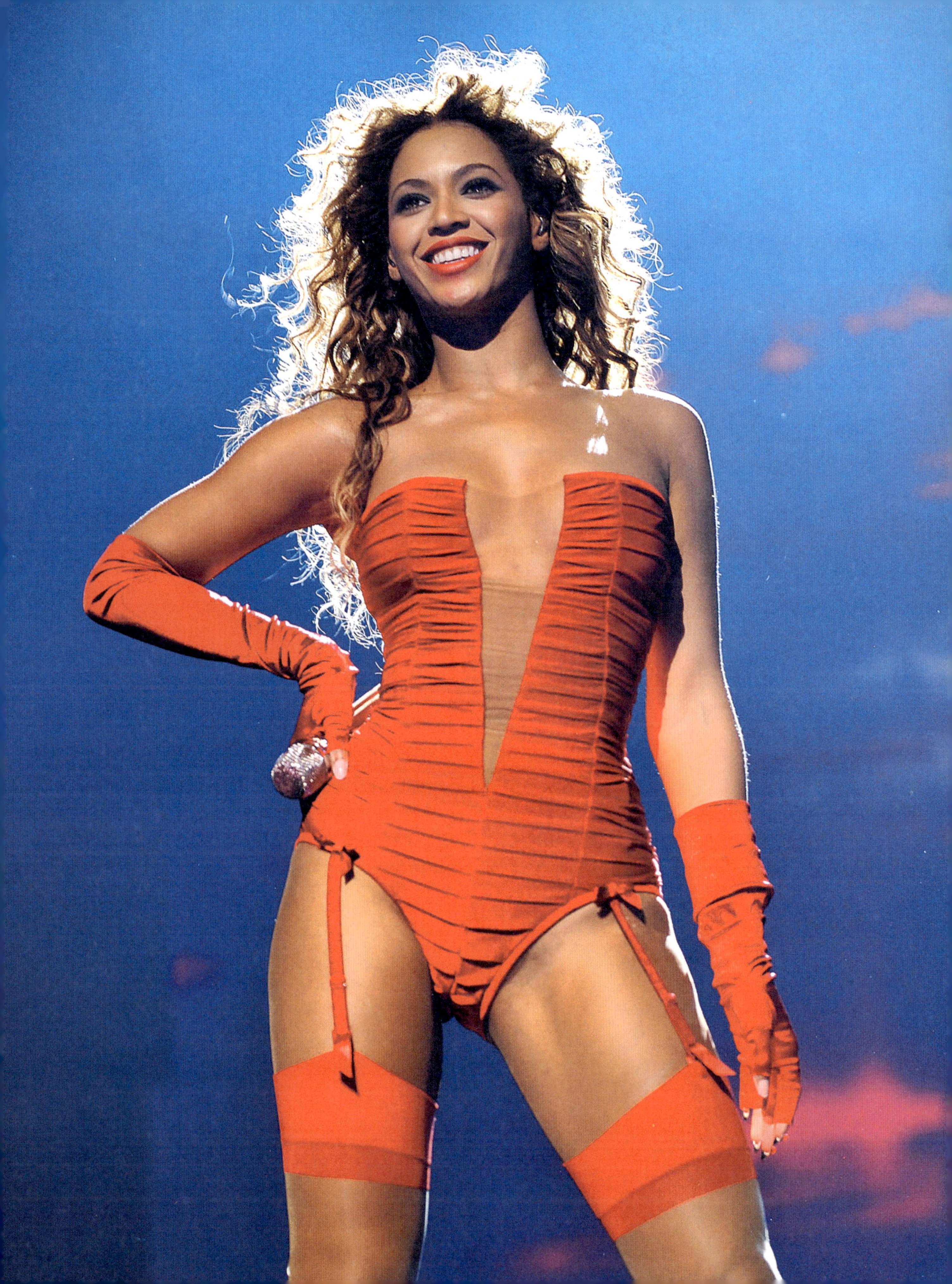

The singer Usher, who was once a babysitter for Beyoncé and her sister Solange when they were teenagers.

LOVE IN THIS CLUB PART II
(USHER, FEATURING BEYONCÉ AND LIL WAYNE)

(Raymond IV, Dwayne Carter Jr., Jamal Jones, Lamar Taylor, Jay Jenkins, Ryon Lovett, Keith Thomas, Darnell Dalton, Thomas Bell, Linda Creed, Keri Hilson/5'09)

Musicians: Usher: vocals / Beyoncé Knowles: vocals / Lil Wayne: rap / Karl Heilbron: guitar / Ray Holten: guitar / **Recording:** Hitland Studios, Alpharetta: 2007 to 2008 / The Record Plant, Los Angeles: 2007 to 2008 / **Technical team:** Producer: Soundz / **Usher *Here I Stand* (album)** / Released in the USA by Laface Records: 13 May 2008 (CD ref.: 88697-23388-2)

You could superimpose the vocal line of *Dilemma*, a single by Nelly and Kelly Rowland released in 2002, over the instrumental—identical in all respects—of *Love in this Club Part II*, yet different producers are behind each song. In the case of *Love in this Club Part II*, which is on *Here I Stand*, Usher's fifth album, it was Kenneth Charles Coby, aka Soundz, who was in charge. Unusually, Beyoncé's performance is not credited, even though she is accustomed to adding her name to the credits of all musical works in which she has been involved—as Soundz himself described, without pulling any punches in explaining this strange habit. "She's the best in the game at promoting a record and when she does one of your records you'll get a single, radio, commercials, and movies. There are so many different types of money that comes with Beyoncé when you do a record for her so it's kind of like the price of admission—the price to get all the other aspects is that you have to pay a little bit. She'll want a little publishing and that's guaranteed; she's going to ask for it and you're going to give it to her; no ifs, ands, or buts. She's going to make that record the biggest hit in the world so give her that publishing. She'll take about 20%."[205] Young producers and composers—you have been warned!

SINGLE

JUST STAND UP

(Kenneth "Babyface" Edmonds, Ronnie "Preach" Walton/3'37)

Musicians: Ashanti: vocals, backing vocals / **Beyoncé Knowles:** vocals, backing vocals / **Carrie Underwood:** vocals, backing vocals / **Ciara:** vocals, backing vocals / **Fergie:** vocals, backing vocals / **Kenya Ivey:** backing vocals / **Keyshia Cole:** vocals, backing vocals / **LeAnn Rimes:** vocals, backing vocals / **Leona Lewis:** vocals, backing vocals / **Mariah Carey:** vocals, backing vocals / **Mary J. Blige:** vocals, backing vocals / **Melissa Etheridge:** vocals, backing vocals / **Miley Cyrus:** vocals, backing vocals / **Natasha Bedingfield:** vocals, backing vocals / **Rihanna:** vocals, backing vocals / **Sheryl Crow:** vocals, backing vocals / Ronnie "Preach" Walton: programming, synthesizers / Kenneth "Babyface" Edmonds: programming, synthesizers / **Recording:** Brandon's Way Recording, Los Angeles: 2008 / Starstruck Studios, Nashville: 2008 / Chicago Recording Company, Chicago: 2008 / Legacy Studios, New York: 2008 / Roc the Mic Studios, New York: 2008 / Capitol Studios, Los Angeles: 2008 / **Technical team:** Producers: Kenneth "Babyface" Edmonds, Antonio "L. A." Reid, Ronnie "Preach" Walton / **Executive producer:** Antonio "L. A." Reid / **Recording engineers:** Paul Boutin, Brian Garten, Alejandro Venguer, Marcos Tovar / ***Just Stand Up* (single)** / Released in the USA by Island Def Jam Music Group: 2 September 2008 (ref.: B0012228-32) / **Best chart ranking in the USA:** 11

Twenty years after they last worked together, the two star producers Kenneth "Babyface" Edmonds and Antonio "L. A." Reid were reunited for a good cause: to produce the single for an all-female charity group made up of the biggest stars of the moment, including Ashanti, Fergie (from Black Eyed Peas), Miley Cyrus, Mariah Carey, and, of course, Beyoncé. The song was recorded in 2008 as part of the national campaign Stand Up to Cancer, with the aim of raising funds to combat the disease. With the exception of Sheryl Crow, LeAnn Rimes, and Melissa Etheridge, the song's various performers came together on 5 December 2008 on stage at Radio City Music Hall in New York to sing *Just Stand Up* together for a special broadcast devoted to the noble cause.

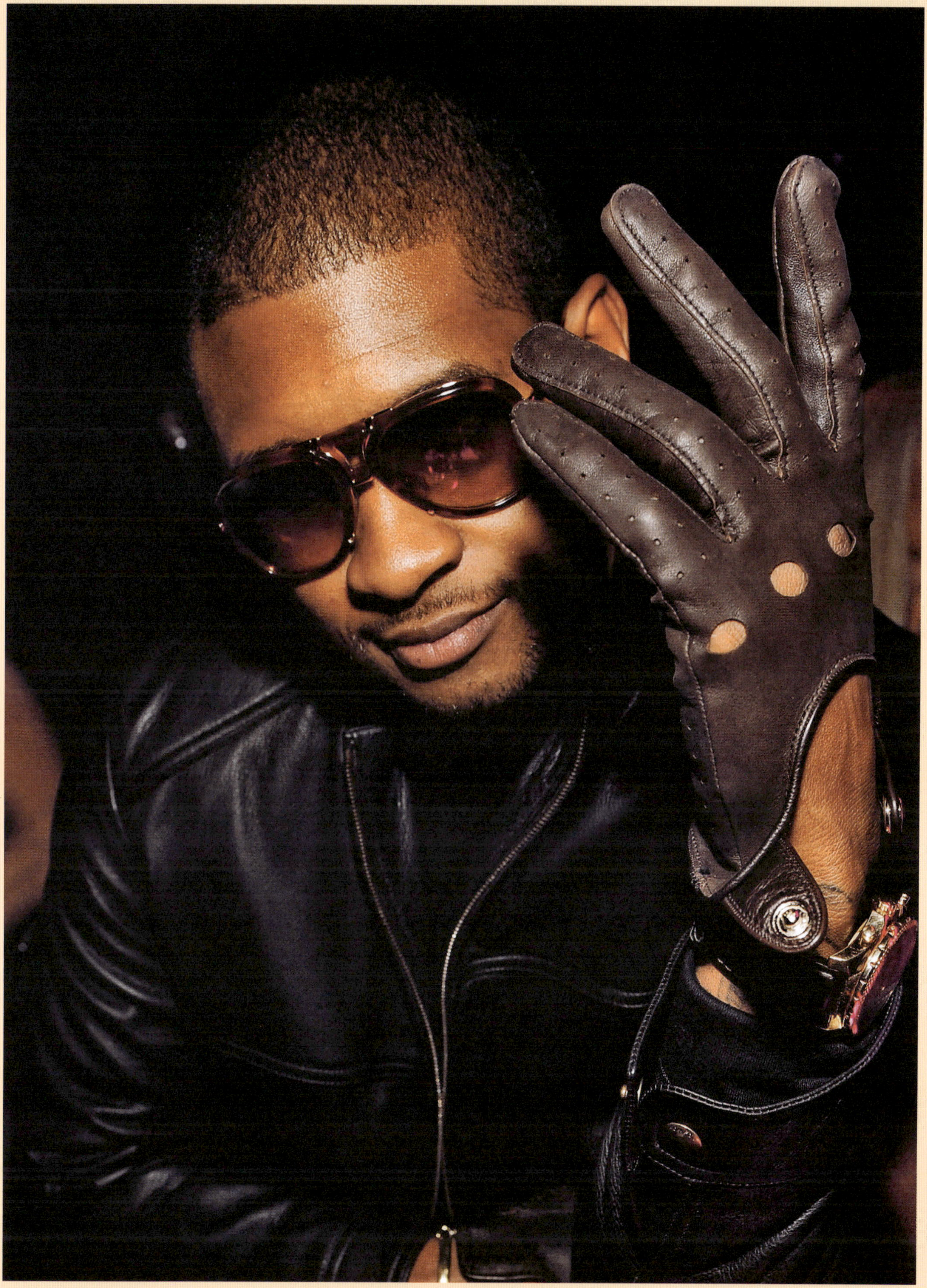

SING A SONG
(THE WUBB GIRLZ FEATURING BEYONCÉ AS SHINE)

(Bob Boyle, Brad Mossman, Beyoncé Knowles/1'36)

Musician: Beyoncé Knowles: vocals / **Recording:** BMossman Productions, Torrance: 2008 to 2009 / Music World Studios, Houston: 2008 to 2009 / Roc the Mic Studios, New York: 2008 to 2009 / **Technical team:** Producers: Beyoncé Knowles, The Bama Boyz / **Executive producer:** Mathew Knowles / **Recording engineers:** Brad Mossman, Jim Caruana, Rommel Nino Villanueva / **Wow! Wow! Wubbzy! Sing a Song (album)** / Released in the USA by Legacy: April 2009 (CD ref.: 59116)

Beyoncé lends her voice to the character Shine in *Wubb Idol*, an animated television special based on the *Wow! Wow! Wubbzy!* series, created by Bob Doyle in 2006. Along with her friends Shimmer and Sparkle, Shine is part of a successful musical group. Beyoncé's participation in this song, which would play over the opening credits, offered welcome visibility to the feature-length film, which was broadcast on the children's channel Nickelodeon on 1 May 2009. The making of *Sing a Song* involved Eddie "E-Trez" Smith III, Jesse J. Rankins, and Jonathan D. Wells, otherwise known as The Bama Boyz, who had already produced *Home for the Holidays* for Destiny's Child in 2005 and had just made *Why Don't You Love Me* for Beyoncé. The latter would appear on an EP that featured some unreleased material from the sessions for *I Am…Sasha Fierce*, logically entitled *I Am…Sasha Fierce—The Bonus Tracks*.

VENUS VS MARS
(JAY-Z)

(Timothy Mosley, Jerome "J-Roc" Harmon, Shawn Carter/3'10)

Musicians: Jay-Z: rap / Beyoncé Knowles: vocals / **Recording:** Roc the Mic Studios, New York: 2009 / **Technical team:** Producers: Jerome "J-Roc" Harmon, Timbaland / **Executive producers:** Kanye West, Shawn Carter / **Recording engineer:** Chris Godbey / **Jay-Z The Blueprint 3 (album)** / Released in the USA by Roc Nation: 8 September 2009 (LP ref.: 520856-1, CD ref.: 520856-2)

Jay-Z's fans know the anecdote; Beyoncé's may not. When the rapper recorded *Venus vs Mars* in 2009, he invited the singer, model, and actor Cassie Ventura to add a few words in the choruses. Although she is credited in the sleeve notes, no doubt so as not to offend her and/or deprive her of some royalties, it is in fact the voice of Beyoncé Knowles that can be heard on the album. Mrs Knowles Carter appears for only a few seconds here and there in the song, but her presence makes all the difference, for it is a hip-hop smash of the kind the duo of Kanye West and Jay-Z knew how to make. The same album, *The Blueprint 3*, released on 8 September 2009, also features *Empire State of Mind*, an international hit recorded with Alicia Keys—an album that any self-respecting hip-hop fan should have in their collection.

SINGLE

TELEPHONE
(LADY GAGA AND BEYONCÉ)

(Beyoncé Knowles, Lady Gaga, LaShawn Daniels, Lazonate Franklin, Rodney Jerkins/3'40)

Musicians: Lady Gaga: vocals, backing vocals / Beyoncé Knowles: vocals, backing vocals / **Recording:** Darkchild Studios, Los Angeles: 2009 / 2nd Floor Studios, Los Angeles: 2009 / Studio Groove, Osaka: 2009 (Beyoncé's voice) / **Technical team:** Producers: Rodney "Darkchild" Jerkins, Lady Gaga / **Executive producer:** Vincent Herbert / **Recording engineers:** Paul Foley, Mike Donaldson, Hisashi Mizoguchi / **Assistant recording engineer:** Takayuki Matsushima / **Lady Gaga The Fame Monster (EP)** / Released in the USA by Streamline Records/Interscope Records: 18 November 2009 (LP ref.: B0013821-01, CD ref.: B0013872-02) / **Best chart ranking in the USA:** 3

This single by Lady Gaga, accompanied by Beyoncé, was one of the biggest hits of 2009. How could anyone not nod their head in time or even dance on the counter of their favorite bar upon hearing this unavoidable hit? This is doubtless what Beyoncé thought when the singer of *Bad Romance* suggested they work together on this offering from the incomparable Rodney "Darkchild" Jerkins. Jerkins produced nothing less than the greatest R&B hits in history, including *The Boy Is Mine* by Brandy & Monica, *It's Not Right But It's Okay* by Whitney Houston, *Say My Name* by Destiny's Child, *If You Had My Love* by Jennifer Lopez, and *He Wasn't Man Enough* by Toni Braxton—which made him a safe bet for any star worthy of the name. Beyond the undeniable effectiveness of its melody and production, the clip of *Telephone*, directed by Jonas Åkerlund, contributed to its success, as well as to the triumph of the highly talented Lady Gaga. For the occasion, Åkerlund even borrowed from Quentin Tarantino the Pussy Wagon, the vehicle driven by Uma Thurman in the movie *Kill Bill: Volume 1* in 2003. "Gaga is my girl!" Beyoncé said in 2011. "I'm her biggest fan. When I first saw her perform, I actually called her and said, 'You are great!' That was before her popularity hit, and we had a natural connection. Later, she asked me to do her video, and I said, 'I trust you, Gaga. I'll do whatever you want me to do.'"[206] A duo at the highest level, whom one dreams of seeing reunited.

Stefani Germanotta, alias Lady Gaga, at the start of her career, riding the wave of the success of her hits *Just Dance*, *Paparazzi*, and *Poker Face*.

BEYONCÉ: ALL THE SONGS 281

Alicia Keys and Beyoncé on stage at Madison Square Garden, New York, 17 March 2010.

PUT IT IN A LOVE SONG
(ALICIA KEYS FEATURING BEYONCÉ)

(Alicia Keys, Kasseem Dean/3'15)

Musicians: Alicia Keys: vocals, Fender Rhodes, piano / **Beyoncé Knowles:** vocals / Carlos Alomar: electric guitar / Steve Mostyn: bass guitar / Swizz Beatz: programming / **Recording:** Oven Studios, New York: 2009 / Conway Recording Studios, Los Angeles: 2009 / Germano Studios, New York: 2009 / MSR Studios, New York: 2009 / **Technical team:** Producers: Alicia Keys, Swizz Beatz / Recording engineer: Ann Mincieli / Assistant recording engineers: Chris Soper, George Fullan, Miki Tsutsumi / **Alicia Keys *The Element of Freedom* (album)** / Released in the USA by J Records: 11 December 2009 (LP ref.: 88697-46571-1, CD ref.: 88697-46571-2)

If there was a second pretender to the throne of the most talented female R&B singer at the very end of the 2000s, it was definitely Alicia Keys. Discovered in 2001 with the single *Fallin'*, from her first album, *Song in A Minor*, which she followed with a series of hits (*You Don't Know My Name* in 2003, *If I Ain't Got You* in 2004, and *Empire State of Mind* with Jay-Z in 2009), the young woman was not, however, a rival to Beyoncé, but rather a close friend. Fans of neo soul, Alicia Keys's specialty, therefore eagerly awaited a duet from these two divas with divine voices; *Put It in a Love Song* made it a done deal. The song was co-produced by Swizz Beatz, who would marry Keys on 31 July 2010 following a two-year romance, even though the two artists had known each other since their teens.

SINGLE

SEE ME NOW
(KANYE WEST, FEATURING BEYONCÉ, CHARLIE WILSON, AND BIG SEAN)

(Brenda Russell, Brian Russell, No I. D., Beyoncé Knowles, Kanye West/6'04)

Musicians: Kanye West: rap / Beyoncé Knowles: vocals / Big Sean: rap / Charlie Wilson: vocals / **Recording:** ?: August 2010 / **Technical team:** Producers: Kanye West, Lex Luger, No I. D. / Executive producers: Antonio "L. A." Reid, Gee Roberson, Kanye West, Kyambo Joshua, Shawn Carter / **Kanye West *My Beautiful Dark Twisted Fantasy*—iTunes Store Bonus Track** / Released in the USA by Roc-A-Fella Records: 22 November 2010 (LP ref.: B0014695-01, CD ref.: B0014695-02)

Although in the eyes of the wider public Kanye West's music is often eclipsed by his escapades and his controversial statements, it must be admitted that the rapper and producer, a close friend of Jay-Z and Beyoncé, has considerable talent and exceptional skill in production, being a real magician when it comes to manipulating the faders on a console. When he was a guest of the presenter Angie Martinez on her show on the New York radio station WQHT, to announce the imminent release of his new album *My Beautiful Dark Twisted Fantasy*, West declared that a bonus track, the recording of which had just been completed at five o'clock that morning with vocal takes by Beyoncé, would soon be available to be downloaded legally on the iTunes platform. Beyoncé sang the choruses, and another distinguished guest was present in the shape of Charlie Wilson, former vocalist of The Gap Band.

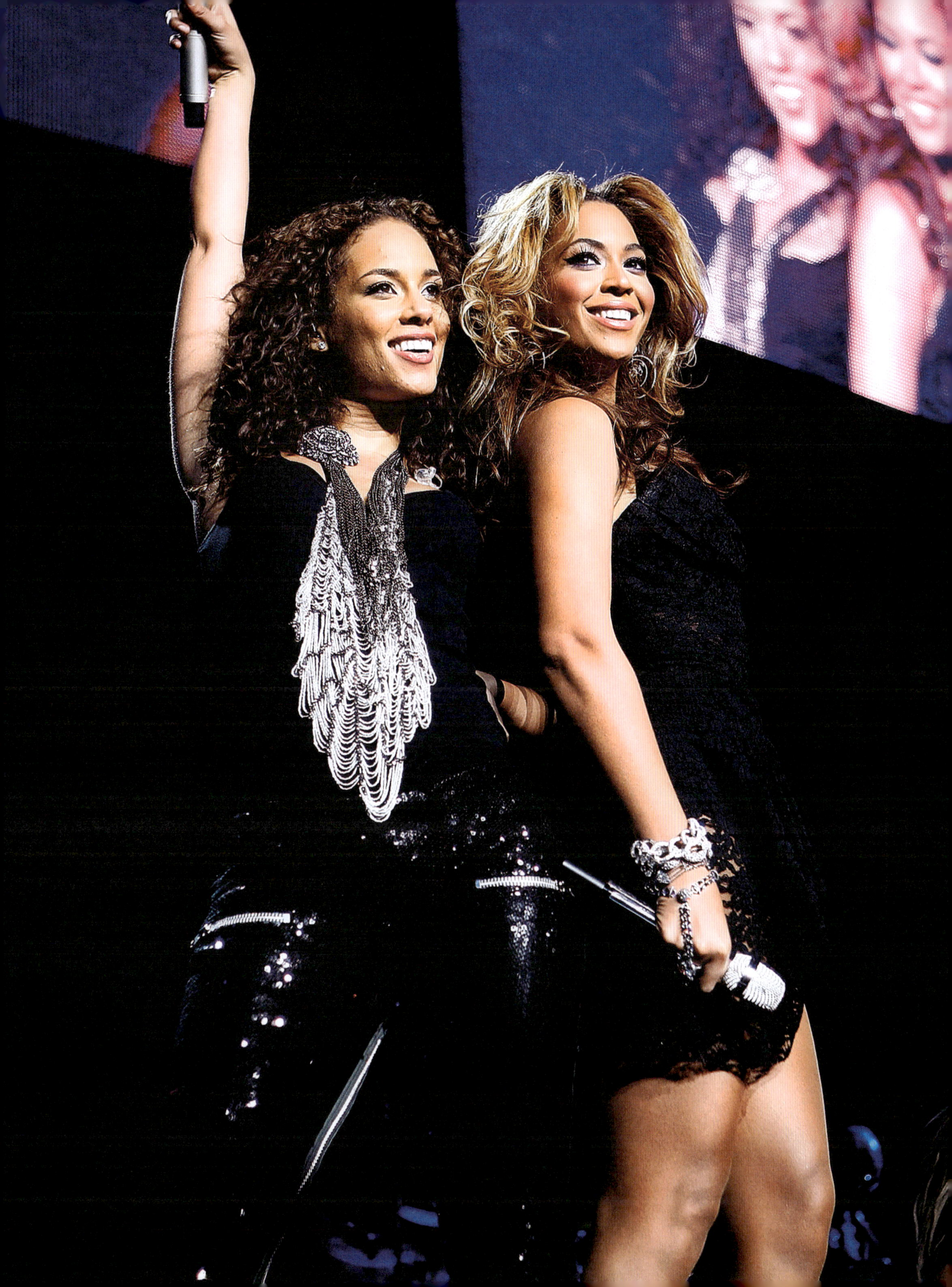

Solange and Beyoncé Knowles in New York, January 2010.

OUTTAKES

HELLO

(Beyoncé Knowles, David Quiñones, Evan "Kidd" Bogart, Ramon Owen/4'17)

Musician: Beyoncé Knowles: vocals, backing vocals / **Recording:** The Campground, Los Angeles: 2008 / Electric Lady Studios, New York: 2008 / **Technical team: Producers:** Beyoncé Knowles, REO / **Executive producers:** Beyoncé Knowles, Mathew Knowles / **Recording engineers:** David Quiñones, Jim Caruana (vocals) / *I Am…Sasha Fierce Deluxe Edition* **(album)** / Released in the USA by Music World Music/Columbia: 18 November 2008 (CD ref.: 88697 40980 2)

Graphic designer, film director, plastic artist, musician, and producer, Ramon "REO" Owen had already lived a thousand lives when he was diagnosed with Hodgkin lymphoma. As he underwent multiple chemotherapy sessions over more than six months, the young man found the strength to battle the illness by taking refuge in his love of art, and especially music, which he practiced assiduously. "Remarkably, during my journey of recovery, some of the music I created during my illness reached the ears of a major label executive, resulting in a publishing deal. Shortly thereafter, I achieved a significant milestone: my first major label placement on Beyoncé's album *Sasha Fierce*. It was a cosmic sign that not only did I belong in this world, but I also had so much more of life left to experience and share through my art."[207] After he had defeated the illness and worked with Beyoncé on *Hello*, REO worked successfully with Keyshia Cole, Lil Wayne, and Ludacris.

EGO

(Beyoncé Knowles, Elvis Williams, Harold Lilly/3'56)

Musicians: Beyoncé Knowles: vocals, backing vocals / Philip Margiziotis: horns / Donald Hayes: saxophone / Dontae Winslow: trumpet / **Recording:** Tree Sound Studios, Atlanta: 2008 / Roc the Mic Studios, New York: 2008 / **Technical team: Producers:** Beyoncé Knowles, Elvis "Blac Elvis" Williams, Harold Lilly / **Executive producers:** Beyoncé Knowles, Mathew Knowles / **Recording engineers:** Mack Woodward, Jim Caruana (vocals) / *I Am…Sasha Fierce Deluxe Edition* **(album)** / Released in the USA by Music World Music/Columbia: 18 November 2008 (CD ref.: 88697 40980 2)

What is Beyoncé referring to when she sings: "It's too big, it's too wide, it's too strong, it won't fit, it's too much, it's too tough"? To her boyfriend's ego, of course—in this song initially composed and produced by the duo of Elvis Williams and Harold Lilly for the singer Chrisette Michele, who had a hit in 2009 with the single *What You Do*. When she turned down *Ego*, it was rescued by Beyoncé, who with her version created yet another quality piece. Even so, it would never go above number 39 on *Billboard*, when it was released as a single featuring rap parts by Kanye West.

Singer Jon McLaughlin, who wrote the first version of *Smash Into You*, initially entitled *Smack Into You*.

SCARED OF LONELY

(Beyoncé Knowles, Crystal Johnson, LaShawn Daniels, Rico Love, Rodney Jerkins, Solange Knowles/3'43)

Musicians: Beyoncé Knowles: vocals, backing vocals / **Rodney Jerkins:** additional instruments / **Recording:** 2nd Floor Studios, Orlando: 2008 / Electric Lady Studios, New York: 2008 / **Technical team:** Producers: Beyoncé Knowles, Rodney Jerkins / **Executive producers:** Beyoncé Knowles, Mathew Knowles / **Recording engineers:** Mike Donaldson, Roberto Vasquez, Jim Caruana (vocals) / *I Am…Sasha Fierce Deluxe Edition* **(album)** / Released in the USA by Music World Music/Columbia: 18 November 2008 (CD ref.: 88697 40980 2)

Rodney Jerkins once again uses his imitation of a harpsichord (which he had employed on Jennifer Lopez's *If You Had My Love* in 1999) to create a quality new song for Beyoncé. In it, she sings of her fear of loneliness, at a tempo perfectly cut out for the dancefloor. Co-written with her sister Solange, *Scared of Lonely* contains an inevitably autobiographical message, given that the singer had declared that *I Am…Sasha Fierce* was like an intimate journal she was revealing to the world. "People would be surprised as to the lack of experiences I've had," she declared in 2008 regarding her relations with men. "When I was 12, 13, I had my first boyfriend, and he was my boyfriend till I was 17 […] That was my only experience with a guy, and since then I've only had one other boyfriend in my life—Jay. I wrote my lyrics from growing up in my mother's hair salon and hearing stories from women there. Women would come in and they'd talk about what was going on in their lives. I would hear about this woman who was shy, and this woman who liked men with money, and this one's into football players, and this woman's been married 20 years and her husband's doing this and that… Those were the stories I heard."[193]

SMASH INTO YOU

(Beyoncé Knowles, Terius Nash, Thaddis Harrell, Christopher Stewart/4'32)

Musicians: Beyoncé Knowles: vocals, backing vocals / **Steve Jordan:** drums / **Recording:** The Boom Boom Room, Burbank: 2008 / Germano Studios, New York: 2008 / Roc the Mic Studios, New York: 2008 / **Technical team:** Producers: Beyoncé Knowles, Terius "The-Dream" Nash, C. "Tricky" Stewart / **Executive producers:** Beyoncé Knowles, Mathew Knowles / **Recording engineers:** Brian "B-LUV" Thomas, Jim Caruana, Kuk Harrell / *I Am…Sasha Fierce Deluxe Edition* **(album)** / Released in the USA by Music World Music/Columbia: 18 November 2008 (CD ref.: 88697 40980 2)

This song, which initially bore the title *Smack Into You*, was produced by Terius "The-Dream" Nash and Christopher "Tricky" Stewart and recorded by Jon McLaughlin for his fourth album, *OK Now*. Eventually it was removed from that album's tracklisting and offered to Beyoncé, who changed two letters in its title and added her name to the credits—which observers, even those who were great admirers of her work, did not fail to point out. Despite the harmonic progression that is rather too similar to that of *If I Were a Boy*, *Smash Into You* is a quality song, and features on the deluxe version of *I Am…Sasha Fierce*.

BEYONCÉ: ALL THE SONGS   285

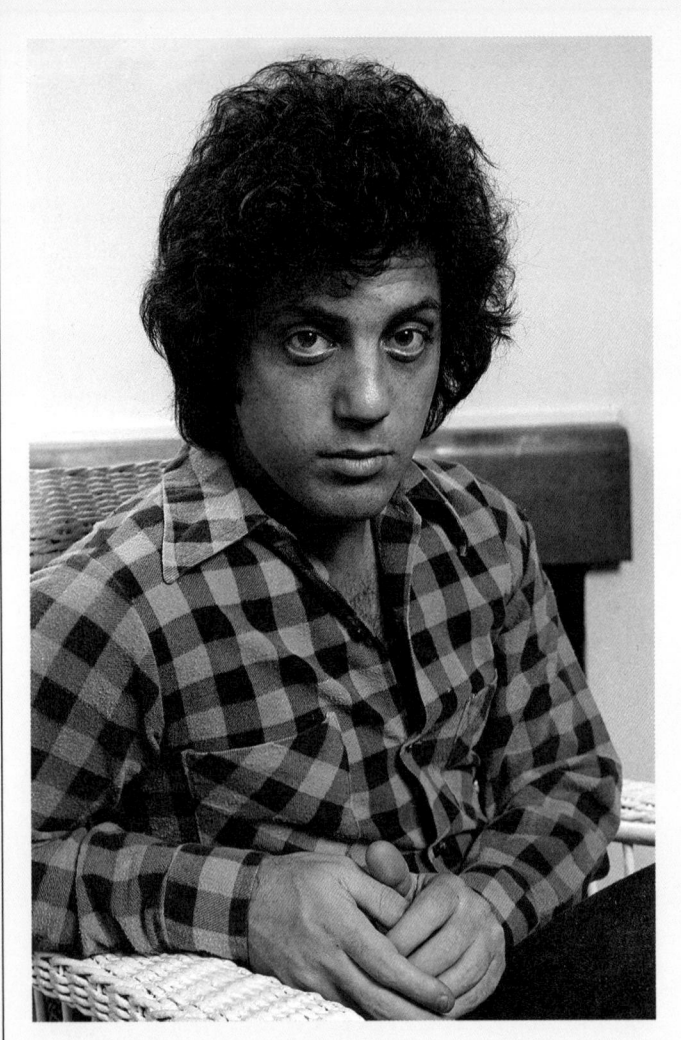

Billy Joel at the time of the success of his single *Honesty*, 1978.

SAVE THE HERO

(Beyoncé Knowles, James Scheffer, Rico Love, Alexandra Tamposi/4'33)

Musicians: Beyoncé Knowles: vocals, backing vocals / **Jim Jonsin:** backing vocals / **Rico Love:** backing vocals / **Recording:** South Beach Studios, Miami Beach: 2008 / Roc the Mic Studios, New York: 2008 / **Technical team:** Producers: Jim Jonsin, Rico Love, Beyoncé / Executive producers: Beyoncé Knowles, Mathew Knowles / **Recording engineer:** Jim Caruana / *I Am…Sasha Fierce* **bonus track** / **Digital release on iTunes:** November 2008

Put together by Rico Love and Jim Jonsin (who is credited under his real name, James Scheffer), *Save the Hero* is an obvious reference to Beyoncé's love of gospel music. It was worked on by the producers at South Beach Studios in Miami Beach, and enhanced with Beyoncé's voice under the technical expertise of recording engineer Jim Caruana, one of the few technicians granted the privilege of recording her voice. After working in public television in Syracuse, Jonsin got himself noticed when he worked as a recording engineer at Full Sail University in Winter Park, Florida, and then was the in-house recording engineer at Sony Music Studios in New York from 1994 to 2007. Now a freelance technician, Caruana could choose the projects that appealed to him, while remaining completely faithful to Beyoncé, whose voice he recorded from 2001 to 2008.

THAT'S WHY YOU'RE BEAUTIFUL

(Andrew Hey, Beyoncé Knowles, James Fauntleroy II/3'40)

Musicians: Beyoncé Knowles: vocals, backing vocals / **Andrew Hey:** additional instruments / **Recording:** Roc the Mic Studios, New York: 2008 / **Technical team:** Producers: Beyoncé Knowles, Andrew Hey / Executive producers: Beyoncé Knowles, Mathew Knowles / **Recording engineers:** Jim Caruana, Andrew Hey / Assistant recording engineer: David Boyd / *I Am…Sasha Fierce Deluxe Edition* **(album)** / Released in the USA by Music World Music/Columbia: 18 November 2008 (CD ref.: 88697 40980 2)

Although he was once part of the team of writers/composers/producers The Underdogs, who were in charge of the soundtrack of *Dreamgirls* in 2006, here Andrew Hey worked with Beyoncé on his own. Featuring a series of chords played on bass guitar by Hey himself, *That's Why You're Beautiful* is a ballad perfectly suited to the part of the album conveying our singer's most unassuming side.

HONESTY

(Billy Joel/3'46)

Musician: Beyoncé Knowles: vocals, backing vocals / **Recording:** South Beach Studios, Miami Beach: 2008 / **Technical team:** Producers: Scott Storch, Beyoncé Knowles / Executive producers: Beyoncé Knowles, Mathew Knowles / *I Am … Sasha Fierce Platinum Edition* **(album)** / Released in the USA by Music World Music/Columbia: 20 October 2009 (CD ref.: 88697 56937 2)

Although *Honesty*, a ballad arranged by the hit-maker Scott Storch, had "success" written all over it, Beyoncé could not claim authorship, because it was one of the American singer Billy Joel's most famous songs. Drawn from his sixth album, *52nd Street*, released in 1978, *Honesty* was one of the hits of 1979 when it was released as a single. Written by Joel and produced by Phil Ramone, it is now a classic in many countries, but it was in France that it became a legendary slow-dance number and inspired the famous composer Vladimir Cosma when he set to work on *Reality*, the cult ballad in the movie *La Boum*, directed by Claude Pinoteau in 1980. Cosma explained that he had asked SACEM [the French society of authors, composers, and publishers of music] for a list of the slow-dance numbers that had been most successful between 1960 and 1980, and had then studied them as one studies a Beethoven symphony, analyzing their construction, their tempo…It was *Honesty*, with its sadness and effective melody, that inspired him to write *Reality*, 29 years before Scott Storch and Beyoncé got hold of it and made an appealing reinterpretation of it.

WHY DON'T YOU LOVE ME

(Angela Beyincé, Eddie Smith III, Jesse Rankins, Jonathan Wells, Solange Knowles, Beyoncé Knowles/3'38)

Musician: Beyoncé Knowles: vocals, backing vocals / **Recording:** Music World Studios, Houston: 2008 / Roc the Mic Studios, New York: 2008 / **Technical team: Producers:** Beyoncé Knowles, The Bama Boyz / **Executive producers:** Beyoncé Knowles, Mathew Knowles / **Recording engineers:** The Bama Boyz, Jim Caruana / *I Am…Sasha Fierce—The Bonus Tracks* **(EP)** / Digital release by Music World Music/Columbia: 12 November 2009

Here, Beyoncé sings of a woman's inability to seduce the man she loves despite her qualities and physical attributes, which she lists in the song. The instrumental passage in *Why Don't You Love Me* is the work of The Bama Boyz, a trio comprising Eddie "E-Trez" Smith III, Jesse J. Rankins, and Jonathan D. Wells. They had just produced the song *ChampagneChroniKnightCap* for Solange Knowles, who asked them for something she could offer to her sister, then in the midst of preproduction of *I Am…Sasha Fierce*. The Bama Boyz passed *Why Don't You Love Me* to the younger Knowles sister, who hastened to write the vocal line and lyrics before sending it to Beyoncé. "When we heard Solange's demo," Jonathan Wells explained, "we were excited because that track was more our true sound than any of the others, but we still kinda didn't believe Beyoncé would cut it… but we hoped!"[208] Against all expectations, Beyoncé was charmed by the song, with its very soul sound (its snare drum struck every beat is one of the signatures of the Motown Sound), and recorded a sublime version that immediately calls to mind her performance in the movie *Dreamgirls*. A video was even shot when Beyoncé decided to make it into a promotional single. "We are excited," Eddie Smith III said, "because it went from being a song that didn't make it to the album to a song that's now a bonus on the album, to a single, a video, and now we get to go overseas and be a part of the promotion. It's a rollercoaster."[209]

POISON

(Beyoncé Knowles, Johntá Austin, Mikkel S. Eriksen, Tor Erik Hermansen/4'05)

Musicians: Beyoncé Knowles: vocals, backing vocals / **Mikkel S. Eriksen:** additional instruments / **Tor Erik Hermansen:** additional instruments / **Recording:** Roc the Mic Studios, New York: 2009 / **Technical team: Producers:** Beyoncé Knowles, Stargate / **Executive producers:** Beyoncé Knowles, Mathew Knowles / **Recording engineers:** Mikkel S. Eriksen, Jim Caruana, Carlos Oyanedel, Damien Lewis / *I Am … Sasha Fierce—The Bonus Tracks* **(EP)** / Digital release by Music World Music/Columbia: 12 November 2009

Yet another successful joint effort for Beyoncé and Stargate, *Poison* recalls the heyday of R&B and would doubtless have secured her another hit had it been released as a single. When asked in August 2010 about the songs on her iPod (for the benefit of younger readers, the iPod, made by Apple, was the Rolls-Royce of audio players during the 2000s), the rapper Nicky Minaj mentioned this song, honoring it with a well-deserved compliment: "I love the melody, I love the cadence. It's playful, but it's just so in-your-face. It's dope and it's creative."[210] Interviewed by Paul Tingen of the website soundonsound.com in 2010, Stargate's Mikkel S. Eriksen described his duo's way of working, jamming together in their studio, each behind his own keyboard, and generally starting with a melody or a chord progression rather than a beat: "We get sounds and we start playing melodic ideas and feels, and when one of us gets something the other likes, the other might say, 'Oh, do that again,' or 'Why not try this chord instead?' and so on. We're going for a unique feel, or melody, or chord progression, or an interesting sound, anything can be an inspiration…We put a lot of thought and attention to having strong melodies in our tracks, and the feedback we get from singers and lyricists is that they love that there are already so many melodies in the track, which they can use."[163]

Cadillac Records (Music from the Motion Picture) **(compilation)**
Released in the USA by Columbia/Music World Music: 2 December 2008
(LP ref.: 88697369361, CD ref.: 88697 41352 2)

In order to play Etta James in *Cadillac Records*, Beyoncé immersed herself completely in the character.

Cadillac Records (2008)

1. **I'm A Man** – Jeffrey Wright
2. **At Last** – Beyoncé*
3. **No Particular Place To Go** – Mos Def
4. **I'm Your Hoochie Coochie Man** – Jeffrey Wright
5. **Once In A Lifetime** – Beyoncé*
6. **Let's Take A Walk** – Raphael Saadiq
7. **6 O'clock Blues** – Solange
8. **Nadine** – Mos Def
9. **The Sound** – Mary Mary
10. **Last Night** – Little Walter
11. **I'd Rather Go Blind** – Beyoncé*
12. **My Babe** – Columbus Short
13. **Bridging The Gap** – Nas Featuring Olu Dara
14. **Maybelline** – Mos Def
15. **Forty Days And Forty Nights** – Buddy Guy
16. **Trust In Me** – Beyoncé*
17. **Juke** – Soul 7 Featuring Kim Wilson
18. **Smokestack Lightnin'** – Eamonn Walker
19. **Promised Land** – Mos Def
20. **All I Could Do Is Cry** – Beyoncé*
21. **My Babe** – Elvis Presley
22. **I Can't Be Satisfied** – Jeffrey Wright
23. **Come On** – Mos Def
24. **Country Blues** – Jeffrey Wright and Bill Simms Jr
25. **Evolution Of A Man** – Q-Tip Featuring Al Kapone
26. **Radio Station** – Terrence Blanchard

* *Cadillac Records (Music from the Motion Picture)* features tracks by several artists; only those performed by Beyoncé are discussed here.

HOMAGE TO ANOTHER SOUL ICON

"I want to be the first Black woman to win an Oscar, a Tony, and a Grammy," Beyoncé declared in 2006.[211] It was thus with this goal in mind that she pursued, in 2008, her quest for the role that would make her a star of the big screen: she played the soul singer Etta James in Darnell Martin's *Cadillac Records*. The movie told the story of the rise of Chess Records, the Chicago label founded by Leonard Chess, which had introduced to the world many artists who later became iconic. In order to get inside the skin of the singer of *At Last* and *I'd Rather Go Blind*, famous for her talent but also for her plain speaking and addiction to heroin, Beyoncé—who was also the film's executive producer—decided to spend a few days in The Phoenix House, a detoxification center in Brooklyn, in order to meet drug addicts. "I never tried drugs in my life so I didn't know about it all," she explained. "It was hard to go there. In the beginning I didn't want to offend anyone, I didn't want to ask the wrong questions or seem judgmental. They were so honest, though, and I am so thankful. I don't think I could have understood that level of pain or need."[212] Featuring a star-studded cast that included Adrien Brody as Leonard Chess, Jeffrey Wright as Muddy Waters, Cedric the Entertainer as Willie Dixon, and Mos Def as Chuck Berry, *Cadillac Records* was released on 5 December 2008, two weeks after *I Am…Sasha Fierce*, and thus contributed to the media coverage of Beyoncé's new album. "I'm the most proud of that movie, more than anything I've done so far," she said in 2008. "More than anything, it changed me. It changed my art. It changed my way of looking at everything; my approach to the songs I chose and the way I sang. I kept it a lot cleaner and lot more simple."[212]

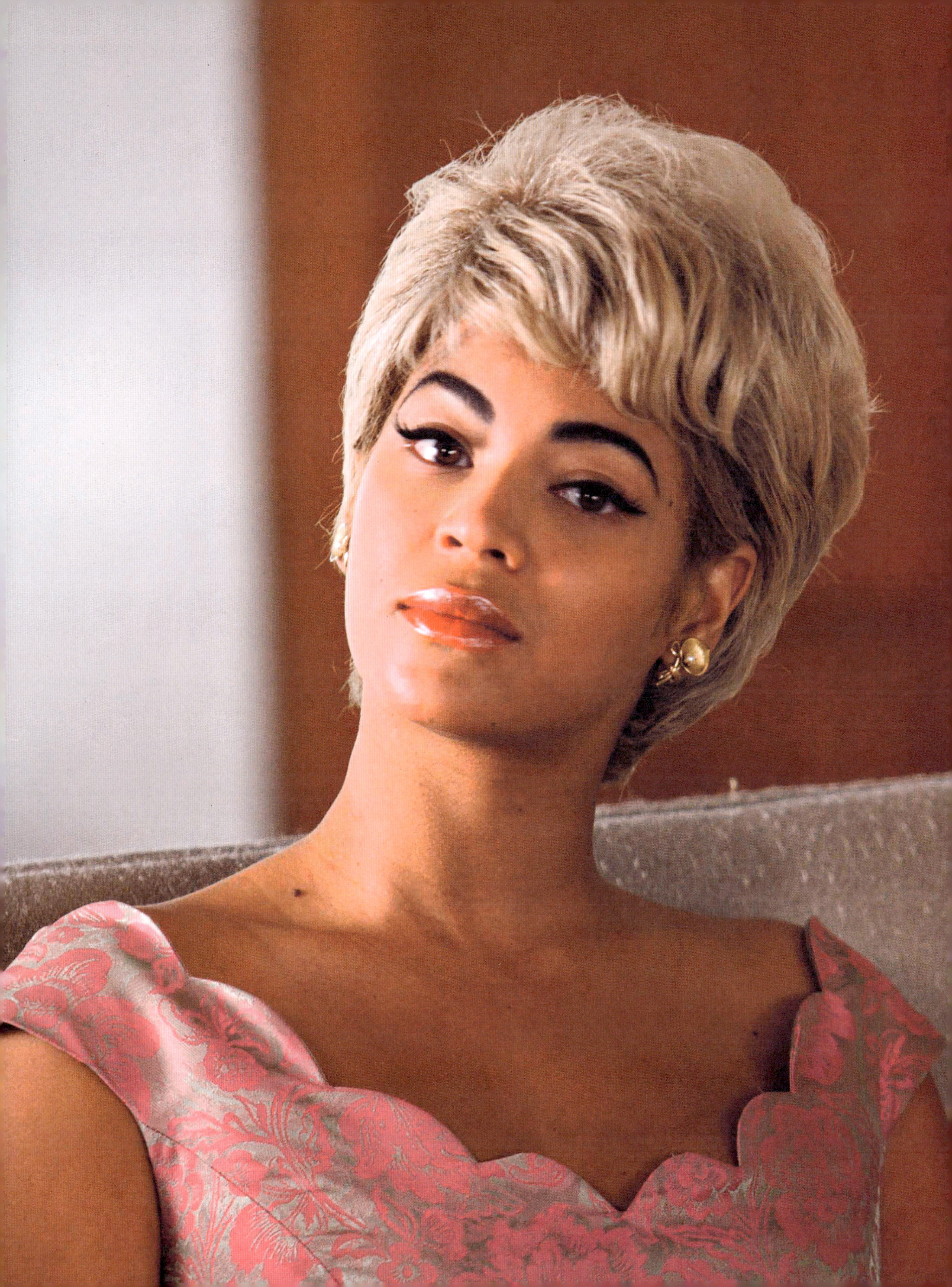

Beyoncé Knowles performs *At Last* at the gala that followed the inauguration of President Barack Obama, 20 January 2009.

AT LAST

(Harry Warren, Mack Gordon/3'01)

Musicians: Beyoncé Knowles: vocals / Billy Flynn: guitar / Danny Kortchmar: guitar / Larry Taylor: bass guitar / Steve Jordan: drums / Leon Pendarvis: piano / **Recording:** Avatar Studios, New York: 2008 / **Technical team:** Producer: Steve Jordan / **Executive producers:** Mathew Knowles, Marshall Chess, Beth Amy Rosenblatt / **Recording engineer:** Niko Bolas / **Assistant recording engineer:** Brian Montgomery / **String arrangements:** Howard Drossin

Composed in 1941 by Mack Gordon and Harry Warren for the film *Orchestra Wives*, *At Last* is better known for its numerous covers than for its original version. The many recordings of the song include those by Glenn Miller and his orchestra for the movie *Sun Valley Serenade* in 1941 and by Céline Dion for her album *A New Day Has Come* in 2002. Despite this history, since 1960 the song has been inextricably linked to the work of its most iconic performer: Etta James, who recorded it that year for her first album, *At Last!*, and appropriated this timeless soul ballad for good. In 2008, Beyoncé made it her own, even going so far as to perform it on 20 January 2009 for President Barack Obama and his wife Michelle's first dance at the Neighborhood Inaugural Ball, the traditional gala that follows the inauguration of the President of the United States. Although Beyoncé's performance was praised by the critics, it was not to the taste of Etta James, who made her feelings on the matter clear: "The great Beyoncé…Like I said, she ain't mine…I can't stand Beyoncé. She has no business up there, singing up there on a big ol' president day, gonna be singing my song that I've been singing forever."[213] James's family got the message. For her funeral, on 28 January 2012, they invited Christina Aguilera to perform *At Last* before an audience of celebrities who had come to bid farewell to the soul star.

CINEMA

290 CADILLAC RECORDS (2008)

BEYONCÉ: ALL THE SONGS 291

CINEMA

As well as being a respected drummer, Steve Jordan is also a talented producer.

A meeting of two superstars: Beyoncé and Tina Turner at the Grammy Awards in Los Angeles, 10 February 2008.

ONCE IN A LIFETIME

(Amanda Ghost, Beyoncé Knowles, James Dring, Ian Dench, Jody Street, Scott McFarnon/4'00)

Musician: Beyoncé Knowles: vocals / **Recording:** Roc the Mic Studios, New York: 2008 / **Technical team:** Producers: Amanda Ghost, The Rural, Ian Dench, Beyoncé Knowles / **Executive producers:** Mathew Knowles, Marshall Chess, Beth Amy Rosenblatt / **Recording engineers:** Jim Caruana, Marcos Tovar

The co-producers of *Once in a Lifetime* include the duo The Rural, consisting of Jody Street and James Dring, who earned their reputation notably through their work with Gorillaz and are also co-writers of the song. The Rural succeeded in modernizing a soul structure that is identifiable from the first few seconds, playing the traditional guitar arpeggios on synthesizers and beating out the rhythm in triplets with a drum machine. The song, which features in the second part of the movie's closing credits, is effective, and brings a contemporary touch to the film as a whole, in the process giving Beyoncé welcome visibility.

I'D RATHER GO BLIND

(Billy Foster, Ellington Jordan/3'10)

Musicians: Beyoncé Knowles: vocals / Lisa Fischer: backing vocals / Billy Flynn: guitar / Danny Kortchmar: guitar / Larry Taylor: bass guitar / Steve Jordan: drums / Leon Pendarvis: organ / Lenny Pickett: saxophone / Earl Gardner: trumpet / **Recording:** Avatar Studios, New York: 2008 / Germano Studios, New York: 2008 / **Technical team:** Producer: Steve Jordan / **Executive producers:** Mathew Knowles, Marshall Chess, Beth Amy Rosenblatt / **Recording engineer:** Niko Bolas / **Assistant recording engineer:** Brian Montgomery

Although he was a session drummer well known for his work with Sheryl Crow, Neil Young, and Alicia Keys (the extraordinarily languorous rhythm of *If I Ain't Got You* is his), Steve Jordan was also a producer famous for his work with John Mayer and Herbie Hancock. Having been invited to work on the soundtrack of *Cadillac Records*, he contributed, among other things, *I'd Rather Go Blind*, which is carried along by an organ melody that one imagines was recorded on a keyboard of the Italian brand Farfisa. A real gem, destined to become a soul classic, which perfectly suits Beyoncé's powerful voice.

CADILLAC RECORDS (2008)

TRUST IN ME

(Jean Schwartz, Milton Ager, Ned Wever/3'44)

Musicians: Beyoncé Knowles: vocals / Billy Flynn: acoustic guitar / Danny Kortchmar: guitar / Larry Taylor: bass guitar / Steve Jordan: drums / Leon Pendarvis: piano **Recording:** Avatar Studios, New York: 2008 / Germano Studios, New York: 2008 / Roc the Mic Studios, New York: 2008 / **Technical team: Producer:** Steve Jordan / **Executive producers:** Mathew Knowles, Marshall Chess, Beth Amy Rosenblatt / **Recording engineers:** Niko Bolas, Jim Caruana / **Assistant recording engineer:** Brian Montgomery / **Arrangements:** Riley Hampton / **String arrangements:** Howard Drossin

Although it evokes the career of Etta James, this soul song also calls to mind the beginnings of another American star: Tina Turner, who started her career in a very soul vein, notably in the music of her husband, the brilliant but controversial Ike Turner. Beyoncé accompanied Tina Turner on stage at the 2009 Grammy Awards ceremony, performing with her the classic *Proud Mary* in a splendid version, which left Beyoncé with a moving memory. "This was kind of like seeing my ideal future," she said. "Like, if I could be 70 and touring around the world and still have that spirit that she has, this young spirit. I mean, she was out-dancing me in her heels! It was a great learning experience for me, and it definitely gave me hope that you can be around for as long as you want to be and still be so positive and so hot and sexy. She's the ultimate."[214]

ALL I COULD DO IS CRY

(Berry Gordy, Gwen Gordy Fuqua, Roquel Davis/3'10)

Musicians: Beyoncé Knowles: vocals / Meegan Voss: backing vocals / Billy Flynn: guitar / Danny Kortchmar: guitar / Larry Taylor: bass guitar / Steve Jordan: drums, backing vocals / Leon Pendarvis: piano / Lenny Pickett: flute / **Recording:** Avatar Studios, New York: 2008 / Germano Studios, New York: 2008 / **Technical team: Producer:** Steve Jordan / **Executive producers:** Mathew Knowles, Marshall Chess, Beth Amy Rosenblatt / **Recording engineer:** Niko Bolas / **Assistant recording engineer:** Brian Montgomery

A classic among classics, *All I Could Do Is Cry* was recorded by Etta James in 1960 and written by a crack trio consisting of Berry Gordy Jr, founder of Detroit's Motown label, his sister Gwen Gordy, and her boyfriend Billy Davis. Over the years, Davis would become a respected songwriter, especially with Motown; he subsequently joined Chess Records in Chicago, where he was artistic director while continuing to write for the artists he signed, such as Chuck Berry and Jackie Wilson.

ALBUM

4

1+1 • I Care • I Miss You • Best Thing I Never Had • Party • Rather Die Young • Start Over • Love On Top • Countdown • End Of Time • I Was Here • Run The World (Girls)

Released in the USA by Parkwood Entertainment/Columbia: 24 June 2011 (CD ref.: 88697908242)
Best chart ranking in the USA: 1

2011

With *4*, Beyoncé declared her artistic independence and her taste for the music of the 1980s and '90s.

BEYONCÉ'S MANY INFLUENCES

As her I Am Tour (sometimes also called the I Am…World Tour) came to an end, Beyoncé made a surprising announcement. "I don't need Sasha Fierce anymore, because I've grown, and I'm now able to merge the two. I want people to see me. I want people to see who I am."[65] On 20 November 2009, she announced on stage at Nottingham's Trent FM Arena in England that she would be back a year later with a new album. She then decided to take a few months off while some of her closest collaborators, including producer Rodney Jerkins, started work on the follow-up to *I Am…Sasha Fierce*.

The winds of change

Although Beyoncé was resting between two albums, she was kept busy, to say the least. In late 2009, her parents divorced, issuing a press release to forestall any malicious gossip: "The decision to end our marriage is an amicable one. We remain friends, parents, and business partners. If anyone is expecting an ugly messy fight, they will be sadly disappointed."[215] One break-up often leads to another, and Beyoncé decided to end her long-standing collaboration with her father Mathew, who had managed her since the start: "I believe that parents prepare their kids for the moment that they're on their own," Beyoncé explained. "At this point, I'm taking everything my dad and my mother have taught me, and I'm able to do things my way. We were at a point where we'd learned so much from each other, and now it's exciting for me to do this on my own and hire my own team."[216]

A salutary break

It would be almost a year before Beyoncé's next album after *I Am…Sasha Fierce* was released. Although her mind may have been occupied by the new album under production, she also made a deliberate effort to slow down and take time out from the frenetic pace of work she had maintained since the early days of Destiny's Child. "I'm approaching 30," she said when she came back afterwards, "and finally took a break in my life […]. I traveled around, spent time with my husband, woke up in my own bed, ate whatever I wanted, went to museums and Broadway plays, watched documentaries, and just had life experiences."[216] Beyoncé also used this downtime to explore new musical styles. She went to numerous festivals and concerts, hearing for the first time the melodious rock of Muse and the incendiary fusion of Rage Against the Machine; she rediscovered the repertoires of Earth, Wind & Fire, DeBarge, Lionel Richie, Teena Marie, New Edition, Prince, and Michael Jackson, and kept a weather eye on new pop stars, including Britain's Adele and Florence + the Machine. In October 2009, she saw the musical *Fela!*, directed by Bill T. Jones at the Eugene O'Neill Theatre in New York (and co-produced by Jay-Z), and began studying the work of its subject, the Nigerian singer, musician, political activist, and king of Afrobeat, Fela Kúti, who had died in 1997.

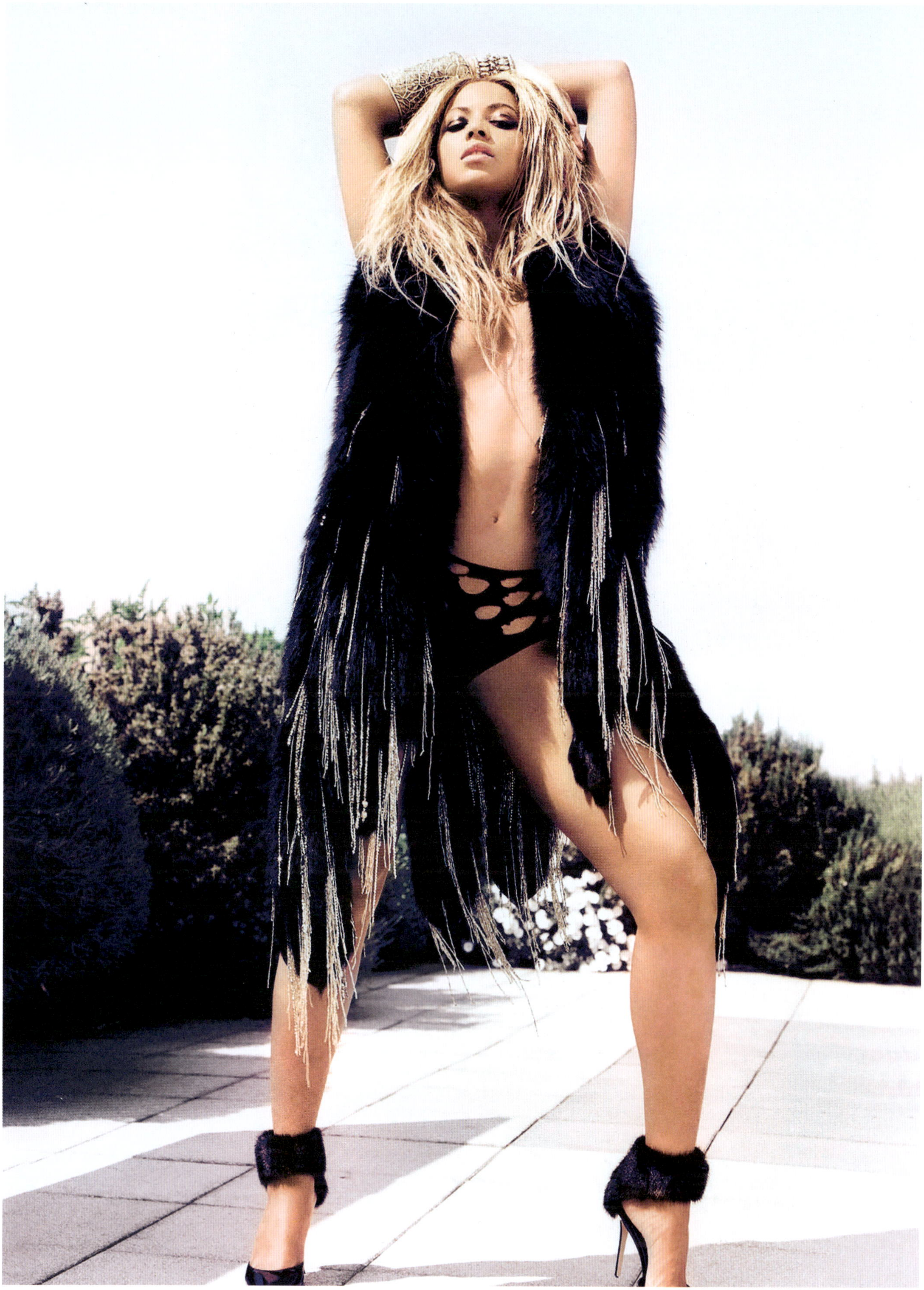

The music of Fela Kúti inspired Beyoncé, who paid homage to the Nigerian artist's African instrumentations and sounds.

Jordan "DJ Swivel" Young, who did invaluable work for Beyoncé on *4*.

The influence of Fela Kúti

In spring 2010, Beyoncé connected with recording engineer Jordan "DJ Swivel" Young, who would work with her on the production of her new album. The two met in April, when Beyoncé headed back to the studio to record a new song, *Party*, and called up Young on the recommendation of a friend, Omar Grant, who had previously worked for Destiny's Child. "I came in," Young recalled, "and she told me, at the end of the day, that I did a great job. A few months later, I got a callback to do more sessions."[217] These new sessions gave Beyoncé the opportunity to work for a few days at New York's MSR Studios alongside the musicians from *Fela!* "We were experimenting with horns, percussion, drums, guitars, and keys," Young explained. "We'd be taking loops, like a section of percussion—congas, for example—and then using them on a completely different record; and that record might be a completely different tempo or in a different key, so we'd literally be pitching it as we went [...] Having fun is the best way I can put it; there were no rules. Okay, it's not the most orthodox way of doing things, but it was very freeing, and having the ability to do whatever you want and whatever she wants was a very cool way to start."[218]

Around the world with Jordan "DJ Swivel" Young

Once the experimenting was done and numerous songs had been recorded with the *Fela!* musicians—it's rumored there is an entire album of African sounds slumbering somewhere in Beyoncé's archives—work on the new album could begin. Most sessions took place in New York, at the MSR, KMA, and Roc the Mic studios, although, for the first time in her career, Beyoncé also recorded outside the United States. After laying down a few tracks at Real World Studios, Peter Gabriel's recording complex in Box, England, Beyoncé took inspiration from the album that Jay-Z and Kanye West were then recording together. "We rented a mansion in Australia," Jordan "DJ Swivel" Young said. "In one room Kanye West and Jay-Z were doing their *Watch the Throne*, and we were in another room. It was incredible. Jay and Kanye recorded in a living room… so we shipped all the gear in, rented what we needed to, and built two studios."[217] While Young would be the main recording engineer on the album, the tracks on it were written by a whole bunch of producers, most of whom were well known to Beyoncé fans: Terius "The-Dream" Nash, Christopher

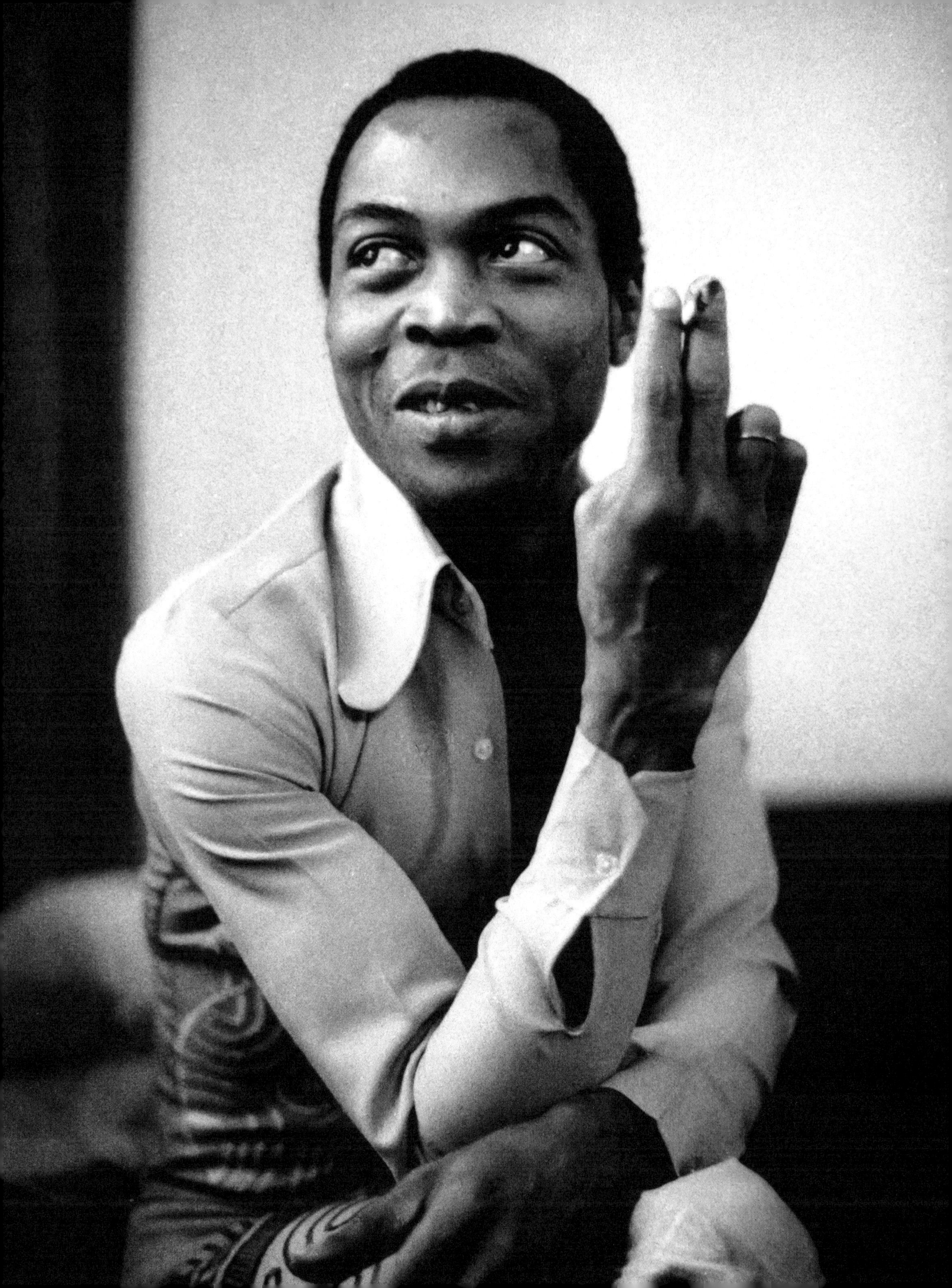

"Tricky" Stewart, Shea Taylor, Babyface, Kanye West, and Ryan Tedder. By the time the sessions were wrapped up, over 70 tracks had been recorded, a sign of how much energy and enthusiasm Beyoncé put into her work. "We pretty much worked every day nonstop," Young revealed. "B's a machine. We recorded more than 70 songs. It was by far the greatest experience I've had in the studio. I spent more time with Beyoncé in the last year than I have spent with my own family in six years."[217]

A disrupted release

Beyoncé's new album was slated for release in late June 2011, but a pirated version began circulating on the internet from 7 June, disrupting the official release and taking the edge off the surprise effect Beyoncé was hoping to create with her new songs. She posted a well-worded message on her Facebook page, expressing her feelings to her followers: "My music was leaked and while this is not how I wanted to present my new songs, I appreciate the positive response from my fans."[219] When the album was finally released, it met with a mixed reception, with even Beyoncé's label being concerned about the lack of decent singles in the tracklisting. They suggested to her that she re-record some more effective songs, which she categorically refused to do. Simply called 4, the album is surprising for its synthetic textures, which are simultaneously modern (the rhythms and new-found energy) and vintage (the omnipresent 1980s and '90s feel). Although some of the singles achieved the kind of success that's not to be sniffed at, *Run the World (Girls)*, *Best Thing I Never Had*, *Party*, *Love On Top*, *Countdown*, *I Care* and *End of Time* wouldn't have the impact on the public that singles such as *Crazy in Love*, *Beautiful Liar*, *Halo*, *Single Ladies (Put a Ring on It)*, and *End of Time* had had, failing to make it into the *Billboard* Hot 100. The new Beyoncé was apparent not just in her music, but also on the album cover, in the shots taken by photographer Greg Gex on the roof of Le Meurice Hotel in Paris on 23 April 2011. The title of the album refers to the number of solo albums Beyoncé had released, as well as expressing one of her strongly held beliefs: "We all have special numbers in our lives, and 4 is that for me. It's the day I was born. My mother's birthday, and a lot of my friends' birthdays, are on the fourth; April 4 is my wedding date."[216]

Beyoncé in the eye of a storm

As Beyoncé was promoting 4, she also became embroiled in a number of controversies. In March 2011, she triggered a salvo of criticism from the American media after blacking up for a photoshoot in tribute to Fela Kúti that featured on the cover of the Paris fashion magazine *L'Officiel*. Shortly before that, she had been sued by video game publisher Gate Five after

Jay-Z on stage at the Staples Center in Los Angeles, 11 December 2011.

Beyoncé shows her bump at the MTV Video Music Awards in Los Angeles, 28 August 2011.

terminating a partnership to develop the game Starpower: Beyoncé. And finally, to conclude this litany of disasters, she stood accused of making an obscene amount of money out of performing for a member of the family of Muammar Gaddafi at a time when the Libyan people had experienced decades of poverty under his dictatorship. She wasn't alone in this, as other artists, including Mariah Carey, 50 Cent, and Usher, had done the same (with Carey reportedly earning a million dollars for her performance in 2008). However, Beyoncé managed to turn this bad press around by announcing a happy event to her fans. On 28 August 2011, as she was about to perform *Love On Top* on the set of the MTV Video Music Awards, she made the following statement: "I want you to stand up on your feet. I want you to feel the love that's growing inside me,"[220] before, at the end of the track, revealing her round belly, the sign of a well-advanced pregnancy. From then on, the pop world only had eyes for the mother-to-be and her husband, Jay-Z; the announcement even boosted album sales.

A star is born

Beyoncé was insatiable when it came to being in the movies, and was fully committed to the offer she'd received to join the cast of Clint Eastwood's new film, an adaptation of *A Star Is Born*. The original William A. Wellman film had been released in 1937 and there had since been three remakes, including a 1976 version directed by Frank Pierson and starring Barbra Streisand and Kris Kristofferson. "It's a dream come true; I'm still in shock that it's really going to happen," Beyoncé confessed at the time. "Clint Eastwood is clearly the absolute best, and I'm so honored and humbled."[216] Unfortunately, the project never came to fruition, as Beyoncé's pregnancy required her to take a break that was incompatible with the movie schedule. The film was postponed and eventually made with Bradley Cooper directing and starring as the male lead, and the part of young singer Ally going to Lady Gaga. However, in 2012, Beyoncé brought into the world the only star that really mattered to her, a daughter named Blue Ivy Carter, born on 7 January at Lenox Hill Hospital in New York.

Beyoncé on the legendary Pyramid Stage of the Glastonbury Festival in the UK, 26 June 2011.

1+1

(Beyoncé Knowles, Terius Nash, Christopher Stewart/4'33)

Musicians: Beyoncé Knowles: vocals, backing vocals / **Nikki Glaspie:** drums / **Pete Wolford?:** electric guitar / **Steven Dennis?:** electric guitar / **Lee Blaske:** synthesizers / **Recording:** Studio at the Palms, Las Vegas: 2010 to 2011 / Triangle Sound Studios, Atlanta: 2010 to 2011 / MSR Studios, New York: 2010 to 2011 (voice) / **Technical team: Producers:** Beyoncé Knowles, Terius "The-Dream" Nash, C. "Tricky" Stewart / **Executive producer:** Beyoncé Knowles / **Recording engineers:** Brian "B- Luv" Thomas, Pat Thrall, Jordan "DJ Swivel" Young (vocals) / **Assistant recording engineers:** Jason Sherwood, Mark Gray, Pete Wolford, Steven Dennis

From the guitar arpeggios played in triple meter to the Hammond organ and Beyoncé's particularly soulful interpretation, everything about *1+1* shows the influence that filming *Cadillac Records* had had on her, the song being an obvious reference to the soul tracks produced by Chess Records as well as by Berry Gordy's Motown. The lyrics in the second verse, in which Beyoncé sings *I don't know much about guns* and *I don't know much about fighting*, are an obvious nod to Sam Cooke's *Wonderful World*, released in 1960 on Keen Records, in which the soul man fervently lists all the things he doesn't know about in order to underscore the one thing he is sure of: the world would be a better place if he was at his sweetheart's side. As the opening song on the standard edition of *4*, this is a great start for Beyoncé and points to the many influences that listeners would get the opportunity to explore over the course of the album.

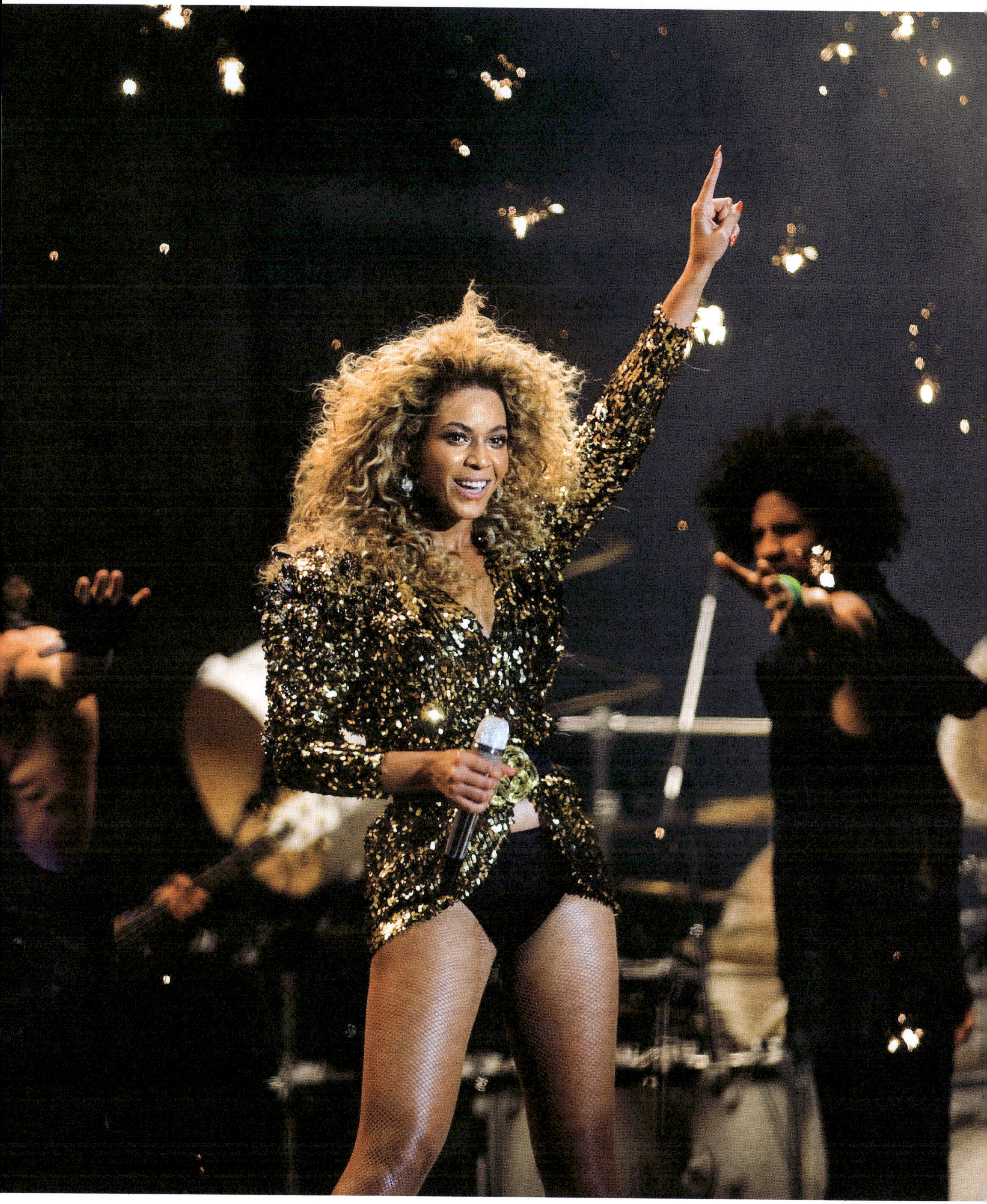

Jeff Bhasker, highly gifted producer and Beyoncé's collaborator of choice for *I Care*.

I CARE

(Beyoncé Knowles, Chad Hugo, Jeff Bhasker/3'59)

Musicians: Beyoncé Knowles: vocals, backing vocals / Billy Kraven: backing vocals / Drew Sayers: saxophone / Nikki Glaspie: drums / Chad Hugo: electric guitar / Jeff Bhasker: synthesizers, electric guitar, programming / **Recording:** The Record Plant, Los Angeles: 2010 to 2011 / Enormous Studios, Los Angeles: 2010 to 2011 / MSR Studios, New York: 2010 to 2011 (voice) / **Technical team: Producers:** Beyoncé Knowles, Jeff Bhasker / **Executive producer:** Beyoncé Knowles / **Recording engineers:** Jeff Bhasker, Mitch Kenny, Jordan "DJ Swivel" Young (vocals) / **Assistant recording engineer:** Ryan Kelly

One of the top songs of 2011 was undoubtedly *We Are Young*, recorded by the band Fun with Janelle Monáe. The song, mostly penned by the talented Jack Antonoff, was also the work of producer Jeff Bhasker, who had collaborated with Kanye West on his albums *808s & Heartbreak* in 2008 and *My Beautiful Dark Twisted Fantasy* in 2010, as well as working on Kanye's and Jay-Z's joint album *Watch the Throne* in 2011. So Beyoncé and Bhasker were fated to meet as she worked on her new album. While Bhasker was putting the finishing touches to his solo album *Born on the Fourth of July*, which he planned to release under the pseudonym Billy Kraven, he offered Beyoncé Beyoncé one of the songs from the album. Called *I Care*, it was produced by Bhasker and Beyoncé, and handed to recording engineer Jordan "DJ Swivel" Young for mixing—a task which took the patience and skill of a watchmaker as Young sifted through the 75 tracks that had been recorded, 40 of which were solely Beyoncé's vocals. Among them, the one she recorded over Bhasker's solo guitar is undoubtedly the standout. "One of the cool things on that song is she riffed the entire guitar solo," Young said, "so her vocal is matching the guitar solo perfectly. It's a genius idea and she totally pulls it off. She's pushing the boundaries of music and experimenting with all sorts of things."[221]

I MISS YOU

(Beyoncé Knowles, Frank Ocean, Shea Taylor/2'59)

Musician: Beyoncé Knowles: vocals, backing vocals / **Recording:** MSR Studios, New York: 2010 to 2011 / **Technical team: Producers:** Beyoncé Knowles, Shea Taylor / **Executive producer:** Beyoncé Knowles / **Recording engineer:** Jordan "DJ Swivel" Young / **Assistant recording engineer:** Gloria Kaba

These days Frank Ocean is an alternative R&B superstar with albums that hit the top of the *Billboard* charts without the help of the traditional labels—his 2016 album *Blonde* went to number 1 in the US—but in 2011 the young man was a complete unknown. He had just independently released his first mixtape, *Nostalgia, Ultra*, and had attracted the attention of one Shawn Carter, aka Jay-Z. "Jay had a CD playing in the car one Sunday when we were driving to Brooklyn," Beyoncé recalls. "I noticed his tone, his arrangements, and his storytelling. I immediately reached out to him—literally the next morning. I asked him to fly to New York and work on my record."[222]

In March 2011, Ocean posted a photo on his Facebook account, revealing his collaboration with Beyoncé, along with these words: "This is the room I'm working in this day. Not to brag but man, this is surreal. Like…she's singing my songs. If time were to stop right now, the past couple weeks would be near the top of the highlight reel for my short time on Earth."[223] Beyoncé and Ocean created the track *I Miss You* alongside producer Shea Taylor. It is one of the highlights of *4*, which Ocean would perform solo on stage at The Wiltern theatre in Los Angeles on 17 July 2012. Ocean also appeared on two tracks on Jay-Z's and Kanye West's 2011 album *Watch the Throne*: the haunting *No Church in the Wild* and *Made in America*.

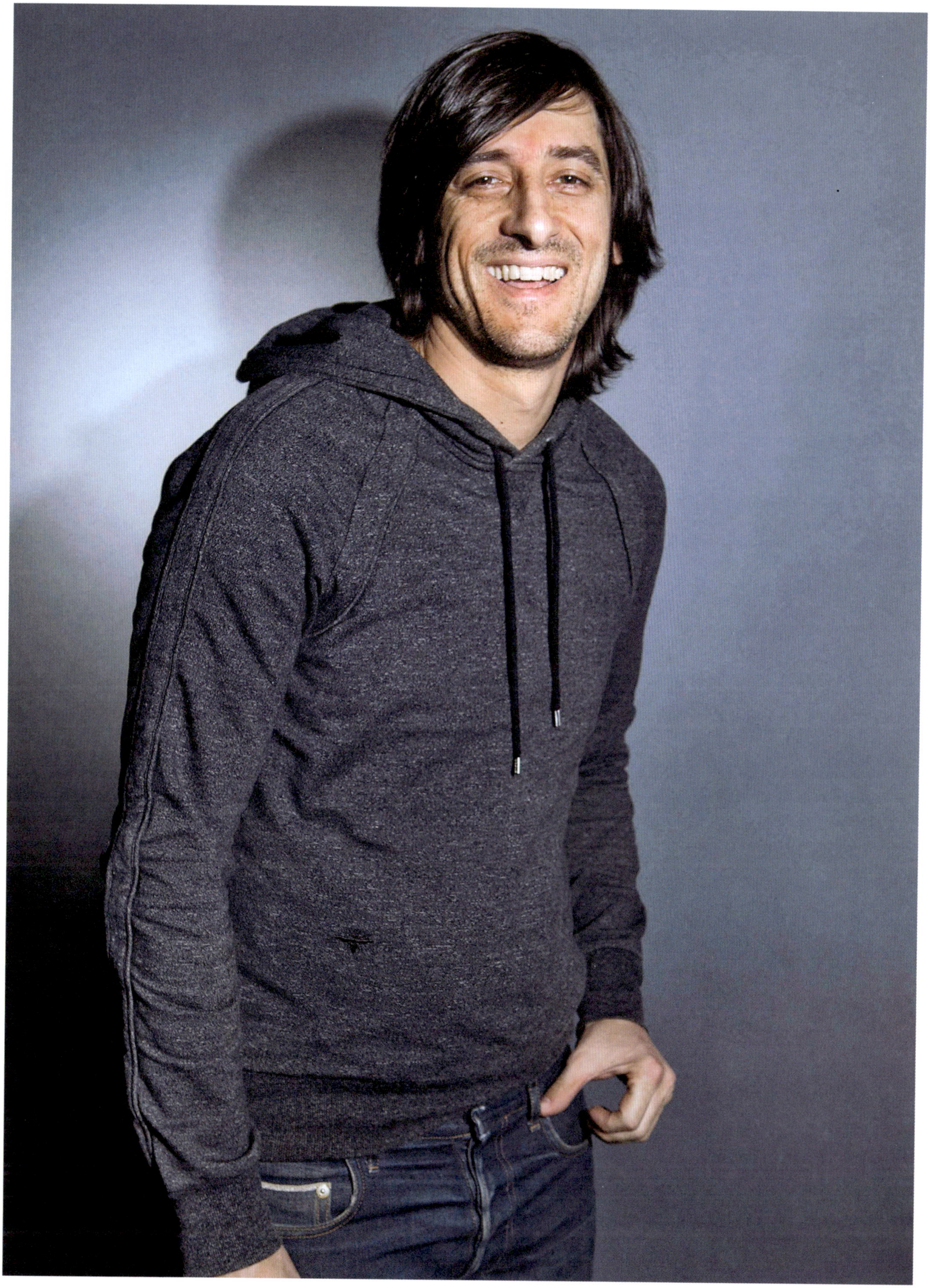

SINGLE

BEST THING I NEVER HAD

(Antonio Dixon, Beyoncé Knowles, Caleb McCampbell, Kenneth Edmonds, Larry Griffin Jr, Patrick Smith, Shea Taylor/4'13)

Musicians: Beyoncé Knowles: vocals, backing vocals / Rob Suchecki: guitar / **Recording:** MSR Studios, New York: 2010 to 2011 / KMA Studios, New York: 2010 to 2011 / **Technical team: Producers:** Antonio Dixon, Beyoncé Knowles, Caleb McCampbell, Kenneth "Babyface" Edmonds, Shea Taylor, S1 / **Executive producer:** Beyoncé Knowles / **Recording engineer:** Jordan "DJ Swivel" Young / **Assistant recording engineers:** Gloria Kaba, Pete Wolford, Serge Nudel / **Single:** Digital distribution by Parkwood Entertainment/Columbia: 1 June 2011 / **Best chart ranking in the USA:** 16

After the danceable *Run the World (Girls)*, Beyoncé's second single from *4* is the mid-tempo ballad *Best Thing I Never Had*. Written by Patrick "J. Que" Smith and produced by Antonio Dixon during a session in California, the song was then polished by the master, Kenneth "Babyface" Edmonds himself, as Smith explained: "After a day or so, Tony [Dixon] and I really sat down and we got into *The Best Thing I Never Had* record. But Kenny came along afterwards, heard it and made some changes. You know—a word here, a word there, a melody here, and all of a sudden the record had a completely new life. He [Babyface] is absolutely masterful at what he does. And I'm super honored to be working with dude."[224] Once the demo of the track—built around a sample of *The Show*, a 1985 single recorded by Doug E. Fresh & The Get Fresh Crew—was finished, the trio were invited to work with Beyoncé herself in New York's MSR studios: "I remember the night she came in and recorded *The Best Thing I Never Had*," Smith said, "she got to the studio at maybe 9 pm. She came off of the plane, and walked into the studio. We played the record. She loved it! She jumped in the studio and knocked out three records that night."[224] As for Babyface, he spoke about Beyoncé in glowing terms, making no attempt to hide his respect for her: "What is the definition of perfection or the closest thing to it? Beyoncé. Icons are made. Stars are born. From the moment Beyoncé took her first breath, her star was shining."[225]

SINGLE

PARTY
(FEATURING ANDRÉ 3000)

(Beyoncé Knowles, Dexter R. Mills, Douglas Davis, Jeff Bhasker, Kanye West, Ricky Walters/4'05)

Musicians: Beyoncé Knowles: vocals, backing vocals / André 3000: rap / **Consequence:** backing vocals / Kanye West: backing vocals / Nick Videen (The Superpower Horns): saxophone / Drew Sayers (The Superpower Horns): saxophone / Alex Asher (The Superpower Horns): trombone / Cole Kamen-Green (The Superpower Horns): trumpet / Josiah Woodson: trumpet / Morgan Price: saxophone / **Recording:** Avex Honolulu Studios, Honolulu: 2010 to 2011 / KMA Studios, New York: 2010 to 2011 (vocals) / Roc the Mic Studios, New York: 2010 to 2011 (vocals) / Strong Mountain Studio, Stone Mountain: 2010 to 2011 (vocals André 3000) / **Technical team: Producers:** Beyoncé Knowles, Kanye West, Jeff Bhasker / **Executive producer:** Beyoncé Knowles / **Recording engineers:** Andrew Dawson, Jordan "DJ Swivel" Young / **Assistant recording engineers:** Christian Mochizuki, Edwin Delahoz, Gaylord Holomalia, Serge Nudel / **Single:** Digital distribution by Parkwood Entertainment/Columbia: 30 August 2011 / **Best chart ranking in the USA:** 50

André 3000, one half of the duo Outkast, who had been a big star since the group's hit singles, *Ms. Jackson* in 2000 and *Hey Ya!* in 2003, was the only artist invited to sing on *4*. Here, he and Beyoncé combine their talents to sing about their love for partying on a Kanye West production put together by recording engineer Jordan "DJ Swivel" Young. "That was the first record I ever cut with her, before we even started the album," Young recalled. "Kanye sent it to her…that early-'90s inspiration was already there. Beyoncé was experimenting…with everything."[217] The song was initially heading in a very different direction, as rapper J. Cole had originally recorded vocals for it. "I did a version of that before her album even came out," he revealed. "I did two verses. I love these verses too, but they ended up going with André's verse and André killed it."[226] To make amends, Beyoncé invited J. Cole to record a few extra lines on the remix of the song, and the video was posted on her YouTube page.

The inimitable producer Babyface, formerly dubbed the Quincy Jones of the 1990s on account of his numerous successes.

Luke Steele, flamboyant front man of the group Empire of the Sun.

RATHER DIE YOUNG

(Beyoncé Knowles, Jeff Bhasker, Luke Steele/3'42)

Musicians: Beyoncé Knowles: vocals, backing vocals / Billy Kraven: backing vocals / Luke Steele: guitar, backing vocals / Jeff Bhasker: synthesizers, programming / Nick Videen (The Superpower Horns): saxophone / Drew Sayers (The Superpower Horns): saxophone / Alex Asher (The Superpower Horns): trombone / Cole Kamen-Green (The Superpower Horns): trumpet / Josiah Woodson: trumpet / Morgan Price: saxophone / **Recording:** Enormous Studios, Los Angeles: 2010 to 2011 / KMA Studios, New York: 2010 to 2011 (vocals) / Roc the Mic Studios, New York: 2010 to 2011 (vocals) / **Technical team: Producers:** Beyoncé Knowles, Luke Steele, Jeff Bhasker / **Executive producer:** Beyoncé Knowles / **Recording engineers:** Jeff Bhasker, Jordan "DJ Swivel" Young (vocals) / **Assistant recording engineers:** Pete Wolford, Ryan Kelly, Serge Nudel / **Brass arrangements:** Shea Taylor

Beyoncé wanted a change when she launched production of 4. "Figuring out a way to get R&B back on the radio is challenging," she revealed in 2011. "Everything sounds the same on the radio. With 4 I tried to mix R&B from the '70s and the '90s with rock 'n' roll and a lot of horns to create something new and exciting. I wanted musical changes, bridges, vibrata, live instrumentation, and classic songwriting."[222] To this end, Beyoncé called in star producer Jeff Bhasker, as well as Luke Steele, half of the flamboyant and extravagant duo Empire of the Sun, whose singles *Walking on a Dream* and *We Are the People* had been hits in 2008.

START OVER

(Beyoncé Knowles, Ester Dean, Shea Taylor/3'19)

Musician: Beyoncé Knowles: vocals, backing vocals / **Recording:** MSR Studios, New York: 2010 to 2011 / Jungle City Studios, New York: 2010 to 2011 / **Technical team: Producers:** Beyoncé Knowles, Shea Taylor / **Executive producer:** Beyoncé Knowles / **Recording engineer:** Jordan "DJ Swivel" Young / **Assistant recording engineers:** Pete Wolford, Ramon Rivas

In winter 2011, with production of the album well underway, Beyoncé and her recording engineer Jordan "DJ Swivel" Young decided to move the sessions to a brand new studio. "In January, an amazing new facility called Jungle City Studios opened in New York," explained Young, "and they agreed to open up a week early to accommodate us. We absolutely loved the space, so we worked there up until the record was finished, pretty much."[218] Co-produced by Shea Taylor, *Start Over* is a testament to the powerful sound Beyoncé was seeking for her fourth solo album. "Shea Taylor was sort of the day-to-day producer, so a lot came from him," Young explained. "If B wanted to add a bridge section, she would give it to Shea and he would go and add the parts. He wasn't one of the guys who came in for just a couple of weeks; he was there every day. But B ultimately produced the album. She's very hands-on with everything, lyrically and musically. If there's something she doesn't like about a track, we're pulling the track apart and fixing it. A lot of it is B getting her ideas out and then having a team around her to help execute those ideas. But everything was very collaborative and open. It was sort of like the best idea wins."[221]

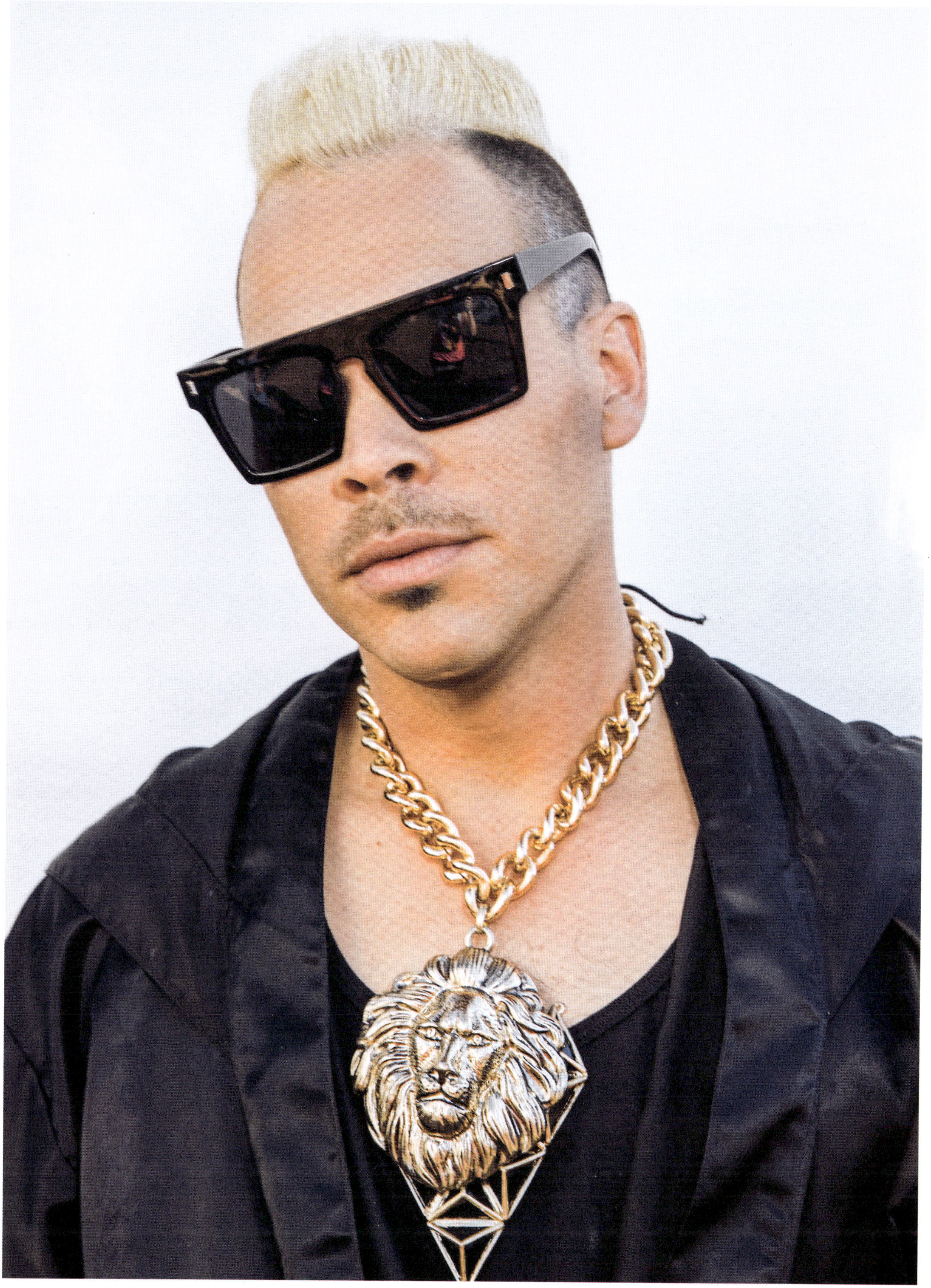

Beyoncé performs Love on Top *on stage at the MTV Video Music Awards in Los Angeles, 28 August 2011.*

SINGLE

LOVE ON TOP

(Beyoncé Knowles, Shea Taylor, Terius Nash/4'27)

2011

Musicians
Beyoncé Knowles: vocals, backing vocals
Shea Taylor: saxophone
Nikki Glaspie: drums
Robert "R.T." Taylor: guitar
Pat Thrall: guitar
Nick Videen (The Superpower Horns): saxophone
Drew Sayers (The Superpower Horns): saxophone
Alex Asher (The Superpower Horns): trombone
Cole Kamen-Green (The Superpower Horns): trumpet
Josiah Woodson: trumpet

Recording
Real World Studios, Box: 2010
Legacy Recording Studios, New York: 2010 to 2011
MSR Studios, New York: 2010 to 2011

Technical team
Producers: Beyoncé Knowles, Shea Taylor
Executive producer: Beyoncé Knowles
Recording engineer: Jordan "DJ Swivel" Young
Assistant recording engineers: Pete Wolford, Scott Barnett

Single
Digital distribution by Parkwood Entertainment/Columbia: 12 September 2011
Best chart ranking in the USA: 20

Genesis

Inspired by the vocal performances of Etta James, the woman she had just played on screen, Beyoncé recorded this very '90s-sounding track, clearly wishing to pay tribute to the new jack swing of her youth, and in particular to New Edition, the first of the successful boy bands, comprising Ricky Bell, Bobby Brown, Johnny Gill, Ralph Tresvant, Michael Bivins, and Ronnie DeVoe. Before most other American singers revisited late 1980s and '90s sounds (with Bruno Mars and The Weeknd leading the charge), Beyoncé once again got in there first, combining on *4* the R&B style that had made her famous with nu soul, new jack swing, and pop. Wanting to push the tribute to the extreme, Beyoncé shot a music video to accompany *Love On Top* at New York's Canoe Studios, making explicit reference to the video for *If It Isn't Love*, the New Edition single released in 1988. "I have worked very hard on this video," Beyoncé revealed to her fans on her website on 16 October 2011. "This song is special to me and I had an idea for the video based on some of my favorite male groups. I remember seeing videos from New Edition, The Jackson 5, and the Temptations, bands I love for their beautiful harmonies, and precise choreography."[227]

Production

It was in New York's Legacy Recording Studios (formerly Right Track Studios) that *Love On Top* came into being. While DJ Swivel was in studio A with Beyoncé recording her vocal tracks, Shea Taylor, the track's main producer, was hard at work creating the beats in a vocal booth, and others, including The-Dream, were busy composing in studio B. When Shea Taylor presented the *Love On Top* instrumental to Beyoncé, she immediately made it her own, loving the harmonic semitone rise at the end of the track, a technique that gives pop songs a surge of power. Once the modulation was recorded, the insatiable Beyoncé asked Swivel to add a third, a semitone higher. "We do the next half step up and she records it, sounds great as always, and then she says, 'Do another one, let's do a fourth.'"[228] The technician, worried that Beyoncé would strain her voice, alerted her to the dangers, but she asked for it to go even higher, recording a fifth and then a sixth version. "The lesson that she taught me in that whole process," said DJ Swivel, "is that there are no rules in music."[228]

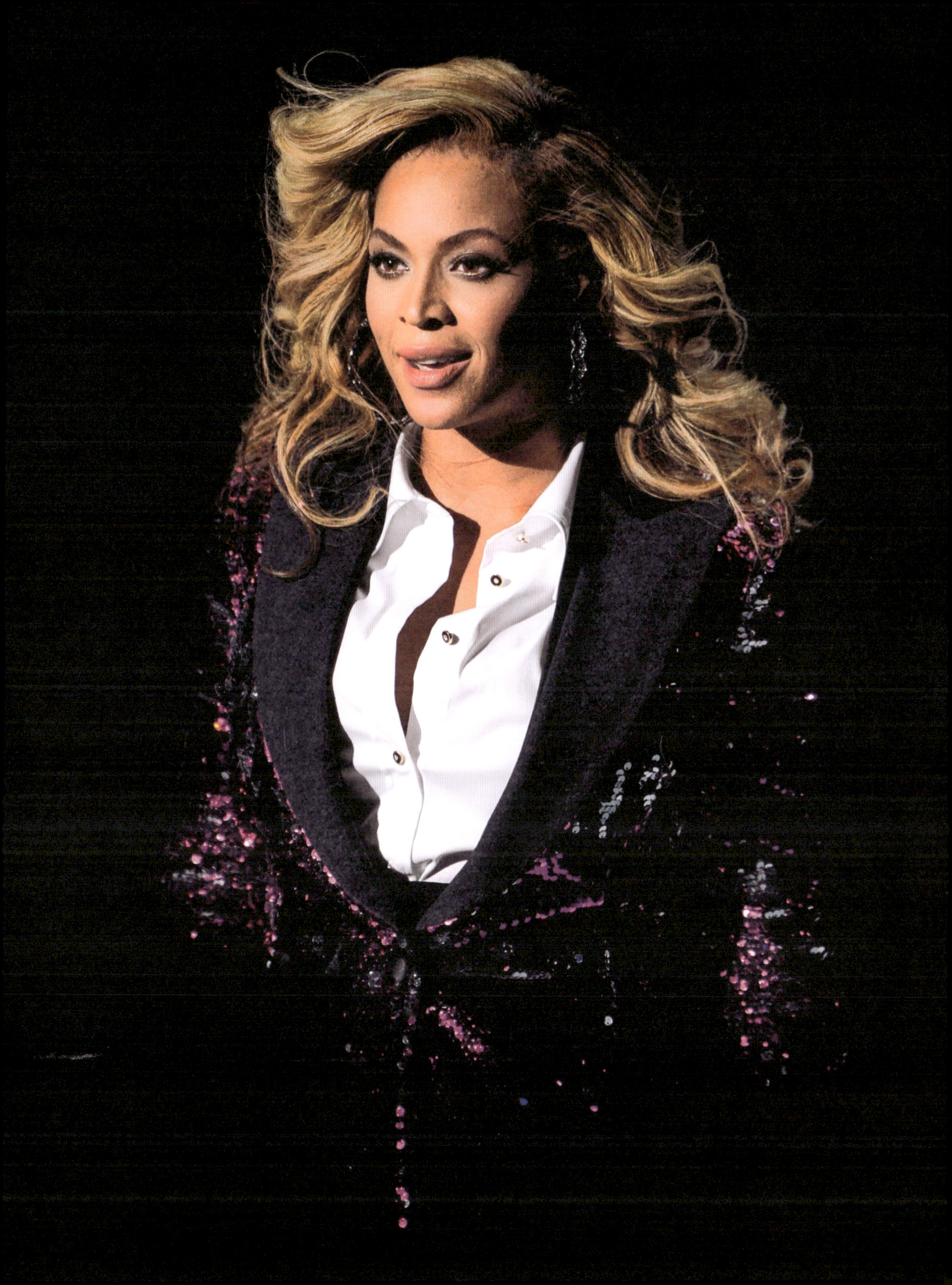

Boyz II Men, sampled by Beyoncé in *Countdown*, are still one of her biggest influences.

SINGLE

COUNTDOWN

(Beyoncé Knowles, Cainon Lamb, Ester Dean, Julie Frost, Michael Bivins, Nathan Morris, Shea Taylor, Terius Nash, Wanya Morris/3'33)

Musicians: Beyoncé Knowles: vocals, backing vocals / Nick Videen (The Superpower Horns): saxophone / Drew Sayers (The Superpower Horns): saxophone / Alex Asher (The Superpower Horns): trombone / Cole Kamen-Green (The Superpower Horns): trumpet / Josiah Woodson: trumpet / **Recording:** MSR Studios, New York: 2010 to 2011 / **Technical team:** Producers: Beyoncé Knowles, Shea Taylor / Executive producer: Beyoncé Knowles / Recording engineer: Jordan "DJ Swivel" Young / Assistant recording engineers: Pete Wolford, Ryan Kelly / **Single:** Digital distribution by Parkwood Entertainment/Columbia: 4 October 2011 / Best chart ranking in the USA: 71

Despite being one of the biggest flops of Beyoncé's career, struggling to only 71st place on the *Billboard* Hot 100, *Countdown* is not without interest. This mostly lies in the different musical styles that structure its main beat: reggae, dancehall, and R&B, all copiously doused with omnipresent brass lines played by The Superpower Horns. The song includes a sample from Boyz II Men's 1991 single *Uhh Ahh*, as Beyoncé wanted to reference her old idols for whom Destiny's Child had been the support act in 1998. "They showed us how to treat an opening act and I will never forget that," she said in 2013, adding jokingly, "That was 15 years ago! Wow, 15 years! I'm old!"[225]

SINGLE

END OF TIME

(Beyoncé Knowles, David Taylor, Shea Taylor, Terius Nash/3'44)

Musicians: Beyoncé Knowles: vocals, backing vocals / Terius "The-Dream" Nash: spoken voice / Jack Daley: bass / Nick Videen (The Superpower Horns): saxophone / Drew Sayers (The Superpower Horns): saxophone / Johnny Butler: saxophone / Alex Asher (The Superpower Horns): trombone / Cole Kamen-Green (The Superpower Horns): trumpet / Josiah Woodson: trumpet / **Recording:** MSR Studios, New York: 2010 to 2011 / **Technical team:** Producers: Beyoncé Knowles, Terius "The-Dream" Nash, Switch / Executive producer: Beyoncé Knowles / Recording engineers: Pat Thrall, Jordan "DJ Swivel" Young (vocals) / Assistant recording engineers: Chris Soper, Pete Wolford / **Single:** Digital distribution by Parkwood Entertainment/Columbia: 23 April 2012 / Best chart ranking in the USA: did not make the charts

Even worse than *Countdown*, which reached only number 71 on the *Billboard* Hot 100, *End of Time* didn't make it into the US charts at all, as it brought up the tail end of the promotion of *4* and signaled Beyoncé's return to the studio. Nevertheless, the song, particularly influenced by Beyoncé's work with the musicians from the musical *Fela!*, was a turning point in her career and she would go on to incorporate percussion and brass instruments in future productions. "It very much has a Fela thing going on," explained Jordan "DJ Swivel" Young. "It started with The-Dream, and then Switch added elements of electronic music, chopped some vocals in there, created an interesting synth intro sound which is actually a Dream vocal."[229] "We did a whole Fela album that didn't go up," The-Dream explained. "It was right before we did *4*. We did a whole different sounding thing, about twenty songs. She said she wanted to do something that sounds like Fela. That's why there's so much of that sound in the *End of Time*."[230]

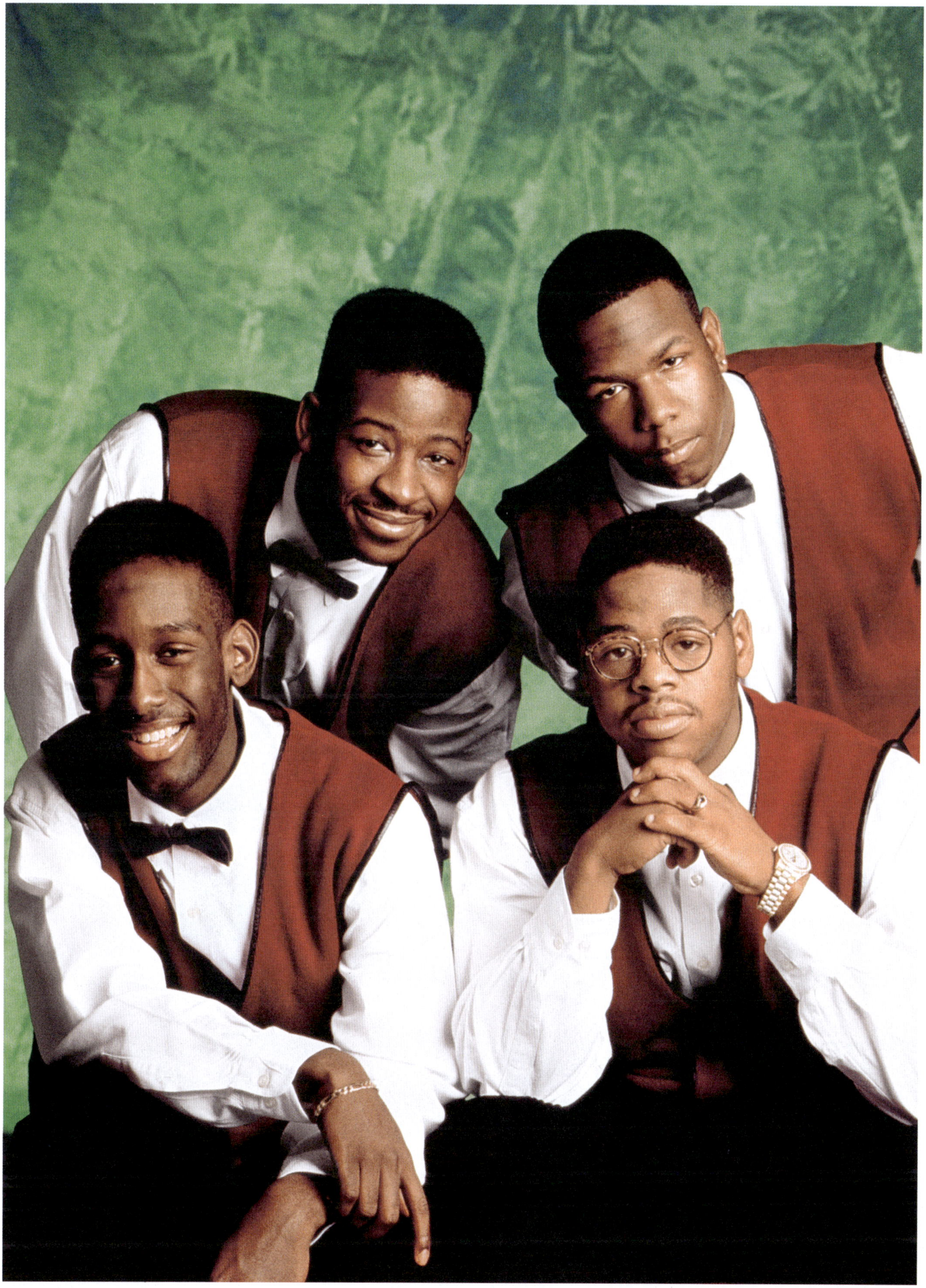

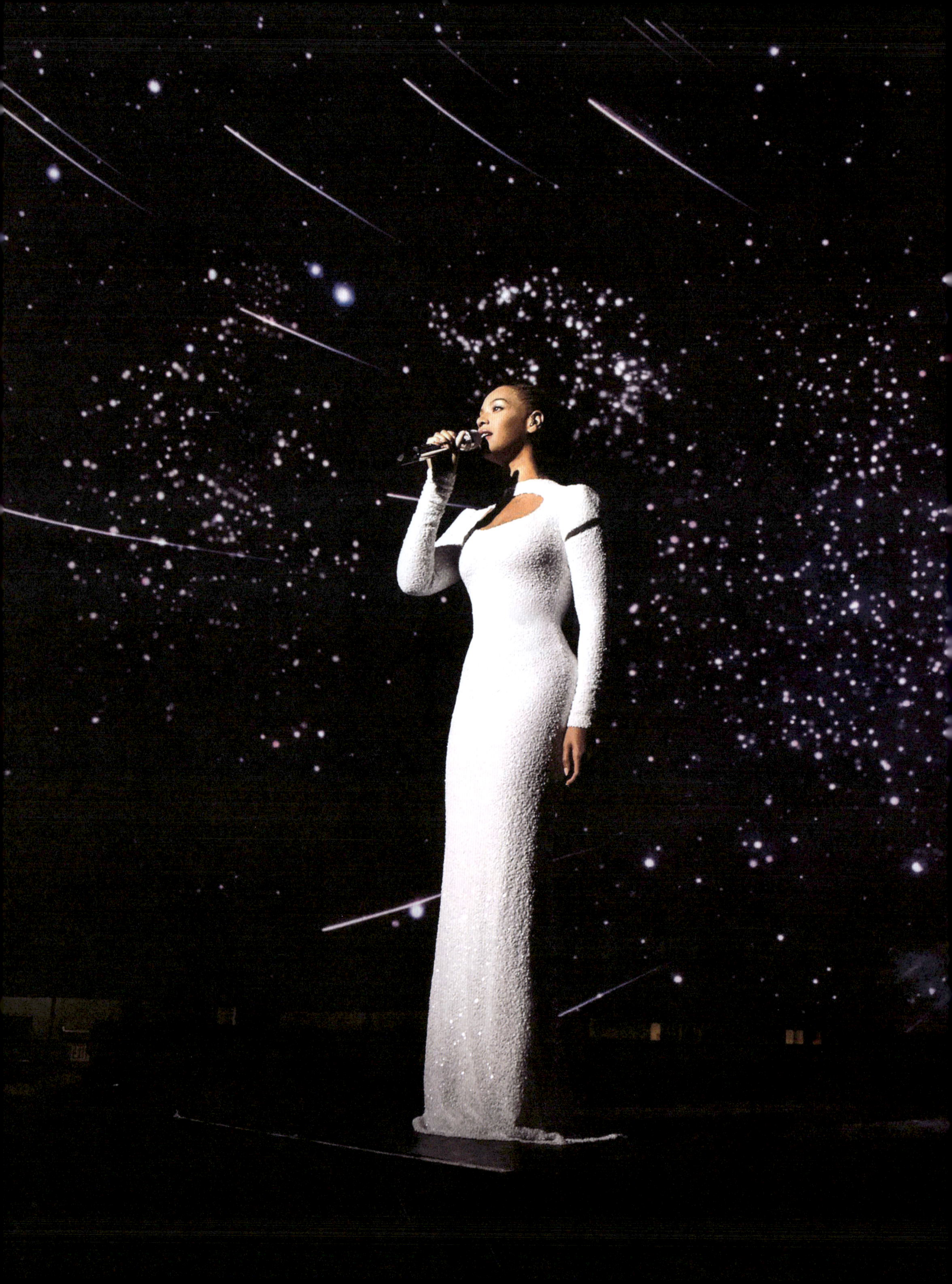

Beyoncé performs *I Was Here* in the hall of the United Nations General Assembly in New York, 10 August 2012.

I WAS HERE

(Diane Warren/3'59)

Musicians: Beyoncé Knowles: vocals, backing vocals / **Ryan Tedder:** backing vocals, drums, piano, programming / **Brent Kutzle:** guitar, cello, piano, programming / **Recording:** Patriot Studios, Denver: 2011 / Boston Harbor Hotel, Boston: 2011 / Conway Recording Studios, Los Angeles: 2011 (vocals) / **Technical team: Producers:** Beyoncé Knowles, Kuk Harrell, Brent Kutzle, Ryan Tedder / **Executive producer:** Beyoncé Knowles / **Recording engineers:** Brent Kutzle, Ryan Tedder, Kuk Harrell (vocals) / **Assistant recording engineers:** Eric Aylands, Jon Sher, Smith Carlson

It's 2011. Diane Warren, one of America's songwriters of the moment (Tina Turner's *Don't Turn Around*, Milli Vanilli's *Blame It on the Rain*, and Toni Braxton's *Un-Break My Heart* were just some of the hits she had penned), is waiting for a friend who is running late. She picks up her guitar and in a few short minutes composes *I Was Here*, a tribute to the victims of the 9/11 terrorist attacks in New York. She immediately records a demo and sends it to Simon Cowell, agent to the stars, imagining that it would work for Susan Boyle or Leona Lewis, two of the many artists he represents. But then she picks up the phone, calls Jay-Z and plays him the track down the line so that he'll speak to Beyoncé about it. The rapper tells her that his wife is in mid-air on a plane but she will call as soon as she lands.

Beyoncé didn't hang around. "Okay, this is Monday, my album is supposed to come out Friday. I'm recording that song. I'm stopping my album."[231] So she added the track at the very last minute, just as Cowell's team was contacting Warren to refuse it (having already rejected *Halo* in 2008!). Warren kept her cool and instantly responded to the message with a cheeky email: "And so I wrote back, 'Funnily enough, I was in the studio last night with probably the biggest artist on the planet. And it went all the way for her.' With a smiley face. So that was a fun email to write," she admitted later.[231]

Beyoncé gives a now-legendary performance of *Run the World (Girls)* at the *Billboard* Music Awards in Las Vegas, 22 May 2011.

SINGLE

RUN THE WORLD (GIRLS)

(Adidja Palmer, Beyoncé Knowles, David Taylor, Nick Van de Wall, Terius Nash, Wesley Pentz/3'56)

Musician
Beyoncé Knowles: vocals, backing vocals

Recording
MSR Studios, New York: 2010 to 2011

Technical team
Producers: Beyoncé Knowles, Shea Taylor, Switch, Terius "The-Dream" Nash
Executive producer: Beyoncé Knowles
Recording engineers: Jordan "DJ Swivel" Young, Pat Thrall
Assistant recording engineer: Pete Wolford

Single
Digital distribution by Parkwood Entertainment/Columbia: 21 April 2011
Best chart ranking in the USA: 29

Genesis

Who makes the world go round? Girls, of course. That's the message Beyoncé wanted to drive home in the single that immediately preceded the release of her new album. Like *End of Time*, *Run the World (Girls)* blended Fela Kúti-inspired African percussion with ultramodern rhythms. It was the work of producers David "Switch" Taylor, Shea Taylor and Terius "The-Dream" Nash, who took their cue from Beyoncé to experiment with all kinds of musical formats. "It's definitely riskier than something a bit more…simple," she commented in May 2011. "I just heard the track and loved that it was so different: it felt a bit African, a bit electronic and futuristic. It reminded me of what I love, which is mixing different cultures and eras—things that typically don't go together—to create a new sound."[216] It cannot be emphasized enough what a turning point these sessions inspired by the Nigerian musician would mark in Beyoncé's music, both in terms of the arrangements of her songs—the use of multiple percussion and brass instruments in her shows like the one at Coachella Valley Music and Arts Festival in April 2018—and the lyrics, where she increasingly asserted her pro-female stance (2016's *Formation* was the apogee of this). The video for *Run the World (Girls)*, directed by Francis Lawrence, presented Beyoncé as more powerful than ever. "In the video, most of all I wanted to show that I'm proud to be a woman," she said. "I had read about powerful African men who have hyenas as pets, and I wanted to create a world where women run the world, so in the video I have these hyenas as pets."[93] Beyoncé's now-legendary performance at the *Billboard* Music Awards on 22 May 2011, in which she performed the song complete with a choreography replicated by dancers and dozens of Beyoncés projected onto a giant screen, confirmed the new direction she was taking, more politically committed than ever.

Production

Beyoncé was listening to *Pon de Floor*, a 2009 single by Major Lazer, and had a revelation. "I heard that sample," she told *Billboard* magazine in June 2011, "and Dream, who is amazing, started humming '… girls' and it evolved into the song it is now."**232** Entirely constructed around *Pon de Floor* (and not just based on a sample from the track), *Run the World (Girls)* came as something of a surprise to Diplo, one of the founding members of Major Lazer (the other being David "Switch" Taylor, who left the group in 2011 and worked on *4* that same year); he wondered why Beyoncé was using a track that had been released as a single a relatively short time before. "When Beyoncé sampled *Pon de Floor* it was already in the clubs two years earlier and I told her that," said the DJ and producer. "She said to me 'No, but do people know this s***?' So I was like 'fine go ahead'. I don't care. I'm in my own world."**233**

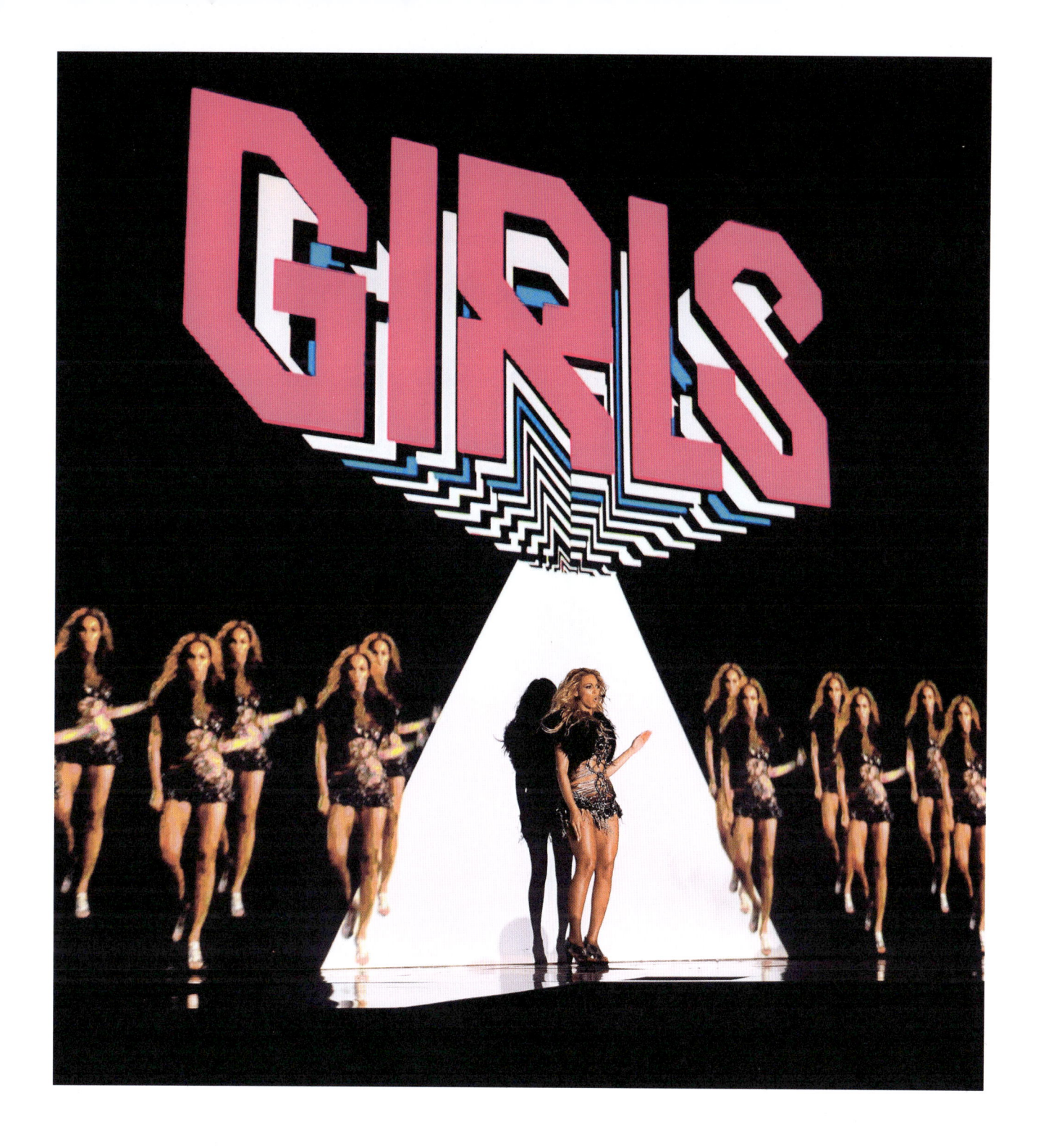

The paths of Mary J. Blige, queen of R&B, and another queen, her friend Beyoncé, have crossed frequently.

SINGLE

LOVE A WOMAN
(MARY J. BLIGE FEATURING BEYONCÉ)

(Beyoncé Knowles, Mary J. Blige, Menardini Timothee, Sean "The Pen" Garrett/4'31)

Musicians: Mary J. Blige: vocals, backing vocals / **Beyoncé Knowles:** vocals, backing vocals / **Recording:** ?: 2011 / **Technical team:** Producers: Kendu Isaacs, Bridge, Sean "The Pen" Garrett / Executive producer: Mary J. Blige / Recording engineer: Mike "Snotty" Miller / Assistant recording engineer: Pete Wolford / **Mary J. Blige** *My Life II…The Journey Continues (Act 1)* **(album)** / Released in the USA by Geffen Records: 21 November 2011 (CD ref.: B0016318-02)

Mary J. Blige takes us on a journey back in time with this R&B track, a genre for which she has long been the best-known female ambassador. Produced by Kendu Isaacs, Bridge, and Sean Garrett, it was originally intended for *4*. Beyoncé—correctly—felt it didn't suit her highly experimental album, which was more a musical melting pot than her usual R&B style, and so she offered it to Blige. "Both these women are two iconic female figures in the world," explained Garrett, "and what would be better than putting those two on a record? We felt it would be a really iconic move. We did a throwback '90s type of feel with the track. We wanted to give people who grew up with Mary and Beyoncé that real feel that they could reminisce on."[234] The original plan was to release it as a single, but in the end it became a kind of niche song—if one can use the word "niche" for the album *My Life II…The Journey Continues (Act 1)*, which sold 500,000 copies in the US and played an active role in showcasing the considerable impact the two R&B queens have had on American popular music.

SINGLE

LIFT OFF
(JAY-Z AND KANYE WEST FEATURING BEYONCÉ)

(Bruno Mars, Jeff Bhasker, Mike Dean, Pharrell Williams, Seal/4'26)

Musicians: Jay-Z: rap / **Kanye West:** rap / **Beyoncé Knowles:** vocals / Anthony Kilhoffer: programming / Hit-Boy: programming / LMFAO: programming / **Recording:** Barford Estate, Sydney: 2011 / **Technical team:** Producers: Jeff Bhasker, Kanye West, Mike Dean, Pharrell Williams, Q-Tip, Don Jazzy / Recording engineers: Noah Goldstein, Pawel Sek / **Jay-Z & Kanye West** *Watch the Throne* **(album)** / Released in the USA by Roc-A-Fella Records: 8 August 2011 (album ref.: B0016010-01, CD ref.: B0015427-02)

If there was one duo that couldn't be ignored in 2011, it was Jay-Z and Kanye West, whose album *Watch the Throne*, released under both their names, was a big event for all self-respecting hip-hop fans. The album's rare guests include The-Dream, Frank Ocean, and, of course, Jay-Z's wife Beyoncé, who performs the choruses on *Lift Off* that were originally due to be sung by Bruno Mars, the song's co-writer. But *Lift Off* was actually the brainchild of Jeff Bhasker, whom Jay-Z and Kanye West asked to travel out to Australia with them when they were recording their album. Bhasker had a bad cold when he arrived in Sydney, so the two rappers asked him to go through his hard drive to find a potential hit, or at least an instrumental to build a track around. The producer had already proved his worth as far as West was concerned when he wrote the unforgettable *Runaway* for *My Beautiful Dark Twisted Fantasy* in 2010. Bhasker then played a theme that he had just written on the piano, which caused collective hysteria in the room, with Jay-Z immediately embracing the melody and Beyoncé singing the hook in the choruses. *Lift Off* was released as a single on 23 August 2011.

HEADPHONES AT THE READY

The voice of Jack King can be heard at 3'13 on *Lift Off*. King was Chief of the Public Information Office at NASA during the historic 1969 Apollo 11 launch, and Jay-Z and Kanye West used a sequence taken from the recording.

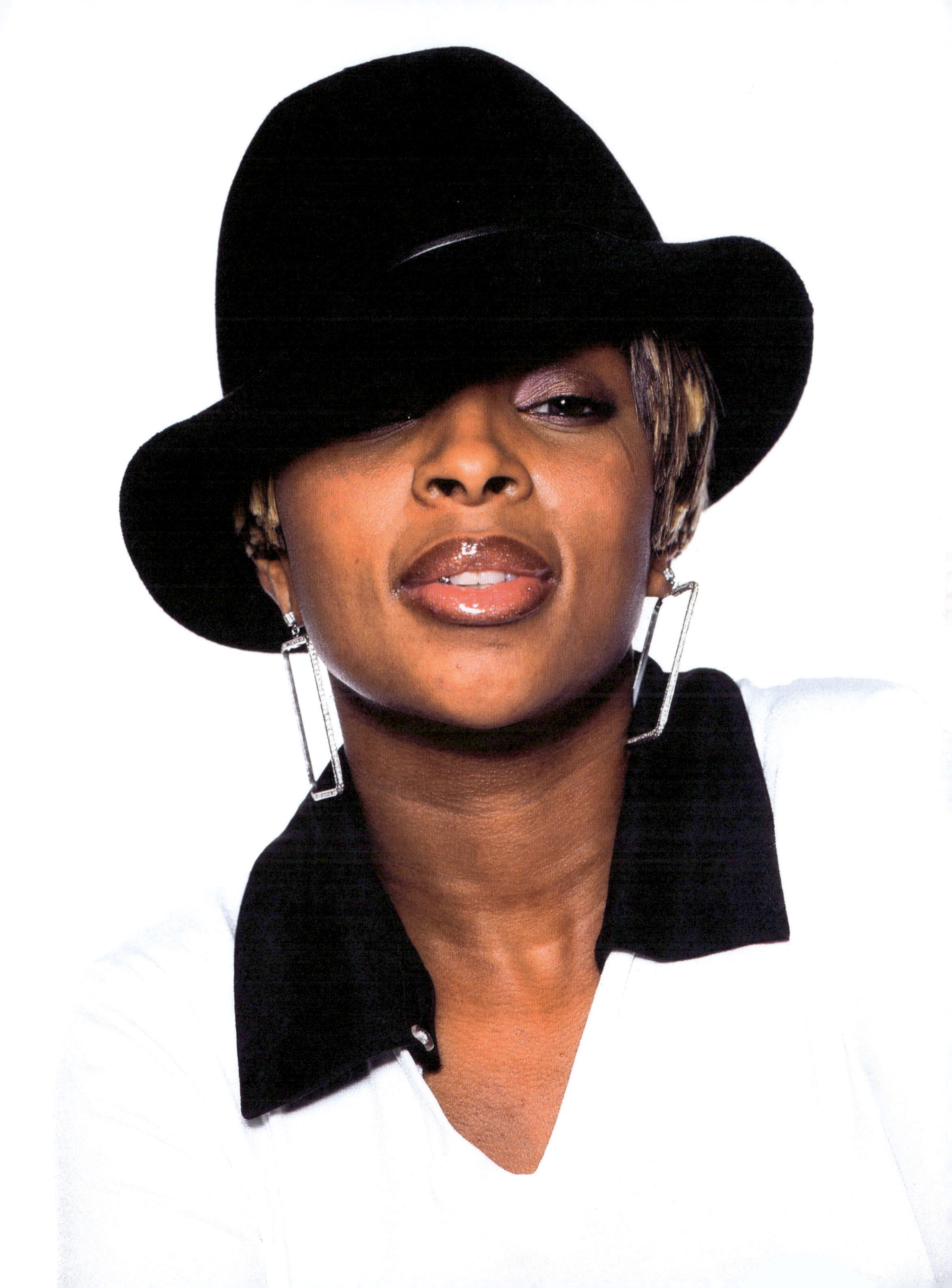

The hit-maker Sean Garrett in Atlanta, December 2007.

Jay-Z and Beyoncé, in love, at the men's singles final of the US Open tennis tournament, 12 September 2011.

LAY UP UNDER ME

(Beyoncé Knowles, Mikkel Eriksen, Sean Garrett, Shea Taylor, Tor Erik Hermansen/4'13)

Musician: Beyoncé Knowles: vocals / **Recording:** ?: 2010 to 2011 / **Technical team: Producers:** Beyoncé Knowles, Shea Taylor / *4 (Target Exclusive)* **(album)** / Released in the USA by Parkwood Entertainment/Columbia: 28 June 2011 (CD ref.: CK1-792999)

When *4* was released, the Target retail chain offered its customers an exclusive version of the album with six additional tracks: three remixes of *Run the World (Girls)* by Kaskade— *Run the World (Girls) (Kaskade Club Remix)*, Jens Bergmark— *Run the World (Girls) (Redtop Club Remix)*, and Julian Napolitano— *Run the World (Girls) (Jochen Simms Club Remix)*—as well as three previously unreleased songs from the album sessions: *Lay Up Under Me, Schoolin' Life,* and *Dance for You*. Composed by Stargate, Shea Taylor, and Sean Garrett, who recorded the first version in 2008 for their album *Turbo 919*, the song heavily features late 1990s dance sounds from a time when R&B artists were unashamedly mixing their groove with dance beats in order to appeal to DJs, notably in tracks such as Janet Jackson's *Together Again* (1997) and Jennifer Lopez's *Let's Get Loud* (1999). This is a song that echoes with the vibes of summer and Californian pool parties.

SCHOOLIN' LIFE

(Beyoncé Knowles, Carlos McKinney, Shea Taylor, Terius Nash/4'53)

Musician: Beyoncé Knowles: vocals / **Recording:** ?: 2010 to 2011 / **Technical team: Producers:** Shea Taylor, Terius "The-Dream" Nash, Beyoncé Knowles, Los Da Mystro / *4 (Target Exclusive)* **(album)** / Released in the USA by Parkwood Entertainment/Columbia: 28 June 2011 (CD ref.: 88697922992)

Beyoncé sings about her childhood and schooldays in this track that sounds more 1980s than ever. This is a direction Jordan "DJ Swivel" Young is totally comfortable with as he shoulders the heavy responsibility of mixing a track produced by The-Dream and featuring personal touches from Shea Taylor and Carlos McKinney, alias Los Da Mystro. "It has a Prince vibe," Young said. "The-Dream wrote and produced it, and it's basically a song about life and growing up. We recorded that toward the end of the project. As soon as I heard it I told B, 'That's the one…I love that song.'"[217] The magic happened at New York's Jungle City Studios, after Young had selected which tracks to retain from the hundred or so recorded for the song, half of which were Beyoncé's vocals. Young didn't hesitate to add reverb to the strikes on the snare drum to give them that emblematic 1980s texture. All the instruments, including the drums, in this song are electronic, which was also typical of the 1980s' sound.

320 OUTTAKES

DANCE FOR YOU

(Beyoncé Knowles, Terius Nash, Christopher Stewart/6'17)

Musician: Beyoncé Knowles: vocals / **Recording:** Real World Studios, Box: 2010 / MSR Studios, New York: 2010 to 2011 / **Technical team:** Producers: Beyoncé Knowles, Terius "The-Dream" Nash, C. "Tricky" Stewart / **4 (Target Exclusive) (album)** / Released in the USA by Parkwood Entertainment/Columbia: 28 June 2011 (CD ref.: 88697922992)

Beyoncé recorded the vocal tracks for *Lift Off* in Australia, but this wasn't the first time she had worked in a studio outside America: she had previously recorded *Dance for You* in Peter Gabriel's legendary Real World Studios in Box, England. This recording complex is known for its architecture and the many artists who have traveled from far and wide to record there (Björk, Kylie Minogue, Sia) as well as the British bands who recorded some of the greatest pop rock albums of the 1990s and 2000s there (Placebo's *Without You I'm Nothing* in 1998, Muse's *Origin of Symmetry*, and Stereophonics' *Just Enough Education to Perform* in 2001). "Peter Gabriel has a studio in a village that looks like *The Lord of the Rings* called Real World Studios," DJ Swivel said. "Beyoncé and I were in Gabriel's private room…It has every musical instrument that he ever collected hanging on the walls. It looks like a madhouse for music…a really creative space."[235]

DREAMING

(Antonio Dixon, Beyoncé Knowles, Kenneth "Babyface" Edmonds, J. Que/4'39)

Musician: Beyoncé Knowles: vocals / **Recording:** ?: 2011 / **Technical team:** Producers: Antonio Dixon, Beyoncé Knowles, Kenneth "Babyface" Edmonds / **4 (Japanese edition) (album)** / Released in Japan by Sony Music Japan: 29 June 2011 (CD ref.: SICP 3185-6)

Dreaming appears on the Japanese version of *4*, giving Beyoncé the opportunity to sing of her love for her husband, Jay-Z, and liken her life to a dream. At the time, the two were recently married, and she was often asked about her relationships with men, as in the April 2011 *Cosmopolitan* interview when she was asked to give her advice on seduction: "Put on good music and something that makes you feel great. I love a pair of high, sexy stilettos with a beautiful dress, but you have to find what works for you […]. And never be predictable. Mix it up, surprise him, change your hair—be the woman he knows with a little bit of a twist."[236]

Songwriter Lee Greenwood, author of *God Bless the U.S.A.*, in 1984.

GOD BLESS THE U.S.A.

(Lee Greenwood/2'43)

Musician
Beyoncé Knowles: vocals, backing vocals
Recording
?: 2008
Technical team
Producer: Beyoncé Knowles
Recording engineer: ?

Single
Digital distribution on iTunes: 6 May 2011
Best chart ranking in the USA: did not make the charts

A song for the nation

God Bless the U.S.A. was recorded in 2008 to be used for the presidential campaign of Illinois senator Barack Obama. It was finally released in May 2011, four days after the head of the al-Qaeda terrorist organization, Osama Bin Laden, was killed following a decade-long manhunt for the man who had masterminded the attacks on New York's World Trade Center in September 2001. The song was originally written and sung by Lee Greenwood in 1984, and became a patriotic anthem after the US invasion of Iraq in 2003. Although Senator Obama had always opposed the Iraq war, his fervent supporter decided to release her version of the song, with profits donated to the widows and orphans of New York City's police and firefighters. On 5 May 2011, the day before the song was released as a legal download, Beyoncé performed it on CNN's *Piers Morgan Tonight*, which reassured fans—who had been left somewhat flummoxed by the style of her new single *Run the World (Girls)*—that she hadn't lost her vocal powers.

A patriotic anthem

Lee Greenwood talked about how this song, celebrated as one of the most patriotic in the American repertoire, came into being. "I wrote it on my keyboard—it's hinged inside the back of the bus […] I wrote most of the song in one day…it flowed pretty well. I waited until I got home to make sure I got the lyrics right. I wanted to mention all the states and cities in the song: Minnesota, Tennessee, Texas, Detroit, Houston, New York, and LA. When I got back to Nashville, I played it for my producer, Jerry Crutchfield, and he liked it. It wasn't in the mainstream of what I usually do, but Universal Records heard it and decided to go with it. The record […] became a hit, and it was eventually named the CMA [Country Music Association] Song of the Year." [237]

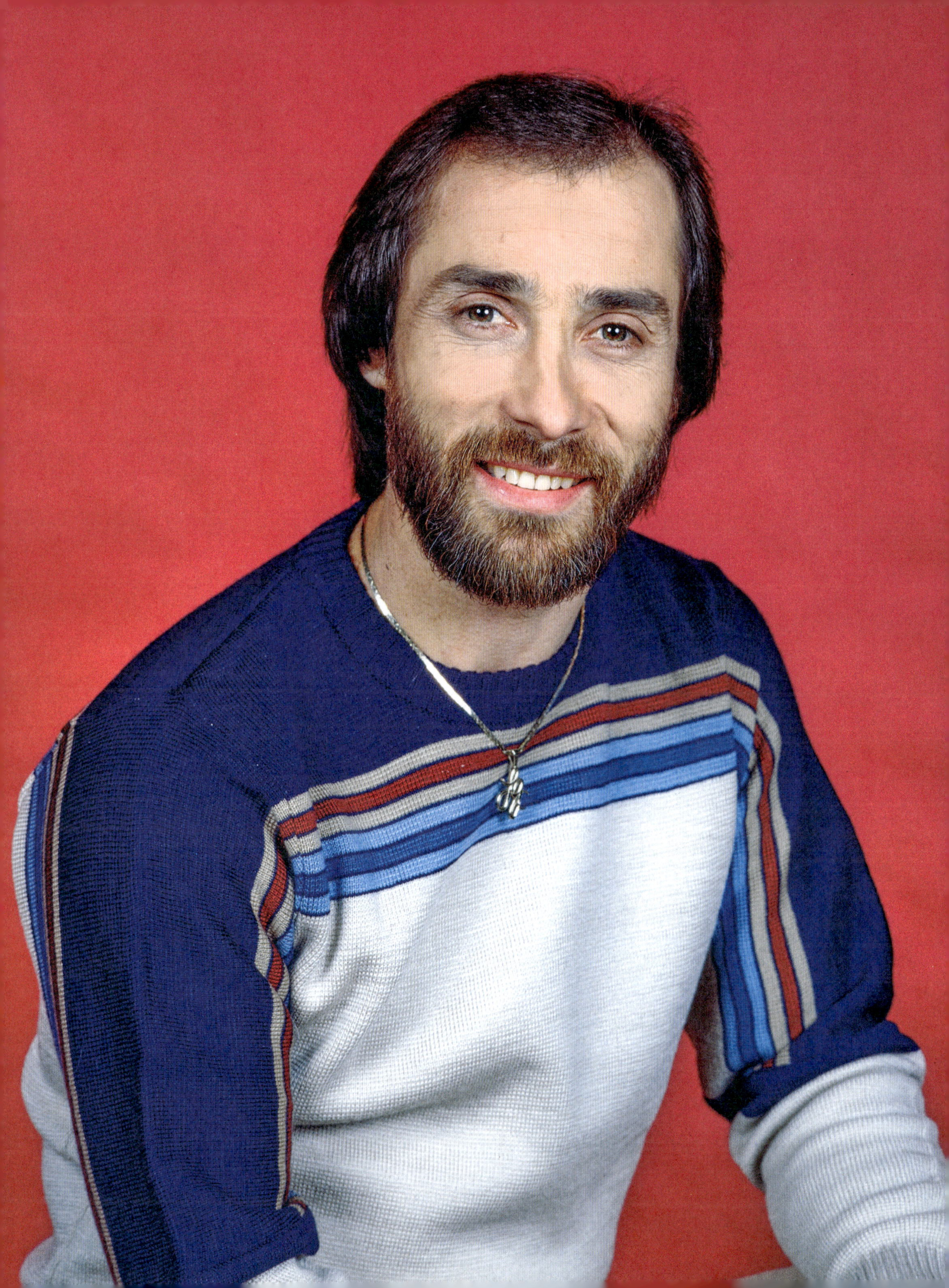

ALBUM

Beyoncé

Pretty Hurts • Haunted • Drunk In Love • Blow • ~~Angel~~ • Partition • Jealous • Rocket • Mine • XO • ***Flawless • Superpower • Heaven • Blue

Digital distribution on iTunes, by Parkwood Entertainment/Columbia: 13 December 2013
Released in the USA by Parkwood Entertainment/Columbia: 20 December 2013 (CD ref.: 88875038422)
Best chart ranking in the USA: 1

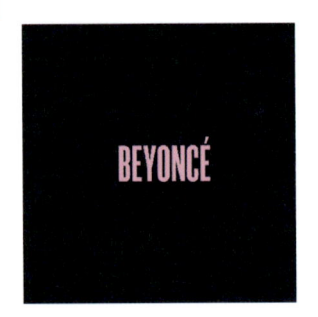

Darker and more mature, the album *Beyoncé* revealed a singer who feared nothing.

BEYONCÉ AND HER TIMES

In March 2012, barely two months after the birth of her first child, Beyoncé announced a three-night concert residency for the official opening of Atlantic City's Revel Resort in April. On 25, 26, and 27 May, she performed three sold-out shows, with the firm intention of showing her fans that motherhood would not put a stop to her career. She further demonstrated this in the months following the Atlantic City concerts, launching production of her new album in August in a sprawling mansion called the Sand Castle that she and her husband rented in Bridgehampton, north-east of New York. A number of hand-picked producers and songwriters were invited, including The-Dream, Shea Taylor, Hit-Boy, and the female star of the moment, Australian singer-songwriter Sia Furler, whose fifth album, *We Are Born*, had been a huge success in 2010. After *Diamonds*, the smash hit she wrote for Rihanna, Furler went on to become one of the most in-demand songwriters and composers.

Surrounded by her family, her long-standing collaborator Teresa LaBarbera Whites, her producer friends, and a slew of technicians and assistants, Beyoncé got her first Writing Camp underway, reproducing on a larger scale the process adopted in 2006 for the writing of *B'Day* at New York's Sony Music Studios. "She flies us all in and puts us all up," Sia said. "We all live in a house together—like five producers and five topline writers. She visits each room and will contribute and let us know what she's feeling and what she's not feeling. Lyrically, melodically, anything."[238] "It was kind of like *Survivor*," joked Melissa Vargas, brand manager at Parkwood Entertainment, who also stayed in the property, which cost $400,000 a month to rent. "We slept in there. Everyone had a room. There was only a certain amount of people that could come, so if you were vibing with her and everything was going great, you would stay for longer. We had a chef and every single person in that house sat down at dinner with Jay and Beyoncé. It didn't matter if you were the assistant engineer, the producer, or a writer."[239]

Enter Jordy "BOOTS" Asher

As summer 2012 drew to a close, around 80 songs formed the basis of Beyoncé's next album, with news about its production kept strictly under wraps. After relocating to New York, Beyoncé and her team—comprising recording engineer Stuart White and a revolving cast of producers presenting their work, including the likes of Hit-Boy, Caroline Polachek, Ryan Tedder, Timbaland, Key Wane, and Pharrell Williams—continued making the album in the privacy of New York's Jungle City and Oven Studios. While Beyoncé captained the ship, a new second-in-command came on board to handle most of the album's production. Behind the pseudonym BOOTS lay a young, formerly homeless prodigy whom Jay-Z had just signed to Roc Nation. His real name was Jordy Asher and when he was introduced to Beyoncé, she immediately embraced his new ideas and sharp ear for songwriting. BOOTS soon became the main man on the project, working closely with Beyoncé to put the new album together.

Beyoncé, Super Bowl queen

On 20 January 2013, Beyoncé was invited to sing *The Star-Spangled Banner* at the closing ceremony of President Barack Obama's second inauguration. For a reason that still eludes

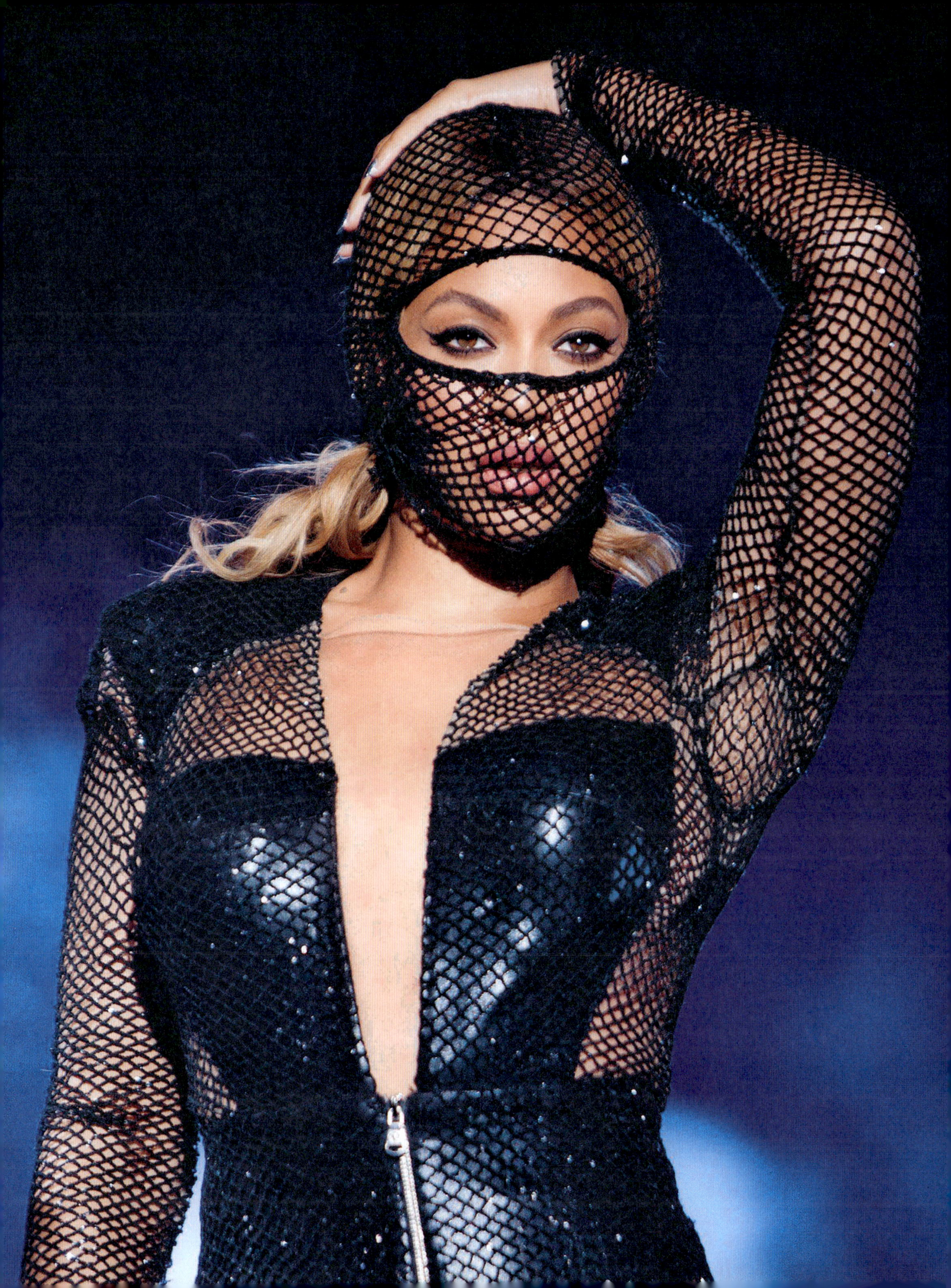

2013

Above: Like Michael Jackson before her, Beyoncé was a faithful ambassador for the Pepsi brand.
Opposite: Jordy "BOOTS" Asher, ready to step out of the shadows.

observers of America's greatest female star, she lip-synched to a pre-recorded track. "I am a perfectionist," she said shortly afterward, to justify her actions against the deluge of criticisms. "One thing about me, I practice until my feet bleed, and I did not have time to rehearse with the orchestra. It was a live television show and a very, very important, emotional show for me—one of my proudest moments. Due to the weather, due to the delay, due to no proper sound check, I did not feel comfortable taking a risk. It was about my president and the inauguration, and I didn't want to take away from that. I decided to go with a pre-recorded track, which is very common in the music industry. And I am very proud of my performance."[240] Shortly afterward, on 31 January, with this contentious episode behind her, Beyoncé silenced the critics when she sang *The Star-Spangled Banner*—live this time—in front of journalists attending the Super Bowl XLVII Halftime Show press conference. She wasn't there out of a desire for revenge: far from it. She had just signed a commercial partnership with Pepsi, the Super Bowl's main sponsor. At the press conference, it was announced that Beyoncé had been invited to perform at half-time during the final on 3 February 2013, which would pit the San Francisco 49ers against the Baltimore Ravens at the Mercedes-Benz Superdrome in New Orleans. Happy for the opportunity to consign her performance at President Obama's inauguration to the dustbin of history, Beyoncé threw herself into this new objective with great gusto, in the knowledge that for her it would also be a celebration of 15 years of uninterrupted success in the music industry. On the day, Beyoncé had the world eating out of her hand, also thrilling fans by inviting her former Destiny's Child colleagues Kelly Rowland and Michelle Williams to perform a medley of two of their greatest hits, *Bootylicious* and *Independent Women Part I*.

A well-kept secret

While fans were growing impatient with the latest rumors of a possible new album from their idol, there had been no official conformation of any upcoming release. As production continued, Beyoncé carefully dropped in some new material here and there, not wanting to disappear below the radar for too long. A Pepsi advert featured a few notes from an unreleased track, *Grown Woman*, while the new H&M campaign with

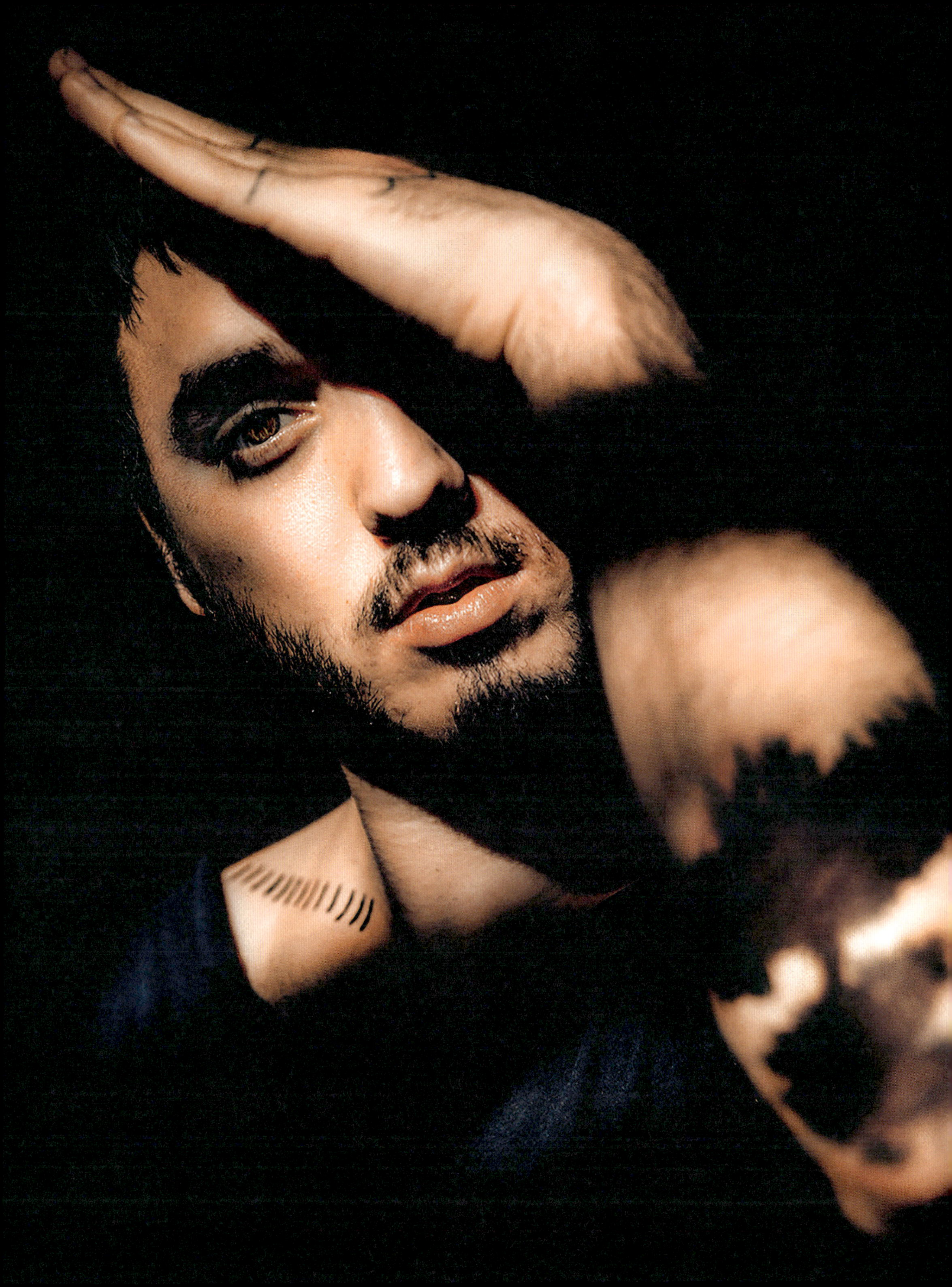

Jay-Z and Beyoncé on stage during the On the Run Tour in 2014.

In 2013, Beyoncé launched the charity foundation BeyGOOD. "I started BeyGOOD to share the mentality that we could all do something to help others, something my parents instilled in me from a young age—to inspire others to be kind, to be charitable, and to be good. We focused on many areas of need, including hurricane relief, education [...], a fellowship program in South Africa, women's rights, support of minority businesses, assisting families with housing needs, water crises, pediatric health care, and pandemic relief."[243]

which she was involved delighted fans with a few seconds from a new song, *Standing on the Sun*. Despite these novelties coming in dribs and drabs, admirers of Queen Bey would have to be patient for a few months more before they were fully satisfied.

Inspired by the massive excitement whipped up by the unannounced release of David Bowie's new single *Where Are We Now?* on the morning of 8 January 2013, ten years after the appearance of his last album, out of the blue Beyoncé released her fifth album on the iTunes Store on 13 December 2013, causing a wave of hysteria among fans. Soberly titled *Beyoncé*, the album sold over 80,000 copies in just three hours and close to a million copies in its first week. The physical version was not released until a week later, and a platinum edition, including two previously unreleased tracks and four remixes, came out on 24 November 2014. The unusually understated cover for *Beyoncé* marked a real break with the singer's previous albums. Beyoncé wanted to create a "visual album" that represented cinematographically what each song meant to her. As the album featured a video to accompany every song, Todd Tourso, its creative director, dropped the dozen or so proposed graphic designs he had been considering in favor of the most pared-back version. "When it's a visual album and it's inundated with imagery, how do you find one that encapsulates it all? It was as simple as not having her face on it. Because that's what everyone would expect, a beauty shot of her. That was the big breakthrough, coming to the conclusion that it doesn't have to have her on it."[241]

A strong visual concept for a dark album

Although Beyoncé had never been as fulfilled as she was in 2013, with her husband, their daughter Blue Ivy, and the huge success she was enjoying, her fifth album was the darkest she had ever recorded. Its productions illustrated her desire to experiment, and the powerful instrumental tracks (thanks to highly present bass and infrabass) blended perfectly with the dark lyrics BOOTS and Beyoncé had written. Opening up as never before, Beyoncé tackled themes such as her own sexuality, women's empowerment in the context of a dominant patriarchy, and her love for her man and her daughter. She also used this album to try to encourage her fans to consume music in a more real way, at a time when people were cramming their iPods with the latest singles and showing little interest in the full content of their favorite artists' albums. "Now people only listen to a few seconds of a song on the iPods and they don't really invest in the whole experience," she explained. "It's all about the single, and the hype. It's so much that gets between the music and the art and the fans. I felt like, I don't want anybody to get the message when my record is coming out. I just want this to come out when it's ready and from me to my fans."[242]

On the road with Mrs Carter

The Mrs. Carter Show World Tour kicked off on 15 April 2013 at Kombank Arena in Belgrade, Serbia. The first leg of the tour, which ended in New York on 22 December, consisted largely of Beyoncé's past repertoire, while the second, which began in Glasgow on 20 February 2014 and toured Europe until 27 March, mostly promoted her new album and saw her performing a number of tracks from *Beyoncé*, including *Blow*, *Partition*, *Drunk in Love*, *Haunted*, *Heaven*, and *XO*. The tour was a triumph, but an even bigger surprise awaited fans. In April 2014, when Beyoncé had just performed 32 concerts while her husband Jay-Z wrapped up his Magna Carter World Tour—promoting his twelfth album, *Magna Carta Holy Grail*—the two stars announced the launch of the phenomenal On the Run Tour, featuring both of them. It would start on 25 June 2014 at the Sun Life Stadium in Miami

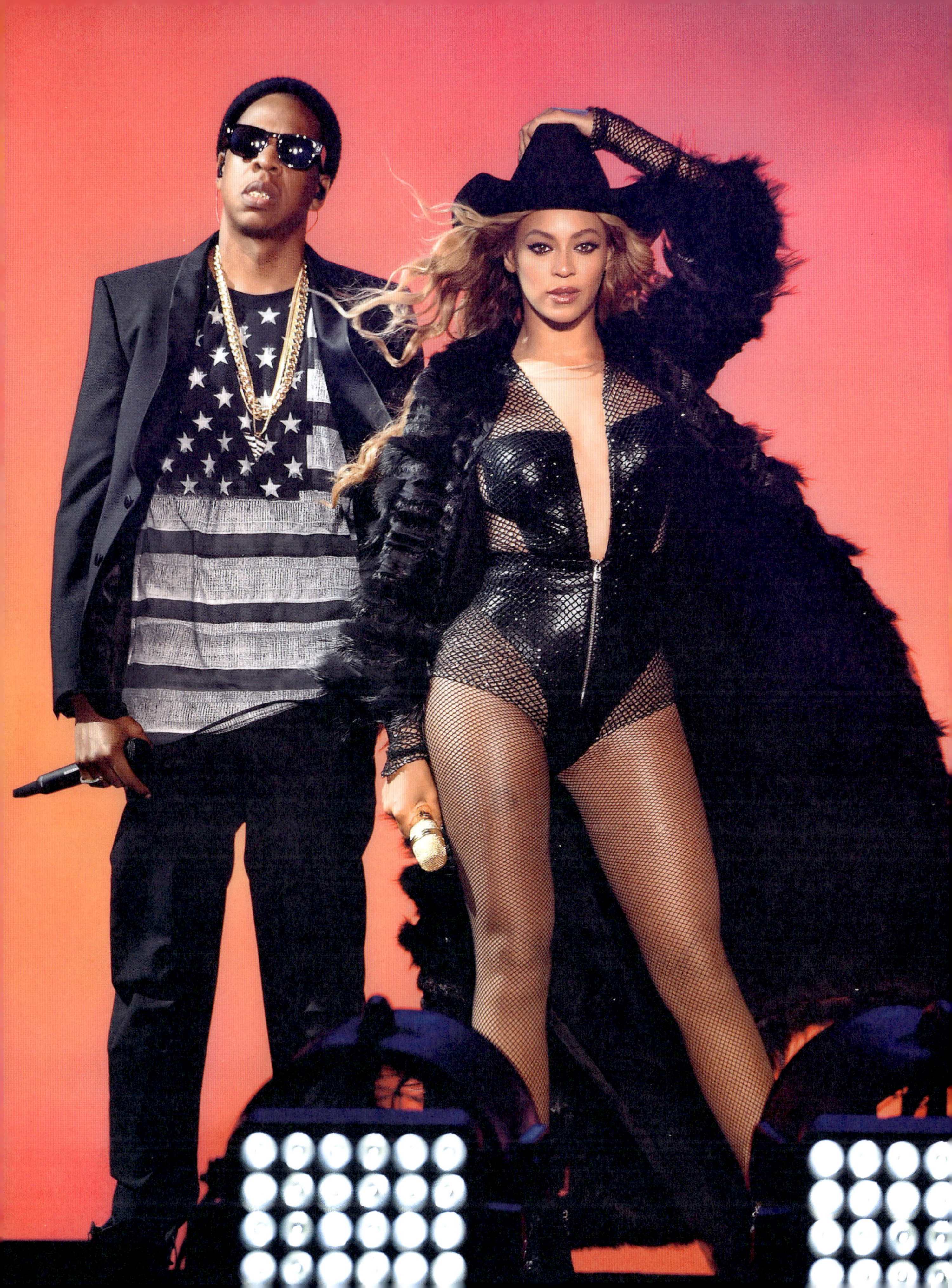

Above: Fans welcome Beyoncé in her native city, Houston, 15 July 2013.
Opposite: Beyoncé during the Mrs. Carter Show World Tour in July 2013.

Gardens, and end on 13 September at the Stade de France in Saint-Denis, Paris, after 21 concerts spanning the two artists' respective careers. Beyond the absolute validation that the success of this tour brought Beyoncé, her fifth album also enabled her to position herself not just as an artist churning out hit after hit, like the many female singers jostling at the top of the *Billboard* 100, but as a key figure who could not be ignored. She was socially and politically committed, supported worthy causes such as women's and LGBT rights (the LGBTQIA+ acronym wouldn't appear until a few years later), and, above all, was able to sell millions of copies of an album that showcased experimental sounds and grown-up, intelligent lyrics. With *Beyoncé*, which was very much a breakthrough album, she established herself as a role model for an entire generation, in a country where instability was lurking and inequality rife.

> The BeyHive community for Beyoncé fans across the world appeared between the albums *4* and *Beyoncé*. The name of the community refers to Beyoncé's nickname Queen B, an amalgam of Queen Bee and Queen Bey.

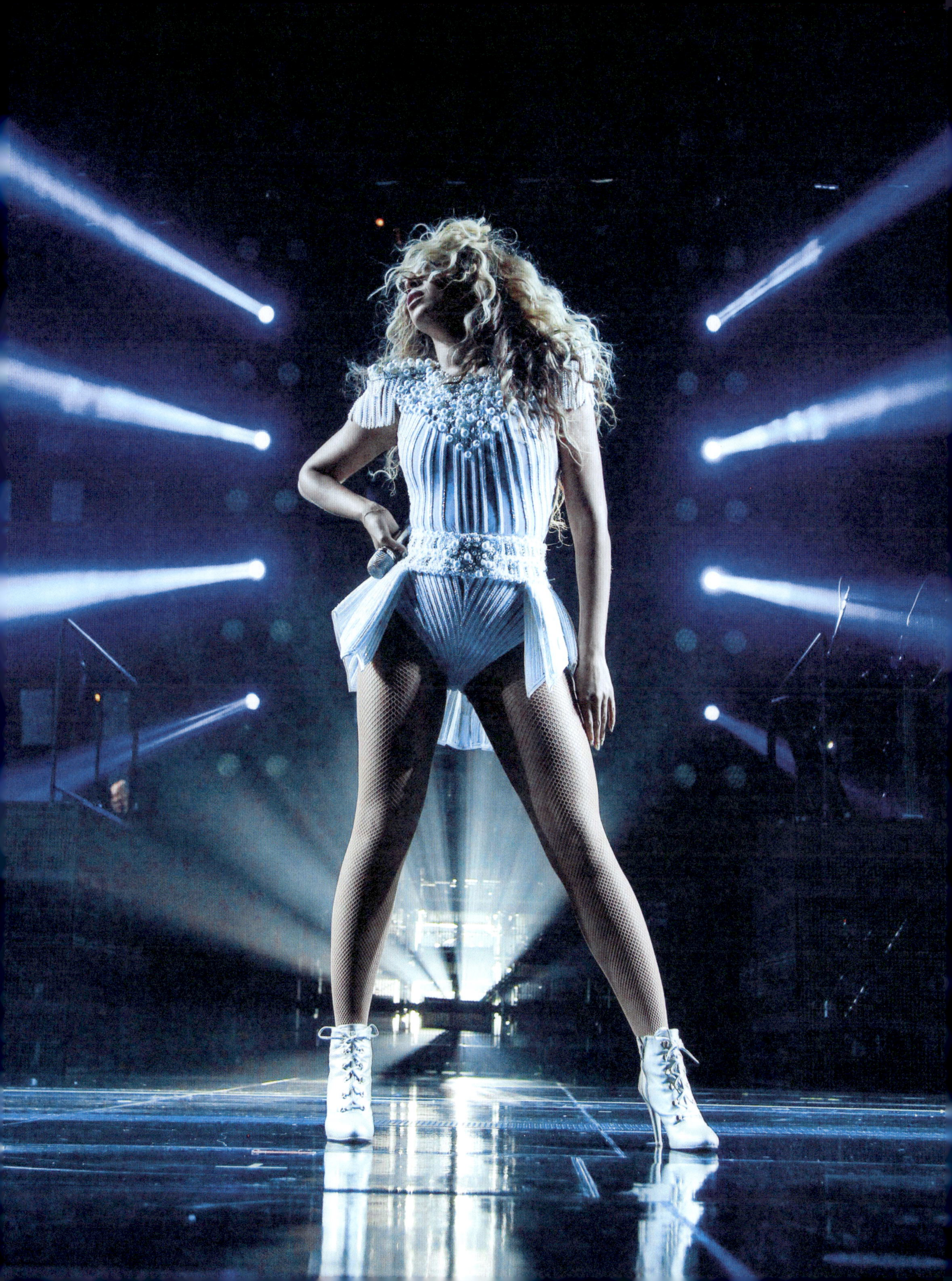

Creator of five fabulous pop albums between 1997 and 2010, Australian singer Sia attained worldwide success in 2014 with her single *Chandelier*.

SINGLE

PRETTY HURTS

(Beyoncé Knowles, Joshua Coleman, Sia Furler/4'17)

Musicians
Beyoncé Knowles: vocals, backing vocals
Derek Dixie: synthesizers

Recording
Kings Landing, Bridgehampton: 2012
Jungle City Studios, New York: 2012 to 2013
Oven Studios, New York: 2012 to 2013

Technical team
Producers: Beyoncé Knowles, Ammo
Executive producer: Beyoncé Knowles
Recording engineers: Stuart White, Ramon Rivas
Assistant recording engineer: Rob Suchecki

Single
Digital distribution by Parkwood Entertainment/Columbia: 10 June 2014
Best chart ranking in the USA: did not make the charts

Genesis

It was in her apartment in Angelino Heights, Los Angeles, that Sia Furler wrote *Pretty Hurts*, just after she and her producer Ammo had recorded her vocals for the track *Titanium*, sent to her by David Guetta. It was 2011 and the Australian artist was basking in the success of her fifth album, *We Are Born*, an excellent pop record featuring the hits *Clap Your Hands* and *Bring Night*. Furler leafed through her address book full of prestigious names and emailed the track to her friend Katy Perry, an international superstar who had scored a string of hits in 2010 with *California Gurls*, *Teenage Dream*, *Firework*, and *Last Friday Night (T.G.I.F.)*. Having received no answer, Sia decided to send the song to Rihanna's manager, who chose *Diamonds* instead. Shortly afterward, Beyoncé found out about the track and quickly expressed her interest. "The second I heard the song, I'm like, 'I have to sing this song, I don't care how hard I have to fight for this song, this is my song!'"[244] Dr. Luke, one of Katy Perry's producers, heard Beyoncé's version of *Pretty Hurts* and played it to Perry, who fired off a disgruntled text to Sia, saying: "I'm pretty hurt you never sent me this song,"[245] to which Furler simply replied: "Check your email."[245] Perry hadn't opened the email containing the track, so she could only bemoan her luck. Fortunately, she proved herself a good loser, with the remark: "It was meant to be with Beyoncé, of course."[245]

Lyrics and video with a strong message

Besides loving the melody to *Pretty Hurts*, Beyoncé was drawn to the message of the lyrics. Their subject—namely the overriding importance of beauty that is drummed into young girls, the beauty contests some are forced to enter, and, more broadly, the physical standards to which women are held all their lives—is perfectly in line with the general spirit of *Beyoncé*, whose main theme is the right to be imperfect. To illustrate the song, Beyoncé made a video with director Melina Matsoukas. "I immediately saw the vision and I thought about pageants and I thought about the most humiliating, judgmental place you can be as a woman," Beyoncé said. "I feel like sometimes the world is a big contest, we're all being judged. I wanted to capture how humiliating and insecure that makes you feel. Melina was able to capture that emotion and capture the extremes we feel we have to go to to please the people that judge us."[246] The scene in which Beyoncé destroys all the trophies on the shelves in the background was undoubtedly the key one for her, as she explained in 2013: "I had this image of this trophy and me accepting these awards, trying in myself to be this champion and at the end of the day when you go through all of these things, is it worth it? Well, you get this trophy and you're like 'I basically starved, I have neglected people that I love, I conformed to what everybody else thinks I should be and I have this trophy. What does that mean?' The trophy represents all the sacrifices I made as a kid, all the time that I lost being on the road, in the studios as a child, and I just wanted to blow that shit up."[247]

Production

Although Sia Furler has stopped showing her face, her writing is instantly recognizable. Until 2012 she was a multifaceted pop artist, but from 2013 her style became more homogenous, as is shown by the songs she wrote for others (*Diamonds* by Rihanna, *Pretty Hurts* by Beyoncé, *Beautiful Pain* by Eminem, *Beautiful People* by Wiz Khalifa) and by her own hits, international successes such as *Elastic Heart* in 2013, *Chandelier* in 2014, and *Unstoppable*, *Cheap Thrills*, and *The Greatest* in 2016. In August 2013 Beyoncé invited Sia to work with her in Southampton, Long Island, where she was very prolific, as always, and happy to discuss her music with Beyoncé, who had recently discovered and loved *Pretty Hurts*. "She's very Frankenstein when she comes to songs. She'll say, 'I like the verse from that. I like the pre-chorus from that. Can you try mixing it with that?' In the end, she had maybe 25 songs of mine on hold, and I was very excited to get a couple of them back. Definitely one is on the album."[238] Sia Furler is a talented songwriter with a string of hits to her name and she certainly doesn't mince her words, as she proved when she came up with a great metaphor for journalists about writing songs for successful pop artists: "You're basically throwing spaghetti at a wall and hoping it will stick."[238]

Beyoncé reveals her bobbed hairstyle at the Grammy Awards in Los Angeles, 26 January 2014.

HAUNTED

(BOOTS, Beyoncé Knowles/6'09)

Musicians
Beyoncé Knowles: vocals, backing vocals
Kwane Wyatt: backing vocals
BOOTS: additional instruments, backing vocals
Hit-Boy: programming

Recording
Jungle City Studios, New York: 2012 to 2013
Oven Studios, New York: 2012 to 2013

Technical team
Producers: BOOTS, Beyoncé Knowles
Executive producer: Beyoncé Knowles
Recording engineers: BOOTS, Stuart White, Ramon Rivas

Genesis

After denouncing the obstacles American women face, here Beyoncé takes aim at the terrible state of record companies, once run by visionary music lovers but by then in the hands of immoral businessmen, driven only by the bottom line. Young producer BOOTS wrote the lyrics for this song, the first segment of which (up to 2'54) is called *Ghost* and was inspired by a meeting with artistic directors to whom he presented the tracks he had composed for Beyoncé. "The things people say in those meetings would take your breath away," BOOTS said. "After a while, I didn't even feel like I was talking to people anymore, I was just talking to chairs. So I went home, it was five in the morning, and I just started typing shit out—everything I hear on the radio isn't inspiring; I'm not inspired by anything I'm doing; these people have no idea what's happening. It was just a stream-of-consciousness. I woke up the next day and realized I needed to do something with that. That's what eventually became that rap."[248]

Production

Beyoncé instantly loved *Ghost*, whose lyrics reflected her own thinking about the music business at the time. She recorded the rap part of the track, then decided to add a second segment called *Haunted*, a ballad also written by BOOTS. His voice can be heard when he improvises on the backing vocals from 3'04 to 3'08, and the piano part he played on the demo version was also retained in the final mix. "I recorded the piano with my iPhone as a voice memo and that shit made it onto the damn album, by the way. It was a loose idea, but the feeling was there. I had written a bunch of songs that could have been 'Beyoncé songs,' whatever that had meant before now, but she wasn't interested in those. There was something about what I had to say that resonated with her."[248]

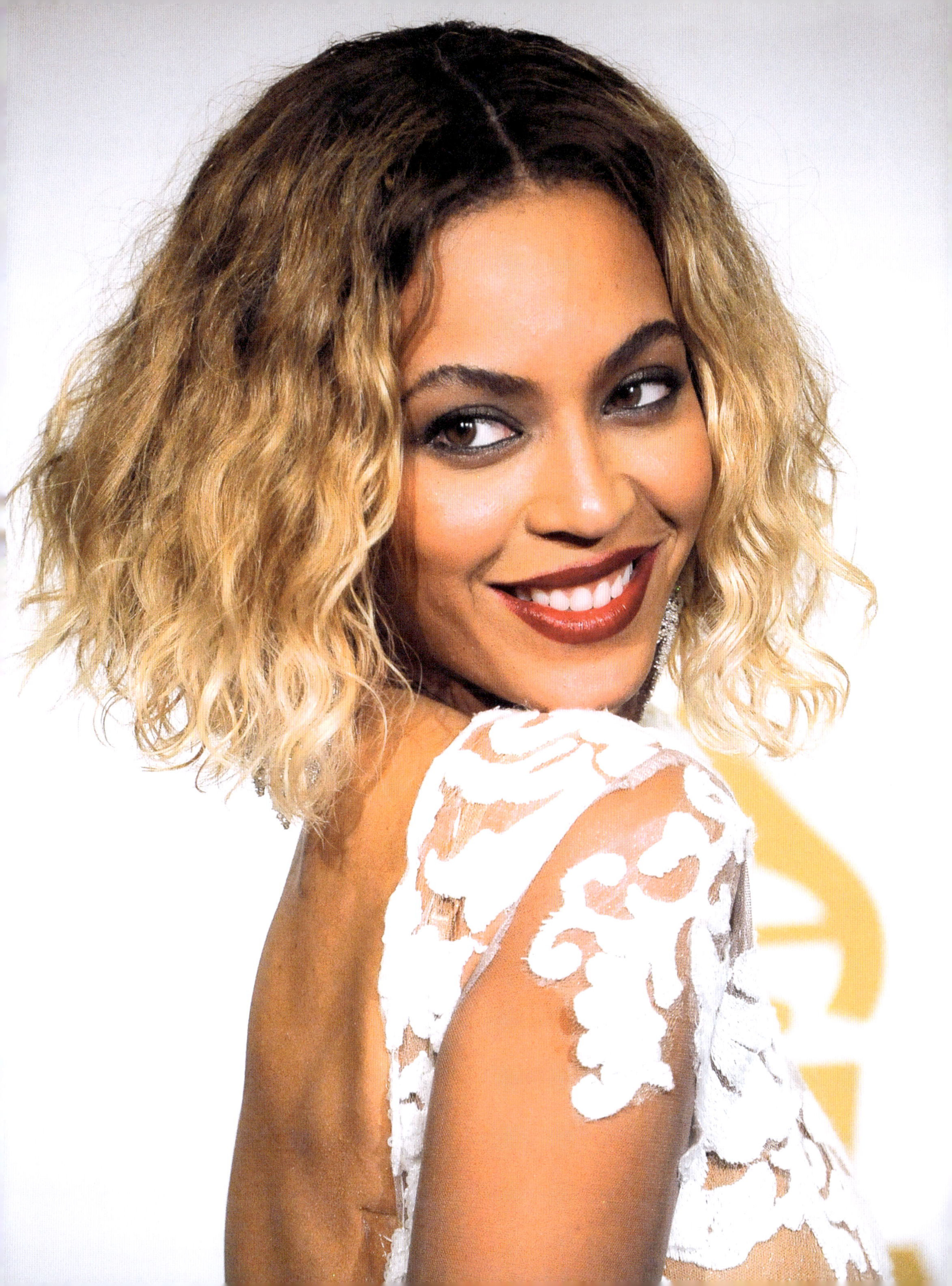

A faithful associate of Jay-Z, the producer Future wrote the vocal line of *Drunk in Love*.

SINGLE

DRUNK IN LOVE
(FEATURING JAY-Z)

(Andre Eric Proctor, Beyoncé Knowles, Brian Soko, Jerome Harmon, Noel Fisher, Rasool Diaz, Shawn Carter, Timothy Mosley/5'23)

Musicians
Beyoncé Knowles: vocals, backing vocals
Jay-Z: rap
BOOTS: additional instruments, backing vocals
Derek Dixie: synthesizers

Recording
Jungle City Studios, New York: 2012 to 2013
Oven Studios, New York: 2012 to 2013

Technical team
Producers: Beyoncé Knowles, Noel "Detail" Fisher, Brian Soko, Jerome Harmon, Timbaland, BOOTS
Executive producer: Beyoncé Knowles
Recording engineers: Stuart White, Ramon Rivas

Single
Digital distribution by Parkwood Entertainment/Columbia: 17 December 2013
Best chart ranking in the USA: 2

Genesis
When Noel "Detail" Fisher, a producer who had worked with Akon, Lil Wayne, and Ray J, wrote the instrumental that would become *Drunk in Love*, he invited his friend, the rapper Future (also a close friend of Jay-Z), to record vocals on the demo track. When he presented the song to Beyoncé, she immediately appropriated it. Meanwhile, Future—who was totally unaware of Fisher's approach to Beyoncé—was busy recording *Good Morning*, a track that featured the same vocal line as *Drunk in Love*, slated to appear on his upcoming album *Honest*. It wasn't until he listened to *Beyoncé* in December that Future discovered his vocal line on the track. "I was like, 'What I'mma do with *Good Morning* now?' This one of our favorite songs."[249] Not only had he not been informed about the production of *Drunk in Love*, his name doesn't even appear on the track's credits.

Production
Drunk in Love was very much a joint effort, with Noel "Detail" Fisher writing the instrumentals, Future the vocal line, and Timbaland adding a few synth lines. Jay-Z then came in to record his improvised rap on the track, causing controversy with the lines *I'm Ike Turner, turn up, baby, no I don't play/ Now eat the cake, Anna Mae!*, an explicit reference to a scene in Brian Gibson's 1993 Tina Turner biopic *What's Love Got to Do With It*, in which Ike Turner assaults his wife in the middle of a restaurant, smashing a piece of cake into her face. This inappropriate quote apart, the track is a success, and the result of an interesting production decision taken by Beyoncé, as recording engineer Stuart White explained: "I remember I mixed it with Tony [Maserati] and at the last minute, she liked the demo better. She liked the way the drums were mixed in the version we did in his studio. But, she wanted everything from the original demo put back in. I was at Tony's studio and literally had to import all the vocals, and music tracks from the original session, and mixing it into what we had made, and make this new version at the last second before we had to turn in the album." Then he added with a laugh: "I re-did the mix hours before we turned the album in."[250]

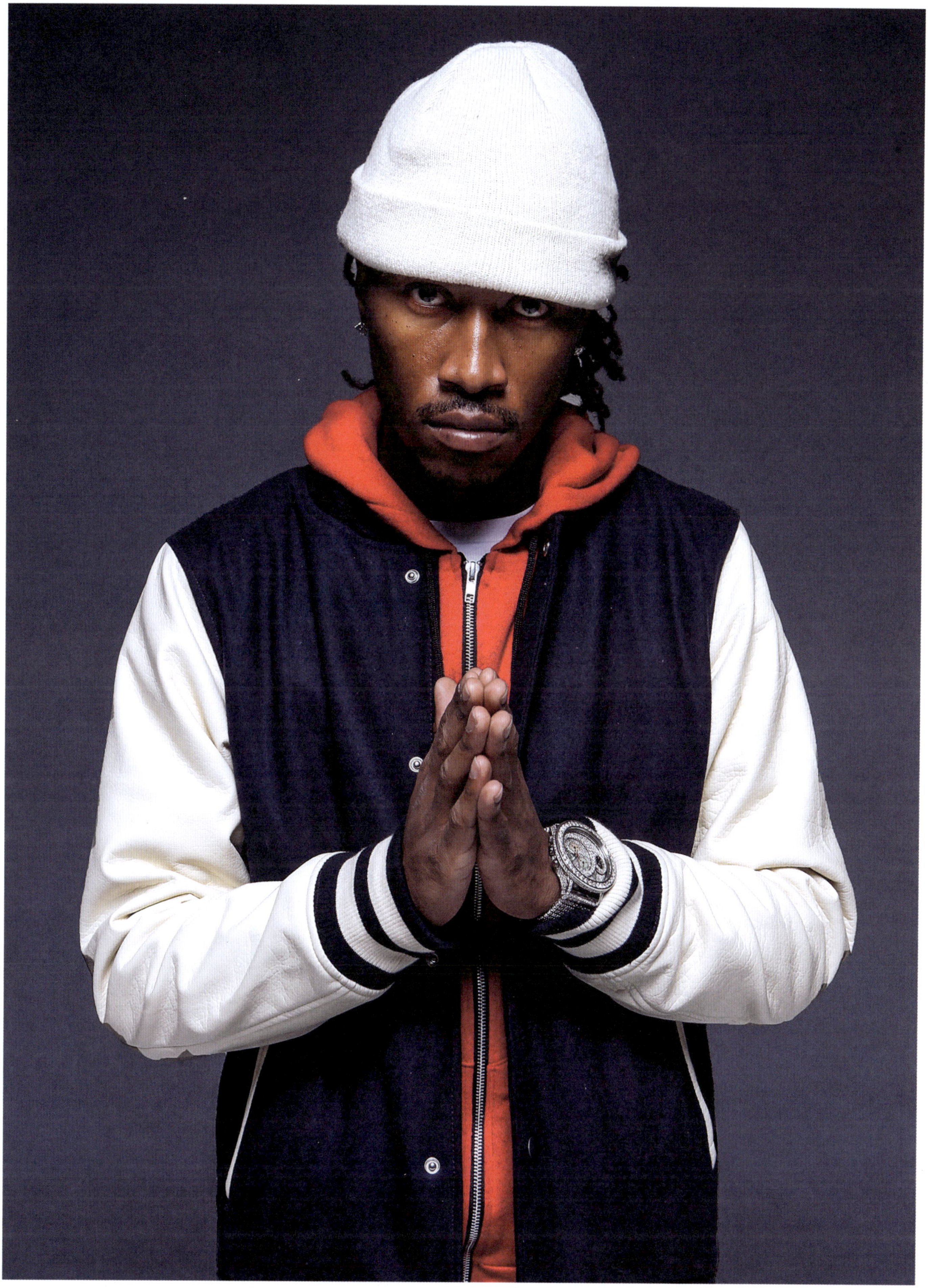

2013

A renowned composer, Caroline Polachek met with immense success in 2023 with her single *Sunset*.

BLOW

(Beyoncé Knowles, James Fauntleroy, Jerome Harmon, Justin Timberlake, Pharrell Williams, Timothy Mosley/5'09)

Musicians: Beyoncé Knowles: vocals, backing vocals / Pharrell Williams: backing vocals / Timbaland: backing vocals / Adison Evans: saxophone / Crystal Torres: trumpet / Katty Rodriguez: saxophone / **Recording:** Jungle City Studios, New York: 2012 to 2013 / Oven Studios, New York: 2012 to 2013 / **Technical team: Producers:** Beyoncé Knowles, Pharrell Williams, Jerome Harmon, Timbaland / **Executive producer:** Beyoncé Knowles / **Recording engineers:** Stuart White, Chris Godbey, Bart Schoudel, Andrew Coleman, Ramon Rivas / **Assistant recording engineer:** Matt Weber / **Brass arrangements:** Derek Dixie

It would be hard not to instantly recognize the styles of Timbaland (one of the song's producers and writers) and Justin Timberlake in *Blow*, a track highly reminiscent of Timberlake's *SexyBack*, written by both men and Nate "Danja" Hills in 2006. The resemblance lies in the 1980s-sounding drum machine—probably a Roland TR-808—of the kind Timbaland used extensively in his productions. It is probably no coincidence that director Hype Williams also chose to give the video a feel close to the decade in which Beyoncé grew up. Even the film location—Houston's FunPlex, an indoor fun center with a roller rink—references her childhood, as it is somewhere she used to go as a teenager. "It was so strange because it was one of my first dates with one of my first boyfriends at FunPlex. And now I got the whole FunPlex that I rented out and I thought I was balling. I'm like 'Man, this FunPlex is just for me!' But it was beautiful to be back there and to shoot with Hype Williams."[246]

ANGEL

(Beyoncé Knowles, Caroline Polachek, James Fauntleroy/ 3'48)

Musicians: Beyoncé Knowles: vocals, backing vocals / Caroline Polachek: synthesizers, programming / **Recording:** Russell's of Clapton, London: 2012 to 2013 / Fetalmaus Studio, New York: 2012 to 2013 / Jungle City Studios, New York: 2012 to 2013 / Oven Studios, New York: 2012 to 2013 / **Technical team: Producers:** Beyoncé Knowles, Caroline Polachek, BOOTS / **Executive producer:** Beyoncé Knowles / **Recording engineers:** Caroline Polachek, Stuart White, Ramon Rivas

Caroline Polachek is now internationally famous for her singles *Bunny Is a Rider*, *Billions*, and *Sunset*, released between July 2021 and October 2022, but she was still a complete unknown when she worked with Beyoncé in 2012. Polachek was spotted by Solange Knowles, who introduced her to her sister, and she was invited to participate in the writing sessions at Jungle City Studios in New York. Polachek had lots of ideas to share, but it was one that had been lying dormant in her computer for two years and that she had recorded at five in the morning in a hotel room, that she wanted to offer to Beyoncé: "I was like, 'Well that song is so sexy. It's gotta go in the pile.' So I rewrote the verse lyrics and sent it to her. It had this minute-and-a-half-long instrumental in the middle of it, and I was like 'I'm sure

> On the album cover, the track appears as *Angel*, and is intended to be read as "No Angel."

340 BEYONCÉ

The French dancer Hajiba Fahmy performed with Beyoncé and is the sensual voice in *Partition*.

they're gonna cut that out, and replace it with something else. There's no way she's gonna let a minute-and-a-half-long instrumental fly.' They kept it."[251] As was her custom, Beyoncé didn't inform her writers and producers of the final tracklisting of her album in advance, so several months later, on the morning of 13 December 2013, Caroline Polacheck couldn't believe it when she got a message from one of her friends: "A friend texted me and was like 'It's out.' And I was like 'What's out?' And they were like, 'Your song is Track 4.'"[251]

SINGLE

PARTITION

(Beyoncé Knowles, Dwane M. Weir, Jerome Harmon, Justin Timberlake, Mike Dean, Terius Nash, Timothy Mosley/5'19)

Musicians: Beyoncé Knowles: vocals, backing vocals / **Hajiba Fahmy:** spoken voice / **Justin Timberlake:** backing vocals / **Terius "The-Dream" Nash:** backing vocals / **Derek Dixie:** synthesizers / **Niles Hollowell-Dhar:** synthesizers / **Recording:** Jungle City Studios, New York: 2012 to 2013 / Oven Studios, New York: 2012 to 2013 / **Technical team:** Producers: Beyoncé Knowles, Jerome Harmon, Justin Timberlake, Key Wane, Timbaland, BOOTS, Mike Dean / **Executive producer:** Beyoncé Knowles / **Recording engineers:** Stuart White, Chris Godbey, Ann Mincieli, Bart Schoudel, Ramon Rivas / **Assistant recording engineer:** Matt Weber / **Single:** Digital distribution by Parkwood Entertainment/Columbia: 25 February 2014 / Best chart ranking in the USA: 23

Just as *Haunted* consists of two segments, *Ghost* and *Haunted*, so *Partition* is constructed from two distinct sections: *Yoncé* from 0'01 to 2'04, and *Partition* from 2'05 to the end of the track. "*Yoncé* is such an incredible song," Beyoncé explained. "I love it because it's really organic and the drumbeat was actually done in the studio by Justin Timberlake. He just started beating on these buckets and The-Dream started coming up with this little chant. And it's so exciting when something naturally happens that way."[246] On the subject of the lyrics, French dancer Hajiba Fahmy, a member of the dance troupe on Beyoncé's Mrs. Carter Show World Tour and On the Run Tour, gives a sensual rendition in French of some lines from the 1998 Joel and Ethan Coen film *The Big Lebowski* in which Maude (Julianne Moore) asks Jeffrey "the Dude" Lebowski (Jeff Bridges) if he likes sex. Because that's what the song is about, as Beyoncé reveals a highly erotic side that she worried might shock her nearest and dearest. "I didn't have a pen or paper, I got to the mic and I said, 'Press Record.' [...] I was so embarrassed after I recorded the song cause I'm just talking shit and I'm like 'I can't play that for my husband'. I still haven't played it for my mum, she's gonna be very mad at me."[252]

Jay-Z and Beyoncé in front of the Metropolitan Museum of Art in New York, May 2015.

JEALOUS

(Andre Eric Proctor, BOOTS, Beyoncé Knowles, Brian Soko, Lyrica Anderson, Noel Fisher, Rasool Diaz/3'04)

Musicians: Beyoncé Knowles: vocals, backing vocals / **BOOTS:** additional instruments, backing vocals / **Recording:** Jungle City Studios, New York: 2012 to 2013 / **Oven Studios, New York:** 2012 to 2013 / **Technical team:** Producers: Beyoncé Knowles, Noel "Detail" Fisher, Andre Eric Proctor, BOOTS, Hit-Boy / **Executive producer:** Beyoncé Knowles / **Recording engineers:** Stuart White, Ramon Rivas, Rob Suchecki / **Assistant recording engineer:** Carlos Perez D'Anda

Behind this R&B ballad with a poignant chorus sung by BOOTS himself ("It seemed like a shame something more melodic didn't happen in the song," he observed[248]) lies another song with lyrics that were unfortunately prophetic. Beyoncé sings that she is jealous and soon her worst nightmare would come to pass. In 2014, a number of tabloids published stories about an alleged affair between Jay-Z and Casey Cohen, one of the stars of the reality show *Princesses: Long Island*, whom the rapper had allegedly met in the New York club 1 Oak, where she worked as a hostess. A few months after the release of *Beyoncé*, rumors of a divorce between the two icons were doing the rounds, and culminated in a series of events that the tabloid press lapped up. On 5 May 2014, an incident occurred while the Carters and Solange Knowles were attending the Met Gala after-party at the Standard Hotel in New York. It would have remained private, had a hotel employee not sold CCTV footage to the website TMZ.com for $250,000. The three artists can be seen entering an elevator, and then Solange attacks Jay-Z with Beyoncé looking calmly on, before a bodyguard steps in to stop the star's younger sister. Although much was made of the incident, the couple gave no official reason for it, fueling rumors that Solange Knowles was taking revenge for her brother-in-law's alleged infidelity. The three artists quickly issued a press release to deny the tabloid gossip, declaring: "Jay and Solange each assume their share of responsibility for what has occurred. They both acknowledge their role in this private matter that has played out in public. They both have apologized to each other and we have moved forward as a united family."[253]

ROCKET

(Beyoncé Knowles, Jerome Harmon, Justin Timberlake, Miguel Jontel Pimentel, Timothy Mosley/6'31)

Musicians: Beyoncé Knowles: vocals, backing vocals / **Justin Timberlake:** backing vocals / **Dwayne Wright:** bass / **Mike Scott:** guitar / **Recording:** Jungle City Studios, New York: 2012 to 2013 / **Oven Studios, New York:** 2012 to 2013 / **Technical team:** Producers: Beyoncé Knowles, Timbaland, Jerome Harmon / **Executive producer:** Beyoncé Knowles / **Recording engineers:** Stuart White, Chris Godbey, Ramon Rivas / **Assistant recording engineer:** Matt Weber

In a neo-soul register perfectly suited to the lyrics of the song, Beyoncé is more sensual than ever. The singer describes a striptease performed for her partner, using a series of metaphors that decency prevents us from reproducing here, even though Beyoncé is completely comfortable with her body and her sexuality, as she revealed in an interview she gave to promote the album. "I don't at all have any shame about being sexual and I'm not embarrassed about it and I don't feel like I have to protect that side of me."[252] She also admitted that she trained very hard to get her pre-pregnancy body back, saying that women shouldn't feel less sensual just because they have carried a baby. This is one of the major themes of the album, with Beyoncé once again staking her claim to be the standard-bearer of the unapologetic and self-confident femininity that she talked about in interviews: "I'd like to believe that my music opened up that conversation. There is unbelievable power in ownership, and women should own their sexuality. There is a double standard when it comes to sexuality that still persists. Men are free and women are not. That is crazy. The old lessons of submissiveness and fragility made us victims. Women are so much more than that. You can be a businesswoman, a mother, an artist, and a feminist—whatever you want to be—and still be a sexual being."[254]

HEADPHONES AT THE READY

To give the *Jealous* instrumental some bite, BOOTS added a few electric guitars at the back of the mix at Beyoncé's request after she showed him the video for *Roach Cock* by the Californian Hanni El Khatib and asked him to give her song a garage-rock touch.

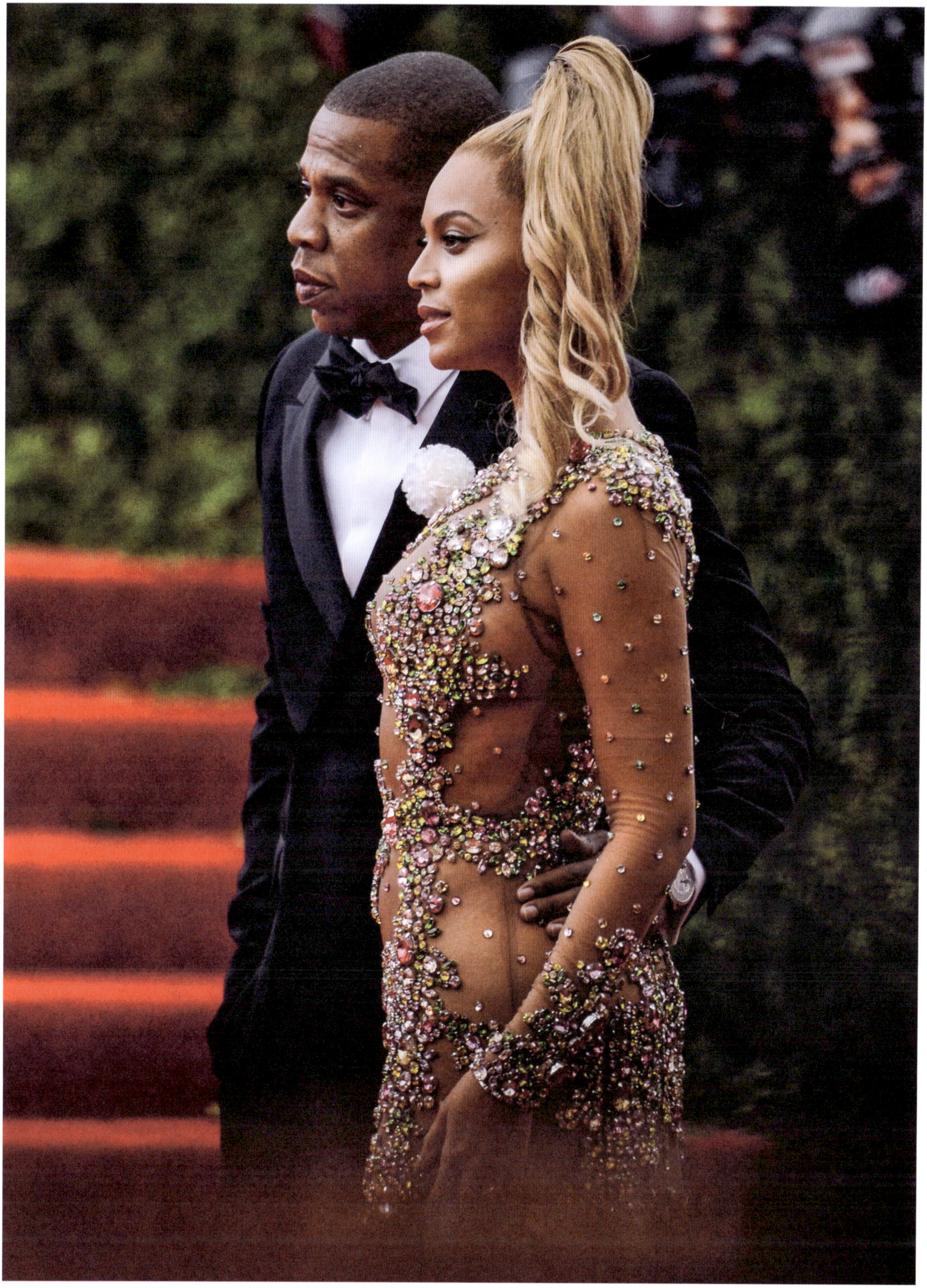

Canadian rapper and singer Drake in August 2005.

MINE
(FEATURING DRAKE)

(Aubrey "Drake" Graham, Beyoncé Knowles, Dwane M. Weir, Jordan Kenneth Cooke Ullman, Noah Shebib, Sidney "Omen" Brown/6'18)

Musicians: Beyoncé Knowles: vocals, backing vocals / Drake: vocals, rap / Omen: programming / Key Wane: synthesizers, programming / **Recording:** Jungle City Studios, New York: 2012 to 2013 / Oven Studios, New York: 2012 to 2013 / **Technical team:** Producer: Noah "40" Shebib, Majid Jordan, Sidney "Omen" Brown / Executive producer: Beyoncé Knowles / **Recording engineers:** Noah "40" Shebib, Noel Cadastre, Stuart White, Ramon Rivas

Canada's Drake was by now one of the most famous rappers on the planet, and it was inevitable that he would one day sing with Beyoncé. It was he who engineered the meeting between himself and the equally famous American singer, as he explained in 2013, shortly after the release of *Beyoncé*: "I reached out to her and asked if I could come and be a part of her project and she was kind enough to invite me out there. And we did some work together."[255] As a devoted admirer of Beyoncé, Drake even went so far as to release a single called *Girls Love Beyoncé* in April 2013, in which he covered the chorus of Destiny's Child's *Say My Name*: "I'm a Beyoncé believer," he confessed at the time. "I really believe strongly in her talent and her position in our generation. I think she's one of the biggest stars ever, but especially for these girls right now. I feel like they need Beyoncé."[255] Under pressure from the teams at Parkwood Entertainment, who had set the release date for the digital version of the album for 20 December 2013, Noah "40" Shebib, one of Drake's long-standing collaborators who was in charge of mixing and mastering *Mine*, said: "They were pressuring me: 'We need this mix. We got to get it done. ASAP, ASAP!' I fight some people sometimes: 'Don't give me the pressure. You're going to get it. Everybody will be okay. Relax.'"[256]

SINGLE

XO

(Beyoncé Knowles, Ryan Tedder, Terius Nash/3'35)

Musicians: Beyoncé Knowles: vocals, backing vocals / Ryan Tedder: backing vocals / The-Dream: backing vocals / Ryan Tedder: additional instruments, programming / Terius "The-Dream" Nash: piano / **Recording:** Trackdown Studios, Sydney: 2012 to 2013 / Tritonus Studios, Berlin: 2012 to 2013 / Jungle City Studios, New York: 2012 to 2013 / Oven Studios, New York: 2012 to 2013 / **Technical team:** Producers: Beyoncé Knowles, Ryan Tedder, Terius "The-Dream" Nash, Hit-Boy / Executive producer: Beyoncé Knowles / **Recording engineers:** Ryan Tedder, Stuart White, Bart Schoudel, Ramon Rivas / Assistant recording engineer: Justin Hergett / **Single:** Digital distribution by Parkwood Entertainment/Columbia: 16 December 2013 / Best chart ranking in the USA: 45

When Beyoncé recorded *XO*, whose title—standing for Extra Old—refers to the labels on bottles of prestigious spirits such as cognac, armagnac, and certain rums, she was not in great physical shape. "I was sick with a bad sinus infection," she explained. "I recorded it in a few minutes just as a demo and decided to keep the vocals. I lived with most of the songs for a year and never re-recorded the demo vocals. I really loved the imperfections, so I kept the original demos. I spent the time I'd normally spend on backgrounds and vocal production on getting the music perfect."[254] Co-written by Ryan Tedder, who had penned *Halo* in 2008, *XO* was released as a single on 16 December 2013. Unfortunately, it took until 4 January 2014 to reach the *Billboard* Hot 100 and had to settle for 45th place, struggling to better the singles of the moment: *Counting Stars* by OneRepublic (whose lead singer was none other than Ryan Tedder!), *The Monster* by Eminem and Rihanna, as well as *Timber* by Pitbull and Ke$ha. It was a real disappointment for Beyoncé, though she would do better with *Drunk in Love*, which reached number two in the American charts in February 2014.

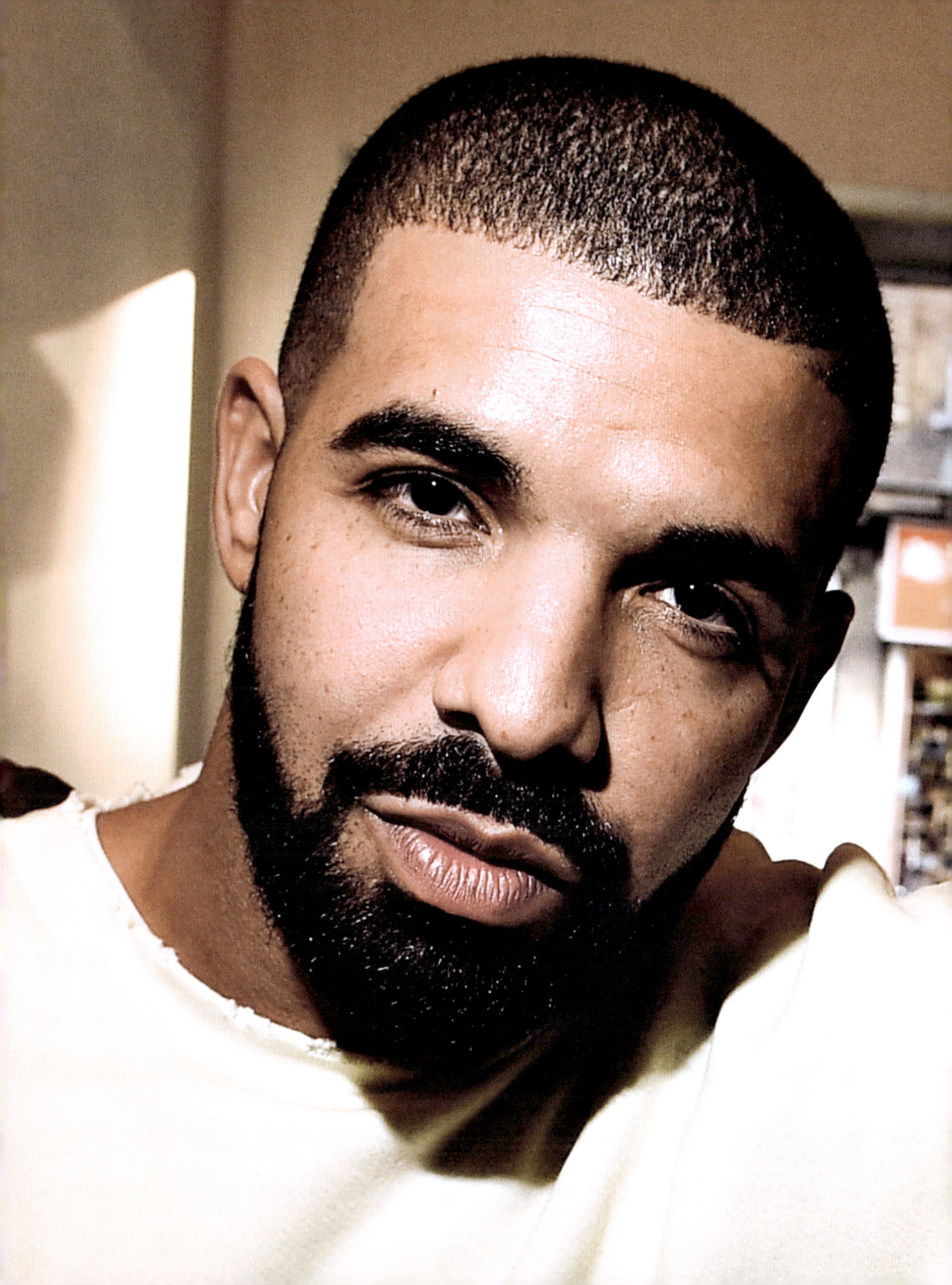

Author and activist Chimamanda Ngozi Adichie in New York, May 2017.

2013

***FLAWLESS
(FEATURING CHIMAMANDA NGOZI ADICHIE)

(Beyoncé Knowles, Chauncey Hollis, Rey Reel Music, Terius Nash, Chimamanda Ngozi Adichie / 4'10)

Musicians
Beyoncé Knowles: vocals, backing vocals
Chimamanda Ngozi Adichie: spoken voice

Recording
Kings Landing, Bridgehampton: 2012
Jungle City Studios, New York: 2012 to 2013
Oven Studios, New York: 2012 to 2013

Technical team
Producers: Beyoncé Knowles, Hit-Boy, Rey Reel Music, BOOTS
Executive producer: Beyoncé Knowles
Recording engineers: Stuart White, Jordan "DJ Swivel" Young, Ramon Rivas, Rob Suchecki
Assistant recording engineer: Tyler Scott
Arrangements: BOOTS

HEADPHONES AT THE READY

It was with the November 1992 defeat of Girls Tyme on *Star Search* in mind that Beyoncé wrote *Bow Down*, which became ***Flawless*. In the intro to the latter, you can hear the voice of presenter Ed McMahon introducing the girl band as they come on stage.

Genesis

On 17 March 2013, as the interminable silence around the progress of a possible new Beyoncé album had fans in a froth, Beyoncé posted a new song on her website: *Bow Down* (sometimes also called *Bow Down/I Been On*), accompanied by a photo of herself as a little girl, taken in front of a fireplace full of trophies, which we guess are the awards she had won as a child star two decades earlier. But once the surprise effect had worn off, the track caused controversy for lyrics that were the antithesis of the feminist Beyoncé claimed to be and vulgar in a way we had never known her to be before. "The reason I put out *Bow Down* is because I woke up, I went into the studio, I had a chant in my head, it was aggressive, it was angry, it wasn't the Beyoncé that wakes up every morning. It was the Beyoncé that was angry. It was the Beyoncé that felt the need to defend herself! And if this song never comes, okay I said it! I listened to it after I finished and said, 'THIS IS HOT! Imma put it out! I'm not going to sell it, I'm just going to put it out!' People like it? great, they don't? they don't."[246] When she began work on her new album, she decided to rework the song, which was included in *Beyoncé* under the name ***Flawless*.

Production

****Flawless* consists of two distinct segments: *Bow Down* and *Flawless*. While BOOTS was largely responsible for the second half of the track, it was Hit-Boy who produced the first. "I was basically trying to make a 'N— in Paris,' female version. With that bounce, with that synth. Obviously you look at the lyrics, she's talking crazy, talking rapper shit. So just to bring that energy out and go to her stadium shows and see the reaction is like, wow."[257] *Bow Down* and *Flawless* are separated by the insertion of a text read by Nigerian author Chimamanda Ngozi Adichie from her book *We Should All Be Feminists*. "I was scrolling through videos about feminism on YouTube and I ran across this video of this incredible Nigerian author […]," Beyoncé explained. "Everything she said is exactly how I feel."[247]

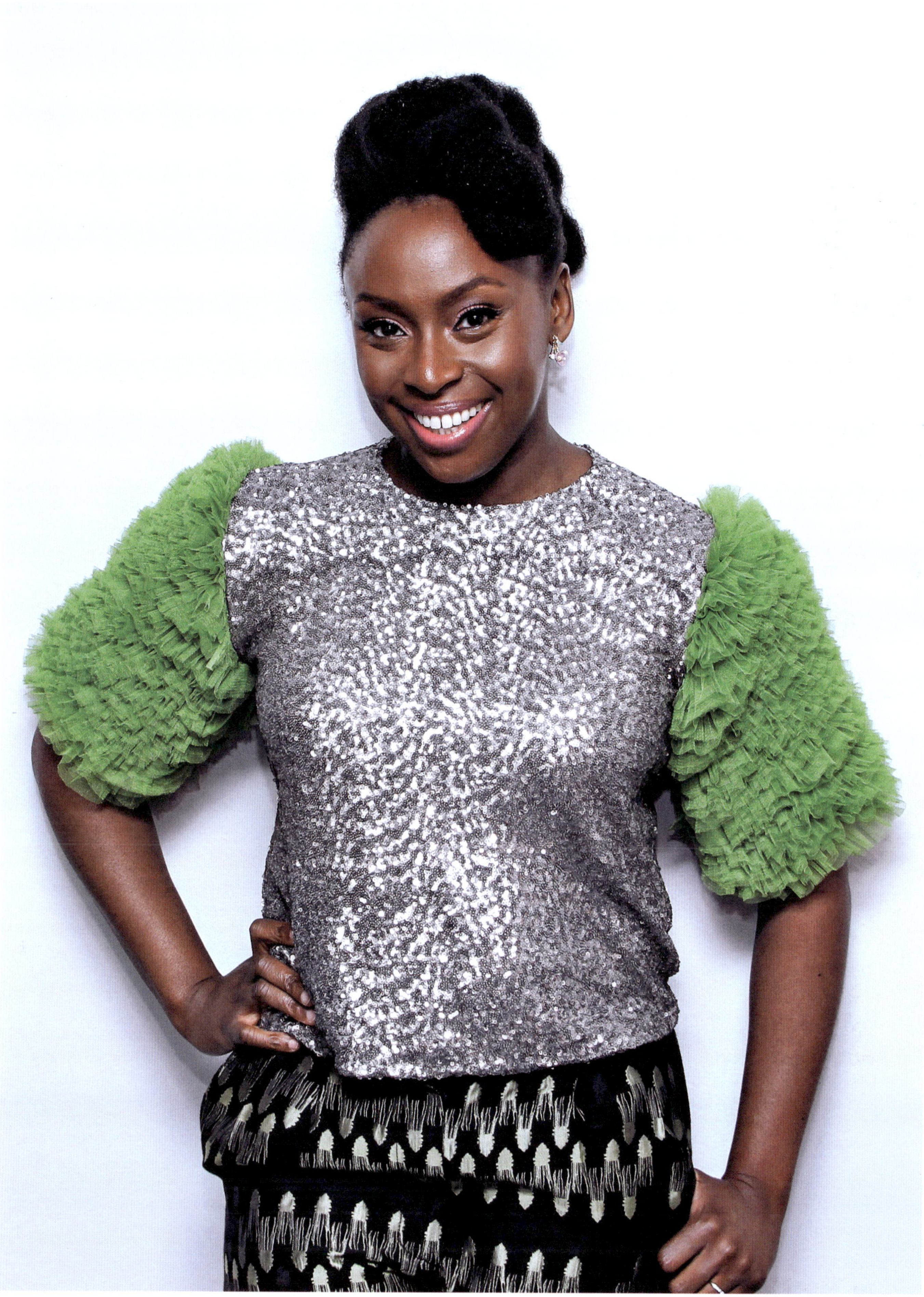

The Carters and their daughter, Blue Ivy, at the MTV Video Music Awards, 24 August 2014.

SUPERPOWER
(FEATURING FRANK OCEAN)

(Beyoncé Knowles, Frank Ocean, Pharrell Williams/4'36)

Musicians: Beyoncé Knowles: vocals, backing vocals / **Frank Ocean:** vocals? backing vocals? / **BOOTS:** backing vocals / **Kelly Rowland:** backing vocals / **Michelle Williams:** backing vocals / **Stefan Skarbek:** backing vocals / **Margot:** violin / **Recording:** Jungle City Studios, New York: 2012 to 2013 / Oven Studios, New York: 2012 to 2013 / Mirrorball Studios, Los Angeles: 2012 to 2013 / **Technical team: Producers:** Pharrell Williams, BOOTS / **Executive producer:** Beyoncé Knowles / **Recording engineers:** Stuart White, Andrew Coleman, Mike Larson, James Krausse, Ramon Rivas, Matt Weber, Jon Castelli / **String arrangements:** Margot

For her reunion with Frank Ocean, who had co-written *I Miss You* on *4,* Beyoncé's languorous vocals perfectly suit the sensuality of her new album. The video for *Superpower* moves away from the theme of the song (the couple as an indestructible entity against the world) and instead features Beyoncé participating in riots that culminate in a stand-off with the police. Directed by legendary videomaker Jonas Åkerlund, the film was shot in a disused shopping mall the team had rented in Los Angeles. "I've been wanting to use it for a long time, I was just waiting for a good thing to use for it," Åkerlund explained. "I don't know if you noticed, but at the end, there's a big area that sort of looks like the freeway. It's fake; some big action movie left it there. It's on top of a garage, but it's a proper five-lane freeway! Only like 400 meters [440 yards] or so, but it's a real freeway."[258]

HEAVEN

(BOOTS, Beyoncé Knowles/3'50)

Musicians: Beyoncé Knowles: vocals, backing vocals / **Melissa Vargas:** spoken voice / **BOOTS:** additional instruments / **Recording:** Westlake Recording Studios, Los Angeles: 2012 to 2013 / Jungle City Studios, New York: 2012 to 2013 / Oven Studios, New York: 2012 to 2013 / **Technical team: Producers:** BOOTS, Beyoncé Knowles / **Executive producer:** Beyoncé Knowles / **Recording engineers:** BOOTS, Stuart White, Rob Cohen, Ramon Rivas

Beyoncé performs *Heaven*, co-written and co-produced with BOOTS, in a piano-vocal style reminiscent of Rihanna's 2012 track *Stay*. It was seeing her mother, Tina Knowles, lose one of her girlfriends that prompted Beyoncé to write these lyrics, in which she tells the deceased: *Heaven couldn't wait for you.* At the end of the track, Melissa Vargas—who worked for Jennifer Lopez at her fashion brand J.Lo before becoming Beyoncé's personal assistant, then going on to work for Parkwood Entertainment as brand manager—recites the first five lines of the Lord's Prayer in Spanish. "I had never worked with someone so focused and committed [as Beyoncé]," Vargas said. "She's just very motivated and driven. She has this adrenaline that's very contagious. [...] She's a very very private person, so she usually will be able to say what she wants to share of her personal life and what she doesn't but you learn that you don't…they're just two separate things: her career and her personal life is that, just very personal."[259]

BLUE
(FEATURING BLUE IVY)

(BOOTS, Beyoncé Knowles/4'26)

Musicians: Beyoncé Knowles: vocals, backing vocals / **Blue Ivy:** spoken voice / **BOOTS:** guitar, synthesizers, piano, programming / **Steven Wolf:** drums / **Margot:** violin / **Recording:** Jungle City Studios, New York: 2012 to 2013 / Oven Studios, New York: 2012 to 2013 / **Technical team: Producers:** BOOTS, Beyoncé Knowles / **Executive producer:** Beyoncé Knowles / **Recording engineers:** BOOTS, Stuart White, Jonathan Lee, Ramon Rivas / **Assistant recording engineers:** Justin Hergett, James Krausse / **String arrangements:** Margot

Beyoncé wrote the lyrics for *Blue*, co-composed with BOOTS, for her little daughter Blue Ivy. "I'm a very protective person," Beyoncé revealed. "I want to make sure that my daughter has a healthy, safe, normal life…she's my top priority. And life's completely different now. I'm still incredibly happy to be able to do what I love, but now everything has more meaning. Now, life's about being a mother."[260] This track by a mother for her daughter was put together by BOOTS in Jungle City Studios in New York, with Blue present at the recording session. "It was such a special day," the producer later said. "Blue was talking so much—from the moment that I met that kid until then, the amount she said tripled. People were watching her making connections."[248] Moved by the little girl's presence, BOOTS decided to add the chirping of birds perched on the studio's window sill to the mix, although you have to listen hard to hear the almost imperceptible sound. "The birds were like a stamp for the song; I wanted to remember that day."[248]

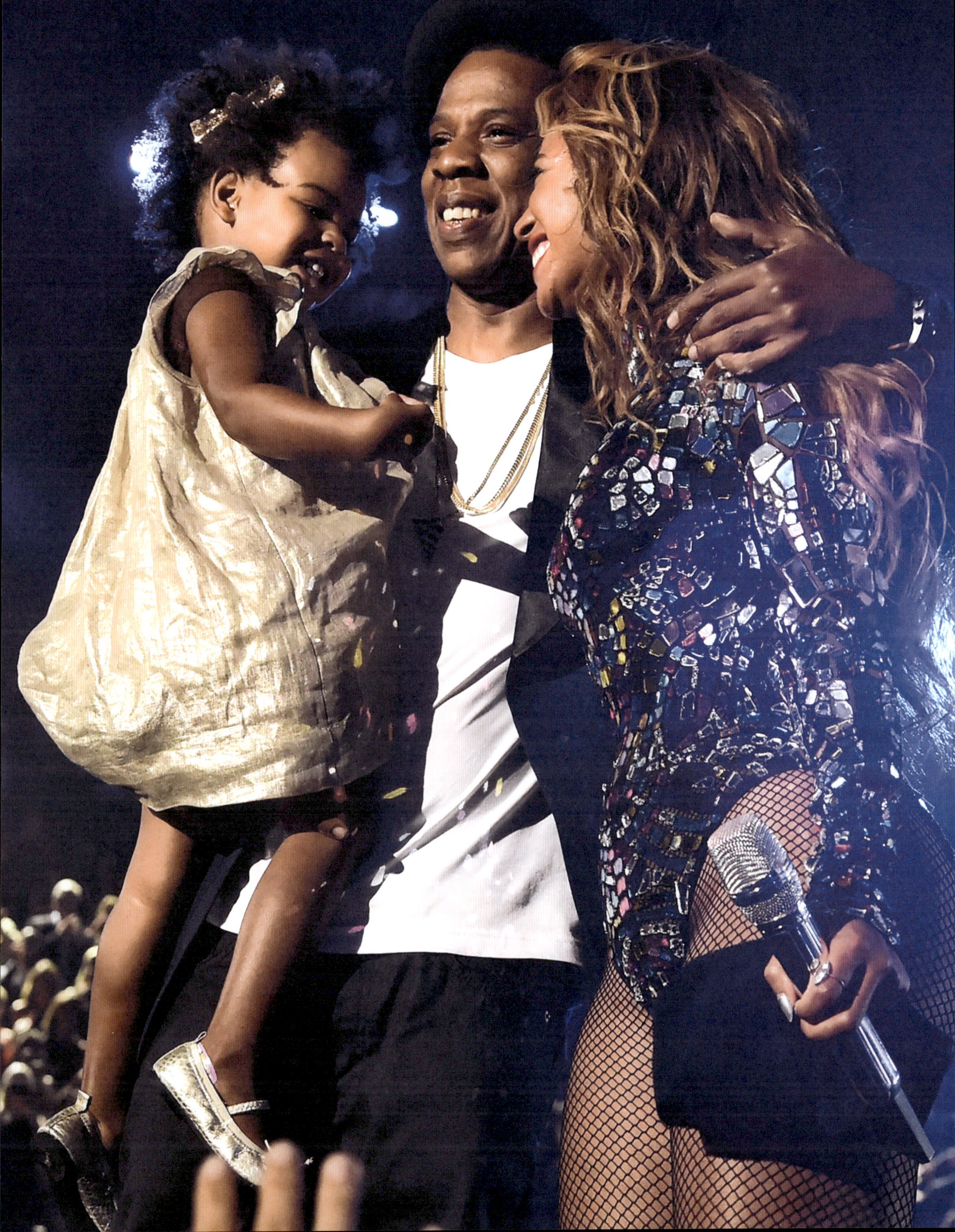

Tina Knowles supported her daughter from the outset, and has remained a valued collaborator.

GOD MADE YOU BEAUTIFUL

(Beyoncé Knowles, Sia Furler, Chris Braide/4'36)

Musician: Beyoncé Knowles: vocals, backing vocals / **Recording:** ?: 2013 / **Technical team:** Producers: Beyoncé Knowles, Christopher Braide / **Recording engineer:** Christopher Braide / **Digital distribution with preorders for** *Life Is But a Dream*: 23 November 2013

Once again, Sia Furler's writing style is recognizable in this previously unreleased track. It was distributed free of charge on 23 November 2013 with preorders for *Life Is But a Dream*, a Beyoncé documentary which had aired on HBO the previous February and came out as a DVD on 25 November 2013. With Christopher Braid—who worked with the likes of Sia Furler, Lana Del Rey, and Afrojack—on co-writing and co-producing duties, Beyoncé had put together a dream team for this song written for little Blue Ivy, born on 7 January 2012. After the release of *Bow Down* in March and the two previously unreleased songs in the Pepsi and H&M campaigns (*Grown Woman* and *Standing on the Sun* respectively), the singer's fans were eagerly anticipating a possible new album from their idol. They would have to wait until the morning of 13 December to enjoy Queen Bey's new songs.

SINGLE

7/11

(Beyoncé Knowles, Noel Fisher, Bobby Johnson/3'34)

Musician: Beyoncé Knowles: vocals, backing vocals / **Recording:** Oven Studios, New York: 2012 to 2013 / The Record Plant, Los Angeles: 2012 to 2013 / **Technical team:** Producers: Beyoncé Knowles, Bobby Johnson, Detail, Sidney Swift, Derek Dixie / **Beyoncé Platinum Edition—More (album)** / Released in the USA by Parkwood Entertainment/Columbia: 24 November 2014 (CD ref.: 88875038442) / **Best chart ranking in the USA:** 13

After the surprise release of *Beyoncé* in December 2013, fans waited many months for the album to be re-released. When it did appear, on 24 November 2014, it came with a DVD entitled *Live*, consisting of ten excerpts from the Mrs. Carter Show World Tour, as well as an extra disc called *More* on which fans could enjoy two previously unreleased songs, *7/11* and *Ring Off*, and four remixes of songs from the original album: *Flawless (Remix)* as a duet with Nicki Minaj, *Drunk in Love (Remix)* with Kanye West, *Blow (Remix)* featuring Pharrell Williams, and finally *Standing on the Sun (Remix)* with Mr. Vegas. *7/11* was produced by Noel "Detail" Fisher and Bobby Johnson, and reached number 13 on the *Billboard Hot 100*.

SINGLE

RING OFF

(Beyoncé Knowles, Mike Caren, William Lobban-Bean, Geoff Early, Charles Hinshaw, Adam Amezaga, Derek Dixie, Stephen Bishop, Chauncey "Hit-Boy" Hollis, Mike Dean, Sidney Swift/3'01)

Musicians: Beyoncé Knowles: vocals, backing vocals / Cornell Dupree: electric guitar / **Recording:** ?: 2013 / **Technical team:** Producers: Mike Caren, Beyoncé Knowles, Cook Classics, Hit-Boy, Mike Dean, Ariel Rechtshaid, Derek Dixie / **Beyoncé Platinum Edition—More (album)** / Released in the USA by Parkwood Entertainment/Columbia: 24 November 2014 (CD ref.: 88875038442) / **Best chart ranking in the USA:** did not make the charts

Before becoming a big shot at Warner Music Group, Mike Caren made a name for himself as a composer and producer for some of the leading pop artists. In 2010 he worked with Kanye West (*Hell of a Life*), in 2011 with David Guetta (*Where Them Girls At*), and in 2013 he offered his services to Beyoncé, writing the dance track *Ring Off* for her. He brought in Cornell Dupree to play the guitar melody extracted from deep in the mix of Stephen Bishop's 1977 single *On and On*, on which Andrew Gold had played six-string. The song's lyrics are as important as the production, with Beyoncé paying tribute to her mother Tina Knowles, whose divorce from her father Mathew had just been finalized. *Mama we can love again/This is where the freedom begins*, she sings, encouraging Tina as she rebuilds her personal life. Tina can actually be heard at 2'46 of the track, in an extract from a speech she gave in 2014 at the launch of the Dallas Women's Foundation (now the Texas Women's Foundation), an organization that provides financial and social support for women, girls, and families.

OUTTAKES

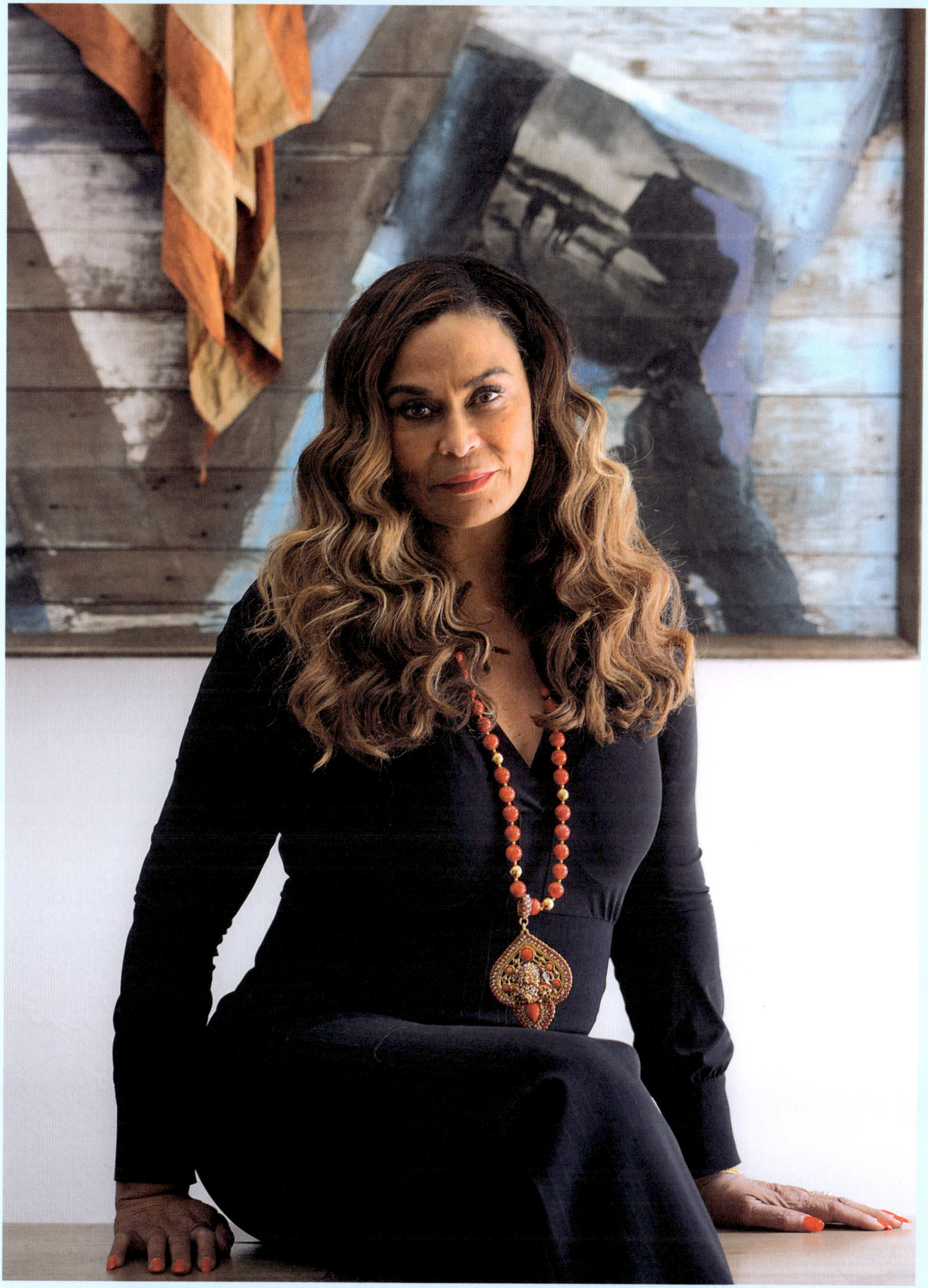

British singer Amy Winehouse in 2004, shortly before the international success of *Back to Black*.

BACK TO BLACK
(BEYONCÉ X ANDRÉ 3000)

(Amy Winehouse, Mark Ronson/3'21)

Musicians: Beyoncé Knowles: vocals / André 3000: vocals / **Recording:** ?: 2012 to 2013 / **Technical team:** Producers: Hollywood Holt, Baz Luhrmann / **Executive producer:** Shawn "Jay-Z" Carter / ***Music from Baz Luhrmann's Film The Great Gatsby* (compilation)** / USA album release by Third Man Records: 7 May 2013 (album ref.: TMR-222) / **USA CD release by** Interscope Records: 7 May 2013 (CD ref.: B0018547-02)

Australian director Baz Luhrmann is as renowned for the eccentricity of his movie productions as for the soundtracks that accompany them. Like Quentin Tarantino or Robert Zemeckis, he has spent decades peppering his movie scores with great songs. In Luhrmann's case, he has even modernized American standards, as he did, for example, with his 2001 film *Moulin Rouge*, set in Paris. When Jay-Z came in as executive soundtrack producer on *The Great Gatsby*—Luhrmann's adaptation of F. Scott Fitzgerald's cult novel that came out in theaters in 2013—he invited his wife to take part in the project, at the request of soundtrack producer Anton Monsted, who wanted to give the second half of the film a darker tone. As production was coming to a close, Jay-Z asked producer Hollywood Holt to come up with an idea for a final song for the soundtrack. Holt suggested a cover version of *Back to Black* by Amy Winehouse, who had died in 2011. "The first time I heard Amy Winehouse," he said, "I felt instantly connected to her. I felt like I knew her, and felt like if we knew each other we'd be good friends. You heard her music and instantly knew that was her. [...] You could not mistake her music for anybody else's."[261] Holt then called in André 3000 from OutKast and put together an astonishing version of the British star's hit. While the first part is somewhat disconcerting because of André 3000's rather intense performance, the segment performed by Beyoncé makes this Knowles-style *Back to Black* well worth a listen. While Mark Ronson, the original producer of this soul hit, praised the performance, Amy Winehouse's father—who had not been asked for his permission to include the track in the film—said he was shocked by the situation and stated on many occasions how much he disliked this new version of his late daughter's hit. On most streaming platforms these days, *Back to Black* does not feature on the tracklisting of the *Great Gatsby* soundtrack.

RISE UP

(Sia Furler, Beyoncé Knowles, Chauncey Hollis, Jesse Woodard/3'25)

Musician: Beyoncé Knowles: vocals, backing vocals / **Recording:** ?: 2012 to 2013 / **Technical team:** Producers: Hit-Boy, Chase N. Cashe / ***Epic—Original Motion Picture Soundtrack* (album)** / Digital distribution by Sony Classical: 21 May 2013 (ref.: 88883735322)

Beyoncé was still pregnant with her first child when she was asked to play the role, at least vocally, of Queen Tara in the animated film *Epic*, loosely adapted from the William Joyce novel *The Leaf Men and the Brave Good Bugs*. The singer took her role extremely seriously, recording her voice alongside a prestigious cast including Colin Farrell, Amanda Seyfried, Christoph Waltz, Aziz Ansari, and Steven Tyler from the group Aerosmith. She also recorded a Sia Furler song, *Rise Up*, which was used to promote the film. Despite its qualities (once again the "Sia style" is very recognizable, arguably to the point of becoming repetitive), the song did not appear on Danny Elfman's soundtrack, but only on the downloadable version, distributed by Sony Classical in May 2013.

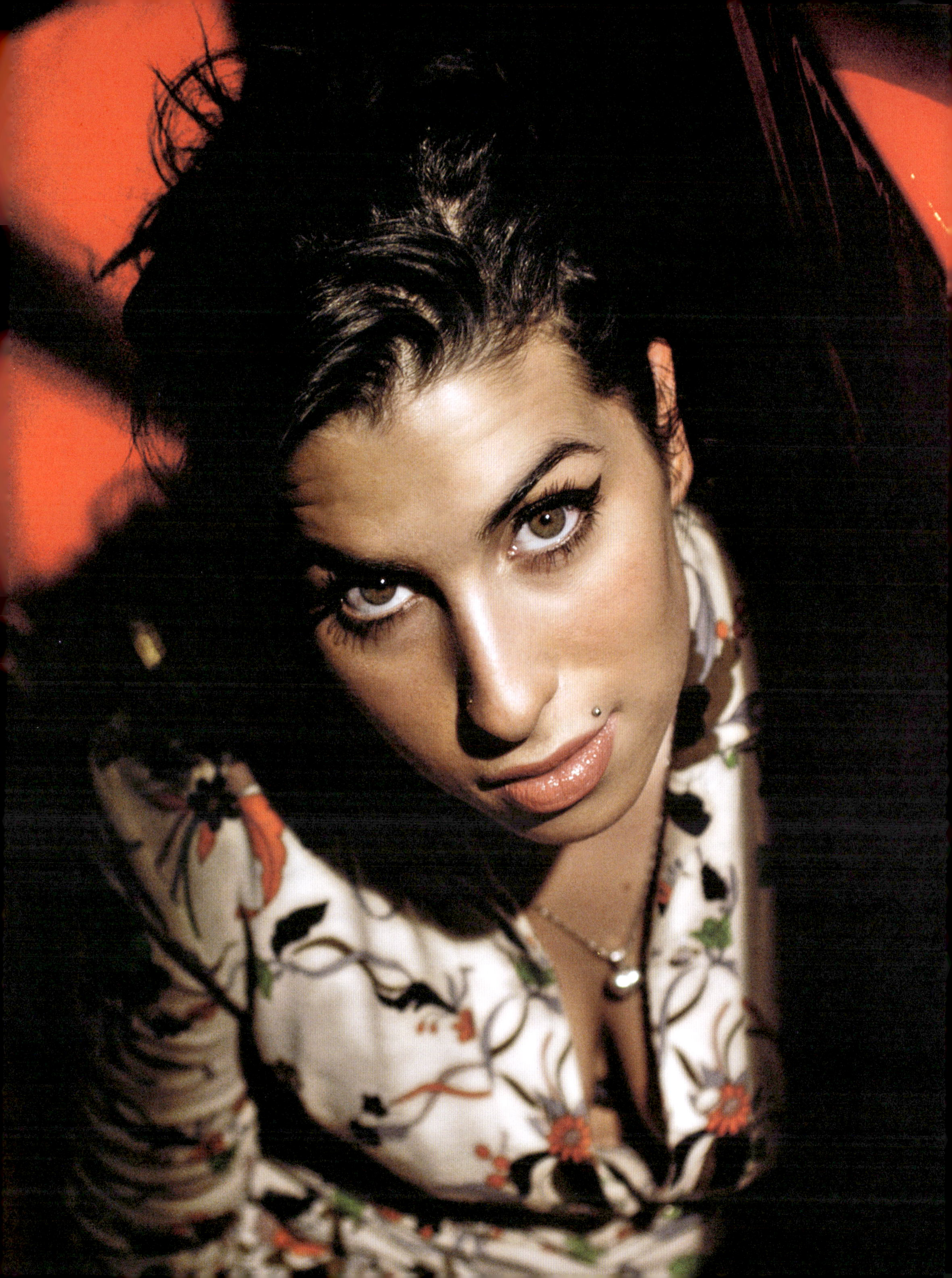

A long-standing associate of Beyoncé, The-Dream invited the singer to feature on his fifth album.

TURNT
(THE-DREAM FEATURING BEYONCÉ AND 2 CHAINZ)

(Terius Nash, Beyoncé Knowles, Tauheed Epps/3'46)

Musicians: The-Dream: rap, vocals / **Beyoncé Knowles:** vocals, rap / **2 Chainz:** vocals / **Recording:** The Sand Castle, Bridgehampton: 2012 / Kings Landing, Bridgehampton: 2012 / Oven Studios, New York: 2013 / Jungle City Studios, New York: 2013 / Deuce Station, Atlanta: 2013 / **Technical team: Producer:** The-Dream / **Executive producers:** The-Dream, Chaka Pilgrim / **The-Dream "IV Play" (album)** / Released in the USA by Def Jam Recordings/Radio Killa Recorders: 28 May 2013 (ref.: B0016721-02)

In 2013, as rumors of a new album were buzzing through the BeyHive—the name for the online community of Beyoncé fans—the singer was appearing in public ever more frequently. This time it was on *IV Play*, the fifth album by one of her favorite collaborators, The-Dream, where she forms a trio with the producer and with rapper 2 Chainz. The latter would be back with Mrs Carter on stage at the Made in America Festival on 31 August 2013, an annual event in the city of Philadelphia, started by Jay-Z the previous year.

YOU CHANGED
(KELLY ROWLAND FEATURING BEYONCÉ AND MICHELLE)

(Courtney Harrell, Kelly Rowland, Harmony Samuels/3'56)

Musicians: Kelly Rowland: vocals / **Beyoncé Knowles:** vocals / **Michelle Williams:** vocals / **Recording:** EastWest Studios, Los Angeles: 2013 / **Technical team: Producer:** Harmony Samuels / **Recording engineers:** Carlos King, Beau Vallis / **Kelly Rowland Talk a Good Game (album)** / Released in the USA by Republic Records: 18 June 2013 (CD ref.: B0018567-02)

Beyoncé needs no persuading when it comes to joining her Destiny's Child colleagues in the studio. After the January 2013 release of the single *Nuclear* and their spectacular reunion at Beyoncé's Super Bowl XLVII Halftime Show on 3 February, they next got together as a threesome on Kelly Rowland's fourth album for a track that was more R&B than ever—*You Changed*, produced by Harmony Samuels. But Kelly went out of her way to clarify the nature of this reunion in an interview with the website Billboard.com: "It's not a Destiny's Child track. It's me featuring Beyoncé and Michelle."[262] In September 2014, the three women reunited again for Michelle Williams's album *Journey to Freedom*, to sing *Say Yes*, also produced by Samuels.

354 COLLABORATIONS

Jay-Z and Beyoncé in Houston during the On the Run Tour.

PART II (ON THE RUN)
(JAY-Z FEATURING BEYONCÉ)

(James Fauntleroy, Jerome Harmon, Shawn Carter, Timothy Mosley/5'34)

Musicians: Jay-Z: rap / Beyoncé Knowles: vocals, backing vocals / **Recording:** Oven Studios, New York: 2013 / **Technical team: Producers:** Timbaland, Jerome "J-Roc" Harmon / **Recording engineer:** Demacio Castellon / **Jay-Z Magna Carta…Holy Grail (album) / Released in the USA by Roc-A-Fella Records/Roc Nation:** 4 July 2013 (CD ref.: B0018877-02)

Part II (On the Run) was produced by Timbaland and J-Roc based on a sample of the piano part from *Believe in Me*, a One Way song from their 1985 album *Wrap Your Body*. It is a follow-up to 2002's *03 Bonnie & Clyde*, which told the story of two lovers who embarked on a crime spree in the US in the 1930s. Here, Jay-Z and Beyoncé give us a first-rate hip-hop score, peppered with references that observers have to listen out for, such as the nod to *Back That Azz Up* by Juvenile, Mannie Fresh, and Lil Wayne from the 1998 album *400 Degreez*, when Jay-Z raps *Push your ma'fucka wig back, I did that/I been wilding since a Juve*, a punchline borrowed from the aforementioned rappers. Beyoncé makes a second, uncredited, appearance on *Magna Carta…Holy Grail*, hidden this time behind the pseudonym Third Ward Trill, as she slips in a few phrases at the end of the thunderous *Tom Ford*.

BEYONCÉ: ALL THE SONGS   355

DREAMS
(BOOTS FEATURING BEYONCÉ)

(BOOTS/4'55)

Musicians: BOOTS: vocals, backing vocals / **Beyoncé:** vocals / **Recording:** ?: 2013 / **Technical team:** Producer: BOOTS / *WinterSpringSummerFall* **(Mixtape)** / Digital distribution USA: 11 April 2014

On 11 April 2014, BOOTS—who had joined the Roc Nation stable and gone from unknown to star producer thanks to his benefactress Beyoncé and his work on her previous album—posted on Twitter (now X) to inform his followers of the release of his first mixtape: *WinterSpringSummerFall*. It consisted of 16 tracks, included artists such as Jeremih, Shlohmo, Kelela, and Son Lux, and was the first official production to appear under the name BOOTS. The release was hotly anticipated by fans, who could now download it. A gift awaited them in the form of a bonus track, recorded by Beyoncé herself, with profits going to charity, as BOOTS explained on his Facebook page a few days later: "So this is the last song on my mixtape. My friend and I recorded it recently and while we were trying to figure out what to do with it, we had an idea. [...] A friend recently told me about a non-profit organization called 'Day One' here in NYC. In their words, 'Day One is the only organization in New York City solely devoted to the issue of teen dating violence.' [...] Every cent made from this song will go directly to Day One. It's hard to put into words how thankful I am for everything and everyone who helped get this together."[263]

As she had done for The-Dream, Beyoncé featured on work by another of her associates, BOOTS, in 2014.

Despite its prestigious lineup (Johnny Rotten from the Sex Pistols, Brandon Boyd from Incubus, and JC Chasez from *NSYNC), the *Jesus Christ Superstar* tour, in which Michelle Williams was to have taken part, was eventually cancelled.

SAY YES
(MICHELLE WILLIAMS FEATURING BEYONCÉ AND KELLY ROWLAND)

(Al Sherrod Lambert, H. "Carmen Reece" Culver, Harmony Samuels, Michelle Williams/4'12)

Musicians: Michelle Williams: vocals, backing vocals / **Beyoncé:** vocals, backing vocals / **Kelly Rowland:** vocals, backing vocals / **Harmony Samuels:** all instruments / **Recording:** London Bridge Studios, Los Angeles: 2014 / **Technical team: Producer:** Harmony Samuels / **Executive producers:** John Dee Hammond, Michelle Williams, Phil Thornton / **Recording engineers:** Jose Cardoza, Carlos King / **Assistant recording engineer:** Chelsye Lifford / **Michelle Williams *Journey to Freedom* (album)** / Released in the USA by eOne Music: 9 September 2014 (CD ref.: LIG-CD-7278)

In 2014, Michelle Williams, still devoted to her gospel repertoire, invited her friends Beyoncé Knowles and Kelly Rowland to sing the praises of Jesus Christ alongside her in the highly danceable *Say Yes*, the last track on her album *Journey to Freedom*. Although Williams and her producer Harmony Samuels added new lyrics to the song, it is very much a Nigerian Christian hymn that our Destiny's Child trio cover here, as the very religious Samuels explains: "I was born in London. My parents are from Nigeria. My family is very multicultural. Half of them are also Jamaican. This is a song we grew up to. Anyone from Africa knows it was an anthem we grew up to and it got us through a lot of hard times."[264] It was during a trip to Nigeria that Samuels persuaded Williams to record her own version of the song, which was put on the back burner. Then one day, Beyoncé and Kelly Rowland heard it and decided to add their vocals. Samuels was convinced that American radio stations would not give it airtime, so he returned it to the archives, until one day it found its way onto the internet: divine intervention, according to Samuels: "I'm waking up in the morning like, '*Say Yes* is leaked' and I'm mad and screaming like who did it. Then Jesus spoke to me like 'Calm down! Watch!' In 24 hours, we had *Rolling Stone*, *Billboard*, and all the high magazines speak about this record. We have Power 105 play it. Hot 97 play it. We had people from all over the world talk about this record like the song says, 'When Jesus Say Yes, Nobody Can Say No.'"[264]

The controversial Nicki Minaj in Antibes, 25 May 2017.

STANDING ON THE SUN (REMIX)
(BEYONCÉ FEATURING MR. VEGAS)

(Sia Furler, Greg Kurstin, Beyoncé Knowles, Noel Fisher, Brian Soko, Rasool Diaz, Andre Eric Proctor/4'33)

Musicians: Beyoncé Knowles: vocals, backing vocals / Mr. Vegas: vocals / **Recording:** Kings Landing, Bridgehampton: 2012 / **Technical team:** Producers: Greg Kurstin, Beyoncé Knowles, Pharrell Williams / Remix: Clifford Smith, Cleveland Browne / ***Beyoncé Platinum Edition—More* (album)** / Released in the USA by Parkwood Entertainment/Columbia: 24 November 2014 (CD ref.: 88875038442)

In March 2013, the new summer advertising campaign for the Swedish brand H&M was unveiled. The face of the brand that year was none other than Beyoncé, who is shown in summer clothing in shots taken by photographers Inez van Lamsweerde and Vinoodh Matadin on a beach in the Bahamas. "I've always liked H&M's focus on fun affordable fashion," she said at the time. "I really loved the concept we collaborated on to explore the different emotions of women represented by the four elements—fire, water, earth, and wind. It was a beautiful shoot on a tropical island. It felt more like making a video than a commercial."[265] To accompany the video that promoted the launch of the campaign, a few seconds of a previously unreleased song, *Standing on the Sun*, aroused the curiosity of fans. Its party feel was perfect for spring, but we would have to wait until 24 November 2014 and the reissue of *Beyoncé* to enjoy *Standing on the Sun*, mostly written by Sia Furler, in its entirety. It also featured vocal parts from dancehall star Mr. Vegas, internationally famous for his 1997 hit single *Heads High*.

FEELING MYSELF
(NICKI MINAJ FEATURING BEYONCÉ)

(Beyoncé Knowles, Chauncey Hollis, Onika Maraj, Solána Rowe/3'57)

Musicians: Nicki Minaj: rap / Beyoncé Knowles: vocals, backing vocals / **Recording:** ?: 2014 / **Technical team:** Producer: Hit-Boy / Recording engineers: Aubry "Big Juice" Delaine, Stuart White / Assistant recording engineer: Ramon Rivas / **Nicki Minaj *The Pinkprint* (album)** / Released in the USA by Young Money Entertainment: 12 December 2014 (ref.: B0022248-02)

Nicki Minaj, who had the whole world dancing in 2012 with her dance hits *Pound the Alarm* and *Starships*, was invited onto the reissue of *Beyoncé* to add her unique vocals to ****Flawless*. Her contribution combines dancehall flow and feminist rhetoric that verges on the politically incorrect. When Minaj came to make her third album, 2014's *The Pinkprint* (after *Pink Friday* in 2010 and *Pink Friday: Roman Reloaded* in 2012), it seemed logical to invite Beyoncé to sing on *Feeling Myself*. The song's similarity to the alternative R&B sounds on *4* and *Beyoncé* meant it was very much in keeping with the new direction Beyoncé was exploring.

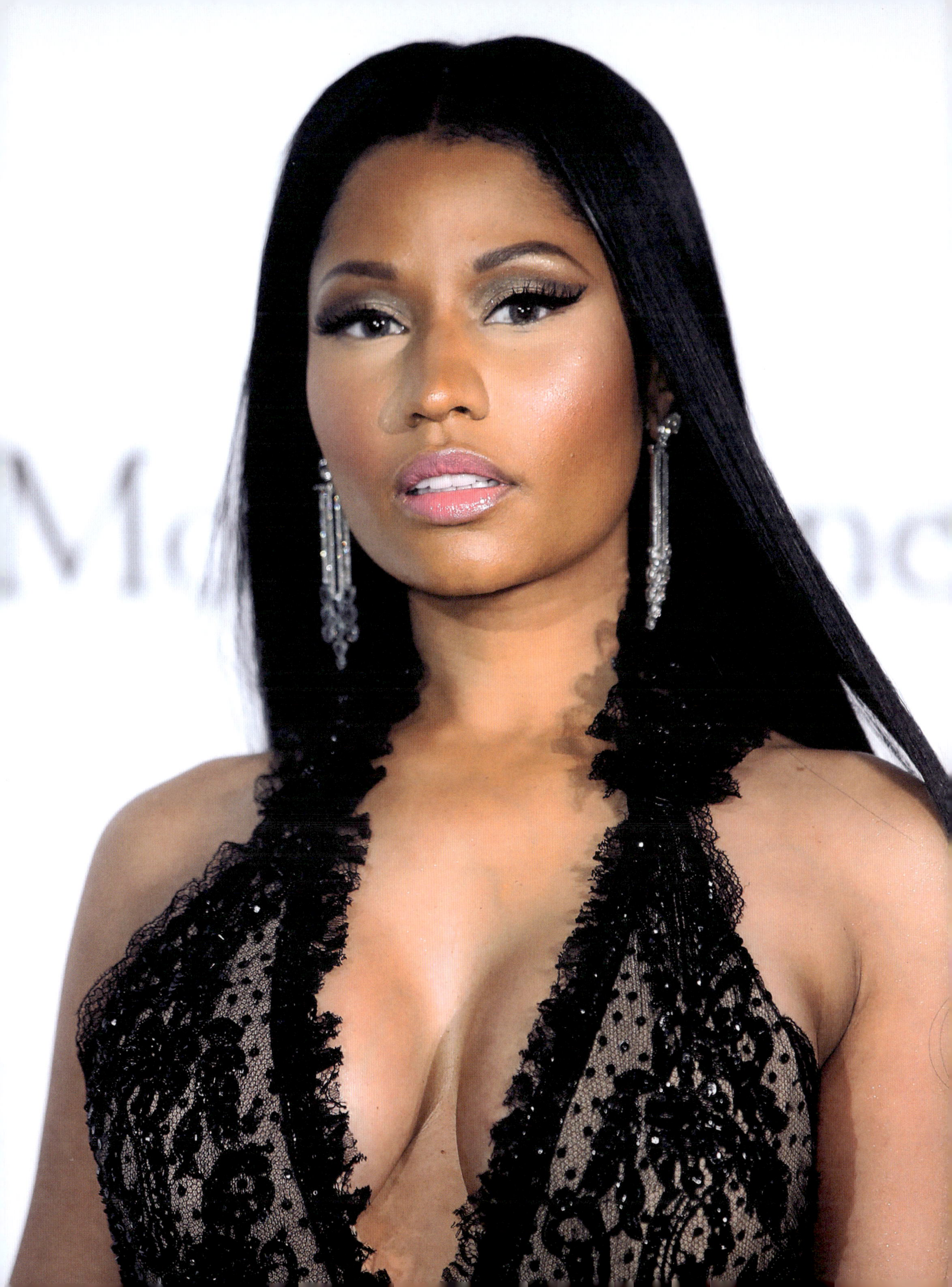

Destiny's Child reunited for the Super Bowl XLVII Half-time Show in New Orleans, 3 February 2013.

NUCLEAR
(DESTINY'S CHILD)

(J. "Lonny" Bereal, James Fauntleroy II, Michelle Williams, Pharrell Williams/3'57)

Musicians
Beyoncé Knowles: vocals, backing vocals
Michelle Williams: vocals, backing vocals
Kelly Rowland: vocals, backing vocals
Pharrell Williams: additional instruments

Recording
South Beach Studios, Miami: 2012
Jungle City Studios, New York: 2012
Westlake Studios, Los Angeles: 2012

Technical team
Producers: Pharrell Williams, Beyoncé Knowles, J. "Lonny" Bereal
Recording engineers: Andrew Coleman, Steve Rusch, Stuart White
Assistant recording engineers: Hart Gunther, Matt Brownlie, Matt Weber, Ramon Rivas, Rob Suchecki

Destiny's Child *Love Songs* (compilation)
Released in the USA by Columbia/Legacy/Music World Music: 25 January 2013 (CD ref.: 88765430182)

The return of Destiny's Child

Once the Destiny's Child reunion at Beyoncé's concert at the Super Bowl XLVII Half-time Show on 3 February 2013 had been announced, Columbia and Music World Music—Mathew Knowles's label, which owns the rights to the trio's music—hurried to release a new compilation, called *Love Songs*. While buyers of the record were pleased to rediscover many of the ladies' hits, they were also delighted to find a previously unreleased track called *Nuclear*. It was built around a well-worn 1980s drum machine sample reworked by producer Pharrell Williams, who was happy to be back working with the R&B superstars. "I was so excited to hear us together again," Beyoncé said. "I just kind of dropped on the floor and felt like a little teenager again when I heard us harmonize. There's nothing like the sisterhood we have."[240]

Three singers in harmony

Nuclear features numerous harmonizations, which were the hallmark of Destiny's Child. "The harmonies and just us stacking [vocals] …," Michelle Williams said. "Beyoncé laid hers first, then I'd go and lay another note to the bottom, and I'm like, 'Wow, this is dope.' I literally got goosebumps. [After hearing it,] Beyoncé sent an email like, 'Man, we sound good together!' I'm like, 'Duh, that's what we do, boo! That's what we do!'"[266]

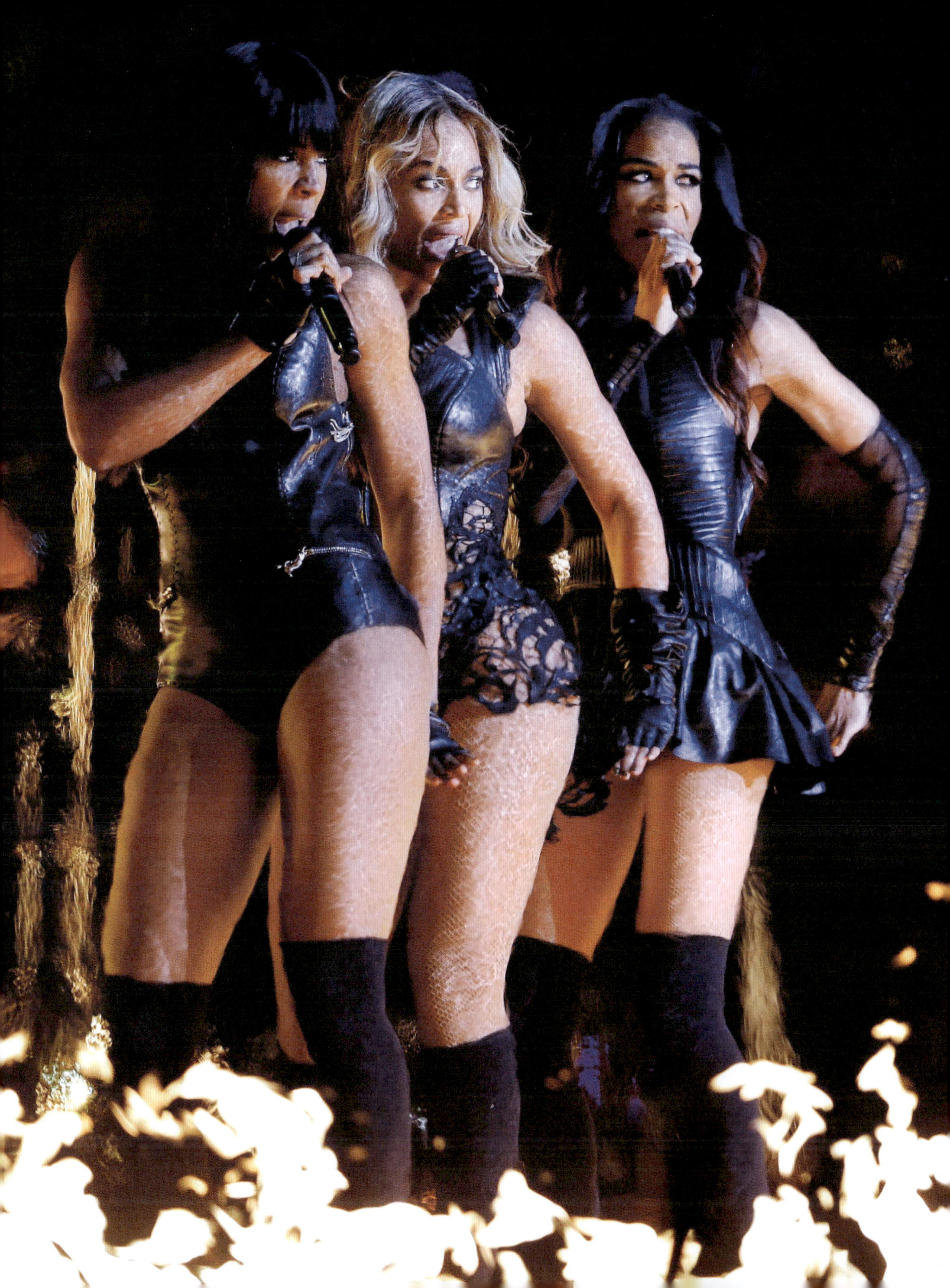

ALBUM

Lemonade

Pray You Catch Me • Hold Up • Don't Hurt Yourself • Sorry • 6 Inch • Daddy Lessons • Love Drought • Sandcastles • Forward • Freedom • All Night • Formation

Available for streaming on Tidal: 23 April 2016
Digital release by Parkwood Entertainment/Columbia: 24 April 2016
Release of CD + DVD in the USA by Parkwood Entertainment/Columbia: 6 May 2016 (ref.: 88985 33682 2)
Release of box set *How to Make Lemonade* by Parkwood Entertainment/Columbia:
18 August 2017 (ref.: 88985446681)
Release of LP in the USA by Parkwood Entertainment/Columbia: 15 September 2017 (ref.: 88985446751)
Best chart ranking in the USA: 1

2016

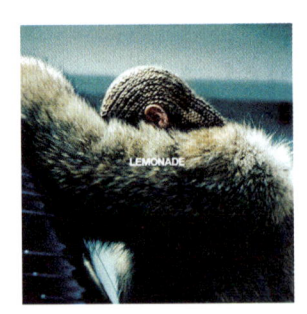

Beyoncé faced her demons and settled scores with *Lemonade*.

> As well as paying homage to her grandmother, whose recipe for lemonade was handed down from mother to daughter in her family, Beyoncé chose the title for her seventh solo album as a reference to the saying "When life gives you lemons, make lemonade"—an encouragement to be optimistic and look on the bright side of life, regardless of the trials encountered.

BEYONCÉ'S CATHARSIS

There are some years that leave their mark because of the events, whether happy or unhappy, that punctuate them. The year 2016—which began with the sudden death of two icons of music, David Bowie and Prince, on 10 January and 21 April respectively—is unquestionably one that will be remembered for discernible changes in behavior within the population of the United States, and the brutal fracturing of the American nation's unity. For 2016 saw the surge in popularity of the billionaire Donald J. Trump and his victory over Hillary Clinton in the US presidential election on 8 November, following an electoral campaign that had deeply divided their fellow citizens. It was thus a fractured country that Beyoncé would now be singing about. She was deeply affected by the increase in racist crimes in the US—some of them attributed to the federal police and denounced by Black Lives Matter. This movement had begun in 2013 and quickly spread across the country, especially condemning police violence that led to the deaths of African Americans such as Trayvon Martin and Rekia Boyd in 2012, Michael Brown and Eric Garner in 2014, and Freddie Gray in 2015. The rift between the communities reached its height on 1 September 2016, when Colin Kaepernick and Eric Reid, two players on the San Francisco 49ers team who had already got themselves noticed by remaining seated on the bench during the US national anthem, decided to take the knee during this moment of national communion, as a sign of protest against police violence. It was an act that eventually cost them their places in the National Football League. Feminist activism also increased in 2016, notably as a reaction to the outrageous statements Trump made about women, which led to the Women's March on Washington on 21 January 2017—a major event that crystallized the fear and anger of American women in response to the numerous openly misogynistic assertions made by the president, who had been inaugurated the previous day. Inspired by this inflamed political and social context, Beyoncé embarked on writing her seventh solo album, which succeeded in synthesizing the feelings of an African-American population in search of justice.

Beyoncé faces her demons

The turmoil her country was experiencing only added to Beyoncé's distress when, on a personal level, she was also going through a very unhappy period. Jay-Z's extramarital affair (previously mentioned in these pages with regard to the song *Jealous*) was now acknowledged privately and was soon to go public. It would shake the convictions of Beyoncé, who until then had resolutely defended the ideal relationship she had had with the rapper from New York since 2003. The trusting Beyoncé would give way to a combative wife, determined not to leave her marriage in the hands of the sensationalist press, and her man to a young woman who was her enemy. It was with a desire to summarize her feelings as a woman betrayed that Beyoncé embarked on the production of the movie *Lemonade*, which would accompany the album of the same name. The two projects were conceived as being inextricably connected, image and sound

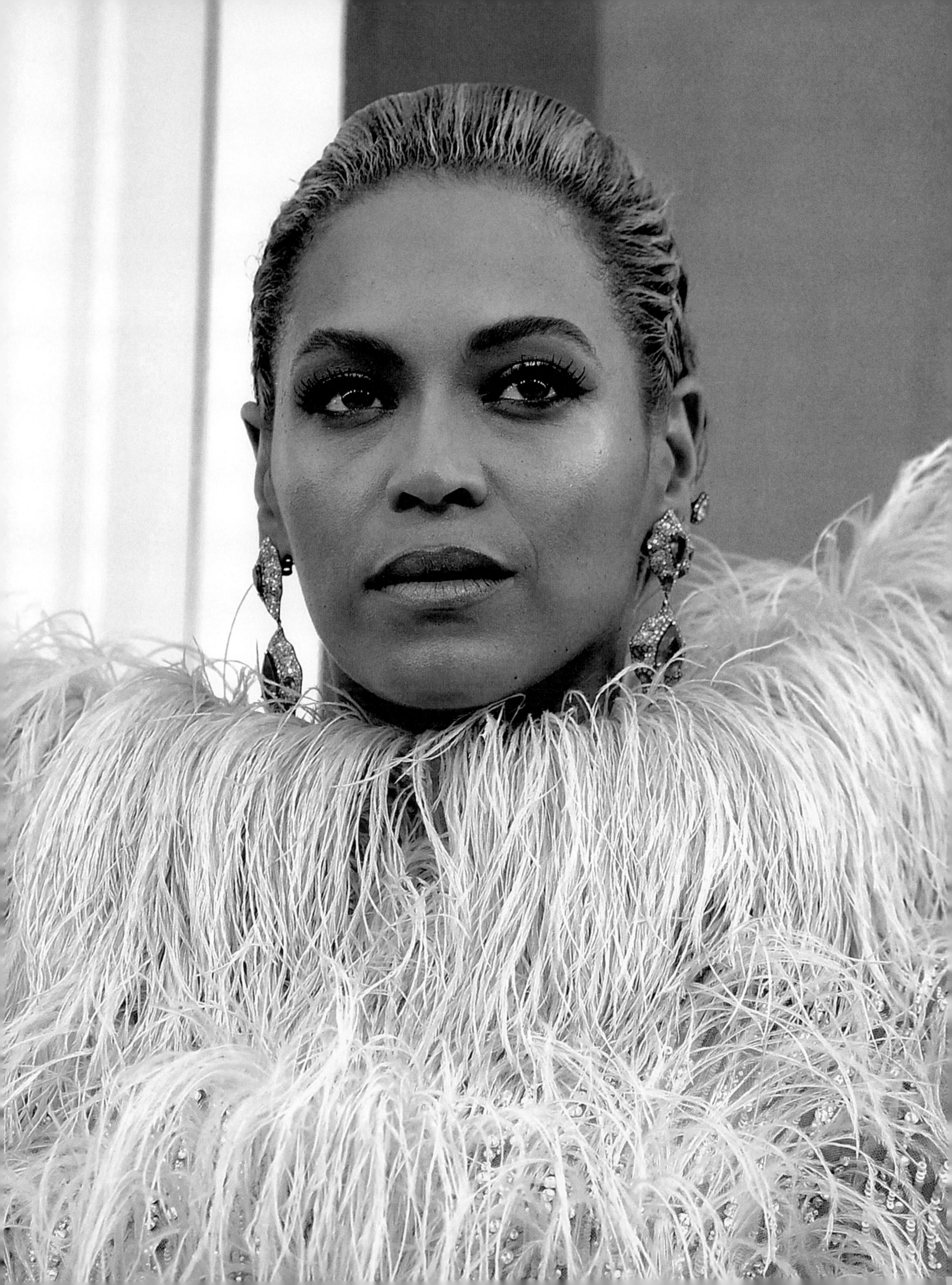

Fans support their idol during an anti-Beyoncé rally in New York in February 2016.

confirming a complementariness that had already been revealed with the release of *Beyoncé* in 2013.

A patchwork of emotions

The genesis of what would become the most important album of Beyoncé's career had begun in 2014. In August she took her place at The Record Plant studios in Los Angeles, accompanied by her faithful sound engineer Stuart White, who would be the centerpiece of the record's production and would guarantee its homogeneity. For, yet again, Beyoncé decided to surround herself with a multitude of associates who worked for her, each in their own corner of the legendary Californian recording studio. The gestation of the album quickly developed into a real artistic epic, for Beyoncé invited a large number of writers and composers to take part in the project, which soon came to resemble a musical patchwork expressing all the emotions she was experiencing. After a month at The Record Plant, followed by a well-earned break, Beyoncé and White transferred the recording of the album for 45 days to Paris, where they set up a recording studio in the Carters' hotel suite. "I tended to work with Bey in one room, while my assistant, Ramon Rivas, would work with Jay-Z in the other room. Bey and J often work at the same time, which is why we needed two systems."[267] In January 2015 the team returned to Los Angeles and moved to the Carter family home, where a studio had been set up for the occasion in the cinema, called The Beehive in the album's sleeve notes. "I lived in a hotel close by her house for a year," White recalled, "and every day they'd text me early in the morning asking me to arrive at a specific time. We would sometimes start as early as eight o'clock. She's a mother, and if her baby is up at seven, she's ready to start work at eight!"[267] Although the themes Beyoncé would address in her songs had not yet been defined, she and White were quickly perfecting the instrumental passages, several months ahead of the lyrics, which would directly convey the artist's state of mind, tormented as she was by the woes of her country and the marital crisis she was experiencing.

A multitude of associates

Across the numerous studios used for recording it (which included Conway Recording Studios, Henson Recording Studios, Pacifique Recording Studios, Capitol Studios in Los Angeles, and Jungle City Studios in New York), *Lemonade* benefited from a gestation that extended over a year, until July 2015, complemented by a few sessions in 2016 for the song *Formation*. With its multiple samples drawn from the American repertoire, texts recited between the songs borrowed from Warsan Shire, a British poet of Somali descent, prestigious guests (The Weeknd, Jack White, Kendrick Lamar, and James Blake), and multiple producers (Kevin Garrett,

Beyoncé and her husband Jay-Z supported Hillary Clinton's campaign during the 2016 US presidential election, which she lost to Donald Trump in November of that year.

Diplo, Ezra Koenig, Derek Dixie, Hit-Boy, MeLo-X, Wynter Gordon, BOOTS, Alex Delicata, PLUSS, and Mike WiLL Made-It), *Lemonade* brings together numerous talents, to offer the BeyHive the most complex and rich album Beyoncé had ever recorded. However, this wasn't enough to quench her thirst for work: alongside the album's production she embarked on the shooting of the movie that would accompany its release, as had been the case with *Beyoncé* in 2013. Inextricably connected to the album, the movie *Lemonade* is divided into 11 chapters representing the various stages of the ordeal Beyoncé endured after discovering that her husband Jay-Z had been unfaithful: "Intuition," "Denial," "Anger," "Apathy," "Emptiness," "Accountability," "Reformation," "Forgiveness," "Resurrection," "Hope," and finally "Redemption." Suffice to say that the Carters' private life no longer held any secrets for Beyoncé's fans, so much did she open up in the album's sometimes very blunt lyrics. Steering a course through her personal existential crisis and her rejection of America's troubles, *Lemonade* is a powerful, major, vital work. As it was sent for pressing and its promotion was being prepared in the greatest secrecy, Beyoncé was unaware that the hardest part lay ahead: convincing an America more divided than ever of the importance of protest, calling for justice, and openness to others. The year 2016, the year of *Lemonade*, was also a year of many battles for the fighter that Beyoncé had become.

Formation and the Super Bowl scandal

On 6 February 2016 the clip of Beyoncé's new single was posted online on Tidal (the streaming platform bought by Jay-Z and launched in the United States in 2015, whose main shareholders were none other than Jay-Z himself, Beyoncé, Daft Punk, Rihanna, Kanye West, and Jack White, as well as Madonna and Usher). Made by the faithful Melina Matsoukas, the video of *Formation* revealed Beyoncé's anger at the social crises referred to above, showing her in the midst of floods that recalled the damage wreaked by Hurricane Katrina,

Rihanna, Alicia Keys, Madonna, and Beyoncé: a dream team assembled for the launch of Tidal in the United States, 30 March 2015.

which had struck Louisiana in 2005, and drew attention to the different ways people were treated according to their race and social background. Police violence was also alluded to when the singer faced lines of police officers clearly about to charge on an African-American child. Barely had fans digested this explosion when, on 7 February, Beyoncé unleashed one of the greatest spectacles ever performed, at a half-time concert at the Super Bowl 50, given by the British group Coldplay, who had invited various artists for the occasion, including Bruno Mars, Mark Ronson, and Beyoncé herself. She performed *Formation* on the pitch of the Levi's Stadium in Santa Clara, California, accompanied by her numerous dancers, all dressed in costumes reminiscent of the Black Panther Party, a black power political movement founded by Bobby Seale and Huey P. Newton in 1966. One of the distinctive features of its uniform was a black beret, which Beyoncé's dancers also wore. Everything about the choreography called the Black Panthers to mind and, when some dancers in the audience were photographed with their fists raised—a Black Panther gesture of protest immortalized on 16 October 1968 by the athletes Tommie Smith and John Carlos at the Olympic Games in Mexico—it was the last straw for Beyoncé's detractors: her use of the symbolic gesture that day seemed an obvious homage to African Americans killed by US police. Indeed, although the performance was hailed all over the world, it was also condemned by some American observers such as Rudy Giuliani—the former mayor of New York, who was close to the candidate Donald Trump—who declared on the Fox News television network: "I thought it was really outrageous that she used it as a platform to attack police officers who are the people who protect her and protect us, and keep us alive. And what we should be doing in the African-American community, and all communities, is build up respect for police officers."[268] Javier Ortiz, president of the Fraternal Order of Police of Miami, went so far as to call for a boycott of the concert Beyoncé was due to give in his city the following 27 April. "I also salute the dozens of law enforcement officers that have been assassinated by members of the Black Panthers," he said.

Beyoncé and her dancers sporting emblematic Black Panthers berets during the half-time concert at the NFL Super Bowl 50 in Santa Clara, 7 February 2016.

BEYONCÉ: ALL THE SONGS

Beyoncé wears a Gucci outfit during the Formation World Tour, Houston, 7 May 2016.

> In order to reserve her album exclusively for the Tidal platform, of which she was a shareholder, Beyoncé decided that *Lemonade* would not be available for streaming until April 2019—three years after its release—on the traditional platforms Spotify, Deezer, and Apple Music.

"We ask all law enforcement labor organizations to join our boycott across the country and to boycott all of her concerts."[269] Fortunately, Ortiz's appeal was ignored, and The Formation World Tour, announced the evening of the Super Bowl 50, would prove a resounding success.

Release to great fanfare

On 23 April 2016 the two components of the *Lemonade* concept were released. The movie—its various segments made by Beyoncé associates such as Jonas Åkerlund, Todd Tourso, and Melina Matsoukas—was broadcast on the television network HBO. As for the album, it was played that day on Tidal, then made available for download on the same platform the following day and on iTunes a few days later. The CD and DVD versions were released on 6 May. On 18 August 2017 a prestigious edition of the album, entitled *How to Make Lemonade*, accompanied by a 600-page book of photographs, was made available to fans. The vinyl version of the album went on sale the following 15 September. Acclaimed from its release, *Lemonade* was praised by the critics for its ambitious blend of genres. Indeed, even though its alternative R&B quality was prevalent throughout the album (*Sorry, 6 Inch, Love Drought, Formation*), its ethereal textures (*Pray You Catch Me, Hold Up*) and its forays into styles that Beyoncé had never visited before (such as country with *Daddy Lessons* and garage rock with *Don't Hurt Yourself*) gave it a very special place in the singer's discography and demonstrated a welcome boldness at this stage in her career.

A painful end to the year

It was thus a tract against attacks on women and minorities that Beyoncé made here, even if it meant leaving by the wayside some detractors who had not yet said their last word. For at the end of 2016, when The Formation World Tour drew to a close, the unity of the American nation was to suddenly break apart. Although this social crisis reached a peak on 8 November 2016, with the election of Donald Trump to the presidency of the United States, another event had drawn Beyoncé's ire a few days earlier, and called into question the faith in her country that was nevertheless firmly rooted within her. On 2 November 2016, she performed an exceptional version of *Daddy Lessons* on stage at the Country Music Awards, accompanied by the no less exceptional Dixie Chicks, queens of country who had been deposed following criticism of George W. Bush by their vocalist Natalie Maines on 10 March 2003, during a concert at the Shepherd's Bush Empire in London. For, while crowned by the success of their country album *Home*, released in 2002, The Dixie Chicks had experienced a boycott of unprecedented ferocity after the incident. This sad journey through the wilderness was described in the unmissable documentary by Barbara Kopple and Cecilia Peck, *Dixie Chicks: Shut Up and Sing*, released in 2006, and related in their seventh album, the introspective *Taking the Long Way*, released the same year. Although the Country Music Awards ceremony was supposed to mark the return of this trio of unmatched virtuosity and prodigious output (the three artists amply deserved to be showered with

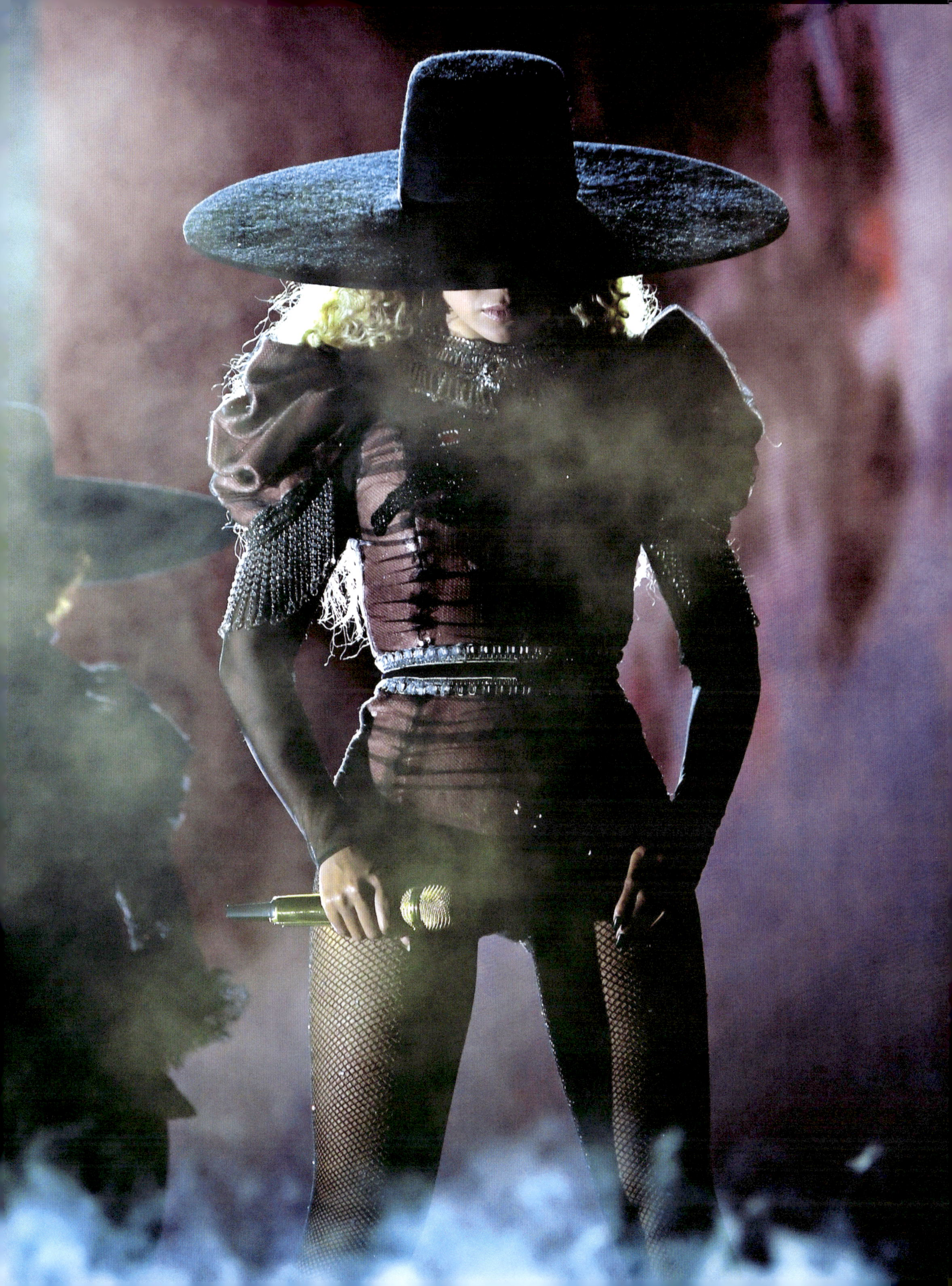

Beyoncé on the water-covered stage at the BET Awards in Los Angeles, June 2016.

such superlatives), on the contrary it celebrated obscurantism and racism. The organizer, the Country Music Association, considered that a Black singer could not attain the status of country artist, and deleted from its various web pages the sequence showing the meeting between Beyoncé, Natalie Maines, and the other Dixie Chicks, Martie Maguire and Emily Strayer. Despite clumsily back-pedaling on this, the CMA did not succeed in obliterating the scandal of this intolerable censorship. The incident had a profound effect on Beyoncé, who tried to get her revenge in 2024 with her country album *Cowboy Carter*. As for the brave Dixie Chicks, they changed their name in 2020, dropping "Dixie," which referenced their Southern roots, certainly, but also the Southern states of the US, which had for the most part opposed the abolition of slavery during the Civil War. Now called The Chicks, the three singers are still today one of the most talented American country music groups.

Despite a major album built on an appeal to protest and awareness, the road to equality and brotherhood seemed to become obscured for Beyoncé, who would make this battle a priority in years to come.

FOR BEYONCÉ ADDICTS

Although eagerly awaited by fans, the vinyl edition of *Lemonade*, released in September 2017, experienced a surprising setback. The entire A-side of the European edition, made of yellow vinyl and pressed in the factory of Celebrate Records in Germany, contained the songs of the Canadian punk group ZEX, which were meant to appear on their album *Uphill Battle*.

BEYONCÉ: ALL THE SONGS 373

A newcomer to the world of Beyoncé, Kevin Garrett added feeling and darkness to her repertoire.

PRAY YOU CATCH ME

(Beyoncé, James Blake, Kevin Garrett / 3'16)

Musicians
Beyoncé: vocals, backing vocals
James Blake: bass guitar
Kevin Garrett: piano
Crystal Alforque, Charlie Bisharat, Susan Chatman, Daphne Chen, Ryan Cross, Lisa Dondlinger, Terry Glenny, Eric Gorfain, Neel Hammond, Gina Kronstadt, Marisa Kuney, Songa Lee, Serena McKinney, Grace Park, Radu Pieptea, Katie Sloan, Ina Veli, Josefina Vergara, Amy Wickman, Yelena Yegoryan: violin
Briana Bandy, Denise Briese, Anna Bulbrook, Alma Fernandez, Leah Katz: viola
Richard Dodd, Vanessa Fairbairn-Smith, Ira Glansbeek, John Krovoza, Ginger Murphy, Geoff Osika, Rodney Wirtz, Adrienne Woods: cello
Eric Gorfain: conductor

Recording
Henson Recording Studios, Los Angeles: 2014 to 2015
Apex Studio, Burbank: 2014 to 2015
Conway Recording Studios, Los Angeles: 2014 to 2015

Technical team
Producers: Beyoncé, Kevin Garrett
Executive producer: Beyoncé Knowles-Carter
Recording engineers: Eric Caudieux, John Cranfield, Ramon Rivas, Greg Koller, Stuart White, Arthur Chambazyan
String arrangements: Jon Brion

Genesis

Beyoncé and Kevin Garrett met at a party organized by the latter's record label, Jay-Z's Roc Nation. Garrett, who had just released his first EP, *Mellow Drama*, was petrified when the superstar was introduced to him, to the point that when she told him he was a talented artist the young composer could think of nothing more appropriate to say than that she was too, provoking laughter among those present—a story Garrett liked to tell in interviews. It was in 2014 that the 23-year-old singer had sent his demos out to the whole music industry, hoping to land a contract with a record label. Through Roc Nation, Beyoncé then came across the song *Pray You Catch Me*, which Garrett had composed in his bedroom using a guitar and a Line 6 DL4 looper pedal. "I got a call saying that she wanted it. It was out of nowhere. I knew who had the song and where they worked, but the expectation was never for it to go to another artist, especially not someone like that. When I got that call, I was kinda more confused than anything else. I thought I was getting pranked."[270]

Production

When it came to spotting new talent, Beyoncé was formidable. She got hold of the song, which she soon re-recorded with Kevin Garrett and James Blake, to add it to her new album. But it was only on the day the movie *Lemonade* was screened on the HBO network, 23 April 2016, that Garrett became aware that his song had been chosen not only to begin the record, but also to open the film of the same name. The young composer, then living in Pittsburgh, visited a friend who subscribed to HBO, to watch the movie. On realizing that *Pray You Can Catch Me* opened Beyoncé's film, Garrett paid attention to every detail of the opening scene, to which his song was closely synchronized. "It was amazing. To see the film open with that song and to hear her sing that song—I didn't even realize that my friend was still in the room watching. Nothing else existed for those couple of minutes."[271]

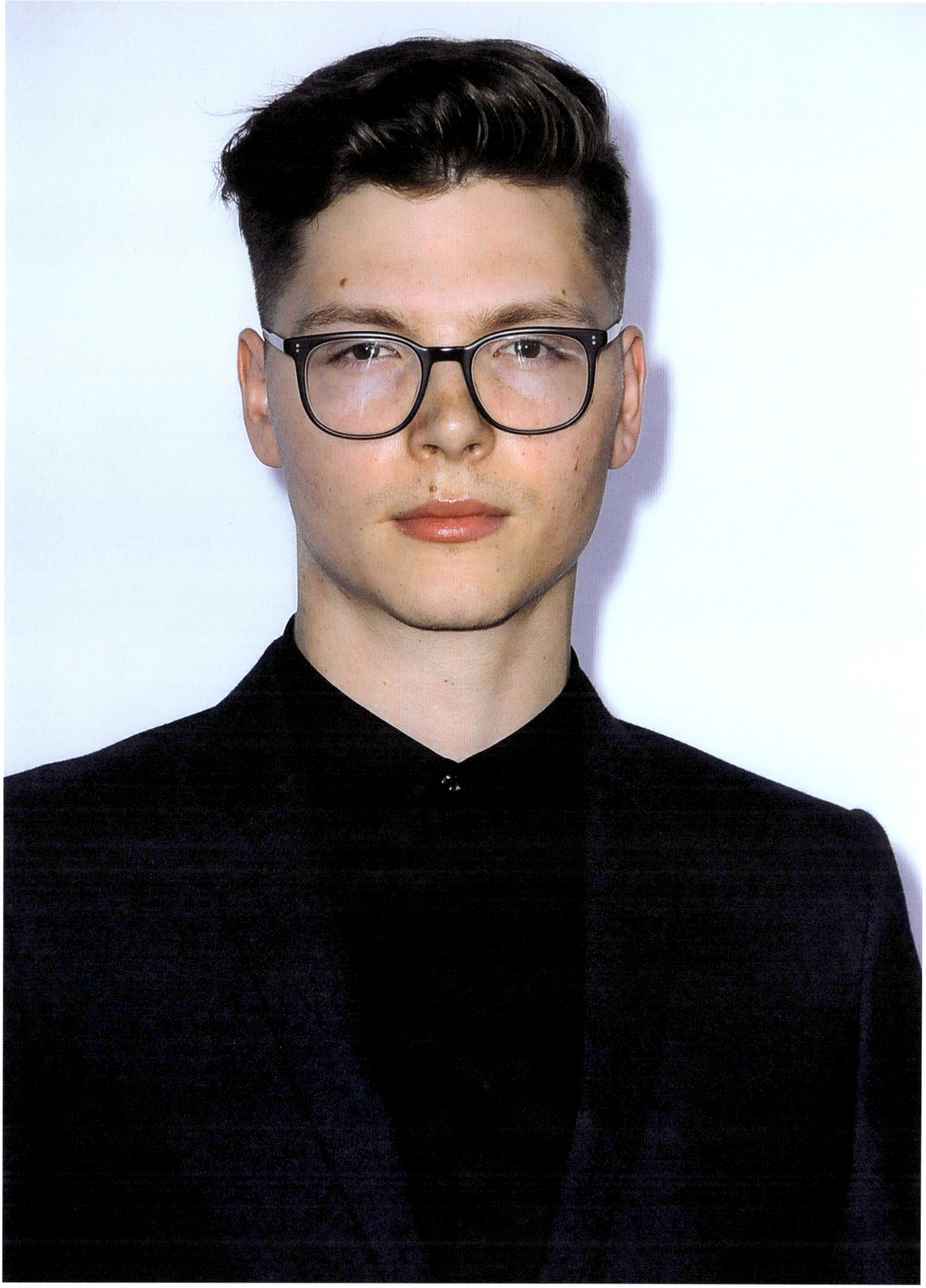

2016

The British producer MNEK played a part in *Hold Up*, one of the highlights of *Lemonade*.

SINGLE

HOLD UP

(Antonio Randolph, Beyoncé, Brian Chase, DeAndre Way, Doc Pomus, Emile Haynie, Ezra Koenig, Joshua Tillman, Karen Orzolek, Kelvin McConnell, Mort Shuman, Nick Zinner, Sean Rhoden, Uzoechi Emenike, Thomas Wesley Pentz/3'41)

Musicians
Beyoncé: vocals, backing vocals
MeLo-X: backing vocals
Diplo: programming
Jr Blender: guitar, programming

Recording
The Record Plant, Los Angeles: 2014 to 2015
Mad Decent Studios, Burbank: 2014 to 2015

Technical team
Producers: Beyoncé, Diplo, Ezra Koenig
Executive producer: Beyoncé Knowles-Carter
Recording engineers: Jon Schacter, Ramon Rivas, Stuart White

Single
Digital release by Parkwood Entertainment/Columbia: 27 May 2016
Best chart ranking in the USA: 13

Genesis

Besides being the most collaborative song on *Lemonade*, *Hold Up* is also one of the cleverest, playing mischievously on the ambivalence of a joyful melody superimposed on a reggae rhythm and cutting lyrics aimed at Jay-Z, into which Beyoncé pours her rage at her unfaithful spouse. To understand the process of this song's creation, it is necessary to go back to 2011, when Ezra Koenig, vocalist with Vampire Weekend, wrote a tweet asking his followers about the idea of changing the main hook of *Maps*, a single by the Yeah Yeah Yeahs released in 2003—*Wait, they don't love you like I love you*—into *Hold up, they don't love you like I love you*. In 2014, while Koenig was working with Diplo, one of the leading lights of the group Major Lazer, on a new song, built around a sample from *Can't Get Used to Losing You*, a single released by Andy Williams in 1963, the idea of using this phrase came back to him. The song *Hold Up* then saw the light of day, and was accompanied by a video by Jonas Åkerlund that shows Beyoncé destroying everything in her path with a baseball bat, as if to make her rage clear.

Production

Even at the demo stage, *Hold Up* had its reggae quality. First of all Josh Tillman, aka Father John Misty, was invited to work on the song, which he enhanced with lyrics and a melody in the first verse. Then, the British producer MNEK came and added the bridge, working closely with Beyoncé herself. "The way Beyoncé works, the song is a jigsaw piece and then she will piece various elements," MNEK explained. "It could be a bit that she's written, a bit that someone else has written and she'll make that the bridge; a bit I've written she'll make the middle eight, that kind of construction."[272] Finally, the American producer and DJ Sean "MeLo-X" Rhoden was invited to work on the track. "I heard the track and was very excited about it because I'm Jamaican," he explained. "And anything that sounds anywhere near Jamaica is kind of my lane, I would say. [...] I just wrote a bunch of things from my perspective and my tone of voice or how I would sing it if I was an ill reggae artist, like Barrington Levy singing on that track."[273]

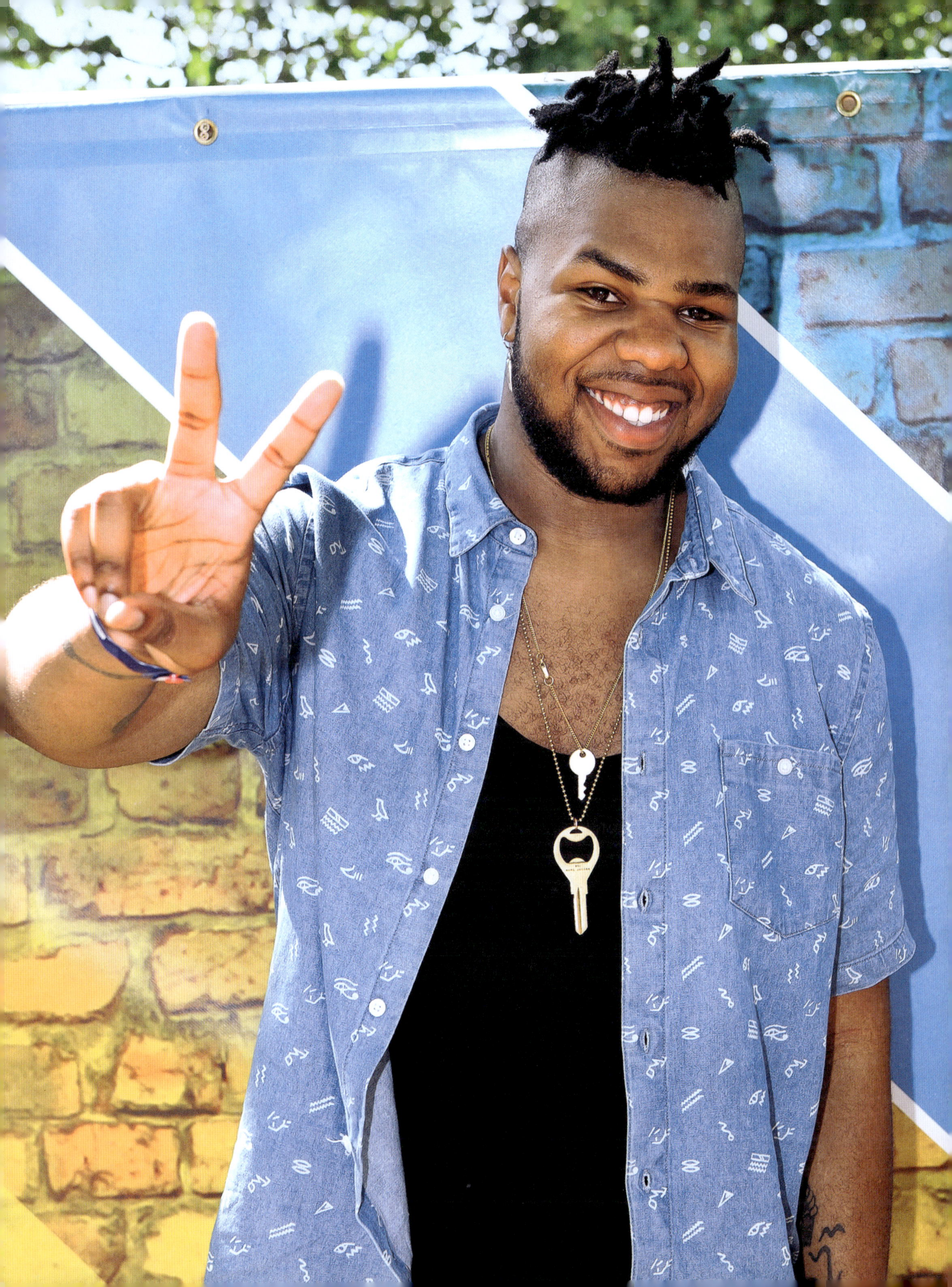

2016

Musician, songwriter, producer, and businessman Jack White is talented, but keeps a low profile in the media.

DON'T HURT YOURSELF
(FEATURING JACK WHITE)

(Beyoncé, Diana "Wynter" Gordon, Jack White, James Page, John Bonham, John Paul Jones, Robert Plant/3'54)

Musicians
Beyoncé: vocals, backing vocals
Jack White: vocals, bass guitar
Ruby Amanfu: backing vocals
Derek Dixie: programming
Patrick Keeler: drums
Mark Watrous: Hammond organ
Crystal Alforque, Charlie Bisharat, Susan Chatman, Daphne Chen, Ryan Cross, Lisa Dondlinger, Terry Glenny, Eric Gorfain, Neel Hammond, Gina Kronstadt, Marisa Kuney, Songa Lee, Serena McKinney, Grace Park, Radu Pieptea, Katie Sloan, Ina Veli, Josefina Vergara, Amy Wickman, Yelena Yegoryan: violin
Briana Bandy, Denise Briese, Anna Bulbrook, Alma Fernandez, **Leah Katz:** viola
Richard Dodd, Vanessa Fairbairn-Smith, Ira Glansbeek, John Krovoza, Ginger Murphy, Geoff Osika, Rodney Wirtz, **Adrienne Woods:** cello
Eric Gorfain: conductor

Recording
Third Man Studio, Nashville: 2014
Henson Recording Studios, Los Angeles: 2014 to 2015
Skip Saylor Recording, Los Angeles: 2014 to 2015
Jungle City Studios, New York: 2014 to 2015

Technical team
Producers: Beyoncé, Jack White, Derek Dixie
Executive producer: Beyoncé Knowles-Carter
Recording engineers: Eric Caudieux, Joshua V. Smith, Greg Koller, Ramon Rivas, Lester Mendoza, Stuart White
Assistant recording engineer: Ed Spear
String arrangements: Jon Brion

Genesis
If Beyoncé was the queen of R&B, Jack White was the king of garage rock, a style he had excelled at since 1997, having single-handedly led The White Stripes, The Raconteurs, and The Dead Weather between 1997 and 2019, while delighting his fans with a series of solo albums, each more brilliant than the last, from 2012 to 2024. He made *Seven Nation Army*, which won The White Stripes acclaim in 2003—but the man from Detroit was unquestionably not a one-hit person. With fingers in many pies, a multi-instrumentalist and an archivist acting as guarantor of America's musical memory—having applied himself to the resurrection of icons such as Loretta Lynn in 2004 and Wanda Jackson in 2011—White was active on all fronts. His working with Beyoncé nevertheless came as a surprise, so much did the raw, abrasive musical style he championed differ from hers. However, it is enough to listen just once to *Don't Hurt Yourself* to understand that here Beyoncé is using the anger and aggressiveness of Jack White's productions to pour out her rage at her unfaithful husband. "You know, I just talked to her and she said, 'I wanna be in a band with you,'" White explained, with a laugh. "I said, 'Really? Well, I'd love to do something.'"[274] Although Beyoncé did not replace the great Alison Mosshart in The Dead Weather, she nevertheless excelled in the thunderous *Don't Hurt Yourself*, venting her fury like the funk singer Betty Davis flirting with the corrosive rock of the alchemist Jack White.

Production
On receiving the tapes of *Don't Hurt Yourself*, recorded by Joshua V. Smith on an eight-track analog tape recorder at Jack White's Third Man Studio in Nashville, Stuart White, Beyoncé's recording engineer, faced several technical challenges. Bleed (a term denoting the inadvertent and undesirable picking up of one instrument's sound by another instrument's microphone during a live recording) was such that he had to juggle the song's different tracks to produce a coherent mix. "I love bleed, as it helps glue the track together and creates depth,"[267] said the technician, always ready to meet a new challenge, seated at his console. Managing to skillfully integrate Beyoncé's voice, recorded using a Shure SM58 microphone and overlaid with a very violent distortion effect, the recording engineer brought the song into being, without ever adulterating the work of its

378 LEMONADE

creator, the brilliant Jack White. When asked to enhance the song with discreet but essential backing vocals, the singer Ruby Amanfu, a friend of White's, executed her task in masterly fashion, singing in operatic style, as she had in *Love Interruption*, a single from White's first solo album *Blunderbuss*, released in 2012. "I think that people are still discovering that it's me singing on *Don't Hurt Yourself*," Amanfu said with amusement. "If you haven't read the credits, the truth is, you wouldn't know."[275]

2016

Singer The Weeknd in April 2016, a few months before the international success of his hits *Starboy* and *I Feel It Coming*.

SINGLE

SORRY

(Beyoncé, Diana "Wynter" Gordon, Sean Rhoden/3'53)

Musicians: Beyoncé: vocals, backing vocals / Chrissy Collins: backing vocals / B. Carr: programming / **Recording:** The Beehive, Los Angeles: 2014 to 2015 / **Technical team:** Producers: Hit-Boy, Beyoncé, MeLo-X, Wynter Gordon, Stuart White / **Executive producer:** Beyoncé Knowles-Carter / **Recording engineers:** Stuart White, Ramon Rivas / **Single:** Digital release by Parkwood Entertainment/Columbia: 3 May 2016 / **Best chart ranking in the USA:** 11

After a career in EDM (electro dance music) under the pseudonym Wynter Gordon, in 2014 the lyricist Diana Gordon worked with Beyoncé, co-writing three sets of lyrics for *Lemonade*, including those for *Sorry*, produced chiefly by Hit-Boy and MeLo-X. The song drew much press comment because of its scathing lyrics, in which Beyoncé yet again settles scores with her adulterous spouse, singing: *Looking at my watch/He shoulda been home/Today I regret the night I put that ring on*. While the lyrics are explicit, it is a phrase at the end of the song—*He better call Becky with the good hair* (the name being a reference to an American racist slang term for a rich, superficial white woman)—that unleashed a veritable witch hunt among fans, the Beyhive being determined to find the woman who had dared to do so much wrong to Beyoncé. Is "Becky" used here only as an expression, or is it a reference to a woman with that name? Interrogated on the subject, Gordon denied her lyrics were based on a true situation, and declared: "I laughed, like this is so silly. Where are we living? I was like, 'What day in age from that lyric do you get all of this information?' Is it really telling you all that much, accusing people?"[276] Given that one of the themes that Beyoncé openly addressed in *Lemonade* is adultery, the fans were justified in taking Gordon's lyrics at face value. As for the—unproven—theories regarding the—unidentified—young woman, they remain an open question.

6 INCH
(FEATURING THE WEEKND)

(Abel "The Weeknd" Tesfaye, Ahmad "Belly" Balshe, Ben Diehl, Beyoncé, BOOTS, Brian Weitz, Burt Bacharach, Danny Schofield, Dave Portner, Hal David, Noah Lennox, Terius "The-Dream" Nash/4'20)

Musicians: Beyoncé: vocals, backing vocals / The Weeknd: vocals / Belly: backing vocals / Derek Dixie: additional instruments / **Recording:** The Record Plant, Los Angeles: 2014 to 2015 / **Technical team:** Producers: Ben Billions, Beyoncé, BOOTS, DannyBoyStyles, Derek Dixie / **Executive producer:** Beyoncé Knowles-Carter / **Recording engineers:** Stuart White, Ramon Rivas

Although he was not yet the global superstar he would become after working with the French musicians Daft Punk on *I Feel It Coming* and *Starboy* in 2016, Abel Tesfaye, aka The Weeknd, had already made two clever, avant-garde albums, mischievously blending an alternative R&B sound with his irresistible voice, often compared to Michael Jackson's. Having just released two excellent singles, *The Hills* and *Can't Feel My Face* (if you don't know them, you should lose no time in listening to them), The Weeknd was invited to work with Beyoncé, who brought him in for *6 Inch*, a song that refers to a woman working in a club, perched on heels that high; she is attracted to money and practices a profession that is not spelt out but is clearly that of an escort. Is this a barb aimed at a presumed girlfriend of Jay-Z? No one can be certain…Nor can anyone be certain that the resemblance between *6 Inch* and *My Girls*, sung by the Baltimore group Animal Collective in 2009, was not deliberate, even though BOOTS, co-writer of *6 Inch*, denied any such borrowing. "[This] amalgamation was accidental. Similar to when George Harrison got sued for *My Sweet Lord*. [In 1981 the ex-Beatle was found to have plagiarized the whole of *He's So Fine* by The Chiffons, released in 1963, for his song *My Sweet Lord*, released in 1970.] You write it and sing it and think 'that's fucking great!!!' and everyone high fives and you're all geniuses for fourteen seconds but it turns out it's great because someone else already fucking wrote it."[277]

380 Lemonade

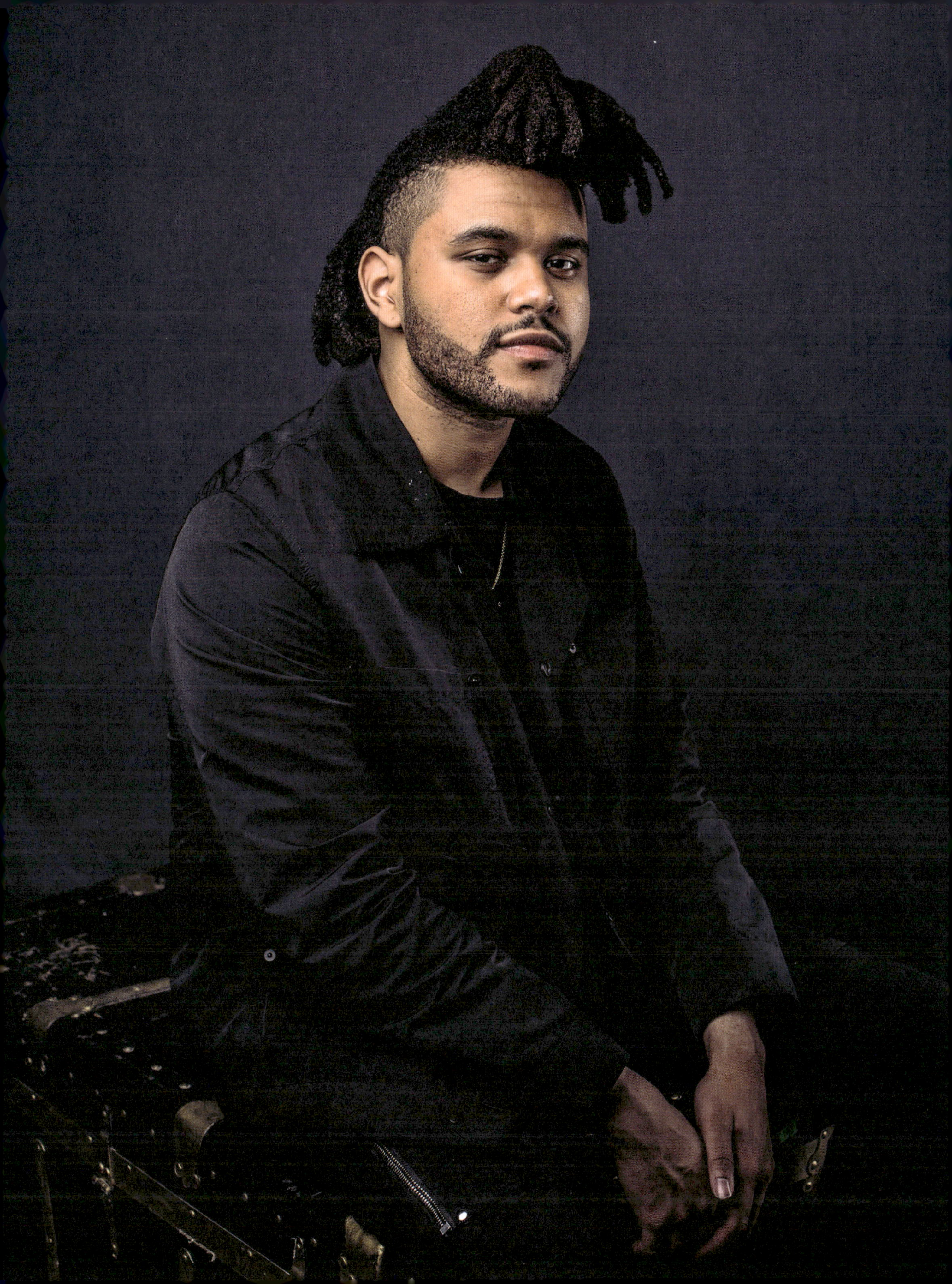

DADDY LESSONS

(Alex Delicata, Beyoncé, Diana "Wynter" Gordon, Kevin Cossom/4'48)

Musicians
- **Beyoncé:** vocals, backing vocals
- **Derek Dixie:** drums, programming
- **Eric Walls:** guitar
- **Courtney Leonard:** bass guitar
- **Patrick Williams:** harmonica
- **Leo Pellegrino (Too Many Zooz):** saxophone
- **Matt Muirhead (Too Many Zooz):** trumpet
- **David Parks (Too Many Zooz):** drums
- **Christopher Gray:** trumpet
- **Peter Ortega:** saxophone
- **Randolph Ellis:** saxophone
- **Richard Lucchese:** trombone

Recording
- Skip Saylor Recording, Los Angeles: 2014 to 2015
- The Beehive, Los Angeles: 2014 to 2015

Technical team
- **Producers:** Beyoncé, Alex Delicata, Derek Dixie
- **Executive producer:** Beyoncé Knowles-Carter
- **Recording engineers:** Lester Mendoza, Ramon Rivas, Stuart White
- **Assistant recording engineer:** Derek Dixie

Genesis

The story of *Daddy Lessons* begins in 2014. While jamming in his Miami apartment with his friends the guitarist Alex Delicata and the songwriter Diana Gordon, producer Kevin Cossom played a part in creating a folk song that made quite an impression on those present. "[Alex] played the guitar, wrote it and we pretty much pressed record on the laptop and sang it down—harmonies, stomping and clapping, and that was the vibe," Cossom explained. "We probably did it a few times till we got it right. We knew that we had something."[278] Diana Gordon, who knew Beyoncé personally, insisted on offering her the song, which did not yet have any lyrics. In order to write them, Gordon seemingly drew on her own experience (although she later denied the lyrics were autobiographical). Abandoned by her father when she was very young, and raised by a mother who was psychologically unstable and a stepfather who made the little girl, as well as her brothers and sisters, join the Pentecostal church, Diana Gordon bore the scars of a childhood lived in terror. "I grew up with a lot of fear from an early age. I would be trembling if my mom would come near me."[279] In the lyrics for *Daddy Lessons*, she portrayed the relationship between a young girl and her father, who teaches her to protect herself in the face of adversity, in an environment reminiscent of those described in classic country songs—the man trains his children like soldiers, pours whisky in his tea, plays blackjack, rides motorbikes, and shoots a revolver. Using these clichés, Gordon unwittingly created a country anthem that was to become one of the highlights of *Lemonade*.

Production

When Diana Gordon played *Daddy Lessons* to her, Beyoncé immediately responded. "When I played it for her, I was like, 'This is one of my favorite songs,'" Gordon recalled. "She was like, 'This is my life.' I told her, 'You know what, take it, do what you want with it.'"[276] Beyoncé re-recorded the song, added a break, and made it completely her own, changing some lines in the lyrics and making explicit reference to her own Texas childhood. Given that the song's autobiographical nature was undeniable—and not denied by the person involved—the idea of adding a fanfare typical of New Orleans soon materialized, for its sound, characteristic of that Louisiana

Matt Muirhead, David Parks, and Leo Pellegrino of Too Many Zooz in New York in 2019.

city, was dear to Beyoncé, whose roots were there. As well as various hand-picked, talented instrumentalists, Beyoncé called on a New York trio who went by the name Too Many Zooz: saxophonist Leo Pellegrino, trumpet player Matt Muirhead, and drummer David Parks. "Basically Beyoncé saw some videos of us in the subway and she decided to get us in the studio," Pellegrino explained. "We recorded over her country track *Daddy Lessons* and later that year she asked us to perform with her and The Dixie Chicks at the CMAs [Country Music Awards]—A dream come true, she is one of the best performers of our time."[280]

HEADPHONES AT THE READY

At 4'42 in *Daddy Lessons*, young Blue Ivy Carter is heard to say: "Good job, Bey!" to her mother, who replies with a tender, knowing laugh.

Vincent Berry II, the original creator of *Sandcastles*, in Los Angeles, February 2017.

LOVE DROUGHT

(Beyoncé, Ingrid Burley, Mike Dean/3'57)

Musicians: Beyoncé: vocals, backing vocals / Mike Dean: synthesizers, programming / **Recording:** Jungle City Studios, New York: 2014 to 2015 / **Technical team: Producers:** Beyoncé, Mike Dean / **Executive producer:** Beyoncé Knowles-Carter / **Recording engineers:** Mike Dean, Stuart White, Ramon Rivas

Here is a song that is 100 per cent "made in Houston." For behind *Love Drought*—with lyrics that, yet again, denounce an adulterous spouse—there is a trio, each of whose members hails from the famous Texan city. Although Beyoncé is of course the first to be credited, production and composition were also the work of Mike Dean, a renowned beat-maker who once worked for Nate Dogg and 2Pac before becoming a faithful associate of Kanye West. The third member of the team was Ingrid Burley. A vocalist with the hip-hop group Trio when she was only 11 years old, as a teenager she benefited from the advice of Mathew Knowles, who was Trio's manager. "He's the person that made me question every last thing that I put down on the record before I let anybody hear it because the number one thing that he wants you to be is the best version of yourself,"[281] Burley recalled with affection. It must be said that the young woman was very close to the Knowles family, for her mother and Tina Knowles were good friends, as were Ingrid and Tina's daughter Solange. Having pursued her musical career, Burley took part in the Bridgehampton writing camp during the summer of 2012, and was then invited to work again with the person who had sometimes babysat her when she was a child. Working alongside Beyoncé proved enriching for Burley, one of whose songs was kept for the final tracklisting of *Lemonade*.

SANDCASTLES

(Beyoncé, Malik Yusef, Midian Mathers, Vincent Berry II/3'03)

Musicians: Beyoncé: vocals, backing vocals / Jack Chambazyan: synthesizers / Vincent Berry II: piano / **Recording:** The Beehive, Los Angeles: 2014 to 2015 / **Technical team: Producers:** Beyoncé, Vincent Berry II / **Executive producer:** Beyoncé Knowles-Carter / **Recording engineer:** Stuart White

Originally from Chicago, the producer Malik Yusef first worked with Queen Bey on the platinum edition of *Beyoncé*, released in November 2014, making the remix of *Drunk in Love*, which was enhanced with the voice of Kanye West. When he bumped into Beyoncé at the 64th NBA All-Star Game in New York on 15 February 2015, the reunion quickly led to a discussion about each other's work. "It's an ongoing, perpetual process," Yusef explained. "Every conversation leads to art. You talk about parenting, it leads to art. You talk about politics, it leads to art."[282] The idea of working together again soon came up, although Beyoncé was very evasive as to what she expected of Yusef. "She just explained she was looking for greatness. Sometimes the artist doesn't say what's in their heart. Sometimes you have to reach out and touch the artist."[282] In order to touch Beyoncé's heart, Malik Yusef worked with a composer friend, Vincent Berry II, who was struggling to recover from a recent, painful breakup. The

The talented James Blake, photographed by Shaun Bloodworth in 2011.

song's melody, and some ideas for the lyrics, came to Yusef on 16 May 2013 as he was driving his car. He immediately recorded them on his smartphone and then sent them to Berry, who suggested the theme of sandcastles washed away by the sea as a metaphor for a romantic relationship swept away with a wave of the hand. "I said, 'You know what, this is my last time writing a song about this girl. I'm putting it all in this,'"[283] the jilted lover declared. A short time later, Berry met Midian Mathers, backing vocalist for Justin Bieber, who was immediately charmed by the song. The young woman made her contribution to it and presented the new version of *Sandcastles* to Teresa LaBarbera Whites, who was then in search of new talents for the production of Beyoncé's sixth album. The rest is history: Beyoncé retained the song for *Lemonade*, after having modified a few lines of the lyrics, and—an occurrence rare enough to be worth noting—Vincent Berry II retained the rights to the song, while nevertheless sharing the royalties with Beyoncé, Mathers, and Yusef. "When someone sings your song, it's incredible," said Berry. "But when the biggest artist in the world sings your song, it's really a defining moment for yourself that you know you're supposed to be doing what you're doing."[283]

FORWARD

(featuring James Blake) (Beyoncé, James Blake/1'19)

Musicians: Beyoncé: vocals / James Blake: vocals, piano / **Recording:** Conway Recording Studios, Los Angeles: 2014 to 2015 / **Technical team: Producer:** Beyoncé / **Executive producer:** Beyoncé Knowles-Carter / **Recording engineers:** Stuart White, Ramon Rivas / **Assistant recording engineer:** John Cranfield

Although *Forward* seems more like a musical interlude than a proper song, it is of fundamental importance in the sequencing of *Lemonade*. For while the first seven songs on the album reveal Beyoncé's anger, and the eighth, *Sandcastles*, all her suffering, *Forward* addresses the theme of resilience, and guides us towards a better time. Faith in the future is therefore the subject of this ethereal track, sung mostly by James Blake, with Beyoncé appearing as a backing vocalist only at the end. Blake was given the lyrics at a meeting with the production team where the concept of the album was explained to him. But when he got together with Stuart White and his assistant Ramon Rivas at Conway Recording Studios in Los Angeles to work on the song, he decided not to follow his employer's instructions. "I've never sung anybody else's lyrics. So I just assumed that's not [what] I was going to be doing. So I got my phone out and sang some of my own lyrics that were about something else and about somebody else. But it fit somehow into the song and it fit into the album, and I'm just honored that they used it."[284]

SINGLE

FREEDOM
(FEATURING KENDRICK LAMAR)

(Alan Lomax, Arrow Benjamin, Beyoncé, Carla Williams, Frank Tirado, John Lomax Sr, Jonathan Coffer, Kendrick Duckworth/4'50)

Musicians: Beyoncé: vocals, backing vocals / **Kendrick Lamar:** rap / **Arrow Benjamin:** backing vocals / **Big Freedia:** backing vocals / **Marcus Miller:** bass guitar / **Canei Finch:** piano / **Just Blaze:** programming, synthesizers / **BOOTS:** programming / **Myles William:** programming / **Recording:** The Beehive, Los Angeles: 2014 to 2015 / **Technical team: Producers:** Beyoncé, Jonny Coffer, Just Blaze / **Executive producer:** Beyoncé Knowles-Carter / **Recording engineers:** Stuart White, Ramon Rivas / **Single:** Digital release by Parkwood Entertainment/Columbia: 9 September 2016 / **Best chart ranking in the USA:** 35

As Beyoncé had just finished recording her vocals for *Runnin' (Lose It All)* by Naughty Boy, the idea of a new joint project with the song's producer, Jonny Coffer, came up. With this in mind, Coffer embarked on some writing sessions, but nothing seemed to him good enough for the new album, until an idea for a powerful rhythm suddenly came back to him. He showed it to two composer friends with whom he was working at the time, Carla Marie Williams and Arrow Benjamin; both were attracted to the song's energy and hastened to work on it. Nevertheless, it required the input of a fourth person before the production of the demo of *Freedom* was completed. Egon, real name Eothen Aram Alapatt, the founder of Now-Again Records, advised the team to include a sample from *Let Me Try*, a song by the psychedelic group Kaleidoscope, for whom he had just reissued an obscure eponymous album: 200 copies had been pressed in 1969 for Mexican radio stations, in order to introduce that style of music to their listeners. Once *Freedom* had been sent to Beyoncé, it was entrusted to the producer Just Blaze, whose task it was to transform the demo into a powerful song. "I just added my own synths, programming additional drums, additional keyboards, making it feel like more like it was a live band as opposed to just a sample loop."[285] Beyoncé quickly secured the services of Kendrick Lamar, a rising star of hip-hop, and herself called the rapper Big Freedia to ask him to provide some backing vocals in the song. As well as being one of the outstanding songs on *Lemonade*, *Freedom* became an anthem used by Democratic candidate Kamala Harris during her campaign for the United States presidency in November 2024.

SINGLE

ALL NIGHT

(Akil King, André Benjamin, Antwan Patton, Beyoncé, Ilsey Juber, Jaramye Daniels, Patrick Brown, Ricky Anthony, Theron Thomas, Timothy Thomas, Thomas Wesley Pentz/5'22)

Musicians: Beyoncé: vocals, backing vocals / **Diplo:** backing vocals, programming / **Henry Allen:** backing vocals, guitar, programming / **Marcus Miller:** bass guitar / **Derek Dixie:** programming, additional instruments / **Christopher Gray:** trumpet / **Peter Ortega:** saxophone / **Randolph Ellis:** saxophone / **Richard Lucchese:** trombone / **Crystal Alforque, Charlie Bisharat, Susan Chatman, Daphne Chen, Ryan Cross, Lisa Dondlinger, Terry Glenny, Eric Gorfain, Neel Hammond, Gina Kronstadt, Marisa Kuney, Songa Lee, Serena McKinney, Grace Park, Radu Pieptea, Katie Sloan, Ina Veli, Josefina Vergara, Amy Wickman, Yelena Yegoryan:** violin / **Briana Bandy, Denise Briese, Anna Bulbrook, Alma Fernandez, Leah Katz:** viola / **Richard Dodd, Vanessa Fairbairn-Smith, Ira Glansbeek, John Krovoza, Ginger Murphy, Geoff Osika, Rodney Wirtz, Adrienne Woods:** cello / **Eric Gorfain:** conductor / **Recording:** Jungle City Studios, New York: 2014 to 2015 / Conway Recording Studios, Los Angeles: 2014 to 2015 / Mad Decent Studios, Burbank: 2014 to 2015 / Henson Recording Studios, Los Angeles: 2014 to 2015 / Apex Studio, Burbank: 2014 to 2015 / Skip Saylor Recording, Los Angeles: 2014 to 2015 (brass) / **Technical team: Producers:** Beyoncé, Diplo, Henry Allen / **Executive producer:** Beyoncé Knowles-Carter / **Recording engineers:** Stuart White, Eric Caudieux, Greg Koller, Ramon Rivas, Lester Mendoza / **Assistant recording engineer:** John Cranfield / **Brass arrangements:** Derek Dixie / **String arrangements:** Jon Brion / **Single:** Digital release by Parkwood Entertainment/Columbia: 2 December 2016 / **Best chart ranking in the USA:** 38

The brothers Theron and Timothy Thomas—songwriters, composers, and producers who had achieved notable successes working with Ariana Grande, Nicki Minaj, and Rihanna—wrote the instrumental part of what would become *All Night* with Rihanna in mind. Now known as R. City, the Thomases worked at the time with the cream of pop and electro music, including the group Jack Ü, which comprised two superstars of the genre: Skrillex and Diplo. It was during a session with the latter for Jack Ü's next album that Theron and Timothy played a demo of the song destined for the famous singer from Barbados. Diplo immediately suggested a Caribbean-style rhythm, and straight afterward offered the song to Beyoncé, with whom he was now working frequently. At that point, the song featured only an electric guitar playing a series of chords steeped in reverb, very discreet drums, some strings, and a sample from *SpottieOttieDopaliscious*, a song by OutKast featured on their album *Aquemini*, released in 1998. The final version of *All Night* eventually saw the light of day after being worked on by Beyoncé and the producer Henry Allen.

Kendrick Lamar attends the MTV Video Music Awards at the Forum in Inglewood, 27 August 2017.

SINGLE

FORMATION

(Asheton Hogan, Beyoncé, Khalif Brown, Michael L. Williams II/3'26)

Musicians
Beyoncé: vocals, backing vocals
Big Freedia: backing vocals
Swae Lee: backing vocals
Matt Doe: trumpet

Recording
The Beehive, Los Angeles: 2014 to 2015
?, New York: 2015

Technical team
Producers: Beyoncé, Mike WiLL Made-It, PLUSS
Executive producer: Beyoncé Knowles-Carter
Recording engineer: Stuart White
Brass arrangements: Derek Dixie

Single
Digital release by Parkwood Entertainment/Columbia: 6 February 2016
Best chart ranking in the USA: 10

Genesis

In April 2014, the producer and rapper Mike WiLL Made-It (real name Michael Len Williams II) was driving to the Coachella Valley Music and Arts Festival (commonly referred to simply as Coachella) with his friends Swae Lee and Slim Jxmmi, of the duo Rae Sremmurd. Mindful of the fact that a short time earlier Beyoncé had requested some songs from him for her next album, Mike WiLL Made-It, whose recent work (including *No Lie* by 2 Chainz, *Pour It Up* by Rihanna, and *We Can't Stop* by Miley Cyrus, to name but a few) had met with international success, played an instrumental passage in the car, and invited each of his companions to improvise over it. At that point Swae Lee said: "OK, so now let's get in formation." Struck by this effective motif, Mike WiLL Made-It asked his friend to change it to "OK, ladies, now let's get in formation." Convinced by this hook, the producer asked Lee to record it on Voice Memos on his iPhone. Some time later, when they were back in Los Angeles, working on the production of *Drink on Us*, a single which Mike WiLL Made-It would release with Swae Lee and The Weeknd in 2015, Lee retrieved the famous phrase from his archives and re-recorded it in a demo of a song that was part trap, part bounce music, which his friend had just worked on, adding some well-judged punchlines. Having sent the song to Beyoncé, Mike WiLL Made-It heard back from her that it would benefit from a clip that was being made, and would be performed at the Super Bowl 50 half-time show—the work being done in record time, because the event was only two weeks away. "She did it," said an astonished Mike WiLL Made-It. "She did exactly what she said. The exact dates and everything, it dropped, and it just broke."[286]

Production

Before introducing it to the whole world, Beyoncé reworked *Formation* in New York during a two-day session with Mike WiLL Made-It, in which she told him about *Lemonade* and its concept. Once the voice of Big Freedia had been added and the song edited and mixed, Beyoncé asked Melina Matsoukas to make the clip in just two days, the week before the Super Bowl 50 half-time show. Shot in Los Angeles, the video of the song is as powerful as its lyrics, mocking racist prejudices against African Americans one by one and emphasizing Beyoncé's pride in belonging to that community. A few days

An LGBTQ+ icon and queen of bounce music, Big Freedia played a part in the success of *Formation*.

before the scandal at the Super Bowl erupted, with Beyoncé's dancers dressed like Black Panthers, she had already shocked the defenders of the US police by releasing her new clip—notably because of a scene in which she slowly drowns while lying on the roof of a police vehicle. The sequence, shot in a swimming pool in the studio, and featuring a green background representing Louisiana invaded by floodwaters following Hurricane Katrina in 2005, attained legendary status. "Anyone who perceives my message as anti-police is completely mistaken," Beyoncé told *Elle USA*. "I have so much admiration and respect for officers and the families of officers who sacrifice themselves to keep us safe. But let's be clear: I am against police brutality and injustice. Those are two separate things. If celebrating my roots and culture during Black History Month made anyone uncomfortable, those feelings were there long before a video and long before me. I'm proud of what we created and I'm proud to be a part of a conversation that is pushing things forward in a positive way."[33]

Eddie Vedder and Beyoncé on stage at the Global Citizen Festival in New York, 26 September 2015.

REDEMPTION SONG
(EDDIE VEDDER AND BEYONCÉ)

(Bob Marley/2'18)

Musicians: Eddie Vedder: vocals, acoustic guitar / Beyoncé Knowles: vocals / **Recording:** Global Citizen Festival, Great Lawn, Central Park, New York: 26 September 2015 / **Technical team:** Recording engineer: John Harris / 2015 Ten Club Annual Single *Wishing Well/Redemption Song* (single) / Released in the USA by Monkeywrench Records: 2015

Started in 2012, the Global Citizen Festival has been, since its foundation, a major charitable event, whose aim is to combat poverty in the world. In 2015, its third year, the festival, held in Central Park, New York, boasted a prestigious program featuring Beyoncé, Coldplay, Pearl Jam, Ed Sheeran, and Fall Out Boy. Among the guests lending their support to this noble cause by singing along with the stars or giving a speech were the singer Ariana Grande, the presenter Stephen Colbert, the actor Leonardo DiCaprio, and the then US vice-president Joe Biden. Although Eddie Vedder—the charismatic vocalist of Pearl Jam, one of the groups that founded grunge in the early 1990s—had not performed this particular number on stage since 1995, that day he chose to perform an acoustic version of the Bob Marley and the Wailers classic *Redemption Song*. For the occasion, Vedder was accompanied by Beyoncé on vocals, and the song included a speech by Nelson Mandela, former president of South Africa. As part of Ten Club Holiday Singles—exclusive singles offered every year to members of Ten Club, the Pearl Jam fan club—the group pressed, via its own label, Monkeywrench Records, a single with on its A-side a cover of Free's *Wishing Well*, and on its B-side the cover of *Redemption Song*: it's a record that every self-respecting Beyoncé fan should buy without delay.

RUNNIN' (LOSE IT ALL)
(NAUGHTY BOY FEATURING BEYONCÉ AND ARROW BENJAMIN)

(Arrow Benjamin, Beyoncé, Carla Marie Williams, Jonny Coffer, Shahid Khan / 3'33)

Musicians: Beyoncé: vocals, backing vocals / **Arrow Benjamin:** vocals, backing vocals / **Recording:** ?: 2015 / **Technical team: Producers:** Naughty Boy, Jonny Coffer / ***Runnin' (Lose It All)*** **(single)** / **Digital release by Virgin:** 17 September 2015

A huge success in the UK, where it went to the top of the charts, the single *Runnin' (Lose It All)* was yet another triumphant collaboration for Beyoncé. It must be said that she was no longer getting herself talked about in 2015; the last time her voice had been heard was alongside Nicki Minaj in the song *Feeling Myself*, in December of the previous year. So now Queen Bey was back, thanks to this duet with the British DJ Naughty Boy. The song had been co-written by Jonny Coffer, who would soon work with Beyoncé on *Freedom*. That partnership had not yet been formed when Coffer played the demo of *Runnin' (Lose It All)* to Jon Platt, Beyoncé's publisher, during a recording session. Charmed, Platt sent a copy to Beyoncé, who soon said she wanted to record her voice on it. Apart from the success this collaboration earned the single in the UK (the song passed almost unnoticed in the US), it allowed Beyoncé and Coffer to get to know each other better and, soon, to envisage working together on the *Lemonade* album.

Shahid Khan, alias Naughty Boy, in London in 2016.

THE GIRL IS MINE
(99 SOULS FEATURING DESTINY'S CHILD AND BRANDY)

(Angela Beyincé, Beyoncé Knowles, Brandy Norwood, Donald Davis, Edward Robinson, Fred Jerkins III, Japhe Tejeda, Kelendria Rowland, LaShawn Daniels, Tenitra Williams, Patrick Douthit, Rodney Jerkins / 3'33)

Musicians: Beyoncé Knowles: vocals / **Kelly Rowland:** vocals / **Michelle Williams:** vocals / **Elisa Caleb:** vocals / **Brandy:** vocals / **Vula Malinga:** vocals / **Jo Caleb:** electronic drums, guitar, synthesizer, programming / **Hal Ritson:** programming / **Recording:** ?: 2014 / **Technical team: Producers:** 99 Souls, Guy Buss, Hal Ritson / **Executive producer:** Mathew Knowles / **Recording engineers:** Jo Caleb, Todd Hurtt / ***The Girl Is Mine*** **(single)** / **Digital release in the UK by Resilience Records/Nothing Else Matters:** 6 November 2015 / **Best chart ranking in the USA:** did not make the charts

It took the producer Jo Caleb, half of the duo 99 Souls, almost a year to finally release a song that would soon top numerous charts around the world. It must be said that this British producer likes to play with fire. Indeed, when, in December 2014—without securing authorization beforehand—he uploaded on Soundcloud a dance number that combined *Girl* by Destiny's Child (2004) with one of the biggest R&B hits of the 1990s, *The Boy Is Mine* by Brandy & Monica (1998), he did not for an instant expect the success it would achieve. Almost three million plays later, he had to acknowledge that his mash-up had been a colossal hit. But this soon attracted the attention of those who held the rights to the two original works, who hastened to block the streaming of *The Girl Is Mine*. It took Caleb several months of negotiations with them before *The Girl Is Mine* could finally be made available officially—this time enhanced with a new vocal line by Brandy. As for Monica, she refused to take part in this new version of her greatest hit, preferring to leave in the past what belonged in the past. On 6 November 2015, 99 Souls posted the following message on their Facebook page: "*The Girl Is Mine* is finally available! 30,288 miles & a stomach full of bleeding ulcers later, Resilience Records has done what the music industry said was impossible. 99 Souls featuring Destiny's Child & Brandy...Yep, official at long last."[287]

Chris Martin and Beyoncé at the party following Jay-Z's concert at the Royal Albert Hall in London, 27 September 2006.

SINGLE

HYMN FOR THE WEEKEND
(COLDPLAY)

(Guy Berryman, Jon Buckland, Will Champion, Chris Martin/4'18)

Musicians
Chris Martin: vocals, piano
Beyoncé Knowles: vocals, backing vocals
Jon Buckland: guitar
Guy Berryman: bass guitar
Will Champion: drums
Tim Bergling: programming
The Regiment Horns: brass

Recording
Lyndhurst Hall, Air Studios, London: 2015
The Bakery, London: 2015
The Beehive, London: 2015
Henson Recording Studios, Los Angeles: 2015
The Village, Los Angeles: 2015
Woodshed Recording, Malibu: 2015

Technical team
Producers: Digital Divide, Rik Simpson, Stargate
Recording engineers: Bill Rahko, Daniel Green, Miles Walker, Robin Baynton

Coldplay *A Head Full of Dreams* (album)
Released in the USA by Atlantic/Parlophone: 4 December 2015
(CD ref.: 553301-2)

Genesis

Coldplay—the British rock group who have sold 100 million albums—are known worldwide for their mainstream pop rock, catchy tunes, and concerts held in the planet's biggest stadiums. In 2014, while they were working on their new album, Chris Martin, their vocalist, wanted to write an anthem in praise of partying, to which clubbers the world over could dance. "I thought I'd like to have a song called 'Drinks on Me' where you sit on the side of a club and buy everyone drinks because you're so f—ing cool," Martin explained. "I was chuckling about that, when this melody came—'drinks on me, drinks on me'—then the rest of the song came out."[288] The problem was, the rest of the group did not agree. Since Coldplay worked as a democracy, each had their say in the writing, and Martin's colleagues and friends Jon Buckland, Guy Berryman, and Will Champion wasted no time in telling him that under no circumstances would they let him sing those words. The vocalist reconsidered, and changed the phrase to "drink on me," which fitted the more spiritual theme of the new lyrics, in which Martin sings of his love of life and the presence of an angel who has come down from heaven to guide him.

Production

As an old friend of Beyoncé, Chris Martin invited her to record a few vocal lines for the song, the production of which was a collaborative effort between the Norwegian duo Stargate, with whom Coldplay had long wanted to work; Digital Divide, another duo, consisting of Mareike Barutzki and Vernon Chaney; and finally Coldplay's faithful recording engineer and producer, Rik Simpson. Although most of *Hymn for the Weekend* was recorded in the group's two London studios, The Bakery and The Beehive, Beyoncé's voice was recorded at Chris Martin's East Coast home in the Hamptons. "We built a vocal booth for her in the bedroom of Chris' kids," laughed Rik Simpson. "I just came in with a laptop and an Avalon mic pre, and she favours a Telefunken 251."[289] In passing, Beyoncé also recorded some backing vocals for *Up&Up*, the last song on Coldplay's new album, *A Head Full of Dreams*.

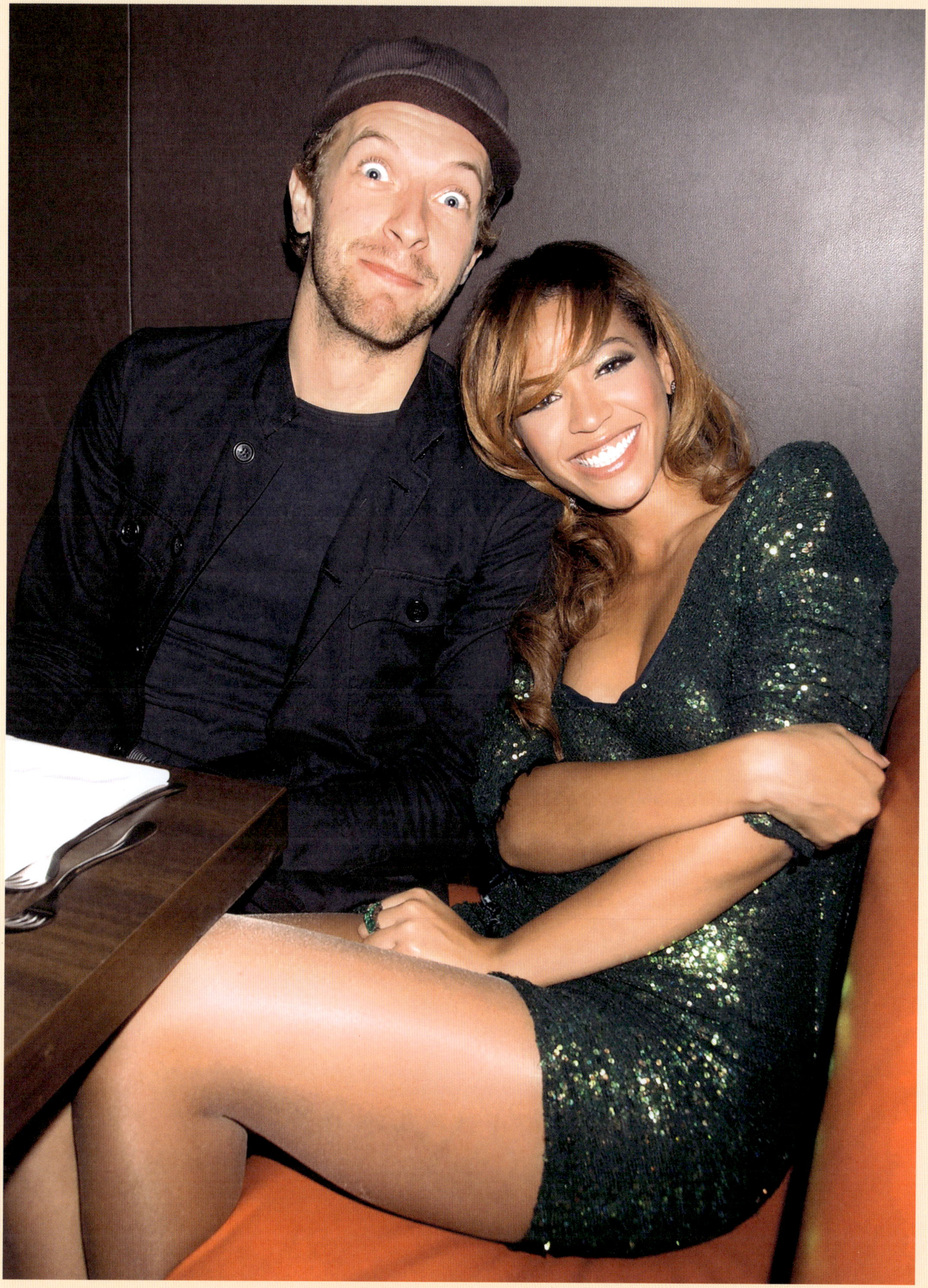

Frank Ocean, the king of alternative R&B, in 2013.

The Chicks (formerly The Dixie Chicks) during the promotion of their seventh studio album, *Taking the Long Way*, in 2006.

White emphasizes the romanticism of its writer, who mixes to perfection his harmonious voice with the modern sounds of alternative R&B, of which he is one of the leading exponents. Beyoncé's almost imperceptible voice brings an extra element of voluptuousness to the song, co-produced by Pharrell Williams.

DADDY LESSONS
(FEATURING THE DIXIE CHICKS)

(Alex Delicata, Beyoncé Knowles, Diana Gordon, Kevin Cossom, Darrell Scott/6'25)

Musicians: Beyoncé: vocals / **Natalie Maines:** vocals, acoustic guitar / **Emily Strayer:** banjo, backing vocals / **Martie Maguire:** fiddle, backing vocals / **Recording:** ?: October 2016 / **Technical team:** Producers: Beyoncé, Derek Dixie, Alex Delicata / **Beyoncé featuring the Dixie Chicks** *Daddy Lessons* **(single)** / Digital release in the USA by Parkwood Entertainment, on Beyonce.com: 2 November 2016

Some collaborations leave their mark on the history of music, just as certain events punctuate the careers of great artists. This is the case with *Daddy Lessons*, which would be a comfort to Beyoncé in her battle against the ubiquitous injustice in an America that struggled to open up to its minorities.

In October 2016, as Beyoncé invited Natalie Maines, Emily Strayer, and Martie Maguire of the trio The Dixie Chicks (since renamed The Chicks) to record with her a revised version of her *Daddy Lessons*, she also planned to perform it on 2 November on stage at the Country Music Awards, which were celebrating their 50th year. This performance would be highly significant for various reasons. First of all, The Dixie Chicks, once the undisputed queens of country music, had not played at the ceremony since 2003, when they fell from grace after Natalie Maines declared at a concert in Britain that she was ashamed President George W. Bush came from the same state as she did. The three women endured a veritable witch hunt, being banned from most country radio stations, threatened, insulted, and criticized by many country musicians. Beyoncé also invited to the 2016 ceremony Leo Pellegrino, Matt Muirhead, and David Parks of the group Too Many Zooz, who proudly proclaimed their pro-LGBT activism (the abbreviation LGBTQIA+ did not appear until later). Finally—and it should be stressed that this

PINK + WHITE
(FRANK OCEAN)

(Christopher Breaux, Pharrell Williams/3'05)

Musicians: Frank Ocean: vocals / **Beyoncé Knowles:** backing vocals / **Pharrell Williams:** programming, synthesizers / **Crystal Alforque, Charlie Bisharat, Susan Chatman, Daphne Chen, Ryan Cross, Lisa Dondlinger, Terry Glenny, Eric Gorfain, Neel Hammond, Gina Kronstadt, Marisa Kuney, Songa Lee, Serena McKinney, Grace Park, Radu Pieptea, Katie Sloan, Marcy Vaj, Ina Veli, Josefina Vergara, Amy Wickman, Chris Woods, Yelena Yegoryan:** violin / **Briana Bandy, Denise Briese, Anna Bulbrook, Alma Fernandez, Leah Katz, Stefan Smith:** viola / **Alisha Bauer, Richard Dodd, Vanessa Fairbairn-Smith, Stefanie Fife, Ira Glansbeek, Simon Huber, John Krovoza, Ginger Murphy, Geoff Osika, Rodney Wirtz, Adrienne Woods:** cello / **Eric Gorfain:** conductor / **Recording: Henson Recording Studios:** 2014 to 2016 / **Technical team: Producers:** Frank Ocean, Pharrell Williams / **Recording engineers:** Eric Caudieux, Greg Keller / **String arrangements:** Benjamin Wright, Jon Brion / **Frank Ocean** *Blonde* **(album)** / Released in the USA by Boys Don't Cry/XL Recordings: 20 August 2016 (album ref.: 862160000302, CD ref.: 862160000302)

After Californian singer Frank Ocean had written for Beyoncé the moving and effective *I Miss You*, which features on *4*, and had sung alongside her in *Superpower* in 2013, it was her turn to return the favor by playing a prestigious part in the song *Pink + White*, on *Blonde*, Ocean's second album. *Pink +*

394 COLLABORATIONS

should not even warrant a line in these pages, so unimportant is it—Beyoncé is an African-American singer. The evening of 2 November, after their appearance on stage had made a lasting impression thanks to the spectacular performance, alchemy between the artists, and absolute perfection of the ensemble of musicians, the Country Music Awards organization decided to remove the video of the show from all its websites and social media. The Dixie Chicks were subjected to a torrent of racist insults, and cowardly commentators declared en masse their opposition to the fact that a Black singer could take ownership of the country music style in that way. Faced with growing controversy, the organizers back-pedaled, reinstated the video on their various websites, and tried to explain themselves as best they could. But the damage had been done, and Beyoncé harbored a bitterness from this episode that in 2024 she would process and convert into a high-quality country album, the excellent *Cowboy Carter*. As for The Dixie Chicks, they were invited to present the 51st Country Music Awards—an invitation to which they replied with a stinging tweet, in a tone that earned Natalie Maines fame: "Unfortunately I've got a thing that night so, no."[290] The Chicks got their revenge by releasing the marvelous *Gaslighter* in 2020. Produced largely by Jack Antonoff, Taylor Swift's faithful producer, the record allowed Natalie Maines to settle scores with a fair few of her detractors. Long live The Chicks!

SHINING
(DJ KHALED FEATURING BEYONCÉ AND JAY-Z)

(Burt Bacharach, Jahron Brathwaite, Ingrid Burley, Shawn Carter, Hal David, Floyd Hills, Khaled Khaled, Beyoncé Knowles/4'43)

Musicians: DJ Khaled: rap / Beyoncé Knowles: vocals, backing vocals / Jay-Z: rap / **Recording:** We The Best Studios, Miami: 2016 / **Technical team: Producers:** DJ Khaled, Danja / **Executive producer:** Asahd Tuck Khaled / **Recording engineer:** Juan "Wize" Peña / **DJ Khaled Grateful (album)** / Available for streaming on Tidal: 13 February 2017 / Released in the USA by Epic/We The Best: 23 June 2017 (album ref.: 889854466510, CD ref.: 88985446652)

When DJ Khaled played the instrumental part of Shining to his friend Jay-Z, the latter's reaction was immediate: he moved his head in time to the song's rhythm, which convinced the producer from Florida of the quality of his work. At that point, he decided to go for broke: "I know the answer's no but if you wanna play this to your wife, man that'd be dope, but I know the answer's no!"[291] Always on the lookout for good productions to pass on to his talented wife, Jay-Z nonetheless agreed, arousing the interest of Beyoncé, who quickly accepted Shining. Most of the lyrics she sang on it were the work of PartyNextDoor, a Canadian songwriter, composer, rapper, and producer who had worked with Drake, Big Sean, and Usher. As for the instrumental part, it was built round a sample from Dionne, a song recorded by Osunlade in 2013, which itself contained a sample from Walk the Way You Talk, sung by Dionne Warwick in 1971 and written and produced by Burt Bacharach and Hal David.

FAMILY FEUD
(JAY-Z FEATURING BEYONCÉ)

(Beyoncé Knowles, Dion Wilson, Elbernita Clark, Shawn Carter/4'11)

Musicians: Jay-Z: rap / Beyoncé Knowles: backing vocals / **Recording:** ?: 2017 / **Technical team: Producer:** No I.D. / **Executive producers:** Shawn "Jay-Z" Carter, No I.D. / **Recording engineers:** Gimel "Young Guru" Keaton, Stuart White (Beyoncé's voice) / **Jay-Z 4:44 (album)** / Released in the USA by Roc Nation: 7 July 2017 (CD ref.: B0027184-02)

In December 2017, Beyoncé posted on her Instagram account a series of photographs taken behind the scenes on the shoot of the clip of Family Feud, whose release as a single was scheduled for the following 26 January. It was the third track taken from the new album from Jay-Z, 4:44, released on 7 July 2017. Although the rapper twisted the knife in the wound by mentioning the renowned Becky, presumed wrecker of the relationship, whose acts were described at length in Sorry, on Lemonade, he nevertheless extolled his unconditional faithfulness to his wife Beyoncé, taking the opportunity to emphasize their status as a "power couple," a description often applied to them by the press. The proof lay in this more than explicit line, which doubtless led the couple's fans to wonder about their own financial situation: What's better than one billionaire? Two. Jay-Z was of course referring to their immense fortunes which, combined, were valued at more than a billion dollars. However, Beyoncé's part in the song is minor, for she confines herself to some backing vocals inspired by the main motif of the song Ha-Ya (Eternal Life), sung by The Clark Sisters in 1980.

Beyoncé fans were determined to settle scores with the mysterious Becky.

French producer Willy William, author of *Mi Gente*, which Beyoncé would transform into a global hit.

SINGLE

MI GENTE
(J BALVIN, WILLY WILLIAM FEATURING BEYONCÉ)

(Alejandro Ramírez, Andres David Restrepo Echavarría, Ashadally Adam, Beyoncé Knowles-Carter, José Álvaro Osorio Balvin, Mohombi Nzasi Moupondo, Terius "The-Dream" Nash, Willy William/3'29)

Musicians: Beyoncé Knowles: vocals, backing vocals / J Balvin: vocals / Willy William: vocals / Blue Ivy Carter: spoken voice / **Recording:** Jungle City Studios, New York: 2017 / **Technical team: Producers:** Jean Rodríguez, Beyoncé Knowles, Willy William / **Recording engineer:** Stuart White / **Assistant recording engineer:** Ramon Rivas / **Single:** Digital release by Scorpio Music/Universal Music Latin/Republic Records/Columbia/Parkwood Entertainment: 28 September 2017

Here is a song that underwent several incarnations before becoming one of the high points of the concerts Beyoncé gave at the Coachella Valley Music and Arts Festival on 14 and 21 April 2018. It was created in France in April 2017, sung by its writer, the producer Willy William, and distributed by Scorpio Music. Wanting to benefit from the interest in *Despacito*—the single by Luis Fonsi and Daddy Yankee which was released in January and would become the summer hit of 2017—Rebecca Leon at Universal Music Latin, Scorpio Music's distributor, suggested to J Balvin that a remix be made, playing on the Hispanic flavor of the piece, soon to be enhanced by lyrics in English and Spanish. Once *Voodoo Song* had been transformed into *Mi Gente*, which sounded like a potential reggaeton hit in tune with the times, all the song lacked was a first-rank guest artist. The logical choice was the world's greatest star: Beyoncé. Motivated largely by the fact that her young daughter Blue Ivy loved the song, Beyoncé agreed to take part in the venture, calling on Jean Rodríguez, Luis Fonsi's brother, for help with pronunciation of the Spanish lyrics. On 28 September, when the song was released, Beyoncé posted the following message on Instagram: "I am donating my proceeds from this song to hurricane relief charities for Puerto Rico, Mexico, and the other affected Caribbean islands."[292] She wanted to do something following the devastating passage of hurricanes Harvey and Maria. The song was accompanied by a clip consisting of images of anonymous people and celebrities dancing to it, thus sharing in its success.

HEADPHONES AT THE READY

When, at 3'07 in *Mi Gente*, Beyoncé asks: "Azul, are you with me?" she is addressing her young daughter Blue Ivy (*azul* means "blue" in Spanish). The little girl answers in person at 3'11: "Ho, yes I am."

BEYONCÉ: ALL THE SONGS 397

THE CARTERS

ALBUM

Everything Is Love

Summer • Apeshit • Boss • Nice • 713 • Friends • Heard About Us • Black Effect • Lovehappy

Made available for streaming on Tidal by Parkwood Entertainment/Roc Nation/S.C. Enterprises: 16 June 2018
Released for streaming by Parkwood Entertainment/Roc Nation/S.C. Enterprises: 18 June 2018
Released in the USA by Parkwood Entertainment/Roc Nation/S.C. Enterprises: 6 July 2018
(album ref.: ROC3374, CD ref.: ROC337)
Best chart ranking in the USA: 2

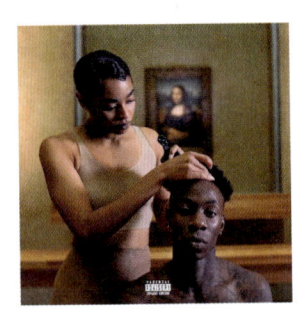

Having left behind their problems in the past, the Carters were absolutely determined to retain their crown.

THE CARTERS IN PARIS

After the stormy times of the past few years, the Carters' married life became peaceful once more. Beyoncé and Jay-Z rediscovered the loving tranquility of their young years, yet were nonetheless busy as parents after, on 13 June 2017, the twins Sir and Ru were born. The news had created a stir on 1 February when the future mother posted a photograph of herself, pregnant, taken by the American artist Awol Erizku. In March 2018, after several months spent caring for her babies, Beyoncé announced the On the Run II Tour, which would once more allow fans to see Beyoncé and Jay-Z together on the greatest stages in Europe and North America, as well as South Africa—for the tour was scheduled to finish the following 2 December at the FNB Stadium in Johannesburg. Always generous with making announcements, Beyoncé got herself talked about well before the start of this series of concerts. Having declared in January 2017 that she would take part in the Coachella Valley Music and Arts Festival in April, Beyoncé eventually had to give up the idea and make way for Lady Gaga, in order to rest and end her pregnancy in safety. Determined to make her return, on 3 January 2018 she was announced as one of the three artists who had top billing at that year's festival, along with The Weeknd and Eminem.

An audience of 125,000 for Beychella

The Coachella festival, popular with stars of all kinds, was an important occasion for Beyoncé, so she did everything imaginable to make this event—held, according to tradition, over two consecutive weekends (in this case, 14 and 21 April 2018 for Queen Bey)—unforgettable for her audience. On the big day, she was surrounded by a hundred dancers and a band of several dozen musicians performing with her, one after the other, her greatest hits—*Crazy in Love, Run the World (Girls), Single Ladies (Put a Ring on It)*—and her most effective recent songs (*Mi Gente, Formation*), all at a relentless pace, with choreography by Chris Grant and JaQuel Knight. "I had a clear vision for Coachella," Beyoncé said. "I was so specific because I'd seen it, I'd heard it, and it was already written inside of me."[293] Accompanied successively on stage by Kelly Rowland, Michelle Williams, her sister Solange, and her husband Jay-Z, Beyoncé performed two unforgettable concerts, which left their mark on the history of pop music and were even privileged to be renamed "Beychella" by Beyoncé's friend DJ Khaled.

In the sealed private rooms of the U Arena

Once the two concerts were over, Beyoncé could devote herself to the On the Run II Tour, scheduled to start on 6 June. With this in mind the Carters flew to Paris, where they had reserved the U Arena—which would become the Paris La Défense Arena in June 2018—in the Parisian suburb of Nanterre, to rehearse the show. Inaugurated on 16 October 2017 with a provisional name, the building was then the biggest venue in Europe. A rugby stadium that was home to the Racing 92 club, it could be converted for musical events, providing 40,000 seats for a concert, and seemed perfectly suited to the gigantic scale of the tour of Beyoncé and Jay-Z, who set up there in May 2018. Aside from the preparations for the show, in between two rehearsals the two artists took advantage of their stay to embark on something they had envisaged for a long time: their first album as a duo. They had

2018

400 EVERYTHING IS LOVE

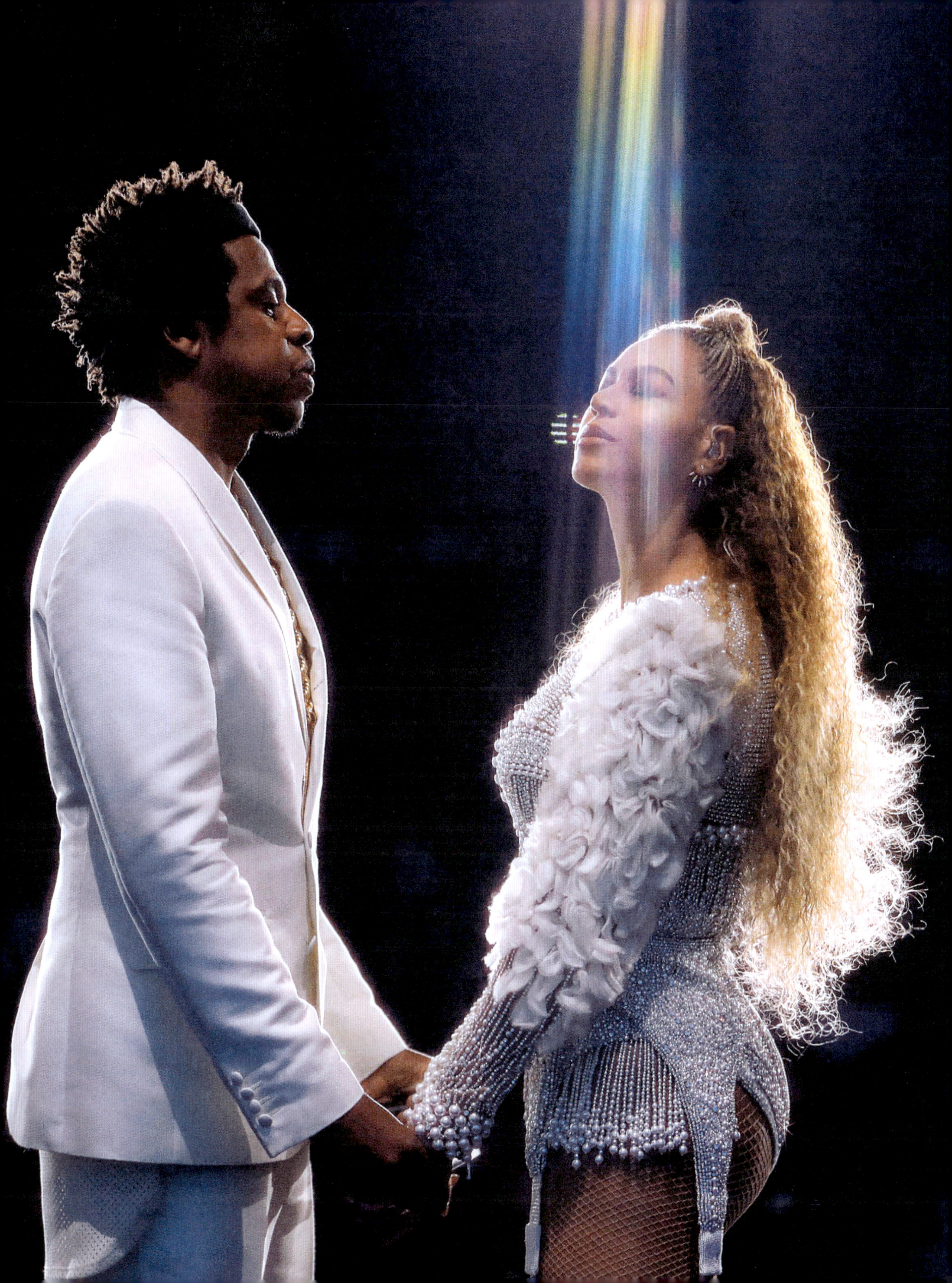

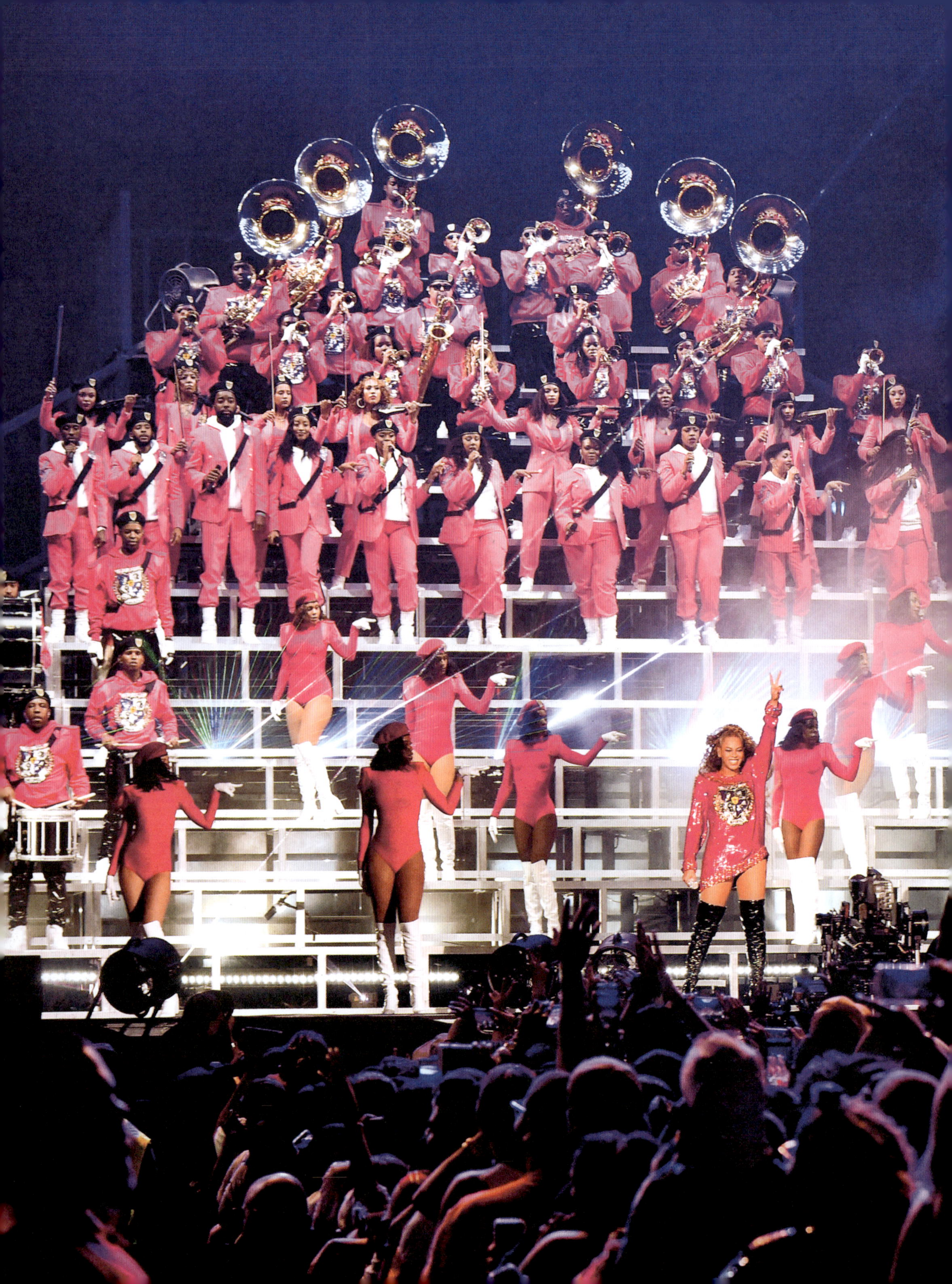

Beyoncé left her mark on the Coachella Festival with the sheer scale of her show and her unforgettable performance.

embarked on the project some time before their departure for France, following a meeting between Jay-Z and his friend the producer Marcello "Cool" Antonio Valenzano, one half of the duo Cool & Dre (the other half being Andre "Dre" Christopher Lyon). Cool's work with Fat Joe, The Game, and Lil Wayne had caught Jay-Z's attention; he invited the producer to Los Angeles to play him his latest work. Cool played the instrumental part of *Salud!*, and Jay-Z fell under the spell of this beat with its trap sounds. In return, he had Cool listen to some demos of songs in which he and Beyoncé blended their voices. When the two artists parted that day, Jay-Z asked his guest to remain available in anticipation of a future collaboration. In May 2018, as his employer was preparing to leave for Europe, Gimel "Young Guru" Keaton, Jay-Z's faithful recording engineer, suggested they take Cool & Dre with them in order to take advantage of rehearsal sessions to record a few ideas for songs. What was supposed to last only a few days went on for several weeks, the time needed to create the Carters' first album.

On the road to London

Initially installed in a Paris hotel room, Cool & Dre were quickly invited to move into one of the private rooms in the U Arena. With an open view onto the stage where Jay-Z and Beyoncé were rehearsing, the two producers worked tirelessly to come up with several songs, including *Summer*, *713*, and *Black Effect*. Beyoncé and Jay-Z joined them between rehearsal sessions to guide them in their work and record a few lines of vocals or rap. "The smartest thing we did was take our ass to that motherfucking arena and create," Dre said. "Us being there was key. [Beyoncé and Jay-Z] would give us direction: 'Dre, go in the vocal booth. Say this, sing this.' We immediately get it done."[294] After three weeks of rehearsals, the team decamped to Cardiff, Wales, where the tour was to start on 6 June. For a week, while the Carters were putting the finishing

BEYONCÉ: ALL THE SONGS   403

The Carters on stage at NRG Stadium in Houston, 16 September 2018.

touches to their show, Cool & Dre fine-tuned their songs. They were joined by another duo of composers and producers: Nova Wav, consisting of Brittany "Chi" Coney and Denisia "Blu June" Andrews. After having worked for Rihanna (*Loveeeeeee Song* in 2012), Ariana Grande (*Best Mistake* in 2014), and Britney Spears (*Hard to Forget Ya* in 2016), the two women, whom Jay-Z had met through Hit-Boy (who had produced *Ni**as in Paris* for him and Kanye West in 2011), were a safe pair of hands on the pop and hip-hop scenes. Once the tour was underway, production of the album went ahead, and was completed backstage at the London Stadium, where Beyoncé and Jay-Z performed on 15 and 16 June. "An hour and a half before showtime," Dre explained, "Bey and Jay were still cutting up vocals. Three hours later it was released to the world. There are no rules when it comes to those two."[295] Indeed, it was at the London concert on 16 June that the immediate release of *Everything Is Love* was announced. After a showing of a clip of the song *Apeshit*—shot in the corridors of the Louvre in Paris—on a giant screen, the two announced to the astounded audience, "New album out," causing hysteria among the fans, as amateur videos shot by audience members show. A step ahead of the media and their own fan base, the two artists surprised and delighted their hordes of admirers. *Everything Is Love* was initially available for streaming, then for download on Tidal on 16 June 2018, before being circulated more widely in the following days. However, the physical version of the album, enhanced by a sleeve showing two of the couple's dancers, Jasmine Harper and Nicholas "Slick" Stewart, posing in front of Leonardo da Vinci's *Mona Lisa*, would have to wait until 6 July 2018.

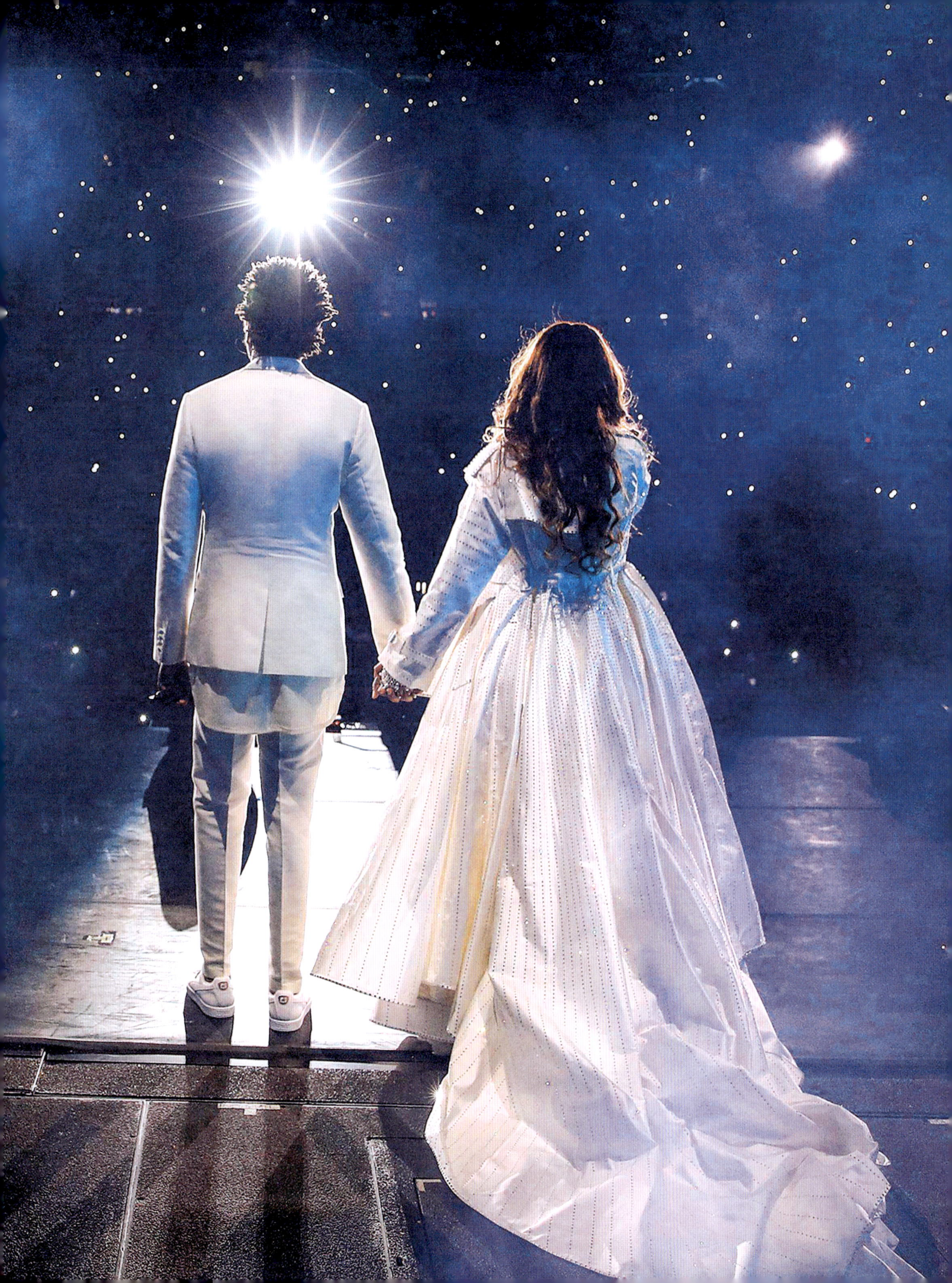

SUMMER

(Andre Christopher Lyon, Beyoncé, Homer Steinweiss, James Fauntleroy II, Leon Michels, Marcello Valenzano, Michael Herard, Shawn Carter, Thomas Brenneck/4'45)

Musicians: Beyoncé: vocals, backing vocals / **Jay-Z:** rap / **Anthony Wilmot:** vocals / **Rorystonelove:** vocals / **Recording:** U Arena, Nanterre: May 2018 / The Church Studios, London: June 2018 / **Technical team: Producers:** Beyoncé, Cool & Dre, Jay-Z, El Michels Affair / **Executive producers:** Beyoncé, Jay-Z / **Recording engineers:** Stuart White, Gimel "Young Guru" Keaton

In 2017 the multi-talented producer and musician Leon Michels recorded (with two members of his group El Michels Affair—the drummer Homer Steinweiss and the guitarist and bass guitarist Thomas Brenneck) a series of instrumental tracks to send to American hip-hop producers, who were always looking for new samples to use for their clients. Among these recordings was a soul gem, which caught the keen ear of Mike Herard, artistic director at Shady Records, Eminem's label. Herard hastened to send this sound, worthy of an instrumental by Curtis Mayfield, to Cool & Dre, two producers who had contributed greatly to the success of 50 Cent, a superstar with Shady/Aftermath—a combination of Shady Records and Dr. Dre's label, Aftermath Entertainment. In May 2008, Leon Michels got a call from Cool & Dre, who told him that one of his instrumental parts had been retained for a project that was underway. "We used one of your samples," the producers told him. "It's for a giant artist. We can't tell you who it is. You have to approve it now. And you can't hear it, but it's going to change your life. It's coming out in two weeks."[296] The song in question, *Summer*, was therefore in large part built around this sequence borrowed from Leon Michels and his musicians. The inspiration for its general tone came to Cool & Dre during the Paris sessions, when they could see from their recording studio, set up in one of the private rooms at the U Arena, the giant screen at the back of the stage on which were shown images of the Carters filming themselves on a beach with a Super 8 camera, more in love than ever. It was Beyoncé herself who decided to add strings to the song, and *Summer* would be performed in concerts during the On the Run II Tour: in Chicago on 11 August and in Detroit on 13 August 2018.

FOR CARTER ADDICTS

This was not the first time Leon Michels had worked with Jay-Z. In 2007 the rapper from New York had used a sample from the song *Make the Road by Walking* by the group Menahan Street Band, whose members included…Leon Michels, Thomas Brenneck, and Homer Steinweiss.

SINGLE
APESHIT

(Beyoncé, Kiari Kendrell Cephus, Pharrell Williams, Quavious Keyate Marshall, Shawn Carter/4'26)

Musicians: Beyoncé: vocals, rap, backing vocals / **Jay-Z:** rap / **Offset:** rap / **Quavo:** rap / **Recording:** U Arena, Nanterre: May 2018 / **Technical team: Producers:** Pharrell Williams, Beyoncé, Jay-Z, Stuart White / **Executive producers:** Beyoncé, Jay-Z / **Recording engineers:** Stuart White, Gimel "Young Guru" Keaton / **Single:** Digital release by Parkwood Entertainment/Roc Nation: 16 June 2018 / **Best chart ranking in the USA:** 13

When working in the studio with the prestigious producer Pharrell Williams, you never know what will become of the song you just recorded. This was the experience of the artist Quavo, rapper, producer, standard-bearer of trap music, and founder—with his partners Takeoff and Offset—of the group Migos. While working with Williams, Quavo wrote two songs with him: first *Stir Fry*, then *Apeshit*—all in the space of an hour. Williams was the beat-maker in charge of the instrumental part, while Quavo recorded his flow on both tracks. The session over, Quavo left the premises, leaving the two pieces with Williams who, as an alchemist of sound, was to take charge of producing and mixing the songs. Once he had finished the job, Williams sent the mix of *Stir Fry* to Quavo, who then reworked it with his Migos associates to include it on their third album, *Culture II*, due to be released in January 2018. As for *Apeshit*, Quavo simply forgot about it, remembering it only when Pharrell Williams informed him that it had been chosen for a big project, namely, the Carters' first album. If the only single from *Everything Is Love* left an impression on people's minds, it was not because of its hard-hitting trap style and numerous profanities, but rather because of its iconic clip, made by Ricky Saiz in the corridors of the Louvre in Paris. It shows Beyoncé, Jay-Z, and their dancers wandering through the world's biggest museum and posing in front of the legendary works it contains, such as *The Winged Victory of Samothrace*, Jacques-Louis David's *The Coronation of Napoleon*, Théodore Géricault's *The Raft of the Medusa*, and Leonardo da Vinci's *Mona Lisa*. The video of *Apeshit* has attained such legendary status that, since July 2018, the Louvre has offered visitors a circuit entitled "In the Footsteps of Beyoncé and Jay-Z," which retraces the route taken by the two stars.

Quavo, of the group Migos, at the Onyx nightclub in Atlanta, 5 April 2021.

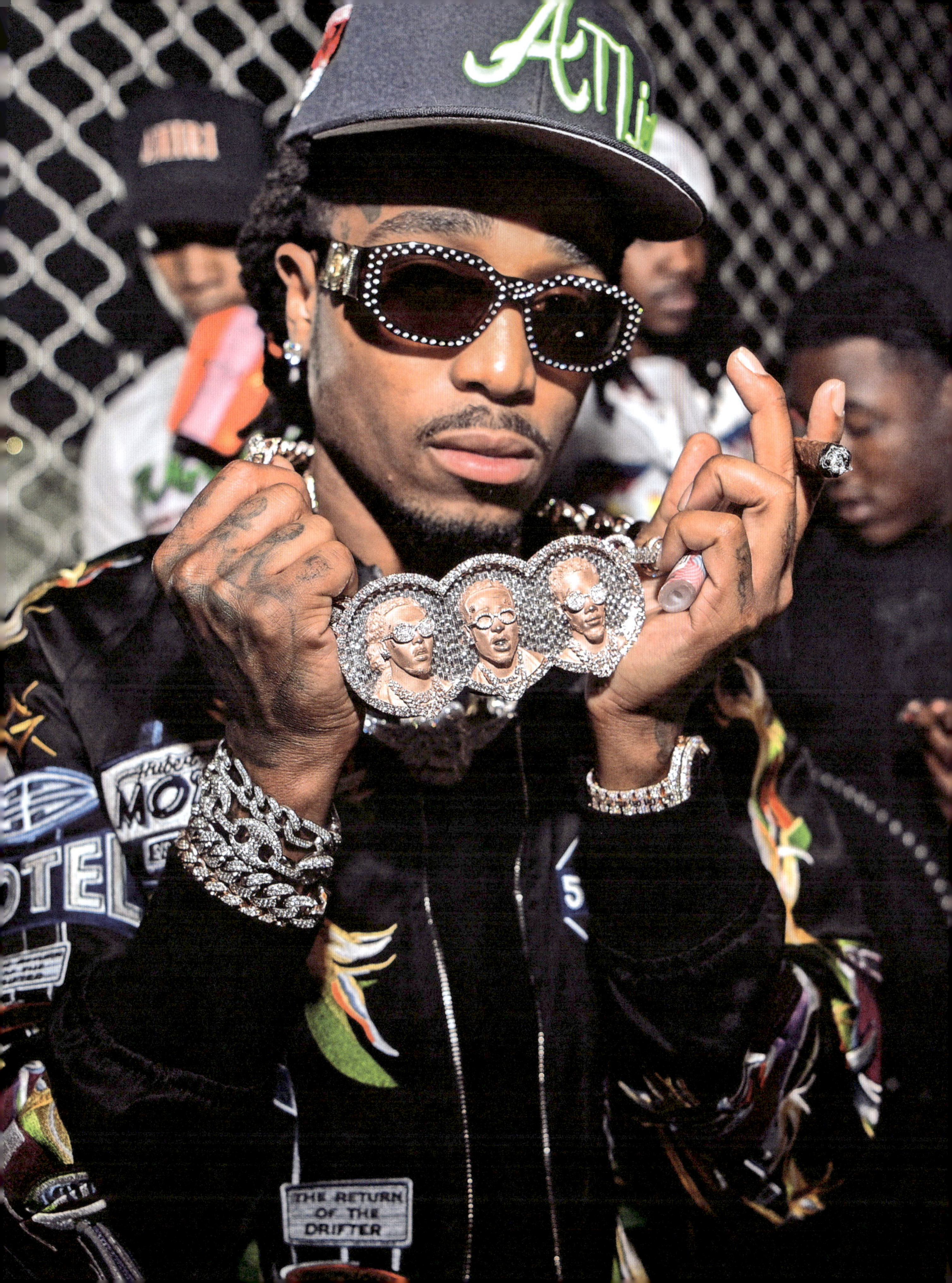
THE RETURN
OF THE
DRIFTER

The rapper Ty Dolla $ign in Los Angeles, 17 September 2017.

BOSS

(Beyoncé, Dernst "D'Mile" Emile II, Shawn Carter, Tyrone "Ty Dolla $ign" Griffin Jr/4'05)

Musicians: Beyoncé: vocals, backing vocals / Jay-Z: rap / Blue Ivy Carter: spoken voice / Ty Dolla $ign: backing vocals / **Recording:** U Arena, Nanterre: May 2018 / **Technical team:** Producers: Beyoncé, D'Mile, Jay-Z, Derek Dixie, MeLo-X, Mike Dean, Stuart White / **Executive producers:** Beyoncé, Jay-Z / **Recording engineers:** Stuart White, Gimel "Young Guru" Keaton

Boss was written and produced by the producer Dernst "D'Mile" Emile II and the rapper Ty Dolla $ign. A virtuoso multi-instrumentalist, D'Mile became, over the years, one of the most influential American producers, working for artists such as Bruno Mars, Mary J. Blige, T-Pain, H.E.R., and Janet Jackson. When he and Ty Dolla $ign wrote the instrumental part of *Boss*, however, they did not know the song would meet such a fate, it being originally destined for Rihanna. "We wrote it, and I think Beyoncé heard it from our publisher," D'Mile explained. "She loved it, and then she kept it for a while and held it for the right time to come out."[297] During the production of *Everything Is Love*, two other artists had a hand in the song: MeLo-X, who reworked the rhythmic programming and added brass tracks produced using a software program, then Mike Dean, a recording engineer who had made his name by working alongside Kanye West and having co-written and co-produced *Love Drought*, on *Lemonade*, for Beyoncé. But D'Mile, the original writer of the song, would know nothing of this development process. "I had no idea. I was getting texts: this sounds like you. I was like, 'What are you talking about?' When people hit me up, that's when I found out."[294]

NICE

(Beyoncé, Brittany Coney, Denisia Andrews, Pharrell Williams, Shawn Carter/3'53)

Musicians: Beyoncé: vocals, backing vocals / Jay-Z: rap / Pharrell Williams: rap, vocals / **Recording:** U Arena, Nanterre: May 2018 / The Church Studios, London: June 2018 / **Technical team:** Producers: Pharrell Williams, Beyoncé, Jay-Z / **Executive producers:** Beyoncé, Jay-Z / **Recording engineers:** Stuart White, Gimel "Young Guru" Keaton

Co-produced by the unavoidable Pharrell Williams, *Nice* allowed Beyoncé to settle scores with her detractors, notably those in the music industry who reproached her for having reserved the release of *Lemonade*, in April 2016, for the streaming and downloading platform Tidal, of which she was one of the shareholders. Over a rap rhythm, enhanced with the voice of Williams himself, the song reveals an artist who is wild, adult, and angry—far from the accommodating R&B singer of times past. Although Williams was at the controls, the chief recording engineer for the song—indeed for the whole album—was Gimel "Young Guru" Keaton. A faithful associate of Jay-Z, in 2009 Young Guru described, on the website soundonsound.com, the way his friend worked on his lyrics and prepared his recording sessions: "Jay doesn't write his ideas down, he does everything in his head. But because he has eight different jobs in one day and there are many distractions, to help him memorize an idea he'll pull out his laptop and will recite it into GarageBand, without worrying about the quality or background noise. It's like a sketchpad, he's just reciting things into it, so he won't lose them. And then he's onto the next thing […] I've given him Dictaphones and things like that, and he loses them—but he's not going to lose his computer!"[298]

408 EVERYTHING IS LOVE

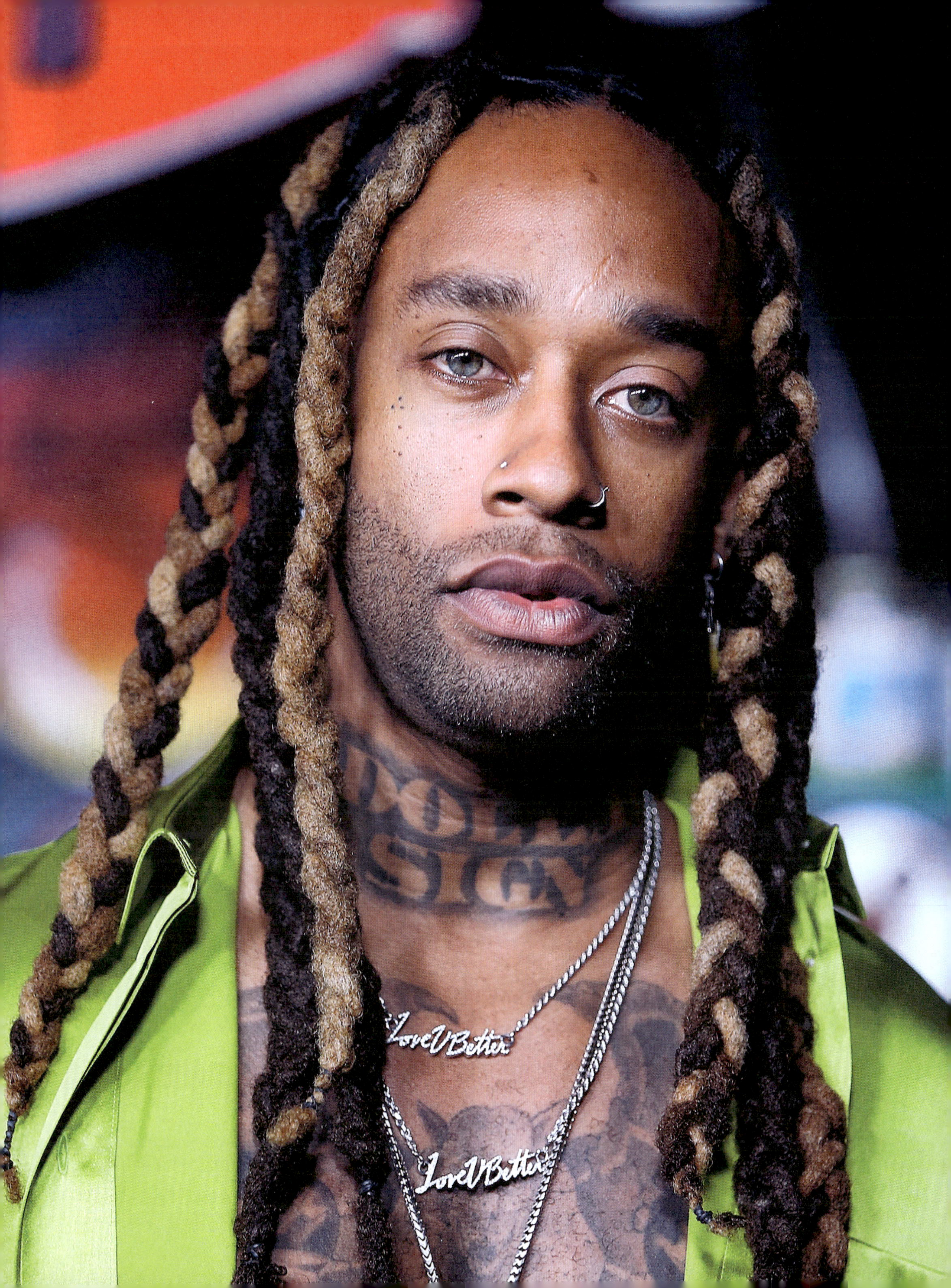

713

(Andre Christopher Lyon, Beyoncé, Marcello Valenzano, Rayshon Cobbs Jr, Shawn Carter/3'13)

Musicians: Jay-Z: rap / **Beyoncé:** vocals, backing vocals / **Recording:** U Arena, Nanterre: May 2018 / **Technical team: Producers:** Beyoncé, Cool & Dre, Jay-Z, 808-Ray, Fred Ball / **Executive producers:** Beyoncé, Jay-Z / **Recording engineers:** Stuart White, Gimel "Young Guru" Keaton

When Beyoncé asked Cool & Dre to think about a hip-hop song celebrating her love story with Jay-Z, it was with *I'll Be There for You/You're All I Need to Get By*, an iconic single by the duo Mary J. Blige/Method Man, released in 1995, in mind. The two producers then came up with an instrumental part made with a young artist going by the name of 808-Ray, whom they had found on the Soundcloud platform some time earlier. When the three musicians produced the song, they had aimed to make a West Coast track like those Dr. Dre produced at the end of the 1990s. To do that, what could be better than to quote from *Still D.R.E.*, the Doctor's most famous hit, which featured on his masterpiece *2001*, released in 1999? All the more since the lyrics of *Still D.R.E.* had been written in their entirety by Jay-Z himself—both Snoop Dogg's parts and Dr. Dre's. Accordingly, Andre "Dre" Christopher Lyon envisaged a quotation everyone could agree on. "I was like, 'What if we come with the "I'm representin' for the hustlers all across the world?'" You know Jay-Z wrote that shit for Dr. Dre? Let's pitch the idea to him and see if Beyoncé will do it for *713*."[299] Before Beyoncé even recorded her voice in the song, Jay-Z had recorded all his rap parts for it, opening up as never before about his meeting, in the early 2000s, the woman who would become his wife and the mother of his children. It was only after having heard her husband's touching lyrics that, in the improvised studio at the U Arena, Beyoncé would add her vocal tracks to the piece, whose title, *713*, is a nod to the telephone code for Houston and the surrounding area.

The duo Cool & Dre, architects of the sound of *Everything Is Love*.

Jay-Z and his closest friends and associates, mentioned in *Friends*: Emory Jones (left) and Tyran "Ty Ty" Smith.

FRIENDS

(Amir "Cash" Esmailian, Beyoncé, Brittany Coney, Denisia Andrews, Jahaan Sweet, Matthew Samuels, Navraj Goraya, Rupert Thomas Jr, Shawn Carter, Tavor Javon Holins/5'45)

Musicians: Beyoncé: vocals, backing vocals / **Jay-Z:** rap /
Recording: Kings Landing Studios West, Los Angeles: 2018 /
Technical team: Producers: Beyoncé, Jahaan Sweet, Jay-Z, Nav, Sevn Thomas, Fred Ball / **Executive producers:** Beyoncé, Jay-Z /
Recording engineers: Stuart White, Gimel "Young Guru" Keaton

By reason of its theme—Jay-Z's total devotion to his friends—*Friends* is unquestionably the most poignant song on the album. On this occasion, the rapper casts his wife into the shade—even though she is omnipresent in the song—mentioning, one by one, those he considers his real friends, and assuring the listener of his total loyalty to them. Jay-Z's long-standing friends are mentioned in turn: Tyran "Ty Ty" Smith, co-founder of Roc Nation; Emory Jones, whom Jay-Z had helped on his release from jail by offering him a job with his ready-to-wear company Roc Apparel Group; Jay Brown, co-founder and chairman of the board of Roc Nation, and Kawanna Brown, his wife; Juan "OG" Perez, head of Roc Nation Sports, and Desiree, his wife, head of operations at Roc Nation; Chaka Pilgrim, in charge of the film and television branch of Shawn Carter Enterprises; and finally Lawrence "Law" Parker, artistic director of Roc Nation. After years of loyalty to Shawn Carter, these faithful friends were rewarded with a name check in this very moving song, *Friends*.

HEARD ABOUT US

(Anderson "Vinylz" Hernandez, Beyoncé, Jahaan Sweet, Matthew Samuels, Nija Charles, Ramon "!llmind" Ibanga Jr, Shawn Carter/3'10)

Musicians: Beyoncé: vocals, backing vocals / **Jay-Z:** rap /
Recording: U Arena, Nanterre, France: May 2018 / **Technical team: Producers:** Beyoncé, Boi-1da, !llmind, Jahaan Sweet, Jay-Z, Vinylz, Fred Ball / **Executive producers:** Beyoncé, Jay-Z /
Recording engineers: Stuart White, Gimel "Young Guru" Keaton

Invited to Paris for the recording sessions of *Everything Is Love* at the U Arena in May 2018, the producers Boi-1da and !llmind—who had been working together for some years, notably on Drake's mixtape *If You're Reading This It's Too Late*, released in 2015—joined Cool & Dre with one goal: to produce the best album possible for their employers Jay-Z and Beyoncé. !llmind—real name Ramon Ibanga Jr—explained his way of working with Matthew Jehu Samuels, aka Boi-1da: "I'll send him melodies; he'll send me drums; we'll go back and forth. That track was just another collaboration amongst probably 30 or 40 we have together that exist right now."[294]

So, after Cool & Dre and Nova Wav, here at the Carters' service was a new ace duo who would offer them the surprising *Heard About Us*, a piece that broke the linear nature of the album, in which the trap style had hitherto been omnipresent, as !llmind explained: "It's cool because the *Heard About Us* record that I did comes in as track seven. On the album it kind of changes the tempo a little, and it's got a nice pop feel to it."[300] Later enhanced with overdubs by Jahaan Sweet and Vinylz, the song brought a little freshness to the sequence of tracks on *Everything Is Love*.

Brittany "Chi" Coney (left) and Denisia "Blu June" Andrews, who made up the duo Nova Wav.

BLACK EFFECT

(Alexander Smith, Andre Christopher Lyon, Beyoncé, Brittany Coney, Denisia Andrews, Marcello Valenzano, Rayshon Cobbs Jr, Shawn Carter/5'15)

Musicians: Beyoncé: vocals, backing vocals / **Jay-Z:** rap / **Dr Lenora Antoinette Stines:** spoken voice / **Recording:** Kings Landing Studios West, Los Angeles: 2018 / **Technical team: Producers:** Beyoncé, Cool & Dre, Jay-Z / **Executive producers:** Beyoncé, Jay-Z / **Recording engineers:** Stuart White, Gimel "Young Guru" Keaton

When they flew to Paris in May 2018, Cool & Dre took with them a few instrumental parts to play to Jay-Z and Beyoncé. Among these was the one that would be used for *Black Effect*, a manifesto for the defense of the African-American community—a cause dear to the two artists' hearts. The co-writers of the song's lyrics, Brittany "Chi" Coney and Denisia "Blu June" Andrews—the duo Nova Wav—were honored to tackle this important theme, for they themselves felt affected by the injustices that were inflicted on their community. "We understand each other's struggles," Andrews explained. "I understand what they mean when they're like hands up, don't shoot. I'm just a Black woman or Black man walking across the street. I did nothing wrong. We understand those struggles, so it's easy to understand when I walk in the store and you're looking at me and you think I'm stealing but I got more money in my pocket than you do. I think it's a natural flow of things, we understand everything that they were speaking about and everything that they wanted to say."[301] Jay-Z told Cool & Dre, who had worked on the instrumental part in Miami before their departure, that he wanted a sample containing some vocals in the song. Their friend and regular work partner, the producer Smitty Beatz, as a professional "digger," would be given the task of finding the rare gem. "He's great at finding samples," said Dre. "He digs all day. I was like, 'yo, you got anything in your stash with someone singing some pain shit?'"[299] With this instruction in mind, Smitty Beatz supplied a sample from *Broken Strings*, released by the Japanese rock group Flower Travellin' Band in 1973. Although the original instrumental part had a hip-hop rhythm, at Jay-Z's request 808-Ray, who worked with Cool & Dre, replaced it with a more trap beat. As for the song's introduction, it contained a monologue by the Jamaican narrator and choreographer Dr. Lenora Antoinette Stines.

Initially recruited by the Carters in March 2018 to provide them with dancers for a promotional clip for *Everything Is Love*, Stines took part in the shoot, providing a monologue on her vision of love; her voice was recorded to be incorporated into the video. Astonished to discover that her input had been used for the song *Black Effect*—and allegedly without her consent (the agreement she had signed regarded only the clip)—the 67-year-old artist took legal action against Beyoncé and Jay-Z, demanding damages, a credit as a co-author of the song, and reimbursement of her legal costs. An agreement was probably reached between the two parties, since no outcome of the affair was subsequently revealed.

LOVEHAPPY

(Beyoncé, Brittany Coney, David Andrew Sitek, Denisia Andrews, Nija Charles, Shawn Carter/3'49)

Musicians: Beyoncé: vocals, backing vocals / **Jay-Z:** rap / **Recording:** U Arena, Nanterre: May 2018 / **Technical team: Producers:** Beyoncé, David Andrew Sitek, Jay-Z, Nova Wav / **Executive producers:** Beyoncé, Jay-Z / **Recording engineers:** Stuart White, Gimel "Young Guru" Keaton

After so many conjugal torments revealed in minute detail on *Lemonade*, but also on *4:44*, an album released by Jay-Z in 2017 (the rapper admitted his wrongdoing and movingly made his apologies in the title track), it seemed that these troubles were now part of the past for the Carters, and *Lovehappy* was there to bear witness to this. With its multiple samples borrowed here and there (*Victory Is Certain* by APC, *Love of my Life (An Ode to Hip Hop)* by Erykah Badu and Common, and *The Jam* by Graham Central Station), the song reconnected with a traditional hip-hop that fans would appreciate from the outset. "It's about surviving, going through tumultuous situations but coming out on the bright side of it," explained Denisia Andrews of the duo Nova Wav, who co-wrote the lyrics. "That's what love is."[294] Although the hatchet was now definitively buried, Beyoncé nevertheless declared several times in interviews that her husband would not get a second chance, and although she was able to forgive, on the other hand forgetting was beyond her capabilities. Let everyone take it as read!

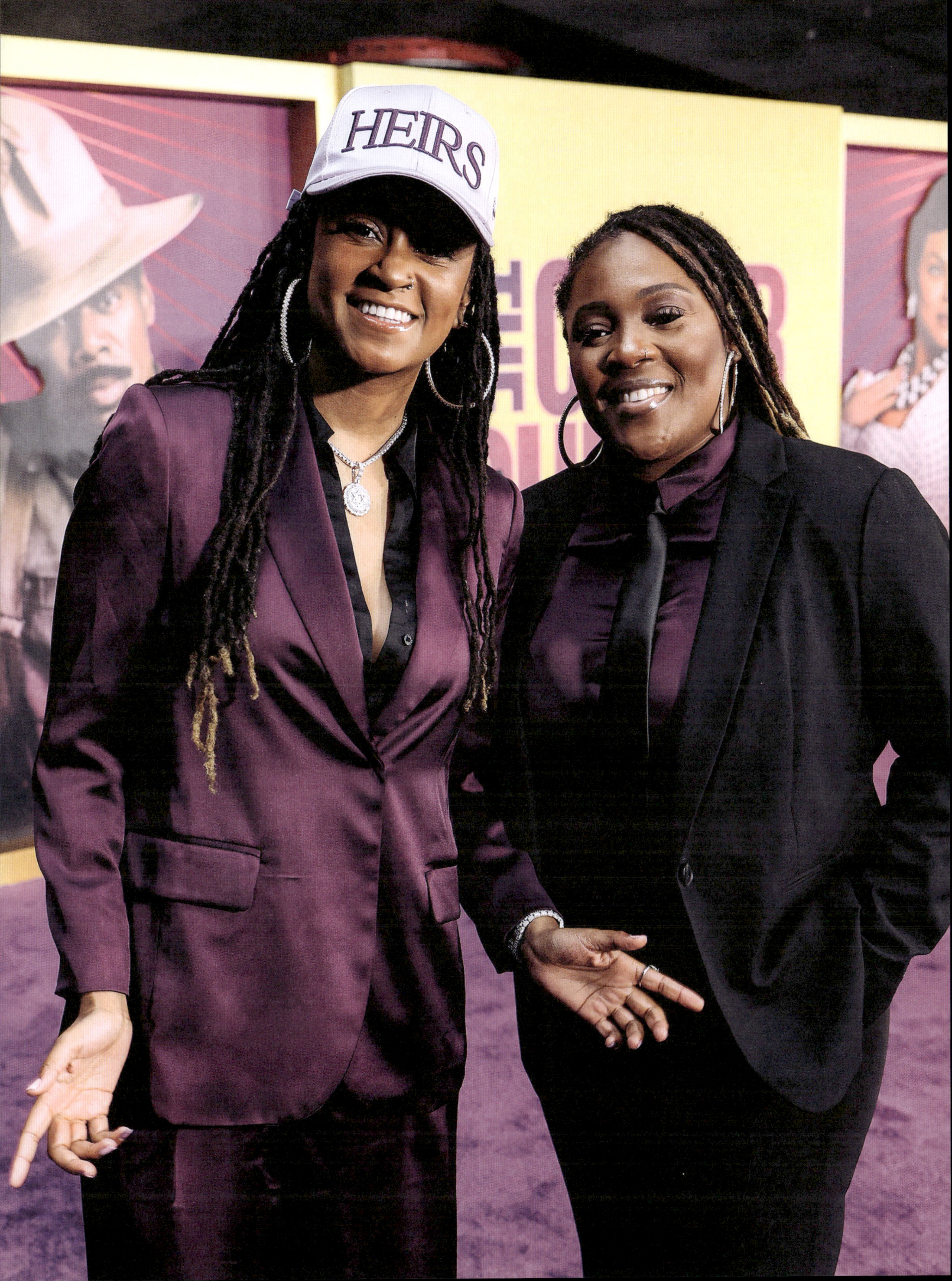
HEIRS

Ed Sheeran and Beyoncé during Stevie Wonder: Songs in the Key of Life—An All-Star Grammy Salute, at the Nokia Theatre in Los Angeles, 10 February 2015.

SINGLE

PERFECT DUET
(ED SHEERAN AND BEYONCÉ)

(Ed Sheeran, Beyoncé/4'19)

Musicians
Ed Sheeran: vocals, acoustic guitar
Beyoncé: vocals
John Tilley: organ, piano

Recording
Abbey Road, London: 2016
?: September 2017

Technical team
Producers: Ed Sheeran, Will Hicks, Benny Blanco
Recording engineers: Chris Sclafani, Joe Rubel, Stuart White
Assistant recording engineers: George Oulton, Jack Fairbrother, Johnny Solway, Matt Jones, Paul Pritchard

Perfect Duet (single)
Digital release by Atlantic/Asylum Records: 1 December 2017

Genesis

Even though it went to the top of the charts the world over on its release as a single in September 2017, the ballad *Perfect*, written by the Brit Ed Sheeran, was somewhat eclipsed by the (even more) colossal success of another of his hits: *Shape of You*, released the previous January, was unquestionably the greatest hit of 2017. Determined not to allow his tune to be buried so quickly, the singer and acoustic guitarist suggested to Beyoncé that she accompany him in the song, to re-release it in December as a duet, logically renamed *Perfect Duet*. It should be pointed out that the two artists knew and admired each other, for they had sung together on stage twice in 2015: the first time at the Global Citizen Festival, where they performed *Drunk in Love*, and the second at a concert in homage to Stevie Wonder, where they revisited together his legendary reggae hit released in 1980, *Master Blaster (Jammin')*. "Rehearsing with her, hearing her sing up close is just a thing to marvel," Sheeran said. "Even if my career ended tomorrow, I'll still be able to tell my grandkids that I got to sing with Beyoncé."[302]

Production

Ed Sheeran and Beyoncé started working on *Perfect Duet* in May 2017, before the latter gave birth to her twins, Sir and Rumi, in June. The song was therefore completed the following September. *Perfect*—which featured fairly complete instrumentation, consisting of drums, bass guitar, organ, and electric guitar—was reworked on Beyoncé's advice: she suggested keeping only the Farfisa organ part recorded by John Tilley, and replacing the guitar with a folk one playing arpeggios. After Beyoncé had recorded her voice with her faithful recording engineer Stuart White, the mixing of the song was entrusted to Tony Maserati. "My job was to get the best sound for Beyoncé's voice, and give it more life; so it breathed more in a way Beyoncé is used to hearing. This meant doing a lot of fader riding. The other thing is that the organ and acoustic guitar start right at the top, and they're very static throughout the song. Instead of everything remaining flat from beginning to end, I did a lot of dynamic rides with the organ and guitar, lowering and raising them all the time, to give space for the vocals."[303] The song went to number 1 in the *Billboard* chart, in the process sweeping aside another hit of the moment, *Havana* by Camila Cabello featuring Young Thug.

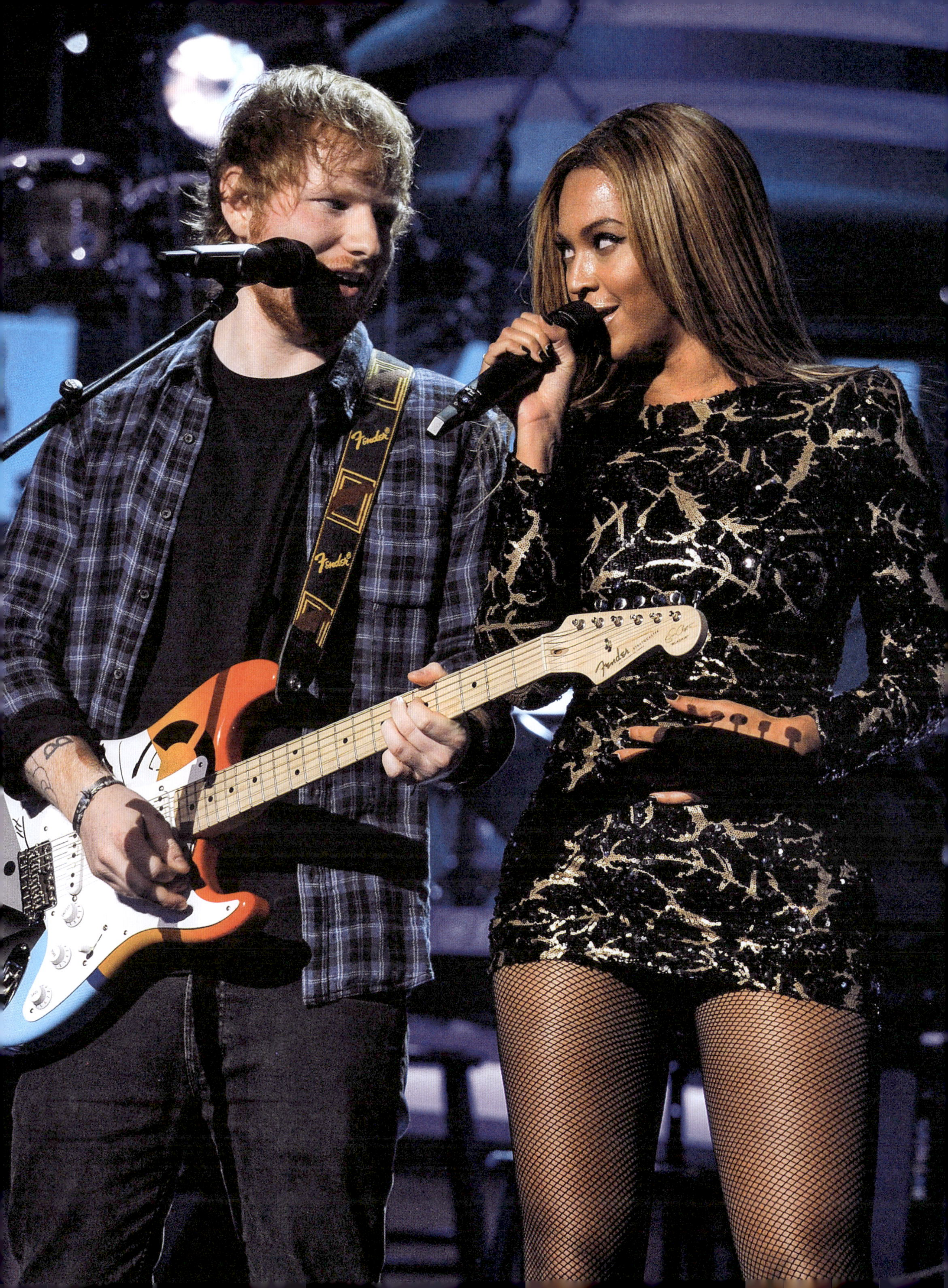
Fender
Fender
Fender

Eminem attends the installation of his friend 50 Cent's star in the Walk of Fame on Hollywood Boulevard in Los Angeles, 30 January 2020.

SINGLE

WALK ON WATER
(EMINEM FEATURING BEYONCÉ)

(Beyoncé Knowles, Holly Hafermann, Marshall Mathers/5'04)

Musicians
Eminem: rap
Beyoncé Knowles: vocals
Skylar Grey: piano
Jason Lader: bass guitar, programming, synthesizer
The Section Quartet: strings

Recording
Effigy Studios, Detroit: 2016 to 2017
Shangri-La, Malibu: 2016 to 2017

Technical team
Producers: Rick Rubin, Skylar Grey
Executive producers: Dr. Dre, Rick Rubin
Recording engineers: Joe Strange, Mike Strange

Eminem *Revival* (album)
Released in the USA by Shady Records/Aftermath Entertainment/Interscope Records: 15 December 2017 (CD ref.: B0027762-02)

Genesis

Eminem, the world's most famous rapper, had long wanted to work with Beyoncé. "It's been on my wish list for a long time," explained the musician from Detroit. "But I never really had a song that I felt like would be right to present to her. So, I was kinda waitin'."[304] Known as much for his vitriolic humor as for his inimitable ultra-rapid flow, Eminem is also seen as a sensitive, honest rapper who never fears to lay himself bare in his lyrics, in contrast to the machismo of most of his hip-hop peers. When he wrote the lyrics to *Walk on Water*, in which he describes the pressure he's subjected to as an idolized artist, but also reminds listeners that he is a mere mortal, not a god as some fans see him (*I walk on water/But I ain't no Jesus/I walk on water/But only when it freezes*, the chorus goes), he decided to take the plunge and suggest to Beyoncé that she sing certain parts. This was doubtless in the hope of repeating the feat of 2010, when Rihanna had elevated *Love the Way You Lie*, earning him another international hit. The two songs also have something else in common: their composer.

Production

Like *Love the Way You Lie* before it, *Walk on Water* is the work of Holly Hafermann, better known by her pseudonym, Skylar Grey. Despite having a CV that puts plenty of other American writers and composers to shame, Grey declared she was overjoyed to have written this song. "This is the song I've been trying to write since age six. Every time I wrote a song I hoped it would be this good. I am truly proud of everything I've created, but this is the one."[305] Thrilled by the chorus Skylar Grey had sent him, Eminem—real name Marshall Mathers—played it to Rick Rubin, a star producer who had worked with him since *The Marshall Mathers LP 2* album, released in 2013. It was Rubin who played the song to Jay-Z, with the idea that Beyoncé sing the choruses. Always up for a top-level duet, Beyoncé quickly added her voice to the song. It met with a decent success, but a disappointing one—it reached only number 14 in the *Billboard* chart, which actually counted as a flop for two stars of that caliber. The fact remains that the song, in its modest way, really works, and is a reminder of the talent of the far-too-unassuming and underestimated Skylar Grey.

416 COLLABORATIONS

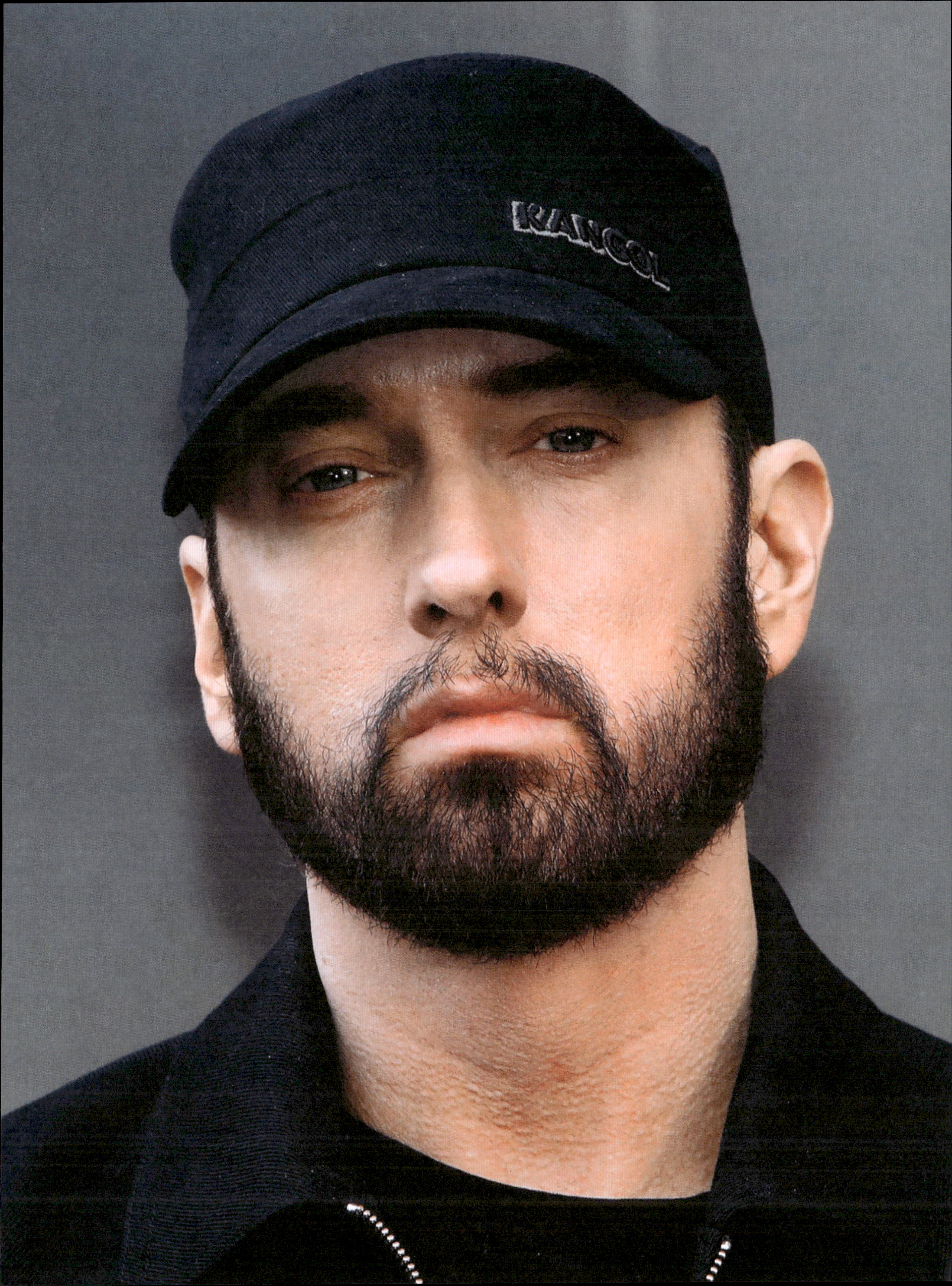
KANGOL

TOP OFF
(DJ KHALED FEATURING JAY-Z, FUTURE, AND BEYONCÉ)

(Beyoncé Knowles-Carter, Brittany Coney, Denisia Andrews, Joseph Zarrillo, Khaled Khaled, Nayvadius Wilburn, Shawn Carter/3'50)

Musicians: DJ Khaled: spoken voice / **Beyoncé Knowles:** vocals, rap, backing vocals / **Future:** rap / **Jay-Z:** rap / **Recording: ?:** 2019 / **Technical team: Producers:** DJ Khaled, Joe Zarrillo / **Executive producers:** Allah Mathematics, Asahd Tuck Khaled, DJ Khaled / **Recording engineers:** Chris Galland, Gimel "Young Guru" Keaton, Juan Peña / **Assistant recording engineers:** Robin Florent, Scott Desmarais / **DJ Khaled** *Father of Asahd* **(album) /** Released in the USA by Epic/We The Best: 17 May 2019 (CD ref.: 19075843972)

A little less than two years after their first collaboration with their friend DJ Khaled, Beyoncé and Jay-Z contributed to the DJ and producer's 11th album, *Father of Asahd*. This time it was in the company of Future, a close associate of Jay-Z, that the Carters came to slum it in this brutal trap song, which Beyoncé made completely her own when she performed it on stage at the Coachella Valley Music and Arts Festival in April 2018. DJ Khaled reported that the recording of *Top Off* took place in the same way as that of *Shining*, for which he had timidly requested Beyoncé's participation through Jay-Z.

"On *Top Off*, I came to Jay-Z to get on it. He get on it and when he played me his verse I was like 'I got an idea: why don't you bring the queen in right here?' That's a crazy question to ask. You gotta be strong to ask this question. I was scared but you know what? I wouldn't be Khaled without trying."[306]

CAN I
(DRAKE FEATURING BEYONCÉ)

(Aubrey Graham, Beyoncé Knowles, Johnny Marr, Noah Shebib/3'09)

Musicians: Drake: rap, vocals / **Beyoncé Knowles:** spoken voice / **Recording: ?:** 2010 to 2016 / **Technical team: Producer:** Noah Shebib / **Drake** *Care Package* **(compilation) /** Released for streaming by OVO Sound: 2 August 2019

When Drake released his very first compilation, *Care Package*, in August 2019, fans were beyond delighted. Available on the OVO Sound label, which the Canadian rapper had founded in 2012 with his producer Noah Shebib and manager Oliver El-Khatib, *Care Package* offered fans mostly unreleased songs, such as the mysterious *Can I*, which is built around a sample of Beyoncé's voice. Aside from its pared-down production, which is rather troubling for a song featuring our singer, the

DJ Khaled and Future in Miami in 2018.

real curiosity of this track is the presence of Johnny Marr, legendary guitarist with The Smiths and The Pretenders, in the song's credits. Indeed, despite their tenacity, fans failed to establish why the Brit had been invited to figure on the list of the song's composers, especially as there is no sample at any point in this unreleased track.

SAVAGE REMIX
(MEGAN THEE STALLION FEATURING BEYONCÉ)

(Bobby Session Jr, J. White Did It, Megan Thee Stallion, Beyoncé Knowles/4'02)

Musicians: Megan Thee Stallion: rap / **Beyoncé Knowles:** rap / **Recording:** ?: 2019 to 2020 / **Technical team: Producer:** J. White Did It / **Megan Thee Stallion** *Good News* **(album)** / Released in the USA by 1501 Certified/300 Entertainment: 20 November 2020

Released for her first EP on 6 March 2020—a mere few days before the world's population went into lockdown because of the COVID-19 pandemic—*Savage*, by Megan Thee Stallion, was a stunning success during that period, thanks especially to the social media platform TikTok, always ready to help promote a new hit. When, after lockdown ended in the US, the rapper, originally from Houston, was working on her first album, she took the chance and suggested to the most famous of all Texans to come and record two verses in her song. "I didn't believe she was actually doing it, but she did it, and my mind was blown. I called my granny."[307] But before working with Megan Thee Stallion, who was well known for her coarse vocabulary, Beyoncé had a request. "Beyoncé was like 'Could you please make your verse a little bit cleaner?' I went in my living room, and I recorded it right then. Beyoncé didn't have to tell me twice!"[307] All the profits from this collaboration went to Bread of Life, the association in Houston that since 1992 had offered meals to the disadvantaged in the city, who were especially affected by the COVID-19 epidemic in 2020.

SORRY NOT SORRY
(DJ KHALED FEATURING NAS, JAY-Z, JAMES FAUNTLEROY, AND HARMONIES BY THE HIVE)

(DJ Khaled, Nasir Jones, Shawn Carter, James Fauntleroy II, Beyoncé Knowles-Carter, Cossom/4'18)

Musicians: DJ Khaled: rap, spoken voice / **Nas:** rap / **Jay-Z:** rap / **James Fauntleroy:** rap / **The Hive (Beyoncé Knowles):** backing vocals / **Recording:** ? / **Technical team: Producers:** DJ Khaled, Streetrunner, Tarik Azzouz / **DJ Khaled** *Khaled Khaled* **(album)** / Released in the USA by Epic/We The Best Music: 30 April 2021 (CD ref.: 19439900532)

Beyoncé and DJ Khaled's third collaboration, *Sorry Not Sorry* was largely performed by Jay-Z and the legendary rapper Nas. Beyoncé, whose part was confined to a few backing vocals hidden in the background of the mix, is here credited as "The Hive." Elegance being a question of detail, the singer's crystal-clear voice brings a touch of grace (and femininity) to this testosterone-boosted song.

FOR BEYONCÉ ADDICTS

Although it did not benefit from an official release, and therefore does not belong in these pages, it is nevertheless worth mentioning that Beyoncé's collaborations include the elegant cover of Henry Mancini and Johnny Mercer's *Moon River*, initially sung by Audrey Hepburn in the 1961 Blake Edwards movie *Breakfast at Tiffany's*. Beyoncé recorded her own version of this iconic and melancholy song as part of the jeweler Tiffany & Co's advertising campaign "About Love," of which Jay-Z and Beyoncé were the new face.

BEYONCÉ: ALL THE SONGS 419

Kirby Lauryen poses backstage at the Forecastle Festival in Louisville, 29 May 2022.

DIE WITH YOU
(Kirby Lauryen Dockery, Beyoncé Knowles/3'36)

Musician: Beyoncé Knowles: vocals, piano / **Recording:** ?: 2015 / **Technical team: Producer:** Beyoncé Knowles / **Die with You (single)** / Released for streaming on Tidal by Columbia/Parkwood Entertainment: 4 April 2017 / **Best chart ranking in the USA:** did not make the charts

On Saturday 4 April 2015, Beyoncé fans—at least, those who subscribed to the Tidal music platform—could watch a video of their idol introducing a completely new song. Wearing a T-shirt with an image of Michael Jackson and a cap jammed onto her head, Mrs Carter performed *Die with You* at the piano, played four hands with the future R&B star Kirby Lauryen. The date was not chosen at random, for that day Beyoncé celebrated the seventh anniversary of her marriage to Jay-Z. Two years later, on 4 April 2017, the song made a big comeback with a completely new video, this time enhanced by personal images of the couple, who wanted to demonstrate to fans the longevity of their relationship, which was then celebrating nine years of marriage. Highly appreciated by fans for its moving quality, *Die with You* is a song that stands out as much for its simplicity as for the tender message Beyoncé addresses to her spouse.

SALUD!
(THE CARTERS)

(Beyoncé, Shawn Carter, Marcello Valenzano, Andre Lyon, Eliot Dubock, Terius Nash/3'33)

Musicians: Beyoncé Knowles: vocals, rap / **Jay-Z:** rap / **Dre:** vocals / **Recording:** Kings Landing Studios West, Los Angeles: 2017 to 2018 / **Technical team: Producers:** Beyoncé, Cool & Dre, Jay-Z / **Executive producers:** Beyoncé, Jay-Z / **Recording engineers:** Stuart White, Gimel "Young Guru" Keaton / **The Carters Everything Is Love (bonus track)** / Released for streaming on Tidal: June 2018

In the course of 2017, Andre "Dre" Christopher Lyon, of the duo Cool & Dre, was invited to Jay-Z and Beyoncé's Los Angeles home. The two men talked about music. Jay-Z played a few ideas for songs that he had just recorded with Beyoncé, and invited Dre to work with him on new ones. The session lasted all night and, as it drew to a close, Dre decided to try his luck, and asked his host: "Jay, can I play you one more record. I gotta play it. If I don't play it, Cool is going to kill me."[308] After just 30 seconds listening to *Salud!*, which the duo had earlier put together in their studio, Jay-Z cried, thrilled as never before: "You trying to tell me that you wait until the very end of the night to play me this?"[308] Dre then hastened to add to the song a hook that had been going through his head for a while (the famous *Put It on Ice*), which the duo would retain at the mixing stage. The arrival of Beyoncé in the studio only confirmed the couple's interest in the song. Soon afterwards they embarked on the recording of their first joint album, with Cool & Dre. In June 2018, the song *Salud!* would be offered to Tidal account holders as a bonus track on *Everything Is Love*.

BE ALIVE
(Beyoncé Knowles, Darius "Dixson" Scott/3'40)

Musician: Beyoncé: vocals / **Recording:** ?: 2021 / **Technical team: Producer:** Darius "Dixson" Scott / **Recording engineer:** Stuart White / **Assistant recording engineer:** Matheus Braz / **Single:** Released for streaming by Columbia/Parkwood Entertainment: 13 November 2021

On 19 November 2021 the movie *King Richard* was released in the United States. Directed by Reinaldo Marcus Green, it tells the story of the journey of Richard Williams, father of the famous tennis players Venus and Serena Williams, who devoted his life to his daughters' success. The movie's soundtrack was the work of the ingenious composer Kris Bowers, who used a prepared piano—one whose workings have been modified to obtain new sounds from it—with the single aim of giving viewers an experience akin to the Williams sisters' playing—hard-hitting and spirited. "I knew I wanted to limit the sound palette to sounds that reflected the game of tennis in a somewhat literal way with strings and having felt on them,"[309] Bowers explained. In order to do this, he modified his piano by adding nails, clothes pegs, and ping-pong balls. In a less-experimental manner, Beyoncé featured on the soundtrack, whose title, *Be Alive*, sent a universal message, which corresponded perfectly to the mainstream nature of Green's movie, in which Will Smith plays Richard Williams.

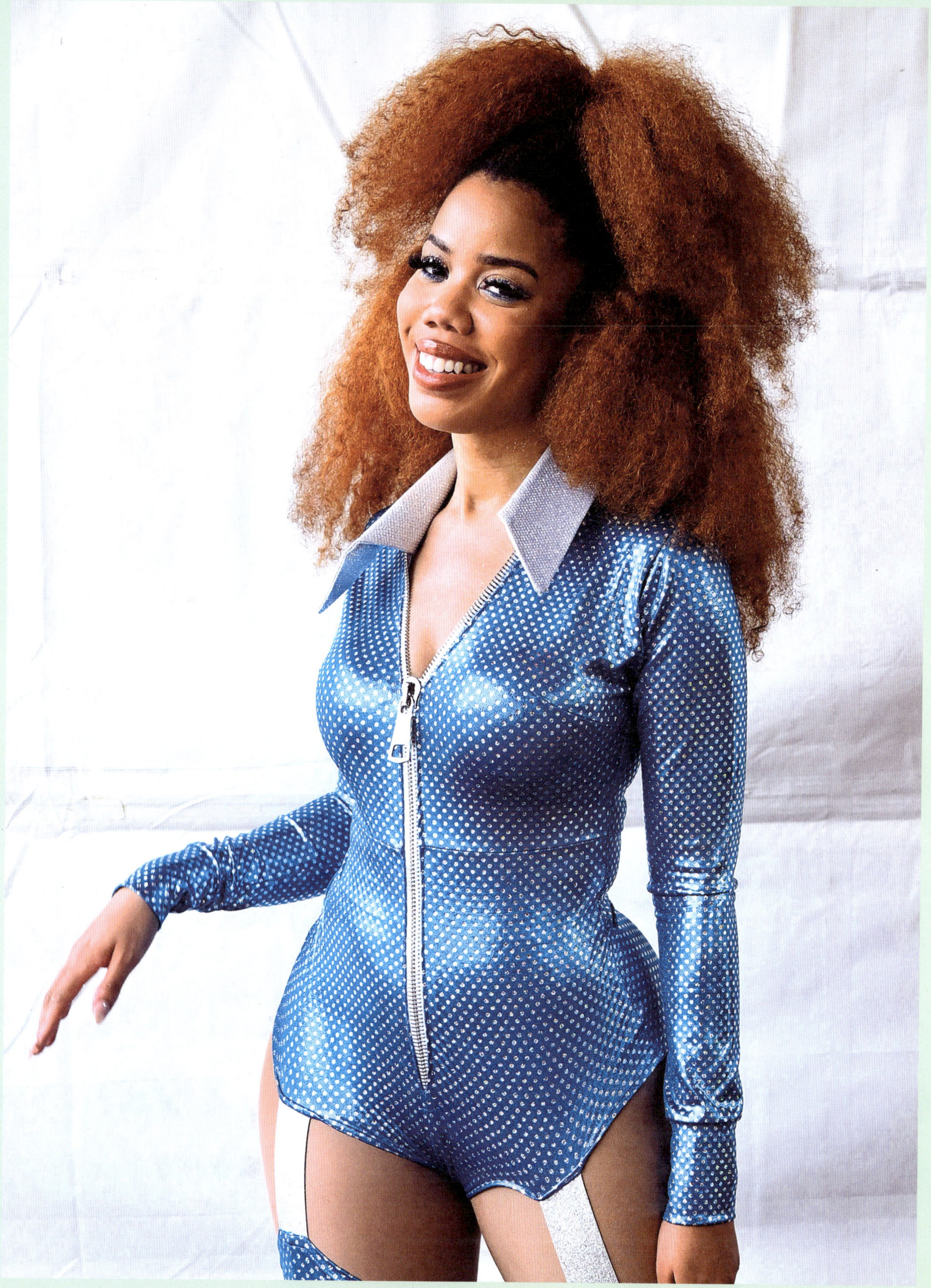

ALBUM

The Lion King: The Gift

Balance (Mufasa Interlude)—James Earl Jones • Bigger—Beyoncé • The Stars (Mufasa Interlude)—James Earl Jones • Find Your Way Back—Beyoncé • Uncle Scar (Scar Interlude)—Chiwetel Ejiofor • Don't Jealous Me—Tekno, Yemi Alade, Mr Eazi, Lord Afrixana • Danger (Young Simba & Young Nala Interlude)—JD McCrary, Shahadi Wright Joseph • Ja Ara E—Burna Boy • Run Away (Scar & Young Simba Interlude)—JD McCrary, Chiwetel Ejiofor • Nile—Beyoncé, Kendrick Lamar • New Lesson (Timon, Pumbaa & Young Simba Interlude)—Billy Eichner, Seth Rogen, JD McCrary • Mood 4 Eva—Beyoncé, Jay-Z, Childish Gambino, Oumou Sangaré • Reunited (Nala & Simba Interlude)—Beyoncé, Donald Glover • Water—Salatiel, Pharrell Williams, Beyoncé • Brown Skin Girl—Beyoncé, SAINt JHN, Wizkid, Blue Ivy Carter • Come Home (Nala Interlude)—Beyoncé • Keys to the Kingdom—Tiwa Savage, Mr Eazi • Follow Me (Simba & Rafiki Interlude)—Donald Glover, John Kani • Already—Beyoncé, Shatta Wale, Major Lazer • Remember (Mufasa Interlude)—James Earl Jones • Otherside—Beyoncé • War (Nala Interlude)—Beyoncé • My Power—Tierra Whack, Beyoncé, Moonchild Sanelly, Nija, DJ Lag, Yemi Alade, Busiswa • Surrender (Simba & Scar Interlude)—Donald Glover, Chiwetel Ejiofor • Scar—070 Shake, Jessie Reyez • I'm Home (Mufasa Interlude)—James Earl Jones, Alfre Woodard, Donald Glover • Spirit (from Disney's The Lion King)—Beyoncé

The Lion King: The Gift features songs by many artists; only those performed by Beyoncé are dealt with here.

**Released for streaming by Parkwood Entertainment/Columbia: 19 July 2019
Best chart ranking in the USA: 2**

Beyoncé was able to reinvent herself and pay homage to her African roots with a diverse, danceable album.

A CELEBRATION OF AFRICAN MUSICAL CULTURES

Although she did not appear on a movie set after taking part in the film *Obsessed*, released in 2009, during the 2000s Beyoncé had embarked on a fine career in movies, with a series of parts in comedies, dramas, and thrillers, as in the film mentioned here. Instead of pursuing this career path the singer decided, on the contrary, to go behind the camera, offering her fans real immersive experiences with multiple videos, more like short films than music clips, of her albums *Beyoncé* and *Lemonade*. She may have stepped back from the classic Hollywood way of working, but her involvement on returning to it was still a powerful experience, verging on the spiritual. From Diana Ross to Etta James, all the characters she played had had an impact on her state of mind—she herself declared that she emerged overwhelmed after playing these different roles on the big screen. Her part in Jon Favreau's 2019 version of *The Lion King* was no exception. Once the recording of Nala's voice for the movie was complete, Beyoncé decided to continue the experience by affirming her emotional attachment to Africa. Keen to continue experimenting with Afrobeat, as she had during the recording of *4* in 2010, she embarked in 2019 on the production of a whole album devoted to paying homage to African culture, to coincide with the release of *The Lion King*. It was presented as an alternative soundtrack to the one released by Walt Disney Records, and consisted mostly of the movie's score, written by Hans Zimmer. "This soundtrack is a love letter to Africa, and I wanted to make sure we found the best talent from Africa, and not just use some of the sounds and did my interpretation of it," she said, of *The Lion King: The Gift*. "I wanted it to be authentic to what is beautiful about the music in Africa."[310]

Distinguished guests

To achieve her goal Beyoncé invited a multitude of artists, chosen individually by Kwasi Fordjour, the creative director of Parkwood Entertainment, to join her in Los Angeles and make the album. These included the Nigerians Burna Boy, Tiwa Savage, Tekno, Mr Eazi, Bankulli, Yemi Alade, and Wizkid, the Ghanaian Shatta Wale, the Cameroonian Salatiel, and the South Africans Moonchild Sanelly and Busiswa. "I wanted to put everyone on their own journey to link the storyline," Bëyoncé explained. "Each song was written to reflect the film's storytelling that gives the listener a chance to imagine their own imagery, while listening to a new contemporary interpretation. It was important that the music was not only performed by the most interesting and talented artists but also produced by the best African producers. Authenticity and heart were important to me."[311]

Black Is King

Inspired by the record she was working on, Beyoncé embarked on the production of a feature-length film celebrating the richness of her cultural heritage. Shot over a period of almost a year and made by six male directors and two female ones, one of them Beyoncé herself, *Black Is King* was released on the Disney+ platform on 31 July 2020. "It started out simple, in my backyard," she said. "I wanted to do one or two videos for *The Gift* album, then it just grew. Before we knew it, we were shooting in Nigeria, Ghana, London, Los Angeles, Johannesburg, and KwaZulu-Natal, South Africa […] *Black Is King* was a huge production that employed a large number of brilliant artists who may not typically see themselves working on a Disney project."[312]

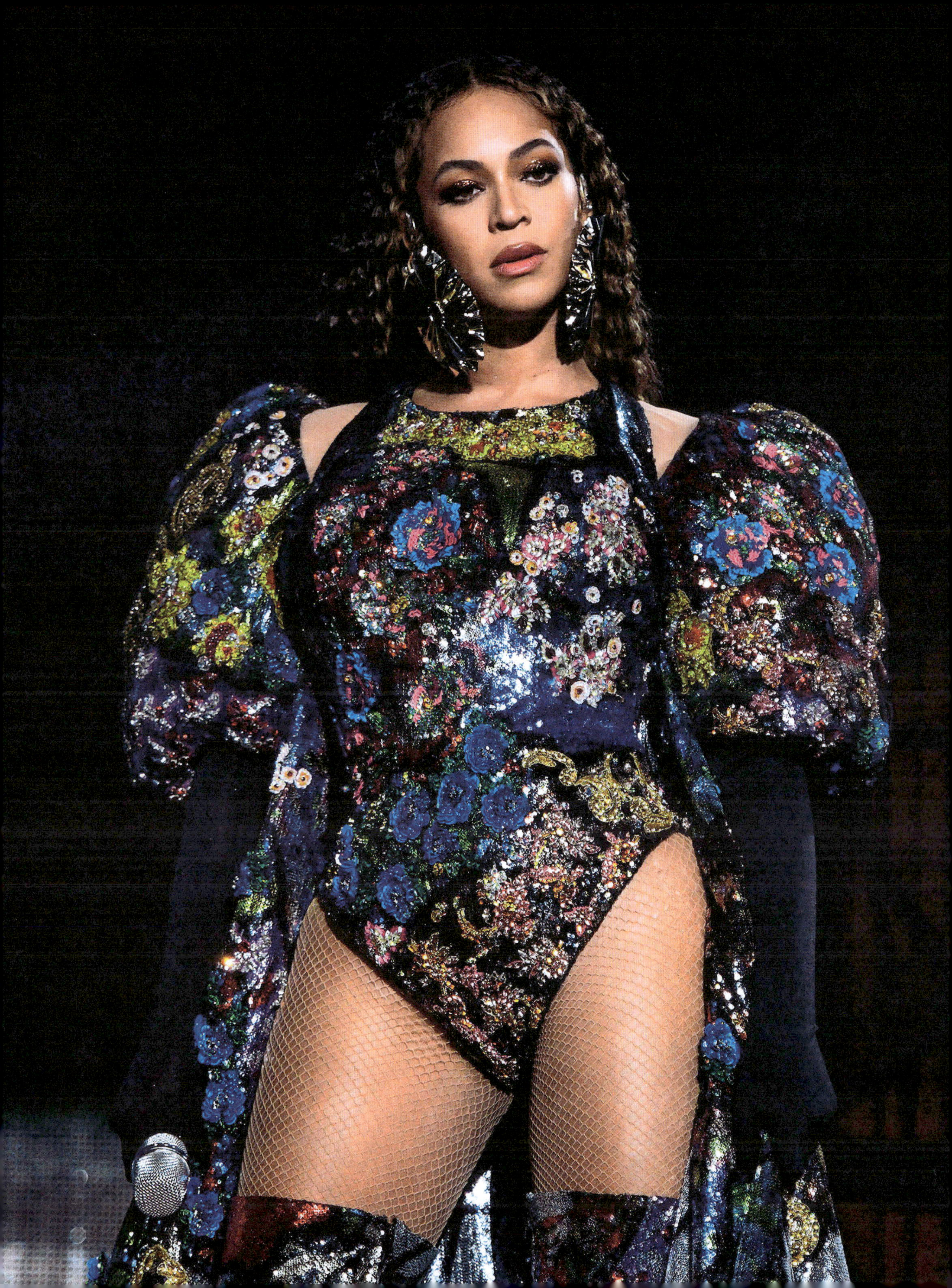

BLACK PARADE

(Beyoncé Knowles, Derek James Dixie, Akil King, Brittany Coney, Denisia Andrews, Kimberly Krysiuk, Rickie Tice, Shawn Carter/4'41)

Musicians: Beyoncé Knowles: vocals, rap / Hailey Niswanger: flute / Arnetta Johnson: trumpet / Cameron Johnson: trumpet / Chris Johnson: trombone / Christopher Gray: trumpet / Crystal Torres: trumpet / Lemar Guillary: trombone / Pete Ortega: saxophone / **Recording:** ?: 2020 / **Technical team:** Producers: Beyoncé Knowles, Derek Dixie / Recording engineer: Stuart White / **The Lion King: The Gift Deluxe Edition (album)** / Released in the USA by Columbia/Parkwood Entertainment: 19 June 2020

Some causes are always worth fighting for. This is certainly true of the one Beyoncé has tirelessly championed: unbiased justice for the African-American community, all too often trampled upon, and whose victims, frequently killed in the course of police violence, continued to accumulate. On 25 May 2020 the murder of the African American George Floyd by a white policeman, who had no pity for the man he had just arrested, renewed the suffering of a community already mourning the recent death of many of its fellow citizens. This tragedy had the effect of reviving the Black Lives Matter movement, when the country had barely emerged from the lockdown due to the COVID-19 pandemic.

On 19 June 2020, when Beyoncé had just released *The Lion King: The Gift*, an album that declared her love for her fellows and was inspired by her experience in recording her voice for *The Lion King*, she also issued the single *Black Parade*, which would feature on the deluxe version of the album. Championing the victories and struggles of African Americans over the years, here the singer made a song that featured the claims made in *Lemonade* and the trap quality of *Everything Is Love*. A powerful, essential track, which reminds us that, though the road to equality is long, we must all take it.

Eric Reid and Colin Kaepernick take the knee during the US national anthem in Charlotte, 18 September 2016.

Songwriter Tim Rice and composer Elton John enjoy the success of *Can You Feel the Love Tonight* in 1995.

CAN YOU FEEL THE LOVE TONIGHT

(Beyoncé Knowles, Donald Glover, Billy Eichner, Seth Rogen)
(Elton John, Tim Rice/3'02)

Musicians: Beyoncé Knowles: vocals / **Billy Eichner:** spoken voice, vocals / **Donald Glover:** spoken voice, vocals / **Seth Rogen:** spoken voice, vocals / **Hollywood Studio Symphony:** orchestra / **Re-Collective Orchestra:** orchestra / **Recording: ?:** 2018, 2019 / **Technical team: Producers:** Hans Zimmer, Jon Favreau, Stephen Lipson, Pharrell Williams, Beyoncé Knowles / **Recording engineers:** Richard Mitchell, Khotso Thahane, Thando Magwaza, Tommy Vicari, Kevin Globerman, Alan Meyerson, Seth Waldmann, Stuart White (Beyoncé's vocals) / **The Lion King Original Motion Picture Soundtrack (album) / Released in the USA by Walt Disney Records:** 11 July 2019 (CD ref.: D003166302)

In 1994, with *Rudyard Kipling's The Jungle Book*, Walt Disney Pictures embarked on a series of remakes that combined live-action shots with computer-generated ones and digital optical effects. In 2019 this continued with the remaking of one of their biggest successes, *The Lion King*. The first version, released in June 1994 in the US, was unquestionably one of the most successful animated films ever, because of the quality of its animation and screenplay, and also thanks to its music: an instrumental score by Hans Zimmer and songs by Elton John and Tim Rice. Some even became legendary—like *Circle of Life*, *Hakuna Matata*, and, of course, *Can You Feel the Love Tonight*, performed by the animals of the savannah and sung by Elton John himself during the closing credits. In 1995, this version won John and Rice an Oscar for Best Original Song, a Grammy Award for Best Male Pop Vocal Performance, and a Golden Globe for Best Original Song. Directed by Jon Favreau (who had made a live-action remake of *The Jungle Book* in 2016), the new version of *The Lion King* is enhanced by prestigious voices, namely those of Donald Glover as Simba, Seth Rogen as Pumbaa, Chiwetel Ejiofor as Scar, and Beyoncé as Nala, Simba's young lioness friend. It was therefore entirely logical that Beyoncé should voice Nala in 2019 and perform *Can You Feel the Love Tonight*. The song would feature on the soundtrack of *The Lion King*, released by Walt Disney Records in July 2019.

BEYONCÉ: ALL THE SONGS 427

Composer Stacy Barthe, who worked with Rihanna, Katy Perry, and Beyoncé.

BIGGER

(Akil King, Richard Lawson, Stacy Barthe, Rachel Keen, Derek Dixie/3'46)

Musicians: Beyoncé: vocals, backing vocals / Rachel "Raye" Keen: backing vocals / Stephanie Matthews: violin / Bianca McClure: violin / Crystal Alforque: violin / Marta Honer: violin / Stephanie Yu: violin / Rhea Hosanny: viola / Jonathan Richards: cello / Tahirah Whittington: cello / Adrienne Woods: cello / **Recording:** NRG Recording Studios, Los Angeles: 2019 / **Technical team: Producers:** Beyoncé, Derek Dixie / **Executive producer:** Beyoncé / **String arrangements:** Stephanie Matthews, Derek Dixie

After the introduction to the record, narrated by the actor James Earl Jones, Beyoncé sings *Bigger*, a ballad written with several new talents, who need to be introduced. Stacy Barthe, who already had under her belt *Hummingbird Heartbeat* by Katy Perry (2010), *Everywhere You Go* for Kelly Rowland (2010), and *Cheers (Drink to That)* by Rihanna (2011), had almost given up music before she met Beyoncé, who urged her to persevere and helped her to do so. "I was tired of being broke!" she said "When I wrote *Cheers* for Rihanna, I didn't have gas to get to the studio."[313] Another singer who needed a helping hand was the Briton Rachel "Raye" Keen, one of the writers sought out by Beyoncé and invited to take part in the Los Angeles sessions. "A cut like that is life-changing," Raye explained. "It means now that in all songwriting conversations, I'm taken seriously—throughout genres. I wrote a lot of songs for that project. I was one of the first to arrive and the last to leave: I put the shift in. And it paid off, thank the Lord."[314]

FIND YOUR WAY BACK

(Beyoncé, Brittany Hazzard, Osabuohien Osaretin, Bubele Booi, Robert Magwenzi, Abisagboola Oluseun/2'42)

Musicians: Beyoncé: vocals, backing vocals / Abisagboola "Bankulli" Oluseun: backing vocals / **Recording:** NRG Recording Studios, Los Angeles: 2019 / **Technical team: Producers:** Beyoncé, Bubele Booi, Robert Magwenzi, Abisagboola "Bankulli" Oluseun, GuiltyBeatz, Derek Dixie / **Executive producer:** Beyoncé

Invited to Los Angeles to work on Beyoncé's new project, the Ghanaian DJ and producer GuiltyBeatz, who was living in London at the time, embarked on the production of songs in the highlife style, which comes from Ghana and has softer, more delicate textures than Afrobeat—which is just as danceable but more hard-hitting. "I'm Ghanaian, so I wanted to bring that cultural sound highlife. Highlife is more guitar-based, slower, with shakers and more percussion elements like congas and bongos," the producer explained.[315] With this goal in mind, he decided to make *Find Your Way Back* using a sample from *Maradona*, recorded by the Nigerian singer Niniola in 2017. "There have been samples [of African music in American pop] here and there, things like Drake and Wizkid collaborating [on *One Dance*]," GuiltyBeatz said. "But it's just been little things. Now that Beyoncé released a whole album, this will open the gateway."[315]

428 THE LION KING: THE GIFT

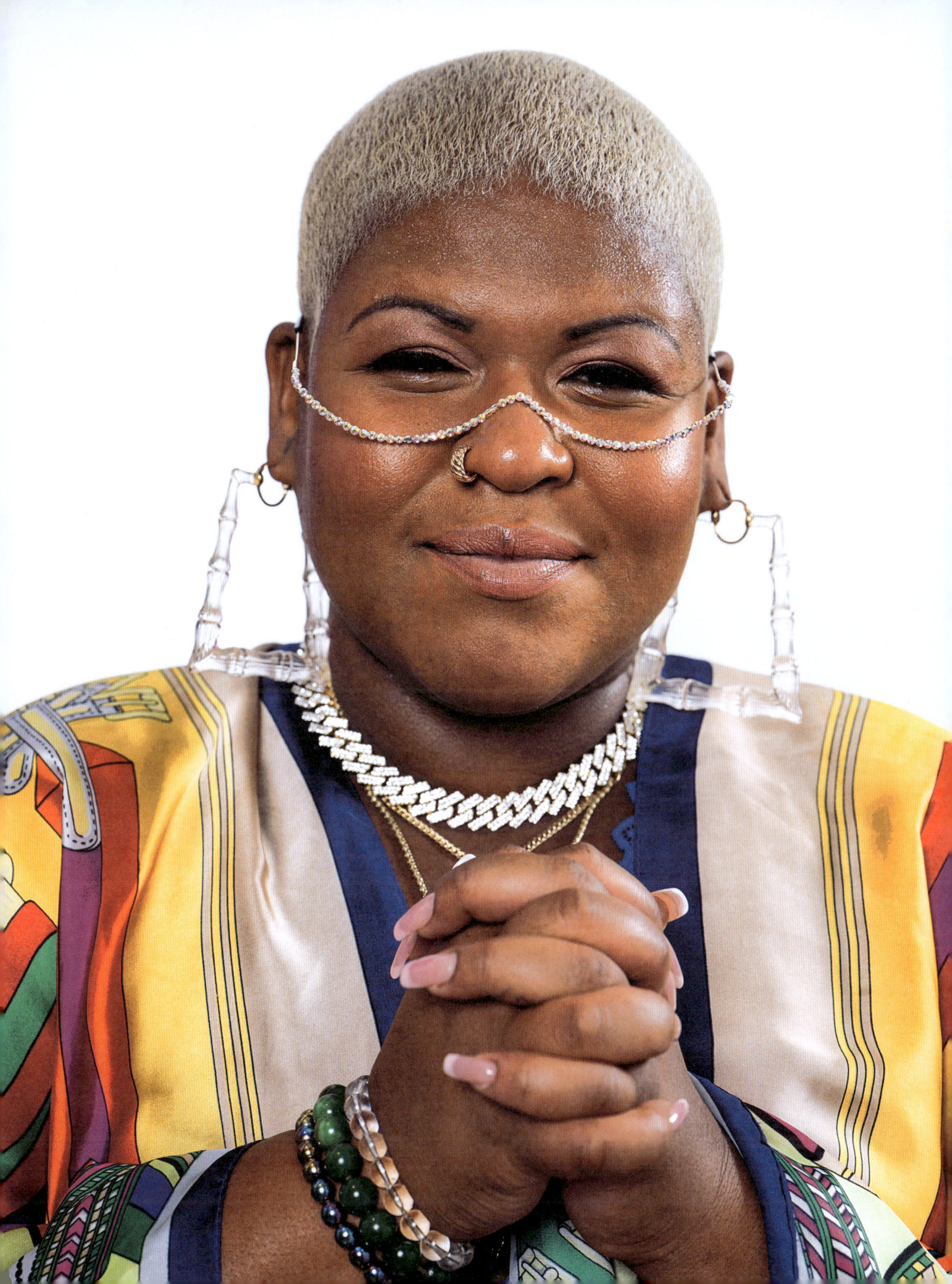

Donald Glover, aka Childish Gambino, whose single *This Is America* won universal acclaim in 2018.

NILE
(WITH KENDRICK LAMAR)

(Beyoncé, Kendrick Lamar, Brittany Coney, Denisia Andrews, Keanu Dean Torres, Hykeem Carter, Sounwave/1'47)

Musicians: Beyoncé: vocals, rap, backing vocals / **Kendrick Lamar:** rap / **Recording:** NRG Recording Studios, Los Angeles: 2019 / **Technical team:** Producers: Beyoncé, Keanu Beats, Hykeem Carter, Sounwave / **Executive producer:** Beyoncé

It is more a matter of trap music than of Afrobeat in *Nile*, performed as a duet by Beyoncé and Kendrick Lamar, which incidentally is more like an interlude at the heart of the album than a song in its own right, as Beyoncé explained: "It's more than just the music, it's a soundscape. It's sonic cinema and it leaves space for you to put yourself in the film. And I think that's really powerful."[316]

SINGLE

MOOD 4 EVA
(WITH JAY-Z, CHILDISH GAMBINO, OUMOU SANGARÉ)

(Beyoncé, Anathi Bhongo Mnyango, Ant Clemons, Brittany Coney, Denisia Andrews, Jeff Kleinman, Michael Uzowuru, Teo Halm, Oumou Sangaré, Childish Gambino, Jay-Z, DJ Khaled, Danja/4'32)

Musicians: Beyoncé: vocals, rap, backing vocals / **Jay-Z:** rap / **Childish Gambino:** rap / **Recording:** NRG Recording Studios, Los Angeles: 2019 / **Technical team:** Producers: Beyoncé, DJ Khaled, Danja / **Executive producer:** Beyoncé / **Single:** Released for streaming by Parkwood Entertainment/Columbia: 19 July 2019 / **Best chart ranking in the USA:** 90

Although some observers cried cultural appropriation on hearing *The Lion King: The Gift* (as they had in 2015 on seeing Beyoncé in a sari, outrageously made up and miming an Indian dance in the clip of Coldplay's *Hymn for the Weekend*), it has to be said that she attained her goal, which was to pay homage to African musical cultures and traditions. Some songs on the album, like the single *Mood 4 Eva*, even make it into the ranks of Beyoncé's best songs. The track is built around a sample from *Diaraby Nene*, recorded in 1991 by the Malian singer Oumou Sangaré for her first album, *Moussolou*. The showcasing of such a talented artist had many plus points according to the producer Michael Uzowuru, who took part in the writing of *Mood 4 Eva* and believed *The Lion King: The Gift* enabled Beyoncé's audience to discover an Afrobeat style that until then they had been totally unaware of. "This will give a great reference point for people to get into that music who haven't before. People need something like this to understand the rhythm, the melodies, the grooves. Beyoncé made a great job of making it accessible."[15] It is worth noting the presence on the song of Childish Gambino, real name Donald Glover. At the time of the recording of *The Lion King: The Gift* he was enjoying exceptional renown thanks to the colossal success of his 2018 single *This Is America*, which denounced police violence and which, well before Beyoncé did the same thing, combined hip-hop, trap, African sounds, and a gospel feel.

WATER
(WITH SALATIEL, PHARRELL WILLIAMS)

(Beyoncé, Pharrell Williams, Alastair O'Donnell, Nana O. Afriyie, Nija Charles, P2J/2'32)

Musicians: Beyoncé: vocals, backing vocals / **Salatiel:** vocals / **Pharrell Williams:** vocals / **Moonchild Sanelly:** backing vocals / **Recording:** NRG Recording Studios, Los Angeles: 2019 / **Technical team:** Producers: Beyoncé, P2J / **Executive producer:** Beyoncé

Although Pharrell Williams is behind its production, the real star of *Water* is the Cameroonian singer Salatiel. While researching African artists, Beyoncé and her associate Kwasi Fordjour came across two songs by Salatiel that caught their attention. The first was *One Day Na One Day*, which the artist had written for the soundtrack of the television series *Bad*

Angel, broadcast in Cameroon on the Canal 2 International network; the second the single *Toi & Moi*, which Salatiel had released in 2017. When Beyoncé contacted him to invite him to take part in *The Lion King: The Gift* and join her in Los Angeles, the Cameroonian was in mid-tour and could not make himself available. The three therefore worked together remotely: Beyoncé in California, Pharrell Williams in his home studio, and Salatiel in his native country. Although *Water* gave prominence to African sounds, the song provoked a barrage of criticism; its detractors felt that Beyoncé had not incorporated enough Cameroonian musical elements into the song. "I don't know what people mean by a Cameroonian sound," Salatiel replied. "Nothing is more Cameroonian than the makossa guitars in the song. Nothing is more Cameroonian than [its rhythm], so I would say those who make these criticisms do not know Cameroonian music—simple as that."[317]

SAINt JHN enjoyed success with his hit *Roses*, remixed by Imanbek in 2019.

SINGLE

BROWN SKIN GIRL
(WITH SAINT JHN, WIZKID, BLUE IVY CARTER)

(Beyoncé, SAINt JHN, P2J, Anathi Bhongo Mnyango, Bipolar Sunshine, Jay-Z, Michael Uzowuru, Stacy Barthe/4'08)

Musicians: Beyoncé: vocals, backing vocals / SAINt JHN: vocals / Wizkid: vocals / Blue Ivy Carter: vocals / **Recording:** NRG Recording Studios, Los Angeles: 2019 / **Technical team:** Producers: Beyoncé, Derek Dixie, P2J / **Executive producer:** Beyoncé / **Single:** Released for streaming by Parkwood Entertainment/Columbia: 23 July 2019 / Best chart ranking in the USA: 76

Despite its commercial failure, the single *Brown Skin Girl* is undoubtedly one of Beyoncé's greatest artistic successes. In extolling the beauty of African Americans' skin color, here she addresses as much her young daughter Blue Ivy, who has been invited to sing, as she does the entire community. "When I see fathers singing *Brown Skin Girl* to their daughters," she explained, "to know that my daughter can have the same opportunities and feel confident and feel like she doesn't have to take her braids down, she can comb her Afro out, she can glisten in her brown skin."[318] In order to create this very beautiful song, with its simple, enchanting, and haunting melody, Beyoncé called on the services of SAINt JHN, the singer of Guyanese descent whose single *Roses*, initially released in 2016, was a global hit in 2019 in a version remixed by the Kazakh DJ Imanbek. SAINt JHN, who wrote the first version of *Brown Skin Girl*, left Beyoncé to rework it, also thinking she would be a better messenger than him to deliver the song's lyrics to Black women the world over.

ALREADY
(WITH SHATTA WALE, MAJOR LAZER)

(Beyoncé, Shatta Wale, GuiltyBeatz, Clément Picard, Diplo, Maxime Picard, Brittany Hazzard, Toumani Diabaté/3'42)

Musicians: Beyoncé: vocals, backing vocals / **Shatta Wale:** vocals / **Recording:** NRG Recording Studios, Los Angeles: 2019 / **Technical team:** Producers: Beyoncé, GuiltyBeatz, Clément Picard, Diplo, Maxime Picard / **Executive producer:** Beyoncé

Behind the very dancehall *Already* there is a top-level team. First of all, the Ghanaian producer GuiltyBeatz came from his home in London to record several instrumental parts—without having the slightest idea what would become of his work. "I didn't know who would end up on which song,"[319] he said. Diplo, of the group Major Lazer, was also involved. His style, which combined ultra-modern sounds with Jamaican ones, was unmistakable. Two other new talents were invited to work on the song: the French duo Picard Brothers—Clément and Maxime Picard. They were friends with Diplo, who had helped them make their name, and had worked on a glorious series of collaborations with Silk City (a group formed by Diplo and the star producer Mark Ronson), Dua Lipa, and Madonna. The pair, who came from the town of Coulommiers to the east of Paris, began to work with Diplo in the Los Angeles sessions. This led to them meeting Mark Ronson, with whom they worked on creating his excellent fifth album, *Late Night Feelings*, released in 2019.

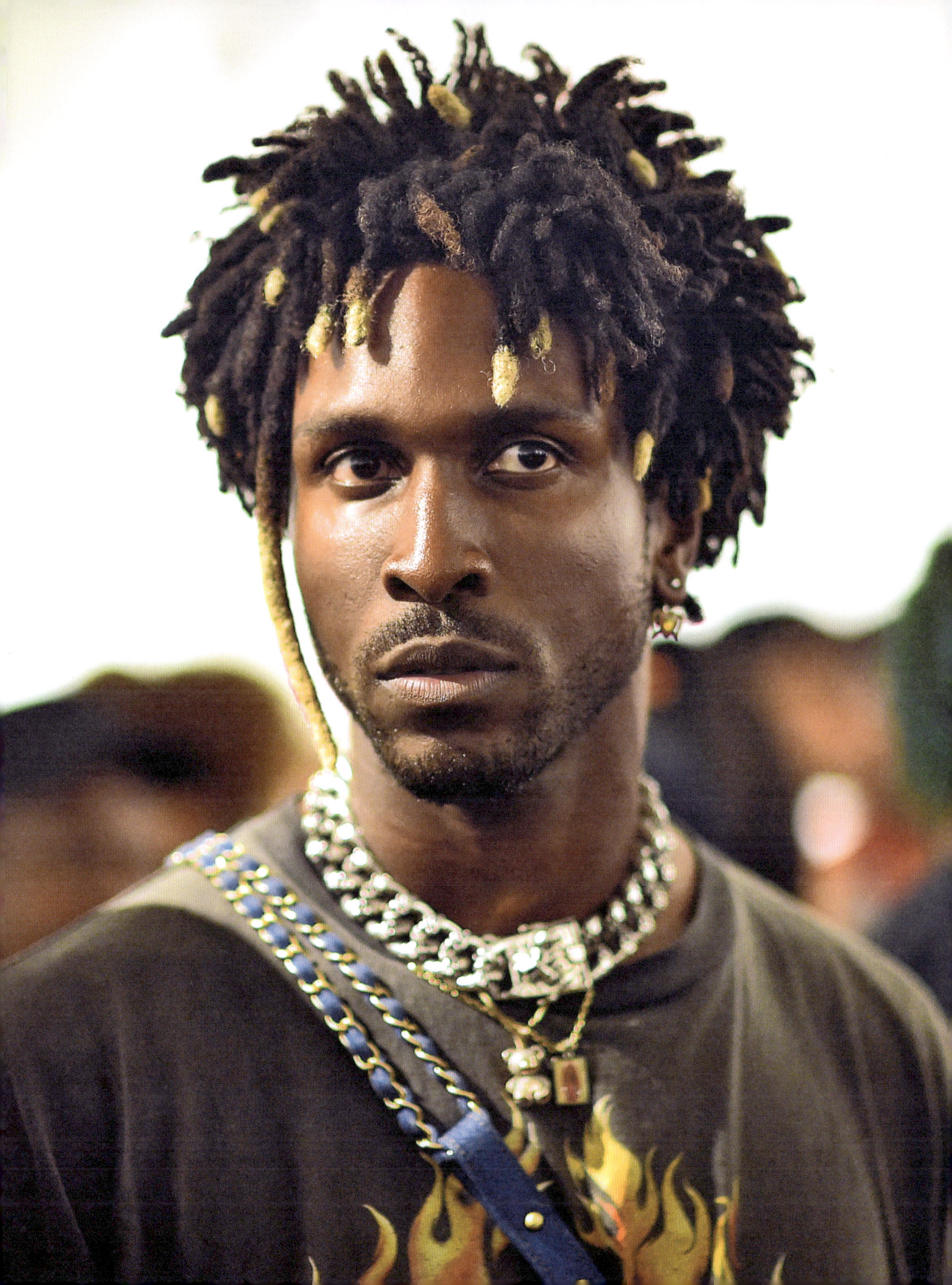

The South African singers Busiswa Gqulu (left) and Moonchild Sanelly.

OTHERSIDE

(Beyoncé, Dave Rosser, Abisagboola Oluseun, Nick Green, Sydney Bennett/3'39)

Musicians: Beyoncé: vocals, backing vocals / Abisagboola "Bankulli" Oluseun: backing vocals / **Recording:** NRG Recording Studios, Los Angeles: 2019 / **Technical team:** Producers: Beyoncé, Derek Dixie, Nicky Davey, Sydney Bennett / **Executive producer:** Beyoncé

Produced in collaboration with Nicky Davey and Sydney "Syd" Bennett, *Otherside* offers a break full of feeling, at the heart of the very danceable *The Lion King: The Gift*. Accompanied by a subtle instrumental part, Beyoncé and the Nigerian singer Abisagboola "Bankulli" Oluseun decided to deliver a refined interpretation of the song—Bankulli inspired by God and Beyoncé by her family. "When you're a mother," she explained, "there's a love that you experience with your kids that's deeper than anything you can imagine. The love is beyond earth and beyond time and space and it's a connection that will be constant. And *Otherside* is that tenderness."[316] James Blake would revisit the song in 2020 in *When We're Older*, on his EP *Covers*, which also features covers of Billie Eilish, Frank Ocean, and Stevie Wonder.

MY POWER
(WITH TIERRA WHACK, MOONCHILD SANELLY, NIJA, DJ LAG, YEMI ALADE, BUSISWA)

(Beyoncé, Busiswa, Moonchild Sanelly, Nija, Tierra Whack, Yemi Alade, Brittany Coney, Denisia Andrews, DJ Lag/4'19)

Musicians: Beyoncé: vocals, backing vocals / Busiswa: vocals / Moonchild Sanelly: vocals / Nija: vocals / Tierra Whack: vocals / Yemi Alade: vocals / **Recording:** NRG Recording Studios, Los Angeles: 2019 / **Technical team:** Producers: Beyoncé, Derek Dixie, DJ Lag / **Executive producer:** Beyoncé

On Sunday 2 December 2018, Beyoncé and Jay-Z performed at the Global Citizen Festival: Mandela 100 in Johannesburg, South Africa. In mid-show Beyoncé and her dancers performed a routine on *Trip to New York*, one of the hits by Lwazi Asanda Gwala, aka DJ Lag, the South African king of gqom—an electronic music sub-genre that had originated in Durban, South Africa, at the start of the decade and of which Gwala is one of the most famous exponents. Shortly after the performance, Kwasi Fordjour, who had been dispatched by Beyoncé to find her the biggest African talents, asked the South African to work on instrumental parts for an as-yet-undefined project. "I tried not to get too excited, as the likelihood of this coming through was, I guess, pretty small. Knowing that my music was being listened by and considered by the world's biggest artist was a huge honor in itself," DJ Lag said.[320] After sending Fordjour six instrumental parts, he was invited to work with Beyoncé's team in Los Angeles, where he then discovered that the project was well advanced. "They already had chosen what they wanted," the DJ explained. "The only thing I did at the studio was work with the voices and add Busiswa's part on the beat."[315] In addition to Busiswa, the artists recorded for the song included her fellow South African Moonchild Sanelly, the Americans Nija Charles and Tierra Whack, and the Nigerian Yemi Alade. The last of these had the fright of her life on arriving in Los Angeles to work with Beyoncé, when she realized she could not sing the slightest note. "I couldn't understand what had happened to me. I could talk, but I couldn't even hit the lowest key. [...] I jacked up on vitamin C. I went in on lemon and ginger. I felt like an herbalist, I was going in on everything."[315]

434 THE LION KING: THE GIFT

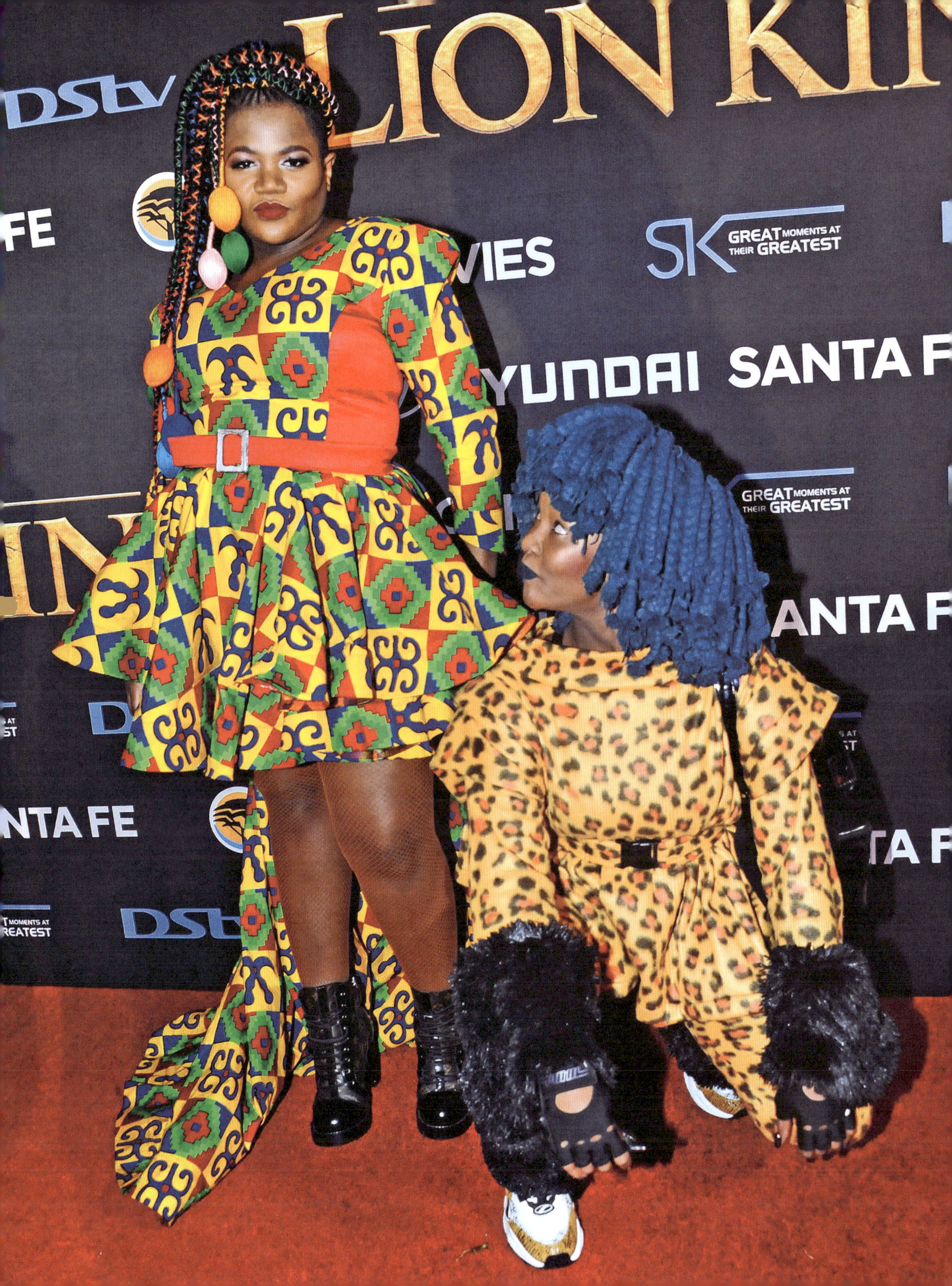
DStv
SK
GREAT MOMENTS AT THEIR GREATEST

Composer and producer Timothy "Labrinth" McKenzie in Glasgow, November 2014.

SINGLE

SPIRIT
(FROM DISNEY'S THE LION KING)

(Beyoncé, Ilya Salmanzadeh, Timothy "Labrinth" McKenzie/4'37)

Musicians
- **Beyoncé:** vocals, backing vocals
- **Andre Washington:** backing vocals
- **Derrick Charles:** backing vocals
- **Donald Paige:** backing vocals
- **Edward Lawson:** backing vocals
- **George Young:** backing vocals
- **ILYA:** backing vocals, percussion, drums, programming
- **Jamal Moore:** backing vocals
- **Jason Morales:** backing vocals
- **Jerome Wayne:** backing vocals
- **Johnny Gilmore:** backing vocals
- **Mabvuto Carpenter:** backing vocals
- **Marcus Eldridge:** backing vocals
- **Maurice Smith:** backing vocals
- **Steve Epting:** backing vocals
- **Stevie Notes:** backing vocals
- **TJ Wilkins:** backing vocals
- **Vernon Burris:** backing vocals
- **Derek Dixie:** drums, programming
- **Labrinth:** percussion, drums, programming, backing vocals
- **Ilya Salmanzadeh:** drums
- **Jeremy Lertola:** percussion
- **Jeff Lorber:** piano

Recording
NRG Recording Studios, Los Angeles: 2019

Technical team
- **Producers:** Beyoncé, Derek Dixie, Labrinth, Ilya Salmanzadeh
- **Executive producer:** Beyoncé
- **Recording engineers:** Stuart White, Daniel Pampuri, Lester Mendoza
- **Assistant recording engineers:** Andrea Roberts, Cory Bice, Jeremy Lertola, Sam Holland, Steven Xai

Single
Released for streaming by Parkwood Entertainment/Columbia: 10 July 2019
Best chart ranking in the USA: 98

Genesis
Hans Zimmer, composer of the film score for *The Lion King*, first met Beyoncé the day the latter went to present him with the song she had just recorded for the movie *Spirit*. Although she was a star of international renown, the singer knew Zimmer's résumé: he had written some of the most significant film soundtracks of the past 40 years, including *True Romance* (Tony Scott, 1993), *Gladiator* (Ridley Scott, 2000), *The Dark Knight* (Christopher Nolan, 2008), and, of course, the original version of *The Lion King*, released in 1994. "At the last moment," Zimmer recalled, "she comes to the room and basically shows us a diamond and goes, 'If you want it, you can have it.' [...] We absolutely adored it. It was absolutely perfect for the film."[321] After several attempts at incorporating it into different sequences of the movie, the song was finally synchronized with the closing credits, and released as a single on 10 July 2019, ten days before Jon Favreau's movie came out.

Production
In early 2019, Walt Disney Studios contacted Ilya Salmanzadeh and Timothy "Labrinth" McKenzie, who had created the song, to work on a track that could represent the movie. Immediately the two producers thought of working with Beyoncé, and set about coming up with a song that might win her over. "We kind of sent a rough demo over to her," Labrinth recalled. "She heard the song and she loved the vibe. She was like, 'Okay, I'm going to get in on it with you.' She started helping us write the rest of the record. It was just like, 'This is incredible.' It was just one of those moments where it was like, 'Okay, I think God's blessing me now.'"[322] Once the melody had been composed and the lyrics written, the two men concentrated on the song's production, aiming to respect the spirit of the film. After diligently studying percussion instruments and other traditional African instruments, then the Swahili language in order to write the introduction, the team put the finishing touches to the track with Hans Zimmer, with the aim of giving *Spirit* a production perfectly in keeping with the maestro's work.

436 THE LION KING: THE GIFT

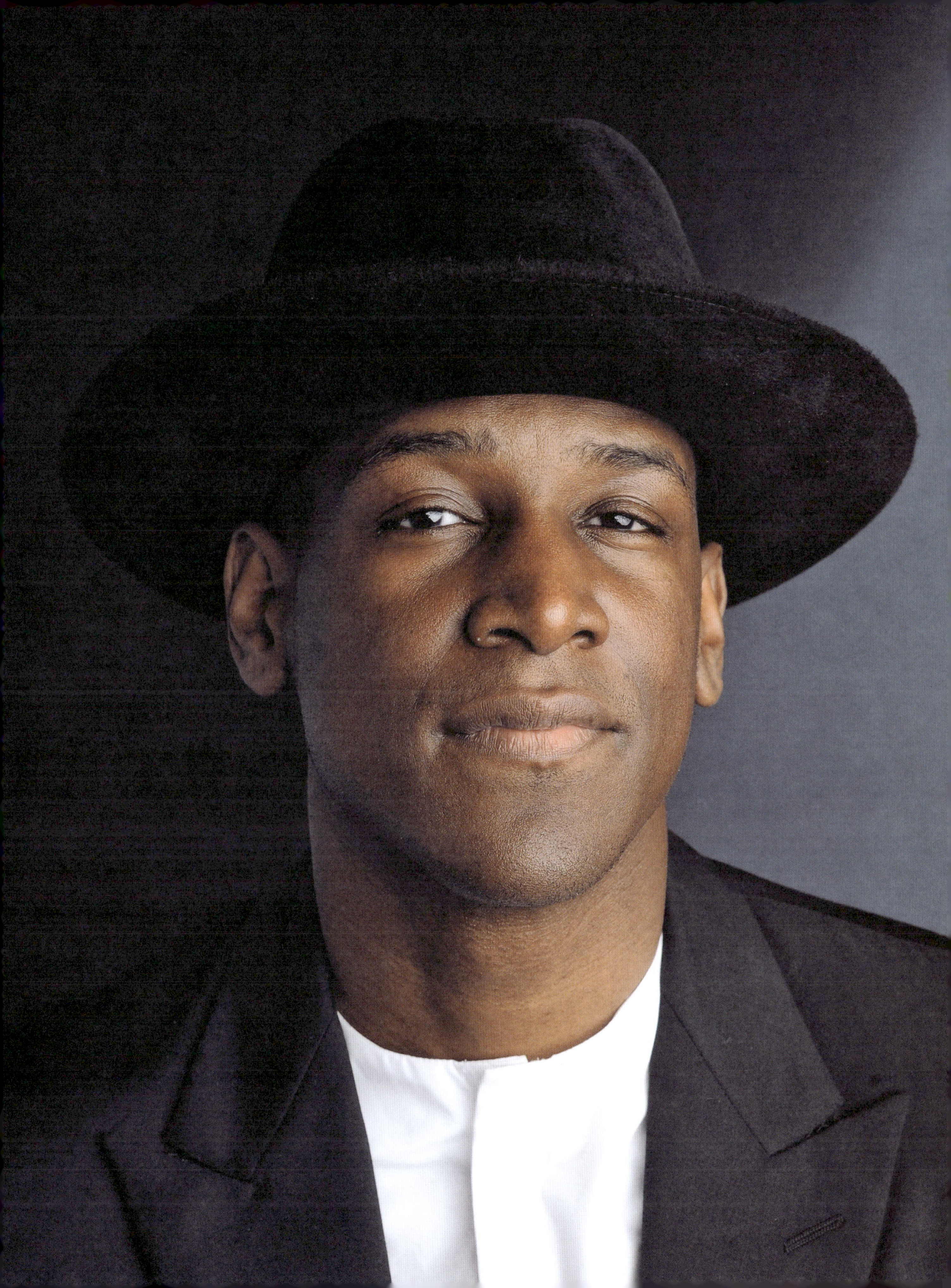

Frankie Beverly, of the group Maze, at the start of the 1980s.

BEFORE I LET GO

(Frankie Beverly, Larry Blackmon, Tomi Jenkins/4'01)

Musician: Beyoncé Knowles: vocals, backing vocals / **Recording:** NRG Recording Studios, Los Angeles: 2020 / **Technical team: Executive producer:** Beyoncé Knowles-Carter / **Recording engineers:** Daniel Pampuri, Lester Mendoza / **Homecoming: The Live Album (album)** / Released in the USA by Columbia/Parkwood Entertainment: 4 December 2020 (album ref.: 19075959261)

Frankie Beverly, founder and vocalist of the group Maze, wrote *Before I Let Go* in 1981, in homage to a young woman with whom he could not succeed in building a lasting relationship. "It was just up and down, and by the end of it I wrote a song because I was feeling I needed to get out of it," the soul singer said. "I was so into the girl, but it just wasn't working out. I was thinking, 'What am I gonna do?' and that thought inspired the song. I was going to try to do all of these things 'before I let go.'"[323] When Beyoncé decided to release a record telling the story of the Coachella Valley Music and Arts Festival, where she gave two legendary concerts in April 2018, it was quickly decided also to produce a video version. Entitled *Homecoming: A Film by Beyoncé*, it was released on Netflix on 17 April 2019. Beyoncé then added two studio songs, *Before I Let Go* and *I Been On*, in order to give her admirers a treat and offer exclusive content to buyers of the audio version of the concert: *Homecoming: The Live Album*. Revisiting the Maze classic (enhanced with a sample from *Candy*, a single released by Cameo in 1986), Beyoncé paid homage to its composer, Frankie Beverly, whom she had known personally since her teens, often rubbing shoulders with him at his concerts in Houston. "She's a great friend of mine, but I didn't know she was going to do this," Beverly said. "I was hearing stuff, but I didn't even want to approach her about it."[323] *Before I Let Go* features in the closing credits of the movie *Homecoming: A Film by Beyoncé*.

I BEEN ON

(Beyoncé Knowles, Jamal Jones, Timothy Mosley, Jonathan "Anonymous" Solone-Myvett, Theron Thomas, Timothy Thomas, Sonny Corey Uwaezuoke/2'25)

Musician: Beyoncé Knowles: spoken voice / **Recording:** NRG Recording Studios, Los Angeles: 2020 / **Technical team: Producers:** Beyoncé Knowles, Timbaland, Jerome Harmon / **Executive producer:** Beyoncé Knowles-Carter / **Recording engineers:** Daniel Pampuri, Lester Mendoza / **Homecoming: The Live Album (album)** / Released in the USA by Columbia/Parkwood Entertainment: 4 December 2020 (album ref.: 19075959261)

Beyoncé made headlines in the music press on 17 March 2013 when she released the song *Bow Down* (sometimes called *Bow Down/I Been On*) on her website. In subsequent months, while she was involved in the production of her sixth solo album, she revisited the song, keeping only certain sections, and it was reborn as a new track: ****Flawless*. The remainder, *I Been On*—co-produced by Timbaland and Jerome "J-Roc" Harmon, with Beyoncé's voice distorted to a very low pitch (as Prince had done in 2001 on his *The Rainbow Children*)—was then set aside in Beyoncé's archives. Determined to offer her fans exclusive content, the singer enhanced the audio version of *Homecoming* with this rarity, which here saw its very first official release.

OUTTAKES

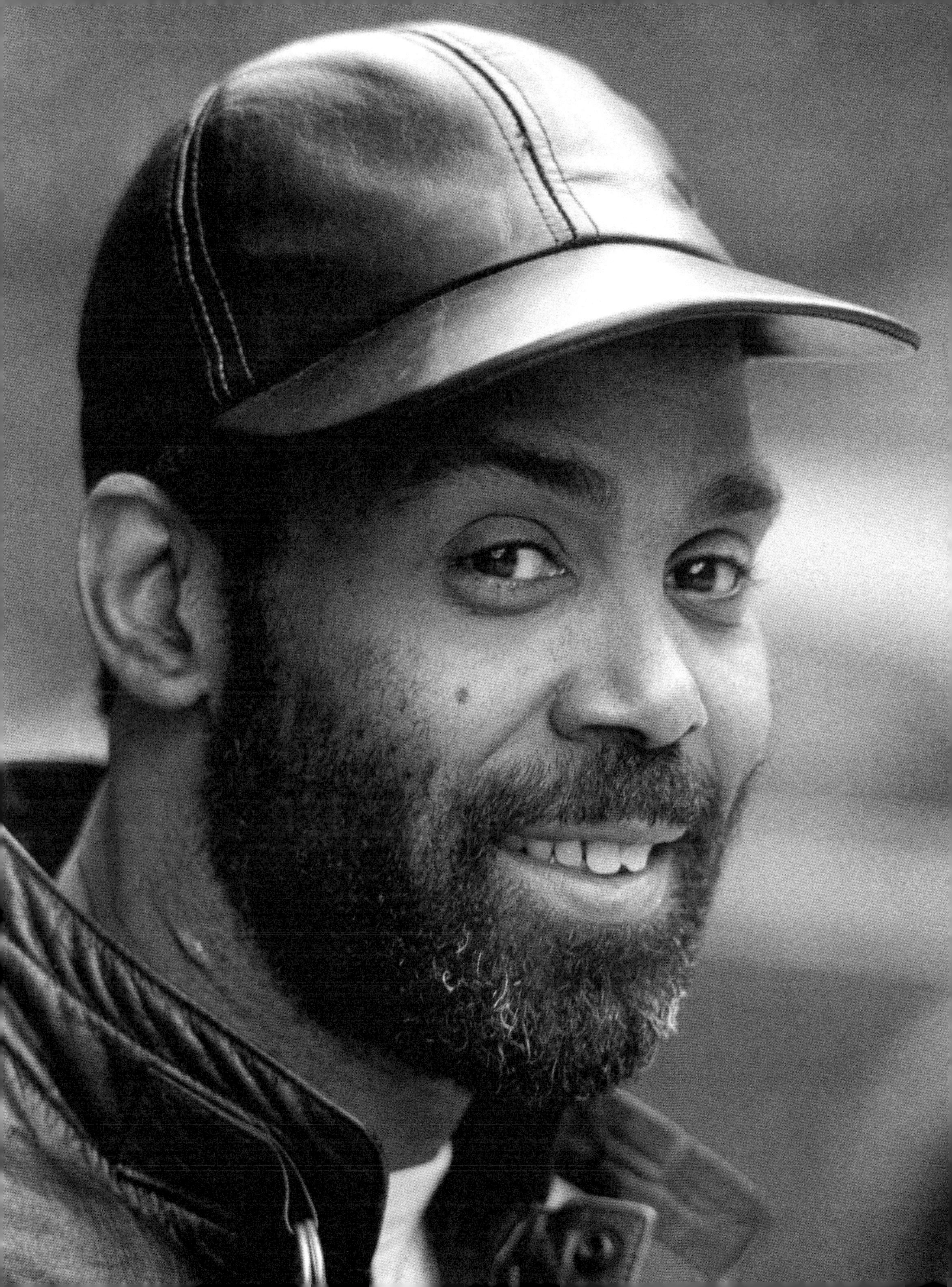

ALBUM

Renaissance

I'm That Girl • Cozy • Alien Superstar • Cuff It • Energy • Break My Soul • Church Girl • Plastic Off the Sofa • Virgo's Groove • Move • Heated • Thique • All Up in Your Mind • America Has a Problem • Pure/Honey • Summer Renaissance •

Streaming by Parkwood Entertainment/Columbia: 29 July 2022
Released in the US by Parkwood Entertainment/Columbia: 29 July 2022
(album ref.: 19658747571, CD ref.: 19658744502)
Best chart ranking in the USA: 1

More charismatic than ever, Beyoncé was determined to make a planet that had finally come out of the 2020 lockdown dance.

A TRIBUTE TO THE 1980S CHICAGO UNDERGROUND SCENE

In 2020, the COVID-19 pandemic struck almost the entire planet, forcing most countries to implement strict quarantine procedures. This particularly affected artists, depriving them of tours, recording sessions, and promotional activities other than through massive use of social media. Many put their careers on hold. But for some, self-isolation proved beneficial, allowing them to work on projects they wouldn't have had time for in normal circumstances. Among the many albums that emerged from lockdown, inspired by these difficult times, were Taylor Swift's *Folklore* and *Evermore*, Metallica's *72 Seasons*, *Carnage* by Nick Cave and Warren Ellis, and Elton John's aptly named *The Lockdown Sessions*. Beyoncé was no exception and used the time to work at home developing a unique album. Like everyone else, she used the technology available to communicate with her collaborators and get ideas down on tape while she waited for better days to come.

Discretion is the name of the game
The ball really got rolling on production of Beyoncé's seventh solo album (*Everything Is Love* and *The Lion King: The Gift* are considered collaborative albums) in May 2020, at a time when some American states were announcing a gradual relaxation of lockdown. As for many others, this enforced quarantine had led Beyoncé to profoundly reappraise her career and pace of work, and to see things from a different perspective. "I truly cherish this time with my family," she said to *Vogue* in November 2020, "and my new goal is to slow down and shed stressful things from my life. I came into the music industry at 15 years old and grew up with the world watching, and I have put out projects non-stop. [...] Now, I've decided to give myself permission to focus on my joy."[312] No one would dare contradict the superstar, but everyone knew that she was incapable of twiddling her thumbs for long. As soon as lockdown was lifted, she launched production of her new album at her own pace. It proved a lengthy business and took almost two years. For the first time, the production was shrouded in mystery after Beyoncé decided not to reveal her creative process to the press (also requiring contributors to remain largely silent) and to grant very few interviews during the promotion of *Renaissance*.

A tribute to life
Beyoncé's first decision was an artistic one. She wanted her next album to celebrate partying, revival, and the feeling of

2022

442 RENAISSANCE

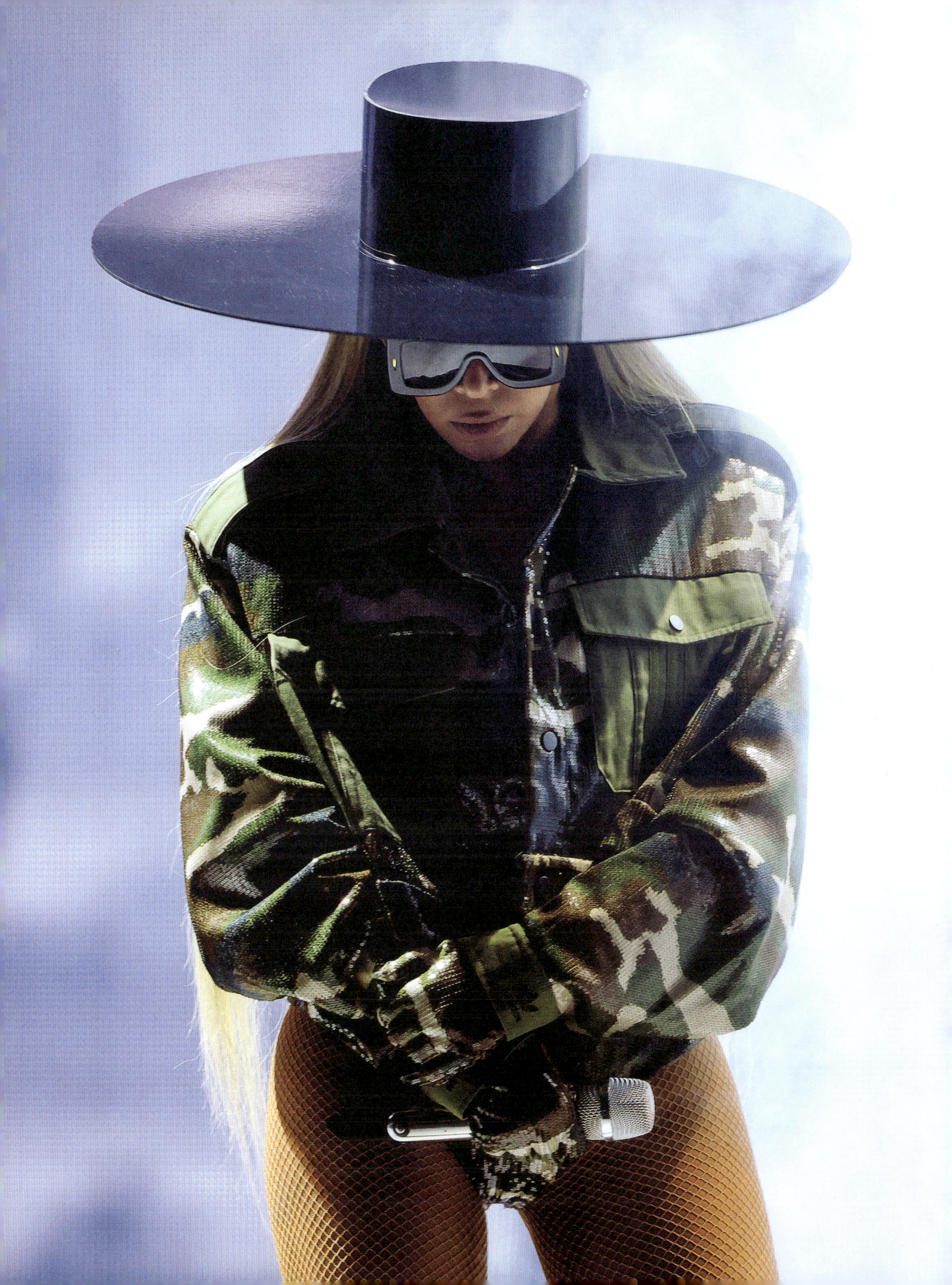

Singer Adeva, whose hit *Warning!* made the whole world dance in 1989.

Superstar DJ Honey Dijon, an important guest on *Renaissance*.

new-found freedom shared by many as summer 2020 approached. She worked with some of her most loyal songwriters and producers (The-Dream, Raphael Saadiq, and Hit-Boy) and expanded her inner circle to invite in artists whose work suited the textures she was seeking for the record. Artists such as Nile Rodgers, co-founder of Chic, who was enjoying a comeback since working with French band Daft Punk in 2013; Grace Jones, former disco queen; Sheila E., the percussionist and drummer forever associated with Prince, for whom she played for many years; as well as the American king of electro and ambassador of dubstep, Skrillex. Other collaborators representing house music—an underground trend spawned in the bowels of niche Chicago clubs in the mid-1980s before it became mainstream and evolved to cater to larger audiences—assisted Beyoncé with the album, a hybrid work that celebrates frivolity and joy. Other names worth mentioning include superstar DJ Honey Dijon, and Terry Hunter, who contributed a remarkable remix of the single *Break My Soul*.

Referencing three years of hits

Although observers broadly describe *Renaissance* as a tribute to 1980s house music and 1990s dance music, it's helpful to look in more detail at the artistic thread that Beyoncé and her producers wove across the record. Some tracks stick to the Afrobeat of *Lion King: The Gift* (*Move*, *Heated*), while others adopt a highly modern production method (*Virgo's Groove*, *Thique*). The album's overarching aesthetic references productions dating from between 1988 and 1991, i.e. the mainstream period of house music and the very start of dance music. While 1988 sounded the death knell for the new wave era, and 1992 saw the birth of a dance style based on the glacial textures of synthesizers and a return to nightclub culture, the period in between was characterized by danceable productions that also featured a soul heritage, one of the hallmarks being frequent use of piano, real or synthesized. Beyoncé's influences on this album include the many songs to emerge from this important period, as she sets out to pay tribute to the plethora of hits that jostled for space in the Top Ten—hits such as Joe Smooth's *Promised Land* (1987), Yazz's *The Only Way Is Up* (1988), Adeva's *Warning* (1989), Madonna's *Vogue* (1990), Londonbeat's *I've Been Thinking About You* (1990), CeCe Peniston's *Finally*, Crystal Waters' *Gypsy Woman (She's Homeless)*, *Crucified* by Army of Lovers, and Nomad's *I Wanna Give You Devotion*, all in the charts in 1991. And that's just a short selection from this glorious period.

The first part of a trilogy

On 28 July 2022, Beyoncé announced on her website the upcoming release of her new album *Renaissance*, the first part of a forthcoming trilogy. Entitled *Act i: Renaissance* on some versions, the album consists largely of songs designed for dancefloors and celebrates life starting up again after several months of enforced lockdown. "Creating this album allowed me a place to dream and to find escape during a scary time for the world," Beyoncé declared in a press release. "It allowed

444 RENAISSANCE

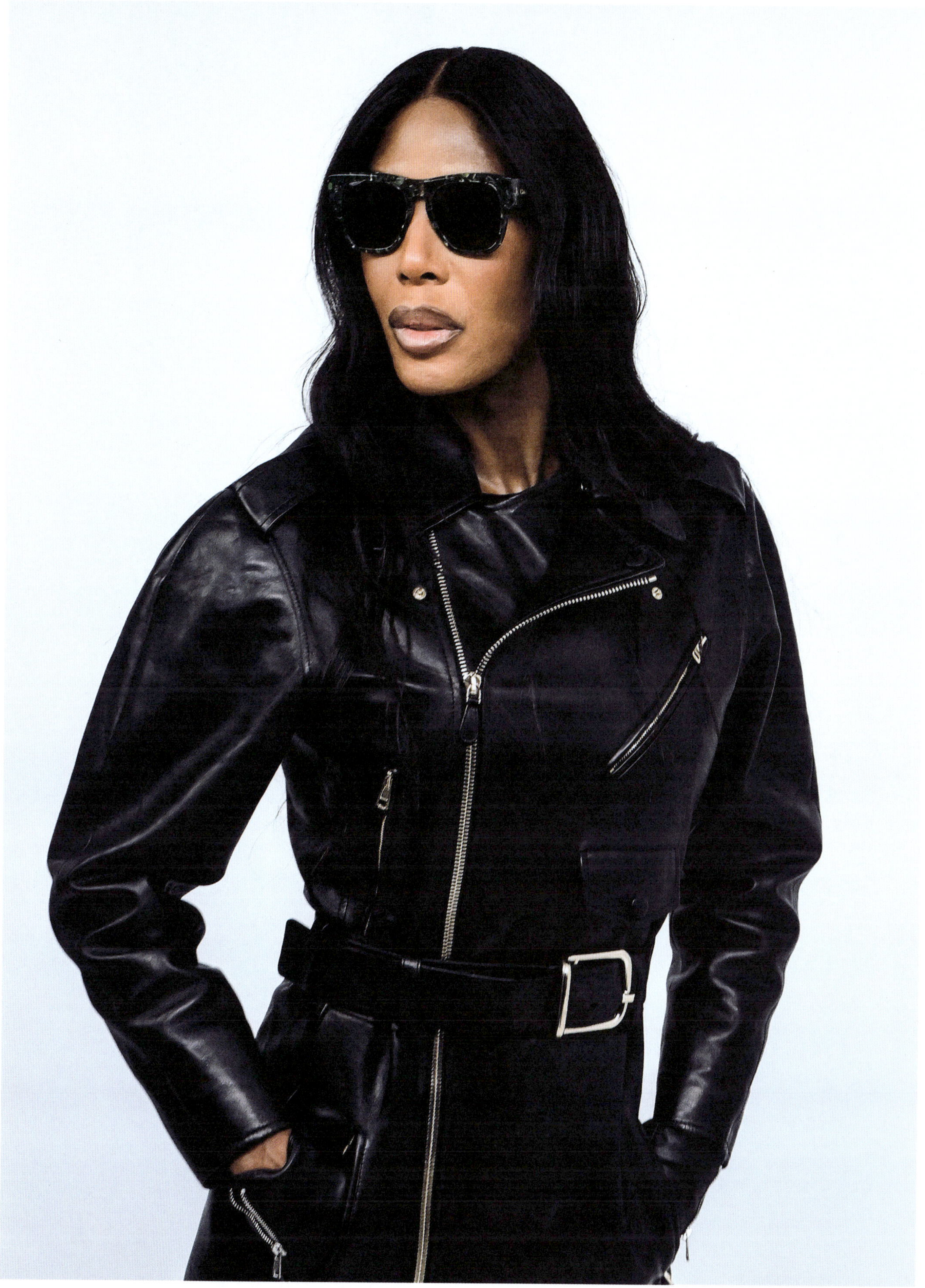

There was an abundance of effects for Queen Beyoncé on the Renaissance World Tour.

me to feel free and adventurous in a time when little else was moving. My intention was to create a safe place, a place without judgment. A place to be free of perfectionism and overthinking. A place to scream, release, feel freedom."[324] Accompanied by the single *Break My Soul*, *Renaissance* met with a spectacular reception when it was released on 29 July 2022, shooting to the top of *Billboard*, and topping the charts in Australia, Canada, France, New Zealand, and the UK. This level of success prompted Beyoncé to revise her plans and get back down to work. On 1 February 2023, she announced the launch of the Renaissance World Tour, a gigantic 56-date tour to promote the album. At the same time, she postponed the release of the album's music videos, but on 25 November 2023 fans would be able to console themselves with the premiere of the documentary *Renaissance: A Film by Beyoncé*, which followed the progress of the tour.

2022

FOR BEYONCÉ ADDICTS

The cover of *Renaissance* pays tribute to British artist John Collier's 1897 painting *Lady Godiva*, depicting the legend of the woman who, in the 11th century, rode naked through the streets of Coventry to persuade her husband, Leofric, Earl of de Mercia, to reduce the townspeople's taxes. Some also see it as a nod to a famous 1977 photo of Bianca Jagger astride a horse in the Studio 54 club on her 32nd birthday.

446 **RENAISSANCE**

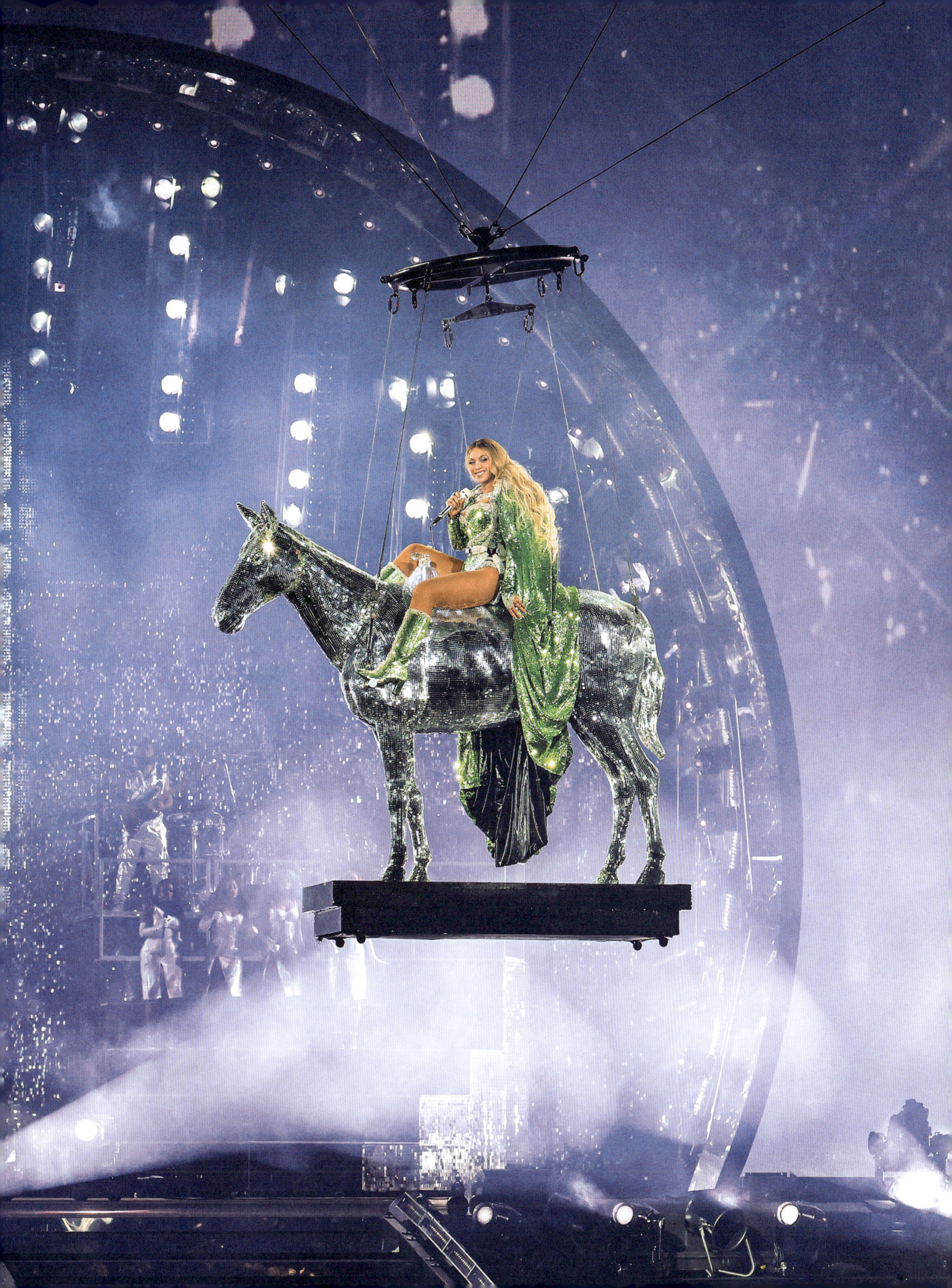

The-Dream got back to basics to make Beyoncé fans dance.

I'M THAT GIRL

(Andrea Yvette Summers, Beyoncé, Kelman Duran, Mike Dean, Terius Nash/3'28)

Musicians
Beyoncé: vocals, backing vocals, programming
Terius "The-Dream" Nash: backing vocals
Kelman Duran: programming
Mike Dean: synthesizers
Stuart White: programming

Recording
The Trailer, East Hampton: 2020 to 2022
The Juicy Juicy, Los Angeles: 2020 to 2022
Parkwood West, Los Angeles: 2020 to 2022

Technical team
Producers: MWA, Mike Dean, Beyoncé, Kelman Duran, Jameil Aossey, S1A0, Stuart White
Executive producer: Beyoncé Knowles-Carter
Recording engineers: Stuart White, Brandon Harding, Andrea Roberts, John Cranfield
Assistant recording engineer: Matheus Braz

Genesis

On the eve of the album's release, Beyoncé posted on her website: "To all of the pioneers who originate culture, to all of the fallen angels whose contributions have gone unrecognized for far too long. This is a celebration for you."[324] Following on from this, the first track on *Renaissance* starts with a sample from rapper Tommy Wright III, an active member of the Memphis hip-hop community. Taken from the track *Still Pimpin* on his 1995 album *Runnin-N-Gunnin*, the sample also pays homage to the song's co-singer, Andrea Summers, aka Princess Loko, a former Memphis rap star with an inimitable flow who died largely forgotten in 2020 at the age of 40. "I have a feeling that they wanted to promote underground culture on this album," said Kelman Duran, producer on the track, "just based on the samples that they had chosen. So I'm sure Beyoncé knows who Tommy Wright is, who Princess Loko is. And I'm sure that they know that she still hasn't been given her due."[325]

Production

While there are numerous producers credited on *I'm That Girl*, the Dominican Kelman Duran was the one behind the track's instrumental. When Beyoncé was working on the production of *The Lion King: The Gift*, Duran received an email from Parkwood Entertainment asking him if he would be interested in presenting some demos. "I didn't know what Parkwood was, and then I saw it was Beyoncé's company. I had a feeling it was for *The Lion King*. Me being cynical, I was like, 'this is probably not going to work.'"[325] History would prove him wrong, as his instrumental was chosen to open the album.

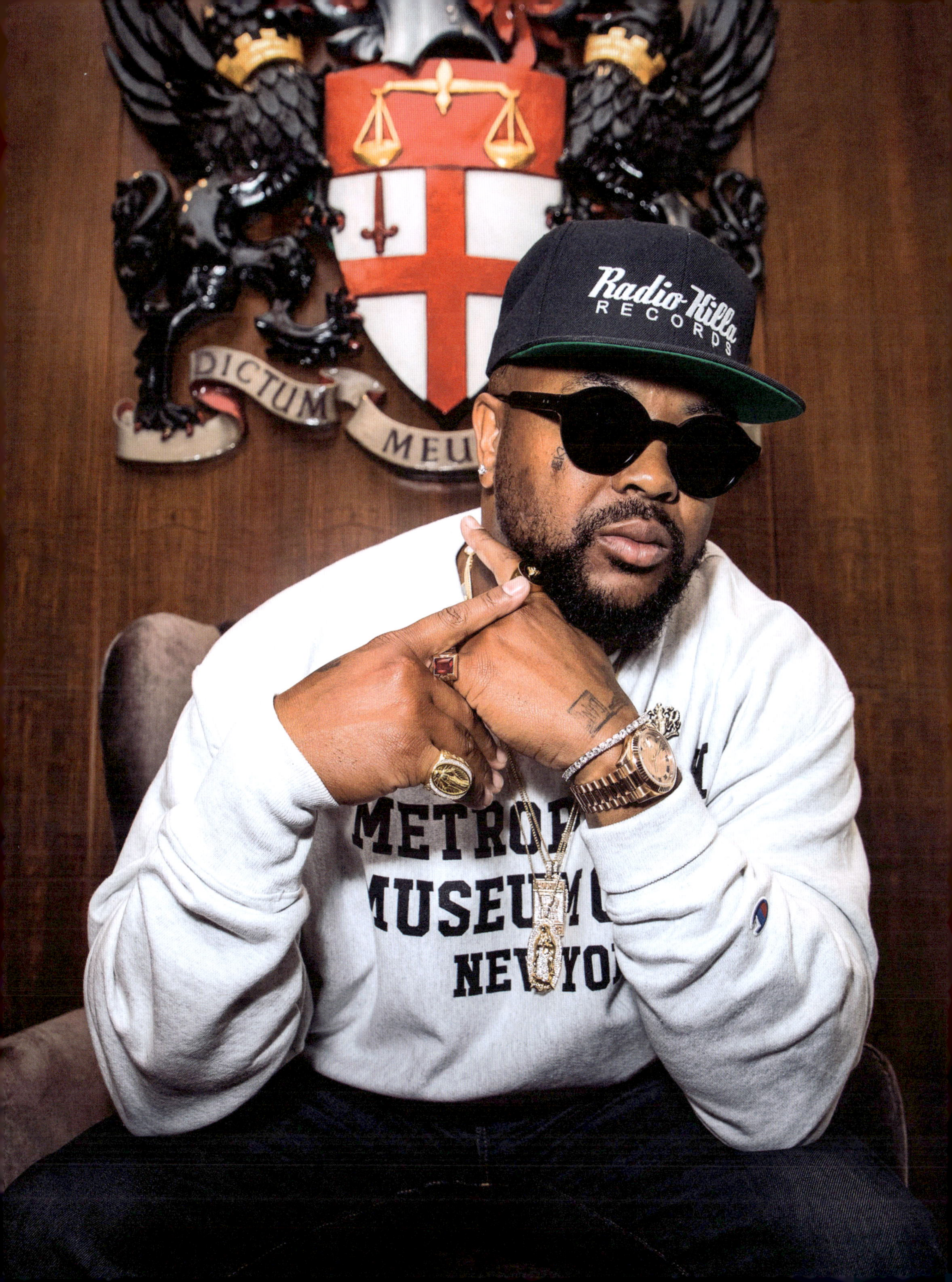
DICTUM
MEU
Radio Killa
RECORDS
METRO
MUSEUM
NEW YO

Fred Fairbrass (left) and Richard Fairbrass of the duo Right Said Fred in 1992.

COZY

(Beyoncé, Christopher Lawrence Penny, Dave Giles II, Honey Redmond, Luke Francis Matthew Solomon, Mike Dean, Nija Charles, Terius Nash/3'30)

Musicians: Beyoncé: vocals, backing vocals / **Nija Charles:** backing vocals / **Dave Giles II:** vocals / **Chris Penny:** programming / **Honey Dijon:** programming / **Luke Solomon:** programming / **Mike Dean:** synthesizers / **Recording:** The Trailer, East Hampton: 2020 to 2022 / The Juicy Juicy, Los Angeles: 2020 to 2022 / Parkwood West, Los Angeles: 2020 to 2022 / **Technical team:** Producers: Beyoncé, MWA, Mike Dean, Chris Penny, Honey Dijon, Luke Solomon / **Executive producer:** Beyoncé Knowles-Carter / **Recording engineers:** Matheus Braz, Andrea Roberts, John Cranfield, Stuart White

One of the stars of *Renaissance* is Honey Dijon, an internationally famous DJ. Originally from Chicago, the LGBTQIA+ activist and proud trans woman delivers here an instrumental that could be straight out of one of her sets. Honey Dijon thus brings her expertise to bear on Beyoncé's *Renaissance*. Having lived through the emergence of house music in the mid-1980s, and then the birth of dance music and techno a few years later, Dijon helped Beyoncé navigate the thickets of this music style and its sub-genres. She also shared her knowledge of the queer scene, kicking off their collaboration by presenting Beyoncé with a copy of Lucas Hilderbrand's book about the 2013 documentary film *Paris Is Burning*, which explores the involvement of African-American and Latino communities in New York's drag ball scene in the 1980s. "My role for her in creating this album, I wanted to do the community justice,"[326] the DJ later said. So she drew on her vast musical culture to pay homage to certain classics such as Lidell Townsell & M.T.F.'s *Get With U*, with the remix by David Morales inspiring the bass line, which itself references 1986's seminal acid house hit *No Way Back* by the American Adonis.

ALIEN SUPERSTAR

(Atia Boggs, Beyoncé, Brittany Coney, Christopher Lawrence Penny, Danielle Balbuena, David Hamelin, David Debrandon Brown, Denisia Andrews, Honey Dijon, Levar Coppin, Leven Kali, Luke Francis Matthew Solomon, Mike Dean, Rami Yacoub, Saliou Diagne, Shawn Carter, Timothy Lee McKenzie, Barbara Ann Teer, Christopher Abbott Bernard Fairbrass, Richard Peter John Fairbrass, Robert Francis Anthony Manzoli, John Michael Holiday, Kim Cooper, Peter Rauhofer/3'35)

Musicians: Beyoncé: vocals, backing vocals / **Blu June:** backing vocals / **Mike Dean:** synthesizers / **Terius "The-Dream" Nash:** synthesizers / **Chris Penny:** programming / **Honey Dijon:** programming / **Luke Solomon:** programming / **Recording:** The Juicy Juicy, Los Angeles: 2020 to 2022 / Parkwood West, Los Angeles: 2020 to 2022 / The Record Plant, Los Angeles: 2020 to 2022 / **Technical team:** Producers: Beyoncé, Mike Dean, Terius "The-Dream" Nash, Chris Penny, Honey Dijon, Luke Solomon, Nova Wav / **Executive producer:** Beyoncé Knowles-Carter / **Recording engineers:** Andrea Roberts, John Cranfield, Chi Coney, Stuart White / **Assistant recording engineer:** Matheus Braz

Like *Energy*, *Alien Superstar* sparked copyright controversy. Right Said Fred, the famous house music duo remembered for their early 1990s single *I'm Too Sexy*, claimed Beyoncé had not sought permission to borrow parts of their vocal line, unlike two other superstars, who had requested permission through the proper channels: Taylor Swift for *Look What You Made Me Do* in 2017 and Drake for *Way 2 Sexy* in 2021. Just as in 2017 Ed Sheeran had been forced to admit having been inspired by the chorus of TLC's *No Scrubs* (1999) for the pre-chorus of his hit *Shape of You*, so Beyoncé readily admitted the nod to *I'm Too Sexy*. But she also insisted (in a statement issued through *Entertainment News* on 7 October 2022) that

2022

450 RENAISSANCE

the appropriate permission had been sought and obtained from the song's publisher, and that Right Said Fred's claims were "erroneous and incredibly disparaging." Another *Alien Superstar* incident involved Diane Warren and her rather ham-fisted comments on Twitter (renamed X in 2023). The successful composer and songwriter who had penned *I Was Here* for Beyoncé in 2011 asked her followers: "How can there be 24 writers on a song?"[327] Following a storm of protest from the BeyHive, Warren was "reprimanded" by The-Dream, the track's co-producer, in an online exchange that quickly descended into a playground dispute. The facts, as explained by The-Dream, were simple. The number of writers and composers credited on the track corresponded to the rights holders of the many tracks sampled on the song. Diane Warren issued a humble apology on Twitter, pointing to Beyoncé's many qualities.

The years pass, but the inimitable style of the guitarist Nile Rodgers stays forever young.

SINGLE

CUFF IT

(Beyoncé, Brittany Coney, Denisia Andrews, Morten Ristorp, Nile Rodgers, Raphael Saadiq, Terius Nash, Allen Henry McGrier, Mary Christine Brockert/3'45)

Musicians
- **Beyoncé:** vocals, backing vocals
- **Beam:** backing vocals
- **Nile Rodgers:** guitar
- **Raphael Saadiq:** bass, drums, synthesizers, Hohner Clavinet, Arp String Ensemble
- **Chris Penny:** programming
- **Honey Dijon:** programming
- **Luke Solomon:** programming
- **Sheila E.:** percussions
- **Daniel Crawford:** piano
- **Terius "The-Dream" Nash:** synthesizers
- **Scott Mayo:** saxophone
- **Lemar Guillary:** trombone
- **Jamelle Adisa:** trumpet

Recording
- **The Trailer, East Hampton:** 2020 to 2022
- **The Juicy Juicy, Los Angeles:** 2020 to 2022
- **Parkwood West, Los Angeles:** 2020 to 2022
- **Tree Sounds Studios, Atlanta:** 2020 to 2022
- **Blakeslee Studio, Los Angeles:** 2020 to 2022
- **Nightbird Recording Studios, Los Angeles:** 2020 to 2022
- **Le Crib, Westport:** 2020 to 2022

Technical team
- **Producers:** Rissi, Terius "The-Dream" Nash, Beyoncé, Nova Wav, Raphael Saadiq
- **Executive producer:** Beyoncé Knowles-Carter
- **Recording engineers:** Hotae Alexander Jang, Steve Rusch, Brandon Harding, Chi Coney, Andrea Roberts, John Cranfield, Stuart White, Russell Graham
- **Assistant recording engineer:** Matheus Braz

Single
- **Streaming by Parkwood Entertainment/Columbia:** August 2002
- **Best chart ranking in the USA:** 6

Genesis

On 6 February 2023, the 65th Grammy Awards were held in Los Angeles. Beyoncé, who was due to receive four awards, was a notable absentee, arriving very late after being stuck in the city's traffic jams. Nile Rodgers, eminent guitarist and producer, founder of Chic and author of many timeless hits, had been invited that evening to present her with the Grammy Award for Best R&B Song for *Cuff It*. In her absence, he stood on stage and shared an anecdote about the track, for which he had recorded a funky guitar line. "When I got called to play on this song, it was the most organic thing that ever happened to me. I heard the song and I just said, 'I wanna play on that. Right now.' And it was one take, I promise. I played it, it was one take and I never even got 'Well, Nile, maybe you should do this, maybe you should do that?' It was just what I felt in my heart."[328]

Production

The first version of *Cuff It* was the work of Raphael Saadiq, who had earmarked it to sing with his legendary band Tony! Toni! Toné! on their reunion tour, the Just Me and You Tour 2023. The producer, who had worked with Beyoncé on many occasions, then thought about offering the song to her, and she enthusiastically accepted. *Cuff It* was passed on to The-Dream, who put it through a detailed production process, calling in Chi and Blu June from the duo Nova Wav to contribute to the track and write the lyrics. But with the recording session at Atlanta's Tree Sound Studios already underway, the two women had zero inspiration. So to clear their heads they decided to slip out to a local strip club, which is where they found inspiration for the song's theme. It was 3am by the time they returned to the studio, rolled their sleeves up, and got down to work. Two other tracks emerged from the Atlanta work sessions: *Energy* and *Summer Renaissance*.

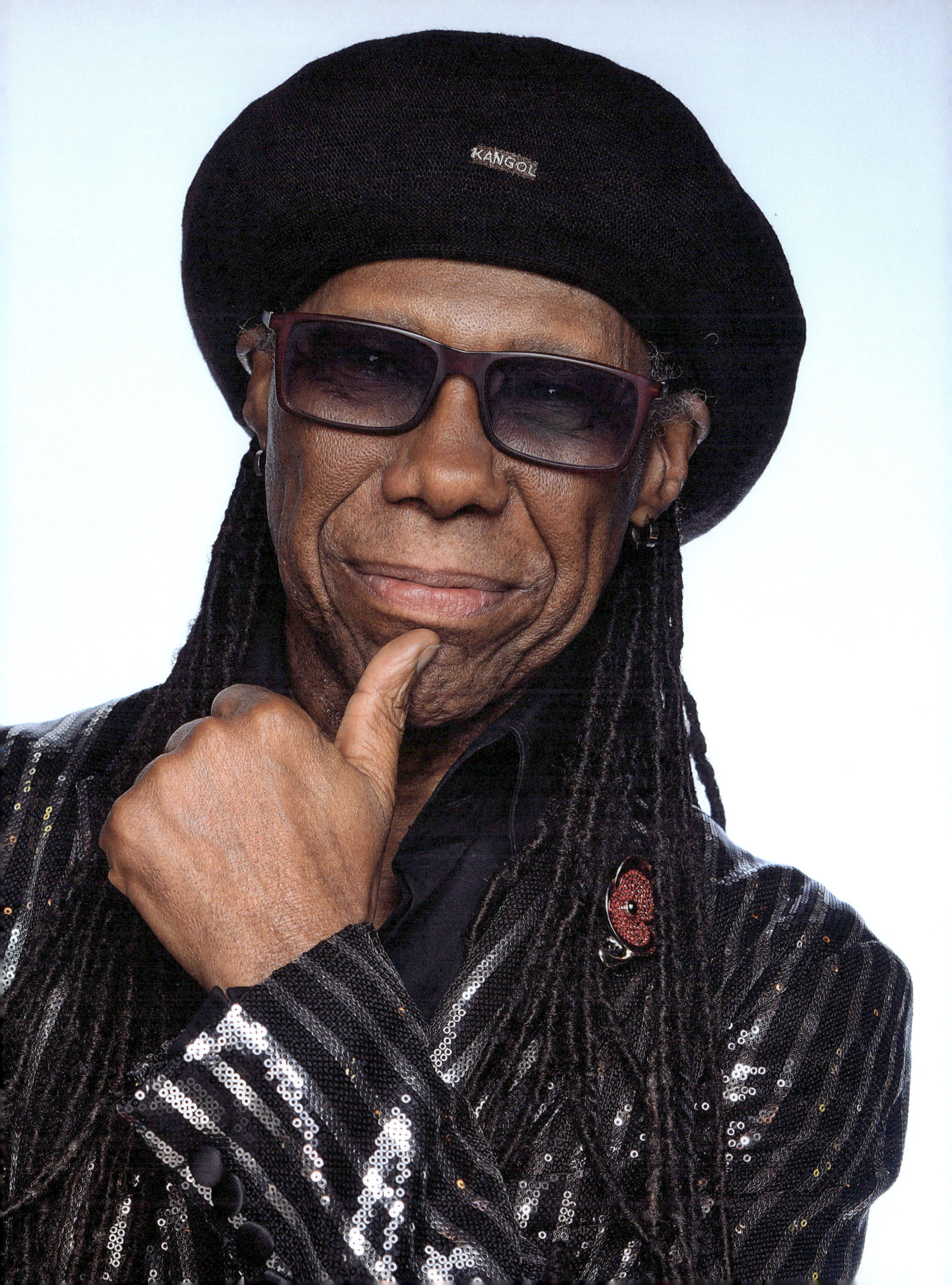
KANGOL

The sample borrowed from Milkshake, by Kelis, was discreetly removed from the mix of Energy.

ENERGY

(Almando Cresso, Beyoncé, Brittany Coney, Denisia Andrews, Jordan Douglas, Sonny Moore, Terius Nash, Tizita Makuria, Tyshane Thompson, Adam James Pigott, Freddie Ross, Chad Hugo, Pharrell Williams, Allen Henry McGrier, Mary Christine Brockert/1'56)

Musicians: Beyoncé: vocals, backing vocals / **Beam:** vocals, backing vocals, programming / **Nova Wav:** synthesizers / **Al Cress :** programming / **Skrillex:** programming / **Recording:** Kings Landing Studios West, Los Angeles: 2020 to 2022 / The Juicy Juicy, Los Angeles: 2020 to 2022 / Parkwood West, Los Angeles: 2020 to 2022 / **Technical team: Producers:** Beyoncé, Al Cress, Beam, Skrillex, Nova Wav / **Executive producer:** Beyoncé Knowles-Carter / **Recording engineers:** Andrea Roberts, John Cranfield, Brandon Harding, Chi Coney, Beam, Stuart White / **Assistant recording engineer:** Matheus Braz

Samples abound in this excellently produced track, featuring the rapper and singer Beam, but one particular one was quickly removed from the mix due to yet another copyright issue. When the singer Kelis first listened to *Renaissance*, she noticed that *Energy* included a segment borrowed from her song *Milkshake*, released on her 2003 album *Tasty*. The song was written and produced by Chad Hugo and Pharrell Williams, then of the duo The Neptunes, and is their property, since, as Kelis explained, the contract she'd signed at the time prohibited her from claiming ownership of the piece. Nevertheless, Kelis was offended by the tactlessness shown by Beyoncé and her teams, who hadn't deemed it necessary to ask her permission to use the sample. After heavy criticism from the BeyHive, Kelis posted a simple and sincere message on Instagram on 22 July 2022 (*Renaissance* having leaked onto the internet a few days before its official release, Kelis had already listened to *Energy*), explaining that she was deeply hurt by the lack of courtesy shown by Beyoncé's teams. As a gesture of reconciliation, Queen Bey removed the *Milkshake* sample from *Energy*, though to this day Hugo and Williams are still credited on the track.

SINGLE

BREAK MY SOUL

(Beyoncé, Shawn Carter, Terius Nash, Christopher A. Stewart, Adam James Pigott, Freddie Ross, George Allen, Fred Craig McFarlane/4'38)

Musicians
Beyoncé: vocals, backing vocals
Big Freedia: vocals? backing vocals?
Kaye Fox (The Samples): backing vocals
Jawan McEastland (The Samples): backing vocals
Peaches West (The Samples): backing vocals
Nikki Grier (The Samples): backing vocals
Alexandria Griffin: backing vocals
Anthony McEastland: backing vocals
Ashley Washington: backing vocals
Ashly Williams: backing vocals
Caleb Curry: backing vocals
Chelsea Miller: backing vocals
Chris McLaughlin: backing vocals
Danielle Withers: backing vocals
Deanna Dixon: backing vocals
Erik Brooks: backing vocals
Fallynn Rian: backing vocals
Herman Bryant: backing vocals
Jamal Moore: backing vocals
Jasmine Patton: backing vocals
Javonte Pollard: backing vocals
Jonathan Coleman: backing vocals
Jorel Quinn: backing vocals
Kim Johnson: backing vocals
Kristen Lowe: backing vocals
Naarai Jacobs: backing vocals
Porcha Clay: backing vocals

Recording
The Trailer, East Hampton: 2020 to 2022
The Juicy Juicy, Los Angeles: 2020 to 2022
Parkwood West, Los Angeles: 2020 to 2022
Henson Recording Studios, Los Angeles: 2020 to 2022

Technical team
Producers: Beyoncé, Jawan McEastland, Nikki Grier, Jens Christian Isaksen, Terius Nash, C. "Tricky" Stewart
Executive producer: Beyoncé Knowles-Carter
Recording engineers: Andrea Roberts, John Cranfield, Brandon Harding, Stuart White, Chris McLaughlin
Assistant recording engineer: Matheus Braz

Single
Streaming by Parkwood Entertainment/Columbia: 20 June 2022
Best chart ranking in the USA: 1

Genesis

On 20 June 2022, Robin Jackson Maynard's phone was full of missed calls, including several from her son: "When I asked him, he says, 'You're trending everywhere, all over the place. Look at your phone!' And then when I saw it, honestly, I didn't know whether to scream; I didn't know whether to cry. I was in disbelief."[329] The lady, it has to be said, isn't a complete unknown, as she was once a house music star who released two albums under the pseudonym Robin S. between 1993 and 1997. Her biggest hit, *Show Me Love*, brought her fame in 1993 when Swedes StoneBridge and Nick Nice did a remix, the original 1990 version having passed totally under the radar. When Beyoncé decided to produce an album in homage to the glory days of house music, a nod to *Show Me Love* was pretty much inevitable. *Break My Soul*, with its very characteristic house music-style production, was an outstanding success when it was released, giving Beyoncé her first solo number one on the Hot 100 since 2008's *Single Ladies (Put a Ring on It)*, also co-produced by Christopher "Tricky" Stewart. Wednesday 3 August 2022 saw the release of an EP comprising four remixes of *Break My Soul*, co-produced by will.i.am, Terry Hunter, Honey Dijon, and Nita Aviance. Three days later, fans were treated to *Break My Soul (The Queens Remix)*, featuring a very special guest: Madonna, with samples of *Vogue*, her house hit from 1990, added to the remix.

Production

Although Beyoncé didn't sample the 1993 version of *Show Me Love*, instead reinterpreting various parts, such as the signature synthesizer notes, it was a different story with *Explode* by rapper Big Freedia, segments of which appeared on *Break My Soul*. Beyoncé took the trouble to invite the Louisiana-born rapper to join her in Los Angeles to see what she had created using his 2014 single. Big Freedia suggested they re-record his vocals, but Beyoncé preferred to keep the original sample, so the rapper settled for approving the addition of samples from his lyrics, which urged listeners to free themselves from whatever was holding them back. "At the time when I wrote *Explode*," the rapper explained, "I was thinking about all of those things I wanted to release […] Sometimes you want to explode, all the things that you're going through. So I wanted to release all those things."[330]

The producer Syd, a member of the collective The Internet, took part in the production of *Plastic Off the Sofa*.

CHURCH GIRL

(Beyoncé, Ralph MacDonald, Eldon D. Anderson, Ernest Wilson, Jerome T. Temple, Terius Nash, William Salter, Elbernita Clark-Terrell, Orville Erwin Hall, Phillip Glen Price, James Brown, Derrick Robert Ordogne, Dion Lamont Norman, Jimi Stephen Payton/3'44)

Musicians: Beyoncé: vocals, backing vocals / **Stuart White:** programming / **Terius "The-Dream" Nash:** programming / **Recording:** The Trailer, East Hampton: 2020 to 2022 / The Juicy Juicy, Los Angeles: 2020 to 2022 / Parkwood West, Los Angeles: 2020 to 2022 / **Technical team: Producers:** Beyoncé, No I.D., Terius Nash, Stuart White / **Executive producer:** Beyoncé Knowles-Carter / **Recording engineers:** Andrea Roberts, John Cranfield, Brandon Harding, Stuart White / **Assistant recording engineer:** Matheus Braz

"Church is my sanctuary, the place I go to let go,"[16] Beyoncé had revealed in 2003. She has always been open about her Christian faith, so it seems only natural that the tracklisting for *Renaissance* should include a track called *Church Girl*. As Beyoncé never does anything the way others do, this isn't a profession of faith as you'd expect, but instead a song about the ways these so-called church girls sometimes behave—maybe not completely wild, but at least free of moral constraints. The lyrics, along with the addition of a sample from the American gospel repertoire (namely *Center of Thy Will* by The Clark Sisters), weren't to the taste of certain pious, somewhat conservative minds, such as Patrick L. Wooden Sr, a pastor from North Carolina who accused Beyoncé of having sold her "soul to the devil"[331] with lyrics he described as libidinous and sacrilegious. The song was written by one of Jay-Z's loyal collaborators, the producer No I.D., who had originally worked on the piece's instrumental for Jay-Z during a work session at the New Yorker's home. "And he was rapping to it, it was for him. And he just put it in the computer, I never thought about it again, I literally forgot about it. And then one day, I just get a call. When you get 2-3 calls from people in a row, you know it's something. 'Hey, do you have this idea? Beyoncé got somethin' to it.' And Jay jokingly tells me, 'Man, she stole my beat. She was like, "Remember that idea in the computer that you didn't finish?"'"[332]

PLASTIC OFF THE SOFA

(Beyoncé, Nick Green, Sabrina Claudio, Sydney Bennett/4'14)

Musicians: Beyoncé: vocals, backing vocals / Sabrina Claudio: backing vocals / **Derek Renfroe:** guitar / **Patrick Paige II:** bass / **Leven Kali:** synthesizers / **Recording:** Kings Landing Studios West, Los Angeles: 2020 to 2022 / The Juicy Juicy, Los Angeles: 2020 to 2022 / Parkwood West, Los Angeles: 2020 to 2022 / **Technical team: Producers:** Beyoncé, Syd, Leven Kali / **Executive producer:** Beyoncé Knowles-Carter / **Recording engineers:** Andrea Roberts, John Cranfield, Stuart White / **Assistant recording engineer:** Matheus Braz

With a drum beat reminiscent of the 1976 Tina Charles hit *I Love to Love (But My Baby Loves to Dance)*, *Plastic Off the Sofa* is a resolutely disco track, the work of two producers with a marked taste for groove. First up is the track's main producer, Leven Kali, who earned his stripes alongside Drake in 2017. Among the musicians hired to give the track a more organic texture than the album's synthetic house pieces were close friends of producer Sydney Bennett, aka Syd (formerly Syd tha Kyd), all members of the band The Internet, which incorporated former members of the hip-hop collective Odd Future. One of them, bassist Patrick Paige II, here showcases his groovy playing style. Leven Kali spoke about the public reception of *Renaissance*: "I've been at different parties where it's people listening to that album from beginning to the end. It just has this infectious, uplifting and coming-together effect on people that I feel is an element of R&B and Black music that used to be around all the time and has been missing. That really inspired me to have some of my own records kind of give that same energy."[333]

2022

456 **RENAISSANCE**

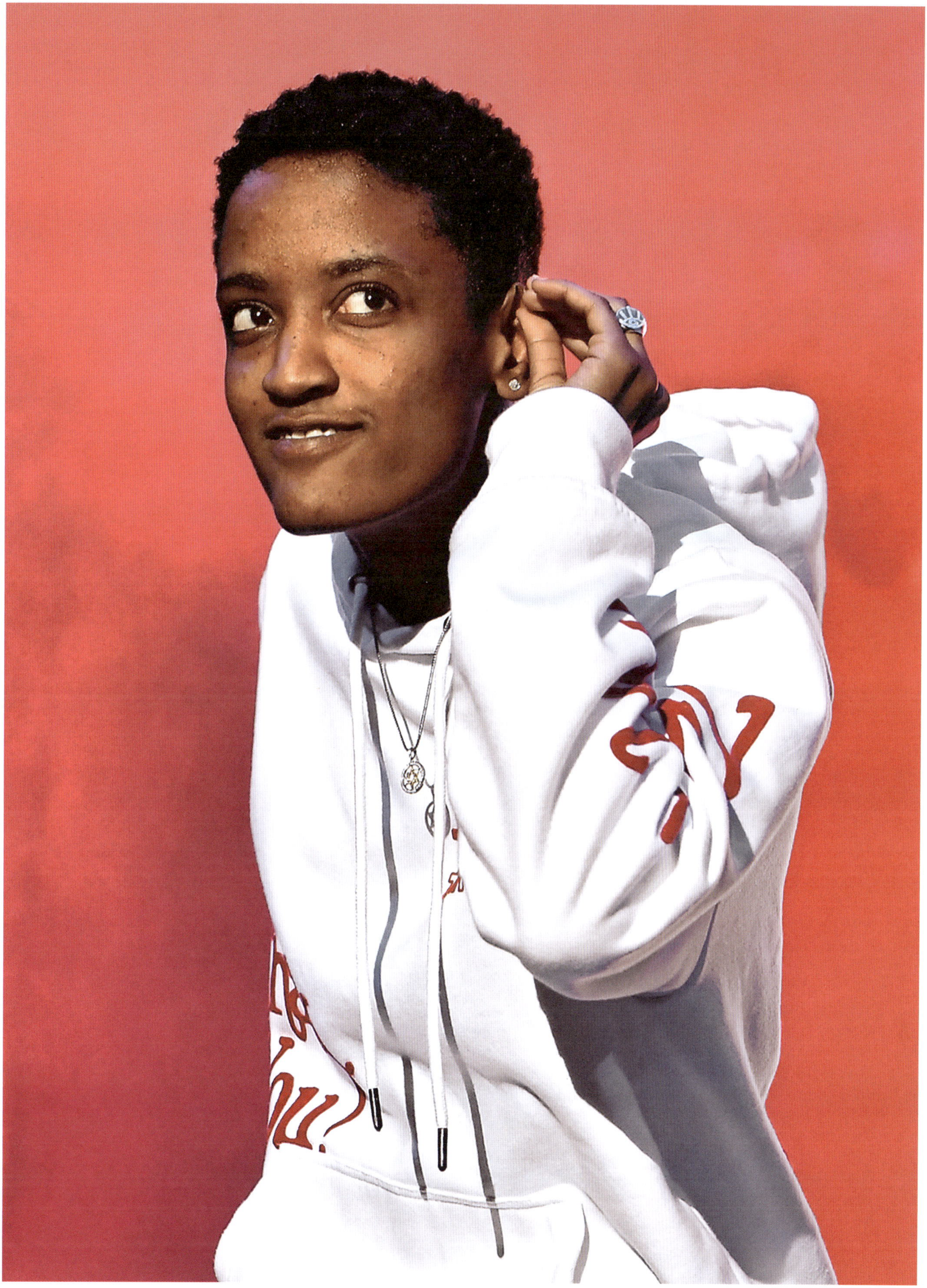

How could you pay homage to the spirit of nightclubs without inviting the iconic Grace Jones to sing in *Move*?

SINGLE

VIRGO'S GROOVE

(Beyoncé, Daniel Memmi, Darius Dixson, Dustin Bowie, Jesse Wilson, Jocelyn Donald, Leven Kali/6'08)

Musicians: Beyoncé: vocals, backing vocals / Leven Kali: backing vocals / Terius "The-Dream" Nash: synthesizers / **Recording:** Kings Landing Studios West, Los Angeles: 2020 to 2022 / The Juicy Juicy, Los Angeles: 2020 to 2022 / Parkwood West, Los Angeles: 2020 to 2022 / **Technical team:** Producers: Beyoncé, Leven Kali, Terius "The-Dream" Nash / **Executive producer:** Beyoncé Knowles-Carter / **Recording engineers:** Andrea Roberts, John Cranfield, Stuart White / **Assistant recording engineer:** Matheus Braz / **Single:** Streaming by Parkwood Entertainment/Columbia: 2 June 2023 / Best chart ranking in the USA: 43

Although most of those involved in the production of *Renaissance* respected the instructions about its conception—don't say anything to the press about it—interviews that some of them granted to the media afford us some insights. In an article in *Variety*, we discover that three old high-school friends, Leven Kali, Daniel Memmi, and Sol Was (although, oddly, the last of these isn't credited on the track), worked together to write *Virgo's Groove*, a disco track that celebrates Beyoncé's astrological sign, a theme already touched on in *Gift from Virgo* from 2003's *Dangerously in Love*. According to Kali, the song is a tribute to his musical culture, predominantly funk. "I feel like a lot of my music […] aligns with that big characteristic of funk, it's all in the bass lines," he explained. "When we all work together, we kind of come in with this fantasy of house, funk, R&B and jazz being fused together. The background vocals and the bassline is something that for me is like a signature."[334]

MOVE

(Ariowa Irosogie, Beyoncé, Brittany Coney, Denisia Andrews, Richard Isong, Ronald Banful, Temilade Openiyi/3'23)

Musicians: Beyoncé: vocals, backing vocals / Grace Jones: vocals / Ari PenSmith: backing vocals / Tems: vocals / **Recording:** Kings Landing Studios West, Los Angeles: 2020 to 2022 / The Juicy Juicy, Los Angeles: 2020 to 2022 / Parkwood West, Los Angeles: 2020 to 2022 / Zak Starkey Studio, Ochi Rios: 2020 to 2022 / **Technical team:** Producers: Beyoncé, P2J, Guiltybeatz, MeLo-X, Stuart White, Terius Nash, Ivor Guest / **Executive producer:** Beyoncé Knowles-Carter / **Recording engineers:** Delroy "Phatta" Pottinger, Andrea Roberts, John Cranfield, Stuart White, Guiltybeatz / **Assistant recording engineer:** Matheus Braz

When asked by *Variety* about their involvement in the writing process on *Move*, and more particularly about Grace Jones's participation, Blu June and Chi from Nova Wav made no attempt to hide their excitement. "It's a dream come true. It's like, the Grace Jones," said Blu June. "Just witnessing her greatness—you can never really plan for moments like this, so when it happens it feels like a big surprise. You feel like a fan all over again, and we're just super humbled."[335] "On my 2021 vision board, Grace Jones is on there and it says 'icon' on top of it," added Chi. "So to be able to cross off things with our vision boards has been so amazing as well."[335] Jones, the Jamaican-born fashion icon who released ten albums between 1977 and 2008, was happy to participate in the *Renaissance* venture after several insistent requests from Beyoncé. She did, however, require a non-negotiable addition to her contract, namely that no auto-tune would be used on her voice, as she wanted her listeners to instantly recognize her timbre.

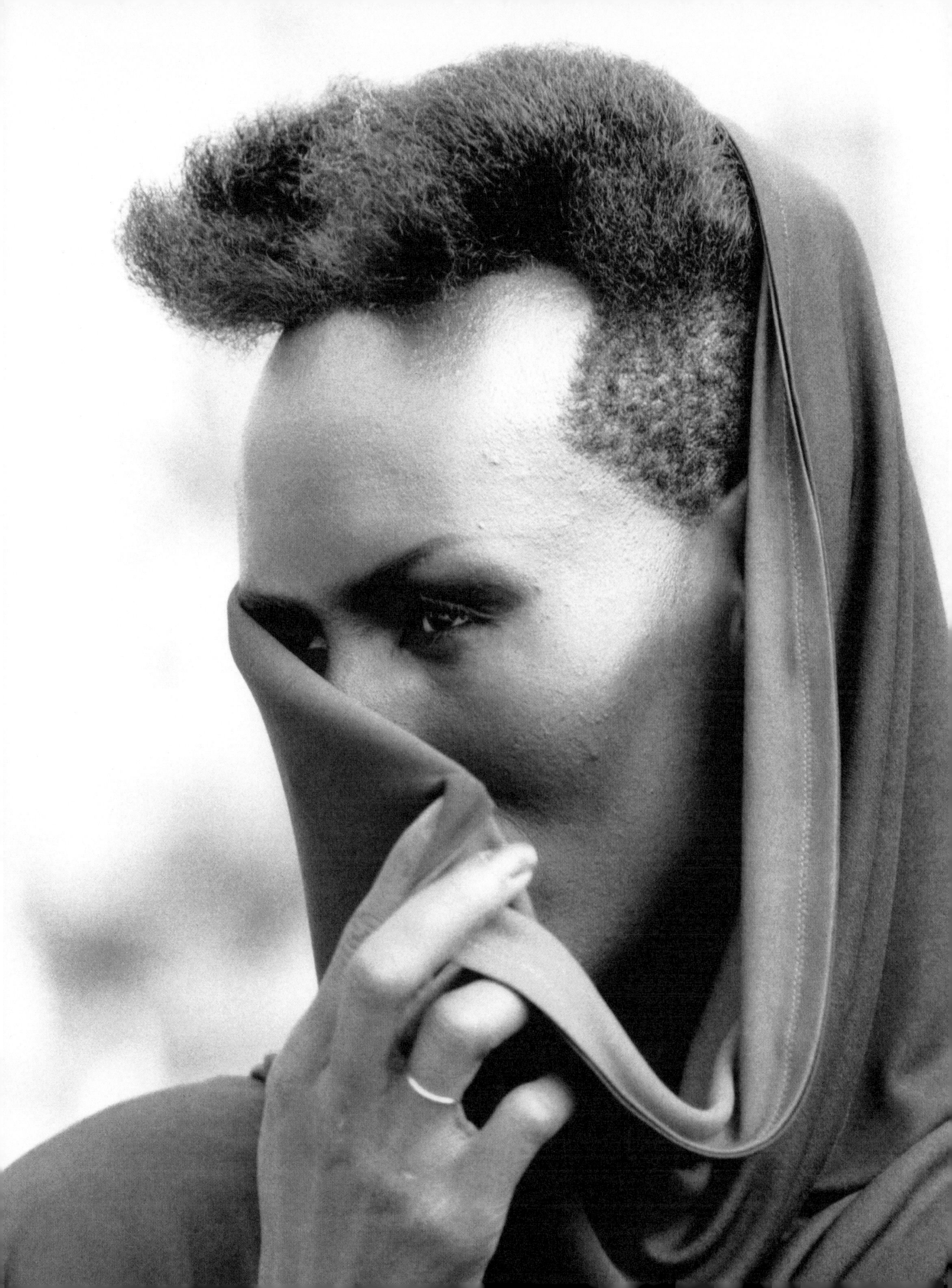

HEATED

(Aubrey Drake Graham, Beyoncé, Brittany Coney, Denisia Andrews, Jahaan Sweet, Matthew Samuels, Ricky Lawson, Rupert Thomas Jr, Sean Seaton/4'20)

Musicians: Beyoncé: vocals, backing vocals / Beam: backing vocals / Tatiana "Tatu" Matthews: backing vocals / Terius "The-Dream" Nash: backing vocals / Cadenza: programming / Kelman Duran: programming / Stuart White: programming / **Recording:** Kings Landing Studios West, Los Angeles: 2020 to 2022 / The Trailer, East Hampton: 2020 to 2022 / The Juicy Juicy, Los Angeles: 2020 to 2022 / Parkwood West, Los Angeles: 2020 to 2022 / Henson Recording Studios, Los Angeles: 2020 to 2022 / **Technical team:** Producers: Beyoncé, Boi-1da, Jahaan Sweet, Neenyo, Sevn Thomas, Cadenza, Kelman Duran, Stuart White / **Executive producer:** Beyoncé Knowles-Carter / **Recording engineers:** Andrea Roberts, Chi Coney, John Cranfield, Stuart White / **Assistant recording engineer:** Matheus Braz

Producers Jahaan Sweet, Matthew "Boi-1da" Samuels, and Sevn Thomas were in the middle of a work session when they created the instrumental for the song that would become *Heated*. Beyoncé received the demo and decided to change it to make it her own, as she so often does in her creative process. And as is often the case, the song's creators discovered on the day of its release that it had been retained for the upcoming album, as Jahaan Sweet explains: "I couldn't even believe it. When I produce with 1da, we just in our own world making ideas. Things get sent to one person, then the next person. Next thing you know, boom, something happens."[336] Beyoncé, who had already had her fair share of controversies related to *Renaissance*, received backlash from associations representing the families of disabled people for the line *Spazzin' on that ass*, spaz being an offensive term to describe seizure symptoms associated with spastic cerebral palsy. Beyoncé asked her sound engineers to remove the offending term from *Heated*, as she had done for Kelis's *Milkshake* sample in *Energy*.

THIQUE

(Atia Boggs, Beyoncé, Chauncey Hollis Jr, Cherdericka Nichols, Jabbar Stevens, Julian Martrel Mason, Terius Nash/4'04)

Musicians: Beyoncé: vocals, backing vocals / Hit-Boy: programming / Lil Ju: programming / Stuart White: programming / **Recording:** Kings Landing Studios West, Los Angeles: 2020 to 2022 / The Trailer, Easy Hampton: 2020 to 2022 / The Juicy Juicy, Los Angeles: 2020 to 2022 / Parkwood West, Los Angeles: 2020 to 2022 / **Technical team:** Producers: Beyoncé, Hit-Boy, Lil Ju, Stuart White / **Executive producer:** Beyoncé Knowles-Carter / **Recording engineers:** Andrea Roberts, John Cranfield, Stuart White / **Assistant recording engineer:** Matheus Braz

In 2014, Hit-Boy, who had produced *Ni**as in Paris* for Jay-Z and Kanye West in 2011, worked with Beyoncé during some informal studio sessions from which two tracks emerged. The first, *Feeling Myself,* was released in December 2014 as a duet between Beyoncé and Nicki Minaj. The second, which became 2022's *Thique*, was shelved for years before Beyoncé rescued it from the archives. "I had to sit on that beat for eight years!"

460 RENAISSANCE

Matthew Jehu Samuels, aka Boi-1da, in Toronto, January 2023.

said Hit-Boy. "That's the way the game goes sometimes. I've had a lot of ups and downs in the game and certain people will perceive like, 'Oh, where's Hit-Boy been? What's Hit-Boy been doing?' But then I'm sitting on stuff like *Thique* that just hasn't materialized yet. Y'all don't even know how ahead I really am…I've been holding onto legendary stuff, and there's plenty more."[337]

ALL UP IN YOUR MIND

(Alexander Guy Cook, Beyoncé, Cherdericka Nichols, Jabbar Stevens, Jameil Aossey, Larry Griffin Jr, Michael Tucker, Mike Dean/2'49)

Musicians: Beyoncé: vocals, backing vocals / **Bah:** programming / **BloodPop:** programming, synthesizers / **Jameil Aossey:** programming / **Mike Dean:** programming, synthesizers / **S1aO:** programming / **Terius "The-Dream" Nash:** drums / **Recording:** The Juicy Juicy, Los Angeles: 2020 to 2022 / Hardcover, Los Angeles: 2020 to 2022 / **Technical team: Producers:** Bah, Beyoncé, BloodPop, Jameil Aossey, Mike Dean, S1AO, Terius "The-Dream" Nash / **Executive producer:** Beyoncé Knowles-Carter / **Recording engineers:** Jabbar Stevens, Andrea Roberts, John Cranfield, Stuart White / **Assistant recording engineer:** Matheus Braz

Connoisseurs of the independent London label PC Music were probably surprised to discover A. G. Cook (Alexander Guy Cook, to give him his full name), the label's founder, on the list of writers of *Renaissance*. The chemistry between the two artists' musical universes, which couldn't be more different, is blatantly obvious when you listen to *All Up in Your Mind*. It makes you wonder what would have come out of a collaboration between Beyoncé and other legendary British artists, in particular those at the forefront of the 1990s trip-hop movement such as Tricky, Massive Attack, Portishead, and Archive. Unfortunately, time travel is impossible, but Beyoncé is nevertheless happy to play the game of massively overusing the auto-tune, one of A. G. Cook's trademarks, which is why you'd swear you can hear a second singer on *All Up in Your Mind*. More mainstream than Cook, American producer BloodPop (then known as Blood Diamonds), whose résumé couldn't be more impressive (he has worked with Britney Spears, Justin Bieber, Madonna, and Lady Gaga), gives the track a more accessible feel. The question that remains to be asked is what would this magnificent *All Up in Your Mind* have sounded like had it been produced solely by sound wizard A.G. Cook?

SINGLE

AMERICA HAS A PROBLEM

(Andrell D. Rogers, Beyoncé, Mike Dean, S. Carter, Terius Nash, Kilo, Tino Santron McIntosh/3'18)

Musicians: Beyoncé: vocals, backing vocals / **Mike Dean:** synthesizers / **Terius "The-Dream" Nash:** programming / **Recording:** The Trailer, East Hampton: 2020 to 2022 / **Technical team: Producers:** Beyoncé, Terius "The-Dream" Nash, MWA, Mike Dean / **Executive producer:** Beyoncé Knowles-Carter / **Recording engineers:** Brandon Harding, Andrea Roberts, John Cranfield, Stuart White / **Assistant recording engineer:** Matheus Braz / **Single:** Streaming by Parkwood Entertainment/Columbia: 19 May 2023 / **Best chart ranking in the USA:** 69

Beyoncé puts aside late-1980s house music for this tribute to '90s rap, turning her attention to hip-hop productions from a time when the new drum machines from Japanese firm Roland and its subdivision Boss had invaded recording studios the world over. The models that came out toward the end of the decade (such as the BOSS Dr. Rhythm DR-550 and Roland R-8 Human Rhythm Composer), recognizable from their glacial sounds far removed from those of the TR-909 and TR-707, were used by many rappers. Here, Beyoncé and her producers The-Dream and Mike Dean revive the great epoch of American rap with a production that is unusual in the singer's repertoire, built largely around several segments from the 1990 track *America Has a Problem (Cocaine)* by the duo Kilo.

The great Donna Summer in 1976, basking in the international success of her second album, *Love to Love You Baby*.

PURE/HONEY

(Beyoncé, Brittany Coney, Darius Dixson, Denisia Andrews, Michael Pollack, Michael Tucker, Moi Renee, Raphael Saadiq, Terius Nash, Joseph P. Barlow, Michael D. Cox, Vejai Marcel Alston/4'48)

Musicians: Beyoncé: vocals, backing vocals, programming / **Dixson:** backing vocals / **BloodPop:** programming / **Stuart White:** programming / **Terius "The-Dream" Nash:** programming / **Kenneth Whalum:** saxophone / **Keyon Harrold:** trumpet / **Recording:** Kings Landing Studios West, Los Angeles: 2020 to 2022 / The Juicy Juicy, Los Angeles: 2020 to 2022 / Parkwood West, Los Angeles: 2020 to 2022 / The Record Plant Recording Studios, Los Angeles: 2020 to 2022 / **Technical team: Producers:** Beyoncé, BloodPop, Nova Wav, Raphael Saadiq, MWA, Mike Dean, Stuart White, Terius "The-Dream" Nash / **Executive producer:** Beyoncé Knowles-Carter / **Recording engineers:** Chi Coney, Andrea Roberts, John Cranfield, Stuart White, Hotae Alexander Jang / **Assistant recording engineers:** Hotae Alexander Jang, Matheus Braz / **Brass arrangements:** Beyoncé, Raphael Saadiq

It's back to business with *Pure/Honey*, a very house track overloaded with samples that showcase the musical culture of the many producers who collaborated on its production. An attentive ear will detect samples from *Cunty (Wave Mix)* by drag queen Kevin Aviance and *Feels Like (featuring Kevin JZ Prodigy)* by MikeQ. The song has two parts—"Pure" and "Honey"—with the second being the work of Nova Wav. "Honey" was the final production that the duo's members, Blu June and Chi, would record for *Renaissance*. "We were trying to sit down with B and catch some of her energy and where her headspace was, but she was in and out of town," Chi explained. "But we were actually able to create the idea in her studio, so that gave us the energy."[335] "We wanted something that felt modern, but also gave you that throwback, retro, disco feel," Blu June added. "I remember getting on the keyboard and playing some chords…it just felt cool, it felt funky."[335] The last sample, added to the track by Beyoncé herself, is an excerpt from *Miss Honey* by Moi Renee, released in 1992. As luck would have it, the sample is in the same key as *Pure/Honey*, adding polish to the production of this track designed for dancefloors.

SUMMER RENAISSANCE

(Atia Boggs, Beyoncé, Brittany Coney, Denisia Andrews, Levar Coppin, Leven Kali, Mike Dean, Ricky Lawson, Saliou Diagne, Terius Nash, Donna Summer, Giorgio Moroder, Pete Bellotte/4'34)

Musicians: Beyoncé: vocals, backing vocals / **Leven Kali:** backing vocals / **Mike Dean:** programming, synthesizers / **Recording:** Kings Landing Studios West, Los Angeles: 2020 to 2022 / The Juicy Juicy, Los Angeles: 2020 to 2022 / Parkwood West, Los Angeles: 2020 to 2022 / Tree Sound Studios, Atlanta: 2020 to 2022 / **Technical team: Producers:** Beyoncé, Nova Wav, Mike Dean, Leven Kali, Terius "The-Dream" Nash / **Executive producer:** Beyoncé Knowles-Carter / **Recording engineers:** Chi Coney, Stuart White

If the first few notes of *Summer Renaissance* sound familiar to you, it's because they're borrowed from the biggest disco hit ever written: *I Feel Love* by Donna Summer, created in 1977 by the diva and her favorite songwriters and founding fathers of disco, Giorgio Moroder and Pete Bellotte. The legendary bass line on *I Feel Love* (played on the Moog synthesizer) provides the intro to Beyoncé's track, before she sings the main hook *It's so good, it's so good, it's so good, it's so good*. The title *Summer Renaissance* is therefore a nod to Donna Summer, the undisputed queen of the disco movement, whom Beyoncé wanted to introduce to her younger fans. This she succeeded in doing with the help of the two young women who make up the duo Nova Wav. They did some research before launching production of the track, starting by typing the word "disco" into a search engine, which inevitably directed them towards Donna Summer. "Even Donna Summer being a pioneer of disco—some people don't know that back story," Blu June later explained, "so we wanted to make people dance, but also give them a little history, too, and say, 'Hey, look, we have roots in this.' Being two women of color, to be able to bring that to the forefront is something that we really wanted to do."[335]

2022

Was Beyoncé singing metaphorically or not in the line *All the boys want my honey from me* on *Pure/Honey*? It's a good question, because the singer they call Queen Bey had recently been living up to her nickname. She had become an amateur beekeeper, owning two hives and around 80,000 bees, including two queens. "We make hundreds of jars of honey a year. I started the beehives because my daughters, Blue and Rumi, both have terrible allergies, and honey has countless healing properties," their mother explained.[312]

462 RENAISSANCE

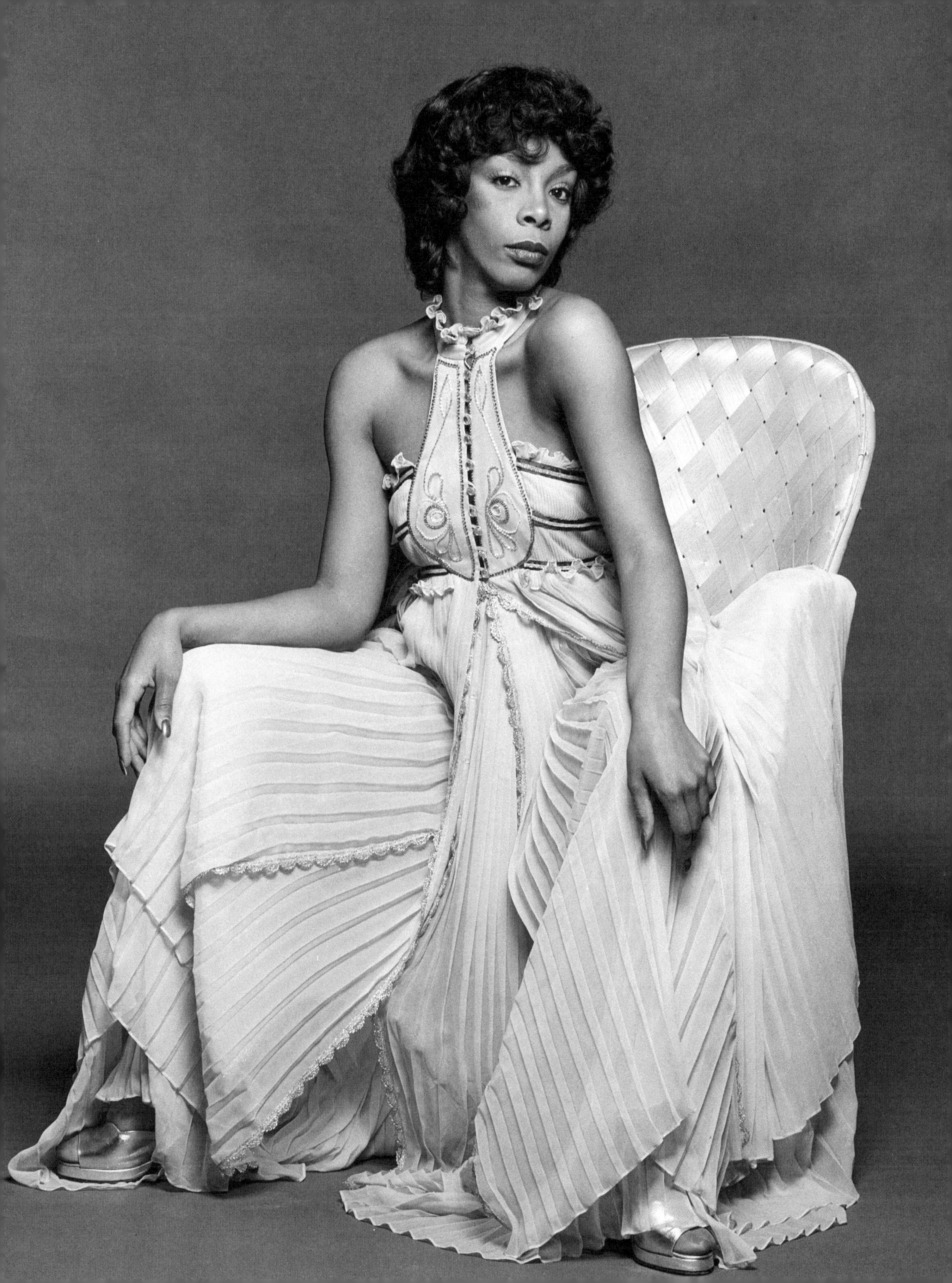

A feminist and immensely talented artist, Janelle Monáe has released four albums since 2010.

SAY HER NAME (HELL YOU TALMBOUT)
(JANELLE MONÁE, KIMBERLÉ CRENSHAW, BEYONCÉ, ALICIA KEYS, CHLOE X HALLE, TIERRA WHACK, ISIS V., ZOË KRAVITZ, BRITTANY HOWARD, ASIAHN, MJ RODRIGUEZ, JOVIAN ZAYNE, ANGELA RYE, NIKOLE HANNAH-JONES, BRITTANY PACKNETT-CUNNINGHAM, AND ALICIA GARZA)

(Janelle Robinson, Nate Wonder, Charles Joseph II, Jidenna Mobisson, Roman GianArthur, Alexe Belle, Isis Valentino, George 2.0/17'42)

Musicians: Janelle Monáe: vocals, spoken voice / Kimberlé Crenshaw: vocals, spoken voice / Beyoncé Knowles: vocals, spoken voice / Alicia Keys: vocals, spoken voice / Chloe x Halle: vocals, spoken voice / Tierra Whack: vocals, spoken voice / Isis V.: vocals, spoken voice / Zoë Kravitz: vocals, spoken voice / Brittany Howard: vocals, spoken voice / Asiahn: vocals, spoken voice / Mj Rodriguez: vocals, spoken voice / Jovian Zayne: vocals, spoken voice / Angela Rye: vocals, spoken voice / Nikole Hannah-Jones: vocals, spoken voice / Brittany Packnett-Cunningham: vocals, spoken voice / Alicia Garza: vocals, spoken voice / Roman GianArthur: vocals, spoken voice, piano, organs, synthesizers, percussions / Nate Wonder: vocals, spoken voice, bass, guitar, drums / Kellindo Parker: guitar / Terrence L. Brown: organ / Lance Powlis: trumpet / **Recording:** Wondaland Studios, Atlanta: 2015, 2021 / **Technical team: Producers:** Nate Wonder, Roman GianArthur, Janelle Monáe, Chuck Lightning / **Recording engineers:** Nate Wonder, Roman GianArthur, Janelle Monáe / **Streaming by Wondaland Records:** 24 September 2021

Hell You Talmbout was released in 2015 by Janelle Monáe and various artists from her Wondaland collective including Deep Cotton, St. Beauty, and Jidenna. It aimed to make citizens and the authorities aware of police brutality and racist violence against the African-American community. At the Women's March on Washington in 2017, Monáe took to the stage and made a speech in front of almost 500,000 angry demonstrators denouncing this brutality, particularly when it was directed against women. Then in 2021, Monáe re-recorded the vocal parts of *Hell You Talmbout*, with the lyrics focusing on the—tragically long—list of names of 61 Black girls and women killed by the police. She invited a number of female singers, including Beyoncé, to join her in this endeavor, with each singer listing one or several names over the 17 minutes and 42 seconds of *Say Her Name (Hell You Talmbout)*. The title of this reworked version refers to the #sayhername campaign launched by the African American Policy Forum in December 2014, which aimed to raise public awareness of this scourge affecting the United States. "I think the lack of visibility of Black women has changed," Monáe said. "In my opinion, these are our sisters. There's a connection when I see another Black woman, when I see a Black little girl. Older, younger, generational—there's a real unspoken connection and a sense that we need to take care of each other."[338]

A new star of alternative R&B, Travis Scott was a distinguished guest on *Renaissance*.

MAKE ME SAY IT AGAIN, GIRL
(THE ISLEY BROTHERS FEATURING BEYONCÉ)

(Chris Jasper, Rudolph Isley, O'Kelly Isley, Marvin Isley, Ernie Isley, Ronald Isley/7'45)

Musicians: Ronald Isley: vocals, backing vocals / **Beyoncé Knowles:** vocals, backing vocals / **Ernie Isley:** acoustic guitar, drums / **Chris Jasper:** Fender Rhodes, synthesizers / **Recording:** The Trailer, East Hampton: 2021 / Kendun Recorders, Burbank: 2021 / **Technical team: Producer:** Tony Maserati / **Recording engineer:** Tony Maserati / **The Isley Brothers "Make Me Say It Again, Girl" (album)** / Released in the US by BFD: 21 July 2023 (album ref.: BFD493LP, CD ref.: BFD493)

The Isley Brothers, icons of soul and funk, made their comeback in 2023 with the release of *Make Me Say It Again, Girl*, an album that features celebrity guest appearances including Trey Songz, Quavo and Takeoff (two former members of the group Migos), and Snoop Dogg. Tina Knowles, a devoted fan and friend of the Isley Brothers, raised the idea of a collaboration with Beyoncé. This wasn't as incongruous as it sounds, as she had grown up listening to their music. When it was suggested to Beyoncé, she was happy to accept, and a cover version of *Make Me Say It Again, Girl* from the group's 13th album *The Heat Is On* (1975) was quickly mooted. The track was particularly significant for Beyoncé because *Second Nature*, the very first song on the first Destiny's Child album, was a reinterpretation of *Make Me Say It Again, Girl*. "All we can say," singer Kandy Johnson Isley, Ronald's wife and the driving force behind the project, later revealed, "is that God's hands was on this whole project. And the fact that they are giving us permission to put it out at this time is just overly special. Between Beyoncé's undeniable talent and [producer/engineer] Tony Maserati's superb job at blending her and Ronald's voices—he made it sound like she was right there with Ronald in the same room."[339]

DELRESTO (ECHOES)
(TRAVIS SCOTT FEATURING BEYONCÉ)

(Beyoncé Knowles, Chauncey Hollis, Jacques Webster, James Blake, Mike Dean, Allen Ritter/4'34)

Musicians: Travis Scott: rap / **Beyoncé Knowles:** vocals, backing vocals / **Justin Vernon:** vocals / **Recording:** ?: 2023 / **Technical team: Producers:** Travis Scott, Beyoncé Knowles, Hit-Boy, Mike Dean, Allen Ritter / **Recording engineer:** Derek "206" Anderson / **Travis Scott "Utopia" (album)** / Released in the US by Epic/Cactus Jack: 28 July 2023 (album ref.: 1 96588 15041 8, CD ref.: 1 96588 38002 0)

Travis Scott is an "ambient" alternative hip-hop superstar. He has never made any secret of his desire to collaborate with Beyoncé, revealing on the website complex.com in 2005: "I wanna work with Beyoncé. You know, I'm from Houston, she's from Houston. I feel like we—we're definitely in due time to do some music."[340] When *Utopia*, Scott's fourth album, was released on 28 July 2023, it was promoted with the single *Delresto (Echoes)*, performed as a duet with Beyoncé. While fans of both artists claimed to have been taken by surprise, Beyoncé had dropped some hints about this distinguished collaboration during the Renaissance World Tour, broadcasting images from a fictitious newspaper called *The Echo* (although the name is used by several British papers) every night when she performed *America Has a Problem*.

BEYONCÉ: ALL THE SONGS   465

A return to 2013, when *Grown Woman* featured in a Pepsi commercial.

MY HOUSE

(Beyoncé Knowles, Terius Gesteelde-Diamant/4'22)

Musicians: Beyoncé Knowles: vocals, rap / **Recording:** ?: October 2023 / **Technical team: Producers:** Beyoncé Knowles, The-Dream, Khirye Tyler / **Recording engineers:** Stuart White, Brandon Harding / **Assistant recording engineers:** Sean Solymar, Tommy Rush, Matheus Braz / **Streaming by Columbia/Parkwood Entertainment:** 1 December 2023

With a similar feel to 2016's *Formation*, Queen Bey's new single *My House* featured on the credits at the end of *Renaissance: A Film by Beyoncé*, first screened in movie theaters on 1 December 2023. Back in October of that year, Beyoncé and The-Dream had been discussing which song they could synchronize to the end credits. For a while, they considered using an existing track but finally decided to create one that suited their mood at the time: it would be *My House*. "It was beautiful," The-Dream later said. "Me and that girl, man, we just clicked. It's not even work anymore. It is, 'Hey, well, what you doing? What you doing? Good morning, good morning, let's do something. Let's do it.' And then the song's done."[341]

GROWN WOMAN

(Timothy Mosley, Chris Godbey, Garland Mosley, Kelly Sheehan, Terius Nash, Darryl Pearson, Jerome Harmon/5'10)

Musicians: Beyoncé Knowles: vocals, backing vocals / **Ismaël Kouyaté:** vocals / **Drew Sayers:** saxophone / **Nick Videen:** saxophone / **Alex Asher:** trombone / **Cole Kamen-Green:** trumpet / **Recording:** Jungle City Studios, New York: 2013 / Oven Studios, New York: 2013 / **Technical team: Producers:** Beyoncé Knowles, Timbaland, J-Roc / **Recording engineers:** Chris Godbey, Stuart White / **Assistant recording engineers:** Fred Sladkey, Gloria Kaba, Matt Weber / **Brass arrangements:** The Superpower Horns / **Streaming by Parkwood Entertainment/Columbia:** 13 December 2023

In March 2013, Beyoncé appeared in the new Pepsi commercial dancing next to doubles of herself that represented all the women she had been in the past. The slogan of the campaign was: "Embrace your past, but live for now."[342] At the time, fans were praying, in vain, for the unreleased song used in the mini-film *Grown Woman* to be officially released. Instead, they had to make do with the mini-film on the *Beyoncé* DVD that featured all the videos from this famous "visual" album, as Beyoncé called it. Directed by Jake Nava, *Grown Woman* is not without interest, notably thanks to its choreography and heady Afrobeat rhythm, several years before Beyoncé began producing tracks influenced by this style of African music for *The Lion King: The Gift*. To celebrate the tenth anniversary of the *Beyoncé* album, the singer gave fans the track they had been waiting a decade for. *Grown Woman* was officially released on 13 December 2023. It features a very danceable production by Timbaland and J-Roc, Beyoncé's infectious enthusiasm, and a guest appearance from Guinean singer Ismaël Kouyaté.

466 SINGLES

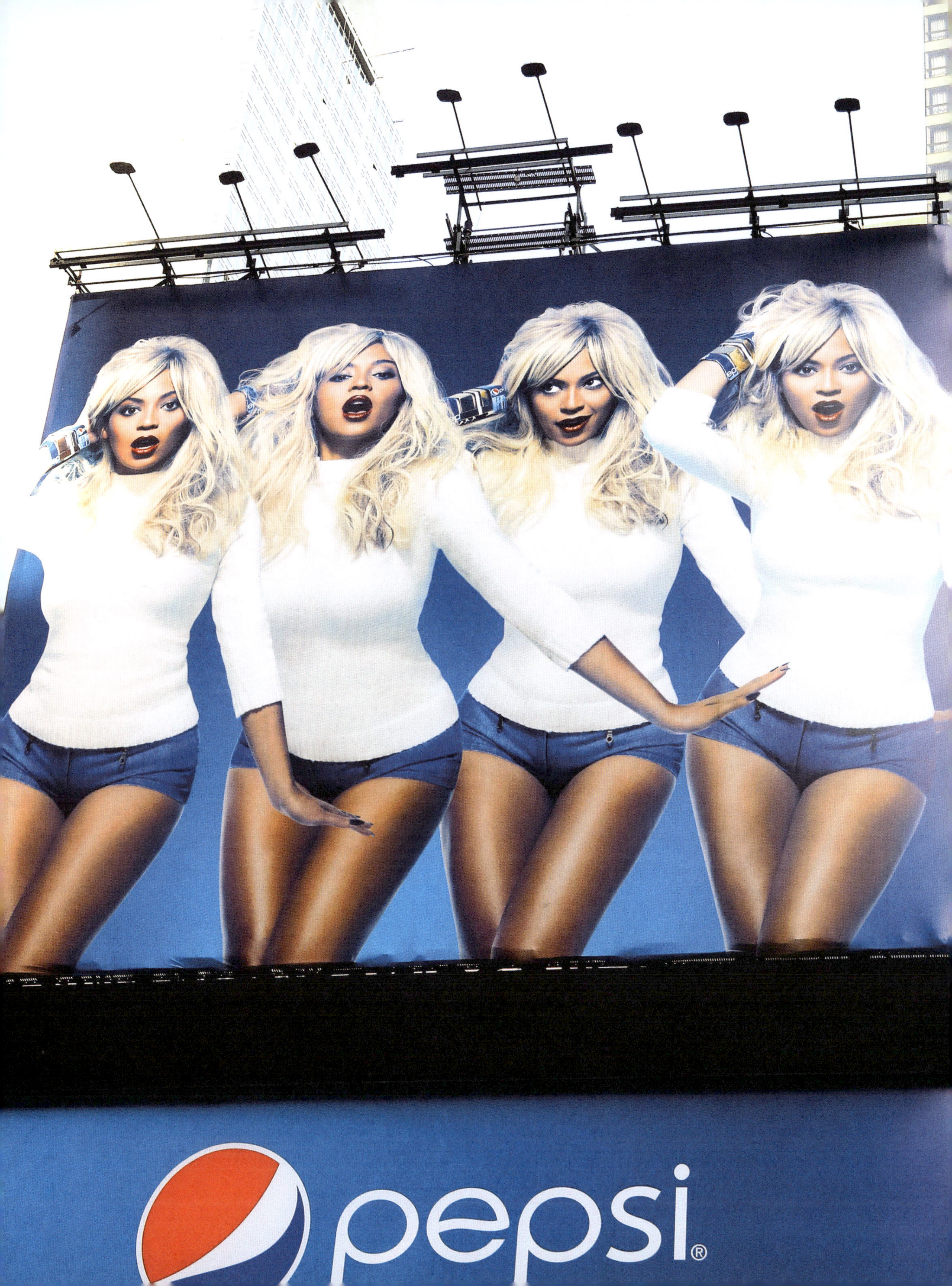
pepsi

ALBUM

Cowboy Carter

Ameriican Requiem • Blackbiird • 16 Carriages • Protector • My Rose • Smoke Hour ★ Willie Nelson • Texas Hold 'Em • Bodyguard • Dolly P • Jolene • Daughter • Spaghettii • Alliigator Tears • Smoke Hour II • Just for Fun • II Most Wanted • Levii's Jeans • Flamenco • The Linda Martell Show • Ya Ya • Oh Louisiana • Desert Eagle • Riiverdance • II Hands II Heaven • Tyrant • Sweet ★ Honey ★ Buckiin' • Amen •

Streaming by Parkwood Entertainment/Columbia: 29 March 2024
Released in the USA by Columbia/Parkwood Entertainment: 29 March 2024
(album ref.: 196588949319, CD ref.: 1965889491252)
Best chart ranking in the USA: 1

Revolutionary, bold, stunning: no shortage of superlatives to describe *Cowboy Carter*.

BEYONCÉ'S COUNTRY MANIFESTO

Does anyone now remember the name of the artist who kept fans entertained during the half-time show at Super Bowl LVIII on 11 February 2024 at Allegiant Stadium in Paradise, Nevada? Historians of American hip-hop would be able to tell us it was the singer Usher, but the eyes of the 29 million TV viewers watching that night would have been directed at two other pop music stars, vying for the crown of biggest female superstar in the world. In one corner, Taylor Swift, taking a break from her Eras tour to support her partner Travis Kelce, tight end with the Kansas City Chiefs, who were playing the San Francisco 49ers. In her role as prestigious supporter, Swift posed next to Kelce with barely disguised delight after his team's victory. In the other corner, Beyoncé, determined not to let her friend Taylor Swift steal the limelight, caused hysteria among her fans when she appeared at half-time in a 59-second commercial for internet service provider Verizon. She is shown doing everything in her power to break the internet. Failing to do so despite all her wacky efforts, at the end of the video she instructs her assistant, played by actor and comedian Tony Hale, to "drop the new music." This announcement, relayed around the world in record time, had an immediate impact, partially overshadowing Usher's performance, despite the fact that his production company was Jay-Z's Roc Nation.

A clever tease

The following day, Beyoncé posted a cryptic video clip on her Instagram account presenting Act ii—3.29. Act ii referred to the second album in the trilogy that began with 2022's *Renaissance* and 3.29 to the release date of this mysterious album: 29 March 2024. The whole world went wild at this revelation of a new Beyoncé album, especially as the Instagram reveal hinted at some most unexpected musical textures. First, we heard the sound of a banjo (played by Rhiannon Giddens, former lead singer and musician with Carolina Chocolate Drops and great champion of African-American country music culture) and then Beyoncé sang, accompanied by country music that was both surprising and very catchy. After revealing the track *Texas Hold 'Em,* followed by another called *16 Carriages*, Beyoncé then waited until 19 March to unveil in another Instagram post what was to follow. "This ain't a Country album. This is a 'Beyoncé' album. This is *act ii Cowboy Carter*, and I am proud to share it with y'all!"[343]

The *Daddy Lessons* scar

Recording of *Cowboy Carter* had begun in 2019, alongside *Renaissance*. "It's been really great to have the time and the grace to be able to take my time with it," Beyoncé said in an official press release on 29 March 2024, the same day that the new album appeared. "I was initially going to put *Cowboy Carter* out first, but with the pandemic, there was too much heaviness in the world. We wanted to dance. We deserved to dance. But I had to trust God's timing."[344] It has to be said that *Cowboy Carter*'s musical aesthetic is at the opposite end of the scale to *Renaissance*. While the latter paid tribute to late 1980s house music, the former shows a previously unknown side to Beyoncé, as she takes us on a journey into the heart of Americana. She had already visited this genre with *Daddy Lessons,* a song she performed with The Dixie Chicks (now

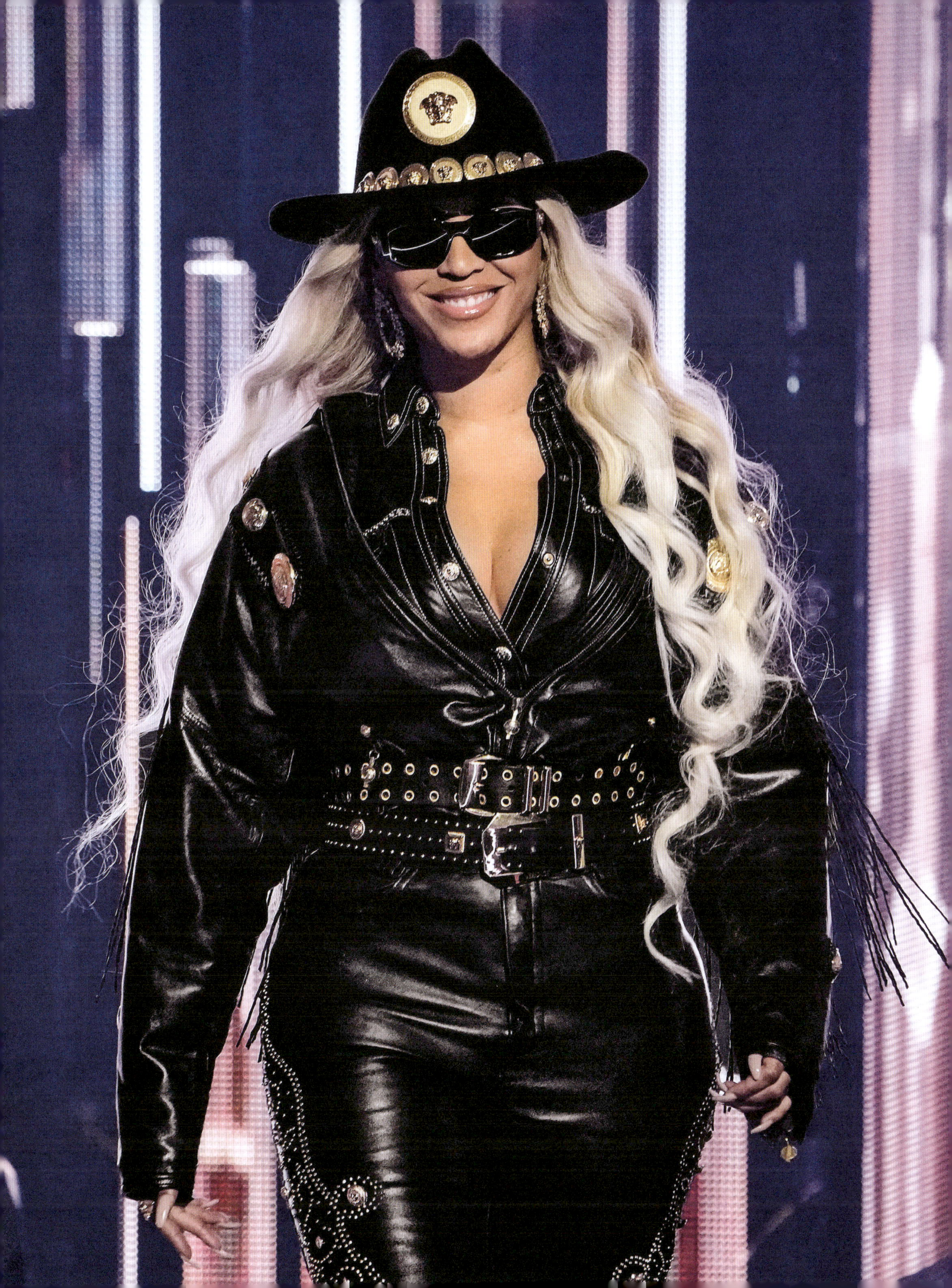

Beyoncé and Jay-Z photographed by Kevin Mazur at the Grammy Awards in Los Angeles, 4 February 2024.

Country star Lainey Wilson supported Beyoncé against her detractors.

renamed The Chicks) at the Country Music Awards Ceremony on 2 November 2016. The way this track was received by the country community, which generally took a very dim view of any incursion of African-American artists into a white-dominated genre, triggered in Beyoncé a real desire to prove her detractors wrong and show she could mix genres in a way that some still resisted. "It was born out of an experience that I had years ago where I did not feel welcomed…and it was very clear that I wasn't. But, because of that experience, I did a deeper dive into the history of Country music and studied our rich musical archive […] The criticisms I faced when I first entered this genre forced me to propel past the limitations that were put on me. *Act ii* is a result of challenging myself, and taking my time to bend and blend genres together to create this body of work."[343]

A frosty reception from the world of country

Just like her other concept albums in the past (*4* themed on the 1980s in 2011, the dark *Beyoncé* in 2013, protest on *Lemonade* in 2016, a love letter to African-American music in *The Lion King: The Gift* in 2019, and the danceable *Renaissance* in 2022), *Cowboy Carter* has undeniable artistic coherence. When it was released, fans and press alike savored an album retracing all of Beyoncé's folk, country, and bluegrass influences, three of the music genres that come under the Americana banner. The artists who supported Queen Bey on the record were as huge as the music revolution it represented, with Beyoncé inviting legends like Dolly Parton, Willie Nelson, Linda Martell, and Stevie Wonder to join her. Other representatives from a younger generation were also invited to the sessions. These included guitarist Gary Clark Jr, singers Post Malone and Shaboozey, and superstar Miley Cyrus. In more than one way, *Cowboy Carter* presents itself as a manifesto from Beyoncé, who was determined to set the record straight, whether some of the more narrow-minded liked it or not. Oklahoma's country radio station KYKC-FM, for example, refused to broadcast *Texas Hold 'Em,* even though its listeners were clamoring for it. Actor John Schneider, an out-and-out patriot famous for playing Bo Duke in *The Dukes of Hazzard,* even went so far as to say that artists who were Democrats (lefties, as he called them) were always trying to monopolize what wasn't theirs in the same way as, in his words, "every dog must mark every tree."[345]

A masterpiece that faced censorship

Despite the sickening controversy and blatant censorship that *Cowboy Carter* suffered at the hands of certain country radio stations, many in the country community supported Beyoncé, starting with the queen, Dolly Parton herself, but also singer Lainey Wilson and Travis Moon, star presenter on Houston's 93Q country radio station, who said of *Texas Hold 'Em:* "We're playing [it] right now. We're actually the first station in America to officially add the song."[346] Beyoncé's parents came out in defense of their daughter, as coverage of her artistic work was somewhat obscured by these controversies so symptomatic of the clear fracture line that divides America. Tina Knowles posted on her Instagram page a montage of images taken from the archives, showing all the times Beyoncé had been involved in the world of country music, while Mathew Knowles said in an interview: "When Beyoncé was a little baby, and I'm talking two–three years old, she would go down and spend the summer with my parents. And her grandfather—my father— loved country music, and he used to sing to her. At an early age, she heard this music. And when you're two, three years old,

Above: Levi's new 2024 advertising campaign featured Beyoncé's song *Levii's Jeans*.
Opposite: A triumphant return for Queen Bey, who electrified NRG Stadium in Houston at half time during the NFL Christmas match, 25 December 2024.

2024

subconsciously music stays in your head."[347] Despite being rejected by part of the country community who don't want to share their heritage with an African-American woman, *Cowboy Carter* shines as much for the risks its author takes as for the quality of its songs. Beyoncé faced down this shameful polemic and won out over her detractors, masterfully putting forward her argument as follows, proving once again that she is highly knowledgeable about the causes she supports. "I wanted everyone to take a minute to research on the word cowboy," she told *GQ* in September 2024. "History is often told by the victors. And American history? It's been rewritten endlessly. Up to a quarter of all cowboys were Black. These men faced a world that refused to see them as equal, yet they were the backbone of the cattle industry. The cowboy is a symbol of strength and aspiration in America. The cowboy was named after slaves who handled the cows. The word cowboy comes from those who were called boys, never given the respect they deserved. No one would dare call a Black man handling cows 'Mister' or 'Sir.'"[348] *Cowboy Carter* is accomplished, well researched, and makes a statement that takes Beyoncé light years beyond the American star system as we know it. It is a bewitching and necessary work, which should rank as one of the artist's best albums; a truly expansive masterpiece, with an audacity never before seen in an artist of this caliber. In a word: indispensable.

FOR BEYONCÉ ADDICTS

The reason the name Beyincé appears on the sleeve of the singer's new album (most pressings don't even include the words *Cowboy Carter*) is that it pays homage to her maternal grandfather Lumis, who bore this surname. An error by the registrar when Tina's birth was registered changed Beyincé to Beyoncé. The future star was then named Beyoncé after her mother's maiden name.

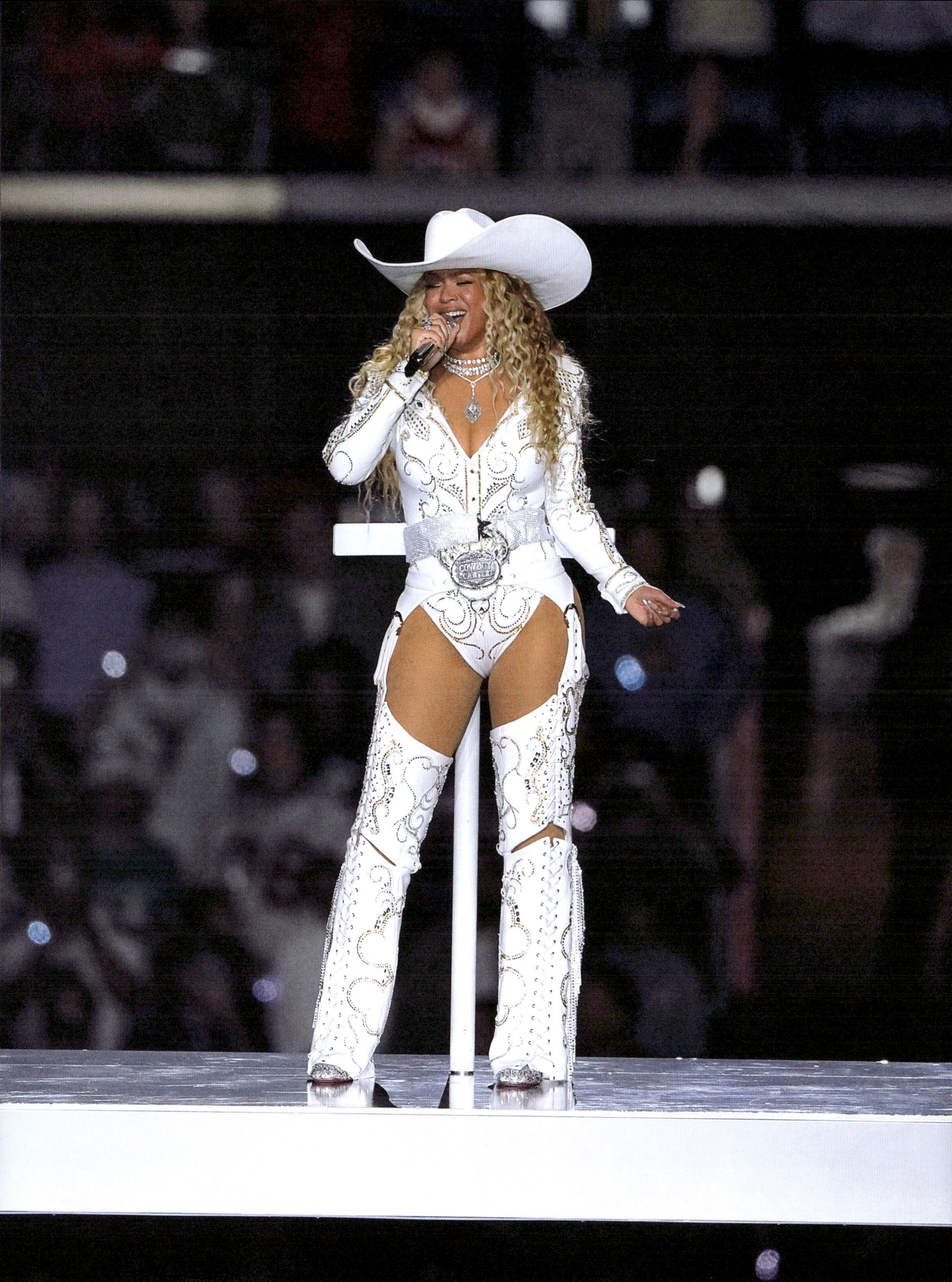

From left: Reyna Roberts, Tanner Adell, Brittney Spencer, and Tiera Kennedy—four of the many artists who worked with Beyoncé on *Cowboy Carter*.

The singer Maya Margarita and Beyoncé at the launch of the whisky brand SirDavis in Paris, 23 September 2024.

AMERIICAN REQUIEM

(Beyoncé, Ernest Dion Wilson, Jon Batiste, Raphael Saadiq, Atia Boggs, Camaron Ochs (Cam), Tyler Johnson, Darius Dixson, Derek Dixie, Shawn Carter, Michael Price, Dan Walsh, Stephen Stills/5'25)

Musicians: Beyoncé: vocals, backing vocals / No I.D.: synthesizers, sitar, guitar / Jon Batiste: synthesizers, sitar, guitar / Khirye Tyler: bass / Raphael Saadiq: drums / Dixson: drums, backing vocals / Khirye Tyler: drums, percussion, synthesizers / Dwanna Orange: backing vocals / Lakeisha Lewis: backing vocals / Camille Grigsby: backing vocals / Nava Morris: backing vocals / Naarai Jacobs: backing vocals / Kiandra Richardson: backing vocals / Phylicia Hill: backing vocals / Storm Chapman: backing vocals / Jenelle Dunkley: backing vocals / Princess Fortier: backing vocals / Brooke Brewer: backing vocals / Chelsea Miller: backing vocals / LaMarcus Eldridge: backing vocals / Cedrit Leonard: backing vocals / George Young: backing vocals / Donald Paige: backing vocals / Mabvuto Carpenter: backing vocals / Jason Morales: backing vocals / Steven Epting: backing vocals / Jerome Wayne: backing vocals / Tanner Adell: backing vocals / Atia "Ink" Boggs: backing vocals / Camaron Ochs (Cam): backing vocals / **Recording:** Kings Landing Studios West, Los Angeles: 2019 to 2024 / The Trailer, East Hampton: 2019 to 2024 / Westlake Recording Studios, West Hollywood: 2019 to 2024 / **Technical team: Producers:** Beyoncé, No I.D., Jon Batiste, Tyler Johnson, Camaron Ochs, Khirye Tyler, Derek Dixie, Tanner Adell, Kuk Harrell / **Executive producer:** Beyoncé Knowles-Carter / **Recording engineers:** Andrea Roberts, Henrique Andrade, Kuk Harrell, Jelli Dorman, Stuart White, John Cranfield, Dani Pampuri, Lester Mendoza, Matheus Braz, Danforth Webster, Patrick Gardner, Jonathan Lopez Garcia, Terena Dawn, Garrett Duncan, Conner McFarland, Nick Sutton, Jeremy Dilli / **Assistant recording engineer:** Matheus Braz / **Choir direction:** Derek Dixie

Beyoncé settles scores right from the intro track of *Cowboy Carter*, whose title *Ameriican Requiem* appears to sound the death knell for an America collapsing under the weight of its contradictions, the land of freedom that is so often divided. *They used to say I spoke too country/Then the rejection came, said I wasn't country 'nough/Said I wouldn't saddle up, but/ If that ain't country, tell me, what is?* This is a thinly disguised allusion to the backlash (see *Daddy Lessons*) that occurred after Beyoncé and The Dixie Chicks' performance at the Country Music Awards in November 2016, and Beyoncé is here to remind us that while she can forgive, she can never forget the harm that was done to her. She also makes an allusion to her grandfather when she sings *Looka there, liquor in my hand/The grandbaby of a moonshine man*. The star, who had just launched her own whisky brand, SirDavis, had recently discovered that her great-grandfather Davis Hogue had been a notorious producer of illegal alcohol during the Prohibition era. "I've always been drawn to the power and confidence I feel when drinking quality whisky and wanted to invite more people to experience that feeling," she revealed in 2024. "Discovering my great-grandfather's moonshine legacy felt like destiny. SirDavis is a tribute to him, uniting us through a shared legacy."[349]

BLACKBIIRD
(FEATURING BRITTNEY SPENCER, REYNA ROBERTS, TANNER ADELL, TIERA KENNEDY)

(Paul McCartney, John Lennon/2'12)

Musicians: Beyoncé: vocals, backing vocals / **Brittney Spencer:** vocals, backing vocals / **Reyna Roberts:** backing vocals / **Tanner Adell:** backing vocals / **Tiera Kennedy:** backing vocals / **Khirye Tyler:** bass, violin, cello / **Recording:** Westlake Recording Studios, West Hollywood: 2019 to 2024 / East Iris Studios, Nashville: 2019 to 2024 / **Technical team:** Producers: Beyoncé, Paul McCartney, Khirye Tyler, Kuk Harrell / **Executive producer:** Beyoncé Knowles-Carter / **Recording engineers:** Stuart White, Kuk Harrell, Jelli Dorman, Matheus Braz, Andrea Roberts, John Cranfield, Henrique Andrade / **Assistant recording engineers:** Matheus Braz, Danforth Webster, Patrick Gardner, Jonathan Lopez Garcia, Terena Dawn, Garrett Duncan, Conner McFarland, Nick Sutton, Jeremy Dilli

On 11 June 1968, when Paul McCartney recorded *Blackbird* on his Martin D-28 guitar at Abbey Road Studios in London, he didn't have in mind a bird with jet-black feathers, as the title of his acoustic masterpiece—which featured on *The Beatles*, known as *The White Album* because of its monochrome sleeve—seems to suggest. He used this metaphor to show his support for the civil rights struggle then raging in the US.

Deeply affected by the assassination of Martin Luther King on 4 April 1968, as well as by images from a documentary showing young Black girls banned from school because of their skin color, the British musician was keen to show his support for the African-American community in their fight for equality. He said to biographer Barry Miles in 1997: "I had in mind a Black woman, rather than a bird. Those were the days of the civil rights movement, which all of us cared passionately about, so this was really a song from me to a Black woman, experiencing these problems in the States: 'Let me encourage you to keep trying, to keep your faith; there is hope.'"[350] Some 56 years after *Blackbird* was first recorded, Beyoncé appropriated the song—which is unfortunately still relevant today—and offered a poignant reinterpretation, produced using the original master tapes from 1968. The ex-Beatle expressed his support for her in a post to his Instagram followers on 4 April 2024, in which he confided how moved he was that Beyoncé had recorded his song: "I am so happy with @beyonce's version of my song *Blackbird*. I think she does a magnificent version of it and it reinforces the civil rights message that inspired me to write the song in the first place […] Anything my song and Beyoncé's fabulous version can do to ease racial tension would be a great thing and makes me very proud."[351]

Robert Randolph and his steel guitar on stage at the Shepherd's Bush Empire in London, 29 June 2011.

SINGLE

16 CARRIAGES

(Beyoncé, Dave Hamelin, Atia Boggs, Raphael Saadiq/3'47)

Musicians: Beyoncé: vocals, backing vocals / **Ink:** guitar / **Justus West:** guitar / **Robert Randolph:** steel guitar / **Justin Schipper:** steel guitar / **Lemar Carter:** drums / **Dave Hamelin:** piano, organ, synthesizers, guitar, drums / **Gavin Williams:** organ / **Ryan Svendsen:** trumpet / **Recording:** Kings Landing Studios West, Los Angeles: 2019 to 2024 / The Record Plant Recording Studios, Los Angeles: 2019 to 2024 / The Trailer, East Hampton: 2019 to 2024 / Parkwood West, Los Angeles: 2019 to 2024 / Dezert Flower Studios, Los Angeles: 2019 to 2024 / **Technical team:** Producers: Beyoncé, Dave Hamelin, Raphael Saadiq, Stuart White / **Executive producer:** Beyoncé Knowles-Carter / **Recording engineers:** Stuart White, Dave Hamelin, Hotae Alexander Jang, Matheus Braz, Andrea Roberts, John Cranfield / **Assistant recording engineer:** Matheus Braz / **Single:** Streaming by Parkwood Entertainment/Columbia: 11 February 2024 / **Best chart ranking in the USA:** 38

Invited to take part in the recording of *Cowboy Carter*, American musician Robert Randolph, whose favorite instrument is the pedal steel guitar, arrived in Los Angeles, where he met up with producer Raphael Saadiq, who was running the session. He was stunned to discover that in the studio that day were keyboardist Khirye Tyler, singer and banjo/fiddle player Rhiannon Giddens, and Beyoncé herself, ready to sing along with them. Saadiq explained to Randolph how the session would go: "Here's what Beyoncé has in her head. And you were hand-picked because you're the only guy who could do this."[352] Other musicians later came in to polish *16 Carriages*, in which Beyoncé opens up about a childhood that was sometimes difficult, torn between the need to not disappoint her parents and to progress her career as a singer and her life as a young woman on the road. One of the musicians, guitarist Justus West, brings a powerful touch to the track. "As soon as I heard the demo version of the song, I knew it would be crucial to add rock elements on the chorus to really emphasize the scale of the song,"[353] he explained. To achieve this, he used his six-string Abasi Larada guitar plugged into the console, with a Neural Plini plug-in digital simulator replacing the amplifier, to which he added reverb and chorusing. "Honestly, the brief in my mind was to make this song as epic as possible."[353] Mission accomplished.

PROTECTOR
(FEATURING RUMI CARTER)

(Beyoncé, Ryan Beatty, Camaron Ochs (Cam), Jack Rochon/3'04)

Musicians: Beyoncé: vocals, backing vocals / **Rumi Carter:** spoken voice / **Ryan Beatty:** backing vocals / **Jack Rochon:** guitar / **Gary Clark Jr:** guitar / **Ryan Svendsen:** trumpet / **Khirye Tyler:** sound effects / **Recording:** Kings Landing Studios West, Los Angeles: 2019 to 2024 / The Trailer, East Hampton: 2019 to 2024 / Parkwood West, Los Angeles: 2019 to 2024 / Westlake Recording Studios, West Hollywood: 2019 to 2024 / **Technical team:** Producers: Beyoncé, Jack Rochon / **Executive producer:** Beyoncé Knowles-Carter / **Recording engineers:** Stuart White, Jack Rochon, Andrea Roberts, Dani Pampuri, Matheus Braz, John Cranfield, Henrique Andrade / **Assistant recording engineers:** Matheus Braz, Patrick Gardner, Danforth Webster, Jonathan Lopez Garcia, Terena Dawn, Garrett Duncan, Conner McFarland, Nick Sutton, Jeremy Dilli

Protector is a declaration of Beyoncé's love for her daughter Rumi, whose voice can be heard at the start of the track. It is a delicious folk ballad carried by the nuanced playing of guitarist Gary Clark Jr. This wasn't the first time the musician had worked with Beyoncé. On 10 February 2015, both artists accompanied Ed Sheeran at the *Stevie Wonder: Songs in the Key of Life—An All-Star Grammy Salute* tribute concert, in which the trio performed the hit *Higher Ground*. Gary Clark Jr., who is no greenhorn when it comes to championing the African-American community—remember his single *This Land*, in which he took on the Woody Guthrie classic *This Land Is Your Land* and sang *This land is mine*—declared, "*Cowboy Carter* was a genius way to shock the system."[354] The guitarist, who also contributed to the tracks *Daughter*, *Desert Eagle*, and *II Hands II Heaven,* then continued: "We do this and we've been doing this forever. Beyoncé can do anything and I think it was great how she pulled people from the country, blues, and gospel realm and took it to a new level [...] She knows that when she releases anything it's going to make an impact culturally."[354]

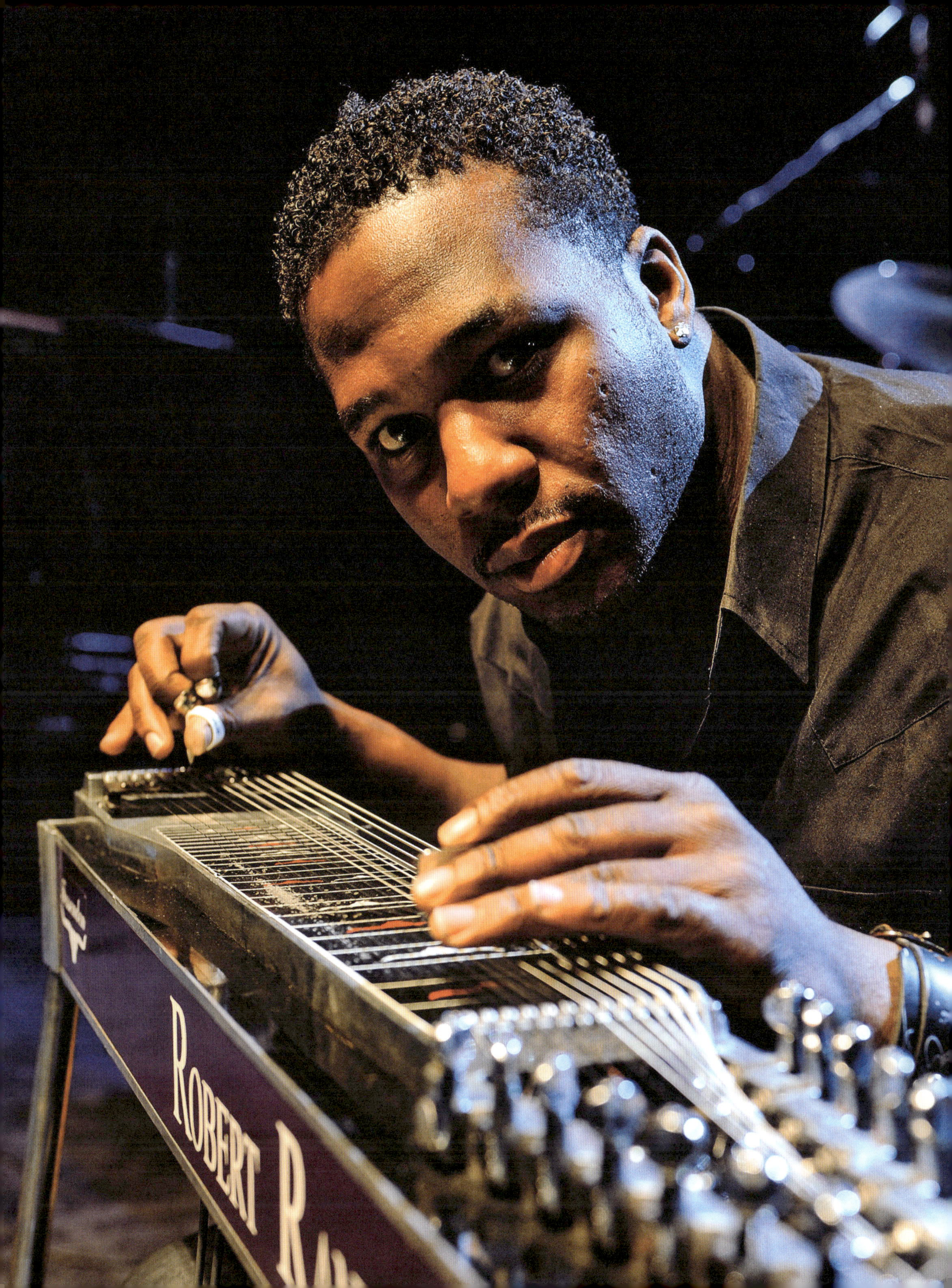
ROBERT

A true icon of country music, Willie Nelson was one of Beyoncé's distinguished guests.

MY ROSE

(Beyoncé, Shawntoni Ajanae Nichols/0'53)

Musician: Beyoncé: vocals, backing vocals / **Recording:** Westlake Recording Studios, West Hollywood: 2019 to 2024 / **Technical team: Producers:** Beyoncé, Mamii / **Executive producer:** Beyoncé Knowles-Carter / **Recording engineers:** Mamii, Stuart White, Matheus Braz, Andrea Roberts, John Cranfield / **Assistant recording engineers:** Matheus Braz, Patrick Gardner, Danforth Webster, Jonathan Lopez Garcia, Terena Dawn, Garrett Duncan, Conner McFarland, Nick Sutton, Jeremy Dilli

My Rose, which is closer to a musical interlude than an actual song, emerged from the collaboration between Beyoncé and a promising artist by the name of Shawntoni Ajanae "Mamii" Nichols. The young woman, whose influences range from Prince to Musiq Soulchild and Tori Kelly, offered her songwriting talents to Beyoncé for this lullaby in triplets, in which Beyoncé sings of her unconditional love for someone she calls "my rose." The secret behind the identity of the person with this sweet nickname was soon revealed. When some of the album's CD editions are inserted into the player, the song's original name appears on the digital display: *Mr. Sir*, in reference to Beyoncé's little boy, Sir Carter.

SMOKE HOUR ★ WILLIE NELSON
(FEATURING WILLIE NELSON)

(Beyoncé, Leah Nardos Takele, Charles Anderson, Son House, Sister Rosetta Tharpe, Chuck Berry, Jesse Stone/0'50)

Musician: Willie Nelson: spoken voice / **Recording:** Westlake Recording Studios, West Hollywood: 2019 to 2024 / **Technical team: Producer:** Beyoncé / **Executive producer:** Beyoncé Knowles-Carter / **Recording engineers:** Stuart White, Matheus Braz, Andrea Roberts, John Cranfield / **Assistant recording engineers:** Matheus Braz, Patrick Gardner, Danforth Webster, Jonathan Lopez Garcia, Terena Dawn, Garrett Duncan, Conner McFarland, Nick Sutton, Jeremy Dilli

Just as the one they called the Man in Black presented his *Johnny Cash Show* from 1969 to 1971, here legendary outlaw Willie Nelson is invited to host his own radio show on the fictitious station KNTRY Radio Texas. Nelson, famous as much for his commitment to worthy causes (which include the legalization of cannabis) and his forthright manner as for his abundant discography, plays the role of a radio host broadcasting excerpts from songs that have obviously been carefully chosen. The five excerpts (interspersed with the typical audible crackling heard when scanning the FM band) are reminders of the impact African-American artists have had on the nation's music culture. Here's a brief overview.

Smoke Hour ★ Willie Nelson is more than just a simple nod: it catalogs the cultural plundering that occurred throughout the 20th century. First up is Charles Anderson's *Laughing Yodel*. Yodeling, a singing technique that originated in 19th-century Europe and became widespread in Switzerland and Austria, reached the US, where it became one of the hallmarks of the virile white cowboy riding across the plains of the Midwest. Beyoncé is here to remind us that well before Kenny Roberts, Gene Autry, and Hank Williams, Black bluesman Charles Anderson had made it his specialty and built his reputation around his mastery of the technique. The next sequence, featuring *Grinnin' in Your Face* by the legendary Son House, emphasizes that without this founding father of blues, Bob Dylan, Keith Richards, Eric Clapton, and Angus Young would probably never have touched a six-string. Next up, the first few notes of Sister Rosetta Tharpe's *Down by the Riverside* more than suffice to give us a glimpse of the tremendous talent of this blueswoman, famous for her repertoire, her playing technique, and the way she wore her Gibson SG electric guitar slung over her shoulder. Dubbed "the Godmother of Rock'n'Roll," Tharpe's musical legacy has yet to be fully recognized. One and a half bars from Chuck Berry's *Maybellene* restore him to his rightful place as the king of American rockers, way ahead of Jerry Lee Lewis or Ricky Nelson. Then comes Roy Hamilton's *Don't Let Go*, reminding us of the impact this famous but much under-estimated Black rocker must have had on the young Elvis Presley when he was writing his first songs. Just as Eminem examines his conscience in his 2002 hit *Without Me*, rapping the lyrics *I am the worst thing since Elvis Presley/To do Black music so selfishly/And use it to get myself wealthy*, Willie Nelson reminds us of the importance of knowing the cultural assets and heritage of one's country to better understand their influence on younger generations.

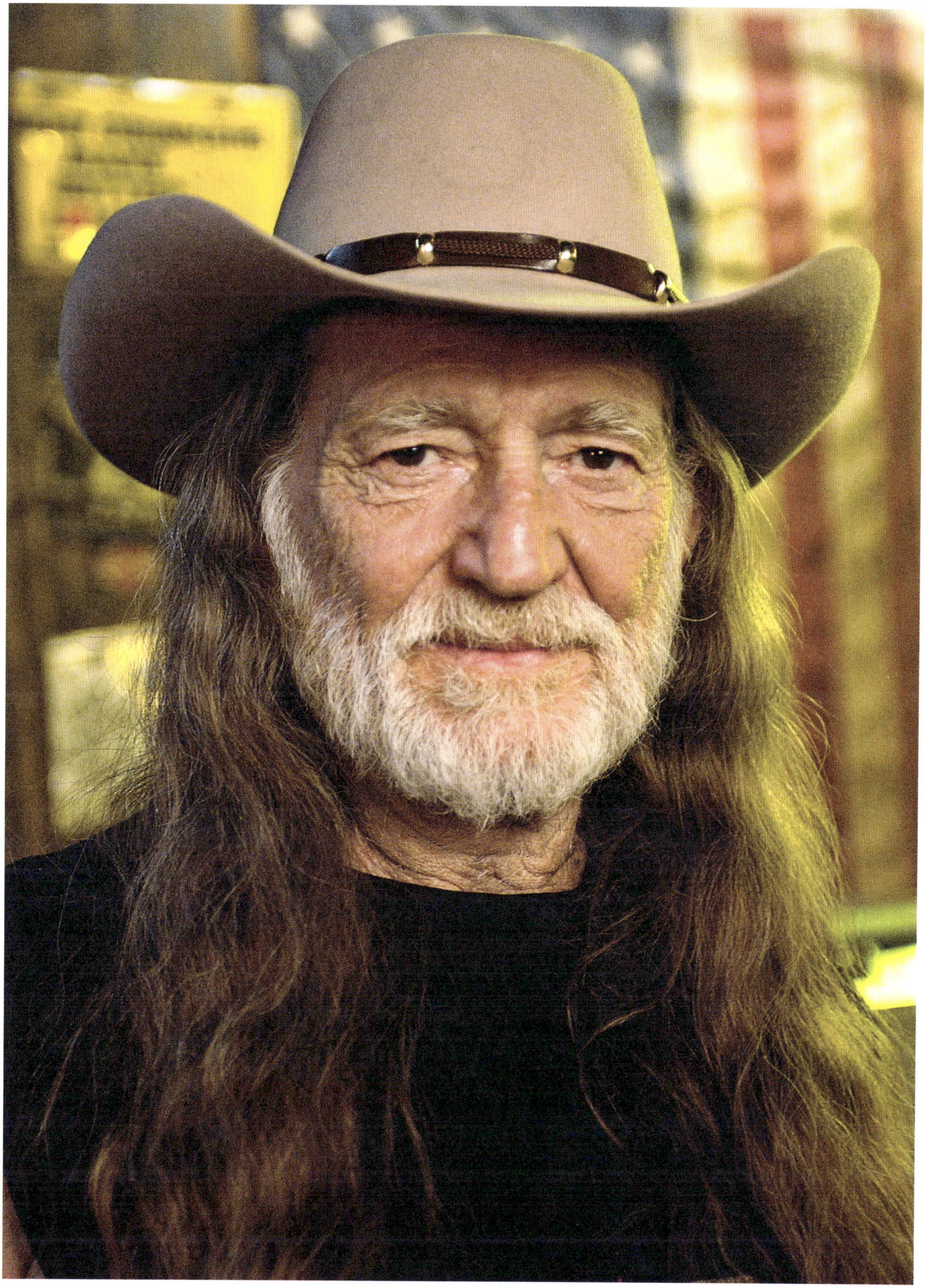

TEXAS HOLD 'EM

(Beyoncé, Elizabeth Boland, Megan Bülow, Brian Bates, Nate Ferraro, Raphael Saadiq/3'53)

Musicians
Beyoncé: vocals, backing vocals
Megan Bülow: backing vocals
Rhiannon Giddens: banjo, viola
Nate Ferraro: guitar, piano, bass
Killah B: drums
Lemar Carter: drums
Raphael Saadiq: piano, bass, drums, Wurlitzer
Lowell Boland: piano
Khirye Tyler: piano, bass
Hit-Boy: synthesizers

Recording
Kings Landing Studios West, Los Angeles: 2019 to 2024
The Trailer, East Hampton: 2019 to 2024
Parkwood West, Los Angeles: 2019 to 2024
Dezert Flower Studios, Los Angeles: 2019 to 2024
Apg Studios, Los Angeles: 2019 to 2024

Technical team
Producers: Beyoncé, Killah B, Nate Ferraro, Raphael Saadiq, Stuart White, Hit-Boy, Mariel Gomerez
Executive producer: Beyoncé Knowles-Carter
Recording engineers: Stuart White, Alex Nibley, Hotae Alexander Jang, Matheus Braz, Andrea Roberts, John Cranfield
Assistant recording engineer: Matheus Braz

Genesis
Following the success of Ariane Grande's single *Positions* in 2020, which he helped write, Brian Vincent Bates, aka Killah B, decided to set up his own music production company and begin seeking new talent. In 2022, he met songwriter Nate Ferraro at a friend's party and told him he was on the lookout for writers. A few weeks later, after listening to a few of Ferraro's songs, Killah B met up with him again, along with two young Canadian artists, Elizabeth Lowell Boland and Megan Bülow. The four of them started playing together as if they'd always known each other and the jam session quickly took a surprising turn. "We did one country idea," explained Killah B, "then we started *Texas Hold 'Em*."[355] With Ferraro on guitar, the other three began working on the track, writing the melody and the lyrics, which Killah B then set about producing. Some time later, one of his circle offered to put him in touch with Mariel Gomerez-Rodriguez, artistic director at Parkwood Entertainment, who was looking for country songs for her employer. Less than a month later, the four creators of *Texas Hold 'Em*, who had been told that Beyoncé was interested in their demo, were asked to send the tapes of the track to Gomerez-Rodriguez and then sign a non-disclosure agreement.

Production
Although Beyoncé was instantly won over by the *Texas Hold 'Em* demo, she wanted to rework it, entrusting the task to her long-standing collaborator, Raphael Saadiq. He added kick drum, bass guitar, and Wurlitzer organ, but the song was still missing the one ingredient that would become its centerpiece. "As soon as Beyoncé puts the banjo on a track my job is done,"[356] the singer, fiddle, and banjo player Rhiannon Giddens had remarked some years before, referring to her mission to acquaint the general public with the history of the banjo, and in particular its African origins. The virtuoso artist, former member of the successful band Carolina Chocolate Drops, who had three solo albums to her name and two others in collaboration with her partner, Sicilian musician Francesco Turrisi, is known both for her music and for her knowledge of music culture, which she explores in the documentary series *The Banjo: Music, History, and Heritage With Rhiannon Giddens*, broadcast on the streaming service Wondrium.

Former vocalist with The Carolina Chocolate Drops, as well as a renowned banjo and fiddle player, Rhiannon Giddens was a safe pair of hands on *Texas Hold 'Em*.

Giddens was called in to join Saadiq and Beyoncé in the studio to record a score with her favorite instrument, but had to keep her participation in the project secret. It wasn't until the morning of 12 February 2024, when Beyoncé posted the video announcing *Texas Hold 'Em* on her Instagram page, that Giddens found out her score had been used in the star's next single. The song would be the first ever by a Black female artist to top the Hot Country Songs *Billboard* chart. "My hope is that years from now, the mention of an artist's race, as it relates to releasing genres of music, will be irrelevant,"[357] Beyoncé stated, as she faced resistance from many country radio programmers, who refused to play the song because of the singer's skin color.

Raphael Saadiq in 2020, photographed by Aaron Rapoport.

BODYGUARD

(Beyoncé, Raphael Saadiq, Ryan Beatty, Elizabeth Lowell Boland, Leven Kali, Shawntoni Ajanae Nichols/4'00)

Musicians: Beyoncé: vocals, backing vocals / **Elizabeth Lowell Boland:** backing vocals / **Ryan Beatty:** backing vocals / **Raphael Saadiq:** piano, synthesizers, guitar, bass / **Lemar Carter:** drums / **Terius "The-Dream" Gesteelde-Diamant:** programming / **Ross Garren:** harmonica / **Recording:** Westlake Recording Studios, West Hollywood: 2019 to 2024 / The Sound Factory, Hollywood: 2019 to 2024 / **Technical team:** Producers: Raphael Saadiq, Beyoncé / **Executive producer:** Beyoncé Knowles-Carter / **Recording engineers:** Stuart White, Hotae Alexander Jang, Henrique Andrade, Matheus Braz, Andrea Roberts, John Cranfield / **Assistant recording engineers:** Matheus Braz, Patrick Gardner, Danforth Webster, Jonathan Lopez Garcia, Terena Dawn, Garrett Duncan, Conner McFarland, Nick Sutton, Jeremy Dilli

With *Bodyguard*, Beyoncé takes a step sideways, abandoning country for a pop-folk worthy of early 1970s Californian productions. "That little bass line, it feels like Fleetwood Mac. Because I love those eras of music,"[358] explains Raphael Saadiq, co-producer and musician on the track. While presenting songs to Beyoncé, he caught her attention with the demo of this piece played on acoustic guitar. Beyoncé added a few lines to the existing melody that reminded Saadiq of Aretha Franklin's and Reba McEntire's vocal timbres, before Elizabeth Lowell Boland, Leven Kali, Shawntoni Ajanae Nichols, and Ryan Beatty were invited to help develop the track, with Beatty notably involved in writing the lyrics. "The line *Sometimes I hold you closer just to know you're real* is one of my favorite lines I wrote for the whole record," he said. "Melody and lyric together can make something feel so much more beautiful."[359]

DOLLY P

(Dolly Parton, Beyoncé, Leah Nardos Takele/0'22)

Musicians: Dolly Parton: spoken voice / **Jack Rochon:** guitar / **Recording:** Westlake Recording Studios, West Hollywood: 2019 to 2024 / The Sound Factory, Hollywood: 2019 to 2024 / **Technical team:** Producers: Beyoncé, Jack Rochon / **Executive producer:** Beyoncé Knowles-Carter / **Recording engineer:** Dolly P's Engineer / **Assistant recording engineers:** Matheus Braz, Patrick Gardner

Before unveiling her cover version of *Jolene*, one of Dolly Parton's best-known standards, which she wrote about a bank clerk who was giving her husband the glad eye, Beyoncé invited the queen of country music to record a short message on the record, as Willie Nelson had done on *Smoke Hour ★ Willie Nelson*. Referring to the mysterious Becky, who had drawn Beyoncé's wrath when she "borrowed" her husband, Parton says: *Hey Miss Honeybee, it's Dolly P/You know that hussy with the good hair you sing about?/Reminded me of someone I knew back when/Except she has flamin' locks of auburn hair/Bless her heart/Just a hair of a different color but it hurts just the same.* Who better to encourage Beyoncé than Dolly Parton herself? And there was more, as she went so far as to declare her support for Beyoncé on Instagram on 23 February 2024: "I'm a big fan of Beyoncé and very excited that she's done a country album. So congratulations on your *Billboard* Hot Country number one single. Can't wait to hear the full album!"[360]

2024

484 COWBOY CARTER

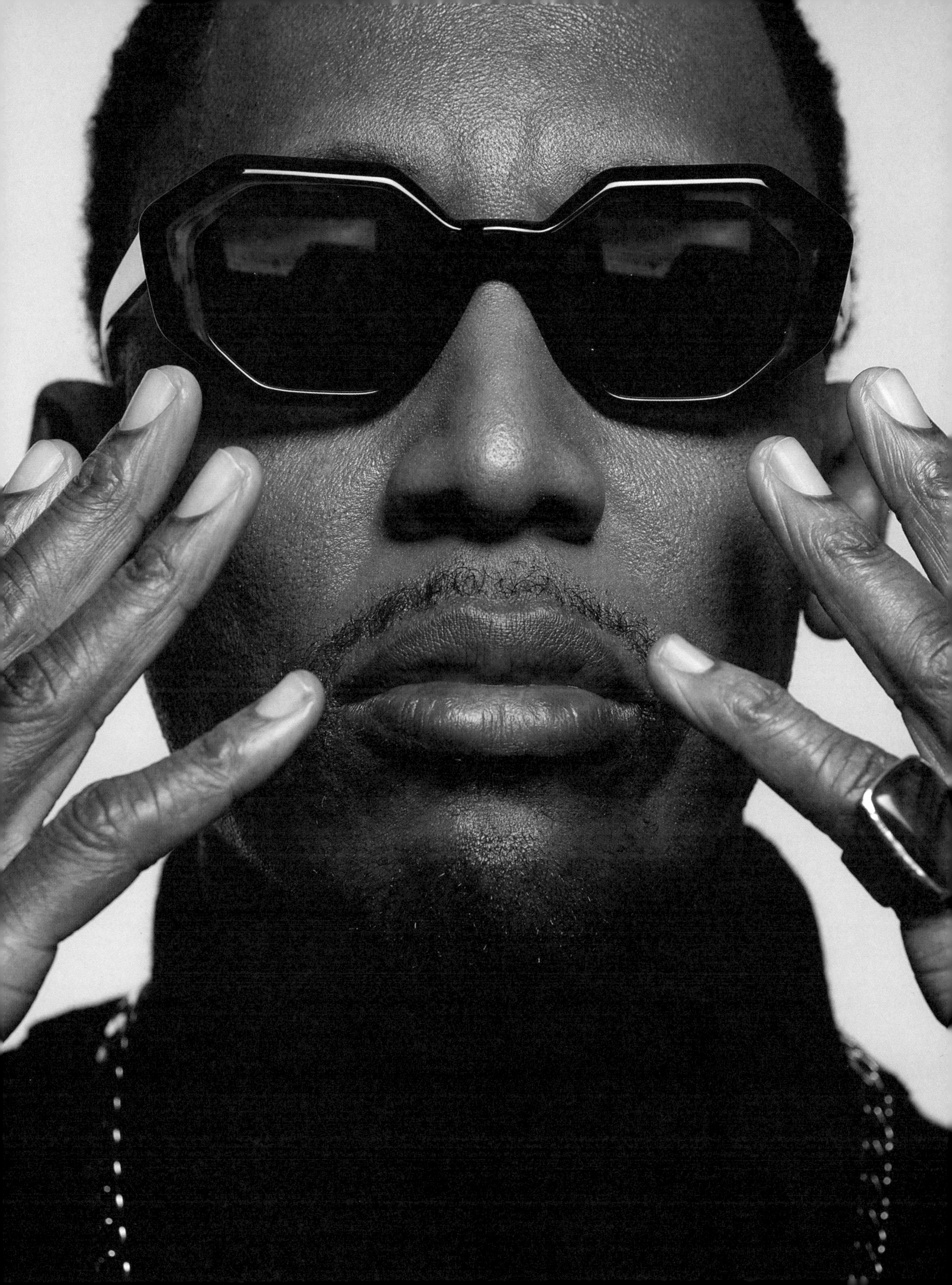

JOLENE

(Dolly Parton, Beyoncé, Denisia Andrews, Brittany Coney, Terius Gesteelde-Diamant/3'09)

Musicians: Beyoncé: vocals, backing vocals, claps / Willie Jones: vocals / Terius "The-Dream" Gesteelde-Diamant: backing vocals, claps / Shawn "Jay-Z" Carter: claps / Dora Melissa Vargas: claps / Denisia "Blu June" Andrews: backing vocals / Steve Epting: backing vocals / Kadeem Nichols: backing vocals / Jerel Duren: backing vocals / Caleb Curry: backing vocals / Michael Shorts: backing vocals / Jamal Moore: backing vocals / Jaden Gray: backing vocals / LaMarcus Eldrige: backing vocals / Stevie Wonder: harmonica / Jack Siegel: guitar / Jack Rochon: guitar / Nova Wav: sound FX / **Recording:** Kings Landing Studios West, Los Angeles: 2019 to 2024 / The Trailer, East Hampton: 2019 to 2024 / Parkwood West, Los Angeles: 2019 to 2024 / Westlake Recording Studios, West Hollywood: 2019 to 2024 / **Technical team:** Producers: Beyoncé, Jack Rochon, Khirye Tyler, Alex Vickery / **Executive producer:** Beyoncé Knowles-Carter / **Recording engineers:** Stuart White, Brandon Harding, Dani Pampuri, Matheus Braz, Andrea Roberts, John Cranfield / **Assistant recording engineers:** Matheus Braz, Patrick Gardner, Danforth Webster, Jonathan Lopez Garcia, Terena Dawn, Garrett Duncan, Conner McFarland, Nick Sutton, Jeremy Dilli / **Choir director:** Nikisha Grier-Daniel

Who could blame Dolly Parton for slightly spoiling the surprise of Beyoncé's cover version of her 1973 classic, *Jolene*? Although all the artists who participated on *Cowboy Carter* seem to have signed and stuck to a non-disclosure agreement relating to their work with Beyoncé, Dolly accidentally dropped a few hints about the project. In 2022, appearing on Trevor Noah's *Daily Show*, she said: "I would just love to hear *Jolene* done in just a big way, kind of like how Whitney [Houston] did my *I Will Always Love You*, just someone that can take my little songs and make them like powerhouses. That would be a marvelous day in my life if she ever does do *Jolene*."[361] On 11 May 2024, at the annual opening of her fun park Dollywood, she let slip a few more revelations about Beyoncé when replying to a question from a Knox News reporter: "I think she's recorded *Jolene* and I think it's probably gonna be on her country album, which I'm very excited about."[361] In the end, the exact nature of the secrets and revelations mattered little, as people will only remember the sheer power of Parton's timeless songs: *Coat of Many Colors*, *I Will Always Love You*, and, of course, *Jolene*, which Beyoncé revisits here with panache, accompanied by, among others, guitarist Jack Rochon, singer Willie Jones, who specializes in a blend of rap and country, and the inimitable Stevie Wonder, who pops in to add a discreet harmonica line to the song.

DAUGHTER

(Beyoncé, Camaron Ochs [Cam], Simon Maartensson, Terius Gesteelde-Diamant, Shawn Carter, Derek Dixie/3'23)

Musicians: Beyoncé: vocals, backing vocals / Simon Maartensson: guitar, bass, drums, piano / Gary Clark Jr: guitar / Rod Castro: guitar / Derek Dixie: sound effects / Khirye Tyler: sound effects / Bianca McClure: violin / Crystal Alforque: violin / Marta Honer: violin / Stephanie Matthews: violin / Stephanie Yu: violin / Rhea Hosanny: viola / Adrienne Woods: cello / Chelsea Gwizdala: double bass / Dwanna Orange: backing vocals / Lakeisha Lewis: backing vocals / Camille Grigsby: backing vocals / Nava Morris: backing vocals / Naarai Jacobs: backing vocals / Kiandra Richardson: backing vocals / Phylicia Hill: backing vocals / Storm Chapman: backing vocals / Jenelle Dunkley: backing vocals / Princess Fortier: backing vocals / Brooke Brewer: backing vocals / Chelsea Miller: backing vocals / LaMarcus Eldridge: backing vocals / Cedrit Leonard: backing vocals / George Young: backing vocals / Donald Paige: backing vocals / Mabvuto Carpenter: backing vocals / Jason Morales: backing vocals / Steven Epting: backing vocals / Jerome Wayne: backing vocals / **Recording:** Kings Landing Studios West, Los Angeles: 2019 to 2024 / The Trailer, East Hampton: 2019 to 2024 / Parkwood West, Los Angeles: 2019 to 2024 / Cave Studios, Nashville: 2019 to 2024 / **Technical team:** Producers: Beyoncé, Camaron Ochs (Cam), Simon Maartensson, Derek Dixie / **Executive producer:** Beyoncé Knowles-Carter / **Recording engineers:** Stuart White, Camaron Ochs (Cam), Matheus Braz, Nick Lobel, Dani Pampuri, Kyle Huffman, Andrea Roberts, John Cranfield / **Assistant recording engineers:** Matheus Braz, Cameron Hogan, Patrick Gardner, Danforth Webster, Jonathan Lopez Garcia, Terena Dawn, Garrett Duncan, Conner McFarland, Nick Sutton, Jeremy Dilli / **String arrangements:** Derek Dixie / **Choral arrangements:** Derek Dixie

Had it featured a harmonica line with a reverb effect, *Daughter* would have sounded like something out of a soundtrack to a Sergio Leone film. During the development of *Cowboy Carter*, Beyoncé immersed herself in the cinema, drawing inspiration from the ambiance of films such as Joel and Ethan Coen's *O Brother, Where Art Thou?* (2000), Quentin Tarantino's *The Hateful Eight* (2015), Michael Matthews' *Five Fingers for Marseilles* (2017), and Martin Scorsese's *Killers of the Flower Moon* (2023). Beyoncé takes us by surprise by including in this wonderful folk ballad her own interpretation of the aria *Caro Mio Ben* by Italian composer Tommaso Giordani, as well as slotting into the heart of the song a segment from *Concerto for Violin No. 1 in D major, Op. 3: Adagio* composed by the man they called the black Mozart, both for the color of his skin and for his sheer talent: French composer Joseph Bologne, Chevalier de Saint-George. "[This adagio] was created in the 1700s," Beyoncé explained. "This is a testament to Chevalier's vision. I hope it inspires artists, as well as fans, to dig deeper and learn more about the Black musical innovators who came before us."[348]

Dolly Parton in 1978—part country, part disco.

Shaboozey at the *Billboard* Music Awards in Las Vegas, 12 December 2024.

SPAGHETTII
(FEATURING LINDA MARTELL, SHABOOZEY)

(Beyoncé, Terius Gesteelde-Diamant, Shawn Carter, Collins Chibueze, Khirye Tyler, DJ Dede Mandrake, Leah Nardos Takele/2'38)

Musicians: Beyoncé: vocals, backing vocals / Linda Martell: spoken voice / Shaboozey: rap / Jack Siegel: guitar / **Recording:** Kings Landing Studios West, Los Angeles: 2019 to 2024 / The Trailer, East Hampton: 2019 to 2024 / Parkwood West, Los Angeles: 2019 to 2024 / Westlake Recording Studios, West Hollywood: 2019 to 2024 / **Technical team: Producers:** Beyoncé, Swizz Beatz, Khirye Tyler / **Executive producer:** Beyoncé Knowles-Carter / **Recording engineers:** Stuart White, Matheus Braz, Henrique Andrade, Andrea Roberts, John Cranfield / **Assistant recording engineers:** Matheus Braz, Patrick Gardner, Danforth Webster, Jonathan Lopez Garcia, Terena Dawn, Garrett Duncan, Conner McFarland, Nick Sutton, Jeremy Dilli

Rapper Shaboozey is without a doubt one of the artists who inspired Beyoncé in the production of *Cowboy Carter*. Like Willie Jones, he magnificently blends country sounds with his blistering hip-hop. His 2022 album *Cowboys Live Forever, Outlaws Never Die* is a skillful blend of trap, rap, and Americana, bringing in acoustic and pedal steel guitars to add a healthy dollop of spaghetti western, a term used to describe a style of western, mostly produced and directed by Italians, that emerged in the 1960s, with director Sergio Leone as their standard-bearer. It's this inspiration that provided the title for this trap song, where the patchwork of influences works perfectly. "Everyone's working at the same time and [in] different rooms," said the rapper about the recording sessions for *Cowboy Carter*, "and I came in a couple of days and recorded some parts. [Beyoncé] heard them later and liked them. It's cool how you don't know until the last moment if your part made it or not."[362]

ALLIIGATOR TEARS

(Beyoncé, Terius Gesteelde-Diamant, Khirye Tyler, Jack Siegel/2'59)

Musicians: Beyoncé: vocals, backing vocals / Jack Siegel: guitar / **Recording:** Westlake Recording Studios, West Hollywood: 2019 to 2024 / **Technical team: Producers:** Beyoncé, Terius "The-Dream" Gesteelde-Diamant, Khirye Tyler / **Executive producer:** Beyoncé Knowles-Carter / **Recording engineers:** Stuart White, Hotae Alexander Jang, Matheus Braz, Andrea Roberts, John Cranfield / **Assistant recording engineers:** Matheus Braz, Patrick Gardner, Danforth Webster, Jonathan Lopez Garcia, Terena Dawn, Garrett Duncan, Conner McFarland, Nick Sutton, Jeremy Dilli

Guitarist Jack Siegel, the song's co-writer and co-producer, met Khirye Tyler on the internet during the 2020 lockdown, which he spent at home in Phoenix. Tyler, who was musical director of Beyoncé's Renaissance World Tour, took Siegel under his wing and invited him to join the production of *Cowboy Carter*. "I was in shock that I had the chance to get music to Beyoncé," said the young musician. "A lot of this industry is last minute. You gotta be ready to execute in really little time. That's where all your prior preparation and skills come in."[363] Siegel worked on *Alliigator Tears*, as well as *Spaghettii*, for which he wrote Shaboozey's vocal section; he also wrote the final part and the outro for *Jolene*.

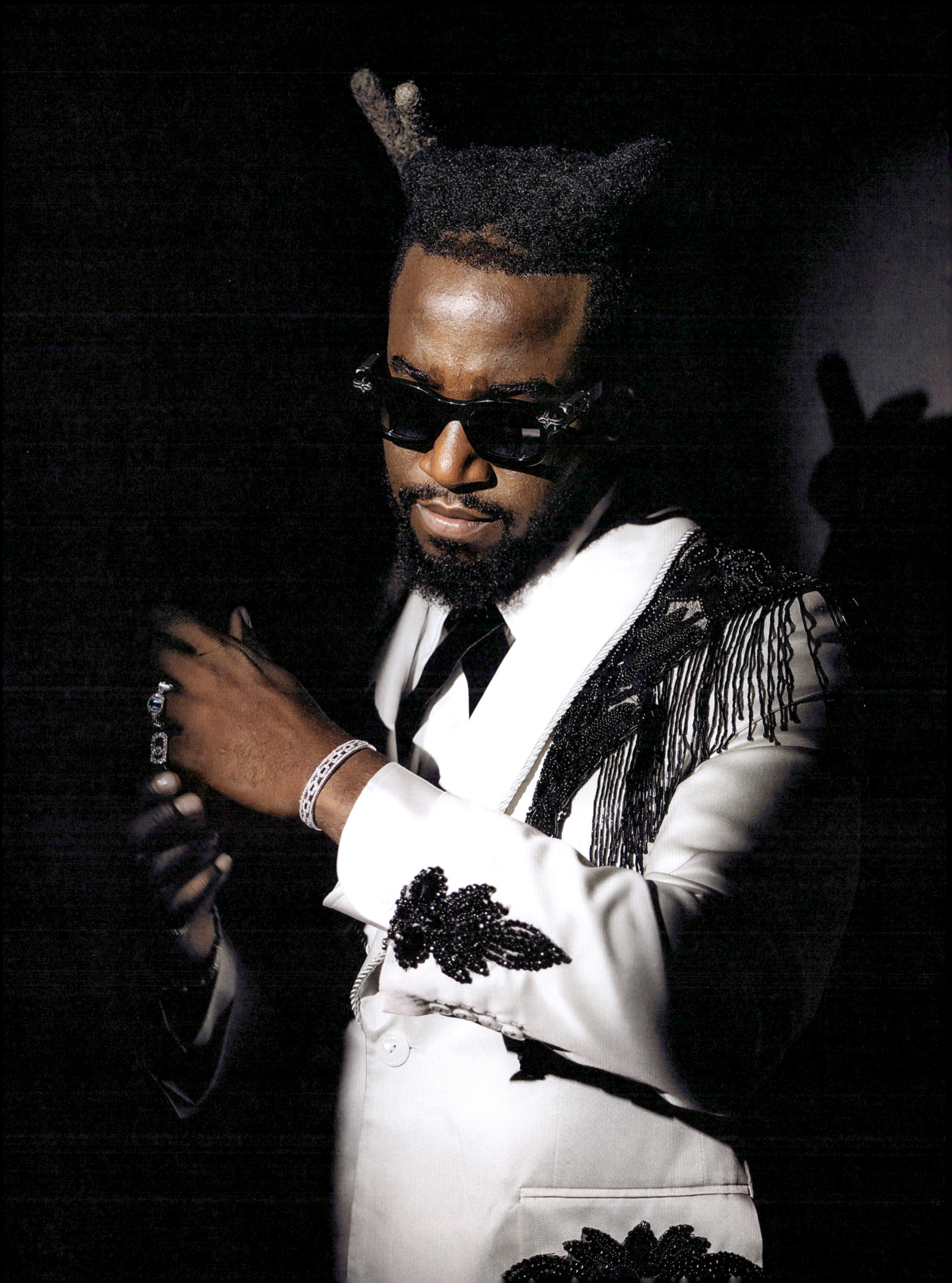

Like Shaboozey and Post Malone, Willie Jones championed quality music that combined rap with country.

SMOKE HOUR II
(FEATURING WILLIE NELSON)

(Beyoncé, Leah Nardos Takele, Dave Hamelin, Jeff Gitelman/0'29)

Musicians: Willie Nelson: spoken voice / Jeff "Gitty" Gitelman: harmonica / Ross Garren: harmonica / Khirye Tyler: sound effects / **Recording:** Dezert Flowers Studio, Los Angeles: 2019 to 2024 / Westlake Recording Studios, West Hollywood: 2019 to 2024 / **Technical team:** Producers: Beyoncé, Dave Hamelin / **Executive producer:** Beyoncé Knowles-Carter / **Recording engineers:** Steve Chadie, Dave Hamelin, Hotae Alexander Jang, Matheus Braz, Andrea Roberts, John Cranfield / **Assistant recording engineers:** Matheus Braz, Patrick Gardner, Danforth Webster, Jonathan Lopez Garcia, Terena Dawn, Garrett Duncan, Conner McFarland, Nick Sutton, Jeremy Dilli / **Arrangements:** Khirye Tyler

As a child, Jeff "Gitty" Gitelman wanted to be a professional basketball player and never imagined that one day he would appear on the album of a music star. A graduate of the prestigious Berklee College of Music, he changed his mind after discovering the firepower of Jimi Hendrix, the rage at the heart of Megadeth and Pantera albums, and the groove from the authentic jazz on Jimmy Smith and Wes Montgomery's album *Jimmy & Wes: The Dynamic Duo*, which his father brought home one day. "I still listen to that record. It's one of the greatest jazz recordings of all time. I remember in that first song, *Down by the Riverside*, the groove was swinging so hard."[364] Now a producer for big-name artists (he has accompanied Lauren Hill and Alicia Keys on stage), Gitelman left his mark on *Cowboy Carter*, supplying harmonica for Willie Nelson's second interlude and helping write the following track, *Just For Fun*.

JUST FOR FUN
(FEATURING WILLIE JONES)

(Beyoncé, Ryan Beatty, Dave Hamelin, Jeff Gitty/3'24)

Musicians: Beyoncé: vocals, backing vocals / **Willie Jones:** vocals, backing vocals / **Khirye Tyler:** guitar, drums / **No I.D.:** drums / **Harv:** drums / **Jeff "Gitty" Gitelman:** harmonica / **Ross Garren:** harmonica / **Dave Hamelin:** bass / **Bianca McClure:** violin / **Crystal Alforque:** violin / **Marta Honer:** violin / **Stephanie Matthews:** violin / **Stephanie Yu:** violin / **Rhea Hosanny:** viola / **Adrienne Woods:** cello / **Chelsea Gwizdala:** double bass / **Ryan Beatty:** backing vocals / **Dwanna Orange:** backing vocals / **Lakeisha Lewis:** backing vocals / **Camille Grigsby:** backing vocals / **Nava Morris:** backing vocals / **Naarai Jacobs:** backing vocals / **Kiandra Richardson:** backing vocals / **Phylicia Hill:** backing vocals / **Storm Chapman:** backing vocals / **Jenelle Dunkley:** backing vocals / **Princess Fortier:** backing vocals / **Brooke Brewer:** backing vocals / **Chelsea Miller:** backing vocals / **LaMarcus Eldridge:** backing vocals / **Cedrit Leonard:** backing vocals / **George Young:** backing vocals / **Donald Paige:** backing vocals / **Mabvuto Carpenter:** backing vocals / **Jason Morales:** backing vocals / **Steven Epting:** backing vocals / **Jerome Wayne:** backing vocals / **Recording:** Kings Landing Studios West, Los Angeles: 2019 to 2024 / The Trailer, East Hampton: 2019 to 2024 / Parkwood West, Los Angeles: 2019 to 2024 / Dezert Flower Studios, Los Angeles: 2019 to 2024 / Cave Studios, Nashville: 2019 to 2024 / The Library, Nashville: 2019 to 2024 / Westlake Recording Studios, West Hollywood: 2019 to 2024 / **Technical team:** Producers: Beyoncé, Dave Hamelin, Alex Vickery / **Executive producer:** Beyoncé Knowles-Carter / **Recording engineers:** Stuart White, Dani Pampuri, Kyle Huffman, Dave Hamelin, Hotae Alexander Jang, Lester Mendoza, Matheus Braz, Andrea Roberts, John Cranfield / **Assistant recording engineers:** Matheus Braz, Cameron Hogan, Patrick Gardner, Danforth Webster, Jonathan Lopez Garcia, Terena Dawn, Garrett Duncan, Conner McFarland, Nick Sutton, Jeremy Dilli / **Choirmaster:** Derek Dixie / **Harmonica arrangements:** Raphael Saadiq

When Willie Jones got a call from his friend Alex Vickery, who was working as a producer on Beyoncé's upcoming album, he couldn't believe his ears. "She's like, 'Are you sitting down?'" Jones recalled. "I was like, 'Yeah.' And she's like, 'You know Beyoncé is working on a country album…[and] she loves your voice.' I was like, 'Are you serious?' She was like, 'Can you come out here tomorrow?' I was like, 'Send the car.'"[365] When he turned up the following day to sing on the track then being recorded, production of *Cowboy Carter* was nearing completion. Jones added his warm, deep vocals to the blues track in question: *Just For Fun*. "I got in the studio and I heard the song," he said, "and I related to it more than d–n near any song I've ever heard in my life. To be on the same track as Beyoncé Giselle Knowles-Carter is definitely a check off my bucket list."[366]

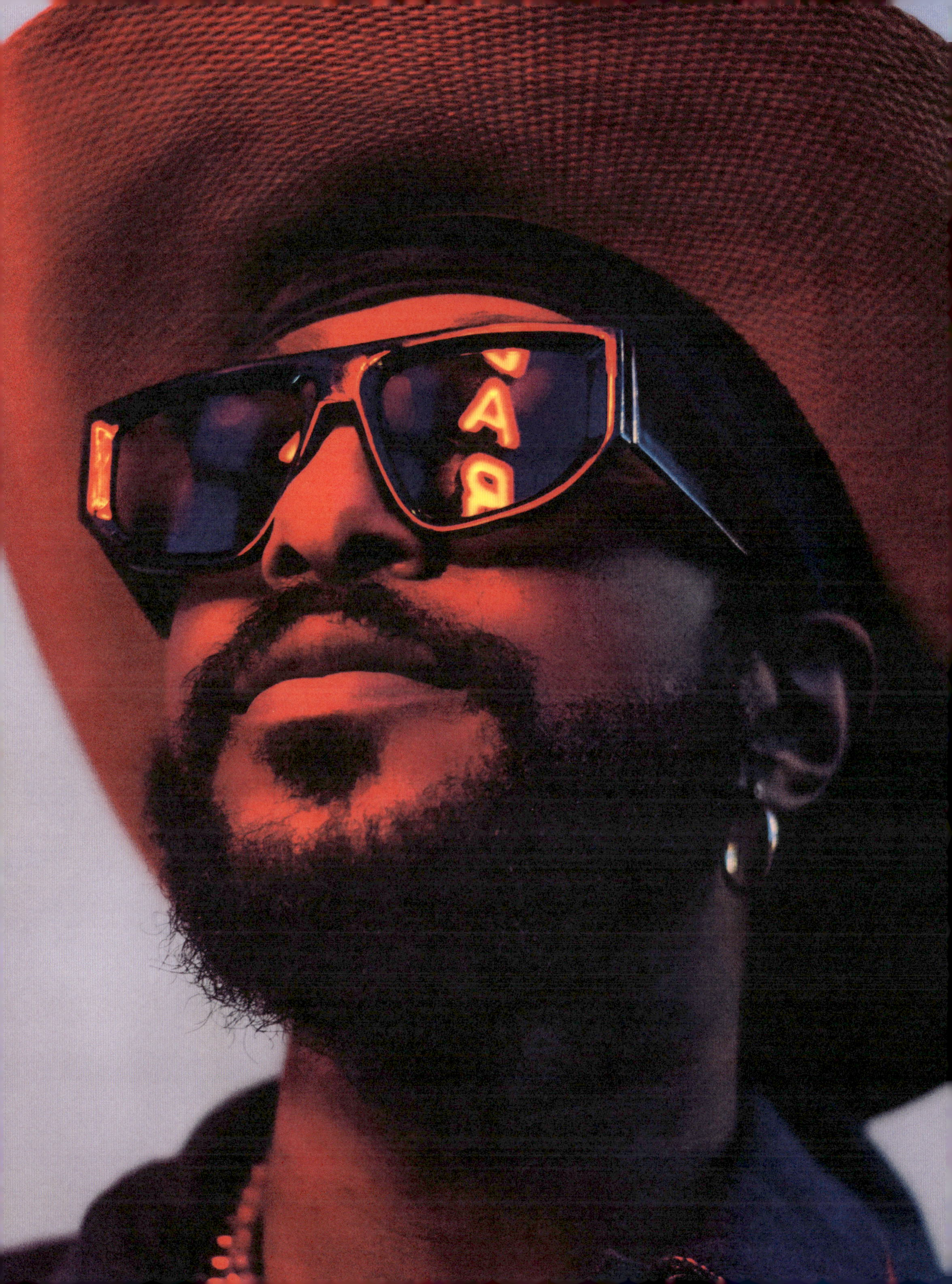

The voice of Post Malone renders one of the finest tracks on the album, *Levii's Jeans*, sublime.

SINGLE

II MOST WANTED
(FEATURING MILEY CYRUS)

(Beyoncé, Miley Cyrus, Michael Pollack, Ryan Tedder/3'28)

Musicians: Beyoncé: vocals, backing vocals / **Miley Cyrus:** vocals, backing vocals / **Jonathan Rado:** acoustic guitar, synthesizers, Wurlitzer, piano / **Sean Watkins:** acoustic guitar / **Adam Granduciel:** electric guitar / **Matt Pynn:** pedal steel guitar / **Pino Palladino:** bass / **Justin Brown:** "Acoustic Guitar Drums" / **Michael Pollack:** Hammond organ / **Sara Watkins:** fiddle / **Recording:** The Village Recording Studios, Los Angeles: 2019 to 2024 / Westlake Recording Studios, West Hollywood: 2019 to 2024 / **Technical team:** Producers: Beyoncé, Shawn Everett, Michael Pollack, Miley Cyrus, Jonathan Rado / **Executive producer:** Beyoncé Knowles-Carter / **Recording engineers:** Stuart White, Pièce Eatah, Shawn Everett, Ian Gold, Ivan Wayman, Matheus Braz, Andrea Roberts, John Cranfield / **Assistant recording engineers:** Matheus Braz, Danforth Webster, Patrick Gardner, Jonathan Lopez Garcia, Terena Dawn, Garrett Duncan, Conner McFarland, Nick Sutton, Jeremy Dilli / **Single:** Streaming by Parkwood Entertainment/Columbia: 12 April 2024 / Best chart ranking in the USA: 6

Who better than Dolly Parton's god-daughter to support Beyoncé in her foray into country? Miley Cyrus and Beyoncé are long-standing friends. They first met on a TV fundraiser for a cancer charity, filmed on 5 December 2008 at New York's Radio City Music Hall. "I was sandwiched between Beyoncé and Rihanna, who were, you know, five feet ten inches and in heels," says Cyrus, with her characteristic humor. "Their hips were, like, up to my shoulders. They were these powerful, fully realized, grown women, and I'm pretty sure I had braces on the back of my teeth."[367] The two singers subsequently became friends and it was inevitable that they would record together one day. So when Beyoncé invited Cyrus to take part in the writing of *Cowboy Carter*, the woman who had performed *Wrecking Ball* and *Flowers* decide to present a song she had written two and a half years earlier. *II Most Wanted*, about the unbreakable bond and close friendship between two women, each ready to do anything for the other, seemed like a fitting song to describe the relationship between the two artists. With its descending chord progression that resembles *Landslide*, Fleetwood Mac's legendary ballad recorded in 1975 and covered by The Dixie Chicks in 2002, *II Most Wanted*

perfectly slots into the general tone of *Cowboy Carter*—so much so that when the two women were recording together and Beyoncé told Miley she wanted to give the track a country flavor, the latter replied: "We don't have to get country; we are country. We've been country. I said, 'You know, between you being from Texas and me being from Tennessee, so much of us is going to be in this song.'"[367]

LEVII'S JEANS
(FEATURING POST MALONE)

(Beyoncé, Austin Post, Terius Gesteelde-Diamant, Nile Rodgers, Shawn Carter/4'17)

Musicians: Beyoncé: vocals, backing vocals / **Post Malone:** vocals, backing vocals / **Nile Rodgers:** guitar / **Khirye Tyler:** sound effects / **Recording:** Westlake Recording Studios, West Hollywood: 2019 to 2024 / Electric Feel Studios, West Hollywood: 2019 to 2024 / **Technical team:** Producers: Beyoncé, Terius "The-Dream" Gesteelde-Diamant, Louis Bell / **Executive producer:** Beyoncé Knowles-Carter / **Recording engineers:** Stuart White, Willie Linton, Brandon Harding, Matheus Braz, Andrea Roberts, John Cranfield / **Assistant recording engineers:** Matheus Braz, Dani Pampuri, Patrick Gardner, Danforth Webster, Jonathan Lopez Garcia, Terena Dawn, Garrett Duncan, Conner McFarland, Nick Sutton, Jeremy Dilli

Great musicians can play anything. It's an adage that absolutely applies to the great Nile Rodgers, who until now had accustomed us to frenzied funk and disco rhythms delivered on one of his famous Fender Stratocaster guitars. Complete change here with *Levii's Jeans*, which is both understated with its soothing feel and flamboyant thanks to its performers' vocal mastery. Rodgers provides the instrumentals for this simple but incredibly effective track, one of the best on *Cowboy Carter*. Beyoncé invited in another superstar: singer and rapper Post Malone, famous in the US for his ability to combine rap, trap, and country. He had never met Beyoncé or even communicated with her except by text. Malone recorded his vocals for the track with the help of his sound engineer Willie Linton, before Beyoncé polished the song with The-Dream and Malone's regular producer, Louis Bell.

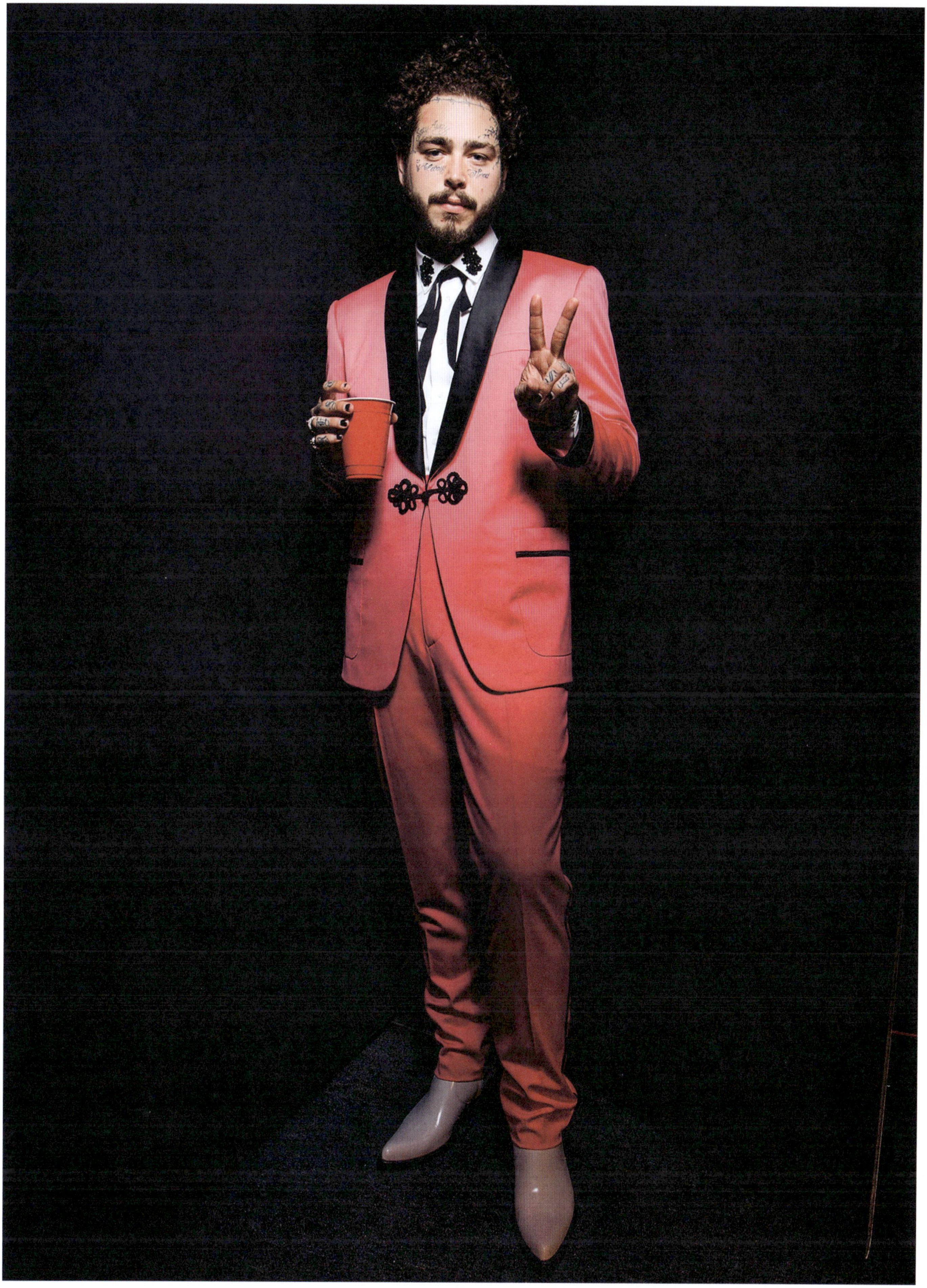

Country singer Linda Martell at the end of the 1960s, shortly before the release of her only album, *Color Me Country*.

FLAMENCO

(Beyoncé, Shawntoni Ajanae Nichols/1'40)

Musicians: Beyoncé: vocals, backing vocals / **Mamii:** guitar / **Khirye Tyler:** sound FX / **Recording:** Westlake Recording Studios, West Hollywood: 2019 to 2024 / **Technical team:** Producers: Beyoncé, Mamii / **Executive producer:** Beyoncé Knowles-Carter / **Recording engineers:** Stuart White, Dani Pampuri, Mamii, Matheus Braz, Andrea Roberts, John Cranfield / **Assistant recording engineers:** Matheus Braz, Patrick Gardner, Danforth Webster, Jonathan Lopez Garcia, Terena Dawn, Garrett Duncan, Conner McFarland, Nick Sutton, Jeremy Dilli / **String arrangements:** Jean Dawson, Johnny May, Itai Shapira, Jonathan Hoskins, Victor Wainstein, Khirye Tyler

Johnny May is an arranger on the new American hip-hop scene, lending his expertise to productions by Kyle Lux, Jean Dawson, and Tyler, The Creator. Here on *Flamenco* he puts his huge talents to great use, arranging the string parts. Young Shawntoni Ajanae Nichols, aka Mamii, the latest entrant in the Roc Nation stable, is co-writer and producer on the track. Her work on the vocal harmonies is particularly noteworthy.

THE LINDA MARTELL SHOW
(FEATURING LINDA MARTELL)

(Beyoncé, Leah Nardos Takele/0'28)

Musicians: Linda Martell: spoken voice / **Khirye Tyler:** sound effects / **Recording:** Westlake Recording Studios, West Hollywood: 2019 to 2024 / **Technical team:** Producer: Beyoncé / **Executive producer:** Beyoncé Knowles-Carter / **Recording engineers:** Dani Pampuri, Matheus Braz, Andrea Roberts, John Cranfield / **Assistant recording engineers:** Matheus Braz, Patrick Gardner, Danforth Webster, Jonathan Lopez Garcia, Terena Dawn, Garrett Duncan, Conner McFarland, Nick Sutton, Jeremy Dilli

Linda Martell, a legend of country music since the early 1960s, is famous both for her talent and for having been the first Black female singer to achieve success in the country genre. This great lady is best known for her wonderful, and only, album, *Color Me Country*, released in 1970. The racial abuse she subsequently received from musicians in Nashville made her decide to leave that emblematic city. Here, following on from Willie Nelson's radio presenter on *Smoke Hour ★ Willie Nelson* and Dolly Parton's announcer on *Dolly P*, Martell plays the role of a TV host on a show featuring the album's next song, *Ya Ya*.

YA YA

(Beyoncé, Terius Gesteelde-Diamant, Shawn Carter, Oliver Rodigan, Harry Edwards, Klara Mkhatshwa Munk-Hansen, Anaïs Marinho, Lee Hazlewood, Brian Wilson, Mike Love/4'34)

Musicians: Beyoncé: vocals, backing vocals / **Terius "The-Dream" Gesteelde-Diamant:** backing vocals / **Raphael Saadiq:** guitar / **Harry Edwards:** guitar, organ, bass, programming / **Robert Randolph:** pedal steel guitar / **Oliver Rodigan:** bass, synthesizers, programming / **Khirye Tyler:** bass, drums, percussions, programming / **Lemar Carter:** drums / **Recording:** Westlake Recording Studios, West Hollywood: 2019 to 2024 / Kings Landing Studios West, Los Angeles: 2019 to 2024 / **Technical team:** Producers: Beyoncé, Terius "The-Dream" Gesteelde-Diamant, Cadenza, Harry Edwards, Khirye Tyler / **Executive producer:** Beyoncé Knowles-Carter / **Recording engineers:** Stuart White, Mathaus Braz, Brandon Harding, Hotae Alexander Jang, Andrea Roberts, John Cranfield / **Assistant recording engineers:** Matheus Braz, Patrick Gardner, Danforth Webster, Jonathan Lopez Garcia, Terena Dawn, Garrett Duncan, Conner McFarland, Nick Sutton, Jeremy Dilli

Ya Ya, built around a sample from Nancy Sinatra's 1966 hit *These Boots Are Made for Walkin'*, written by Lee Hazlewood, sees Beyoncé return to her love for soul, present in the song largely thanks to the drum rhythm that includes strikes on the snare drum on every beat. Musician and producer Raphael Saadiq, who plays guitar on the track, was probably influential here, having himself released two albums inspired by Motown Sound: *The Way I See It* in 2008 and *Stone Rollin'* in 2011. This soul-orientation is likely to have come as much from Saadiq's own musical culture as from the international success of several masterpieces in the genre that were released at the time: Joss Stone's *The Soul Sessions* (2003), Amy Winehouse's *Back to Black* (2006), and Duffy's *Rockferry* (2008). The track takes Beyoncé back to her roots and reminds us that mixing genres is a strength, especially when it is done so masterfully and deliberately.

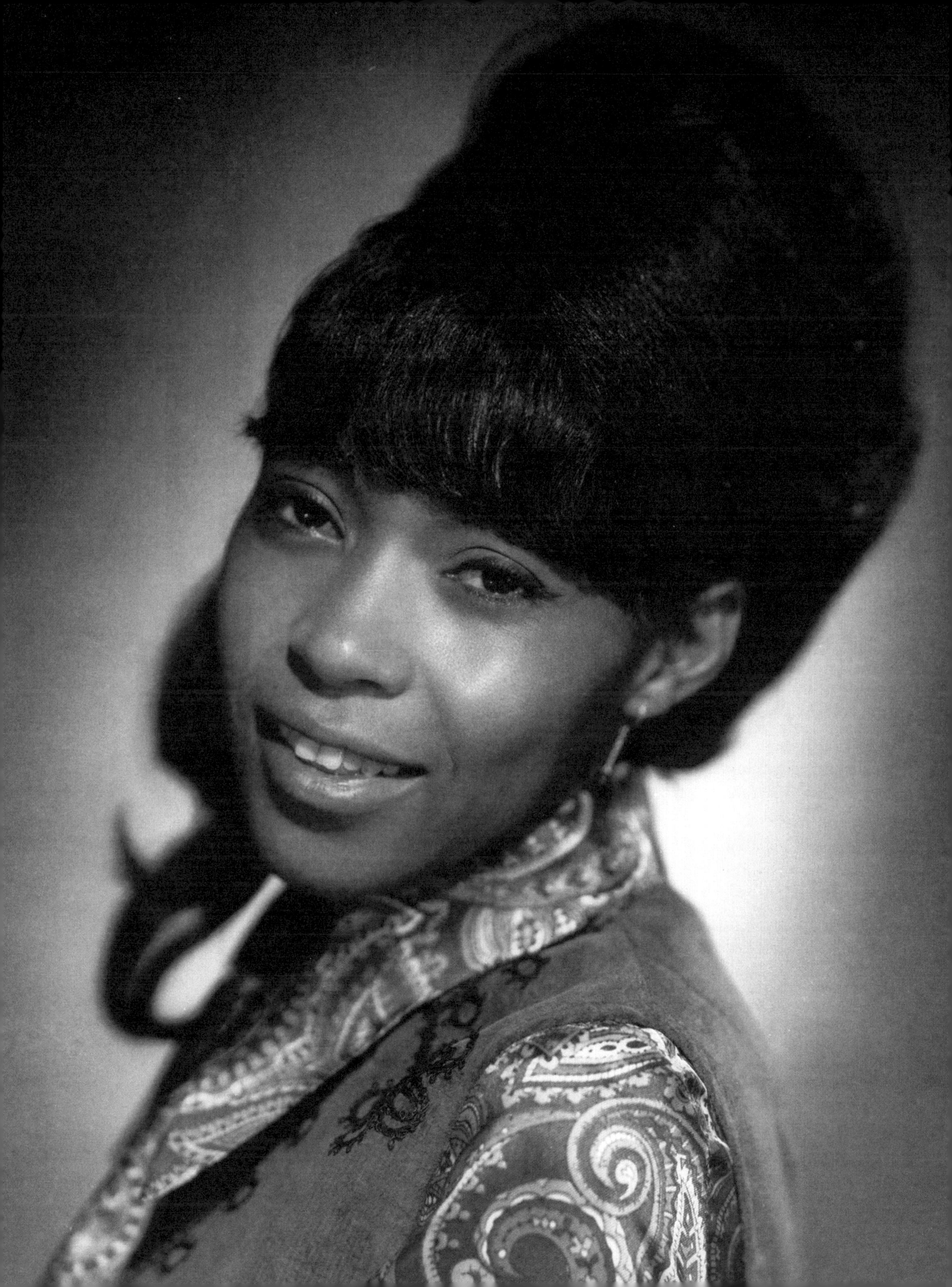

The music of the king of rock'n'roll, Chuck Berry, features twice on Cowboy Carter.

OH LOUISIANA

(Chuck Berry/0'52)

Musicians: Beyoncé: vocals, backing vocals / **Recording:** Westlake Recording Studios, West Hollywood: 2019 to 2024 / **Technical team: Producers:** Beyoncé, Terius "The-Dream" Gesteelde-Diamant / **Executive producer:** Beyoncé Knowles-Carter / **Recording engineers:** Brandon Harding, Matheus Braz, Andrea Roberts, John Cranfield / **Assistant recording engineers:** Matheus Braz, Patrick Gardner, Danforth Webster, Jonathan Lopez Garcia, Terena Dawn, Garrett Duncan, Conner McFarland, Nick Sutton, Jeremy Dilli

In 1971, Chuck Berry recorded *Oh Louisiana* for his album *San Francisco Dues*. It was released by Chess Records, the label whose epic story is told in the 2008 film *Cadillac Records*, in which Beyoncé plays singer Etta James. When the song came out in 1971, it wasn't typical of Berry's repertoire: he was better known for his energetic rock'n'roll output (for the uninitiated, Berry wrote some of the seminal tracks of 1950s rock: *Maybellene, Thirty Days, Roll Over Beethoven*, and, the best known of all, *Johnny B. Goode*) than for his soul, or even funk, numbers, of which *Oh Louisiana* is one. Beyoncé revisits the song, concealing her voice behind an auto-tune effect that raises the pitch. In so doing, she tips her hat to this icon of African-American culture and along the way pays homage to the state of Louisiana, part of her personal heritage.

DESERT EAGLE

(Beyoncé, Jabbar Stevens, Miranda Johnson, Marcus Reddick/1'12)

Musicians: Beyoncé: vocals, backing vocals / Gary Clark Jr: guitar / Bah Christ: guitar / Marcus Reddick: bass / Khirye Tyler: percussions / **Recording:** Westlake Recording Studios, West Hollywood: 2019 to 2024 / **Technical team: Producers:** Beyoncé, Bah, Marcus Reddick / **Executive producer:** Beyoncé Knowles-Carter / **Recording engineers:** Stuart White, Brandon Harding, Dani Pampuri, Matheus Braz, Andrea Roberts, John Cranfield / **Assistant recording engineers:** Matheus Braz, Danforth Webster, Patrick Gardner, Jonathan Lopez Garcia, Terena Dawn, Garrett Duncan, Conner McFarland, Nick Sutton, Jeremy Dilli

Marcus Reddick is a virtuoso arranger, composer, and bassist. In *Desert Eagle*, he delivers a highly precise, technical bass for the full 72 seconds of the track. Although more of an interlude than a song, it also features another appearance on production from Jabbar "Bah" Stevens, whom we saw on *Thique* and *All Up in Your Mind* on *Renaissance*.

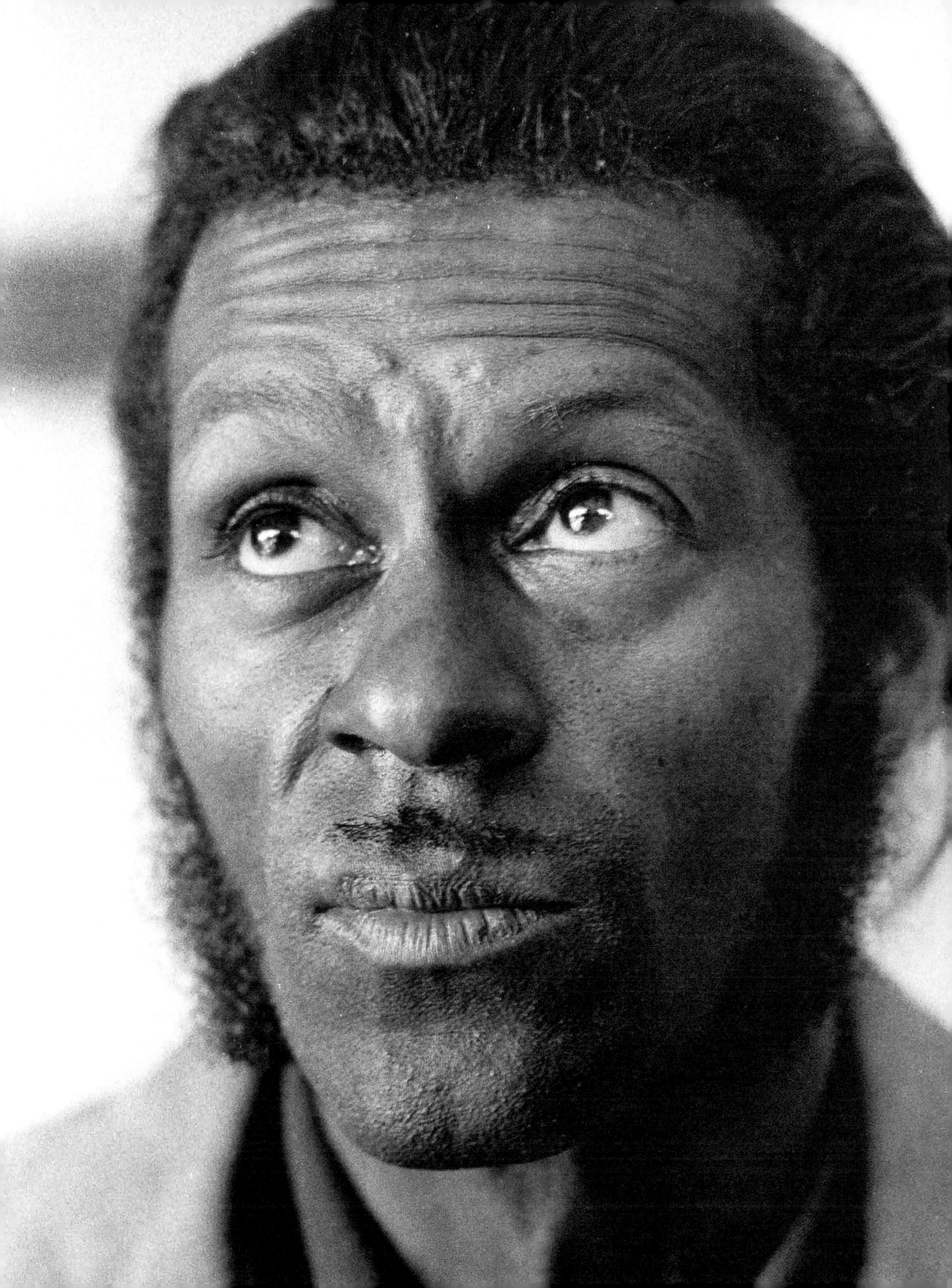

RIIVERDANCE

(Beyoncé, Terius Gesteelde-Diamant, Rachel Keen, Mark Spears/4'12)

Musicians: Beyoncé: vocals, backing vocals, percussions / Terius "The-Dream" Gesteelde-Diamant: guitar, bass, backing vocals / Khirye Tyler: percussion / **Recording:** Westlake Recording Studios, West Hollywood: 2019 to 2024 / **Technical team: Producers:** Beyoncé, Terius "The-Dream" Gesteelde-Diamant / **Executive producer:** Beyoncé Knowles-Carter / **Recording engineers:** Stuart White, Brandon Harding, Matheus Braz, Andrea Roberts, John Cranfield / **Assistant recording engineers:** Matheus Braz, Patrick Gardner, Danforth Webster, Jonathan Lopez Garcia, Terena Dawn, Garrett Duncan, Conner McFarland, Nick Sutton, Jeremy Dilli

Riiverdance, with its acoustic guitar line and title that refers to the famous 1994 Bill Whelan musical, evokes traditional Irish music far removed from the country style of the rest of the album. Beyoncé performs this piece produced by The-Dream and singer Rachel "Raye" Keen, who had previously contributed to the writing of *Bigger* on *The Lion King: The Gift*. After writing numerous hits for other artists, including *Dreamer* for Charli XCX in 2017, *Home With You* for Madison Beer in 2018, and *Sixteen* for Ellie Goulding in 2019, Keen finally achieved the status she deserved, with recognition for her talent and a Grammy nomination in the Best New Artist category.

II HANDS II HEAVEN

(Beyoncé, Dave Hamelin, Ryan Beatty, Jack Rochon, Terius Gesteelde-Diamant, Mark Spears/5'41)

Musicians: Beyoncé: vocals, backing vocals / Gary Clark Jr: guitar / Khirye Tyler: sound effects / Jack Rochon: bass / Terius "The-Dream" Gesteelde-Diamant: programming, percussions, backing vocals / **Recording:** Kings Landing Studios West, Los Angeles: 2019 to 2024 / The Trailer, East Hampton: 2019 to 2024 / Parkwood West, Los Angeles: 2019 to 2024 / Dezert Flower Studios, Los Angeles: 2019 to 2024 / Westlake Recording Studios, West Hollywood: 2019 to 2024 / **Technical team: Producers:** Beyoncé, Dave Hamelin, Jack Rochon / **Executive producer:** Beyoncé Knowles-Carter / **Recording engineers:** Stuart White, Dave Hamelin, Brandon Harding, Matheus Braz, Dani Pampuri, Andrea Roberts, John Cranfield / **Assistant recording engineers:** Matheus Braz, Patrick Gardner, Danforth Webster, Jonathan Lopez Garcia, Terena Dawn, Garrett Duncan, Conner McFarland, Nick Sutton, Jeremy Dilli

In this song that pulses to the rhythm of the iconic Roland TR-808 drum machine, Beyoncé once again raises her glass to her love for whisky, for which she is now an ambassador: she promoted her own brand, SirDavis, alongside *Cowboy Carter*. *Two hands to Heaven/My whiskey up high*, she sings, marketing her brand perfectly. "Making liquor has been in Southern families like mine for many generations," she explains. "The Jack Daniel's famous recipe? That was heavily influenced by a Black man named Nathan 'Nearest' Green. He was a former slave who became Jack Daniel's master distiller."[348]

TYRANT

(Beyoncé, Camaron Ochs, Terius Gesteelde-Diamant, David Doman, Dominik Redenczki, Ezemdi Chikwendu/4'10)

Musicians: Beyoncé: vocals, backing vocals / Reyna Roberts: vocals, backing vocals / Dolly Parton: spoken voice / Brittney Spencer: backing vocals / Tiera Kennedy: backing vocals / Terius "The-Dream" Gesteelde-Diamant: backing vocals / Péter Kovács: violin / Anders Mouridsen: claps / Camaron Ochs (Cam): claps / **Recording:** Cave Studios, Nashville: 2019 to 2024 / Westlake Recording Studios, West Hollywood: 2019 to 2024 / **Technical team: Producers:** Beyoncé, Dave Hamelin, D.A. Got That Dope, Khirye Tyler, Kuk Harrell / **Executive producer:** Beyoncé Knowles-Carter / **Recording engineers:** Stuart White, Brandon Harding, John Cranfield, Nick Lobel, Kristen Hilkert, Kuk Harrell, Jelli Dorman, Matheus Braz, Andrea Roberts / **Assistant recording engineers:** Matheus Braz, Patrick Gardner, Danforth Webster, Jonathan Lopez Garcia, Terena Dawn, Garrett Duncan, Conner McFarland, Nick Sutton

After David "D.A." Doman made his mark as a beat-maker for Eminem (*Godzilla*, as a duet with Juice WRLD, in 2020), Tyga (*Taste*, in 2019), and Megan Thee Stallion (*Cry Baby*, in 2020), he was invited to administer a strong dose of infrabass to *Cowboy Carter* on *Tyrant*, a track that navigates between R&B, hip-hop, and trap. Doman had sent the track's instrumental to his friend The-Dream, who contacted him a year later to tell him it had been selected for Beyoncé's upcoming album and to invite him into the studio to listen to what had become of the track. "Immediately I was like, 'Oh, man, this is fire!' Beyoncé is one of the greatest artists of all time, easily…I'm really picky with songs that are done over my beats, and sometimes I don't love the outcome. But I really love this song."[368] Another top-notch guest on the song is singer Reyna Roberts, whose vocals perfectly complement Beyoncé's and underline the R&B feel while Queen B delivers a thundering rap. "From the very moment I heard my voice on [*Tyrant*], I couldn't believe it," Roberts said. "I'm still so thankful that Beyoncé brought us onto a project and made us a little part of her legacy because people here weren't doing that, but she did."[369] Roberts is referring here to the small group of female artists invited to contribute to the track, including Brittney Spencer and Tiera Kennedy. The three young women, delighted at how well they got on during the work session and how their voices complemented each other, joked that their trio was a kind of mini Destiny's Child.

British singer Rachel "Raye" Keen at the MTV Europe Music Awards in Manchester, 10 November 2024.

The indispensable Pharrell Williams, faithful associate of Beyoncé since the early 2000s.

SWEET ★ HONEY ★ BUCKIIN'
(FEATURING SHABOOZEY)

(Beyoncé, Pharrell Williams, Collins Chibueze, Terius Gesteelde-Diamant, Shawn Carter, Hank Cochran, Harlan Howard/4'56)

Musicians: Beyoncé: vocals, backing vocals / Shaboozey: vocals, backing vocals / Pharrell: backing vocals / Khirye Tyler: programming, sound effects / **Recording:** Westlake Recording Studios, West Hollywood: 2019 to 2024 / **Technical team:** Producers: Beyoncé, Pharrell / **Executive producer:** Beyoncé Knowles-Carter / **Recording engineers:** Stuart White, John Cranfield, Henrique Andrade, Mike Larson, Matheus Braz, Andrea Roberts / **Assistant recording engineers:** Matheus Braz, Danforth Webster, Patrick Gardner, Jonathan Lopez Garcia, Terena Dawn, Garrett Duncan, Conner McFarland, Nick Sutton, Jeremy Dilli

Pharrell Williams returned to Beyoncé's musical universe to produce this track, built around three distinct segments: *Sweet* to 2'02, *Honey* from 2'03 to 2'45, and then *Buckiin'* from 2'46 to the end. Indisputably the weirdest track on *Cowboy Carter*, *Sweet ★ Honey ★ Buckiin'* sees Beyoncé back experimenting, with the help of her friend and producer Pharrell. "My process is that I typically have to experiment," she explains. "I enjoy being open to have the freedom to get all aspects of things I love out and so I worked on many songs. I recorded probably 100 songs. Once that is done, I am able to put the puzzle together and realize the consistencies and the common themes, and then create a solid body of work."[370]

AMEN

(Beyoncé, Dave Hamelin, Danielle Balbuena, Camaron Ochs, Tyler Johnson, Ian Fitchuk, Darius Dixson, Derek Dixie, Sean Solymar, Ricky Lawson/2'25)

Musicians: Beyoncé: vocals, backing vocals / Ian Fitchuk: piano / Dave Hamelin: organ / Tyler Johnson: organ / Omar Edwards: organ / Dave Hamelin: synthesizers / Derek Dixie: synthesizers / Arnetta Johnson: trumpet / Christopher Gray: trumpet / Christopher Johnson: double bass / Crystal Torres: trumpet / Gabrielle Garo: flute / Jesse McGinty: saxophone / Lemar Guillary: trombone / 070 Shake: backing vocals / Camaron Ochs: backing vocals / Ryan Beatty: backing vocals / Dwanna Orange: backing vocals / Lakeisha Lewis: backing vocals / Camille Grigsby: backing vocals / Nava Morris: backing vocals / Naarai Jacobs: backing vocals / Kiandra Richardson: backing vocals / Phylicia Hill: backing vocals / Storm Chapman: backing vocals / Jenelle Dunkley: backing vocals / Princess Fortier: backing vocals / Brooke Brewer: backing vocals / Chelsea Miller: backing vocals / LaMarcus Eldridge: backing vocals / Cedrit Leonard: backing vocals / George Young: backing vocals / Donald Paige: backing vocals / Mabvuto Carpenter: backing vocals / Jason Morales: backing vocals / Steven Epting: backing vocals / Jerome Wayne: backing vocals / **Recording:** Kings Landing Studios West, Los Angeles: 2019 to 2024 / The Trailer, East Hampton: 2019 to 2024 / Parkwood West, Los Angeles: 2019 to 2024 / Dezert Flower Studios, Los Angeles: 2019 to 2024 / Cave Studios, Nashville: 2019 to 2024 / The Library, Nashville: 2019 to 2024 / **Technical team:** Producers: Beyoncé, Dave Hamelin, Tyler Johnson, Camaron Ochs (Cam), Derek Dixie, Ian Fitchuk, 070 Shake, Sean Solymar / **Executive producer:** Beyoncé Knowles-Carter / **Recording engineers:** Stuart White, John Cranfield, Kyle Huffman, Dave Hamelin, Tyler Johnson, Konrad Snyder, Dani Pampuri, Lester Mendoza, Matheus Braz, Andrea Roberts / **Assistant recording engineers:** Matheus Braz, Cameron Hogan, Danforth Webster, Patrick Gardner, Jonathan Lopez Garcia, Terena Dawn, Garrett Duncan, Conner McFarland, Nick Sutton, Jeremy Dilli / **Choirmaster:** Derek Dixie

Amen opens with a gospel ballad featuring a number of the contributors to *Cowboy Carter* and ends in grandiose fashion with a reprise of the album's first track, *Ameriican Requiem*. Beyoncé's ambitious production, experimental sound textures, and prestigious guests mark the culmination of this concept album. The Beach Boys had their *Pet Sounds*, The Beatles their *White Album*, David Bowie his *The Rise and Fall of Ziggy Stardust and the Spiders from Mars*, and Beyoncé Knowles-Carter leaves her mark on music history with this Dantean *Cowboy Carter*.

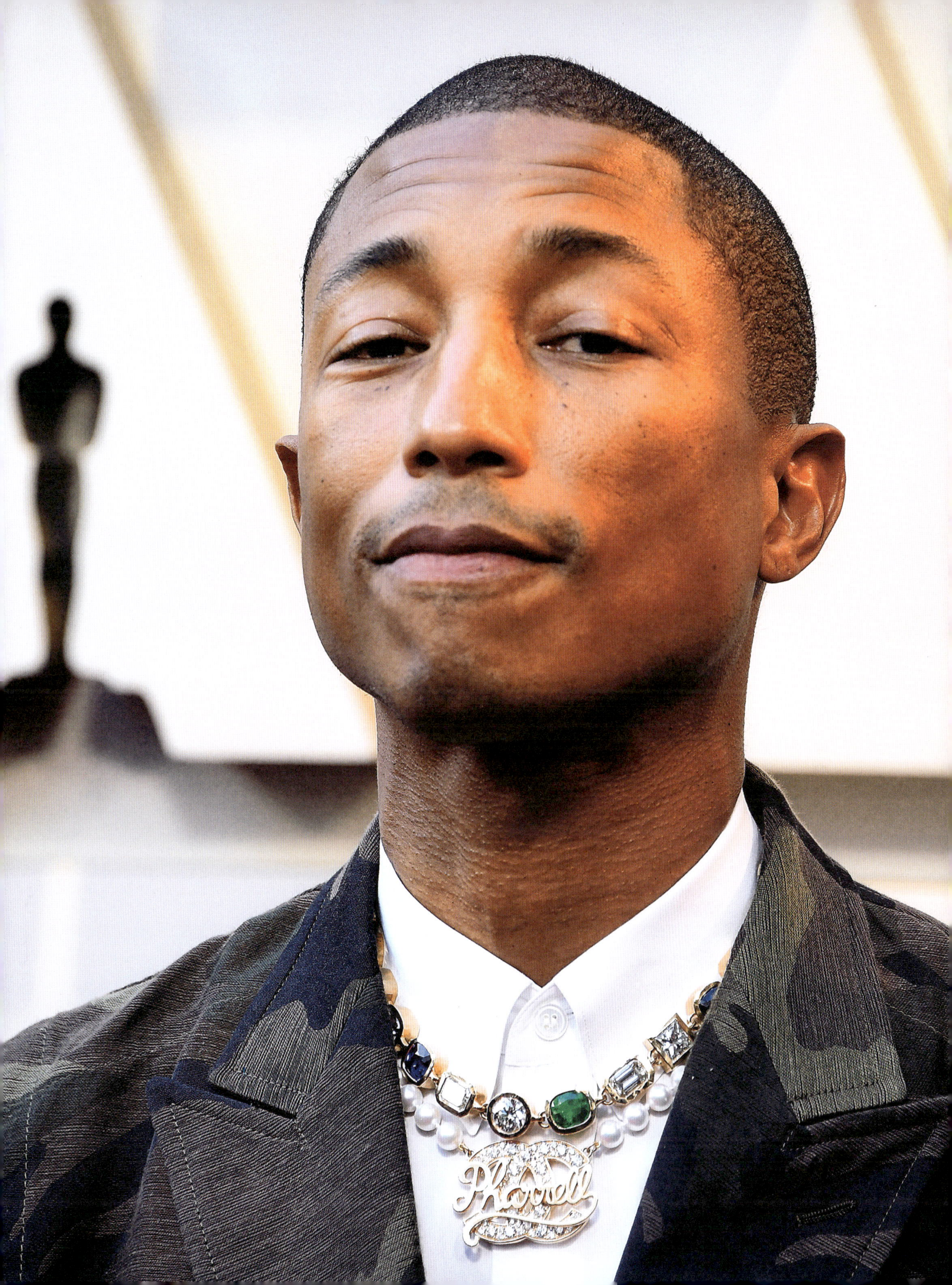
Pharrell

Compilations & Live

COMPILATIONS
This Is The Remix (Destiny's Child)
#1's (Destiny's Child)
Love Songs (Destiny's Child)
Destiny's Child: The Untold Story Presents Girls Tyme

LIVE
Homecoming: The Live Album

Only compilations and live audio albums are discussed here.

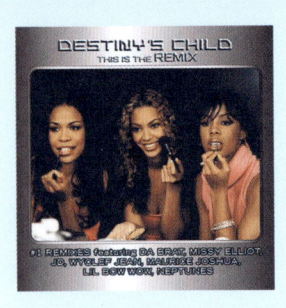

THIS IS THE REMIX
(DESTINY'S CHILD)

No, No, No Part 2 (Extended Version) (4'03)
Emotion (The Neptunes Remix) (4'15)
Bootylicious (Rockwilder Remix) (4'12)
Say My Name (Timbaland Remix) (5'01)
Bug a Boo (Refugee Camp Remix) (3'48)
Dot (The E-Poppi Mix) (3'58)
Survivor (Remix Extended Version) (3'24)
Independent Women Part II (3'42)
Nasty Girl (Maurice's Nu Soul Remix Radio Edit) (4'08)
Jumpin', Jumpin' (Remix Extended Version) (7'16)
Bills, Bills, Bills (Maurice's Xclusive Livegig Mix) (3'23)
So Good (Maurice's Soul Remix) (4'59)
Heard a Word (Michelle Williams) (4'57)

Released in the USA by Sony Music/Columbia: 12 March 2002
(LP ref.: C2 86431, CD ref.: 507627 2)
Best chart ranking in the USA: 29

After the July 2001 release of the EP *Love: Destiny*, comprising a previously unreleased track called *My Song* plus six remixes, available exclusively in Target stores, Destiny's Child, their manager, and the teams at Columbia decided to follow up with *This Is the Remix*, a compilation of different versions of the group's hits. Most had already appeared on the B-sides of singles. As the trio had been waiting in the wings since production of Beyoncé's first solo album had begun, *This Is the Remix* was a good way of reminding fans they existed, although interest in the record was fairly muted. It featured no new tracks, apart from Michelle Williams' single, released on 5 March to promote her first solo album, *Heart to Yours*. As the ladies were all busy with their own artistic projects, it fell to Mathew Knowles to justify the high media presence of his protégées: "I wouldn't want any of my artists to directly compete with each other. They're so multi-talented that while one's working TV, the other can be working a record."[371]

#1'S
(DESTINY'S CHILD)

Stand Up for Love (2005 World Children's Day Anthem) (4'45)
Independent Women Part I (3'36)
Survivor (3'49)
Soldier (4'04)
Check on It (Beyoncé feat. Slim Thug) (3'31)
Jumpin', Jumpin' (3'48)
Lose My Breath (3'33)
Say My Name (4'00)
Emotion (3'55)
Bug a Boo (3'22)
Bootylicious (3'28)
Bills, Bills, Bills (3'45)
Girl (3'26)
No, No, No Part 2 (3'15)
Cater 2 U (4'06)
Feel the Same Way I Do (4'05)

Released in the USA by Sony Music/Columbia: 21 October 2005
(CD ref.: CK 97765)
Best chart ranking in the USA: 1

Fans had already deduced from *This Is the Remix* that Destiny's Child were taking a break, but when the compilation *#1's* was released almost a year after *Destiny Fulfilled*, it became clear that this was their swansong. It offers a retrospective of their career and includes tracks from all their studio albums except *8 Days of Christmas*, which is a shame, as the title track would have slotted in well here. The R&B ladies also gave their fans three rare treats: *Stand Up for Love (2005 World Children's Day Anthem)*, *Check on It*, recorded by Beyoncé in 2005 and featured in the Shawn Levy film *The Pink Panther*, and finally *Feel the Same Way I Do*, produced by the ever-faithful Rodney "Darkchild" Jerkins.

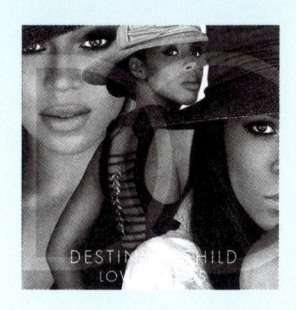

LOVE SONGS
(DESTINY'S CHILD)

Cater 2 U (4'05)
Killing Time (5'07)
Second Nature (5'08)
Heaven (Kelly Rowland) (3'59)
Now That She's Gone (5'33)
Brown Eyes (4'34)
If (4'16)
Emotion (3'56)
If You Leave (4'33)
T-Shirt (4'40)
Temptation (4'03)
Say My Name (Timbaland Remix) (5'01)
Love (4'30)
Nuclear (4'17)

Released in the USA by Music World Music/Columbia:
25 January 2013 (CD ref.: 88765430182)
Best chart ranking in the USA: 72

In a 2006 interview with *Billboard*, Mathew Knowles explained, "When they were little girls, I just remember saying, 'Hey guys, we want to end when we're on top, not going down.' And obviously, they saw the value of that. The beauty of that is ending on a positive note, you can continue the integrity of the brand because there are still opportunities with the Destiny's Child brand [...] because of the way that we've retired the brand, you can go back to it at any time."[19] In 2012, the legendary Destiny's Child manager did just that by supporting Sony Music's release of two new compilations. The first, *Playlist: The Very Best of Destiny's Child*, featured nothing new and was simply part of the record label's *Playlist* collection. The second, *Love Songs*, gave the group an opportunity to offer their fans a brand new single called *Nuclear*, produced by Pharrell Williams.

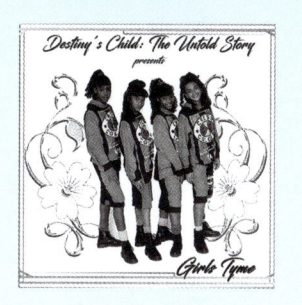

DESTINY'S CHILD: THE UNTOLD STORY PRESENTS GIRLS TYME

God Bless the Child (Intro) (1'25)
I Wanna Be Where You Are (4'03)
Sunshine (4'51)
Say It Ain't So (3'53)
Boy I Want You (3'40)
Girls Tyme Fun (4'07)
632-5792 (4'28)
Boyfriend (4'19)
Teacher Fried My Brain (4'15)
When I Laid My Eyes on You (3'05)
In My City (4'07)
Hip House (3'27)
Blue Velvet (3'52)
Take Em 2 Another Level (3'30)
Talking 'Bout My Baby (3'25)

Download on iTunes, from Trinitee Urban Records:
2 December 2019
Best US chart ranking: did not make the charts

In 2019, as Mathew Knowles was preparing to publish his first book, *Destiny's Child: The Untold Story*, in which he also revealed secrets about his daughter Beyoncé's childhood, he announced the release of a new compilation album. It consisted of songs recorded by Girls Tyme—an early version of Destiny's Child—at Sausalito's Record Plant studios in 1992, under the supervision of Arne Frager, owner of the studio and Knowles's partner at the time the band first rose to fame. In 2000, Mathew Knowles paid Frager $100,000 for the master tapes and rights to these recordings. He also had the 14 other Girls Tyme songs under lock and key, waiting for the opportune moment to come along. That moment came in 2019, alongside the publication of his book. As he said at the time: "Beyoncé and Kelly [Rowland were] the real mainstays of Destiny's Child. They were in this group. The album is mainly Beyoncé, a young lady named Ashley Davis who went on to be a protégée of Prince, went on to go to finals of *The Voice*, and Kelly Rowland. So, I decided to put it out."[372]

Beyoncé delivers a notable performance at the Coachella Valley Music and Arts Festival in Indio, 21 April 2018.

HOMECOMING: THE LIVE ALBUM

Welcome (3'16)
Crazy in Love (2'47)
Freedom (1'54)
Lift Ev'ry Voice and Sing (2'09)
Formation (4'22)
So Much Damn Swag (Interlude) (0'59)
Sorry (6'34)
Kitty Kat (0'42)
Bow Down (1'27)
I Been On (2'40)
Drunk in Love (4'14)
Diva (2'45)
Flawless/Feeling Myself (3'58)
Top Off (1'22)
7/11 (3'04)
Bug a Boo Roll Call (Interlude) (1'57)
Party (3'48)
Don't Hurt Yourself (4'16)
I Care (4'08)
Partition (2'18)
Yoncé (1'08)
Mi Gente (2'56)
Baby Boy (1'32)
You Don't Love Me (No, No, No) (1'11)
Hold Up (0'46)
Countdown (1'43)
Check on It (1'16)
Déjà Vu (4'49)
The Bzzzz Drumline (Interlude) (3'10)
Run the World (Girls) (3'53)
Lose My Breath (1'30)
Say My Name (1'51)
Soldier (2'11)
Get Me Bodied (4'23)
Single Ladies (Put a Ring on It) (3'27)
Lift Ev'ry Voice and Sing (Blue's Version) (1'42)
Love on Top (3'47)
Shining (Thank You) (2'39)
Before I Let Go (Bonus Track) (4'00)
I Been On (Bonus Track) (2'24)

Released in the USA by Parkwood Entertainment/Columbia: 17 April 2019 (LP box set ref.: 19075959261)
Best chart ranking in the USA: 4

A major milestone in Beyoncé's career was her appearance at the Coachella Valley Music and Arts Festival in the Colorado Desert on 14 and 21 April 2018, filmed and broadcast on Netflix as *Homecoming: A Film by Beyoncé*. This was inevitably accompanied by an audio version. *Homecoming: The Live Album* was released by Parkwood Entertainment on the same day as the film and distributed by Columbia. Other Beyoncé concerts have been released on DVD (*Live at Wembley* in 2004, *The Beyoncé Experience Live* in 2007, *I Am…Yours: An Intimate Performance at Wynn Las Vegas* in 2009, and *The I Am…World Tour* in 2010), but *Homecoming: The Live Album* was her very first live recording, released on both CD and vinyl. However, while this audio version gives a sense of Beyoncé's firepower on the gigantic Coachella stage, commandeered two weekends in a row by her many dancers and musicians, it struggles to convey the massive scale of the two shows. As a compilation of her best tracks, it is nonetheless an important record, mixed by the loyal Stuart White, who tore his hair out working on the sheer volume of material provided by the show's musical director, Derek Dixie, and his colleague Lester Mendoza. For total immersion in the show that really crowned Queen Beyoncé, it's best to watch the documentary *Homecoming: A Film by Beyoncé*. It features some of the show's most memorable moments (including the African-American anthem *Lift Ev'ry Voice and Sing,* the thunderous *Formation*, the fiery opening notes of *Mi Gente*, the reunion with Kelly Rowland and Michelle Williams for a Destiny's Child medley, and the *Love on Top* finale) and made Beyoncé one of the legends of the Californian festival.

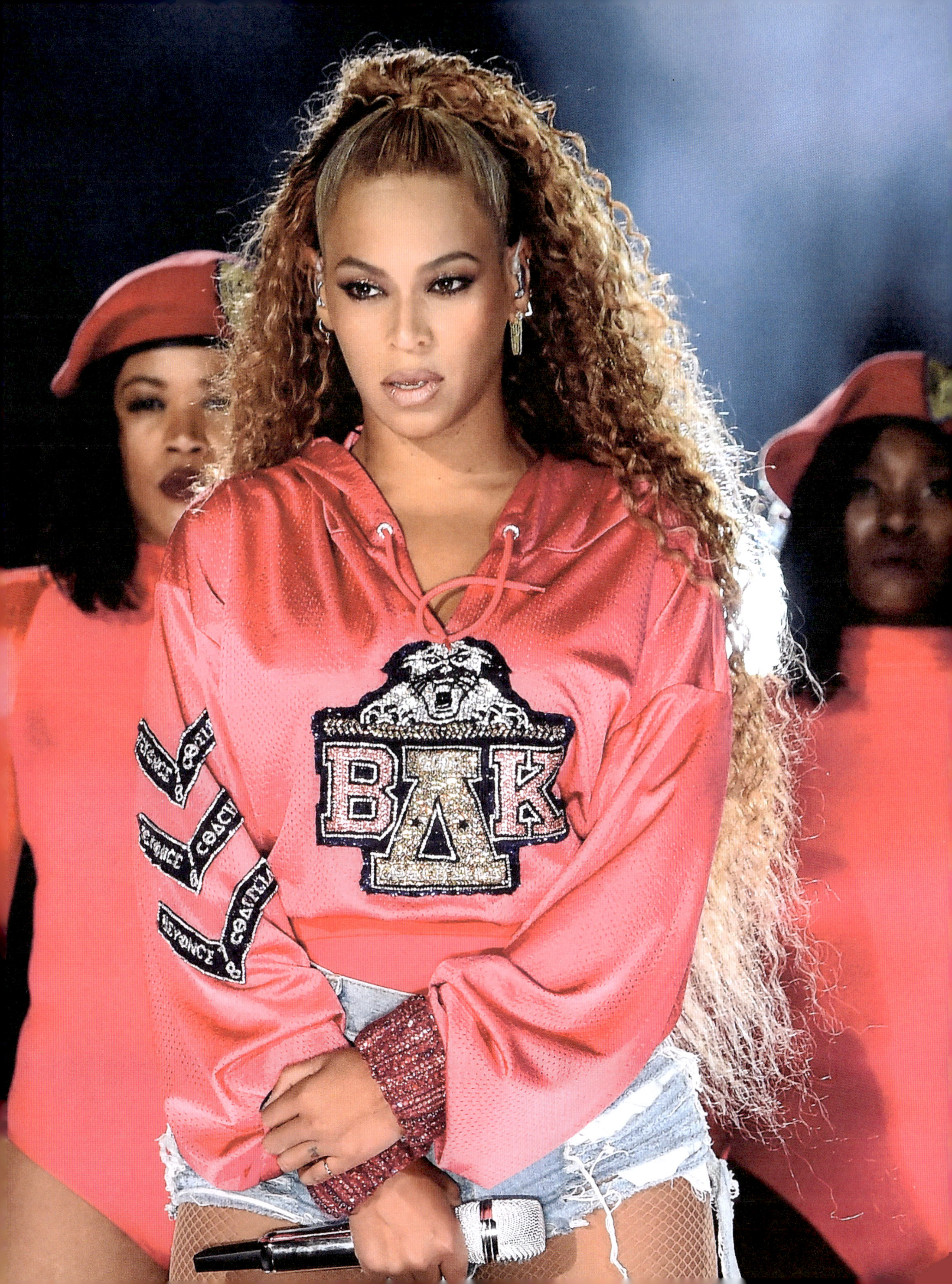
BAK

GLOSSARY

Acid house: a sub-genre of house music, originating in Chicago in the mid-1980s. Its tempo is as fast as that of house music. Acid house was extremely popular in the late 1980s and early 1990s, thanks to artists such as Kraze and Phuture.

Ad-lib: an improvised musical or vocal performance, at the musician's discretion, on an audio recording.

Alternative R&B: a musical sub-genre of R&B championed by artists such as Drake and Frank Ocean, characterized by a sound quality that overrides the traditional verse/chorus structure of R&B songs.

Ambient: a musical genre that is most often instrumental, featuring ethereal, minimalist textures.

Americana (music): a musical genre that blends various styles of music that are part of American culture, such as folk, bluegrass, and country.

Arpeggio: a chord whose notes are played in succession rather than simultaneously.

Auto-tune: music software marketed in 1997 by the American company Antares Audio Technologies that allows the pitch of a note to be modified. Hip-hop producers have since adapted its original use to give vocals a robotic effect.

Battle: a spontaneous or freestyle contest between two rappers in which they rap using boasts, wordplay, and insults aimed at each other.

Beatboxing: in music, a technique that aims to reproduce the different elements of a drumkit and/or other instruments using only the mouth.

Beatmaker: an artist, usually the producer, who creates a beat and a melody on tracks, often using samples from other tracks or other artists' songs.

Bluegrass: a musical sub-genre of country that developed in the 1940s in the United States. It is distinguished by its use of exclusively stringed instruments such as the guitar, double bass, mandolin, banjo, and fiddle.

Bounce music: a musical sub-genre of hip-hop which appeared in New Orleans at the end of the 1980s. It features lyrics and dances in which sensuality and sexual allusions are prominent.

Dancehall: a musical genre which appeared in Jamaica in the 1970s. It is derived from reggae, but its rhythms are faster and more danceable.

Delay: an audio effect that reproduces the acoustic phenomenon of the echo. Incorporated into an effects pedal or a mixing console, it is used on vocals and instruments, which makes it possible to regularly repeat a sound by shifting its signal in time.

Digger: a specialist in searching for rare records.

Distortion: a sound effect created by degrading the quality of an audio signal by saturating a channel on an amplifier using the latter's "distortion" effect, or by the use of a distortion pedal.

Dubstep: a musical sub-genre of EDM (see next entry) that features powerful and strident synthesizer sounds, as well as blends of rhythms influenced by house and hip-hop.

EDM: short for electronic dance music. A term for mainstream dance music aimed at dance venues and radio stations.

Effects pedal: a small electronic device used to transform the sound of an instrument as it is being played.

EP: abbreviation for extended play. A record format that's often around half the length of an album.

Fader: a device for gradually adjusting the volume of the audio channel on each track in a recording.

Fiddle: a violin used in musical genres other than classical music, notably country and bluegrass. Musicians who play fiddles are known as fiddlers.

Flanger: similar to a phaser, a flanger modifies the frequencies of an audio signal to produce an effect that sounds like a "swoosh," which is much appreciated by guitarists and drummers.

Freestyle: a rapping style that is most often improvised and developed around a set theme.

GarageBand: a music creation software program developed by Apple for its computers in 2004.

Grunge: a sub-genre of rock, and a cultural movement, which sprang up in Seattle, Washington, at the beginning of the 1990s. It rejected the sophistication of 1980s rock and metal in favour of aesthetic and musical authenticity, often with the addition of lyrics expressing the malaise of a certain section of American youth.

Hi-hat: two cymbals set one above the other and facing each other, which are operated by the drummer's foot. The drummer also uses a drumstick to set the cadence of his/her rhythmic pattern.

House music: a musical genre that started in Chicago during the 1980s. Danceable and hypnotic, house music (usually referred to simply as "house") had its heyday in nightclubs the world over until the early 1990s; it was then replaced by dance music, which was far more commercial.

Looper: an effect contained in a pedal that allows a sound signal to be recorded and played repeatedly, as well as the addition of other segments that can be superimposed on each other to build a track.

Mainstream: refers to what is considered normal or popular among the majority of people.

Master recordings: all the original recordings (physical or digital) of an audio format. The producer of a record holds the master recordings and uses them as desired, even if they have been recorded by another artist.

Mixtape: a musical project by an artist that allows them more creative freedom and less commercial pressure than when recording a conventional album or EP.

New jack swing: a musical style that appeared at the end of the 1980s, usually referred to simply as "new jack." It offers a reinterpretation of rap in a less aggressive version, because it is driven not by forceful statements but rather by lyrics dealing with love.

Outlaw: an adjective applied to the members of the outlaw country movement, represented notably by Willie Nelson, Kris Kristofferson, Waylon Jennings, and Johnny Cash, and created by these musicians in the face of the cultural and musical restrictions imposed by the country musicians and producers of Nashville at the end of the 1970s.

Outtake: a piece of music recorded in the studio or live that has not been used in the official version of an album. It may be an unreleased song or an alternative version of an existing one, and may be unearthed later for the release of a compilation or a reissue.

Overdubs: all the new sounds (voices and/or instruments) recorded and added to an existing recording.

Pedal steel guitar: similar to a steel guitar, but played while rested on the knees or set on a special support using a bottleneck that the player slides over the strings. It is fitted with pedals that change the pitch of certain strings to enable a more varied sound. Popularly used in country music.

Plug-in: a digital effect used by producers and mixers in the studio to modify a sound signal.

Punchline: the name given to a phrase placed at the heart of spoken or rapped lyrics that stands out from the whole because of its striking and/or provocative character.

Reggaeton: a musical style inspired by Jamaican dancehall, but differing from it in featuring electronic textures.

Reverb: a natural or artificial echo effect given to an instrument or voice during the recording or mixing of a piece.

Sampler: an electronic instrument that records and plays back samples (portions of sound recordings) to create new music.

Stomps: a musical genre that combines elements of blues, folk, and rock and features driving rhythms, a fast tempo, and a heavy beat.

Teasing: the art of releasing snippets of information about a forthcoming event with the intention of arousing the interest of one's audience.

Tracklisting: a list of the songs on an album.

Trap: a musical sub-genre of hip-hop that differs by its minimalist character, the throbbing flow of its performers, and the predominance of the hi-hat in the mixing of its rhythmic base.

Trip-hop: a musical genre that appeared in the UK in the mid-1990s, using hip-hop rhythms without adopting its conventions: the rappers' flow is replaced by sung verses and choruses that are usually very melodious. The British groups Portishead, Massive Attack, and Archive were its chief exponents.

Voice notes: a vocal note recorded in the "dictaphone" app on a smartphone.

Yodel: a singing technique based on the rapid alternation of notes. The earliest records of yodeling date it to the mountains of Europe in 1545; it crossed the Atlantic in the 1830s and became incorporated in the culture of Americana. Numerous American artists—for example, Jimmie Rodgers and Hank Williams—used it in their songs during the 20th century.

BIBLIOGRAPHY

1 "In My Heart with Heather Thomson, Tina Knowles-Lawson: American Business Woman & Fashion Designer", podcast, September 2020.

2 Del Rosario (Alexandra), "Beyoncé's 'Beyincé' Sash Is No Mere Typo: Tina Knowles Offered an Explanation Years Ago", latimes.com, 22 March 2024.

3 Touré, "Beyoncé Talks Fame, Relationships, Starting a Family, Becoming Sasha Fierce", rollingstone.com, 4 March 2004.

4 "Eat, Play, Love!", *Essence*, July 2011.

5 "Solange Brings It All Full Circle with her Sister Beyoncé", interviewmagazine.com, 10 January 2017.

6 "Beyoncé—Interview on Sunday Night", 2011.

7 "Beyoncé's Evolution", harpersbazaar.com, 10 August 2021.

8 "The Ellen DeGeneres Show—Beyoncé in Central Park", 5 September 2006.

9 Pesce (Nicole Lyn) "Beyoncé's Childhood Dance Teacher Tells Moneyish about that Epic Coachella Performance", marketwatch.com, 20 April 2018.

10 Knowles (Mathew), *Destiny's Child, The Untold Story*, Music World Publishing, 2019.

11 Hall (Michael), "It's a Family Affair", texasmonthly.com, April 2004.

12 "Beyoncé Knowles", brewer-international.com

13 Dunn (Jancee), "Date with Destiny", theguardian.com, 10 June 2001.

14 "Family Business", mtv.com, 15 November 2004.

15 Soetan (Sope), "Destiny's Child's Debut Album at 25: How a Neo-Soul Album from Teens Spawned R&B Legends", grammy.com, 16 February 2023.

16 Bandele (Asha), "Tina & Beyoncé", *Essence*, August 2003.

17 "Lynn Norment, The Untold Story of how Tina & Mathew Knowles Created the Destiny's Child Gold Mine", *Ebony*, September 2001.

18 Newman (Melinda), "Knowles on Nurturing the Trio", *Billboard*, 14 January 2006.

19 Mitchell (Gail), "Destiny's Child", *Billboard*, 14 January 2006.

20 Knowles (Beyoncé), Rowland (Kelly), Williams (Michelle), and Herman (James Patrick), *Soul Survivors. The Official Autobiography of Destiny's Child*, New York, Regan Books, 2002.

21 "Destiny's Child (featuring Beyoncé)—'No No No'/Interview", youtube.com, 1998.

22 Flynn (Paul), "Of Course You Can Lose Yourself", theguardian.com, 18 August 2006.

23 "Q & A: Kelly Rowland", cnn.com, 4 October 2006.

24 Norment (Lynn), "Destiny's Child: The Growing Pains of Fame", *Ebony*, September 2000.

25 Kaplan (Ilana), "LaTavia Roberson Announces New Docuseries & Dispels Her Label as the 'Bitter' Former Destiny's Child Member", billboard.com, 11 September 2017.

26 "Beyoncé's First Hit—Wyclef Jean Breaks Down 'No, No, No Part 2' | Behind The Scenes", youtube.com, 16 March 2017.

27 Ruff (Rivea), "LeToya Luckett and LaTavia Roberson Reflect on the Making of 'Destiny's Child' on its 25th Anniversary", essence.com, 17 February 2023.

28 "Producer Rob Fusari Dishes on Lady Gaga, Beyoncé, Craig Marks", billboard.com, 24 February 2010.

29 Ornah, "Interview: Master P Talks Remaining Relevant in Today's Rap Scene and Giving Beyoncé One of Her First Songs", complex.com, 4 March 2013.

30 "Destiny's Child on Master P's Softer Side", mtv.com, 9 July 1998.

31 "Taura 'Aura' Stinson Talks Hits for Destiny's Child & Kelis, Work with Raphael Saadiq, Industry Struggles (Exclusive Interview)", youknowigotsoul.com, 10 April 2011.

32 Parker (Veronika), "Being Beyoncé", *Aspire*, May–June 2006.

33 Gottesman (Tamar), "EXCLUSIVE: Beyoncé Wants to Change the Conversation", elle.com, 4 April 2016.

34 "Destiny's Child among Hottest New Female Groups", *Jet*, 2 August 1999.

35 "Destiny's Child—Behind the Songs Interviews", youtube.com, 2023.

36 "Divas Live!", *Vibe*, February 2001.

37 "For R&B Act Destiny's Child, 2000 Was a 'Jumpin' Year", *Billboard*, 30 December 2000.

38 O'Brien (Lucy), "Destiny's Child: 'We wear nothin' with our butt cheeks out, our boobs out'—a classic interview from the vaults", theguardian.com, 24 April 2013.

39 Masud (Ali), "Michelle Williams", yourlocalguardian.co.uk, 20 May 2004.

40 Cummings (Tony), "Michelle Williams: The Destiny's Child singer sings about The Heart of the Matter", *Cross Rhythm Magazine*, no. 69, July 2002.

41 "Michelle Williams Makes Her Own Destiny!", afterbuzztv.com, 3 April 2024.

42 Nichols (Sara), "Total Access 24/7", *Family Fox*, 1 January 2001.

43 Taraborrelli (J. Randy), *Becoming Beyoncé. The Untold Story*, New York, Grand Central Publishing, 2015.

44 Jones (Marcus), "Kandi Burruss reflects on hits she made with Xscape, Destiny's Child, Pink, *NSYNC, and more", ew.com, 1 April 2021.

45 Callas (Brad), "Kandi Burruss says her ex was dating a member of Destiny's Child when she wrote 'Bills, Bills, Bills' hit", complex.com, 10 July 2021.

46 "Destiny's Child. Hot, sexy singing group soars to the top", *Jet*, 14 May 2001.

47 Biakolo (Kovie), "Kandi Burruss shares the funny story behind writing Destiny Child's 'Bills, Bills, Bills'", glamour.com, 8 July 2021.

48 Associated Press, "Missy Elliott on writing for Aaliyah, Beyoncé and Herself", billboard.com, 29 November 2018.

49 Sparks (Marvin), "Destiny's Child 'The Writing's on the Wall' LP revisited by co-writer Kandi Burruss | Return to the classics", soulculture.com, 4 April 2011.

50 Ornah, "Jermaine Dupri tells all: The stories behind his *Classic Records (Part 1)*", complex.com, 15 March 2013.

51 Jefferson (J'Na), "'Say My Name' 20 years later: Why the Destiny's Child staple is still on everyone's lips", grammy.com, 19 June 2019.

52 "Sweet Sixteen. Jody Watley. Destiny's Child", jodywatley.net, 27 July 2020.

53 Larsen (Crystal), "5 Questions With … Mary Mary", grammy.com, 3 December 2014.

54 "Platinum Inspiration. Darryl Simmons", yamaha.com

55 Dunn (Jancee), "A Date with Destiny", rollingstone.com, 24 May 2001.

56 "Inside the Making of 'Survivor', Jessica Goodman, People—Beyoncé", *The Renaissance Tour*, 2023.

57 Braco (Lorraine), "When Destiny's Child Went to Therapy with Tony Soprano's Shrink", interview, August 2001.

58 Garfield (Simon), "Uh-oh! Uh-oh! Uh-oh!", theguardian.com, 14 December 2003.

59 Goodman (Jessica), "Destiny's Child's Survivor: Oral History", ew.com, 29 April 2016.

60 Vdovin (Marsha), "Analog Dialog: *It's a Family Affair*. Crankin' out the Hits: Producer Corey Rooney and Engineer Peter Wade", uaudio.com, November 2003.

61 "Destiny's Child: 2000 was their year. Now just wait and see what they've got for 2001", *The Face*, January 2001.

62 "Destiny's Child discuss their inspiration for their single 'Survivor'", *MTV News*, 1 January 2001.

63 "Anthony Dent speaks on producing 'Survivor' for Beyoncé", *HBCUmix*, youtube.com, 21 January 2011.

64 Neuman (Maria), "Soul Survivors", *Honey*, May 2001.

65 Hauser (Brooke), "Song of Herself", *Allure*, February 2010.

66 Bradley (Andy) and Wood (Roger), *House of Hits: The Story of Houston's Gold Star/SugarHill Recording Studios*, Austin, University of Texas Press, 2010.

67 Goodman (Jessica), "Inside the Making of Destiny's Child's 'Bootylicious' 15 years later", ew.com, 20 May 2016.

68 "Outtakes: Stevie Nicks on Petty, Prince, Beyoncé, and Harry", ny1.com, 28 October 2020.

69 Stas (Heather) and Cumberpatch (Franklin), "Destiny's Child: Three the Hard Way", vh1.com, April 2002.

70 Kawashima (Dale), "Rob Fusari Co-Writes & Produces Top Hits for Destiny's Child, Will Smith and Other Artists", songwriteruniverse.com, 2005.

71 Dickinson (Alistair), "Staying on the Edge: An Interview with Damon Elliott", popmatters.com, 13 December 2009.

72 "The man behind hits by Beyoncé, Missy Elliot, and more", songhero.com, 12 September 2021.

73 "Beyoncé—Making of *Carmen: A Hip-Hopera (Part 1)*", dailymotion.com, 2014.

74 "Making of *Carmen Hip-Hopera Part 2*", dailymotion.com, 2017.

75 Braxton (Greg), "'Carmen' Gets Hip", latimes.com, 6 May 2001.

76 "Artists Against AIDS Worldwide's New Superstar Version of Marvin Gaye's 'What's Going On' in Stores Tuesday, October 30", hopeforafricanchildren.org, 29 October 2001.

77 "Destiny's Child to take hiatus", billboard.com, 6 December 2001.

78 "Christmas with Destiny's Child interview @ 106 & Park", dailymotion.com

79 "'Do you hear what I hear?': The story behind the song", franciscanmedia.org, 2018.

80 VanHorn (Teri), "Destiny's Child put 'Stank' into Christmas on Holiday Album", mtv.com, 24 September 2001.

81 Zaleski (Annie), *This is Christmas, song by song. The stories behind 100 holiday hits*, New York, Running Press, 2023.

82 Jones (Daisy), "How Destiny's Child changed R&B forever", dazeddigital.com, 12 June 2015.

83 Jacob (Matthew), "'She wanted to be fantastic'. An oral history of Beyoncé in *Austin Powers: Goldmember*, a goofy anomaly in a now-rarefied pop career", vulture.com, 15 July 2022.

84 Moss (Corey), "Beyoncé records song written by Mike Myers for 'Powers' flick", mtv.com, 6 December 2001.

85 VanHorn (Teri), "Destiny's Child Solo CDs Won't Compete With Group, Each Other", mtv.com, 8 December 2000.

86 Otto (Jeff), "Interview: Beyoncé Knowles", ign.com, 9 February 2006.

87 Wartofsky (Alona), "A Child of Destiny", washingtonpost.com, 22 September 2003.

88 "About Dangerously in Love (Part 1)", youtube.com

89 Patterson (Sylvia), "Perfect Diva", *The Face*, October 2003.

90 Schartz (Emma), "Markus Klinko Takes Us Behind the Scenes with Britney and Beyoncé", interviewmagazine.com, 19 July 2023.

91 Moss (Corey), "Beyoncé Smitten by Triplets, Hungry Unknowns at Dance Audition", mtv.com, 7 May 2003.

92 "I Didn't Think About Trying to Make It the Most Commercial Record", *People—Beyoncé The Renaissance Tour*, 2023.

93 "Beyoncé Talks Fashion: *W Magazine* July 2011 Interview: "7 Looks That Shaped Her Career", smartologie.com, 22 June 2011.

94 "Crazy About Beyoncé", billboard.com, 16 June 2003.

95 "Beyoncé Dangerously in Love Making the Album 2003", youtube.com

96 Hiatt (Brian), "Beyoncé's Studio Secrets: Inside the Making of Her Best Songs", rollingstone.com, 29 July 2022.

97 Gomez (Jade), "Usher Recalls 'Babysitting' Teenage Beyoncé", complex.com, 13 August 2023.

98 Watkins (Donovan), "Rolling Stone Magazine List Beyoncé's 70 Best Songs, 'Baby Boy' featuring Sean Paul and 'Standing in the Sun' feat. Mr. Vegas Make the Cut", worldmusicnews.com, 2022.

99 Marie (Erika), "Sean Paul Denies Hooking Up with Beyoncé, Claims She Confronted Him about Rumors", hotnewhiphop.com, 26 September 2022.

100 Moss (Corey), "Genuinely in Love", mtv.com, 2003.

101 Moss (Corey), "Another Beyoncé Solo LP Due Before Destiny's Child Reunite", mtv.com, 1 December 2003.

102 "Dangerously In Love", *Pop Superstars*, "Beyoncé", 2023.

103 "Beyoncé Working It with Missy Elliott on Solo Album", mtv.com, 18 November 2002.

104 Tyrangiel (Josh), "Destiny's Adult", time.com, 22 June 2003.

105 "Beyoncé's Debut Album, Dangerously in Love", thread.co.nz, 24 July 2003.

106 Palmer (Tamara), "'The Miseducation of Lauryn Hill': 25 Facts about the Iconic Album, From its Cover to its Controversy", grammy.com, 25 August 2023.

107 Reid (Shaheem), "Jay-Z Camp Refutes Toni Braxton's Tupac-Biting Claims", mtv.com, 9 October 2002.

108 Lynskey (Dorian), "Missy Elliott—Beyoncé Said: 'If I sound crazy, don't put this out!'", theguardian.com, 14 September 2019.

109 Mayo (Kierna), "Beyoncé Unwrapped", *Essence*, August 2003.

110 Noto (Justin), "IAM se souvient de son featuring avec Beyoncé", intrld.com, 15 October 2020.

111 Waring (Charles), "A Rose By Any Other Name—Ex-Rose Royce Singer Gwen Dickey Talks", soulandjazzandfunk.com, 30 July 2015.

112 Downey (Ryan J.), "Beyoncé transforms into Bohemian, Motherly Nightclub Singer", mtv.com, 21 November 2002.

113 Byrd (Kenya N.), "The Contenders", *Savoy*, September 2003.

114 "Cuba Gooding Jr. and Beyoncé Knowles. Clash and love in movie 'The Fighting Temptations'", *Jet*, September 2003.

115 Reid (Shaheem), "Destiny's Child Attack the Movies, Broadway; Plan New Album", mtv.com, 10 April 2003.

116 Wilbekin (Emil), "Beyond Beyoncé", *Vibe*, October 2002.

117 "Beyoncé Heat—Catch The Fever", beyonceparfums.com, 2011.

118 Devenish (Colin) and Halperin (Shirley), "Destiny's Child Grow Up", rollingstone.com, 24 September 2004.

119 Mitchell (Gail), "Destiny's Return", *Billboard*, 27 November 2004.

120 "Destiny's Child, Back—and even more bootylicious!", *FHM*, February 2005.

121 Devenish (Colin), "Destiny's Child to Split", rollingstone.com, 13 June 2005.

122 "'Breath' of Fresh Air: Destiny's Child Returns", billboard.com, 9 September 2004.

123 "Destiny's Child—The Destiny Fulfilled Interview", DVD *Destiny Fulfilled Australian Tour Version*, November 2004.

124 Moss (Corey), "Beyoncé Healing Fast Thanks to Serena Williams", mtv.com, 6 October 2004.

125 Garrett (Sean), "25 Essential Songs—Destiny's Child 'Soldier' (2004)", complex.com, November 2012.

126 Moss (Corey), "Beyoncé Salutes Jay-Z on Destiny's Child Track 'Soldier'", mtv.com, 29 October 2004.

127 Kramer (Kyle), "Beyoncé and Destiny's Child Changed Lil Wayne's Life with 'Soldier'", vice.com, 13 September 2017.

128 Rotchford (Lesley), "Beyoncé: Fun, Fearless Female of the Year 2006", *Cosmopolitan*, 1 November 2006.

129 Mitchell (Gail), "Destiny's Child, A Golden Dream Shines on for Three Solo Stars, with Film and Music Plans on the Horizon", *Billboard*, 14 January 2006.

130 Cho (Jaeki), "9th Wonder Tells All: The Stories Behind His Classic Records", complex.com, 20 May 2011.

131 Picardi (Phillip), "Kelly Rowland Has Been Holding Back. She'll share the hardest story of her life on her new album", thecut.com, 29 May 2020.

132 Mark Sutherland, "These Relationships Weren't Made by Sending Beats, They Had to Be Built. We Had to Meet and Like Each Other, Go Through Ups and Downs", musicbusinessworldwide.com, 19 June 2023.

133 "Bryan-Michael Cox on Working w/Destiny's Child; Jagged Edge;

Ideal", ThisIs50, youtube.com, 17 March 2014.

134 "Rockwilder Talks about His Life and Career: Redman, 50 Cent, Destiny's Child + More", *The Donnie Houston Podcast,* youtube.com, 27 May 2020.

135 "Erron Williams Still Protects His Baby Sister, Michelle Williams", *The Michael Finkley Show,* youtube.com, 27 July 2021.

136 Sleeve notes "Unity (The Official Athens 2004 Olympic Games Album)", 2004.

137 "Vandross Video Features Famous Friends, Fans", billboard.com, 19 July 2003.

138 "Message From Christian Andréason", katrinacd.com, 2005.

139 Watson (Shane), "Booty Queen", *The Sunday Times Style Magazine,* 5 September 2004.

140 "Destiny's Child Releases New Anthem for World Children's Day at McD's", McDonald's press release, 27 September 2005.

141 Buss (Bryna), "Michelle Williams of Destiny's Child", out.com, 13 February 2006.

142 Reid (Shaheem) and Calloway (Sway), "All Eyes on Beyoncé", mtv.com, 14 August 2006.

143 Moss (Corey), "Want to Wake Up With Beyoncé? Revealing Photo Spread Takes You Inside Her Morning", mtv.com, 12 July 2006.

144 "Superstar Beyoncé Knowles talks about second album 'B'Day' and her life", youtube.com, 16 August 2006.

145 Vineyard (Jennifer), "Beyoncé—Behind the B'Day Videos", mtv.com, 2 April 2007.

146 Reid (Shaheem), "Beyoncé Asks Women to Battle over her for Backing-Band Roles", mtv.com, 19 June 2006.

147 "The Baddest B—News Flash: Beyoncé Knowles Is Not a Girl Anymore", *Vibe,* June 2007.

148 "Dreamgirls, from Broadway to the Big Screen", *Ebony,* December 2006.

149 Hiatt (Brian), "Rodney Jerkins: How We Made Beyoncé's Greatest Song", rollingstone.com, 1 August 2022.

150 Jisi (Chris), "Jon Jon Webb's Complete Bass Line—Beyoncé's Déjà vu", bassplayer.com, December 2006.

151 Amber (Jeannine), "A Fashionable Life", *Essence,* September 2006.

152 Concepción (Mariel), "Beyoncé Rings the Alarm on Vibe.com", vibe.com, 16 August 2006.

153 "For The Record: Quick News on Eminem, Aaliyah, Panic! At The Disco, DMX, Beyoncé, Britney Spears & More", mtv.com, 25 August 2006.

154 Conniff (Tamara), "Beyoncé's Little Secret", *Billboard,* 24 June 2006.

155 Roberts (Dave), "There's Nothing Like Making It in New York. I Know It's a Cliché, But It's True", musicbusinessworldwide.com, 5 April 2023.

156 Reid (Shaheem), "Beyoncé Wants End to Drama over New Drama 'Dreamgirls'; Sets Tour", billboard.com, 12 December 2006.

157 Feeney (Nolan), "Producer duo Stargate share the secrets behind their Rihanna, Katy Perry, and Beyoncé hits", ew.com, 9 April 2018.

158 Maresca (Rachel), "Beyoncé sparks Jay Z cheating rumors during On The Run Tour, changes lyric to 2006 'Resentment' track about infidelity", nydailynews.com, 2 July 2014.

159 "Walter Milsapp III—Biography", fr.yamaha.com.

160 "Beyoncé (Check On It) Behind the Scenes", youtube.com.

161 "Beyoncé Adds Spice and Intrigue to Movie 'The Pink Panther'", *Jet,* 13 February 2006.

162 Morales (Wilson), "Stomp the Yard. An Interview with Ne-Yo", blackfilm.com, 11 January 2007.

163 Tingen (Paul), "The Stargate Writing & Production Team", soundonsound.com, May 2010.

164 Horan (Tom), "Following Her Destiny", nzherald.co.nz, 20 December 2008.

165 "Stars—Alejandro Fernández", *Billboard,* 7 July 2007.

166 Lazerine (Devin), "New Music: Justin Timberlake f/Beyoncé—'Until the End of Time'", rap-up.com, 26 September 2007.

167 Horowitz (Steven J.), "5 Songwriters and Producers Explain their Unreleased Beyoncé Collaborations", thefader.com, 3 March 2016.

168 Smith (Daniel), "Beyoncé kicks off Japan promo for sophomore solo album 'B Day'", accessonline.com, 2006.

169 Balan (Elena), "Beyoncé Special Edition B'Phone by Samsung", softpedia.com, 12 October 2007.

170 Bruno (Antony), "Beyoncé Reveals New Samsung B-Phone", billboard.com, 11 October 2007.

171 Morales (Wilson), "Dreamgirls: An Interview with Beyoncé Knowles", blackfilm.com, 29 January 2006.

172 Otto (Jeff), "Interview: Beyoncé Knowles—Pink Panther's pink diamond-clad starlet talks to IGN", ign.com, 9 February 2006.

173 "Underdogs Begin Busy Year with 'Dreamgirls' Soundtrack", billboard.com, 13 November 2006.

174 "Murphy Muses on Dream Role", aalbc.com, 2006.

175 Morales (Wilson), "Dreamgirls: An Interview with Jamie Foxx", blackfilm.com, 11 December 2006.

176 Morales (Wilson), "Dreamgirls: An Interview with Keith Robinson", blackfilm.com, 11 December 2006.

177 "Beyoncé Reigns Supreme", *InStyle,* January 2007.

178 "Beyoncé Willingly Steps Back in 'Dreamgirls'", timesleader.com, 20 December 2006.

179 Perry (Clayton), "Interview: Sharon Leal—Actress and Singer", crperry84.wordpress.com, 11 April 2012.

180 Sharp (Ken), "Henry Krieger: The Dream Maker", americansongwriter.com, 7 February 2013.

181 Cerasaro (Pat), "Indepth Interview: Henry Krieger Talks Lucky Duck, Dreamgirls, Side Show Revival & More", broadwayworld.com, 15 March 2012.

182 Faraci (Devin), "Interview: Jamie Foxx (Dreamgirls)", chud.com, 18 December 2006.

183 *Larry King Live,* "Interview with Beyoncé", *CNN,* 23 April 2009.

184 "Beyoncé Is Sasha Fierce", oprah.com, 13 November 2008.

185 "Beijing date announced for Beyoncé's 'I AM...' World Tour", chinadaily.com.cn, 13 October 2009.

186 Adler (Shawn), "Beyoncé Writes a Letter to Fans, Saying She Has 'Taken Risks' on Upcoming LP", mtv.com, 2 October 2008.

187 whoissashafierce.com, October 2008.

188 Crosley (Hillary), "Worker B", *Billboard,* 8 November 2008.

189 Widran (Jonathan), "BC Jean Co-Writes #1 Hit 'If I Were a Boy' for Beyoncé, Signs With J Records and Releases Single", songwriteruniverse.com, 21 September 2010.

190 Kawashima (Dale), "Interview with Toby Gad, Hit Writer/Producer for Beyoncé, Alicia Keys, Fergie and Demi Lovato", songwriteruniverse.com, 4 September 2012.

191 Bouwman (Kimbel), "If you have the help of a veteran writer or producer who can help and mentor you then that's as invaluable as getting a big cheque", hitquarters.com, 8 February 2010.

192 "I Am... Sasha Fierce", *Pop Superstars—Beyoncé,* 2023.

193 Horan (Tom), "Beyoncé: dream girl", telegraph.co.uk, 8 November 2008.

194 "How The-Dream Wrote Beyoncé's 'Single Ladies' in 17 Minutes", *Genius,* youtube.com, 31 May 2017.

195 Herndon (Jessica), "Inside Story: The Making of Beyoncé's 'Single Ladies'", people.com, 1 January 2010.

196 Cairns (Dan), "YouTube plays part in Beyoncé Knowles' life", timesonline.com, 10 May 2009.

197 Hughes (Hilary), "10 Years of 'Single Ladies': Beyoncé's Director, Choreographers & More Put a Ring on Her Iconic Music Video", billboard.com, 26 July 2018.

198 Mitchell (Gail), "Beyoncé: The *Billboard* Q & A", billboard.com, 2 October 2009.

199 "The Story Behind Beyoncé's 'Single Ladies', Our American Stories with Lee Habeeb", facebook.com, 21 September 2024.

200 "Beyonce's Fans", *Billboard,* 10 October 2009.

201 "Sean Garrett on Beyoncé: 'She's a Diva'", rap-up.com, 11 September 2008.

202 Lazerine (Devin), "New Music: Beyoncé—'Sweet Dreams

202 "(Acoustic)'", rap-up.com, 12 November 2009.

203 Reid (Shaheem), "Usher, Beyoncé Collaborator Rico Love Talks 'Organic' Songwriting Process", mtv.com, 8 April 2010.

204 Ahmed (Insanul), "Bangladesh Tells All: The Stories Behind His Biggest Hits", complex.com, 1 November 2010.

205 Trent, "That Grape Juice Interviews Soundz", thatgrapejuice.net, 16 December 2010.

206 "Beyoncé Talks Fashion: W Magazine July 2011 Interview '7 Looks That Shaped Her Career'", smartologie.com, 22 June 2011.

207 "Meet Ramon 'REO' Owen", canvasrebel.com, 20 November 2023.

208 "The Story Behind Beyoncé's Why Don't You Love Me", antimusic.com, 12 May 2010.

209 Chinchilla (Wilbert), "From Interns to Beyoncé Hitmakers: The Bama Boyz Journey Inside the Knowles' Music World", houston.culturemap.com, 3 July 2010.

210 Lazerine (Devin), "What's on Nicki Minaj's iPod?", rap-up.com, 10 August 2010.

211 "Beyoncé Knowles: Her Quest for an Oscar", independent.co.uk, 7 March 2006.

212 Boucher (Geoff), "Beyoncé: Lady sings the blues", latimes.com, 16 November 2008.

213 Kaufman (Gil), "Beyoncé Slammed by Etta James for Singing 'At Last' at Inaugural Ball", mtv.com, 5 February 2009.

214 Hauser (Brooke), "Song of Herself", *Allure*, February 2010.

215 "Beyoncé's Mother Tina Knowles Files for Divorce", billboard.com, 19 December 2009.

216 "Beyoncé Q&A: The *Billboard* Music Awards Millennium Artist Discusses Her Career And New Album", billboard.com, 11 May 2011.

217 Murphy (Keith), "6 questions to Jordan 'DJ Swivel' Young", *Billboard*, 25 June 2011.

218 Watson (Paul), "DJ Swivel: Recording Beyoncé's 4", soundonsound.com, October 2011.

219 Beyoncé's Facebook account, 8 June 2011.

220 "Beyoncé—Love on Top Live at the MTV VMA's 2011", youtube.com.

221 "Beyoncé Runs Her World: Inside the Recording of '4'", djswivel.com.

222 Alvarez (Gabriel), "Beyoncé: Mighty Fly", complex.com, 19 July 2011.

223 "Frank spotted in the studio with Beyoncé", blonded.blog, 12 March 2011.

224 Gyant, "'Best Thing I Never Had' Songwriter Inspired by Beyoncé", bet.com, 3 June 2011.

225 "4", *Pop Superstars*—Beyoncé, 2023.

226 Lazerine (Devin), "J. Cole Calls Beyoncé 'Party' Remix a 'Blessing'", rap-up.com, 24 October 2011.

227 "Beyoncé World Premieres 'Love on Top' in Australia", beyonceonline.com, 16 October 2011.

228 "Recording Love on Top for Beyoncé", DJ Swivel's YouTube page, 11 September 2020.

229 Weiss (David), "Engineer Profile: DJ Swivel on the Making of Beyoncé's '4'", sonicscoop.com, 26 June 2011.

230 "End of Time", genius.com

231 Hiatt (Brian), "Diane Warren: Wild Stories Behind Hits for Beyoncé, Cher, Aerosmith and More", rollingstone.com, 6 February 2021.

232 Rogers (Ray), "The *Billboard* Q & A—Beyoncé", *Billboard*, 4 June 2011.

233 Thorogood (Tom), "We always know how to rock a party", thesun.co.uk, 12 July 2013.

234 Lazerine (Devin), "Sean Garrett Calls Mary J. Blige and Beyoncé Duet 'Iconic'", rap-up.com, 16 November 2011.

235 Murphy (Keith), "Beyoncé Experimented 'With Everything' on New Album, Says Engineer", hollywoodreporter.com, 17 June 2011.

236 Gannon (Louise), "Look Who's Back!", *Cosmopolitan*, April 2011.

237 Kawashima (Dale), "Country Singer Lee Greenwood Talks about Writing the Anthem 'God Bless the USA,' the Song's Impact, and Writing His Songs", songwriteruniverse.com, 3 July 2015.

238 Spanos (Brittany), "Sia's Reject Opus: Songwriter on Reclaiming Adele, Rihanna's Unwanted Hits", rollingstone.com, 3 December 2015.

239 Hicklin (Aaron), "Beyoncé: behind the scenes with a superstar", theguardian.com, 20 April 2014.

240 "Beyoncé Sings National Anthem Live at Super Bowl Press Conference", rollingstone.com, 31 January 2013.

241 "Beyoncé", *Pop Superstars*—Beyoncé, 2023.

242 Hampp (Andrew) and Mitchell (Gail), "How Beyoncé's 'Beyoncé' Stayed Secret Until the Day of Release, Its First Singles", billboard.com, 13 December 2013.

243 "The Once & Future of Beyoncé", *Harper's Bazaar*, September 2021.

244 "Beyoncé praises Australian songwriter Sia", smh.com.au, 19 December 2013.

245 Knopper (Steve), "How a Song Written by Sia Furler Becomes a Hit", nytimes.com, 21 April 2014.

246 "Beyoncé Explains the Visual Album on iTunes Radio", ohnotheydidnt.livejournal.com, 14 December 2013.

247 "'Self-Titled': Part 2. Imperfection", Beyoncé's YouTube page, 18 December 2013.

248 Greene (Jayson), "Beyoncé's Muse", pitchfork.com, 21 January 2014.

249 Fleischer (Adam) and Calloway (Sway), "Future Tells the Surprising Story behind 'Drunk In Love'", mtv.com, 28 April 2014.

250 Nelson Jr. (Keith), "Studio Sessions | Stuart White talks being Beyoncé's main engineer, helping Solange finish 'A Seat at the Table' and more", revolt.tv, 31 October 2019.

251 Maher (Natalie), "It's Caroline Polachek's Dream World; We Just Live in It", harpersbazaar.com, 27 March 2020.

252 "'Self-Titled' Part 4. Liberation", Beyoncé's YouTube page, 30 December 2013.

253 Grow (Kory), "Jay Z, Beyoncé, Solange Issue Statement after Met Gala Fight", rollingstone.com, 15 May 2014.

254 Hicklin (Aaron), "Beyoncé Liberated", out.com, 8 April 2014.

255 Lazerine (Devin), "Drake Praises Beyoncé, Reveals Collaboration", rap-up.com, 24 September 2013.

256 Knopper (Steve), "How Did Beyoncé Keep Her Surprise Album a Secret?", rollingstone.com, 13 December 2013.

257 Hiatt (Brian), "Exclusive: Hit-Boy Produced Beyoncé's New Song 'Thique'… Eight Years Ago", rollingstone.com, 12 August 2022.

258 Rosenthal (Jeff), "Director Jonas Åkerlund on 'Haunted,' 'Superpower,' and Beyoncé's Many Virtues", vulture.com, 16 December 2013.

259 "Meet the People behind Beyoncé: Melissa Vargas", out.com, 8 April 2014.

260 Rehlin (Gunnar), "The Scandinavian Connection", *Z Lifestyle*, July 2013.

261 McDermott (Emily), "Holt without Hollywood", interviewmagazine.com, 3 March 2016.

262 Brandle (Lars), "Kelly Rowland, Beyoncé & Michelle Williams Team on 'You've Changed': Listen", billboard.com, 28 May 2013.

263 BOOTS' Facebook page, 22 April 2014.

264 "'Say Yes' producer Harmony Samuels explains song's origin", unexpected-michelle.com, 28 May 2014.

265 Williams (Nakisha), "Beyoncé is the new face of H&M", ew.com, 21 March 2013.

266 Thomas (Rebecca), "Destiny's Child 'Love Songs': Four Key Tracks!", mtv.com, 28 January 2013.

267 Tingen (Paul), "Mix Masters: Beyoncé. Making Lemonade with Beyoncé's Right-Hand Man, Stuart White", audiotechnology.com, 23 September 2016.

268 Cutler (Jacqueline), "Beyoncé's 'Black Power' salute during Super Bowl 50 halftime show slammed by Rudy Giuliani as 'attack' on police", nydailynews.com, 8 February 2016.

269 Legaspi (Althea), "Miami Police Union President Calls for Beyoncé Show Boycott", rollingstone.com, 19 February 2016.

270 Vitagliano (Joe), "Kevin Garrett Shares Stories of Violin Lessons, Writing for Beyoncé, His New Album", americansongwriter.com, 18 January 2024.

271 Vain (Madison), "Kevin Garrett talks Beyoncé's 'Pray You Catch Me'", ew.com, 22 August 2016.

272 Tencic (Nat), "Writer-turned-solo artist MNEK unpacks three of his biggest hits", abc.net.au, 26 April 2018.

273 Strauss (Matthew), "Beyoncé's *Lemonade* Collaborator MeLo-X Gives First Interview on Making of the Album", pitchfork.com, 25 April 2016.

274 "Jack White on Detroit, Beyoncé and Where Songs Come From", npr.org, 10 September 2016.

275 Gale (Alex), "'Lemonade' Backup Singer Ruby Amanfu Talks Beyoncé, Jack White and Racism", billboard.com, 30 April 2016.

276 Goodman (Jessica), "Diana Gordon interview: The 'Becky with the good hair' scribe opens up about new music", ew.com, 2 August 2016.

277 "6 Inch", genius.com.

278 Platon (Adelle), "Beyoncé's Folky 'Lemonade' Track 'Daddy Lessons': Co-Writer Kevin Cossom Shares the Story behind the 'Tough' Song", billboard.com, 28 April 2016.

279 Starling (Lakin), "Diana Gordon Is 'Anti-Formula' and Ready for her Fresh Start", thefader.com, 3 August 2016.

280 "INTERVIEW: Too Many Zooz—'Beyoncé saw some videos of us in the subway and she decided to get us in the studio'", gscene.com, 14 October 2018.

281 Platon (Adelle), "Beyoncé Protege Ingrid on Being Mentored by the Superstar: 'She Challenged Me'", billboard.com, 26 May 2016.

282 Peisner (David), "Making 'Lemonade': Inside Beyoncé's Collaborative Masterpiece", rollingstone.com, 28 April 2016.

283 Kennedy (Gerrick D.), "How a homeless songwriter's story of heartbreak made it into Beyoncé's album", latimes.com, 15 June 2016.

284 "Secret Genius: James Blake", *Spotify*, 24 June 2016.

285 Rys (Dan), "Five Beyoncé Collaborators Explain Their Roles in the Making of 'Lemonade'", billboard.com, 2 May 2016.

286 "Mike WiLL Made-It", redbullmusicacademy.com, 2016.

287 99 Souls Facebook account, 6 November 2015.

288 Platon (Adelle), "Hear Beyoncé on Coldplay's 'Hymn for the Weekend' Preview", billboard.com, 24 November 2015.

289 Tingen (Paul), "Inside Track: Coldplay 'Hymn for the Weekend'", soundonsound.com, March 2016.

290 Natalie Maines's Twitter account, 3 November 2016.

291 "DJ Khaled Tells the Story of How He Got Jay Z and Beyoncé on 'Shining'", *XXL*, youtube.com, 27 April 2017.

292 Beyoncé's Instagram account, 28 September 2017.

293 "Beyoncé in Her Own Words: Her Life, Her Body, Her Heritage", vogue.com, 6 August 2018.

294 Leight (Elias), "Beyoncé, Jay-Z Collaborators Detail How 'Everything Is Love' Came Together", rollingstone.com, 18 June 2018.

295 Feeney (Nolan), "Beyoncé and JAY-Z Collaborators Cool & Dre Detail the Last-Minute Making of 'Everything Is Love'", billboard.com, 18 June 2018.

296 Van Pelt (Carter), "Behind Leon Michels' Hits: From Working with the Carters & Aloe Blacc, to Creating Clairo's New Album", grammy.com, 27 May 2024.

297 Kawashima (Dale), "Grammy & Oscar-Winning Writer/Producer D'Mile Writes Hits with Silk Sonic ('Leave the Door Open', 'Smokin Out the Window') and H.E.R. ('I Can't Breathe')", songwriteruniverse.com, 20 April 2022.

298 Tingen (Paul), "Secrets of the Mix Engineers: Young Guru", soundonsound.com, December 2009.

299 Leight (Elias), "Producers Cool & Dre On What It's Like To Make A Beyoncé and Jay-Z Album", rollingstone.com, 18 June 2018.

300 Ortiz (Edwin), "!!lmind on How He Landed on Beyoncé and JAY-Z's New Album 'Everything Is Love'", complex.com, 17 June 2018.

301 *Views from the Studio: Nova Wav's Seismic Industry Presence Swells with Faith and Confidence*, Camille Augustin, vibe.com, 4 March 2019.

302 Nelson (Jeff), "Ed Sheeran Opens up about his A-List Pals, from his Clapton Collab to Taking Shots with Beyoncé ('She Was So Confused!')", people.com, 15 March 2017.

303 Tingen (Paul), "Mix Masters: Beyonce & Ed Sheeran", audiotechnology.com, 29 March 2018.

304 "Eminem Speaks on Working with Beyoncé", *Shade45*, youtube.com, 17 November 2017.

305 Skylar Grey's Twitter account, 10 November 2017.

306 "#DJKhaled on the making of 'Top Off' feat. #JAYZ, #Beyoncé, and #Future", Tidal's TikTok account, 8 July 2020.

307 Robinson (Ellie), "Beyoncé Asked Megan Thee Stallion to Re-Do Her 'Savage (Remix)' Verse", nme.com, 23 April 2023.

308 Tanzer (Myles), "How Beyoncé and JAY-Z's 'SALUD' Got Made", thefader.com, 27 June 2018.

309 Tangcay (Jazz), "Kris Bowers on How the Prepared Piano Helped Him Ace the 'King Richard' Score", variety.com, 19 November 2021.

310 Giorgis (Hannah), "The Blind Spot of Beyoncé's *Lion King* Soundtrack", theatlantic.com, 19 July 2019.

311 "Beyoncé Produces and Performs on Multi-Artist Album 'The Lion King: The Gift'", prnewswire.com, 9 July 2019.

312 Enninful (Edward), "'I've Decided to Give Myself Permission to Focus on my Joy': How Beyoncé Tackled 2020", vogue.co.uk, 1 November 2020.

313 Johnson (Victoria), "Stacy Barthe on Beyoncé's Advice and Stepping into the Spotlight", parlourtravel.com, 20 March 2013.

314 Levine (Nick), "Five Things We Learned from our in Conversation Video Chat with RAYE", nme.com, 30 November 2020.

315 Leight (Elias), "Inside Beyoncé's Bold Bet to Get Americans to Listen to African Music", rollingstone.com, 19 July 2019.

316 "Beyoncé Making the Gift", youtube.com

317 "4 Questions à Salatiel", *Inspire Afrika Magazine*, facebook.com, 24 September 2019.

318 Aiello (Mckenna), "Beyoncé's *Making the Gift* Special Reveals Intimate Family Moments", eonline.com, 17 September 2019.

319 "The 70 Greatest Beyoncé Songs", rollingstone.com, 1 April 2024.

320 "DJ Soupamodel, Meet the African Artists Beyoncé Collaborated with for 'The Lion King: The Gift'", billboard.com, 25 July 2019.

321 Bradley (Bill), "Here's How Beyoncé's New Song 'Spirit' Wound up in 'The Lion King'", huffpost.com, 11 July 2019.

322 Fekadu (Mesfin), "Labrinth on Working with Beyoncé: 'She's a Perfectionist'", seattletimes.com, 18 July 2019.

323 LeDonne (Rob), "Frankie Beverly Responds to Beyoncé Covering his Maze Hit 'Before I Let Go'", billboard.com, 24 April 2019.

324 Beyoncé.com, 28 July 2022.

325 Lopez (Julyssa), "Kelman Duran Didn't Expect to Be Part of Beyoncé's 'Renaissance'", rollingstone.com, 10 August 2022.

326 Luse (Brittany), "Serving House Music History With Honey Dijon", npr.org, 30 December 2022.

327 Diane Warren's Twitter account, 1 August 2022.

328 Rogerson (Ben), "Nile Rodgers Reveals That He Recorded the Guitar Part for Beyoncé's Cuff It in One Take", musicradar.com, 6 February 2023.

329 Curto (Justin), "Robin S. Is Riding the Wave of Beyoncé's 'Break My Soul'", vulture.com, 27 June 2022.

330 "Rapper Big Freedia Discusses Beyoncé Feature and New Orleans Bounce Music", *CBS mornings*, facebook.com, 29 July 2022.

331 Hiatt (Brian), "How Does One Song Have 24 Writers?... and Other 'Renaissance' Controversies", rollingstone.com, 15 August 2022.

332 Shipley (Al), "We've Got a File on You: No I.D", stereogum.com, 18 October 2023.

333 Samuels (Keithan), "Leven Kali Wants to Inspire Movement on New EP 'Let It Rain': Interview", ratedrnb.com, 28 October 2022.

334 Garcia (Thania), "Fine-Tuning Beyoncé's 'Virgo's Groove': How Three High-School Friends Ended Up Producing a Song on 'Renaissance'", variety.com, 17 August 2022.

335 Shafer (Ellise), "'Renaissance'": Meet Nova Wav, the Songwriting and Producing Duo Behind Half of

Beyoncé's New Album", variety.com, 29 July 2022.

336 Rouhani (Neena), "In Demand: How Producer Jahaan Sweet Became a Secret Weapon for Kendrick Lamar, Beyoncé & More", billboard.com, 25 August 2022.

337 Jones (Damian), "Hit-Boy says Beyoncé's 'Thique' was originally made in 2014", nme.com, 17 August 2022.

338 Fitzgerald (Kiana), "We Can Give Them 17 Minutes", thecut.com, 30 September 2021.

339 Mitchell (Gail), "The Isley Brothers Talk Teaming with Beyoncé, Taking their Career to the Next Phase", billboard.com, 10 August 2022.

340 Price (Joe), "Travis Scott Finally Made his Beyoncé Collab Happen after Manifesting It 8 Years Ago", complex.com, 28 July 2023.

341 Fekadu (Mesfin), "The-Dream on Oscars Shortlist, Why He'd Give his Kidney to Beyoncé and How Losing his Mother Connected Him to 'Color Purple'", hollywoodreporter.com, 9 January 2024.

342 "Beyoncé Pepsi Commercial—Grown Woman", youtube.com, 2016.

343 Beyoncé's Instagram account, 19 March 2024.

344 Official "Cowboy Carter" press release, 29 March 2024.

345 Johnson (Daniel), "'Dukes of Hazzard' Actor John Schneider under Fire for 'Racist' Remarks about Beyoncé Singing Country Music: 'Every Dog Must Mark Every Tree, Right?'", blackenterprise.com, 19 February 2024.

346 Stenzel (Westley), "Will country radio play Beyoncé's new songs? Station managers weigh in", ew.com, 15 February 2024.

347 Wolstenholme (Luke) and Collins (Riyah), "Beyoncé: Renaissance star loved country music as a baby, dad reveals", bbc.com, 21 February 2024.

348 Tharpe (Frazier), "The Business of Being Beyoncé Knowles-Carter", gq.com, 10 September 2024.

349 Selladurai (Shivani), "Beyoncé Launches Sirdavis Whisky as an Homage to her Great-Grandfather", crfashionbook.com, 20 August 2024.

350 Miles (Barry), *Paul McCartney: Many Years from Now*, London, Secker & Warburg, 1997.

351 Paul McCartney's Instagram account, 4 April 2024.

352 Browne (David), "Beyoncé Wanted Some 'Country Fire.' She Knew Just Who To Call", rollingstone.com, 13 February 2024.

353 Borg (Janelle), "'As soon as I heard the demo, I knew it would be crucial to add rock elements': Justus West reveals how he sneaked Tosin Abasi and Plini onto the new Beyoncé album (sort of)", guitarworld.com, 16 May 2024.

354 Kylene (Jazmin), "Gary Clark Jr. Talks Parenthood, Tiktok and 'Cowboy Carter' at his Rockwalk Induction", blavity.com, 5 May 2024.

355 Rogerson (Ben), "'I was leaving the studio, but they were like, 'we're doing country, man!' and I was just like, 'that's different, let's go.' We did one country idea, then we started Texas Hold 'Em': Killah K on the making of a lead single from Beyoncé's Cowboy Carter", musicradar.com, 7 November 2024.

356 Rhiannon Giddens' Instagram account, 13 February 2024.

357 Trapp (Malcolm), "Beyoncé Reveals How Unwelcoming Country Music Experience Inspired 'COWBOY CARTER'", rap-up.com, 19 March 2024.

358 Hiatt (Brian), "Tony! Toni! Toné! Won't Reunite Again—And Six More Things We Learned From Raphael Saadiq", rollingstone.com, 9 September 2024.

359 LeDonne (Rob), "Ryan Beatty on his crazy 2024, from writing with Beyoncé to touring with Noah Kahan & Maggie Rogers", billboard.com, 26 April 2024.

360 Dolly Parton's Instagram account, 23 February 2024.

361 Evans (Greg), "Dolly Parton Teases Beyoncé Version of 1973 Classic 'Jolene'", deadline.com, 11 March 2024.

362 Trapp (Malcolm), "Shaboozey Details 'Very Free-Form' Experience Collaborating with Beyoncé on 'COWBOY CARTER'", rap-up.com, 5 April 2024.

363 Levin (Jordan), "Songwriting for a Superstar—Frost Alum on Beyonce's 'Cowboy Carter'", news.miami.edu, 23 April 2024.

364 Samuels (Keithan), "Producer Jeff 'Gitty' Gitelman on his Musical Journey, Working with R&B Stars: Interview", ratedrnb.com, 11 October 2024.

365 Arnold (Chuck), "Riding with Bey: How Beyoncé got Willie Jones to saddle up in the 'fourth quarter' for 'Cowboy Carter'", nypost.com, 9 April 2024.

366 Nicholson (Jessica), "Willie Jones and Shaboozey on What It's Like to Collab with Beyoncé on 'Cowboy Carter'", billboard.com, 5 April 2024.

367 Hawgood (Alex), "Miley Cyrus Finally Gets Her 'Flowers'", wmagazine.com, 3 June 2024.

368 Thompson (Erica), "Chicago's D.A. Got That Dope produced Beyoncé's 'Tyrant,' the violin-heavy banger on 'Cowboy Carter'", chicago.suntimes.com, 31 March 2024.

369 Denis (Kyle), "Reyna Roberts Talks Beyoncé's 'Cowboy Carter' Impact: "It's So Interesting to See How People Treat Me Now'", billboard.com, 16 June 2024.

370 Horowitz (Steven J.), "Beyoncé Initially Planned to Release 'Cowboy Carter' before 'Renaissance,' but 'There Was Too Much Heaviness in the World'", variety.com, 29 March 2024.

371 VanHorn (Teri), "Destiny's Child—Independent Women of Destiny's Child Coordinate Solo Projects", mtv.com, 11 October 2001.

372 Brow (Jason), "Mathew Knowles Wrote 'Destiny's Child: The Untold Story' to 'Correct All the Misinformation'", hollywoodlife.com, 19 February 2020.

Web Sources

beyonceonline.org
beyoncetribe.it
billboard.com
destinyschild.com
discogs.com
thebeyonceworld.com
whosampled.com
worldradiohistory.com

INDEX

Folios in bold = album openers or spread devoted to a specific track/song

!!!mind 411
#1's [compilation] 206, 232, 503, 504
03 Bonnie & Clyde 89, 146, 152, 154, 166, 355
(Holy Matrimony) Letter to the Firm 103
(There's No Place Like) Home For the Holidays 143
(Why, Why, Why) No Billz 71
*NSYNC [group] 80, 124, 171, 237, 357
****Flawless** 325, **346**, 358, 43
II Hands II Heaven 469, 478, **498**
II Most Wanted 469, **492**
IV Play [album] 354
1+1 295, **302**
16 see Sweet Sixteen
16 Carriages 469, 470, **478**
1975 138
1999 [album] 237
2 Chainz 354, 388
2 Step 205, 206
24/7 Studio 80, 112
2nd Floor Studios 194, 205, 280, 285
2Pac 166, 384
353 Studio 80
3LW [group] 128, 171
4 [album] **294–317**, 318, 320, 321, 332, 348, 358, 394, 472
4:44 [album] 396, 412
400 Degreez [album] 355
50 Cent 90, 164, 168, 174, 234, 237, 301, 406, 416
52nd Street [album] 286
6 Inch 363, 370, **380**
6 o'clock Blues 288
632-5792 241, 505
7/11 350, 506
702 [group] 24, 32, 60, 72, 88, 110, 113
713 399, 403, **410**
72 Seasons [album] 442
8 Days of Christmas 115, 127, **132**
8 Days of Christmas [album] 115, **126–137**, 142, 143, 159, 199, 504
8 Days of Christmas—2005 Reissue [album] 143
808 76
808-Ray see Cobbs Jr., Rayshon
808s & Heartbreak [album] 304
9th Wonder 196, 204, 205
99 Souls 391

A

A "DC" Christmas Medley 127, **132**
A Head Full of Dreams [album] 392
A Jolly Christmas From Frank Sinatra [album] 128
A Milli 274
A New Day Has Come [album] 290
A Night to Remember 85
A Portrait of Melba [album] 196
A Thousand Miles 190
A Tribe Called Quest [group] 44
A Very Special Christmas [album] 134
A Woman Like Me 232, 233

Aaliyah 72, 86, 88, 100, 160, 205, 206
Aaron, Kory 274, 276
Abbey Road Studios 414, 477
Abbiss, Jim 238
Abdul, Paula 54, 92
Abijaoudi II, Victor 233
Act i: Renaissance see Renaissance [album]
Act ii—3.29 see Cowboy Carter [album]
Adele 296
Adam, Adolphe 136
Adams, Yolanda 66
Adderley Jr., Nat 162
Addicted to Love 226
Addictive 156
Adell, Tanner 476, 477
Adeva 444
Adichie, Chimamanda Ngozi 346
Adisa, Jamelle 452
Adonis 450
Aerosmith [group] 352
Afanasieff, Walter 99, 113, 115
Afriyie, Nana O. *see* Lord Afrixana
Afrojack 350
After All is Said And Done 87
Age Ain't Nothing But a Number [album] 88
Agee, Tawatha 162
Agel, Jason 233, 238
Ager, Milton 293
Aguilera, Christina 6, 60, 78, 96, 104, 122, 124, 128, 137, 290
Ain't No Mystery 138
Ain't Nuttin' But Music 174
Åkerlund, Jonas 280, 348, 370, 376
Akhenaton 170
Akon 338
Alade, Yemi 423, 424, 434
Aldridge, Darcy 42
Alejandro 276
Alexander, Jovonn 58, 80
Alexander, Vincent 158
Alfie (What's It All About, Austin?) 138
Alforque, Crystal 374, 378, 386, 394, 428, 486, 490
Ali, Asif 134
Alien Superstar 441, **450–451**
All I Could Do is Cry 288, **293**
All Money is Legal [album] 89
All n My Grill 86
All Night 363, **386**
All That I'm Lookin' For 203
All Up in Your Mind 441, **461**, 496
Allah, Bilal 50
Allen, Debbie 10
Allen, George 455
Allen, Henry 386
Allen, Paul "PDA" 205
Allen, Robert 143
Allen, Tucker 136
Alligator Tears 469, **488**
Almodovar, Roberto 234
Al-Musfi, Omar 234
Alomar, Carlos 282
Already 423, **432**
Already Gone 267
Alston, Vejai Marcel 462
Always Be My Baby 38
Amanfu, Ruby 378, 379

Amazing Grace 57, **85**
Amen 469, **500**
America Has a Problem 441, **461**, 465
America Has a Problem (Cocaine) 461
American Gangster [album] 233
Ameriican Requiem 469, **476**, 500
Amezaga, Adam 350
Amil 89
Amir, Philippe 170
Ammo *see* Coleman, Joshua
Amor Gitano 236, 278
Anastacia 171
And I am Telling You I'm Not Going 242, 248
And I am Telling You I'm Not Going (Dance Mix) 242
Anderson, Charles 480
Anderson, Derek "206" 465
Anderson, Eldon D. 456
Anderson, Lyrica 342
Anderson, Skip 162
Andrade, Henrique 476, 477, 478, 484, 488, 500
André 3000 158, 306, 352. *See also* OutKast [group]
Andréason, Christian 203
Andrews, Delroy 160
Andrews, Denisia *see* Blu June
Angel 130
Angel 325, **340**
Angel of Mine 66
Angelopoulos-Daskalaki, Gianna 200
Animal Collective [group] 380
Another Bad Creation [group] 14
Ansari, Aziz 352
Anthony, Ricky 386
Antonio, Romeo 179
Antonoff, Jack 304, 395
Aossey, Jameil 448, 461
Apeshit 399, 404, **406**
Apex Studio 374, 386
Apg Studios 482
Apple Pie À La Mode 95, 106, **109**
Aquemini [album] 386
Aram Alapatt, Eothen *see* Egon
Archive [group] 461, 509
Are You My Woman (Tell me So) 154
Armstrong, Craig 238
Armstrong, Kymberli 36
Army of Lovers [group] 444
Arnold, Mike 49
Arnold, Paul 49
Arraya, Pablo 134
Arthur, Allen "Al Geez" 216
Ashadaly Adam 397
Ashanti 205, 278
Asher, Alex 306, 308, 310, 312, 466
Asher, Jordy *see* BOOTS
Ashford, Nickolas 250
Asiahn 464
At Last 288, **290**
At Last! [album] 290
Atack, Timothy 238
Atkins-Campbell, Erica 88
Atkins-Campbell, Trecina "Tina" 88
Austin, Dallas 39
Austin, Johnta 287

Autry, Gene 132, 143, 480
Avatar Studios 290, 292, 293
Avex Honolulu Studios 306
Aviance, Kevin 462
Aviance, Nita 455
Avicii 276
Avila, Bobby Ross 180
Aylands, Eric 315
Azzouz, Tarik 419

B

B. Carr 380
BC Jean 258, 264
Baby Boy 110, 145, 149, 156, **157**, 205, 506
Baby Boy (Junior's World Mixshow) 172
Babyface 84, 92, 258, 268, 278, 298, 306, 307, 321
Baby One More Time [album] 87, 228
Bacharach, Burt 380, 396
Back & Forth 160
Back 2 Life 34
Back That Azz Up 355
Back to Black 352
Back to Black [album] 244, 494
Back Up 240
Backstreet Boys [group] 80, 124
Bacon, Rob 202
Bad Boys II 168
Bad Boys II—The Soundtrack [compilation] 168
Bad Habit 183, **197**
Bad Romance 276, 280
Badu, Erykah 42, 412
Bagge, Anders 87
Bah *see* Stevens, Jabbar
Bailamos 200
Baker, Christian 266
Baker, Joséphine 216
Balance (Mufasa Interlude) 423
Balbuena, Danielle 450, 500
Baldwin, Peggy 237
Ball, Fred 410, 411
Ballard, Florence 92
Balmer, Rich 104
Balshe, Ahmad *see* Belly
Baltimora [group] 108
Balvin, J 397
Balvin, José Álvaro Osorio *see* Balvin, J
Bandy, Briana 374, 378, 386, 394
Banful, Ronald *see* Guiltybeatz
Bangladesh Studios 274, 276
Bankulli 424, 428, 434
Baraka, Ras 164
Barba, Reyli 236
Bardani, Ray 162
Bardot, Brigitte 216, 238
Barela, Samie 121
Barford Estate 318
Barlow, Joseph P 462
Barnes, Samuel J 89. *See also* Poke And Tone
Barnes, Sherrod 160
Barnett, Scott 310
Barrymore, Drew 96, 102
Barthe, Stacy 428, 432
Bartkowiak, Andrzej 88
Barutzki, Mareike *see* Digital Divide
Baseline Studios 158, 160, 166

Bassi, Maurizio 108, 110
Bates, Brian Vincent *see* Killah B
Batiste, Jon 476
Batson, Mark 164
Battery Studios 90, 124, 234
Battle, Hinton 245
Baynton, Robin 392
B'Day [album] **208–231**, 233, 234, 240, 241, 258, 270, 326
B'Day Anthology Video Album [DVD] 212, 222, 226, 239
B'Day Deluxe Edition [album] 236, 238, 239, 240, 241
Be Alive 420
Be With You 145, **158**, 200
Be Without You 197
Beam 452, 454, 460
Bearsville Studios 90
Beasley, John 244, 245, 246, 248, 250, 252, 254, 255
Beatty, Ryan 478, 484, 490, 498, 500
Beatz, Smitty 412
Beautiful Liar 212, **234**, 236, 268, 272, 300
Beautiful Pain 335
Beautiful People 335
Beautiful Stranger 140
Beck, Christophe 232
Beckham, David 230
Beckham, Victoria 230
Beckman, Meja 87
Bedingfield, Natasha 278
Bedoya, Carlos 156, 157, 159, 164
Bee Gees [group] 113, 114
Beenie Man 184
Beer, Madison 498
Before I Let Go 438, 506
Belec, Jon 164
Believe in Me 355
Bell, Chris 80
Bell, Louis 492
Bell, Ricky 310
Bell, Thomas 278
Bell Biv Devoe [group] 107
Belle, Alexe 464
Bellotte, Pete 156, 462
Belly 380
Ben Billions *see* Diehl, Ben
Benjamin, André *see* André 3000
Benjamin, Arrow 386, 391
Benning, Brian 237
Bennett, Sydney *see* Syd
Bennett-Smith, Sylvia 49
Benson, Renaldo 124
Bereal, Charlie "Little Charlie" 88
Bereal, J. "Lonny" 360
Bergeron, Wayne 244, 245, 246, 248, 250, 252
Bergling, Tim 392
Bergman, Ola 76
Bergmark, Jens 320
Berlin, Irving 135
Berry, Chuck 288, 293, 480, 496
Berry II, Vincent 384, 385
Berryman, Guy 392
Berz, Karren 104
Best Mistake 404
Best of My Love 46
Best Thing I Never Had 295, 300, **306**
Beverly, Frankie 438

Beyincé, Angela 156, 158, 159, 160, 181, 196, 198, 204, 205, 210, 220, 222, 232, 240, 258, 276, 287, 391
Beyincé, Lumis Albert 10, 474
Beyoncé, Celestine *see* Knowles, Tina
Beyoncé, Lumis Joseph "Skip" 10
Beyoncé [album] **324–350**, 358, 366, 367, 384, 424, 472, 474
Beyoncé Interlude 145, **164**
Beyoncé: Live at Wembley [DVD] 150
Beyoncé Platinum Edition— More [album] 350, 358
BFD 465
Bhasker, Jeff 304, 306, 308, 318
Bice, Cory 436
Biden, Joe 390
Bieber, Justin 385
Bieck, Greg 113, 115
Bienvenue 170
Big Boi 86, 149, 158, 386. *See also* OutKast [group]
Big Drawers 198
Big Freedia 386, 388, 389, 455
Big Girls Don't Cry 264
Big (Jazz Instrumental) 242
Big Momma's House: Music from the Motion Picture [compilation] 89
Big Momma's Theme 89
Big Pimpin' 156
Big Sean 282, 396
Big3 Records 198, 205
Bigger 423, **428**, 498
Bilal 176, 179
Billions 340
Bills, Bills, Bills 57, 60, 62, 64, **70–71**, 74, 78, 102, 159, 504
Bills, Bills, Bills (Maurice's Xclusive Livegig Mix) 504
Bin Laden, Osama 322
Bipolar Sunshine 432
Birchett, Anesha 240
Birchett, Antea 240
Birthday 23, **48**
Bisharat, Charlie 237, 374, 378, 386, 394
Bishop, Stephen 350
Bivins, Michael 310, 312
Bizarre 174
Bizet, Georges 120
Björk 321
Bjørklund, Amund 228
Black, Jully 178, 200
Black & Blue 109
Blackbiird 469, **477**
Blackbird 477
Black Effect 399, 403, **412**
Black Eyed Peas [group] 200, 264, 278
Black is King [film] 424
Blackmon, Larry 438
Black Parade 426
Blacks' Magic [album] 102
Blackwell, Otis *see* Davenport, John
Blades, Rubén 171
Blake, James 367, 374, 385, 434, 465
Blake, Jeff 51
Blake, Leigh 124
Blakeslee Recording Studio 202
Blame It on the Rain 315

516 INDEX

Blanchard, Terrence 288
Blanco, Benny 414
Bland, Ed 241
Blaque [group] 76
Blaske, Lee 302
B.L.A.Z.E. 120
Blaze, Just 386
Blaze Finale 120
Bleek, Memphis 89, 152
Blessed Assurance 66
Blige, Mary J. 6, 48, 50, 103, 124, 128, 168, 181, 197, 202, 270, 276, 278, 318, 408, 410
Blonde [album] 304, 394
Blood Diamonds *see* BloodPop
BloodPop 461, 462
Bloodworth, Shaun 385
Blow 325, 330, **340**
Blow My Buzz 174
Blow (Remix) 350
Blu June 404, 408, 411, 412, 418, 426, 430, 434, 450, 452, 454, 458, 460, 462, 486
Blue 325, 348
Blue Velvet 505
Blue Wave Studio 87
Blunderbuss [album] 379
Blunt, James 234
Blurred Lines 226
BMossman Productions 280
Boadicea 181
Bob Marley & The Wailers [group] 390
Bodin, Ida 237
Bodyguard 469, **484**
Bogart, Evan "Kidd" 266, 284
Boggs, Atia "Ink" 450, 460, 462, 476, 478
Boi-1da 411, 460
Boland, Elizabeth Lowell 482, 484
Bolas, Niko 290, 292, 293
Bologne, Joseph chevalier de Saint-George 486
Bonham, John 378
Bono 124
Boom 120
BOOTS 326, 328, 330, 336, 338, 340, 341, 342, 346, 348, 356, 357, 367, 380, 386
Bootsy's Rubber Band [group] 158
Bootylicious 95, **106–107**, 118, 120, 121, 198, 229, 328, 504
Bootylicious (Love: Destiny Version) 118
Bootylicious (Rockwilder Remix) 504
Borderline *see* Destiny's Child [group]
Born on the Fourth of July [album] 304
Boss 399, **408**
Boston Harbor Hotel 315
Botwin, Will 188
Boutin, Paul 278
Bowden, Jeffrey 42
Bow Down 346, 350, 438, 506
Bow Down/I Been On *see* Bow Down
Bow Wow, Lil' 118, 120, 197
Bowers, Kris 420
Bowie, David 134, 162, 202, 330, 364, 500
Bowie, Dustin 458
Bowman, Randy 62
Boy I Want You 505
Boyd, Brandon 357
Boyd, David 286
Boyd, Rekia 364
Boyfriend 505
Boyle, Bob 280
Boyle, Susan 315
Boynton, Donnie 76
Boys (Co-Ed Remix) 138

Boyz II Men [group] 14, 16, 28, 29, 51, 80, 87, 92, 181, 312
Brackins, Charles 44
Braide, Christopher 350
Branch, Darrell "Digga" 90
Brand New Heavies [group] 42
Brandon, Kevin 237
Brandon's Way Recording 278
Brandy & Monica [group] 58, 82, 280, 391
Brandy (Norwood) 58, 60, 88, 391
Brathwaite, Jahron 396
Bravehearts [group] 156
Braxton, Toni 78, 166, 196, 280, 315
Braz, Matheus 420, 448, 450, 452, 454, 455, 456, 458, 460, 461, 462, 466, 476, 477, 478, 480, 482, 484, 486, 488, 490, 492, 494, 496, 498, 500
Break My Soul 441, 444, 446, **455**
Break My Soul (The Queens Remix) 455
Breathe (Rap Version) 157
Breaux, Christopher 394
Breeding, Carl 42
Brenneck, Thomas 406
Brewer, Brooke 476, 486, 490, 500
Brewer, David Lee 13
Bridge see Timothee, Menardini
Bridgeman, Brian 160
Bridges 23, **39**
Bridges [group] *see* Destiny's Child [group]
Bridges, Jeff 341
Bridging the Gap 288
Briese, Denise 374, 378, 386, 394
Briggs, Kevin "She'kspere" 58, 68, 70, 74, 78, 84, 89
Bring Em Out 192
Bring Night 334
Brion, Jon 374, 378, 386, 394
Brockett, Mary Christine 452, 454
Brockman, Craig 159, 168
Brody, Adrien 288
Broken-Hearted Girl 257, **268**
Broken Strings 412
Brooks, Erik 455
Brotha Part II 181
Broussard, John "Jab" 115, 116, 162
Brown, Al 162
Brown, Bobby 42, 92, 310
Brown, David Debrandon 450
Brown, Foxy 51, 103
Brown, James 140, 159, 456
Brown, Jay 266, 411
Brown, Justin 492
Brown, Kawanna 411
Brown, Khalif *see* Lee, Swae
Brown, Mary 37, 41
Brown, Michael 364
Brown, Patrick 386
Brown, Raphael "Tweety" 80
Brown, Sidney *see* Omen
Brown, Sleepy 158
Brown, Terrance (or Terry) "T-Low" 80
Brown, Terrence L. 464
Brown, Yvette Nicole 122
Browne, Cleveland 358
Brown Eyes 95, **115**, 505
Brownlie, Matt 360
Brown Skin Girl 423, **432**
Brownstein [group] 32, 205
Brungardt, Charles 202
Brunman, Glen 244, 245, 246, 248, 250, 252, 254, 255
Bryant, Herman 455
Bryant, Joy 120
B-Sides [promotional CD] 92

Bubele Booi 428
Buckingham, Lindsey 106
Buckland, Jon 392
Buddah Epitome 51
Bug a Boo 57, 60, 68, **74–75**, 118, 504
Bug a Boo Roll Call (Interlude) 506
Bulbrook, Anna 374, 378, 386, 394
Bulgarian Radio Studios 170
Bulgarian Symphony Orchestra 170
Bullmark [group] 54
Bülow, Megan 482
Bun B 232
Bundy, Laura Bell 245
Bunny is a Rider 340
Burke, Kareem "Biggs" 89, 152, 166
Burks, Jonathan 178
Burley, Ingrid 384, 396
Burna Boy 423, 424
Burris, Vernon 436
Burruss, Kandi 58, 68, 70, 71, 74, 76, 78, 80, 84
Burse, Kim 134, 136
Burton, Michael 204
Busa Rhyme 86
Bush, George W. 99, 124, 370, 394
Busiswa 423, 424, 434
Buss, Guy 391
Busta Rhymes 198, 202
Butler, Johnny 312
Butler, Josh 168
Byrd, Donald 198

C

Cabello, Camila 414
Cabra, Eduardo 234
Cacciurri, Ralph 180
Cactus Jack 465
Cadenza 460, 494
Cadillac Car 242, **245**
Cadillac Records [film] 260, 288, 292, 496
Cadillac Records (Music From the Motion Picture) [compilation] 288
Caesar, Shirley 176
Calderon, Michael 68, 70, 76
Calderone, Victor 105, 114, 118
Caleb, Elisa 391
Caleb, Jo *see* 99 Souls
California Gurls 228, 334
California Love 152
Call My Name 203
Calvin, Billie Rae 174
Calzada, Orlando 104
Cameo [group] 438
Cameron, Carmen 233
Cameron, James 113
Campbell, Glendon 244, 245, 246, 248, 250, 252, 254, 255
Campbell, Gordon 244, 245, 246, 248, 250, 252, 254, 255
Campbell, Scott 246, 248, 250, 252, 254, 255
Campbell, Warryn "Baby Dubb" 87, 88
Cam'Ron 90, 152
Can I Get A… 89
Can You Feel the Love Tonight 427
Candy 438
Candy Shop 90, 234
Cane, Sean 233
Can't Feel My Face 380
Can't Get Used to Losing You 376
Can't Help But Wait 197
Can't Help Myself 92
Can't Hold Us Down 122
Can't Stop 26, **50**

Cantrell, Blu 157
Capitol Studios 237, 246, 248, 250, 252, 254, 255, 278, 366
Cappeau, Placide 136
Car Wash 174
Cards Never Lie 120, **121**
Care Package [album] 418
Caren, Mike 350
Carey, Mariah 16, 18, 38, 60, 72, 87, 113, 128, 171, 181, 278, 301
Cargill, Mark 237
Carlos, John 368
Carlson, Brittany Jean *see* BC Jean
Carlson, Smith 315
Carlton, Vanessa 190
Carmon, Tim 244, 245, 246, 248, 250, 252, 254, 255
Carmouche, Chris 158
Carolina Chocolate Drops [group] 470, 482, 483
Caro Mio Ben 486
Carol of the Bells 137
Carpenter, Mabvuto 436, 476, 486, 490, 500
Carrington, Sean 240
Carson, Ruth 14
Carstarphen, Victor 196
Carson, Aaron 170
Carter, Adnis 152
Carter, Blue Ivy 301, 330, 348, 350, 383, 397, 408, 423, 432, 462
Carter, Dwayne *see* Lil Wayne
Carter, Gloria 152
Carter, Hykeem 430
Carter, James 198
Carter, Lemar 478, 482, 484, 494
Carter, Nick 171
Carter, Rumi 400, 414, 462, 478
Carter, Shawn Corey *see* Jay-Z
Carter, Sir 400, 414, 480
Caruana, Jim 116, 154, 158, 160, 179, 190, 192, 194, 196, 197, 198, 202, 204, 205, 206, 216, 220, 222, 224, 226, 228, 230, 232, 234, 238, 241, 264, 266, 268, 269, 270, 274, 276, 280, 284, 285, 286, 287, 292, 293
Case 64, 76
Casey, Brandon 62, 70
Casey, Brian 62
Casey, Harry Wayne 140
Cash, Johnny 480, 509
Cash Money Studios 192, 205
Cashe, Chase N. 352
Casta, Laetitia 150
Castelli, Jon 348
Castellon, Demacio 355
Castle Oak Studios 49
Castro, Cristian 171
Castro, Rod 486
Cater 2 U 183, **194**, 504, 505
Caterini, Giacomo De 200
Caudieux, Eric 374, 378, 386, 394
Cave, Nick 442
Cave Studios 486, 490, 498, 500
Cedric the Entertainer 288
Celis, Gustavo 234
Center of Thy Will 456
Cephus, Kiari Kendrell *see* Offset
Chadie, Steve 490
Chaffin, Blake 86
Chaikin, Jules 206
Chakrabongse, Hugo 268
Chambazyan, Arthur 374
Chambazyan, Jack 384
Chambers, Gordon 87
ChampagneChronicKnightCap 287
Champion, Will 392
Cha'n André 54
Chandelier 334, 335
Chanderpaul, Shivnarine 157

Chaney, Vernon *see* Digital Divide
Chapman, Storm 476, 486, 490, 500
Charge It 2 Da Game [album] 50
Charles, Derrick 436
Charles, Nija *see* Nija
Charles, Tina 456
Charli XCX 498
Charlie's Angels: Music From the Motion Picture [compilation] 122
Chartmaker Studios 206
Chase, Brian 376
Chase Studios 104, 108
Chasez, JC 357
Chatman, Susan 237, 374, 378, 386, 394
Che Greene 37
Che, Roger 168, 181
Cheap Thrills 335
Check on It 209, 224, **232**, 504, 506
Check on It (Beyoncé Feat. Slim Thug) 504
Cheeks, James 240
Cheers (Drink to That) 428
Chen, Daphne 374, 378, 386, 394
Chess, Leonard 288
Chess, Marshall 290, 292, 293
Chevet, Éric 170
Chi 404, 408, 411, 412, 418, 426, 430, 434, 450, 452, 454, 458, 460, 462, 486
Chibueze, Collins 488, 500
Chic [group] 136, 444, 452
Chicago Recording Company 278
Chicago Trax Recording 86, 136
Chikwendu, Ezemdi 498
Childish Gambino *see* Glover, Donald
Chloe x Halle [group] 464
Choice [group] 84
Chosen Expression [group] 66
Christión 152
Chuban, Ivana 242
Chulalongkorn, King of Siam 268
Chung King Studios 37, 112
Church Girl 441, **456**
Ciara 278
Clapton, Eric 480
Clark Jr., Gary 473, 478, 486, 496, 498
Clarke, Phillipa 237
Clarke, Willie 222
Clarkson, Kelly 267
Clark Terrell, Elbernita 396, 456
Claudio, Sabrina 456
Clay, Porcha 455
Clayton, Jeff 237
Clemons, Ant 430
Cleveland, Alfred 124
Cliché [group] *see* Destiny's Child [group]
Clinton Jr., George 158
Clinton, George 86
Clinton, Hillary 364, 367
Clooney, Rosemary 135
C-Murder 38
Coat of Many Colors 486
Cobbs Jr., Rayshon 410, 412
Coby, Kenneth Charles *see* Soundz
Cochran, Hank 500
COE.BE.3 Studios 159
Coen, Ethan 341, 486
Coen, Joel 341, 486
Coffer, Jonathan (or Jonny) 386, 391
Cofield, Charmelle 232
Cohen, Casey 342
Cohen, Rob 348
Colaiuta, Vinnie 206
Colbert, Stephen 390
Coldplay [group] 233, 368, 390, 392, 430

Cole, Keyshia 278, 284
Cole, Natalie 198
Coleman, Andrew 226, 340, 348, 360
Coleman, Derrick 136
Coleman, Jonathan 455
Coleman, Joshua 334
Collier, John 446
Collins, Bootsy 158, 159
Collins, Chrissy 380
Collins, Kip 121
Collins, William 158
Color Me Badd [group] 14
Color Me Country [album] 494
Combs, Sean *see* P. Diddy
Come Home (Nala Interlude) 423
Come On 288
Commissioned [group] 66
Common 412
Como, Perry 143
Comstock, Frank 112
Concerto pour violon no. 1 en ré majeur, Op. 3: Adagio 486
Condon, Bill 210, 242, 244, 245, 246, 248, 250, 252, 254, 255
Coney, Brittany *see* Chi
Confessions 57, **72**, 86, 160
Confessions of Fire [album] 90
Conley, Robert 113, 115
Conrader, Michael 88, 110, 112
Consequence *see* Mills, Dexter R.
Conway, Chrissy 84
Conway Recording Studios 282, 315, 366, 374, 385, 386
Cook, Alexander Guy 461
Cook Classics *see* Lobban-Bean, William
Cooke, Sam 302
Cool & Dre [group] 403, 404, 406, 410, 411, 412, 420
Cooley, Eddie 179
Coolio 104
Cooper, Bradley 301
Cooper, Gary 158
Cooper, Jim 194
Cooper, Kim 450
Coots, J. Fred 132
Coppin, Levar Ryan 233, 450, 462
Coppola, Francis Ford 68
Coroner [group] 135
Cosma, Vladimir 287
Cossom, Kevin 382, 394, 419
Cottle, Tameka 70
Coulais, Bruno 287
Countdown 295, 300, **312**, 506
Counting Stars 344
Country Blues 288
Covers [album] 434
Cowboy Carter [album] 372, 395, **468–501**
Cowboys Live Forever, Outlaws Never Die [album] 488
Cowell, Simon 266, 315
Cox, Bryan-Michael 89, 197
Cox, Michael D. 462
Cozy 441, **450**
Cracchiolo, Salvator 237
Craig B 42, 50
Cranfield, John 374, 385, 386, 448, 450, 452, 454, 455, 456, 458, 460, 461, 462, 476, 477, 478, 480, 482, 484, 486, 488, 490, 492, 494, 496, 498, 500
Crawford, Daniel 452
Crawford, Shondrae "Bandalasz" 274, 276
Crazy Feelings 86, 160
Crazy in Love 6, 30, 145, 149, **154–155**, 156, 158, 272, 300, 400, 506
CrazySexyCool [album] 24
Creed, Linda 278
Creep 24

Crenshaw, Kimberlé 464
Creole 241
Cress, Al *see* Cresso, Almando
Cresso, Almando 454
Crocker, Tiheem 89
Crooks, Darrell 244, 245, 246, 248, 250, 252, 254, 255
Crosby, Bing 134, 135
Crosby, Fanny Jane 66
Cross, Ryan 374, 378, 386, 394
Crouse, Kevin 88
Crow, Sheryl 278, 292
Crowe, Russel 233
Crucified 444
Crump, HR 168
Crump, Preston 42
Crutchfield, Jerry 322
Cruz, Jasmin 236
Cry Baby 498
Cuff It 441, **452**
Culture Freedom 16
Culver, H. "Carmen Reece" 357
Cunty (Wave Mix) 462
Curry, Caleb 455, 486
Curtain Call 242
Curtis, Greg 179
Cutler, Scott 254
Cyrus, Miley 278, 388, 473, 492

D

D12 [group] 174
D12 World [album] 174
D.A. Got That Dope *see* Doman, David "D.A."
Da Brat 89, 105, 118, 120, 168
Da Costa, Paulinho 206
Da Real World [album] 86, 160
Daddy 145, **164**
Daddy Lessons 363, 370, **382–383**, **394–395**, 470, 472, 476
Daddy Wasn't There 138
Daddy Yankee 397
Daddy's House Recordings 168, 181, 233
Daft Punk [group] 360, 368, 380, 444
Dag [group] 54
Daley, Jack 312
Dallas Sound Lab 80
Dalsemer, Ian 48
Dalton, Darnell 278
Dance for You 320, **321**
Dance With Me 95, **113**
Dance With My Father [album] 202
Danger (Young Simba & Young Nala Interlude) 423
Dangerously in Love 95, **115**, 162
Dangerously in Love 2 145, **162**
Dangerously in Love [album] 68, 72, **144–164**, 170, 172, 174, 179, 184, 188, 205, 260, 458
Daniel, Jack 498
Daniels, Jaramye 386
Daniels, LaShawn 58, 82, 190, 192, 204, 206, 240, 280, 285, 391
Dannyboystyles *see* Schofield, Danny
Dante, Stephen 52
Darkchild *see* Jerkins, Rodney "Darkchild"
Darkchild Studios 280
DARP Studios 70
Dash, Damon 89, 152, 166
Daughter 469, 478, **486**
Davenport, John 179
Davey, Nicky 434
David, Hal 380, 396
David, Jacques-Louis 406
Davis, Ashley Tamar 14, 241, 505
Davis, Billy 293

Davis, Clive 80, 248
Davis, Don[ald] 196, 391
Davis, Douglas 306
Davis, Hal 252
Davis, Katherine K. 134
Davis, Makeda 89, 158
Davis, Roquel 293
Davis, Vidal 196
Dawn, Terena 476, 477, 478, 480, 484, 486, 488, 490, 492, 494, 496, 498, 500
Dawson, Andrew 306
Dawson, Jean 494
DC1 *see* Destiny's Child [group]
DC3 *see* Destiny's Child [group]
De La Soul [group] 44
Deacon, John 200
Dean, Ester 308, 312
Dean, James 154
Dean, Kasseem *see* Swizz Beatz
Dean, Kendrick 391
Dean, Mike 318, 341, 350, 384, 408, 448, 450, 461, 462, 465
Dean, Wayburn 180
DeBarge [group] 296
DeBarge, Eldra 160
DeBarge, Randy 160
DeBourg, Andre 80
Deck the Halls 132
Deep Cotton [group] 464
Déjà Vu 209, 212, **216**, 218, 229, 240, 506
Del Rey, Lana 350
Delahoz, Edwin 306
Delaine, Aubry "Big Juice" 358
Delicata, Alex 367, 382, 394
Delresto (Echoes) 465
Demme, Ted 86
Dench, Ian 234, 258, 268, 269, 292
Dennis, Cheri 233
Dennis, Steven 302
Dent, Anthony 99, 104, 108, 110
Deréon, Agnèz 186
Dernst, Emile II *see* D'Mile
Desert Eagle 469, 478, **496**
Desmarais, Scott 418
Des'ree 238, 239
Destiny Fulfilled [album] **182–199**, 204, 205, 206, 207, 212, 504
Destiny's Child [group] 14, 16, 17, 19, 24, 26, 28, 29, 30, 32, 34, 36, 37, 38, 39, 41, 44, 45, 46, 48, 49, 50, 51, 52, 54, 58, 60, 62, 64, 66, 68, 70, 71, 72, 74, 78, 80, 82, 83, 84, 85, 86, 87, 88, 89, 90, 92, 94, 96, 99, 100, 102, 104, 106, 108, 110, 113, 114, 115, 116, 118, 120, 121, 122, 124, 128, 130, 132, 134, 135, 137, 142, 143, 146, 149, 150, 156, 160, 168, 179, 180, 184, 186, 190, 192, 194, 196, 197, 198, 199, 200, 204, 205, 206, 210, 232, 236, 241, 255, 258, 262, 280, 296, 298, 312, 328, 344, 346, 354, 357, 362, 391, 465, 498, 504, 505, 506
Destiny's Child [album] **22–54**, 58, 103
Destiny's Child: The Untold Story Presents Girls Tyme [compilation] 241, 503, **505**
Detail *see* Fisher, Noel "Detail"
Devereaux, Yvette 237
Devil's Night [album] 174
Devine, Marcus "Da Heat Mizer" 205
DeVoe, Ronnie 310
Devor, Neil 206
Dezert Flower Studios 478, 482, 490, 498, 500
Diabaté, Toumani 432
Diagne, Saliou 450, 462

Diamonds 326, 334, 335
Diana [album] 250
Diana Ross And The Supremes [group] 137, 206, 248
Diaraby Nene 430
Diaz, Cameron 96, 102
Diaz, Rasool 338, 342, 358
DiCaprio, Leonardo 390
Dickey, Gwen 174
Dickey, Steve "Rock Star" 233
Diehl, Ben 380
Die With You **420**
Digital Divide [group] 392
Digital Services Recording Studios 37, 89, 108, 109, 110, 113, 118, 132, 168
Digital Sound 76, 85
Dijon, Honey 444, 450, 452, 455
Dilemma 30, 130, 146, 278
Dilli, Jeremy 476, 478, 480, 484, 486, 488, 490, 492, 494, 496, 498, 500
DiLorenzo, Vincent 196
Dimarco, Wolfram 203
Dion, Céline 113, 171, 202, 290
Dionne 396
Diplo 317, 367, 376, 386, 432
Disappear 257, **268**
Diva 257, **274**, 506
Dixie, Derek James 334, 338, 340, 341, 350, 367, 378, 380, 382, 386, 388, 394, 408, 426, 428, 432, 434, 436, 476, 486, 490, 500, 506
Dixie Chicks *see* The Chicks [group]
Dixon, Antonio 306, 321
Dixon, Deanna 455
Dixon, Willie 288
Dixson, Darius 458, 462, 476, 500
DJ Dede Mandrake 488
DJ Imanbek 432
DJ Khaled 396, 400, 418, 419, 430
DJ Lag 423, 434
DJ Quik 174
D'Mile 408
Do It Again **90**
Do You Hear What I Hear? 127, **134**, 136
Do You Know [album] 66, 205
Do You Know Where You're Going to 85
Dobson, Tamara 138
Doc Pomus 376
Dodd, Richard 374, 378, 386, 394
Dogg, Nate 384
Dolly P 469, **484**, 494
Dolly P's Engineer [group] 484
Doman, David "D.A." 498
Donald, Jocelyn 458
Donaldson, David 80, 112
Donaldson, Mike 280, 285
Donatello, Joey "The Don" 86
Dondlinger, Lisa 374, 378, 386, 394
Don Jazzy 318
Donovan, Tim 90
Don't Fight the Feeling 176
Don't Hurt Yourself 363, 370, **378–379**, 506
Don't Jealous Me 423
Don't Let Go 480
Don't Make Me Wait 34
Don't Stop 'Til You Get Enough 216
Don't Turn Around 315
Doppler Studios 76, 121, 179, 180, 181
Dorman, Jelli 476, 477, 498
Dorsey, Robert "LB" 238
Dot 115, **122**
Dot (The E-Poppi Mix) 504
Douglas, Jordan 454

Douglass, Jimmy 72, 237
Douthit, Patrick *see* 9th Wonder
Down By the Riverside 480, 490
Doyle, Bob 280
Dozier, Reggie 202
Dr. Dre 90, 137, 152, 156, 164, 174, 406, 410
Dr. Luke 334
Drake 344, 396, 411, 418, 428, 450, 456, 460, 509
Drawn [album] 114
Dre 403, 404, 406, 410, 412, 416, 420. *See also* Cool & Dre [group]
Dream [group] 128
Dreamgirls 242, **248**
Dreamgirls [film] 210, 212, 242–255, 286, 287
Dreamgirls (Finale) 242, **255**
Dreaming 321
Dreamlover 87
Dreams 356
Dresdow, Dylan 136
Dring, James 292
Drossin, Howard 290, 293
DRS [group] 44
Drunk in Love 325, 330, **338**, 344, 384, 414, 506
Drunk in Love (Remix) 350
D-Town 274
Dua Lipa 432
Dubock, Eliot 420
Duckworth, Kendrick 386
Duffy 494
Duflot-Verez, Raoul 170
Duke, Bill 176
Duncan, Garrett 476, 478, 480, 484, 486, 488, 490, 492, 494, 496, 498, 500
Dunkley, Jenelle 476, 486, 490, 500
Duplessis, Jerry "Wonda" 37, 46, 86
Dupree, Cornell 350
Dupri, Jermaine 24, 26, 38, 42, 80, 86, 89, 118, 120, 124
Duran, Kelman 448, 460
Duren, Jerel 486
Durst, Fred 124
Dwane M. Weir *see* Wane, Key
Dylan, Bob 480
Dyson, Michael Dywane Jackson 51

E

Early, Geoff 350
Early, James 246
Earth, Wind & Fire [group] 86, 138, 296
East Iris Studios 477
East, Nathan 206, 244, 245, 246, 248, 250, 252, 254, 255
Eastwood, Clint 301
EastWest Studios 354
Eatah, Piéce 492
Edge of Seventeen 106, 107
Edmonds, Kenneth *see* Babyface
Edwards, Blake 419
Edwards, Derek "Grizz" 50
Edwards, Harry 494
Edwards, Omar 500
Edwards Jr., Bernard *see* Focus
Effie, Sing My Song 242
Effigy Studios 416
Ego **284**
Egon 386
Ehrhardt, Ernie 237
Eichner, Billy 423, 427
Eilish, Billie 434
Eiseman, Blake 76, 179, 180, 181

Ejiofor, Chiwetel 423, 427
El Khatib, Hanni 342
El Michels Affair [group] 406
El Sevillano, Paco 236
Elastic Heart 335
Elba, Idris 260
Eldridge, Lamarcus 436, 476, 486, 490, 500
Electric Feel Studios 492
Electric Lady Studios 80, 284, 285
Elektra Entertainment Group 16, 17
Elfman, Danny 352
Elizondo, Michael "Mike" 174
El-Khatib, Oliver 418
Elliot, Michael 120, 121
Elliott, Chad "Dr. Ceuss" 58, 80
Elliott, Damon 99, 110, 130, 135, 140, 179
Ellis, Corte 172, 178, 179, 200
Ellis, Lisa 260
Ellis, Randolph 382, 386
Ellis, Warren 442
Emage [group] 44
Embrya [album] 68
Eminem [group] 86, 90, 137, 164, 174, 335, 344, 400, 406, 416, 480, 498
Emenike, Uzoechi *see* MNEK
Emotion 95, 113, **114**, 115 504, 505
Emotion (The Neptunes Remix) 504
Empire of the Sun [group] 308
Empire State of Mind 280, 282
eMusic Presents NFL Jams [compilation] 51
En Vogue [group] 12, 17, 109
Encore for the Fans 209
Encore Studios 86
Endless Love 255
End of the Road 92
End of Time 295, 300, **312**, 316
Energy 132, 441, 450, 452, **454**, 460
Enormous Studios 304, 308
Enriquez, Joy 170
Enya 181
Epic—Original Motion Picture Soundtrack [album] 352
Epps, Mike 176
Epps, Tauheed *see* 2 Chainz
Epting, Steven 436, 476, 486, 490, 500
Eriksen, Mikkel Storleer 228, 229, 234, 268, 269, 287, 320. *See also* Stargate
Erizku, Awol 400
Esmailian, Amir "Cash" 411
Espionage [group] 228
Estefan, Gloria 171
Etheridge, Melissa 278
Eugene, Jane 50
Evans, Adison 340
Evans, Big D. 233
Evans, Faith 32, 51, 87, 104, 176
Evans, Ray 135
Eve 124, 128, 156, 181
Everett, Shawn 492
Everingham, Dave 39, 48
Evermore [album] 442
Everything 118
Everything I Do 176, **179**
Everything is Love [album] **398–413**, 420, 426, 442
Everywhere You Go 428
Evil Woman 138
Evolution of a Man 288
Exodus [album] 87
Explode 455
Eyen, Tom 244, 245, 246, 248, 250, 252, 254, 255
Eye of the Tiger 106

F

Fahmy, Hajiba 341
Fairbairn-Smith, Vanessa 374, 378, 386, 394
Fairbrass, Christopher Abbott Bernard *see* Fairbrass, Fed
Fairbrass, Fred 450
Fairbrass, Richard Peter John 450
Fairbrother, Jack 414
Faith [album] 132
Fake Your Way to the Top 242, **244**
Fallin' 282
Fall Out Boy [group] 390
Fambro, Ken "K-Fam" 76, 99, 115
Family 242, **246**
Family Feud 68, **396**
Family Portrait 200
Fancy 95, **109**
Fanmail 60, 75
Fanmail [album] 60, 78, 156
Farquhar, Kurt 142
Farrell, Colin 352
Fat Joe 403
Fat Lip 190
Father Figure 132
Father John Misty 376
Father of Asahd [album] 418
Father Shaheed 54
Fauntleroy II, James 286, 340, 355, 360, 406, 419
Favreau, Jon 424, 427, 436
Feel the Same Way I Do 206, 504
Feelin' You Pt. 2 (H-Town Screwed Mix) 168
Feeling Myself 358, 391, 461
Feels Good 76
Feels Like (Featuring Kevin JZ Prodigy) 462
Feist, Mark J. 99, 114
Fela! [musical comedy] 296, 298, 312
Fergie 264, 278
Ferguson, Larry 121
Fernández, Alejandro 236
Fernandez, Alma 374, 378, 386, 394
Ferraro, Nate 482
Fetalmaus Studio 340
Fever 176, **179**
Fiddmont, Frederick 244, 245, 246, 248, 250, 252
Fighting Temptation 176, **178**
Finally 444
Finch, Canei 386
Finch, Richard 140
Find Your Way Back 423, **428**
Fingers, Kay 105
Firework 334
Fischer, Eric 49
Fischer, Lisa 292
Fisher, Noel "Detail" 338, 342, 350, 358
Fitchuk, Ian 500
Fitzgerald, Francis Scott 352
Flack, Roberta 37, 162
Flamenco 469, 494
Flanagan, Sharon 84
Flashback 205
Flawless/Feeling Myself 506
Flawless (Remix) 350
Flaws And All 238
Fleetwood Mac [group] 106, 484, 492
Fleming, Ian 138
Florence + The Machine [group] 296
Florent, Robin 418
Flores, Jaime 236
Flowers 492
Flower Travellin' Band [group] 412
Floyd, Alan 134

Floyd, George 426
Floyd, William "Bar None" 51
Flynn, Billy 290, 292, 293
Flyte Tyme 137
Focus 136, 137, 159
Foley, Paul 280
Folklore [album] 442
Fonsi, Luis 397
Foo Fighters [group] 190
Ford, James 237
Fordjour, Kwasi 424, 430, 434
Forever Starts Today 49
Forman, Steve 49
Formation 316, 363, 366, 367, 368, 370, **388–389**, 400, 466, 506
Fortunate 86
Forty Days And Forty Nights 288
Forward 363, **385**
Fosse, Bob 220, 273
Foster, Billy 292
Foster, David 206
Foster-Gillies, Amy 206
Foulds, David 200
Fox, Kaye 455
Foxx, Jamie 210, 242, 245, 246, 248, 250, 255
Frager, Arne 14, 44, 241, 505
Fragione, Philippe *see* Akhenaton
Frank, David 49
Frankie Lymon And The Teenagers [group] 52
Franklin, Aretha 202, 484
Franklin, Farrah 62, 64, 74, 80, 83, 122, 255
Franklin, Kirk 66, 116
Franklin, Lazonate 280
Franny G 124
Freak Hoes 38
Freakum Dress 209, **226**, 241
Fredriksson, Kris 200
Free 176, 178, 183, **198**
Free [group] 390
Freedom 363, **386**, 391, 506
Freeman 170
Fresh, Doug E. 306
Fresh, Mannie 355
Friedman, Roger 222
Friends 399, **411**
Frierson, Richard 168
Frost, Julie 312
Frosty the Snowman 132
Frye, Brian 38, 89, 124
Frye, John 39
Fu-Gee-La 37
Fugees [group] 37, 46, 84, 181
Fullan, George 282
Full Moon [album] 88
Fun [group] 304
Furler, Sia *see* Sia
Furtado, Nelly 124
Fusari, Rob 24, 37, 38, 41, 54, 86, 99, 106, 109, 113, 116, 130, 132, 137
Futura Productions 234
Future 338, 418
FutureSex/LoveSounds [album] 237

G

Gabriel, Juan 170
Gabriel, Peter 298, 321
Gad, Jens 264
GAD Studios 264
Gad, Toby 258, 264
Gaines, Calvin 37, 41, 54, 86, 99, 113, 116, 137
Galdston, Phil 87
Galland, Chris 418
Gallas, Andy 86
Gamble, Cheryl "Coko" 78

Gamble, Dee Dee Sharp 205
Game Over 204–205
Gangsta Lean 44
Gangsta Shit 168
Gangsta's Paradise 104
Gardner, Earl 292
Gardner, Patrick 476, 477, 478, 480, 484, 486, 488, 490, 492, 494, 496, 498, 500
Garfield, Simon 102
Garner, Eric 364
Garo, Gabrielle 500
Garren, Ross 484, 490
Garrett, Kevin 367, 374
Garrett, Ronnie 84
Garrett, Sean "The Pen" 190, 192, 196, 198, 204, 205, 210, 220, 222, 224, 226, 232, 240, 270, 274, 276, 318, 320
Garrett, Stephen Ellis 206
Garten, Brian 278
Garza, Alicia 464
Gaslighter [album] 395
Gates, Pam 237
Gatica, Humberto 206
Gatson Jr., Frank 155, 242, 273
Gaye, Marvin 124, 226, 246
Gaye, Nona 124
Gayle, Stephanie 64
Geel, Andy 233
Genie in a Bottle 60, 96, 104
George 2.0 464
Géricault, Théodore 406
Germano Studios 266, 282, 285, 292, 293
Germanotta, Stefani *see* Lady Gaga
Gesteelde-Diamant, Terius *see* The-Dream
Get Busy 157
Get Me Bodied 159, 209, 212, **220**, 224, 270, 273, 506
Get on the Bus 52, 86
Get Rich Or Die Tryin' [album] 174
Get Ur Freak On 156
Get With U 450
Geter, Tara 76
Geto Boys [group] 46
Gex, Greg 300
Ghetto Supastar [album] 46
Ghost 336, 341
Ghost, Amanda 234, 268, 269, 292
Ghrib, Nabil 170
GianArthur, Roman 464
Gibb, Barry 114
Gibb, Maurice 114
Gibb, Robin 114
Gibbs, Karen 52
Giddens, Rhiannon 470, 478, 482, 483
Gift From Virgo 145, 160, **164**, 458
Gilbert, Nicci 32
Gildem, Brad 82
Giles II, Dave 450
Giles, Cameron *see* Cam'Ron
Gill, Johnny 310
Gillespie, Haven 132
Gilman, Billy 170
Gilmore, Johnny 436
Gimme the Light 157
Ginuwine 72, 76, 87, 197, 205, 206
Giordani, Tommaso 486
Girl 36, 183, 196, 198, 204, 391, 504
Girl Like Me 118
Girls Can't Do What the Guys Do 222
Girls Love Beyoncé 344
Girls Tyme [group] *see* Destiny's Child [group]
Girls Tyme Fun 505

Gitelman, Jeff "Gitty" 490
Gittens, Rawle 37
Giuliani, Rudy 370
Give Me the Reason [album] 202
Give Me Your Love 88
Gladston McIntosh, Carl 50
Glansbeek, Ira 374, 378, 386, 394
Glaser, Paul Michael 84
Glaspie, Nikki 302, 304, 310
Gleeson, David 115
Glenn Miller And His Orchestra 290
Glenny, Terry 374, 378, 386, 394
Globerman, Kevin 427
Glover, Danny 210, 242
Glover, Donald 423, 427, 430
Glover, Khaliq 237
Go D.J. 192
Godbey, Chris 280, 340, 341, 342, 466
God Bless the Child (Intro) 505
God Bless the USA 322
God Made You Beautiful 350
Godzilla 498
Goin' Downtown 242
Gold, Andrew 350
Gold, Ian 492
Goldmine Inc. 52
Goldstein, Jason 90, 229
Goldstein, Noah 318
Gomerez-Rodriguez, Mariel 482
Gonzalez, Desiree 152
Gonzalez, Troy 102
Good Girl Gone Bad [album] 238
Good Morning 338
Good News [album] 419
Good to Me 88
Goode, Aaron "Goody" 216
Gooding Jr., Cuba 176, 180
Goraya, Navraj 411
Gordon, Diana *see* Gordon, Wynter
Gordon, Mack 290
Gordon, Wynter 367, 380, 382, 394
Gordy, Berry 17, 244, 245, 246, 248, 293, 302
Gordy Fuqua, Gwen 293
Gorfain, Eric 374, 378, 386, 394
Gore, Al 99
Gorillaz [group] 292
Gorfain, Eric 374, 378, 386, 394
Gosnell, Raja 89
Gospel Medley (Dedicated to Andretta Tillman) 95, **116**
Got's My Own 204
Gotta Be 26
Got to Give Up 226
Goude, Jean-Paul 444
Goulding, Ellie 498
Gousse, Max 264
Graham, Aubrey *see* Drake
Graham, Heather 138
Graham, Ricky 200
Graham, Russell 452
Graham Central Station [group] 412
Grande, Ariana 137, 386, 390, 404, 482
Granduciel, Adam 492
Grant, Chris 400
Grant, Gary 244, 245, 246, 248, 250, 252
Grant, Omar 298
Grassi, Andy 121
Grateful [album] 396
Gray, Christopher 382, 386, 426, 500
Gray, Freddie 364
Gray, Jaden 486
Gray, Mark 302
Great Day 233
Great Divide Studios 226
Green, Al 39
Green, Daniel 392
Green, Mean 42

Green, Nathan "Nearest" 498
Green, Nick 434, 456
Green, Reinaldo Marcus 420
Greenwood, Lee 322
Grier, Nikki 455
Grier, Pam 138
Grier-Daniel, Nikisha 486
Griffin, Alexandria 455
Griffin Jr., Larry *see* S1 (Symbolic One)
Griffin Jr., Tyrone *see* Ty Dolla $ign
Griggs, Eric 244, 245, 246, 248, 250, 252, 254, 255
Grigsby, Camille 476, 486, 490, 500
Grinnin' in Your Face 480
Grinstead, Irish 24
Grinstead, LeMisha 24
Groove Me 138
Grown Woman 330, 350, **466**
Gruber, Franz Xaver 134
Gudewicz, Jaime 134
Guest, Ivor 458
Guetta, David 276, 334, 350
Guillary, Lemar 426, 452, 500
GuiltyBeatz 428, 432, 458
Gunther, Hart 360
Guru *see* Young Guru
Guthrie, Gwen 89
Guthrie, Woody 478
Guy, Buddy 288
Gwala, Lwazi Asanda *see* DJ Lag
Gwizdala, Chelsea 486, 490
Gypsy Woman (She's Homeless) 444

H

Hackett, Naimy 108, 110
Hackford, Taylor 245
Hafermann, Holly *see* Skylar Grey
Hailey, Michelle 39
Haldeman, Oakley 132
Halderson, Troy 246, 248, 250, 252, 254, 255
Hale, Tony 470
Hall, Daryl 52
Hall, Orville Erwin 456
Halm, Teo 430
Halo 257, 260, **266–267**, 300, 315, 344
Hamelin, Dave 450, 478, 490, 498, 500
Hamelin, David *see* Hamelin, Dave
Hamilton, Phil 160
Hamilton, Roy 86, 480
Hammerhead 233
Hammond, John Dee 357
Hammond, Neel 374, 378, 386, 394
Hampden, Ivan 162
Hampton, Lisa 237
Hampton, Riley 293
Hancock, Herbie 292
Hangin' on a String (Contemplating) 50
Hannah-Jones, Nikole 464
Hanson 37
Happily Ever After 64, 76
Happy Face 95, 106, **113**, 137
Harbour, Gerald 142
Harding, Brandon 448, 452, 454, 455, 456, 461, 466, 486, 492, 494, 496, 498
Hard Knock Life (Ghetto Anthem) 152
Hard Knock Life (Ghetto Anthem—Dr. Evil Remix) 138
Hard to Forget Ya 404
Hard to Say Goodbye 242, **254**
Hardcover 461
Hardy, Anthony 68

Harmon, Jerome "J-Roc" 280, 338, 340, 341, 342, 355, 438, 466
Harmony—The Official Athens 2004 Olympic Games Classical Album [compilation] 200
Harper, Darryl 166
Harper, Jasmine 404
Harrell, Courtney 354
Harrell, Thaddis "Kuk" 270, 273, 285, 315, 476, 477, 498
Harris, Andre 196
Harris, Calvin 276
Harris, Clifford *see* T.I.
Harris, John 390
Harris, Kamala 386
Harris III, James *see* Jimmy Jam
Harrison, George 380
Harrison, Rich 149, 154, 158, 192, 210, 222, 226, 241
Harrold, Keyon 240, 462
Hartmann Way Sound Studios 88
Harv 490
Harward, Dabling 244, 245, 246, 248, 250, 252, 254, 255
Haseley, Simon 233
Hathaway, Donny 12, 137, 162
Haunted 325, 330, **336**, 341
Havana 414
Have a Holly Jolly Christmas 132
Have Your Way 122
Hawkins, Jamie 36
Hawkshaw, Alan 233
Hayes, Darren 124
Hayes, Donald 284
Hayes, Isaac 46, 252
Haynie, Emile 376
Hazlewood, Lee 494
Hazzard, Brittany 428, 432
H.E.R. 408
He Still Loves Me 176, **180**
He Wasn't Man Enough 78, 280
Heads High 358
Heal L.A. see What More Can I Give
Heard, Andreao 160
Heard About Us 399, **411**
Heard a Word (Michelle Williams) 504
Hearst, Garrison 51
Heartbreak Hotel 113
Heart to Yours [album] 66, 130, 146, 198
Heated 441, 444, **460**
Heat [limited edition CD] 179
Heaven 325, 330, **348**
Heaven (Kelly Rowland) 505
Heaven Knows 176
Heavy 242, **248**
Heilbron, Karl 278
Heintz, Tim 87
Hello 284
Hell of a Life 350
Hell You Talmbout 464
Henriques, Sean Paul *see* Sean Paul
Henry, Neville 52
Henson Recording Studios 232, 246, 248, 250, 252, 254, 255, 366, 374, 378, 386, 392, 394, 455, 460
Herard, Michael *see* Herard, Mike
Herard, Mike 406
Herbert, Vincent 24, 37, 41, 54, 86, 280
Here I Stand [album] 278
Here Comes Santa Claus 132
Hergett, Justin 344, 348
Hermansen, Tor Erik 228, 229, 234, 268, 269, 287, 320. *See also* Stargate
Hernandez, Anderson *see* Vinylz
Hero 113, 200

He's So Fine 380
Hey, Andrew 286
Hey, Jerry 244, 245, 246, 248, 250, 252
Hey Goldmember 138, **140**
Hey Ladies 57, **78**, 159
Hey Mama 200
Hey Ya! 158, 306
Hicks, Will 414
Higgins, Daniel 244, 245, 246, 248, 250, 252
Higher Ground 478
Hilderbrand, Lucas 450
Hill, Faith 228
Hill, Lauryn 46, 84, 87, 103, 164, 176, 490
Hill, Phylicia 476, 486, 490, 500
Hills, Floyd Nate (Nathaniel) *see* Danja
Hilson, Keri 278
Hines, Deni 170
Hinshaw, Charles 350
Hip Hop Star 145, 149, **158**
Hip House 505
HIStory: Past, Present and Future, Book I [album] 171
His Woman His Wife (The Soundtrack) [compilation] 122
Hit-Boy 318, 326, 336, 342, 344, 346, 350, 352, 358, 367, 380, 404, 444, 460, 461, 465, 482
Hitland Studios 278
Hitmen [group] 181
Hoffs, Susanna 138
Hogan, Asheton 388
Hogan, Cameron 486, 490, 500
Hogue, Davis 64
Hold My Beer 118
Hold Up 363, 370, **376**, 506
Holiday, John Michael 450
Holins, Tavor Javon 411
Holland, Sam 436
Holliday, Jennifer 248
Hollis, Chauncey *see* Hit-Boy
Hollowell-Dhar, Niles 341
Hollywood 233, 238
Hollywood Holt 352
Hollywood Studio Symphony 427
Holmes, Donald 68, 72
Holmes, Lenny 72
Holomalia, Gaylord 306
Holten, Ray 278
Holtman, Steve 244
Home 12
Home [album] 370
Home for the Holidays 143, 280
Home With You 498
Homecoming: a Film By Beyoncé [film] 438, 506
Homecoming: The Live Album 438, **506**
Honer, Marta 428, 486, 490
Honesty 286–287
Hooper, Nellee 238
Hoover, James 37, 42, 49, 76, 85, 89, 108, 109, 110, 113, 118, 132
Hope for Haiti Now [album] 267
Horesco IV, John 89, 124
Hosanny, Rhea 428, 486, 490
Hoskins, Jonathan 494
Houlihan, John 102, 105, 140
House of Music 36, 39, 44, 76, 85, 109, 118
House, Son 480
Houston, Cissy 160
Houston, Marques *see* Platinum Status [group]
Houston, Thelma 85
Houston, Whitney 6, 14, 18, 30, 34, 46, 58, 60, 72, 82, 92, 113, 134, 172, 280, 486
Hova *see* Jay-Z
Howard, Brittany 464

Howard, Harlan 500
How Sweet It is (To Be Loved By You) 246
How to Make Lemonade [album] 363, 370
Hudson, Jennifer 242, 244, 245, 246, 248, 250, 255
Huffman, Kyle 486, 490, 500
Huffnagle, Kent 109
Huggar, Robert L. "R.L." 80
Hugo, Chad 114, 140, 172, 226, 304, 454
Hummingbird Heartbeat 428
Hung Up on My Baby 46
Hunter, Eric 198
Hunter, Oshea 80
Hunter, Terry 444, 455
Hurley, Elizabeth 138
Hurts, Truth 156
Hurtt, Todd 391
Hutchison, Graig 120
Hymn for the Weekend **392**, 430

I

I am Changing 242
I Am... Sasha Fierce [album] **256–277**, 280, 284, 285, 286, 287, 288, 296
I Am... World Tour [DVD] 506
I Am... Yours an Intimate Performance at Wynn Las Vegas [DVD] 506
I Been On 438, 506
I Been On (Bonus Track) 506
I Believe I Can Fly 86
I Can't Take No More 172
I Care 295, 300, **304**, 506
I Don't Know No One Else to Turn to 196
I Don't Wanna Know 181
I Feel It Coming 380
I Feel Love 462
I Got That 89
I Gotta Leave You 118
I Kissed a Girl 228
I Know 176, **179**, 200
I Know (Destiny's Child—will.i.am) 200
I Like Funky Music 178
I Like It 160
I Like Your Lovin' (Do You Like Mine?) [album] 154
I Love to Love (But My Baby Loves to Dance) 456
I Meant You No Harm/Jimmy's Rap 242
I Miss You 295, **304**, 348, 394
I Miss You Old Friend 242
I Try 49
I Wanna Be Where You Are 16, 505
I Wanna Give You Devotion 444
I Want You Baby 242, **246**
I Was Here 295, **315**, 451
I Will Always Love You 486
I Wish 107
IAM [group] 170
Ibanga Jr., Ramon *see* !Illmind
Iced Earth [group] 135
I'd Rather Be With You 158
If 183, **198**, 505
If I Ain't Got You 282, 292
If I Ruled the World (Imagine That) 103
If It Isn't Love 310
If I Was Your Girlfriend 166
If I Were a Boy 257, 260, **264**, 272, 285
If Looks Could Kill (You Would Be Dead) 120, **121**
If You Had My Love 82, 103, 280, 285
If You Leave 57, **80**, 505
If You're Reading This It's Too Late [mixtape] 411
Iglesias, Enrique 200
Iglesias, Julio 171
I'll Be Missing You 181
I'll Be There for You/You're All I Need to Get By 410
Illusion 23, **46**
Illusion (Maurice's Radio Mix) 46
ILYA *see* Salmanzadeh, Ilya
I'm a Man 288
I'm Getting Ready 176
I'm Good at Being Bad 156
I'm Home (Mufasa Interlude) 423
I'm Lookin' for Something 242
I'm Ready 34
I'm Somebody 242, **250**
I'm Still in Love With You [album] 39
I'm That Girl 441, **448**
I'm Too Sexy 450
I'm Your Baby Tonight [album] 113
I'm Your Hoochie Coochie Man 288
Imagination [group] 46
Imagine 12
Imhotep 170
Immortal Beloved (Outro) 120
In Da Club 90, 174
In Full Bloom [album] 174
Ja Rule 124
Jasper, Chris 36, 465
Jay-Z 68, 89, 90, 104, 142, 146, 149, 150, 152, 154, 156, 157, 158, 159, 160, 164, 166, 168, 174, 184, 190, 198, 210, 212, 216, 218, 222, 224, 226, 228, 233, 234, 238, 258, 262, 266, 267, 269, 270, 273, 276, 280, 282, 290, 301, 304, 315, 318, 321, 326, 330, 332, 338, 342, 346, 352, 354, 355, 364, 366, 367, 368, 376, 380, 396, 400, 403, 406, 408, 410, 411, 412, 416, 418, 419, 420, 423, 426, 430, 432, 434, 450, 455, 456, 460, 461, 470, 472, 476, 486, 488, 492, 494, 500
Jay-Z—The Blueprint [album] 166
Jazzy *see* Jay-Z
Jealous 325, **342**, 364
Jean, Wyclef 29, 37, 38, 46, 70, 86, 118, 120, 121, 124
Jefferson, LaMarquis "ReMarqable" 124
Jefferson, Storm 37
Jeffries, Anthony 87
Jenkins, Jay 278
Isaacs, Kendu 318
Isaksen, Jens Christian 455
Ishizeki, Jun 216
Isis V. 464
Isley, Ernie 36, 465
Isley, Kandy Johnson 465
Isley, Marvin 36, 465
Isley, O'Kelly 36, 465
Isley, Ronald 36, 465
Isley, Rudolph 465
Isong, Richard *see* P2J
It's All Over 242, **250**
It's Not Right But It's Okay 58, 82, 280
I've Been Thinking About You 444
I've Tried 118
Ivey, Kenya 278
IZ 179, 180, 181

J

J Records 202
J. Wade and The Soul Searchers [group] 222
J. White Did It 419
Ja Ara E 423
In My City 505
In My Lifetime, Vol. 1 [album] 152, 174
In the Zone [album] 200
Incubus [group] 357
Independent Women 96, 98 102, 112, 115, 229
Independent Women Part I 95, 96, **102–103**, 112, 122, 159, 328, 504
Independent Women Part II 95, **112**, 205, 504
Ingram, Ashley 46
Insell-Staack, Judith 164
Inseparable 198
Interscope Records 86, 352, 416
Intro (The Writing's On The Wall) 57, **68**
Invincible [album] 171
Irosogie, Ariowa 458
Irreemplazable [EP] 234, 236
Irreplaceable 209, 212, **228–229**, 236, 264
Is She the Reason 183, **196**, 204, 268
JackÜ [group] 386
Jackson, Alonzo 44, 134
Jackson, Charles 198
Jackson, Curtis 90
Jackson, Eric 244, 245, 246, 248, 250, 252, 254, 255
Jackson, Janet 18, 34, 39, 60, 181, 188, 320, 408
Jackson, Larry 228
Jackson, Michael 10, 11, 17, 18, 128, 149, 171, 216, 296, 328, 380, 420
Jackson, Randy 44
Jackson, Sharon Sheinwold 138
Jackson, Wanda 378
Jackson III, Curtis James *see* 50 Cent
Jackson Dyson, Michael Dywane 51
Jackson Maynard, Robin 455
Jacobs, Naarai 455, 476, 486, 490, 500
Jagged Edge [group] 26, 42, 62, 76, 76, 80, 89, 196
Jagger, Bianca 446
Jake And The Phatman [group] 202
James, Bryton 171
James, Etta 260, 288, 290, 293, 310, 424, 496
James, Rick 42
Jang, Hotae Alexander 452, 462, 478, 482, 484, 488, 490, 494
Jenkins, Nathan 232
Jenkins, Tomi 438
Jennings, Waylon 509
Jeremih 356
Jerkins, Rodney "Darkchild" 58, 82, 83, 190, 192, 194, 204, 206, 210, 212, 216, 240, 258, 280, 285, 296, 391, 504
Jerkins III, Fred 82, 122, 190, 204, 206, 240, 391
Jesus Loves Me 95, 116
Jidenna 464
Jimmy & Wes: The Dynamic Duo [album] 490
Jimmy Jam 50, 179, 180, 181, 202
Jingle Bells 132
Jodeci [group] 50
Joel, Billy 286
John, Elton 202, 427, 442
John, Leee 46
Johnson, Aaron J. 233
Johnson, Arnetta 426, 500
Johnson, Bashiri 162
Johnson, Bobby 350
Johnson, Cameron 426
Johnson, Chris[topher] 426, 500
Johnson, Crystal 285
Johnson, Darlette 11, 12, 13, 14, 49
Johnson, Eric "E-Bass" 166
Johnson, James 244, 245, 246, 248, 250, 252, 254, 255
Johnson, Kim 455
Johnson, Leisa 233
Johnson, Miranda 496
Johnson, Rickey 124
Johnson, Tyler 476, 500
Jolene 469, 484, **486**, 488
Jolley, Steve 46
Jones, Bill T. 296
Jones, Emory 411
Jones, Grace 444, 458
Jones, James Earl 423, 428
Jones, Jamal 278
Jones, John Paul 378
Jones, Loretha 180
Jones, Matt 414
Jones, Mike 172
Jones, Nasir 419
Jones, Shannon 233
Jones, Tommy Lee 26, 44
Jones, Willie 486, 488, 490
Jonsin, Jim 258, 274, 276, 286
Jordan, Ellington 292
Jordan, Etterlene 160
Jordan, Montell 176, 180
Jordan, Steve 285, 290, 292, 293
Jordan, Steven A. *see* Stevie J.
Joseph II, Charles 464
Joshua, Kyambo 282
Joshua, Maurice 46, 105, 114
Journey to Freedom [album] 354, 357
Joyce, William 352
J. Que *see* Smith, Patrick "J. Que"
Jr Blender 376
J-Roc *see* Harmon, Jerome "J-Roc"
Juber, Ilsey 386
Judge, Ronald 216
Juice Wrld 498
Juke 288
Jump 38
Jumpin', Jumpin' 57, **80**, 504
Jumpin', Jumpin' featuring Jermaine Dupri 118
Jumpin', Jumpin' (Remix Extended Version) 504
Jungle City Studios 308, 320, 334, 336, 338, 340, 341, 342, 344, 346, 348, 354, 360, 366, 378, 384, 386, 397, 466
Just an Illusion 46
Just Be Good to Me 50
Just Be Straight With Me 50
Just Dance 276, 281
Just Enough Education to Perform [album] 321
Just for Fun 469, **490**
Just Kickin' It 38
Just Like a Pill 200
Just My Imagination (Running Away With Me) 246
Just Stand Up 278
Juvenile 355
Jxmmi, Slim 388

K

Kaba, Gloria 304, 306, 466
Kadhafi, Mouammar 301
Kaepernick, Colin 364, 427
Kaleidoscope [album] 60
Kaleidoscope [group] 386
Kali, Leven 450, 456, 458, 462, 464
Kamen-Green, Cole 306, 308, 310, 312, 466
Kani, John 423
Kapone, Al 288
Karlin, Kenneth *see* Soulshock & Karlin
Karpells, Chip 168
Kaskade 320
Katz, Leah 374, 378, 386
Kaycee 42, 54
KC & The Sunshine Band [group] 140
Ke$ha 344
Kearney, Sharon 90
Kearney, Walter "Stone" 205
Keaton, Gimel *see* Young Guru
Keeler, Patrick 378
Keen, Rachel *see* Raye
Keep Giving Your Love to Me 168
Kephren 170
Kelce, Travis 470
Kelela 356
Keller, Greg 394
Kelley, Tim 39
Kelly, R. 86
Kelly, Ryan 304, 308, 312
Kelly, Tim 29
Kelly, Tori 480
Kendun Recorders 465
Kennedy, Tiera 476, 477, 498
Kenny, Mitch 304
Kessee, Kelton *see* Platinum Status [group]
Key, Francis Scott 188
Key Beats 110. *See also* Stewart, Rapture and Seats, Eric
Keys, Alicia 88, 124, 164, 181, 197, 230, 280, 282, 292, 368, 464, 490
Key to My Heart 84
Keys to the Kingdom 423
Khaled, Asahd Tuck 396, 418
Khaled Khaled *see* DJ Khaled
Khaled Khaled [album] 419
Khalifa, Wiz 335
Khan, Shahid *see* Naughty Boy
Khéops 273
Khoury, Hanna 234
Kidd, Kelly 203
Kidd, Thom "TK" 84
Kierulf, Brian 90
Kilhoffer, Anthony 318
Killah B 482
Killing Me Softly 37
Killing Me Softly with His Song 162
Killing Time 23, 26, **44–45**, 50, 168, 505
Kilo [group] 461
Kinelski, Rob 216, 220, 222, 224, 226, 228, 230, 234, 241
King, Akil 386, 426, 428
King, Carlos 354, 357
King, Jack 318
King, Martin Luther 477
King, Valerie 237
Kingdom Come [album] 210, 233
Kings Landing 334, 346, 354, 358, 411, 412, 420, 454, 456, 458, 460, 462, 464, 476, 478, 482, 486, 488, 490, 494, 500
Kirby, Bruno 222
Kissing You 238
Kitty Kat 209, 226, 506
Klasfeld, Marc 190
Kleinman, Jeff 430
Kline, Kevin 232
Klinko, Markus 146, 150
KMA Studios 306, 308
Knapp, Phoebe Palmer 66
Knight, JaQuel 273, 282
Knocked Out 92
Know That 54
Knowles, Lou Helen 8
Knowles, Mathew 8, 10, 12, 14, 16, 17, 18, 19, 29, 34, 36, 37, 38, 39, 41, 42, 44, 46, 48, 49, 50, 54, 62, 64, 68, 70, 72, 74, 76, 78, 80, 82, 84, 85, 88, 89, 96, 98, 102, 104, 106, 107, 108, 109, 110, 112, 113, 114, 115, 116, 122, 132, 134, 135, 136, 137, 140, 143, 154, 156, 157, 158, 159, 160, 162, 164, 168, 178, 179, 190, 192, 194, 196, 197, 198, 204, 205, 206, 212, 216, 220, 222, 224, 226, 228, 230, 241, 244, 245, 246, 248, 250, 252, 254, 255, 264, 266, 268, 269, 270, 274, 276, 280, 284, 285, 286, 287, 290, 292, 293, 296, 360, 384, 474, 504, 505
Knowles, Solange 10, 11, 17, 130, 134, 140, 142, 143, 168, 172, 174, 176, 192, 196, 197, 220, 222, 238, 284, 285, 287, 340, 342, 384, 400
Knowles, Tina 8, 10, 12, 13, 14, 17, 19, 28, 29, 30, 64, 76, 99, 140, 186, 196, 226, 348, 350, 465, 473, 474
Koenig, Ezra 367, 376
Koller, Greg 374, 378, 386
Kopple, Barbara 370
Kortchmar, Danny 290, 292, 293
Kouyaté, Ismaël 466
Kovács, Péter 498
Kozey, Todd 205
Krausse, James 348
Kraven, Billy 304, 308
Kravitz, Zoë 464
Krawiec, Pete 113, 115
Kraze [group] 508
Krazy in Luv (Maurice's Nu Soul Remix) 172
Krieger, Henry 244, 245, 246, 248, 250, 252, 254, 255
Kris Kross [group] 14, 38
Kristofferson, Kris 301, 509
Kronstadt, Gina 374, 378, 386, 394
Krovoza, John 374, 378, 386, 394
KrossWire Studios 38
Krysiuk, Kimberly 426
Kuney, Marisa 374, 378, 386, 394
Kuniva 174
Kurstin, Greg 358
Kushner, Tony 242
Kúti, Fela 296, 298, 300, 312, 316
Kutzle, Brent 315

L

La Marimonda 234
La-La-La 168
LaBelle, Patti 36
Labrinth 436, 450
LaBute, Neil 122
LaCoCo Studios 39
LaDay, Deborah 13, 49
LaDay, Millicent 14
Lady Gaga 194, 230, 276, 280, 301, 400, 461
Lady Love [album] 34
Lady Saw 86
Lair Studios 230
Lallerstedt, Sonny 84
Lamar, Kendrick 367, 386, 387, 423, 430
Lamb, Cainon 312
Lambert, Al Sherrod 357
LaMontagne, Ray 266
Lancaster, Keith 180
Landers, Tim 179
Landslide 492
Larien, Jason 206
Lars, Vincent 39, 85
Larson, Mike 348, 500

Last Friday Night (T.G.I.F.) 334
Last Night 288
Late Night Feelings [album] 432
Late Registration [album] 88
LaToison, Staci 14
Laughing Yodel 480
Laundry Service [album] 234
Laurey, Emily 136
Lauryen Dockery, Kirby 420
Lawrence, Francis 102, 316
Lawrence, Martin 86
Lawrence, Ronald 232
Lawson, Edward 436
Lawson, Richard 428
Lawson, Ricky 244, 245, 246, 248, 250, 252, 254, 255, 460, 462, 500
Lay Up Under Me 320
Le Crib 452
Leal, Sharon 250, 252, 254, 255
L'Ecole du Micro D'Argent [album] 170
Lee, Bill 99, 113, 116, 137
Lee, Casey 120
Lee, Jonathan 348
Lee, Malcolm D. 87, 174
Lee, Peggy 179
Lee, Songa 374, 378, 386, 394
Lee, Spike 87
Lee, Swae 388
Lee-Kitto, Songa 237
Lefèvre, Maxime 170
Legacy Studios 278, 310
Leib, Mitchell 427
Lemonade [album] 60, **362–389**, 391, 396, 408, 412, 424, 426, 472
Lemonade [film] 366, 367
Lennon, John 12, 477
Lennox, Noah 380
Leon, Rebecca 397
Leonard, Cedrit 476, 486, 490, 500
Leonard, Courtney 382
Leone, Sergio 486, 488
Léontovitch, Mykola 137
Lertola, Jeremy 436
Leslie, Ryan 168
Let Me Try 386
LeToya 34
Let's Get It Started 200
Let's Get Loud 320
Let's Get Married 76
Let's Take a Walk 288
Levant, Gayle 246
Levens, Rod 205
Levert Sr., Eddie 176, 180
Levi's Jeans 469, 474, **492**
Levy, Barington 376
Levy, Shawn 232, 504
Lewis, Aaron 124
Lewis, Chris 14
Lewis, Damien 287
Lewis, James 233
Lewis, Jerry Lee 480
Lewis, Lakeisha 476, 486, 490, 500
Lewis, Leona 266, 278, 315
Lewis, Leshan David "L.E.S." 89
Lewis, Ricky "Ric Rude" 194, 206
Lewis, Terry 50, 179, 180, 181, 202
Lidell Townsell & M.T.F. [group] 450
Life is But a Dream 350
Lifford, Chelsye 357
Lift Ev'ry Voice And Sing 506
Lift Ev'ry Voice And Sing (Blue's Version) 506
Lift Off 318, 321
Lighthouse [group] 132
Lightning, Chuck 464
Like Dat 118
Lil' Bow Wow 80, 89

Lil Ju 460
Lil' Kim 72, 86
Lil Wayne 192, 274, 278, 284, 338, 355, 403
Lilly, Harold 284
Lil'O 26, 50
Lincoln, Jay 36, 39, 48
Lind, Espen 228
Linton, Willie 492
Lipson, Stephen 427
Listen 209, 242, 254
Liszt, Franz 269
Little Drummer Boy 127, **134**
Little Richard 52
Little Walter 288
Little Willie John 179
Liu, Lucy 96, 102
Live at Wembley [album] 172, 174, 205
Live at Wembley [DVD] 506
Live Oak Studios 39, 48, 85
Lively, Kevin 84
Livingston, Jay 135
Lizé, Didier 170
LMFAO [group] 318
Lobban-Bean, William 350
Lobel, Nick 486, 498
Lobo Studios 102
Locke, Lyndall 162
Logus, Paul 181
Lomax, Alan 386
Lomax Sr., John 386
London Bridge Studios 357
Londonbeat [group] 444
Look What You Made Me Do 450
Loose Ends [group] 50
Lopes, Lisa "Left Eye" 24, 26, 100
Lopez, Dave 230
Lopez, David 236
Lopez, Jennifer 60, 82, 103, 124, 128, 172, 230, 280, 285, 320, 348
Lopez Garcia, Jonathan 476, 477, 478, 480, 484, 486, 488, 490, 492, 494, 496, 498, 500
Lorber, Jeff 436
Lord Afrixana 423
Lorrell Loves Jimmy/Family (Reprise) 242
Los Da Mystro *see* McKinney, Carlos
Lose My Breath 183, **190**, 192, 194, 205, 504, 506
Losing My Religion 200
Love 183, **198**, 505
Love, Kandice 172
Love, Mike 494
Love, Rico 274, 276, 285, 286
Love a Woman 318
Love: Destiny [EP] 118, 504
Love Drought 363, 370, **384**, 408
Love Hangover 252
Love Interruption 379
Love in This Club Pt. II 192, 278
Love Me Not 118
Love of My Life (An Ode to Hip Hop) 412
Love on Top 295, 300, 301, **310**, 506
Love Songs [compilation] 360, 505
Love the Way You Lie 416
Love to Love You Baby 156
Love to Love You Baby [album] 462
Love Unlimited Orchestra [group] 37
Love You I Do 242
Loveeeeeee Song 404
Lovehappy 399, **412**
Lovely Jane 54
Loves Me Like a Rock 176
Lovett, Ryon 278

Lowe, Kristen 455
Lucas, Reggie 160
Lucchese, Richard 382, 386
Luckett, LeToya Nicole 12, 16, 19, 26, 28, 32, 34, 36, 37, 38, 39, 41, 42, 44, 46, 48, 49, 50, 51, 52, 54, 60, 62, 64, 68, 70, 72, 74, 76, 77, 78, 80, 82, 84, 85, 86, 87, 88, 89, 90, 92, 97, 255
Luckett, Pamela 34
Ludacris 284
Luger, Lex 282
Luhrmann, Baz 239, 352
Lux, Kyle 494
Lyrnon, Frankie 52
Lynch, Eric 168
Lyndhurst Hall 392
Lynn, Jonathan 176, 200
Lynn, Loretta 378
Lyon, Andre "Dre" Christopher *see* Dre
Lyons, John 138

M

Maartensson, Simon 486
MacDonald, Ralph 456
Mack, Karriem 172, 178, 200
Mackin, Riley 244, 245, 246, 248, 250, 252, 254, 255
MacLaine, Shirley 220
Macrae, Joshua J. 200
Mad 192
Mad Decent Studios 376, 386
Madison, Jayms 233
Madonna 18, 368, 432, 444, 455, 461
Magna Carta... Holy Grail [album] 332, 355
Magnus-Lawson, Oreoluwa *see* Lil'O
Maguire, Martie 372, 394
Magwaza, Thando 427
Magwenzi, Robert 428
Mahogany Soul [album] 181
Maines, Natalie 370, 372, 394, 395
Majid Jordan [group] 344
Major Lazer [group] 316, 317, 376, 423, 432
Makaveli *see* 2Pac
Make Me Say It Again, Girl 36, **465**
Make Me Say It Again, Girl [album] 465
Make Me Say It Again, Girl (Part I & II) 36
Make the Road By Walking 406
Makuria, Tizita 454
Malina, William 113
Malinga, Vula 391
Mamii 480, 484, 494
Mancini, Henry 419
Mandela, Nelson 171
Mandell, Caroline 230
Mandler, Anthony 220
Manhattan Ave. Studios 49
Manhattan Center Studios 52
Mansfield Studios 266
Manta Sound 132
Manzoli, Robert Francis Anthony 450
Maps 376
Maradona 428
Maraj, Onika *see* Minaj, Nicki
Marasciullo, Fabian 192
Margarita, Maya 476
Margiziotis, Philip 284
Margot 54
Maria Maria 46
Marinho, Anaïs 494
Marks, Johnny 132, 143
Marley, Bob 87, 390

Marley, Ziggy 171
Marr, Johnny 418, 419
Marrin, Matt 179, 180, 181
Mars, Bruno 310, 318, 368, 408
Marsden, Matthew 52
Marshall, Quavious Keyate *see* Quavo
Martell, Linda 473, 488, 494
Martin, Chris 233, 392
Martin, Darnell 260, 288
Martin, Max 228
Martin, Ricky 171
Martin, Steve 232
Martin, Trayvon 364
Martinez, Angie 282
Mary Jane Girls [group] 42
Mary Mary [group] 88, 176, 288
Maserati, Tony 338, 414, 465
Mason, Julian Martrel *see* Lil-Ju
Mason, Mark 89
Mason Jr., Harvey 244, 245, 246, 248, 250, 252, 254, 255
Mason Sr., Harvey 244, 245, 246, 248, 250, 252, 254, 255
Massive Attack [group] 461, 509
Master Blaster (Jammin') 414
Master P 38, 42, 50
Master Sound Studios 86
Matadin, Vinoodh 358
Mathematics, Allah 418
Mathers, Marshall 416
Mathers, Midian 384, 385
Matsoukas, Melina 220, 222, 334, 368, 370, 388
Matsushima, Takayuki 280
Matthews, Deleno 233
Matthews, Michael 486
Matthews, Stephanie 428, 486, 490
Matthews, Tatiana "Tatu" 460
Maxwell 36, 42, 68, 86, 87
Maxwell's Urban Hang Suite [album] 36
May, Brian 200
May, Johnny 494
May, Robert L. 143
Mayer, John 292
Mayfield, Curtis 88, 230, 406
Mayo, Scott 452
Maze [group] 438
Mazur, Kevin 472
MC Lyte 176, 178
McCalla Jr., Erroll "Poppi" 99, 115, 116, 122, 132, 143, 149, 162, 174
McCampbell, Caleb 306
McCartney, Paul 477
McCary, Michael 171
McClure, Bianca 428, 486, 490
McConnell, Kelvin 376
McCoy, Michael 113, 115, 164
McCracken, Dave 258, 268, 269
McCrary, JD 423
McCrorey, Charles 124
McEastland, Anthony 455
McEastland, Jawan 455
McEntire, Reba 171, 264, 484
McFadden, Gene 196
Mcfarlane, Conner 476, 477, 478, 480, 484, 486, 488, 490, 492, 494, 496, 498, 500
McFarlane, Fred Craig 455
McFarnon, Scott 292
McG 102, 122
McGinty, Jesse 500
McGrier, Allen Henry 452, 454
McIntosh, Tino Santron 461
McKenzie, Timothy Lee *see* Labrinth
McKinley, Raymond 36, 85
McKinney, Carlos 320
McKinney, Serena 374, 378, 386, 394

McKinnor, Nadine 137
Mohr, Joseph 134
McKnight, Brian 171
McLaughlin, Chris 455
McLaughlin, Jon 285
McLeod, Myra 237
McMahon, Ed 16, 346
McSpadden, Wyatt 8
McVay, Swifty 174
Me & My Boyfriend 166
Me Against the Music 200
Me And My Girlfriend 166
Me, Myself and I 145, 156, **159**, 188, 194, 205
Megadeth [group] 490
Megan Thee Stallion 419, 498
Mellow Drama [album] 374
MeLo-X 367, 376, 380, 408, 458
Memmi, Daniel 458
Men in Black 26, 103
Menahan Street Band [group] 406
Mendoza, Lester 378, 382, 386, 436, 438, 476, 490, 500, 506
Mercer, Johnny 419
Mercie, Léofric de 446
Mercury, Freddie 200
Merry Christmas [album] 128
Mereness, Ian 86
Metallica [group] 442
Method Man 410
México-Madrid: En Directo Y Sin Escalas [album] 236
Meyerson, Alan 427
Mi Gente 397, 400, 506
Michael, George 132
Michele, Chrisette 284
Michels, Jordan 406
Middleton, Chuck 222
Midnight Magic [album] 48
Migos [group] 406, 465
Miguel, Luis 170
Mike WiLL Made-It 367, 388
MikeQ 462
Miles, Barry 477
Milkshake 132, 454, 460
Miller, Byron 160
Miller, Chelsea 455, 476, 486, 490, 500
Miller, Colin 238, 240
Miller, Marcus 202, 386
Miller, Michael 274, 276
Miller, Mike "Snotty" 318
Miller, Percy Robert *see* Master P
Millsap III, Walter 230
Milli Vanilli [group] 315
Mills, Dexter R. 68
Mills, Kevin 244, 245, 246, 248, 250, 252, 254, 255
Minaj, Nicki 287, 350, 358, 386, 391, 461
Mincieli, Ann 282
Mine 325, **344**
Ming Tea [group] 138
Minogue, Kylie 321
Mirror Image Recorders 121
Mirrorball Studios 348
Miss Honey 462
Miss Thang [album] 39
Miss You (Dr. Dre Remix 2002) 138
Missy Elliott 52, 58, 72, 86, 89, 115, 149, 156, 159, 168, 176, 178, 206
Mitchell, Richard 427
Mizell, Jordan 406
Mizell, Fonce 198
Mizell, Larry 198
Mizoguchi, Hisashi 280
Mnyango, Anathi Bhongo 430, 432
Mobb Deep [group] 156
Mo B. Dick 50
Mobisson, Jidenna *see* Jidenna
Mocha 86

Mochizuki, Christian 306
Mohr, Joseph 134
Monáe, Janelle 304, 464
Monica 16, 39, 62, 66, 89, 205. *See also* Brandy & Monica [group]
Monkeywrench Records 390
Monroe, Marilyn 238
Monsted, Anton 352
Montgomery, Brian 290, 292, 293
Montrose, Lynn 168
Mood 4 Eva 423, **430**
Moon, Travis 473
Moon River 419
Moonchild Sanelly 423, 424, 430, 434
Moore, Alecia *see* Pink
Moore, Anthony 244, 245, 246, 248, 250, 252, 254, 255
Moore, Chant. 89
Moore, Falonte 99, 106, 109, 113, 130, 132
Moore, Jamal 436, 455, 486
Moore, Julianne 341
Moore, Melba 176, 180, 181, 196
Moore, Rufus 80
Moore, Sonny 454
Moorer, Lana *see* MC Lyte
Moraga, Giovanna 237
Morales, David 450
Morales, Jason 436, 476, 486, 490, 500
Morales, Mark 48
Morales, Michael 134
Morales, Ramon 74, 78, 84, 102, 137
Moroder, Giorgio 156, 462
Morbid Angel [group] 135
More Than a Woman 160
More Than a Woman [album] 166
Morgan, Patrick 237
Morissette, Alanis 264
Morris, Nathan 312
Morris, Nava 476, 486, 490, 500
Morris, Tom 135
Morris, Wanya 312
Morris, Wirlie 134
Morrisound Recording 135
Mos Def 120, 121, 288
Mosley, Garland 466
Mosley, Timothy *see* Timbaland
Moss, Corey 210
Moss, James "J. Moss" 205
Mosshart, Alison 378
Mossman, Brad 280
Mostyn, Steve 282
Motivation 192
Motown Christmas [compilation] 137
Mouridsen, Anders 498
Moussolou [album] 430
Move 242, **244**, 444, **458**
Move Your Body *see Get Me Bodied*
Mowry, Tahj 14
Moynihan, Bobby 273
Mr Eazi 423, 424
Mr. B 160
Mr. Porter 174
Mr. Sir *see* **My Rose**
Mr. Vegas 350, 358
Ms. Jackson 158, 306
MSR Studios 282, 298, 302, 304, 306, 308, 310, 312, 316, 321
Mtume, James 160
MTV's Hip Hopera: Carmen [album] 120, 121, 166
Muirhead, Matt "Doe" 382, 383, 388, 394
Mungo, Vernon 70
Munk-Hansen, Klara 498
Mkhatshwa 494
Murphy, Eddie 86, 210, 242, 244, 245, 246

Murphy, Ginger 374, 378, 386, 394
Murphy, Walter 178
Musa, Naser 234
Muse [group] 296, 321
Music From & Inspired By The Motion Picture Austin Powers in Goldmember [compilation] 138
Music From Baz Luhrmann's Film The Great Gatsby [compilation] 352
Music From the Motion Picture Dreamgirls—Deluxe Edition [compilation] 242
Music From the Motion Picture The Fighting Temptations [compilation] 176
Music Grinder Studios 121
Music Inspired by the Motion Picture Life [compilation] 86
Music World Studios 280, 287
Musiq Soulchild 480
Mussard, Geoffroy *see* Shurik'n
MWA 450, 461, 462
My Babe 288
My Beautiful Dark Twisted Fantasy [album] 282, 304, 318
My First Time 172
My Girls 380
My Heart Still Beats 95, **113**
My Heart Will Go On 113
My House 466
My Life II…The Journey Continues (Act 1) [album] 318
My Love is Your Love 46
My Love is Your Love [album] 60, 113
My Man 205
My Power 423, **434**
My Rose 469, **480**
My Song 118, 504
My Sweet Lord 380
My Sweet Summer Suite [album] 37
My Time Has Come 23, **49**
Mya 46, 72, 104, 171
Myers, Mike 130, 138, 140
Myers, Paul 140

N

Nadine 288
Naive **168**, 174
Napolitano, Julian 320
Nardone, Michele 237
Nas 103, 124, 156, 164, 288, 419
Naslen, John 132
Nasty Girl 95, **108**
Nasty Girl (Maurice's Nu Soul Remix Radio Edit) 504
Nate Dogg 90
Naughty Boy 386, 391
Naughty Girl 145, **156**, 159, 205
Naughty Girl (Calderone Quayle Club Mix) 172
Nav *see* Goraya, Navraj
Nava, Gregory 52, 86
Nava, Jake 155, 272, 466
Ndegeocello, Meshell 42, 87
Neal, Lee 36, 44
Necrosis [group] 135
Neenyo 460
Nelly 30, 124, 128, 130, 146, 278
Nelson, Candice C. 230
Nelson, Marc 87, 89
Nelson, Ricky 480
Nelson, Steve 132
Nelson, Willie 469, 473, 480, 484, 490, 494, 509
Nesby, Ann 176
Nesmith, Dwayne 274
Never Say Never [album]
Nevil, Robbie 87
New Edition [group] 14, 50, 296, 310
New Kids on the Block [group] 14
New Lesson (Timon, Pumbaa & Young Simba Interlude) 423
Newton, Huey P. 368
Newton, John 85
Next [group] 80
Ne-Yo 210, 228, 233, 238
Nibley, Alex 482
Nice 399, **408**
Nichol, Joseph McGinty *see* McG
Nicholas, Zoe 200
Nichols, Cherdericka 460, 461
Nichols, Kadeem 486
Nichols, Shawntoni Ajanae *see* Mamii
Nicks, Stevie 106, 107
Night Whistler 198
Nightbird Recording Studios 452
Nija 411, 412, 430, 434, 450
Nile 423, **430**
Niniola 428
Niño Villanueva, Rommel 280
Niswanger, Hailey 426
No Church in the Wild 304
No Doubt [group] 124, 264
No I.D. 282, 396, 456, 476, 490
No Lie 388
No Matter What Sign You Are 206
No More Rainy Days 86
No, No, No 28, 41, 42
No, No, No Part 1 23, 37, 38, **41**
No, No, No Part 2 **37**, 38, 41, 48, 70, 86, 106, 504
No, No, No Part 2 (Extended Version) 504
No Particular Place to Go 288
No Scrubs 58, 70, 74, 78, 450
No Way Back 450
Noah, Trevor 486
Nobody Could Take Your Place 205
Nomad [group] 444
Nomis Studios 52
Norman, Dion Lamont 456
Nostalgia, Ultra [mixtape] 304
Notes, Stevie 436
Nothing Out There for Me 160, 168
Nova Wav [group] 404, 411, 412, 450, 452, 454, 458, 462, 486
Now Behold the Lamb 95, 116
Now That She's Gone 57, **76**, 505
NRG Recording Studios 428
Nudel, Serge 306, 308
Nzasi Moupondo, Mohombi 397

O

Oakenfold, Paul 138
Oates, John 52
Obama, Barack 220, 262, 290, 322, 328
Obama, Michelle 220
Obsessed [film] 260, 424
Ocean, Frank 304, 318, 348, 394, 434, 509
Ocean of Thoughts And Dreams 196
Ochs, Camaron (Cam) 476, 478, 486, 490, 500
Odd Future [group] 456
O'Dell 42, 50
Oden, Rachel 54
O'Donnell, Alastair 430
Odum, Billy 124
Offset 406
Off the Wall [album] 216
Oh Louisiana 469, **496**
O' Holy Night 127, **136**, 199
OK Now [album] 285
Olivia 234
Olivier, Jean-Claude 89. *See also* Poke And Tone
Olsson, Alex 41
Olu Dara 288
Oluseun, Abisagboola *see* Bankulli
O'Malley, Rory 245
Omen 344
On and On 350
Once in a Lifetime 288, **292**
One in a Million [album] 88
One Night Only 242, **252**
OneRepublic [group] 258, 266, 344
One Way [group] 355
Onorati, Henry 134
On Our Own 92
On the 6 [album] 60
Oochie Wally 156
Openiyi, Temilade *see* Tems
Opera of the Bells 127, **137**
Orange, Dwanna 476, 486, 490, 500
Ordogne, Derrick Robert 456
Origin of Symmetry [album] 321
Ortega, Pete[r] 382, 386, 426
Ortiz, Bill 39, 85
Ortiz, Javier 370
Orzolek, Karen 376
Osaretin, Osabuohien 428
Osika, Geoff 374, 378, 386, 394
Osunlade 396
Otherside 423, **434**
Otis, Shuggie 158, 159, 164
Oulton, George 414
OutKast [group] 149, 158, 306, 352, 386
Outro (Amazing Grace… Dedicated to Andretta Tillman) 57, **85**
Outro (Dc-3) Thank You 95, 106, **116**, 137
Oven Studios 282, 326, 334, 336, 338, 340, 341, 342, 344, 346, 348, 350, 354, 355, 466
Owen, Ramon "REO" 284
Owens, Lashaun 172, 178, 179, 200
Oyanedel, Carlos 287
Ozuna, Bobby 202

P

P2J 430, 432, 458
Packnett-Cunningham, Brittany 464
Pacific Recording 87
Pacifique Studio 82, 366
Page, James 378
Paige, Donald 436, 476, 486, 490, 500
Paige II, Patrick 456
Pajam [group] 205. *See also* Allen, Paul "PDA," Kearney, Walter "Stone," Moss, James "J. Moss"
Pajama Studios 36, 44
Palladino, Pino 492
Palmer, Adidja 316
Palmer, Robert 226
Paltrow, Gwyneth 233
Pampuri, Dani[el] 436, 438, 476, 478, 486, 490, 492, 494, 496, 498, 500
Pantera [group] 490
Papa Michael, Anthony 39
Paparazzi 276, 281
Paranoia 118
Park, Grace 374, 378, 386, 394
Parker, Kellindo 464
Parker, Lawrence "Law" 411
Parks, David 382, 383, 394
Parks, Dean 206
Parks, Gordon 230, 252
Parks Jr., Gordon 230
Parkwood West 448, 450, 452, 454, 455, 456, 458, 460, 462, 478, 482, 486, 490, 498, 500
Part II (On the Run) 355
Partition 325, 330, **341**, 506
Parton, Dolly 473, 484, 486, 487, 492, 494, 498
Party 295, 298, 300, **306**, 506
PartyNextDoor *see* Brathwaite, Jahron
Passe, Suzanne de 14
Patchwerk Recording Studios 42, 160, 164, 168, 274, 276
Patchwork Studios 200
Patience 242
Patience (Composer Demo) 242
Patrick, Cameron 237
Patriot Studios 315
Patton, Antwan *see* Big Boi
Patton, Jasmine 455
Paul, Sean 184
Pausini, Laura 171
Pavlov, Deyan 170
Payton, Jimi Stephen 456
P. Diddy 24, 124, 168, 172, 181, 233
Peaches West 455
Pearl Jam [group] 390
Pearson, Darryl 466
Peck, Cecilia 370
Pellegrino, Leo 382, 383, 394
Peña, Juan "Wize" 396, 418
Pendarvis, Leon 290, 292, 293
Peniston, CeCe 444
Penny, Christopher Lawrence 450, 452
Pensado, Dave 179
Pensmith, Ari 458
Pentz, Wesley 316
Pepsi Music 2004 (Dare for More) [EP] 200
Perez, Desiree 411
Perez, Juan "OG" 152, 411
Perez, Rudy 236
Perez D'Anda, Carlos 342
Perfect 414
Perfect Duet 414
Perfect Man 88, 95, 110
Perfect World 242
Périer, Jean-Marie 171
Perron III, Marius 134
Perry, Clay 236
Perry, Katy 228, 334, 428
Perry, Reggie *see* Syience
Perry, Tyler 164
Personal Conversation [album] 64
Pet Sounds [album] 500
Petty, Tom 171
Pezin, Slim 170
Phifer, Mekhi 120, 121
Phillinganes, Greg 244, 245, 246, 248, 250, 252, 254, 255
Phillips, Justin 168
Phillips, Omar 124
Phos—The Official Athens 2004 Olympic Games Greek Album 200
Phuture [group] 508
Picard, Clément 432
Picard, Maxime 432
Picard Brothers [group] 432
Pickett, Lenny 292, 293
Pickett, Wilson 244
Pieptea, Radu 374, 378, 386, 394
Pierson, Frank 301
Pigott, Adam James 454, 455
Pilgrim, Chaka 354, 411
Pimentel, Miguel Jontel 342
P.I.M.P. 90
Pink 84, 200, 228
Pink + White 394
Pink Friday [album] 358
Pink Friday: Roman Reloaded [album] 358
Pinoteau, Claude 287
Pistilli, Gene 178
Pistol Pistol 174
Pitbull 344
Placebo [group] 321
Plant, Robert 378
Plastic Off the Sofa 441, **456**
Platinum Bells 127, **135**
Platinum Island Studio 54
Platinum Post Studios 89
Platinum Status [group] 78
Platt, Jon 391
Play-Tone 124
Playlist: The Very Best of Destiny's Child [compilation] 505
Please Mr. Postman 246
Plitt, Todd 160
PLUSS 367, 388
Poison 287
Poke And Tone [group] 89, 99, 102, 103
Poker Face 276, 281
Polachek, Caroline 326, 340, 341
Pollack, Michael 462, 492
Pollard, Javonte 455
Pon de Floor 316, 317
Pontier, Claudine 70
Poor Righteous Teachers [group] 54
Porter, Denaun 234
Portishead [group] 461, 509
Portner, Dave 380
Positions 482
Posse on Broadway 76
Post, Austin 492
Post Malone 473, 490, 492
Pottinger, Delroy "Phatta" 458
Pound the Alarm 358
Pour It Up 388
Power of the Dollar [album] 90
Powlis, Lance 464
Pray 233
Pray You Catch Me 363, 370, **374**
Preminger, Otto 120
Presley, Elvis 288, 480
Pretty Hurts 325, 334, 335, 363
Preven, Anne 254
Price, Keli Nicole 216
Price, Michael 476
Price, Morgan 306, 308
Price, Phillip Glen 456
Prince 10, 42, 50, 150, 166, 179, 188, 198, 226, 237, 296, 438, 444, 480, 505
Princess Fortier 476, 486, 490, 500
Princess Loko 448
Pritchard, Paul 414
Proctor, Andre Eric 338, 342, 358
Promised Land 288, 244
Proof 174
Protector 469, **478**
Proud Mary 293
Puff Daddy *see* P. Diddy
Pure/Honey 441, **462**
Purple Rain [album] 237
Pusateri, Joe 179
Pussycats 46
Put It in a Love Song 282
Pynn, Matt 492

Q

Q-Tip 288, 318
Quavo 406, 465
Queen [group] 200
Queen Latifah 202
Queen of the Night 92
Question Existing 238
Quinn, Jorel 455
Quiñones, David 284
Quisiera Ser 236

R

R. City [group] 386
Radio 257, **274**
Radio Station 288
Rado, Jonathan 492
Rae Sremmurd [group] 388
Raekwon 86
Rage Against the Machine [group] 296
Rah Digga 120, 121
Rahko, Bill 392
Rain Down 176
Rainbow [album] 60
Rainy Days 164
Ramírez, Alejandro 397
Ramirez, Juan 134
Ramone, Phil 286
Randolph, Antonio 376
Randolph, Kevin 244, 245, 246, 248, 250, 252, 254, 255
Randolph, Robert 478, 494
Rankins, Jesse J. 143, 287. *See also* The Bama Boyz [group]
Rapoport, Aaron 484
Rashad, Phylicia 10
Rasmus, Rudy 30
Ratajkowski, Emily 226
Rated Next [album] 80
Rather Die Young 295, **308**
Rauhofer, Peter 450
Ray, Anthony 76
Raye 428, 498, 499
Ray J 338
Raymond IV *see* Usher
Razgui, Boujemaa 234
Re-Collective Orchestra 427
Ready Or Not 37, 181
Realest Niggas 168
Reality 287
Real Love 48, 103
Real Love [album] 103
Real World Studios 310
Reasonable Doubt [album] 152
Rechtshaid, Ariel 350
Record, Eugene 154
Record Plant 14, 44, 206, 216, 226, 240, 241, 246, 248, 250, 252, 254, 255, 278, 304, 350, 366, 376, 380, 450, 462, 478, 505
Recording Artists for Hope—The Katrina CD Vol. 1 [compilation] 203
Redd 104
Reddick, Marcus 496
Redding, Otis 52, 244
Redemption Song 390, 394
Redenczki, Dominik 498
Redman 86, 198
Reed, Sharay 136
Reel Music, Rey 346
Refugee Camp *see* Fugees [group]
Regney, Noël 134
Reichenbach, William 244
Reid, Antonio "L.A." 84, 92, 162, 233, 278, 282
Reid, Clarence 222
Reid, Eric 364, 427
Rell 152
R.E.M. [group] 200
Remember (Mufasa Interlude) 423
Remenick, Brian 89
Renaissance [album] **440–463**, 465, 470, 472, 496
Renaissance: A Film By Beyoncé [film] 446, 466
Renee, Moi 462
Renfroe, Derek 456

522 INDEX

Renner, Aaron 244, 245, 246, 248, 250, 252, 254, 255
REO *see* Owen, Ramon "REO"
Resentment 209, **230**
Restrepo Echavarria, Andres David 397
Reunited (Nala & Simba Interlude) 423
Revival [album] 416
Resee Un Printemps [album] 170
Rexha, Bebe 276
Reyez, Jessie 423
Rhoden, Sean *see* MeLo-X
Rhone, Sylvia 17
Rhymes, Busta 156
Rhythm Divine 200
Rian, Fallynn 455
Ric Rude *see* Lewis, Ricky "Ric Rude"
Rice, Geoff[rey] 202, 226, 228, 232
Rice, Marlene 164
Rice, Tim 427
Richards, Aleesha *see* Mocha
Richards, Carol 135
Richards, Jonathan 428
Richards, Keith 480
Richardson, Desmond 273
Richardson, Kiandra 476, 486, 490, 500
Richardson, Latanya 176
Richbourg, Alex "Godson" 179, 180, 181
Richie, Lionel 48, 171, 255, 296
Rickerson, Byron 86, 136
Riddick, Makeba 210, 216, 220, 222, 226, 240, 241, 269
Right Said Fred [group] 450
Right Track Recording 121, 162
Rihanna 194, 224, 238, 266, 270, 278, 326, 334, 335, 344, 348, 368, 386, 388, 404, 408, 416, 428, 492
Riiverdance 469, **498**
Riker, Warren 37
Riley, Tim 202
Riley, Timothy Christian 44
Rimes, LeAnn 278
Ring Off 350
Ring the Alarm 209, 210, 212, **224**
Rise Up 352
Rison, Andre 51
Rissi 452
Ristorp, Morten 452
Ritson, Hal 391
Rittenhouse, Byron 80
Ritter, Allen 465
Rivas, Ramon 308, 334, 336, 338, 340, 341, 342, 344, 346, 348, 358, 360, 366, 374, 376, 378, 380, 382, 384, 385, 386, 397
Roach, Jay 138
Roach, Michael 41
Roach, Ray 138
Roach Cock 342
Roberson, Gee 282
Roberson, LaTavia 12, 14, 16, 19, 26, 28, 30, 32, 34, 36, 37, 38, 39, 41, 42, 44, 46, 48, 49, 50, 51, 52, 54, 62, 64, 68, 70, 72, 74, 76, 78, 80, 82, 84, 85, 86, 87, 88, 89, 90, 92
Roberts, Andrea 436, 448, 452, 454, 455, 456, 458, 460, 461, 462, 476, 477, 478, 480, 482, 484, 486, 488, 490, 492, 494, 496, 498, 500
Roberts, Kenny 480
Roberts, Reyna 476, 477, 498
Robertson, Kathleen 237
Robinson, Andre *see* Cha'n André
Robinson, Bob 24, 39
Robinson, Eddie 196

Robinson, Edward 391
Robinson, Janelle *see* Monáe, Janelle
Robinson, Keith 245, 246, 250
Roc Boys (And the Winner Is)... 233
Roc the Mic 233, 236, 238, 258, 264, 266, 268, 269, 270, 273, 274, 276, 278, 280, 284, 285, 286, 287, 292, 293, 298, 306, 308
Rochon, Jack 478, 484, 486, 498
Rocket 325, **342**
Rockferry [album] 494
Rockwilder 198
Rodgers, Jimmie 509
Rodgers, Nile 444, 452, 492
Rodigan, Oliver 494
Rodriguez, Alejandro 206
Rodriguez, Jean 397
Rodriguez, Katty 340
Rodriguez, Mj 464
Rogen, Seth 423, 427
Rogers, Andrell D. 461
Rogers, Kelly W. 54
Roll Over Beethoven 496
Rollins, Jack 132
Romano, Frankie 132
Romeo Must Die (The Album) (compilation) 88
Romero, Daniel 202
Ronson, Mark 352, 368, 432
Rooney, Cory 48, 99, 102, 103
Rooney, Herb 103
Rorystonelove 406
Rosario, Charlie 105
Rose, Anika Noni 242, 244, 245, 246, 248, 250, 252, 254, 255
Rosenberg, Jamie 226
Rosenblatt, Beth Amy 290, 292, 293
Rose Royce [group] 174
Roses 432
Ross, Bill 206
Ross, Diana 12, 92, 137, 210, 212, 242, 248, 250, 252, 254, 255, 424
Ross, Freddie 454, 455
Ross, Jimbo 237
Rosser, Dave 434
Rotem, Jonathan 109, 118
Rotten, Johnny 357
Rouse, Ricardo 166
Roustom, Kareem 234
Rowe, Solána 358
Rowland, Doris 14, 30
Rowland, Kelendria Trene *see* Rowland, Kelly
Rowland, Kelly 12, 14, 16, 17, 19, 24, 26, 28, 30, 32, 36, 37, 38, 39, 41, 42, 44, 46, 48, 49, 50, 51, 52, 54, 58, 62, 66, 68, 70, 72, 74, 76, 78, 80, 82, 84, 85, 86, 97, 88, 89, 90, 92, 96, 99, 102, 104, 106, 107, 108, 109, 110, 112, 113, 114, 115, 116, 118, 122, 130, 132, 134, 135, 136, 137, 142, 143, 146, 154, 172, 179, 184, 190, 192, 194, 196, 197, 198, 200, 203, 204, 205, 206, 220, 241, 255, 276, 278, 328, 348, 354, 357, 360, 391, 400, 428, 504, 505, 506
Roxx, Divinity 218
Royce Da 5'9" 120
Rubel, Joe 414
Rubin, Rick 237, 238, 416
Rudolph the Red-Nosed Reindeer 143
Ruffin, Jimmy 246
Run Away (Scar & Young Simba Interlude) 423
Runaway 318
Runnin' (Lose It All) 386, **391**
Runnin-N-Gunnin [album] 448

Run the World (Girls) 295, 300, 306, **316–317**, 320, 322, 400, 506
Rusch, Steve 360, 452
Rush, Tommy 466
Russell, Brenda 282
Russell, Brian 282
Russell's of Clapton 340
Rye, Angela 464

S

S1 (Symbolyc One) 306, 448, 461
Saadiq, Raphael 44, 86, 202, 288, 444, 452, 462, 476, 478, 482, 484, 490, 494
Sail On 23, **48**, 103
SAINt JHN 423, 432
Saiz, Ricky 406
Salatiel 423, 424, 430, 431
Salmanzadeh, Ilya 436
Salter, William 456
Salt-N-Pepa [group] 16, 32, 102
Salud! 403, **420**
Samberg, Andy 273
Samuels, Harmony 354, 357
Samuels, Matthew Jehu *see* Boi-1da
Sandcastles 363, **384**, 385, 386
Sandrich, Mark 135
San Francisco Dues [album] 496
Sang, Samantha 114
Sangaré, Oumou 423, 430
Santana [group] 46
Santa Claus is Coming to Town 132
Santana, Carlos 84, 170
Sanz, Alejandro 170, 236
Sarpong, Sam 120, 121
Sasaki, Motonori 137
Satellites 257, 269
Sauder, Steve 89
Savage 419, 424
Savage, Tamara 89
Savage, Tiwa 423
Savage Remix 419
Save the Hero 286
Say Her Name (Hell You Talmbout) 464
Say It Ain't So 505
Say My Name 60, 62, 78, **82**, 83, 118, 122, 190, 240, 280, 344, 504, 505, 506
Say My Name (Timbaland Remix) 504, 505
Say Who [album] 52
Say Yes 354, **357**
Sayers, Drew 304, 306, 308, 310, 312, 466
Scared of Lonely 285
Scarface 10
Schack, Carsten *see* Soulshock & Karlin
Scheffer, James *see* Jonsin, Jim
Schifrin, Lalo 273
Schipper, Justin 478
Schneider, John 473
Schofield, Danny 380
Schoolin' Life 320
Schoudel, Bart 340, 341, 344
Schubert, Franz 269
Schwartz, Jean 293
Schwartz, Joshua M. 90
Sclafani, Chris 414
Scorsese, Martin 486
Scott, Darius "Dixson" 420
Scott, Darrell 394
Scott, LaTocha 32, 70
Scott, Mike 342
Scott, Ridley 436
Scott, Tamika 70
Scott, Tony *see* Platinum Status [group]
Scott, Travis 465
Scott, Tyler 346

S.D.E. [album] 90
Seal 318
Seal, Manuel 38, 42
Seale, Bobby 368
Seals, Denise 13, 14, 49
Sean Paul 149, 157
Searching for Soul, Part 1 222
Seaton, Alexis 168
Seaton, Sean *see* Neenyo
Seats, Eric 88, 99, 110, 112
Secada, Jon 170
Second Nature 23, **36**, 37, 39, 465, 505
Segura, Junella 62
Sek, Pawel 318
Senator Jimmy D *see* Douglass, Jimmy
Sera, Kitten Kay 203
Sermons, Il Saunders H. 240
Serrecchio, Matt 232
Session Jr., Bobby 419
Seven Nation Army 378
Seventh Heaven 89
Sex Pistols [group] 357
Sexy Daddy 95, **110**
Sexy Ladies 237
Sexy Lil' Thug 174
SexyBack 237, 340
Seyfried, Amanda 352
SGC Studio 205
Shaboozey 473, 488, 490, 500
Shacter, Jon 376
Shakira 170, 212, 234, 268
Shakur, Tupac *see* 2Pac
Shalamar [group] 85
Shamello *see* Buddah Epitome
Shangri-La 416
Shape of You 414, 450
Shapira, Itai "Biako" 494
Shayne, Gloria 134
Shchedryk 137
Shebib, Noah "40" 344, 418
She Can't Love You 57, **84**
Sheehan, Kelly 466
Sheeran, Ed 390, 414, 450, 478
Sheila E. 444, 452
Shelter 166
Sher, Jon 315
Sherwood, Jason 302
She's a Bitch 72, 86
She's Gone 52
Shider, Tim 54
Shill, Steve 260
Shining 396, 418
Shining Star 138
Shining (Thank You) 506
Shire, Warsan 367
Shlohmo 356
Short, Columbus 288
Shortie Like Mine 197
Shorts, Michael 486
Show Me Love 455
Show Me the Way 23, **42**, 48
Shropshire, Adonis 168, 181, 233
Shut Up 318
Sia 276, 326, 334, 335, 350, 352, 358
Siegel, Jack 486, 488
Sigel, Beanie 89, 152
Signet Sound 113
Signed, Sealed, Delivered (I'm Yours) 206
Signore, Nunzio 113
Sign o' the Times [album] 166
Signs 145, **160**
Silent Night 127, **134**, 136
Silent Sound Studios 84, 92, 192, 205, 274, 276
Silk City [group] 432
Silkk the Shocker 38, 50

Silver Bells 135
Simmons, Aleese 76
Simmons, Daryl 16, 17, 39, 58, 84, 92, 156
Simmons, LaTrelle 76
Simmons, Lonnie 76
Simmons, Sherry 16
Simms Jr., Bill 288
Simon, Paul 180
Simply Beautiful 39
Simply Deep [album] 146, 154
Simpson, Jessica 87, 128, 194
Simpson, Rik 392
Simpson, Valerie 250
Sinatra, Frank 128
Sinatra, Nancy 494
Sing a Song 280
Sing a Song [album] 280
Singh, Tarsem 200
Single Ladies (Put a Ring on It) 6, 220, 256, 257, 260, **270**, 272, 273, 300, 400, 455, 506
Sir Mix-A-Lot 76
Sisqó 78
Sitek, David Andrew 412
Sixteen 498
Skarbek, Stefan 348
Skarzynski, Peter 241
Skeleton Crew [group] 14
Skip Saylor Recording 378, 382, 386
Skrillex 386, 444, 454
Skunk Juice 241
Skylar Grey 416
Sladkey, Fred 466
Slater, Jason 54
Slim Thug 232
Sloan, Katie 374, 378, 386, 394
Smack Into You *see* **Smash Into You**
Smallwood, Richard 116
Smash Into You 285
Smash Mouth [group] 138
Smith, Alexander 412
Smith, Bruce W. 142
Smith, Bryan 244, 245, 246, 248, 250, 252, 254, 255
Smith, Clifford 358
Smith, John "Jubu" 48
Smith, Joshua V. 378
Smith, Justin Shirley 200
Smith, Maurice 436
Smith, Patrick "J. Que" 306
Smith, Paul 244, 245, 246, 248, 250, 252, 254, 255
Smith, Rashad 90
Smith, Shaffer *see* Ne-Yo
Smith, Tamy Lester 89
Smith, Tommie 368
Smith, Tyran "Ty Ty" 234, 238, 411
Smith, Varick 181
Smith, Will 26, 44, 103, 106, 168, 420
Smith III, Eddie "E-Trez" 143, 287
Smith Jr., LaVelle 154
Smoke Hour ★ Willie Nelson 469, **480**, 484, 494
Smoke Hour II 469, **490**
Smokestack Lightnin' 288
Smokey Robinson & The Miracles [group] 246
Smooth, Joe 444
Snoop Dogg 86, 152, 156, 168, 410, 465
Snyder, Konrad 500
So Amazing 202
So Amazing: An All-Star Tribute to Luther Vandross [compilation] 202
So Anxious 76
So What 84, 228
So Good 57, **68**, 74

So Good (Digital Black-NGroove Club Mix) 118
So Good (Maurice's Soul Remix) 504
So Much Damn Swag (Interlude) 506
So So Def 26, 89
Soft Cell [group] 266
Soho Studios 160
Soko, Brian 338, 342, 358
Sol Was 458
Soldier 183, **192**, 504, 506
Solomon, Luke Francis Matthew 450, 452
Solonne-Myvett, Jonathan "Anonymous" 438
Solo Star [album] 168
Solway, Johnny 414
Solymar, Sean 466, 500
Somethin' Fresh [group] *see* Destiny's Child [group]
Songs in A Minor [album] 88, 282
Son Lux [group] 356
Sonnenfeld, Barry 26
Sony Music Studios 116, 134, 136, 137, 154, 158, 160, 170, 172, 179, 190, 192, 194, 196, 197, 198, 202, 204, 205, 206, 210, 212, 216, 220, 222, 226, 228, 230, 232, 233, 234, 238, 240, 241, 254, 286, 326
Soper, Chris 282, 312
Sorry 363, 370, **380**, 396, 506
Sorry Not Sorry 419
SOS 266
S.O.S. Band [group] 50
Sotolongo, Manelich 102
Soul 7 [group] 288
Soul Diggaz [group] 172, 179
Soul Hooligan [group] 138
Soulshock & Karlin 99, 113
Sound on Sound 106, 109, 113
Soundtrack Studios 88, 110
Soundz 278
Sounwave 430
South Beach Studios 146, 156, 157, 159, 160, 164, 205, 276, 286, 360
SouthSide Studios 89, 121
Spaghettii 469, **488**
Spear, Ed 378
Spears, Britney 6, 78, 87, 124, 138, 200, 228, 238, 404
Spears, Mark 498
Speechless 145, **160**
Spencer, Brittney 476, 477, 498
Spendlove, Randy 244, 245, 246, 248, 250, 252, 254, 255
Spice Girls [group] 230
Spikes, Charles 76
Spilfogel, Chris 244, 245, 246, 248, 250, 252, 254, 255
Spirit Rising Vol. 2: Inspirational [compilation] 122
Sporty Thievz [group] 71
SpottieOttieDopalisciouS 386
Spread a Little Love on Christmas Day 127, **136–137**, 504
Springer, Brian 72, 104, 114, 115, 116, 162
St. Beauty [group] 464
St. Lunatics [group] 128
Stafford Smith, John 188
Stallworth, Kenny 76
Standing on the Sun 330, 350, 358
Standing on the Sun (Remix) 350, 358
Standridge, Glenn 202
Stand Up for Love (2005 World Children's Day Anthem) 206, 504
Stankonia Studios 158

Star Spangled Banner 188. See also The Star-Spangled Banner
Starboy 380
Stargate [group] 210, 228, 229, 234, 258, 268, 269, 270, 287, 320
Starships 358
Starstruck Studios 278
Start Over 295, **308**
Static Major *see* Garrett, Stephen Ellis
Stay **84**, 348
Stay Tuned Studio 115
Stearns, David 234
Steele, Luke 308
Stefani, Gwen 124
Stein-Ross, Nancy 237
Steinweiss, Homer 406
Stephanie, Stephen 132
Step on Over 242, **252**
Steppin' to the Bad Side 242, **245**
Stereophonics [group] 321
Stevens, Jabbar 460, 461, 496
Stevie J. 181
Stewart, Christopher A. "Tricky" 270, 272, 273, 285, 298, 302, 321, 455
Stewart, Nicholas "Slick" 404
Stewart, Nisan 159, 168
Stewart, Rapture 88, 99, 110, 112
Stewart, Shakir 162
Stewart, Tim 194
Still D.R.E. 152, 410
Still in Love (Kissing You) 238–**239**
Still Pimpin 448
Still Waiting 190
Stillman, Al 143
Stills, Stephen 476
Stimulate Me **86**
Stines, Lenora Antoinette (Dr.) 412
Stinson, Dana *see* Rockwilder
Stinson, Taura 44, 54
Stipe, Michael 124
Stir Fry 406
Stockman, Shawn 170
Stokes, Chris 78, 130
Stone, Angie 32, 138, 176, 180, 181
Stone, Jesse 480
Stone, Joss 494
Stone, Sharon 224
Stoneback, Shane 124
StoneBridge and Nick Nice [group] 455
Stone Rollin' [album] 494
Stop That! 120, **121**
Storch, Scott 122, 149, 156, 157, 159, 205, 206, 286, 287
Strange, Joe 416
Strange, Mike 416
Strange Games & Things 37
Strawberry Letter 159
Strawberrybee Productions 264
Strayer, Emily 372, 394
Street, Jody 292
Streetrunner 419
Streisand, Barbra 174, 238, 301
Strickland, Marcus 477
Strong Mountain Studio 306
Stronger 78
Studio 609 196, 205
Studio at the Palms 302
Studio Claudia Sound 170
Studio Groove 280
Studio La Cosca 170
Studio M 134, 135
Studios Zgen 170
Sturm, Larry 136
Suchecki, Rob 306, 334, 342, 346, 360
Suga Mama [group] 209, 215, 218, 262

Suga Mama 209, **222**, 241
SugarHill Recording Studios 68, 74, 78, 84, 102, 106, 107, 114, 115, 116, 137, 162
Sullivan, Matt 244, 245, 246, 248, 250, 252, 254, 255
Sum 41 [group] 190
Summer 399, 403, **406**, 469
Summer, Brian 136
Summer, Donna 156, 202, 462
Summer Renaissance 156, 441, 452, **462**
Summers, Andrea Yvette *see* Princess Loko
Summertime 176, **181**
Sumthin' Sumthin' 36
Sunrise Studios 143
Sunset 340
Sunshine 16, 505
Superpower 325, **348**, 394
Superstition 140
Surrender (Simba & Scar Interlude) 423
Survivor 95, 99, **104–105**, 108, 120, 159, 205, 229, 504
Survivor [album] 68, 72, **94–118**, 120, 122, 128, 137, 146, 162, 184, 205
Survivor [group] 106
Survivor (Remix Extended Version) 504
Sutcliffe, Jess 246, 248, 250, 252, 254, 255
Sutton, Nick 476, 477, 478, 480, 484, 486, 488, 490, 492, 494, 496, 498, 500
Svendsen, Ryan 478
Swails, Joey 44, 76, 85, 118
Swain, Tony 46
Swass [album] 76
Swedien, Bruce 171
Sweet, Jahaan 411, 460
Sweet ★ Honey ★ Buckiin' 469, **500**
Sweet Dreams 257, 260, **276**
Sweet Kisses [album] 87
Sweet Sixteen 58, 85
Swift, Sidney 350
Swift, Taylor 395, 442, 450, 470
Swing Low Sweet Chariot 176, **180**
Swing Mob [group] 206
Switch *see* Taylor, David "Switch"
Swizz Beatz 210, 220, 222, 224, 228, 232, 270, 282
Swope, David 134
SWV (Sisters With Voices) [group] 24, 78
Syd 434, 456
Syd tha Kyd *see* Syd
Syience [group] 233, 238, 264

T

Tainted Love 266
Take Em 2 Another Level 505
Take That [group] 80
Takele, Leah Nardos 480, 484, 488, 490, 494
Takeoff 406, 465
Takin' the Long Way Home 242
Taking the Long Way [album] 370, 395
Talbert, David E. 122
Talk a Good Game [album] 354
Talking 'Bout My Baby 505
Tamposi, Alexandra 286
Tan, Phil 38, 124
Tan, Yen-Hue 124
Tanksley, James 202
Tanksley, Johnny 202
Tañón, Olga 171
Tanto And Devonte [group] 184
Tapley, Tom 192

Tapper, Richard J. 124
Taraborrelli, Randy 68
Tarantino, Quentin 103, 159, 280, 352, 486
Tarzan Boy 108
Taste 498
Tasty [album] 454
Tate, Larenz 52
Taylor, David "Switch" 312, 316, 317
Taylor, Lamar 278
Taylor, Larry 290, 292, 293
Taylor, Nicky 14
Taylor, Nina 14
Taylor, Robert "R.T." 310
Taylor, Roger 200
Taylor, Shea 238, 298, 304, 306, 308, 310, 312, 316, 320, 326
T-Bone 176
Teacher Fried My Brain 505
Teamwork Studios 174
Tedder, Ryan 258, 266, 267, 298, 315, 326, 344, 492
Teenage Dream 228, 334
Teena Marie 296
Teer, Barbara Ann 450
Tejeda, Japhe 391
Tekno 423, 424
Telephone 276, **280**
Tell Me 23, **39**
Temple, Jerome T. 456
Temptation 57, **76**, 505
Tems 458
Terry, Phillip 204
Terry T. 76, 109
Tesfaye, Abel *see* The Weeknd
Tesori, Jeanine 242
Texas Hold 'Em 6, 469, 470, 473, 482
Thahane, Khotso 427
Thalía 171
Thankful [album] 88
Tharpe, Sister Rosetta 480
That's How You Like It 145, **160**
That's the Way It is in My City 14
That's Why You're Beautiful 286
The Bakery 392
The Bama Boyz [group] 143, 280, 287
The Beach Boys [group] 128, 500
The Beach Boys' Christmas Album 128
The Beach House Recording Studios 236
The Beatles [group] 380, 477, 500
The Beehive 366, 380, 382, 384, 386, 388, 392
The Benjamin Wright Orchestra 237
The Best Man (Music From the Motion Picture) [compilation] 87
The Beyoncé Experience Live [DVD] 506
The Blueprint2: The Gift & The Curse [album] 166
The Blueprint 3 [album] 280
The Boom Boom Room 274, 285
The Boss [album] 250
The Boy is Mine 58, 82, 280, 391
The Boy is Mine [album] 60
The Brothers Johnson [group] 159
The Bzzzz Drumline (Interlude) 506
The Campground 284
The Carters [group] 403, 420
The Characters [group] 51
The Chicks [album] 472, 476, 492
The Chicks [group] 370, 372, 383, 394, 395
The Chiffons [group] 380
The Chi-Lites [group] 154
The Clark Sisters [group] 66, 396, 456

The Closer I Get to You 145, **162**, 202
The Commodores [group] 48
The Cutting Room Recording Studios 90
The Dead Weather [group] 378
The Dolls [group] *see* Destiny's Child [group]
The Don Killuminati: The 7 Day Theory [album] 166
The Dramatics [group] 196
The-Dream 258, 270, 273, 270, 285, 298, 302, 310, 312, 316, 317, 318, 320, 321, 326, 341, 344, 354, 356, 380, 397, 420, 444, 448, 450, 451, 452, 454, 455, 456, 458, 460, 461, 462, 466, 484, 486, 488, 492, 494, 496, 498, 500
The Dreamettes [group] 244, 246
The Dynasty: Roc La Familia [album] 166
The Element of Freedom [album] 282
The Emotions [group] 46
The Enterprise 72, 102, 104, 109, 110, 114, 115, 134, 136, 162, 168, 179
The Fame [album] 276
The Fame Monster [album] 276, 280
The Fighting Temptations [film] 176, 178, 179, 180, 200
The First Night 66
The Game 164, 403
The Gap Band [group] 282
The Get Fresh Crew [group] 306
The Girl is Mine 391
The Greatest 335
The Heat is On [album] 465
The Hell Song 190
The Hills 380
The Hit Factory Miami 90, 160, 168, 234
New York 48, 72, 88, 89, 113, 115, 118, 121, 136, 154, 157, 162, 200
The Internet [group] 456
The Introduction 120
The Isley Brothers [group] 36, 103
The Jackson 5 [group] 14, 137, 140
The Jam 412
The JB's [group] 140
The Juicy Juicy 448, 450, 452, 454, 455, 456, 458, 460, 461, 462
The Last Great Seduction 120, **121**
The Library 490, 500
The Linda Martell Show 469, **494**
The Lion King [film] 424, 426, 427, 436
The Lion King Original Motion Picture Soundtrack [album] 427
The Lion King: The Gift [album] 423, **422–437**, 442, 448, 466, 472, 498
The Lockdown Sessions [album] 442
The Marshall Mathers LP 2 [album] 416
The Marvelettes [group] 246
The Miseducation of Lauryn Hill [album] 46, 84
The Monster 344
The Neptunes [group] 114, 130, 140, 168, 172, 226, 454
The Next Episode [album] 80
The Notorious B.I.G. 168, 181
The O'Jays [group] 176, 180
The Only Way Is Up 444
The Pazant Brothers [group] 241
The Pink Panther [film] 232, 233

The Pinkprint [album] 358
The PJs: Music from & Inspired by the Hit Television Series [compilation] 86
The Platters [group] 52
The Pretenders [album] 419
The Primettes [group] 244
The Proud Family (Songs From the Hit TV Series) [compilation] 142
The Proud Family Theme Song 142
The Rainbow Children [album] 438
The Raconteurs [group] 378
The Regiment Horns [group] 392
The Revival [album] 76
The Rise And Fall of Ziggy Stardust And the Spiders From Mars [album] 500
The Rolling Stones [group] 138
The Roots [group] 87, 156
The Rural [group] 292
The Samples [group] 455
The Sand Castle 354
The Score 37, 46
The Section Quartet 416
The Show 306
The Smiths [group] 419
The Soul Sessions [album] 494
The Sound 288
The Sound Factory 484
The South Central Orchestra 202
The Stars (Mufasa Interlude) 423
The Star-Spangled Banner 328
The Stone 176
The Story of Beauty 95, **115**
The Superpower Horns [group] 306, 308, 310, 312, 466
The Supremes [group] 14, 28, 92, 96, 210, 242, 244, 246, 248
The Temptations [group] 96, 137, 246
The Time [group] 50, 181
The Tracks of My Tears 246
The Trailer 448, 450, 452, 455, 456, 460, 461, 465, 476, 478, 482, 486, 488, 490, 498, 500
The Underdogs [group] 244, 245, 246, 248, 250, 252, 254, 255, 286
The Underlab 244, 245, 246
The Undisputed Truth [group] 174
The Veltones [group] 10
The Velvet Rope [album] 60
The Village 392
The Village Recording Studios 492
The Village Recorder 179, 180 181
The Way I See It [album] 494
The Weeknd 310, 367, 380, 388, 400
The White Stripes [group] 378
The Writing's on the Wall [album] 52, **56–85**, 95, 102, 118, 132, 160
The Wubb Girlz [group] 280
Theme from Shaft 252
These Boots Are Made for Walkin' 494
Thicke, Robin 226
Think 230
Thique 441, 444, **460–461**, 496
Third Man Studio 378
Third World [group] 184
Thirty Days 496
This Christmas 127, **137**
This is America 430
This is Not a Test! [album] 178
This is the Remix [compilation] 80, 198, 504
This Land 478
This Land is Your Land 478
This Love 118
This Song's for You 168
Thomas, Brian "B-LUV" 270, 285, 302

Thomas, Candace 160
Thomas Crown Studios 237
Thomas, Damon 244, 245, 246, 248, 250, 252, 254, 255
Thomas, Delisha 216, 240
Thomas, Gerard 68, 72
Thomas, Keith 278
Thomas, Rozonda "Chilli" 24, 26
Thomas, Sevn 411, 460
Thomas, Stayve 232
Thomas, Theron 386, 438
Thomas, Timothy 386, 438
Thomas Jr., Rupert *see* Thomas, Sevn
Thompson, Ahmir "Questlove" 124
Thompson, Marvin 240
Thompson, Michael 244, 245, 246, 248, 250, 252, 254, 255
Thompson, Tyshane 454
Thornton, Phil 357
Thrall, Pat 154, 157, 302, 310, 312, 316
Through With Love 183, **198**
Thug Life 90
Thurman, Uma 280
T.I. 192
Tice, Rickie 426
Tilley, John 414
Tillman, Andretta 14, 23, 49, 57, 85, 95, 116
Tillman, Josh *see* Father John Misty
Tillman, Joshua 376
Tim & Bob [group] 24, 39
Timbaland 52, 86, 130, 206, 230, 237, 270, 280, 326, 338, 340, 341, 342, 355, 438, 466
Timber 344
Timberlake, Justin 171, 188, 237, 273, 340, 341, 342
Time to Come Home 176, **181**
Times Like These 190
Timothee, Merandini 318
Tingen, Paul 287
Tirado, Frank 386
Titanium 334
TK Disc Studios 102
TLC [group] 24, 26, 58, 60, 62, 70, 74, 75, 78, 100, 113, 156, 450
Tocci, Michael 238
To Da River 176
Todd, Andy 238
To Zion 84
Toi & Moi 431
T.O.K. [group] 184
Toledo, Rene Luis 236
Tolot, Francesca 226
Tom Ford 355
Tomlinson, Ralph 188
Tom's Diner 54
Tony! Toni! Toné! [group] 19, 39, 44, 76, 452
Too Close 80
Too Many Zooz [group] 382, 383, 394
Top Off 418, 464, 506
Torres, Crystal 340, 426, 500
Torres, Keanu "Beats" Dean 430
Total 24, 72
Total Praise 95, 116
Tourso, Todd 330, 370
Tovar, Marcos 268, 269, 278, 292
Townsend, Robert 120, 121
Toxic 200
T-Pain 408
Traces of My Lipstick [album] 60
Trackdown Studios 344
Tree Sound Studios 284, 452, 462
Tresvant, Ralph 310
Trey Songz 197, 465

Triangle Sound Studios 68, 74, 78, 84, 302
Tricky see Stewart, Christopher "Tricky"
Trip to New York 434
Tritonus Studios 344
Trouble 200
Trouble [album] 266
Troutman, Larry 172
Troutman, Roger 172
TRU (The Real Untouchables) [group] 38
Tru 2 Da Game [album] 38
True Star (A Private Performance) 174
Trump, Donald J. 364, 367, 370
Trust in Me 288, **293**
T-Shirt 183, **196**, 505
Tsumura, Mari 237
Tsutsumi, Miki 282
Tucker, Michael see BloodPop
Tupac see 2Pac
Turbo 919 [album] 320
Turman, Nycolia 80, 90
Turn Your Lights Down Low 87
Turner, Ike 293, 338
Turner, Kevin 136
Turner, Tina 18, 233, 293, 315, 338
Turnt 354
Turrisi, Francesco 483
Twain, Shania 228
Tweet 168, 206
Ty Dolla $ign 408
Tyga 498
Tyler, Khirye 466, 476, 477, 478, 482, 486, 488, 490, 492, 494, 496, 498, 500
Tyler, Steven 352
Tyler, The Creator 494
Tyrant 469, **498**

U

U Arena 406
U2 [group] 124
Uhh Ahh 312
ULB Studios 121
Ullman, Jordan Kenneth Cooke 344
Umbrella 270
Un-Break My Heart 315
Uncle Louie [group] 178
Uncle Scar (Scar Interlude) 423
Under Construction [album] 160
Understanding 38
Underwood, Carrie 278
United Harmony [group] 66
Unity (The Official Athens 2004 Olympic Games Album) [compilation] 200
Unpretty 78
Unstoppable 335
Until the End of Time 237
Up&Up 392
Upgrade U 158, 209, **222**, 224
Uphill Battle [album] 372
Upside Down 250
Usher 38, 156, 162, 171, 181, 192, 197, 202, 262, 278, 301, 368, 396, 470
Utopia [album] 465
Uwaezuoke, Sonny Corey 438
Uzowuru, Michael 430, 432

V

Vadukul, Max 212
Valdez, Robert 135
Valentino, Isis 464
Valenzano, Marcello "Cool" Antonio see Cool & Dre [group]
Vallis, Beau 354
Vampire Weekend [group] 376

Van Der Saag, Jochem 206
Van de Wall, Nick 316
Vandross, Luther 10, 162, 171, 202
Van Lamsweerde, Inez 358
Vanity 6 [group] 226
Vargas, [Dora] Melissa 326, 348, 486
Vasquez, Devin 140
Vasquez, Roberto 285
Veal, Charles 202
Vedder, Eddie 390
Vega, Suzanne 54
Velasquez, Regine 114
Veli, Ina 374, 378, 386, 394
Venguer, Alejandro 278
Ventura, Cassie 280
Venus vs Mars 280
Verdon, Gwen 273
Vergara, Josefina 374, 378, 386, 394
Verglas, Antoine 130
Verhoeven, Paul 224
Vernon, Justin 465
Vertelney, Reed 49
Vicari, Tommy 427
Vickery, Alex 486, 490
Victory is Certain 412
Videen, Nick 306, 308, 310, 312, 466
Video Phone 257, **276**
Viento a Favor [album] 236
Villanueva, Jeff 190, 194, 206, 216, 240
Vinci, Leonardo da 404, 406
Vinylz 411
Virgo's Groove 160, 441, 444, **458**
Visitante 234
Vita 89
Vogue 444, 455
Vol. 2… Hard Knock Life [album] 89, 152
Voodoo Song see Mi Gente
Voss, Meegan 293

W

Wachtel, Waddy 107
Wainstein, Victor 494
Wake, Ric 136
Waldmann, Seth 427
Wale, Shatta 423, 424, 432
Walk, Aaron 244, 245, 246, 248, 250, 252, 254, 255
Walk, Bryan 244, 245, 246, 248, 250, 252, 254, 255
Walker, A.J. 233
Walker, Eamonn 288
Walker, Hezekiah 66
Walker, Miles 274, 276, 392
Walker, William 85
Walking on a Dream 308
Walk on Water 174, **416**
Walk the Way You Talk 396
Wallace, Cameron 210, 222
Wallace, Stan 160
Waller, Robert 156, 157, 159, 194, 205, 206
Walls, Eric 382
Wally World Studios 113, 115
Walpole, Chuck 76
Walsh, Dan 476
Walters, Ricky 306
Walton, Ronnie "Preach" 278
Waltz, Christoph 352
Wane, Key 326, 341, 344
Warning! 444
Warren, Anne 245
Warren, Diane 315, 451
Warren, Harry 290
Warren G 89
Warwick, Dionne 110, 202, 396

Washington, Andre 436
Washington, Ashley 455
Washington, Carl 42
Washington, Denzel 233
Washington, Rosalie 181
Watch the Throne [album] 298, 304, 318
Water 423, **430**
Waters, Crystal 444
Waters, Muddy 288
Watford, Ricky 180, 181
Watkins, Sara 492
Watkins, Sean 492
Watkins, Tionne "T-Boz" 24, 26
Watley, Jody 85
Watrous, Mark 378
Watts, Cliff 238, 239
Way 2 Sexy 450
Way, DeAndre 376
Wayman, Ivan 492
Wayne, Jerome 436, 476, 486, 490, 500
We Are Born [album] 326, 334
We Are the People 308
We Are the World 171
We Are Young 304
We Can't Stop 388
We The Best Studios 396
We Will Rock You 200
We Will Rock You (Pepsi "Gladiator" Soundtrack Remix 2004) 200
Webb, Jon Jon 216, 218
Webb, Susie 200
Weber, Matt 340, 341, 342, 348, 360, 466
Webster, Danforth 476, 477, 478, 480, 484, 486, 488, 490, 492, 494, 496, 498, 500
Webster, Jacques 465
Weekes, Desree see Des'ree
Weitz, Brian 380
Weitz, Chris 130
Weitz, Paul 130
Welcome 36, 506
Welcome to Hollywood 233, **238**
Wellman, William A. 301
Wells, Jonathan D. 143, 287. See also The Bama Boyz [group]
Wesley Pentz, Thomas 376, 386
West, Chelsea see Peaches West
West, Justus 478
West, Kanye 48, 166, 233, 280, 282, 284, 298, 301, 304, 306, 318, 346, 350, 368, 384, 404, 408, 460
Westlake Recording Studios 348, 476, 477, 478, 480, 484, 486, 488, 490, 492, 494, 496, 498, 500
Weston, John 234
Wever, Ned 293
Whack, Tierra 423, 434, 464
Whalum III, Kenneth 240, 462
What Becomes of the Brokenhearted 246
What It's Gonna Be 205
What More Can I Give 171
What We Gonna Do 120
What You Do 284
Whatever You Want 76
What's Going On 124
What's It Gonna Be 172
Wheeler, Carl 39, 76
Whelan, Bill 498
When I First Saw You 242, 255
When I First Saw You (Duet) 242, **255**
When I Laid My Eyes on You 505
When We're Older 434
Where Are We Now? 330
Where Is the Love? 200
Where My Girls At? 72, 88

Where Them Girls At 350
Where'd You Go 57, **78**
White Album [album] 477, 500
White, Barry 37
White Christmas 127, **135**
White, Jack 367, 368, 378, 379
White, Stuart 326, 334, 336, 338, 340, 341, 342, 344, 346, 348, 358, 360, 366, 374, 376, 378, 380, 382, 384, 385, 386, 388, 396, 397, 406, 408, 410, 411, 412, 414, 420, 426, 427, 436, 448, 450, 452, 454, 455, 456, 458, 460, 461, 462, 466, 476, 477, 478, 480, 482, 484, 486, 488, 490, 492, 494, 496, 498, 500, 506
Whitehead, Amil see Amil
Whitehead, John 196
White-King, Brenda 160
Whites, Teresa LaBarbera 19, 24, 37, 38, 41, 42, 58, 70, 82, 88, 106, 326, 385
Whittington, Tahirah 428
Who am I (What's My Name?) 152
Who Do You Give Your Love To? 134
Why Do Fools Fall in Love: Music From and Inspired by the Motion Picture [compilation] 52
Why Do Fools Fall in Love: Original Versions From the Movie [album] 52
Why Don't You Love Me 158, 280, **287**
Why You Actin' 205
Wickman, Amy 374, 378, 386, 394
Wiggins, Charlie see Saadiq, Raphael
Wiggins, D'Wayne 19, 24, 36, 39, 44, 48, 54, 58, 76, 85, 99, 109, 118
Wilburn, Nayvadius see Future
Wild Wild West 106, 107
Wilkins, TJ 436
Wilkins, Wayne 276
will.i.am 200, 455
William, Myles 386
William, Willy 397
Williams, [Tenitra] Michelle 62, 64, 66, 70, 74, 83, 85, 92, 96, 99, 100, 102, 104, 106, 107, 108, 109, 110, 112, 113, 114, 115, 116, 118, 122, 130, 134, 135, 136, 137, 142, 143, 146, 172, 178, 179, 184, 186, 190, 192, 194, 196, 197, 198, 199, 200, 204, 205, 206, 207, 220, 255, 328, 348, 354, 357, 360, 391, 400, 504, 506
Williams, Andy 376
Williams, Ashly 455
Williams, Carla Marie 386, 391
Williams, Cory 168
Williams, Elvis "Blac Elvis" 284
Williams, Erron 136, 198, 199, 204
Williams, Gavin 478
Williams, Hank 480, 509
Williams, Hype 232, 340
Williams, John 52
Williams, Kameelah 24, 32
Williams, Patrick 382
Williams, Pharrell 114, 140, 168, 172, 210, 226, 318, 326, 340, 348, 350, 358, 360, 394, 406, 408, 423, 427, 430, 431, 454, 500, 505
Williams, Richard 420
Williams, Sekani 121
Williams, Serena 420
Williams, Tenitra 391
Williams, Tony 84
Williams, Venus 420
Williams, Wayne 237

Williams II, Michael L. see Mike WiLL Made-It
Williams Sr., Walter 176, 180
Willis, Wallace 180
Willoughby, Ethan 237
Wilmot, Anthony 406
Wilson, Brian 494
Wilson, Bryce 158
Wilson, Charlie 282
Wilson, Ernest Dion 396, 476
Wilson, Jackie 293
Wilson, Jesse 458
Wilson, Kim 288
Wilson, Lainey 472, 473
Wilson, Mark 54
Wilson, Mary 92
Wilson, Mike 42, 168
Winans, Mario 172, 181, 198, 233
Winans, Marvin 66
Winehouse, Amy 244, 352, 494
Winslow, Dontae 284
Winter Paradise 127, **132**
WinterSpringSummerFall [mixtape] 356
Wirtz, Rodney 374, 378, 386, 394
Wise Intelligent 54
Wishing on a Star 172, **174**
Wishing Well 390
With Me 28, 42
With Me Part I 23, **38**
With Me Part II 23, **42**, 48
Without Me 480
Without You 113
Without You I'm Nothing [album] 321
Wizkid 423, 424, 428, 432
Wolf, Steven 348
Wolford, Pete 302, 306, 308, 310, 312, 316, 318
Woman in Me 87
Wondaland Studios 464
Wonder, Nate 464
Wonder, Stevie 12, 107, 137, 140, 202, 206, 414, 434, 473, 478, 486
Wonderful World 302
Wood, Willie 205
Woodard, Alfre 423
Woodard, Jesse 352
Woodley, Shane "Bermuda" 166, 236, 238
Woods, Adrienne 374, 378, 386, 394, 428, 486, 490
Woodshed Recording 392
Woodson, Josiah 306, 308, 310, 312
Woodward, Mack 284
Work It Out 30, 138, **140**, 146, 172, 176
Workman, Dan 68, 74, 106, 107, 114, 115, 116, 122, 162
Workman, Nioka 164
World Wide Woman 240
Wrap Your Body [album] 355
Wrecking Ball 492
Wrice, Joyce 142
Wrice, Tyrone 166
Wright, Benjamin 24, 44, 48, 202, 237, 394
Wright, Betty 222
Wright, Dwayne 342
Wright, James 179, 180, 181
Wright, Jeffrey 288
Wright, Marie see Free
Wright III, Tommy 448
Wright Joseph, Shahadi 423
Wyatt, Kwane 336
Wyldcard see Dean, Kendrick
Wynn, Juanita 198

X

Xai, Steven 436
XO 325, 330, **344**
Xscape [group] 24, 32, 38, 60, 70, 205
Xzibit 156

Y

Ya Ya 469, **494**
Yacoub, Rami 450
Yancy, Marvin 198
Yazz 444
Yeah Yeah Yeahs [group] 376
Yegoryan, Yelena 374, 378, 386, 394
Yellowhair, Sheldon 244, 245, 246, 248, 250, 252, 254, 255
Yes 145, **159**
Yoba, Malik 122
Yoncé 341, 506
You Changed 354
You Don't Know My Name 282
You Don't Love Me (No, No, No) 506
You Gotta Be 238
You Make Me Wanna 38
Young, Andre Romelle see Dr. Dre
Young, Angus 480
Young, George 436, 476, 486, 490, 500
Young, Jordan "DJ Swivel" 298, 302, 304, 306, 308, 310, 312, 316, 320, 321, 346
Young, Neil 292
Young Americans 202
Young Guru 233, 238, 396, 403, 406, 408, 410, 411, 412, 418, 420
Young Thug 414
Younglord see Frierson, Richard
You're Beautiful 234
You're the Only One 54
You've Been So Good 95, 116
Yu, Stephanie 428, 486, 490
Yusef, Malik 384, 385

Z

Zak Starkey Studio 458
Zane, Lil 176
Zarrillo, Joseph [Joe] 418
Zavala, Jimmy "Z" 179
Zayne, Jovian 464
Zemeckis, Robert 352
ZEX [group] 372
Zimmer, Hans 424, 427, 436
Zinner, Nick 376
Zreik, Wassin 110

ACKNOWLEDGMENTS

Thank you to Marie Laure Miranda and Katia de Azevedo for their help and their kindness.

Thank you, too, to Boris Guilbert, Charlotte Couture, and Lucie Ollagnier of Les Éditions E/P/A, as well as to Sara Quémener and Zarko Telebak of ZS Studio.

And thank you to Rose and Vera.

PICTURE CREDITS

© **TRUNCK ARCHIVE/PHOTOSENSO** Cliff Watts/Trunk Archive/PhotoSenso: p. 7

© **WYATT MCSPADDEN** p. 9

© **GETTY IMAGES** Paul S. Howell/*Houston Chronicle* via Getty Images: p. 10 • Frank Micelotta/ImageDirect: p. 16 • Gilles Petard/Redferns: p. 17, 36 • Smiley N. Pool/*Houston Chronicle* via Getty Images: p. 18–19, 20–21, 25, 38 • Columbia Pictures/Getty Images: p. 26 • Ron Davis/Getty Images: p. 27, 79, 100 • Aaron Rapoport/Corbis/Getty Images: p. 28, 485 • Raymond Boyd/Getty Images: p. 28–29, 81, 87 • Paul Bergen/Redfern: p. 37, 53 • Lynn Goldsmith/Corbis/VCG via Getty Images: p. 39 • Mychal Watts/WireImage: p. 43 • Paul Natkin/Getty Images: p. 45, 71, 451 • Kevin Cummins/Getty Images: p. 47 • *Afro American Newspapers*/Gado/Getty Images: p. 48 • Andrew Savulich/*NY Daily News* Archive via Getty Images: p. 51 • Al Pereira/Michael Ochs Archives/Getty Images: p. 55, 153, 178, 495 • Bob Berg/Getty Images: p. 60 • Pam Francis/Getty Images: p. 65 • Fred Duval/FilmMagic: p. 69 • James Keivom/*NY Daily News* Archive via Getty Images: p. 73 • Steve Granitz/WireImage: p. 84, 337, 501 • Michael Ochs Archives/Getty Images: p. 85, 114, 137, 159 • Gregory Bojorquez/Getty Images: p. 91, 158, 193, 200 • James Kriegsmann/Michael Ochs Archives/Getty Images: p. 93 • Frank Micelotta/Getty Images: p. 98, 171 • Tim Roney/Getty Images: p. 101, 123, 169 • Fryderyk Gabowicz/picture alliance via Getty Images: p. 105, 108, 319, 444 • Fin Costello/Redferns: p. 107 • Ray Tamarra/Getty Images: p. 111 • David Corio/Redferns: p. 117, 439 • Lester Cohen/WireImage: p. 125, 225, 415 • Kevin Mazur/WireImage: p. 133, 151, 157, 261, 262, 263, 277, 311, 317, 481 • George Rinhart/Corbis via Getty Images: p. 135 • Todd Plitt/Getty Images: p. 147, 161 • Jo Hale/Getty Images: p. 148–149 • Michael Putland/Getty Images: p. 156, 231, 286, 463 • David Corio/Michael Ochs Archives/Getty Images: p. 163, 299 • Anthony Barboza/Getty Images: p. 165 • Gary Reyes/*Oakland Tribune* Staff Archives/MediaNews Group/*Bay Area News* via Getty Images: p. 167 • Brian Rasic/Getty Images: p. 173 • Ken Hively/*Los Angeles Times* via Getty Images: p. 175 • Jim Steinfeldt/Michael Ochs Archives/Getty Images: p. 181 • Talaya Centeno/WWD/Penske Media via Getty Images: p. 186 • Jesse D. Garrabrant/NBAE via Getty Images: p. 187 • Focus on Sport/Getty Images: p. 189 • M. Caulfield/WireImage for Columbia Records: p. 191 • Jonathan Wong/*South China Morning Post* via Getty Images: p. 197 • CBS via Getty Images: p. 202 • Johnny Nunez/Getty Images: p. 204 • Mathew Imaging/FilmMagic: p. 207 • Douglas Mason/Getty Images: p. 214–215 • J. Strauss/FilmMagic: p. 217 • Dimitrios Kambouris/WireImage for Conde Nast media group: p. 218–219 • Michael Caulfield/WireImage for BET Network: p. 221 • Central Press/Getty Images: p. 223 • Lynn Goldsmith/Corbis/VCG via Getty Images: p. 227 • Paul Mounce/Corbis via Getty Images: p. 229 • Etienne George/Corbis via Getty Images: p. 232 • John Rogers/Getty Images • p. 235 • Lalo Yasky/WireImage: p. 236 • Jeff Vespa/WireImage for Sundance Film Festival: p. 237 • Martyn Goodacre/Getty Images: p. 239 • James Devaney/WireImage: p. 241 • Harry Langdon/Getty Images: p. 253 • Dagmar Scherf/ullstein bild via Getty Images: p. 259 • Michael Tran/FilmMagic: p. 265 • Cyrus McCrimmon/*The Denver Post* via Getty Images: p. 267 • Justin Goff/UK Press via Getty Images: p. 268 • API/Gamma-Rapho via Getty Images: p. 269 • Jeff Kravitz/FilmMagic: p. 271 • Michael Loccisano/FilmMagic: p. 275 • Denise Truscello/WireImage: p. 279 • Theo Wargo/WireImage: p. 281 • Jeffrey Ufberg/WireImage: p. 283 • Jerritt Clark/WireImage: p. 284 • Fred Hayes/WireImage for Sundance Film Festival: p. 285 • Richard Ecclestone/Redferns: p. 292 • Michael Caulfield/WireImage: p. 293 • Brian van der Brug/*Los Angeles Times* via Getty Images: p. 300 • Kristian Dowling/Getty Images: p. 301 • Samir Hussein/Getty Images: p. 302–303 • Clarence Williams/*Los Angeles Times* via Getty Images: p. 307 • Chelsea Lauren/Getty Images: p. 309 • Chris Carroll/Corbis via Getty Images: p. 313 • Ben Rose/WireImage: p. 320 • Rob Tringali/SportsChrome via Getty Images: p. 321 • CBS via Getty Images: p. 323 • Larry Busacca/PW/WireImage for Parkwood Entertainment: p. 331, 332, 355 • Gilbert Carrasquillo/FilmMagic: p. 335 • Roger Kisby/Getty Images: p. 339 • Taylor Hill/Getty Images: p. 340 • Maria Moratti/Getty Images: p. 341 • Ray Tamarra/GC Images: p. 343 • George Pimentel/WireImage: p. 345 • Donna Ward/Getty Images: p. 347 • Jeff Kravitz/MTV1415/FilmMagic: p. 349 • Kent Nishimura/*Los Angeles Times* via Getty Images: p. 351 • Rob Verhorst/Redferns: p. 353 • Mike Coppola/WireImage: p. 354 • Paul Morigi/WireImage: p. 356 • Christina Horsten/picture alliance via Getty Images: p. 357 • Mike Marsland/Mike Marsland/WireImage: p. 359 • Theo Wargo/MTV1617/Getty Images for MTV: p. 365 • Erik McGregor/LightRocket via Getty Images: p. 366 • Kevin Mazur/Getty Images for Roc Nation: p. 368 • Larry Busacca/PW/WireImage: p. 371, 396 • Kevin Winter/BET/Getty Images for BET: p. 372–373 • Barry King: p. 375 • Joseph Okpako/Redferns via Getty Images: p. 377 • Matt Carr/Getty Images: p. 379 • George Pimentel/WireImage: p. 381 • Stephen Lovekin/WWD/Penske Media via Getty Images: p. 383 • Shaun Bloodworth/PYMCA/Avalon/Getty Images: p. 385 • Jon Kopaloff/FilmMagic: p. 387 • Rick Kern/Getty Images: p. 389 • Kevin Mazur/Getty Images for Global Citizen: p. 390 • Dave J Hogan/Dave J Hogan/Getty Images: p. 391, 453 • Dave M. Benett/Getty Images: p. 393 • Lester Cohen/WireImage: p. 394 • J. Emilio Flores/Corbis via Getty Images: p. 395 • Kevin Mazur/Getty Images for Coachella: p. 402–403, 507 • Prince Williams/Wireimage: p. 407, 433 • Phillip Faraone/Getty Images: p. 409 • Rodrigo Varela/WireImage for Don't Think Twice: p. 410 • Shareif Ziyadat/Getty Images: p. 411 • Eric Charbonneau/Getty Images for Warner Bros: p. 413 • Shareif Ziyadat/Getty Images for Deleon Tequila: p. 418 • Stephen J. Cohen/Getty Images: p. 421 • Amanda Edwards/Getty Images: p. 429 • Kravitz/FilmMagic for Bonnaroo Arts and Music Festival: p. 431 • Oupa Bopape/Gallo Images via Getty Images: p. 435 • Dave Hogan/MTV 2014/Getty Images for MTV: p. 437 • Kevin Mazur/WireImage for Parkwood: p. 443, 446–447, 476 • Stephane Cardinale - Corbis/Corbis via Getty Images: p. 445 • Chris Polk/FilmMagic: p. 454 • Paras Griffin/Getty Images: p. 457 • Chip HIRES/Gamma-Rapho via Getty Images: p. 459 • Steve Russell/*Toronto Star* via Getty Images: p. 460 • Gabriel Olsen/Getty Images for Absolut Elyx: p. 464 • John Shearer/WireImage: p. 465 • Walter McBride/Corbis via Getty Images: p. 467 • John Shearer/Getty Images for CMT: p. 472, 477 • Kevin Mazur/Getty Images for The Recording Academy: p. 473 • Michael Blackshire/*Los Angeles Times* via Getty Images: p. 474 • Kevin Nixon/*Guitarist* magazine/Future via Getty Images: p. 479 • Judith Burrows/Getty Images: p. 483 • Harry Langdon/Getty Images: p. 487 • Carlos Gonzalez/Penske Media via Getty Images: p. 489 • Rich Fury/AMA2018/Getty Images for dcp: p. 493 • Gijsbert Hanekroot/Redferns: p. 497 • Gareth Cattermole/MTV EMA/Gareth Cattermole/Getty Images for Paramount: p. 499

© **HEMIS** Brittany Smith/Alamy/Hemis: p. 12–13 • UPI/Alamy/Hemis: p. 67 • ZUMA Press, Inc./Alamy/Hemis: p. 88 • Entertainment Pictures/Alamy/Hemis: p. 89 • MediaPunch Inc/Alamy/Hemis: p. 99 • AJ Pics/Alamy/Hemis: p. 103, 142, 177 • Trinity Mirror/Mirrorpix/Alamy/Hemis: p. 109, 112 • kpa Publicity Stills, United Archives GmbH/Alamy/Hemis: p. 213, 249 • The Photo Access/Alamy/Hemis: p. 240 • RGR Collection/Alamy/Hemis: p. 243, 247, 251 • Pictorial Press Ltd/Alamy/Hemis: p. 260 • Kathy Hutchins/Alamy/Hemis: p. 417

© **EVERETT COLLECTION** Scott Humbert/© Walt Disney Television/Courtesy: Everett Collection: p. 14

© **AVALON** Wilberto van den Boogaard/Avalon/Avalon: p. 31, 49, 83 • RIP/Avalon/Avalon: p. 33, 35 • Ola Bergman/Avalon/Avalon: p. 77 • Ray Burmiston/Avalon/Avalon: p. 119

© **BRIDGEMAN IMAGES** Everett Collection/Bridgeman Images: p. 40–41

© **STEPHEN MCBRIDE** p. 59, 61, 63, 97

© **IMAGO IMAGES** Fredrik Sandberg/TT/Imago Images: p. 75 • Imago/Famous: p. 199 • Imago/Newscom/GDA: p. 211, 297

© **ANTOINE VERGLAS** p. 129, 130–131

© **WIKIMEDIA COMMONS** p. 136, 143

© **SIPA PRESS** REX features/Sipa: p. 139, 141 • Daniel Moss/Sipa: p. 155 • AP/Sipa: p. 170 • Ronald Grant/Mary Evans/Sipa: p. 180 • Jim Cooper/AP/Sipa: p. 185, 195 • CB2/Zob/wenn.com/Sipa: p. 203 • Jason DeCrow/AP/Sipa: p. 272–273 • Rex Features/REX/Sipa: p. 289 • Elise Amendola/AP/Sipa: p. 290–291 • Amy Sussman/AP/Sipa: p. 305 • Cliff Watts/AP/Sipa: p. 314–315 • Rob Hoffman/Newscom/Sipa: p. 327 • Patrick Demarchelier/AP/Sipa: p. 328 • Robin Harper/AP/Sipa: p. 333 • Marcio Sanchez/AP/Sipa: p. 361 • Andrew Harnik/AP/Sipa: p. 367 • Sean Ryan/IPS/Shutterst/Sipa: p. 369 • Jordan Strauss/AP/Sipa: p. 384 • Maria Laura Antonelli/AGF/Sipa: p. 397 • PicturerGroup/REX/Shutterstock/Sipa: p. 401 • Andrew White/Parkwood/PictureGroup/REX/Shutterstock/Sipa: p. 404–405 • Raven Varona/Parkwood/PictureGroup/REX/Shutterstock/Sipa: p. 425 • Mike McCarn/AP/Sipa: p. 426 • Ron Galella, Ltd./Ron Galella Collection via Getty Images: p. 427 • Vianney Le Caer/Shutter/SIPA: p. 449 • Chris Pizzello/AP/Sipa: p. 471 • Eric Christian Smith/AP/Sipa: p. 475

© **RYAN WEST** p. 298

© **ELIOT LEE HAZEL** p. 329

© **ALEXANDA RAE** p. 491

© **ALL RIGHTS RESERVED** p. 11, 24, 58, 96, 120, 128, 138, 146, 176, 184, 210, 242, 258, 288, 296, 326, 364, 400, 424, 470, 504, 505, 506

An Hachette UK Company
www.hachette.co.uk

Original title: *Beyoncé, La Totale*
Texts: Benoît Clerc
Published by Les Éditions E/P/A–Hachette Livre 2025

This edition first published in Great Britain in 2025 by Cassell,
an imprint of Octopus Publishing Group Ltd
Carmelite House
50 Victoria Embankment
London EC4Y 0DZ
www.octopusbooks.co.uk

The authorized representative in the EEA is Hachette Ireland,
8 Castlecourt Centre, Dublin 15, D15 XTP3, Ireland (email: info@hbgi.ie)

Copyright © 2025 Les Éditions E/P/A–Hachette Livre
Translation copyright © Octopus Publishing Group Ltd, 2025

Distributed in the US by
Hachette Book Group
1290 Avenue of the Americas
4th and 5th Floors
New York, NY 10104

Distributed in Canada by
Canadian Manda Group
664 Annette St.
Toronto, Ontario, Canada M6S 2C8

All rights reserved. No part of this work may be reproduced
or utilized in any form or by any means, electronic or
mechanical, including photocopying, recording or by any
information storage and retrieval system, without the prior
written permission of the publisher.

ISBN 9781788405577

eISBN 9781788405584

A CIP catalogue record for this book is available from the British Library.

Printed and bound in China

10 9 8 7 6 5 4 3 2 1

For this edition:
Publisher: Trevor Davis
Translators: Simon Jones and Andrea Reece
Project Editor: Sarah Reece
Copy Editor: Caroline Taggart
Proofreader: Helena Caldon
Art Director: Yasia Williams
Typesetter: Jeremy Tilston
Assistant Production Manager: Lisa Pinnell

Disclaimers:
All information was correct at the time of printing.
Details that are unknown are marked by "?"; for example, the name
of the recording studios for *With Me Part II* on page 42.